SOCIAL PARTNERSHIPS AND RESPONSIBLE BUSINESS

Cross-sector partnerships are widely hailed as a critical means for addressing a wide array of social challenges such as climate change, poverty, education, corruption, and health. Amid all the positive rhetoric of cross-sector partnerships though, critical voices point to the limited success of various initiatives in delivering genuine social change and in providing for real citizen participation.

This collection critically examines the motivations for, processes within, and expected and actual outcomes of cross-sector partnerships. In opening up new theoretical, methodological, and practical perspectives on cross-sector social inter-actions, this book reimagines partnerships in order to explore the potential to contribute to the social good. A multi-disciplinary perspective on partnerships adds serious value to the debate in a range of fields including management, politics, public management, sociology, development studies, and international relations. Contributors to the volume reflect many of these diverse perspectives, enabling the book to provide an account of partnerships that is theoretically rich and methodologically varied.

With critical contributions from leading academics such as Barbara Gray, Ans Kolk, John Selsky, and Sandra Waddock, this book is a comprehensive resource which will increase understanding of this vital issue.

M. May Seitanidi is Senior Lecturer in Strategy at Kent Business School at the University of Kent and a Visiting Fellow at the International Centre for Corporate Social Responsibility (ICCSR) at Nottingham University Business School, UK.

Andrew Crane is George R. Gardiner Professor of Business Ethics and Director of the Centre of Excellence in Responsible Business at the Schulich School of Business, York University, Toronto, Canada.

This comprehensive research handbook will become a standard work on cross-sector partnerships as a means for addressing social challenges. The handbook assembles perspectives from many of the leading scholars in this field.

Duane Windsor, Rice University, Texas, USA

Partnerships and collaboration are a too-often neglected aspect of impactful business-society interventions and programmes. This thoughtful and impressive collection provides a gateway to the latest cutting-edge research on cross-sector partnerships and promises to be a vital resource for scholars and engaged practitioners alike.

Stephen Brammer, Professor of Strategy, Birmingham Business School, UK

Social Partnerships and Responsible Business is set to make a worthwhile contribution to the study and practice of social entrepreneurship as well as contemporary debates about the value of democratic organisation in the field of business. Its cross-sector focus will have particular appeal to students interested in alternative business models that challenge the hegemony of the state and corporations in social and economic development.

Dr Rory Ridley-Duff, Senior Lecturer, Sheffield Business School, UK

This book comes at a critical time, as there is no more important mechanism for addressing global sustainability problems than constructive multi-sector relationships: we need to learn our way forward together. *Social Partnerships and Responsible Business* outlines the opportunities and challenges in working across sectors, and offers questions for reflection and dialogue to help us re-imagine possibilities. It is an invaluable resource for people from business, government, academia, and civil society – and since we are all of the above, that means everyone.

Barry Colbert, Associate Professor, Policy & Strategic Management,
Wilfrid Laurier University, Canada

Collaboration is an important frontier for sustainability, as many issues are far greater than any single organization can solve. The range of contributors to this volume will make this an important resource for anyone wanting to embark on collaboration research or collaborative practices.

Dr Tima Bansal, Ivey Business School, Western University, Canada

The book provides a clear picture of where we stand now in terms of research and practice, but additionally it provides provoking visions of what could be … The potential for co-creating social, environmental, and economic value has not yet been fully tapped. This book contributes importantly to the realization of that vital goal.

James E. Austin, the Eliot I. Snider and Family Professor of Business Administration,
Emeritus at Harvard Business School, USA

SOCIAL PARTNERSHIPS AND RESPONSIBLE BUSINESS

A research handbook

Edited by M. May Seitanidi and Andrew Crane

LONDON AND NEW YORK

First published 2014
by Routledge
2 Park Square, Milton Park, Abingdon, Oxon OX14 4RN

and by Routledge
711 Third Avenue, New York, NY 10017

Routledge is an imprint of the Taylor & Francis Group, an informa business

British Library Cataloguing in Publication Data
A catalogue record for this book is available from the British Library

Library of Congress Cataloging in Publication Data
A catalog record has been requested for this book.

ISBN: 978-0-415-67863-6 (hbk)
ISBN: 978-0-415-67864-3 (pbk)
ISBN: 978-1-315-86717-5 (ebk)

Typeset in Stone Sans and Bembo
by FiSH Books Ltd, Enfield.

CONTENTS

FIGURES

TABLES AND BOXES

Tables

Boxes

CONTRIBUTORS

Hadley Archer is Vice President, Strategic Partnerships and Development at WWF-Canada, where he leads the development of a portfolio of corporate, individual, government, and foundation relationships that advance conservation through improved practices, provide funding for WWF's conservation work, and creating opportunities for leadership in the environment. In this capacity, he works with companies such as Loblaw, Coca-Cola, HP, Fairmont, Resolute and CSL to raise the bar on responsible business practices. He joined WWF in Switzerland in 2004, where he worked with companies to adopt policies that favour sustainable use of wood and paper products. Prior to his involvement in the environmental field, Hadley worked for Procter & Gamble for six years in various marketing and finance roles. He has a Bachelor of Commerce degree from the University of Manitoba in his hometown of Winnipeg and a Master of Forest Conservation degree from the University of Toronto.

Marlene Janzen Le Ber is Assistant Professor and Associate Director – Program Development, Interfaculty Program in Public Health at the Schulich School of Medicine and Dentistry, Western University in London, Ontario, Canada. Marlene came to academia with over twenty years of healthcare management experience. A well-seasoned health care executive, she is known in the healthcare community as a leader and change maker who spearheaded numerous system wide changes. Supported by the prestigious doctoral and postdoctoral awards from Canada's Social Sciences and Humanities Research Council (SSHRC), Marlene completed her PhD in Strategy at the Richard Ivey School of Business, Western University in 2010 and her postdoctoral work at the Erb Institute for Global Sustainable Enterprise at the University of Michigan thereafter. Her research, supported by SSHRC as well as Community-University Research Alliances and Ontario Trillium Foundation, centres on the processes of social innovation using the health and social services sectors as the context. Of particular interest are cross-sector partnerships, transdisciplinarity, and hybrid organizations. Marlene's work has been published in several leading academic journals, including Organization, Journal of Business Ethics, and Business and Society, as well as several book chapters and best paper proceedings from the Academy of Management (AOM) and the Administrative Sciences Association of Canada (ASAC).

Jean J. Boddewyn is Emeritus Professor of Marketing and International Business in the Zicklin School of Business of Baruch College, City University of New York, where he taught from 1973 to 2006 after teaching at New York University (1964–1973) and the University of Portland, OR (1957–1964). He holds a Commercial Engineering degree from the University of Louvain (Belgium), an MBA from the University of Oregon and a PhD in Business Administration from the University of Washington (Seattle). His current research interests center on reciprocity as a mode of entry, international business political behavior, public affairs, the regulation and self-regulation of advertising around the world, international business strategy and MNE theory. He received the 2002 Academy of Management's Distinguished Service Award in recognition of his service as editor of *International Studies of Management and Organization* since 1971, his pioneering research on comparative management, foreign divestment, and international business-government relations, and his leadership roles as one of the first Chairs (1974) of the AOM's International Management Division as well as Vice President (1975–1976) and President (1993–1994) of the Academy of International Business. He is a Fellow of the Academy of International Business, the Academy of Management, and the International Academy of Management. He served as Dean of the AIB Fellows from 2005 to 2008. He was the recipient of a Fulbright Award (1951–1952) to study at the University of Oregon and obtained his MBA.

Sonia Bookman is an Associate Professor in the Department of Sociology, University of Manitoba, Manitoba, Canada. She obtained her doctorate in Sociology at the University of Manchester. Her research interests include branding, consumer culture, corporate social responsibility, and urban life. She is currently working on a research project that explores intersections between urban branding, revitalization, and human rights discourses in the city of Vancouver, Canada.

Oana Branzei is Associate Professor of Strategy, the David G. Burgoyne Faculty Fellow, the Building Sustainable Value Research Fellow at the Ivey School of Business, Western Ontario University. In 2012-2014 she is also a Visiting Professor at the Center for Positive Organization Scholarship and the Erb Institute for Global Sustainable Enterprise at the Ross School of Business, University of Michigan. She holds a doctorate from University of British Columbia. Her current research focuses on the pro-social functions of business, especially on the social dynamics of social change, social innovation and social enterprise. Her field work in Kenya, Tanzania, Sudan, Rwanda, Uganda, Brazil, Peru, India, and Bangladesh documents the incidence, resilience, and persistence of positive social impact of doing business under extreme scarcity, adversity and conflict. She also studies the social micro-processes of positive agency and especially the balancing acts between public good and private gain across organizational forms (from manufacturing firms to R&D alliances and creative communities) and contexts (from clean energy to sustainable cuisine and ethical fashion). Her research projects have been supported by grants from Canada's Social Sciences and Humanities Research Council, the Canadian International Development Agency (CIDA), the Association of African Universities (AAU), the Association of Universities and Colleges in Canada (AUCC), the International Development Research Centre (IDRC), and the Investment Climate and Business Environment Research Fund (ICBE RF). Her work has appeared in the top journals in strategy, entrepreneurship, and international business; she also contributed to numerous books and handbooks. Her first edited book, *Critical Perspectives on the Third Sector*, was published by Emerald in 2011.

Amelia Clarke has been working on environment and sustainability issues since 1989. She is now a faculty member in the School of Environment, Enterprise and Development (SEED) at the University of Waterloo and is Director of the Master of Environment and Business (MEB) executive-education online program. She sits on the editorial board of the *Academy of Management Learning and Education* journal, and is an executive member of the Social Responsibility Division of the Administrative Science Association of Canada. She holds a PhD in Management from McGill University. Her research interests and publications are in the areas of: sustainable development strategies; collaborative strategic management; cross-sector social partnerships; corporate social and environmental responsibility; campus environmental management; and youth-led social entrepreneurship.

Andrew Crane is the George R. Gardiner Professor of Business Ethics and Director of the Centre of Excellence in Responsible Business at the Schulich School of Business, York University, Toronto. Over the past decade he has been at the forefront of efforts to integrate social, ethical, and environmental issues into global management research and education. He is the co-author or editor of 11 books, including *Corporate Social Responsibility: Readings and Cases in a Global Context*, second edition recently published by Routledge. He has published widely on business ethics and CSR in scholarly management journals, sits on the editorial board of several international journals, and regularly presents on the subject at conferences in Europe, North America, Asia, Africa, and Latin America. He is a frequent contributor to the media, and co-writes (with Dirk Matten) the Crane and Matten blog which is widely regarded as a leading voice in the CSR debate. In 2011, he was selected as a finalist in the Aspen Institute Faculty Pioneers Awards.

Tina Dacin is the E. Marie Shantz Professor of Strategy and Director of the Center for Responsible Leadership at the Queen's School of Business. She received her PhD from the University of Toronto. Her research interests include cultural heritage, traditions, institutions, social entrepreneurship, and the social architecture of collaboration. Her work has been published in leading management journals and she has served these journals in a variety of editorial positions.

Jonathan Doh is the Rammrath Chair in International Business, Faculty Director of the Center for Global Leadership, and Professor of Management at the Villanova School of Business. He teaches, conducts research, and consults on international business and corporate responsibility. Jonathan is author and co-author of more than 60 articles, 30 book chapters, and seven books. Recent articles have appeared in *Academy of Management Review, Business Ethics Quarterly, California Management Review, Journal of International Business Studies, Organization Science, Sloan Management Review*, and *Strategic Management Journal*. His latest books are *International Management: Culture, Strategy, and Behavior, (8th edition, McGraw-Hill Irwin, 2012), the leading international management text, and NGOs and Corporations: Conflict and Collaboration* (Cambridge University Press, 2009). In 2012, he was elected to a five-year term that will culminate as Chair of the Academy of Management Organizations and Natural Environment Division. He holds a PhD in strategic and international management from George Washington University.

Barbara Gray is a Professor and Executive Programs Faculty Fellow Emerita in the Smeal College of Business at Penn State University. She also served as Director of the Center for Research in Conflict and Negotiation. She has studied organizational and environmental conflict, framing and sensemaking, collaborative partnerships and institutional processes for over 35 years. She has published three books and over 90 articles in journals such as *Administrative Science Quarterly, Academy of Management Journal, Academy of Management Review*, and *Organization Science*. Her research has been funded by NSF, EPA, NIH, and the Hewlett Foundation. She has served as an organizational consultant, mediator and trainer for many private, public and non-governmental organizations worldwide including Greenpeace International, the Dutch Ministry of Environment, Union Carbide, and US Steel and many others. She recently was awarded a grant from the Network for Business Sustainability to study cross-sectoral partnerships for sustainability. She has a BS in Chemistry from University of Dayton and a PhD in Organizational Behavior from Case Western Reserve University.

Roberto Gutiérrez holds a PhD in Sociology from Johns Hopkins University, and is Associate Professor in the School of Management of the Universidad de los Andes (Bogotá, Colombia). From 2003 to 2008, he chaired the Social Enterprise Knowledge Network (www.sekn.org). He has published articles about alliances, social enterprises, education, and development in popular media and academic journals including the *American Sociological Review*, the *Review of Educational Research*, the *Journal of Management Education*, the *Harvard Business Review* (Latin America edition), and the *Stanford Social Innovation Review*.

Ralph Hamann is Research Director and Associate Professor at the University of Cape Town Graduate School of Business. His research is on organisational responses to complex social-ecological problems, such as climate change and food security. Additional roles include Academic Director of the Network for Business Sustainability: South Africa, and Chair of the Southern Africa Food Lab.

Cathy L. Hartman, PhD, is a Professor of Marketing and Co-director of the Center for the Market Diffusion of Renewable Energy and Clean Technology at the Jon M. Huntsman School of Business at Utah State University. She teaches both graduate and undergraduate classes on buyer behavior, and her research focuses on the relationship and management issues of collaborations among environmental stakeholders, and how they influence the diffusion of cleaner technology and business practices. She and her colleague Edwin R. Stafford are co-principal investigators on a $2.25 million US Department of Energy program to study the diffusion of wind power development in Utah and the West.

Lucian J. Hudson is Director of Communications, the Open University. A champion and practitioner of collaboration, he is author of the UK government's first international report on what makes for effective cross-sector collaboration, *The Enabling State: Collaborating for Success* (FCO, 2009). He has also held top communications roles in four government departments, including Director of Communication, Foreign and Commonwealth Office, and the UK government's first-ever Director of e-Communications. Before joining the Open University, he was a Partner and the first Managing Director of Cornerstone Global Associates, providing international strategic consultancy to government, business, and civil society organizations. He was a senior television executive and journalist with the BBC and ITV for 17 years, and was Head of Programming, International Channels, BBC Worldwide. He has served as Chairman of three nonprofit organizations, including the Tavistock Institute of Human Relations.

Surinder Hundal After a career in the corporate sector where she led work on communications, strategy, marketing, and partnerships in global businesses such as Nokia and BT, Surinder Hundal is now working specifically in the field of cross-sector partnerships, partnership brokering, and partnership evaluation. An accredited partnership broker, she works as an independent consultant through Rippleseed (www.rippleseed.com). She is also a Director of the Partnership Brokering Association (http://partnershipbrokers.org) and an Associate of the Partnering Initiative (http://thepartneringinitiative.org). Surinder holds a post-graduate certificate in Cross-sector Partnerships from the University of Cambridge; a MBA from the Cass Business School in London; and a B.Sc. Honors in Life Sciences from the University of Westminster. Surinder was awarded her PhD in pharmacology from the University of London.

Ans Kolk is a Full Professor at the University of Amsterdam Business School, the Netherlands. Her research has focused on corporate responsibility and sustainability in relation to international business firms, and their interactions with local, national, and international stakeholders. Topics of research have included poverty and international development; bottom of the pyramid and subsistence markets; partnerships; codes of conduct and non-financial reporting; stakeholders and governance; climate change and energy. She has published numerous articles in international journals, as well as book chapters, and also books. In 2009, she received the Aspen Institute Faculty Pioneer European Award (Lifetime Achievement Award) (www.anskolk.nl; akolk@uva.nl).

Diana Mangalagiu is Professor at Reims Management School, France and Visiting Fellow at the Smith School for Enterprise and the Environment, University of Oxford. She has a dual background, in both natural sciences and social sciences. Her interest is in sustainability and in the articulation of environmental and economic policies in corporate and public policy settings addressed through modelling, social experimentation and foresight. She is a lead author of the Global Environmental Outlook, UNEP and her book, *Reframing the Problem of Climate Change* (with Jaeger et al.), was published by Earthscan in 2012.

Patricia Márquez holds a PhD in Social Anthropology from the University of California Berkeley, and is Associate Professor of Management at the University of San Diego. She is the Faculty Director of the USD Changemaker HUB. Her current research is on the role business can play in alleviating poverty worldwide. She is an active participant of the Social Enterprise Knowledge Network (SEKN), a network of prestigious business schools across the Americas and Spain focusing on advancing knowledge and influencing practice. Her research has been published in journal articles, teaching cases, and numerous books.

Cheryl Martens holds a PhD from the University of Manchester and has published work on the politics of global branding and corporate social responsibility as well as the branding of HIV/AIDS communication. She has lectured on branding and brand communications as Senior Lecturer at Bournemouth University and currently teaches methodology and communications courses in the Latin American Faculty for Social Sciences (FLACSO), Ecuador. Her research interests include social partnerships, corporate social responsibility, media and globalization.

Barbara Nijhuis is an independent not for profit/charity expert, currently based in Amsterdam. She has gained her professional experience in various commercial and not-for-profit organizations with a strong focus on and extensive field experience in Guatemala. In 2000 she started the foundation "Amigos de San Juan" (www.amigosdesanjuan.org). Starting in 2007 she worked several years as the Executive Director of Safe Passage/Camino Seguro in Guatemala City (www.safepassage.org), where she initiated and promoted various international and local partnerships. Recent activities include contract negotiating and developing strategies for the worldwide partnership between UNICEF and ING.

John Peloza is an Associate Professor of Marketing at the College of Business, Florida State University. His research focuses on corporate social responsibility, and in particular the financial and business impacts from investments in CSR. He is the editor of the Valuing Sustainability knowledge forum at the Network for Business Sustainability (www.nbs.net). He has published numerous articles in top marketing and management journals including *Journal of Marketing, Journal of Management, California Management Review, Journal of the Academy of Marketing Science*, and *Journal of Business Ethics*.

Stella Pfisterer is a Research Associate at the Partnerships Resource Centre at the RSM Erasmus University Rotterdam in the Netherlands. Her work for the past eight years, as a practioner and academic, has mainly concentrated on cross-sector collaboration for sustainable development. She is particularly interested in the effectiveness of partnerships with the private sector embedded in international development cooperation. Her areas of expertise include development policy analysis; inter-organizational relationships (in particular governance and management of collaborations) and institutional development. Stella developed a series of training and teaching modules related to effective partnership management.

Jill Purdy is an Associate Professor in the Milgard School of Business at the University of Washington Tacoma, where she served as the Academic Director of the Center for Leadership and Social Responsibility from 2007–2012. Her scholarly work focuses on understanding multi-level institutional dynamics and their impact on how cross-sectoral issues are interpreted and addressed. Her research appears in such journals as *Academy of Management Journal, International Journal of Conflict Management, Public Administration Quarterly*, and *Academy of Management Learning and Education*, and she serves on the editorial board of *Negotiation and Conflict Management Research*. Current research projects include a study of regional and national systems supporting the development of social enterprise. In addition to research and teaching, she works with business, government, and nonprofit organizations to facilitate problem solving, strategic planning and collaboration. She earned her doctorate in Management and Organization from Pennsylvania State University in 1994.

Ezequiel Reficco holds a PhD in Law and Diplomacy from the Fletcher School, Tufts University, and is an Associate Professor at the School of Management of the Universidad de Los Andes (Bogotá, Colombia). He worked at Harvard Business School from 2001–2008 as a Post-doctoral Fellow and Senior Researcher. He co-authored *Social Partnering in Latin America* (Cambridge, MA, 2004). He has published numerous book chapters and various articles in popular media and academic journals such as *Business and Society*, the *Stanford Social Innovation Review*, and the *Harvard Business Review* (Latin America edition).

Carlos Rufín is Associate Professor of International Business at Suffolk University in Boston. He holds a BA in Economics from Princeton University, an MA in Economics from Columbia University, and a PhD in Public Policy from Harvard University. The focus of his research is the strategic management of multinationals' relations with governments and of their environmental and social impacts. One of his specific interests is the development of business models combining profitability and poverty alleviation, as suggested by the concept of the Base of the Pyramid. On this subject, he has published several papers and co-edited the book *Private Utilities and Poverty Alleviation* (Cheltenham, UK, 2011).

Miguel Rivera-Santos is Associate Professor at EMLYON Graduate School of Management, France, and at Babson College, US. His current research focuses on cross-partnerships for poverty alleviation. Specific topics include, among others, the governance of cross-sector partnerships; the interaction between institutional environments and partnership structure at the Base of the Pyramid; the structural characteristics of supply chains bridging formal and informal contexts; and the governance of transactions involving formal, informal, and illegal actors. His research has been published in leading journals as well as in a variety of academic books.

Jana Schmutzler started as a PhD student at the School of Management of the Universidad de los Andes (Bogotá, Colombia), and is now affiliated with the Schumpeter Business School at the Bergische University of Wuppertal, Germany. Her research interests lie in the area of entrepreneurship and innovation, with a specific focus on collaboration patterns.

M. May Seitanidi (FRSA) is Associate Professor of Strategy at Kent Business School, University of Kent and Visiting Fellow at the International Centre for Corporate Social Responsibility (ICCSR) at Nottingham University Business School, University of Nottingham. She has published extensively on cross-sector social partnerships in academic journals as well as popular press. Her work for over 20 years, as a practitioner and academic, focused on all types of cross-sector social interactions, previously on philanthropy and socio-sponsorship and currently on social partnerships. She was the founder of the Hellenic Sponsorship Centre (1994), the magazine "Sponsors and Sponsorships" (1995), and more recently of a group (2005) on nonprofit-business partnerships with 400 academic and practitioner members interested in partnerships: http://tech.groups.yahoo.com/group/NPO-BUSPartnerships/. In 2007 she founded the International Symposia Series on "Cross Sector Social Interactions" organized by academics at leading universities around the world. Since 2006 she edits the "Annual Review of Social Partnerships" (ARSP) promoting cross-sector collaboration for the social good. She has served as a consultant and trainer for many private, public, and non-governmental organizations. Books include: *The Politics of Partnerships* (2010, short-listed for the SIM 2013 Best Book Award) and *Creating Value in Nonprofit-Business Collaborations: New Thinking & Practice* (2014, co-authored with James E. Austin).

John W. Selsky is an independent scholar and Consulting Fellow of the Institute for Washington's Future (Seattle). He has a long-standing interest in collaborative responses to turbulent organizational environments, and this is the source of his work in both cross-sector partnerships and futures methods. His Master's and doctoral degrees are from the Wharton School, and he has taught in universities in the United States, Australia, New Zealand, and Turkey. He has published in major American and European management journals. His book, *Mastering Turbulence: The Essential Capabilities of Agile and Resilient Individuals, Teams and Organizations* (with Joe McCann), was published by Jossey-Bass in 2012. He is a co-organizer of the Oxford Futures Forum and co-editor (with Rafael Ramirez and Kees van der Heijden) of *Business Planning for Turbulent Times: New Methods for Applying Scenarios* (Earthscan, 2008, rev.ed. 2010). John can be contacted at jselsky@tampabay.rr.com.

Edwin R. Stafford, PhD, is a Professor of Marketing and Co-director of the Center for the Market Diffusion of Renewable Energy and Clean Technology at the Jon M. Huntsman School of Business at Utah State University. He teaches marketing strategy and researches sustainable entrepreneurship, green marketing, and the diffusion of cleantech innovations in the context of cross-sector social partnerships. He and his colleague Cathy L. Hartman are co-principal investigators on a $2.25 million US Department of Energy program to study the diffusion of wind power development in Utah and the West.

Antonio Tencati is Associate Professor of Management at the Department of Economics and Management, Università degli Studi di Brescia, Italy. Between March 2005 and August 2012 he was Assistant Professor of Management and Corporate Social Responsibility at the Department of Management and Technology, Università Bocconi, Milan, with which he continues to collaborate. He is a member of the Steering Committee and a Research Coordinator at CReSV, the Center for Research on Sustainability and Value at Università Bocconi, and a member of the Business Ethics Faculty Group of the CEMS (Community of European Management Schools – The Global Alliance in Management Education). His research areas include business and society, management of sustainability and corporate social responsibility, environmental management, innovation and operations management.

Rob van Tulder is Full Professor of International Business-Society Management at RSM Erasmus University Rotterdam. He holds a PhD (cum laude) in social sciences from the University of Amsterdam. He has been visiting professor at various universities and consultant to international organizations (such as the UN, the IMF, and the European Union), multinational enterprises, non-governmental organizations and ministries around the world. He is co-founder of the Department of Business-Society Management, one of the leading departments in the world researching and teaching on the contribution of business and leaders towards society. Currently he is also Academic Director of the Partnerships Resource Centre (www.partnershipsresourcecentre.org) that studies the cross-sector partnerships between firms, NGOs, and government for sustainable development. He has published in the *California Management Review, Journal of International Business Studies, Journal of Business Ethics, Journal of World Business*. His latest books include: *Managing the Transition to a Sustainable Enterprise. Lessons from Frontrunner companies (2014), Doing Business in Africa (2013), Corporate Responsibilities in Turbulent Times (Beijing 2012, 2010 in Chinese);Skill Sheets: An Integrated Approach to Research, Study and Management*, (Amsterdam, 2012); *International Business-Society Management*, (London, 2006). For more information, see: www.thepartnershipsresourcecentre.org.

Paul Uys was born and educated in South Africa and has 40 years of retail experience. He is currently a Product Development and Responsible Sourcing Consultant, and was until 2013 Vice President, Sustainable Seafood with Loblaw Companies Limited, Canada. At Loblaw he enjoyed various executive roles in their Control Brand division for over 25 years. Previously, as Vice President of Fresh foods, he played a key role in developing the President's Choice and No Name brands, as well introducing the Loblaws Organic program and their healthy eating line-up, President's Choice Blue Menu.

Clodia Vurro is a Post-doctoral fellow in Business Administration and Management at the Department of Management and Technology, Bocconi University. She is also Senior Research Fellow at the Center for Research on Sustainability and Value (CReSV), Bocconi University and SDA Assistant Professor of Strategy and Entrepreneurship at the SDA Bocconi School of Management. Her research areas comprise management of corporate development processes, learning dynamics of sustainability strategy implementation, corporate social responsibility and social entrepreneurship.

Steve Waddell Responding to the twenty-first century's enormous global challenges and realizing that its unsurpassed opportunities require new ways of acting and organizing, for the past 30 years Steve Waddell has been supporting this with organizational, network, and societal change and development. He does this through consultations, education, research, and personal leadership. For the last ten years he has focused largely on multi-stakeholder global change networks (Global Action Networks). Currently he is deeply engaged with development of GOLDEN for Sustainability, a global network of research centers partnering with business and others to accelerate transformation to sustainable enterprise. His publications include Societal *Learning and Change: Innovation with Multi-Stakeholder Strategies* (2005); and *Networking Action: Organizing for the 21st Century* (2011). He has a PhD in sociology and an M.B.A., and is a Canadian-American living in Boston.

Sandra Waddock is Galligan Chair of Strategy, Carroll School Scholar of Corporate Responsibility, and Professor of Management at Boston College's Carroll School of Management. Author of more than 100 papers and ten books, she received the 2004 Sumner Marcus Award for Distinguished Service (Social Issues in Management,

Academy of Management), the 2005 Faculty Pioneer Award for External Impact (Aspen Institute), and in 2011 the David L. Bradford Outstanding Educator Award (Organizational Behavior Teaching Society). She has been a visiting scholar at Harvard Kennedy School (2006–2007; fall 2012) and University of Virginia Darden Graduate School of Business (2000). Current research interests are corporate responsibility and infrastructure, the problem of growth, wisdom, system change, management education, and intellectual shamans. Books include: *Building the Responsible Enterprise* with Andreas Rasche (2012), *SEE Change: Making the Transition to a Sustainable Enterprise Economy* with Malcolm McIntosh (2011), and *The Difference Makers* (2008, SIM Best Book Award, 2011).

Angela Wilkinson is Director of Strategic Foresight with OECD and formerly the Director of Futures Programmes at the Smith School for Enterprise and the Environment, University of Oxford. She has contributed to over 100 futures initiatives, including the direction of several major and ambitious international programs involving public-private partnerships of UN agencies, international NGOs, and multinational companies. Prior to Oxford, Angela spent a decade as a leading member of Shell International's Global Scenario team. She is core faculty on the Oxford Scenarios program and her interest in environmental issues and sustainable enterprise span nearly three decades.

Sarah Winchester was born in South London in 1978 where she still lives. After school she spent nine months in Northern Nepal teaching English in a rural village. She studied Sociology, Social Anthropology, and Social Policy at Newcastle University. After two and a half years working for Red Letter Days, following a road trip around New England with passionate students from Yale's Department of Forestry and Environmental Studies, Sarah was inspired to seek a role in the Third Sector. Her charity career started with ActionAid, followed by two and a half years at Macmillan Cancer Support in their corporate partnerships team. She started at the Prince's Trust seven and a half years ago as a Corporate Partnerships Manager and has worked her way to Deputy Director of Fundraising. She is now responsible for a team of 40 people and over £15 million worth of income from corporations, individual philanthropists, and trusts and foundations.

Christine Ye is an assistant professor of marketing at Westminster College in Salt Lake City, Utah. She holds a PhD in Marketing from the College of Business, Florida State University. She received her Master's degree in Statistics at Yale University and a Bachelor's degree in Marketing from the Kelley School of Business at Indiana University, Bloomington. She is a Society for Marketing Advances Doctoral Consortium fellow and recipient of the Leslie N. Wilson-Delores Auzenne Fellowship at Florida State University. Her research focuses on understanding the role of trust in a firm-customer relationship, particularly in the domain of CSR and e-commerce. She has presented research papers at numerous national conferences including the Association for Consumer Research, American Marketing Association

Educators, Academy of Marketing Science, and Marketing and Public Policy conferences.

Simon Zadek is Visiting Scholar at Tsinghua School of Economics and Management, Senior Fellow at the Global Green Growth Institute and the International Institute for Sustainable Development, and an advisor on sustainability to the World Economic Forum. He was until recently Senior Visiting Fellow at Harvard's John F. Kennedy School of Government and a Senior Fellow at the Centre for International Governance Innovation. He founded and was until 2009 Chief Executive of the think tank, AccountAbility. He publishes extensively through academic channels and the other media. His book, *The Civil Corporation*, was awarded the Academy of Management's prestigious Best Book on Social Issues in Management, and his *Harvard Business Review* article, "Paths to Corporate Responsibility" is widely used as a reference point in understanding emergent sustainability strategies. Simon has advised many of the world's leading corporations in their adoption of sustainability as a fundamental building block of their core strategies, and advises governments on sustainability aspects of economic policy, most recently including China and South Africa.

Laszlo Zsolnai is Professor and Director of the Business Ethics Center at the Corvinus University of Budapest. He is chairman of the Business Ethics Faculty Group of the CEMS (Community of European Management Schools – The Global Alliance in Management Education). He is Editor-in-chief of *Ethical Prospects* published by Springer. He is also editor of the "Frontiers of Business Ethics" book series at Peter Lang Publishers in Oxford. Laszlo Zsolnai was born in 1958, in Szentes, Hungary. He has a Master's degree in Finance and a doctorate in Sociology from the Budapest University of Economic Sciences. He received his PhD and DSc degrees in economics from the Hungarian Academy of Sciences.

ACKNOWLEDGEMENTS

The idea for this book came initially during the organization of the second International Symposium in Cross Sector Social Interactions (CSSI) that took place on 29 April 2010 at Brunel University in London. The inspirational support of Ans Kolk, the stimulating encouragement of Routledge's Terry Clague and the passionate engagement of colleagues during and after the symposium provided the solid foundations for this book. Contributions were originally invited by presenters at the symposium, among whom Cheryl Martens (Chapter 14) was the winner of the Routledge Best Poster Award in Social Partnership Research 2010 at the symposium (CSSI, 2010). After the symposium, we extended invitations to a wider cohort of academics and practitioners who had significant experience in the field in order to cover a broad area of disciplines, contexts and social issues.

We are delighted by the opportunity to develop this volume which would not be possible without the support of various people. We would like to thank Brunel Business School and the Research Centre BRESE for supporting the organization of the second CSSI Symposium, as well as Terry Clague, David Varley and their team at Routledge for their support in the process of developing the handbook. We are also indebted to Shanthini Jeyakumar, Andrew Crane's assistant at the Centre of Excellence in Responsible Business at the Schulich School of Business, whose professionalism in managing communication and deadlines removed a considerable amount of stress from our shoulders.

It is an honour for the volume to be heralded by the foreword of a highly acclaimed academic and recipient of the Lifetime Achievement Award in Collaboration Research (CSSI, 2012), Professor James E. Austin, whose work provided the inspiration for many in this volume and beyond to work in this field. We are grateful for his insights, outstanding leadership and continued inspiration.

Last, but not least, we express our sincere gratitude to all 39 contributors of the Handbook for their outstanding scholarship, enthusiasm and patience in going through several rounds of revisions, sustaining the energy and continuing the reflective dialogue for achieving high quality outcomes in the field of social partnerships that connects and energizes us for the social good. We thank you all.

Reference

CSSI (2012) Press Release. 2nd International Symposium on Cross Sector Social Interactions: Re-imagining partnerships for the global social good, 7 May 2010. Available from http://works.bepress.com/may_seitanidi/25/

HOW TO USE THIS BOOK

This book has been written primarily – but not only – for a research audience. Many readers will be established or emerging scholars looking to understand the existing research around social partnerships and responsible business and to explore the possibilities for extending, refining or redirecting this research. But we have also edited the book with other audiences in mind. For students and teachers, especially those involved with graduate-level masters and PhD courses, we aspire for this volume to be the first comprehensive study text on social partnerships which will help students familiarize themselves with the relevant literature in all its dimensions. For this purpose, we have structured the book into clear sections and stand-alone chapters that can be deployed as weekly introductory subject readings. For practitioners, this should make it fairly easy to dip in and out of areas of interest in the book. Also, examples from practice are used in many of the chapters to aid understanding of how the ideas presented relate to real-life practice, and in Part D, practitioners bring their experience in the field to bear on various facets of social partnerships and responsible business. At the end of each chapter throughout the book, there are also questions for reflection that will help readers of all stripes – researchers, students, practitioners – think about what has just been discussed and its broader implications. In the conclusion we also offer a series of ideas for reimagining social partnerships that can be used to develop your own landscape of possibilities, whoever you are, and regardless of why you have chosen to pick up the book in the first place.

FOREWORD

James E. Austin
Eliot I. Snider and Family Professor of Business
Administration, Emeritus, Harvard Business School

This book is a timely and significant contribution to the field. Over the past three decades we have witnessed the widespread emergence of corporate social responsibility and the accompanying explosive growth of cross-sector partnering. Both practice and research amply confirm that responsible business is smart business. There are, of course, a multitude of actions that businesses should, can, and do take on their own that are socially beneficial. It is equally clear that the capacity to generate social good is greatly magnified when the business, civic, and public sectors combine their complementary capabilities. The magnitude and complexity of many social, environmental and economic problems confronting the world today can only be addressed meaningfully through such partnerships.

There have been enormous advances in our knowledge about cross-sector social partnering, and this book provides a most useful comprehensive examination of the state of the field. In such undertakings three issues are particularly relevant: which disciplinary lens to use in the examination, whether to emphasize theory or practice, whether to focus on the current state or the future. A great strength of this book is the masterful and productive way each of these has been addressed.

As an academic phenomenon and as an area of practice, social partnering is inherently multidisciplinary and interdisciplinary. The book's contributing authors span disciplines and adeptly integrate them. The complementary power of these heterogeneous perspectives and research methods creates broader and deeper comprehension. Furthermore, the analyses operate at multiple levels: global, national, local, and macro, meso, and micro. Thus, the reader will find multiple windows through which to view social partnering, each offering distinct insights and together constituting a tapestry of richer understanding.

Theory and practice are inescapably interdependent. Each feeds the other. In the relatively young and vigorously growing field of social partnering the interaction is even more important. Appropriately, the book examines the theoretical evolution, compares collaborative, competitive and confrontational paradigms, presents new conceptualizations, and identifies remaining gaps. On the applied side, the book covers a wide range of vital issues ranging from key success factors, critical partnering capabilities, brand roles, interaction dynamics, networks, alliance portfolios, govern-ance approaches, and the influence of contextual forces. Rich experiential insights are offered by the practitioner authors. Importantly, the essays also identify the multitude of challenges that confront the search for successful social partnering. Realities continue to test our theoretical constructs.

The book provides a clear picture of where we stand now in terms of research and practice, but additionally it provides provoking visions of what could be. The collective set of "reimaginings" peer into the future and stimulate our thinking about promising paths of exploration for both researchers and practitioners. The potential for co-creating social, environmental, and economic value has not yet been fully tapped. This book contributes importantly to the realization of that vital goal.

1

SOCIAL PARTNERSHIPS AND RESPONSIBLE BUSINESS

What, why and how?

Andrew Crane and M. May Seitanidi

Introduction

Social partnerships – or the joining together of organizations from different sectors of society to tackle social problems – have been widely hailed as a critical tool for addressing an array of serious challenges facing society. Having first emerged in the guise of public private partnerships (PPPs), initially through the involvement of the private sector in local economic development and urban renewal in the 1980s (Wettenhall, 2003), social partnerships have since become both more encompassing in terms of sectors and issues involved, and more expansive in terms of their global reach. Today, social partnerships cross public, non-profit and private sectors in a range of ways and have been used to tackle everything from climate change and resource conservation to health, education, poverty, local development, and even corruption and organized crime.

The growing attention afforded to social partnerships over the past three decades has culminated in what some commentators have referred to as the emergence of a "partnership society" (Googins and Rochlin, 2002), a "partnership paradigm" (Glasbergen, 2007) or even a "trend with no alternative" (Richter, 2004). Although such proclamations may be premature, there is no denying that social partnerships are no longer viewed as such exotic or iconoclastic arrangements as they once were. Indeed, the trend towards more partnerships across sectors, and more substantial and longer-lasting relationships among such partners, has been widely alluded to in the literature. Although with the exception of PPPs (see for example Rufin and Rivera-Santos, 2012) hard data on the prevalence of social partnerships are actually quite hard to come by, the message from researchers is consistent and persuasive. Almost a decade ago, Selsky and Parker (2005: 2) noted that "the number of [cross-sector social partnerships] has grown very rapidly in recent years" whilst LaFrance and Lehmann (2005: 216) suggested that "corporations have been increasingly pursuing partnerships with public institutions including governments, international organizations and NGOs". More recently, Seitanidi and Lindgreen (2010: 1) have suggested that "interactions across sectors have intensified in recent years" and Koschmann *et al.* (2012: 332) have argued that because of their "prevalence and popularity", social partnerships are "often mandated by funders, expected by local communities, and assumed by policy makers to be the best way of working on social problems."

Along with this apparent escalation in the practice of social partnerships has come a growing body of academic literature dedicated to analysing them. For instance, a recent review of the business-non-profit partnership literature by Laasonen *et al.* (2012: 521) reveals a "sharply increasing amount of publications in recent years". Branzei and Le Ber's (2014) chapter in this volume also provides convincing evidence of an expanding literature dealing with cross-sector partnerships across different academic fields. From no more than one or two published articles a year at the turn of the century, they report more than 25 a year since 2010.

Given that we are in the midst of a rapidly expanding field of theory and practice, it is timely to take stock of where we are and to bring some sense of coherence to some of the various proliferating strands of thinking, researching and acting. This Research Handbook is by no means intended to be a comprehensive account of our current stock of knowledge on responsible business and social partnerships, but it does represent an important attempt to bring together some of the most important and influential voices in the debate and to set out some important pathways through an increasingly diverse and multifaceted literature.

In this introductory chapter, our aim is to examine the field of social partnerships and responsible business in terms of three key questions:

1 What are social partnerships and responsible business?
2 Why do we need to provide a new perspective on social partnerships and responsible business?
3 How can we best understand and characterize this emerging field?

What are social partnerships and responsible business?

There are many phenomena that might or might not be regarded as social partnerships. Much depends on how we define them and where we set the parameters for inclusion and exclusion. At the outset of this chapter we briefly referred to social partnerships as "the joining together of organizations from different sectors of society to tackle social problems". Although this works as a useful summary, it is not precise enough to define the phenomenon with any degree of certainty. What do we mean by "joining together"? Which "different sectors" are we talking about? And what constitutes a "social problem"?

This definitional problem is compounded by the diversity of terminology that is used to refer to a set of overlapping phenomena. Whilst in this book, we primarily refer to social partnerships and cross-sector social partnerships (which we use interchangeably), others refer to "multi-stakeholder" partnerships or relationships (Everett and Jamal, 2004; Pinkse and Kolk, 2012), "cross-sector collaborations" (Bryson *et al.*, 2006), "cross-sector social interactions" (Seitanidi and Lindgreen, 2010), "social alliances" (Berger *et al.*, 2004) or other such variants. Some authors also prefer to examine a sub-set of the phenomenon such as business-non-profit partnerships, or public-private partnerships rather than the whole gamut of cross-sectoral relations.

Extant research on social partnerships has sought to clarify some of these ambiguities. Looking first to the question of what "joining together" means, Austin's (2000) elaboration of the collaboration continuum suggests that we can conceive of interaction as stretching from simple one-way financial or *philanthropic* support, through to two-way *transactional* relationships around specific activities, all the way up to *integrative* strategic alliances and, more recently, to transformational collaborations (Austin and Seitanidi, 2012a and Austin and Seitanidi, 2012b). In this book, we are concerned specifically with the latter two stages of Austin's continuum. This is because the defining characteristic of social *partnerships* are that they require "involvement in the planning and implementation of activities by two or more organizations", "joint-problem solving of participants" and "a resource commitment from all partners" (Waddock, 1991: 483). That is, social partnerships are defined here according to the level of engagement of the participants. Not all relationships across sectors are social partnerships – i.e. they are a specific form of relationship involving a relatively high level of engagement for a considerable amount of time.

The question of which sectors we are referring to under the rubric of social partnerships is also worthy of elaboration. In general, there are four types of cross-sectoral social partnerships – business-non-profit, business-government (also called public-private partnerships), government-non-profit, and tri-partite partnerships that cross all three sectors. As shown in Figure 1.1, we are only concerned in this book with three of these four types, namely partnerships involving business. One reason for this is that our own disciplinary expertise is located in the realm of business and management, and so the partnerships between companies and other social actors is our customary point of departure. Similarly, as Branzei and Le Ber (2014) note in their analysis of the literature in Chapter 12, the business and management field has been the primary source of published research on cross-sector partnerships in recent years. It is also notable that business is itself becoming an increasingly dominant social institution, involved not just in economic activities, but in much broader social, environmental and political affairs. Hence, relationships between businesses and other social actors have taken on a wider significance, including a shift towards greater attention to corporate social responsibility and making a difference (Waddock, 2010) and a "hollowing out" of the state (Skelcher, 2000) with greater private sector involvement in broader societal governance (Cashore, 2002; Matten and Crane, 2005; Pattberg, 2005; Ronit, 2001).

This also explains why, as our title indicates, it is partnerships in the area of *responsible business* that form the principal focus for this book. Businesses can sometimes participate in cross-sector partnerships without any real need to engage

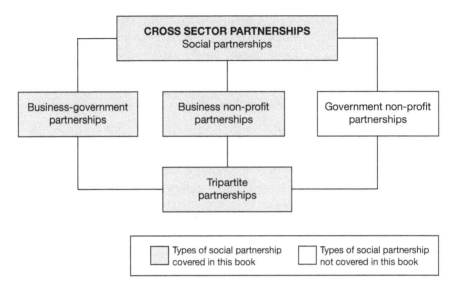

FIGURE 1.1 Types of social partnerships
Adapted from Seitanidi and Crane, 2009

with any notion of responsibility. This would be the case, for example, in private finance initiatives (PFI) whereby companies provide finance for public sector infrastructure projects, typically through debt and/or equity, and then may also provide operational services under contract, but would not typically be involved in decisions regarding the social impact or outcomes of the project. However, the involvement of business in social partnerships is more commonly associated with an explicit attention to the social role and responsibilities of companies.

One approach here is to view partnerships as a means of implementing social responsibility strategies (Husted, 2003; Seitanidi and Crane, 2009; Walters and Anagnostopoulos, 2012). Indeed, partnerships have become a well-established feature of the theory and practice of CSR, such that many CSR textbooks and handbooks will include a chapter or sections on partnerships (e.g. Crane, *et al.*, 2013; Haynes *et al.*, 2013; Kotler and Lee, 2008) whilst companies reporting on their social performance will almost always report on at least some of their cross-sector partnerships.

An alternative perspective would view partnerships as a site where new responsibilities emerge (Seitanidi, 2008). That is, engagement in partnerships brings companies into different territory, raises expectations, and exposes them to new risks. As a result, conceptions of companies' social responsibilities can be reshaped through the practice of partnership. The key point here is that, regardless of approach, our concern is with questions that extend beyond businesses simply fulfilling their contractual obligations in providing finance or building public infrastructure. Rather, we see social partnerships as a site for the expression of responsible business and indeed as a critical lens in which to explore the changing nature and extent of business responsibilities for the social good.

Considerations of the social good bring us to the last of our three initial definitional questions, namely what constitutes a "social problem". The first point to note here is that we are specifically concerned with partnerships focused on addressing social issues – i.e. they must in some way be identified with "a public policy agenda item" (Waddock, 1991: 482). Additionally, although parties may collaborate to address such a problem for self-interested reasons (e.g. a firm may wish to enhance its brand, a government department may be exploring new sources of revenue or a non-profit may be seeking to attract members), a social partnership also requires the articulation of social goals that extend beyond the self-interested goals of the partners (Austin, 2000; Austin and Seitanidi, 2012a; Austin and Seitanidi, 2012b; Seitanidi, 2010) – such as forest protection, provision of affordable housing or guaranteeing human rights. It is this combination of organizational-level and societal-level outcomes that represents one of the most interesting, but most challenging aspects, in both the theory and practice of social partnerships. Therefore, in this book, our concern is with the multi-level outcomes of social partnerships, but with a strong emphasis on how partnerships contribute to the social good. After all, the common ground of cross-sector collaborative efforts is an "imperative to realise benefits for the wider community rather than for special interests" (Skelcher and Sullivan, 2002: 752).

Why do we need to provide a new perspective on social partnerships and responsible business?

There is already considerable literature on social partnerships and responsible business, as well as some excellent review articles assessing the state of the field (e.g. Austin and Seitanidi, 2012a; Austin and Seitanidi, 2012b; Bovaird, 2004; Kourula and Laasonen, 2010; Laasonen et al., 2012; Selsky and Parker, 2005). So why do we need a major research handbook such as this now, and what do we hope to bring that will be unique or unusual?

The most important factor to account for here is that whilst the phenomenon of social partnerships is sufficiently well established that some already speak of a partnership paradigm, there is not a similarly well established scholarly field. In fact, we can characterize social partnerships as essentially *a phenomenon without a field*. This is because the study of social partnerships has taken place in many different disciplines and sub-areas of academic inquiry, often without a shared set of core ideas, concepts or foundational works. Researchers have explored social partnerships from core disciplines of politics and public policy, international relations, development studies, law, business and management, environmental studies, and third sector studies, among others. Even within these disciplines, there is often considerable fragmentation in the scholarly literature with, for example, alternative perspectives being developed in politics from those interested in global governance and those more concerned with new public management. Similarly in management studies, researchers in marketing, strategy, international business, business ethics, and other sub-fields have all explored social partnerships, often with quite limited interaction across the different silos.

Compounding this issue of fragmentation is the fact that, as yet, there is no journal specifically dedicated to social partnerships research, which means that relevant articles are often to be found in disparate publications. Some recent special issues on the subject in journals such as *The Social and Economic Review* (see Ó Riain, 2006), the *Journal of Business Ethics* (see Seitanidi and Lindgreen, 2010) and *Science and Public Policy* (see Turpin and Fernández-Esquinas, 2011) have provided important focal points for research contributions in different disciplines, but these remain the exceptions. So, to date, there is little sense of a well-defined or unified field. Social partnerships remains an emerging scholarly field characterized by intersecting disciplinary lenses.

This state of emergence is also reflected in courses about social partnerships. There are as yet few dedicated courses on the subject, although there have been some limited offerings over the past decade. The University of Cambridge has offered for many years a Postgraduate Certificate in Cross Sector Partnership, whilst the University of Limerick has offered an entire master's degree in Partnership Studies. The Sam M. Walton College of Business and the J. William Fulbright College of Arts and Sciences at the University of Arkansas jointly offer a for-credit master's certificate program in "Cross sector alliances: public, private and nonprofit collaboration" aiming to help future managers from different types of organizations to work together better (Hyatt, 2012). In addition, Portland State University and the Tuck School of Business at Dartmouth College both offer MBA modules dealing with cross-sector partnerships whilst the School of Oriental and Asian Studies at the University of London and the School of Public Affairs at the University of Washington both run courses on public-private partnerships. These are a few examples of a very small but slowly growing collection of specialized courses on social partnerships, but it is worth remembering that partnerships also increasingly feature as a component in a wide range of more general courses, whether in business schools (e.g. courses on CSR, business ethics and strategic management), politics departments (e.g. courses on governance, public policy or public management), geography and environmental studies (e.g. courses on urban regeneration, regional development or sustainable development) and elsewhere.

All this suggests that social partnership does not yet have the features of a distinct academic field – but it also makes the present moment a good time to take stock of the literature and assess where we are and where we are going. At this early stage in its development, it is clear that there have been many important discoveries but also that there are still many gaps in our knowledge about social partnerships. The extant literature has been relatively successful in determining types or forms of social partnership, the antecedents or drivers of social partnerships, some of the different stages that partnerships go through (e.g. design, formation, implementation, and evaluation) as well as assessments of relevant outcomes. A number of scholars have advanced models which seek to capture the phenomenon of social partnerships in a relatively comprehensive way (e.g. Bryson *et al.*, 2006; Gray, 1989; Seitanidi and Crane, 2009), as well as more focused studies of specific stages or critical dynamics (e.g. Seitanidi *et al.*, 2010). There have also been numerous descriptive studies examining specific cases of social partnerships in more detail as well as critical studies examining the societal implications of social partnerships. These have ranged from studies looking at governance (Crane, 2011; Dahan *et al.*, 2010; Rivera-Santos and Rufin, 2010), to value creation (Austin, 2010; Austin and Seitanidi, 2012a; Austin and Seitanidi, 2012b; Le Ber and Branzei, 2010), change (Seitanidi, 2010; Seitanidi *et al.*, 2010; Waddock, 2010), and social justice (Cornelius and Wallace, 2010), among others.

To date, much of the empirical work in the area has been exploratory and case-study based. This has provided numerous important new insights into the emerging phenomenon, but has left us short of much by way of confirmed hypotheses from which we can make definite predictions. Therefore, one major risk at this stage is to take for granted the "received wisdom" that has already built up around social partnerships, but which hasn't been subjected to rigorous empirical testing. This includes assumptions that social partnerships are necessarily the best solution for complex social problems, that partners from different sectors always have cultural differences, the effective CSR requires social partnerships, or even that getting social partnerships right is especially difficult. Of course, these assumptions might be correct, but we simply do not yet have a sufficient body of robust empirical work to demonstrate it with any certainty.

In this book we aim to examine some of this received wisdom by summarizing existing knowledge, as well as bringing new research into the public domain. We take stock of the state-of-the-art research in the field of social partnerships within business and management in order to demonstrate the dimensions, attributes, stages, challenges, methods, theories and practices in social partnerships. Our ultimate goal in all this is to consider the case for *reimagining* social partnerships. That is, given what we already know about social partnerships, should we seek to simply continue on the same path or is it time for some kind of redirection? This is especially germane to our evaluation of social partnerships as contributing to the broader social good – namely, are our existing approaches to thinking about, researching and practising social partnerships sufficient to ensure that genuine social progress is made or do we need new theories, new research methods and new practices? Certainly, for all the hype around them, social partnerships have also received ample criticism on a wide range of issues which suggest that they consist of mechanisms for "window dressing", "green washing" (Kolk and van Tulder, 2005) and "marketing spin-offs" (Crane, 1998). Critics have questioned their democratic performance, transparency, account-ability and openness (Skelcher and Sullivan, 2008); they have highlighted their lack of transferability, mainstreaming and knowledge transfer (Williams and Sullivan, 2009); and have assessed them to be unsystematic and unsustainable (Seitanidi and Crane, 2009). It is clearly time to take stock and evaluate the current trajectory.

How can we understand and characterize the emerging field of social partnerships and responsible business?

As with any area of scholarly research that it still in its relatively early stages, there are numerous ways that we can map out the relevant areas of interest. Without trying to be exhaustive, in this book, we have elected to focus on the four subject areas that we believe provide a good overall introduction to the theory and practice of social partnerships for any researcher interested in this emerging field – and which also provide a solid foundation for its reimagining. Following this introduction, the book is structured into four sections, focusing on contexts, management, theory/method, and practice respectively.

Local, national and global perspectives on social partnerships (Part A). Social partnerships have emerged at various regional levels – and these different contexts give rise to distinct issues and problems as well as particular theoretical and empirical approaches. At a local or regional level, cross-sector partnerships has been explored as a means for, among other things, urban regeneration, economic development, municipal service provision, and community engagement. Local perspectives on partnerships therefore often analyse their potential for, on the one hand, generating efficiencies in service delivery, and on the other, enabling meaningful participation among local communities. At a national level, considerable interest in partnerships has been driven by their emergence in developed countries that have embraced neo-liberal reforms which have resulted in a rolling back of the state and an opening up of welfare service provision to private and civil actors. In developing economies, by contrast, partnerships have been seen as a potential solution to institutional voids in the provision of public goods and the protection of human rights. At the global level, social partnerships have increasingly been positioned as an effective response to complex social problems such as poverty, food security and climate change that cannot be solved by actors from any single sector alone.

Some of the major themes cutting across these different contexts include the shift from public to private authority, the move to market-based and network forms of societal governance, and the development of partnership culture and rhetoric across the sectors. Perhaps most critically though is the question of whether in fact partnerships do actually make a positive contribution to the social good. The contributions in Part A will assess this question from a number of different vantage points, as well as documenting some of the reasons and implications of the emergence of partnerships in various contexts and exploring the key challenges that lie ahead.

Management and governance challenges (Part B). The second part of the book examines some of the key management and governance challenges faced in developing social partnerships. As a relatively new area of practice, social partnerships raise some quite unique management challenges, but there is also quite a lot that can be learnt from our existing stock of knowledge about management practice. In this section, our contributors will address questions such as how organizations develop portfolios of different partnerships to solve particular sets of problems, how social partnerships can be leveraged to create brand value, how conflict is managed in social partnerships and what role entrepreneurship can take in the emergence and institutionalization of cross-sector partnerships. They will also address questions regarding the governance structures necessary for ensuring that partnerships are effective and accountable to those they are supposed to serve. We have selected these particular areas both because they reflect some of the most critical challenges faced by managers of social partnerships in practice, and also because they help to connect up social partnerships research with specific areas of management theory such as marketing, entrepreneurship, corporate strategy, corporate governance, and organizational studies.

Theory and methods (Part C). The third part of the book explores some of the ways in which we have sought to understand social partnerships through different theoretical lenses and methodological approaches, and how we might recast our understanding of partnerships in the future. To date, research on social partnerships has been primarily driven by several different theoretical approaches. According to Selsky and Parker (2005), research has tended to be dominated by resource-dependence perspectives (i.e. organizations collaborate because they lack critical resources such as competencies possessed by actors in other sectors), social issues management (which focuses on the nature and evolution of social in issues and organizations' responses to them) and a societal sector approach (which takes as its starting point the blurring of boundaries between the sectors and its implications). Similarly, as we mentioned earlier, research methods have tended to rely on conceptual and case-study approaches.

Our aim in Part C is to provide an analysis of this extant research (Chapter 12) and to explore some promising avenues where it might be possible to reimagine social partnerships in new and interesting ways. This includes new methodologies such as futures methods (Chapter 13), and new theoretical approaches such as Foucauldian-inspired studies of governmentality in social partnership (Chapter 14). We also explore the potential that lies in an institutional theory perspective since this is fast becoming a dominant paradigm in responsible business research (Chapter 15). Finally, we address the question of whether in fact we need an entirely new theory of the firm to address "partnership society" in a more fundamental way (Chapter 16).

Perspectives on practice (Part D). The final part of the book takes us from theory to practice. As a phenomenon without a field, much of the literature on social partnerships has been phenomenon-driven rather than theory-driven. Therefore it makes sense even in a research handbook to explore what we can learn from the current practice of social partnerships and what might lie in store for the future. To do this, we have assembled one academic highly engaged in practice, and eight practitioners to explore the praxis of social partnerships – namely what researchers can learn from practice and vice-versa. These shorter-length contributions from practitioners highly experienced in designing, implementing and writing about cross-sector partnerships provide some unique insights into current developments from a range of different perspectives and offer the opportunity for researchers as well as practitioners to re-imagine partnerships for the future.

A note on Wordles

In order to capture in a summative and aesthetic way the themes of these sections we present a Wordle at the beginning of each.[1] A Wordle is a word cloud representing the relative frequency of words in a given text (in our case, all the chapters in the respective section). Wordles enable "viewers to have an overview of the main topics and the main themes in a text, and may illustrate the main standpoints held by the writer of the text" (McNaught and Lam, 2010: 630) A Wordle is thus a visualization of the ideas presented in a text and can be used as a "toy" (Feinberg, 2013), a medium for expression and participation (Viegas *et al.*, 2009) and as a supplementary research tool (McNaught and Lam, 2010). Our aim was to provide a visual representation of the main themes of each section that would summarize, inspire, surprise and hopefully provoke further insights for the reimagining of social partnerships and responsible business.

Conclusion

In this chapter we have sought to provide a brief but hopefully illuminating introduction to social partnerships and responsible business, to set out why we believe this book offers a valuable and unique perspective on the subject, and to explain the constituent parts of the book and how they give us a compelling and comprehensive way of understanding the broad field of research. In the conclusion of the book, we will revisit some of these themes and set out some of the key learnings that can be gleaned from the chapters to come – and perhaps most critically of all, tease out some of the ways that we really might be able to reimagine social partnerships for the twenty-first century.

Note

1 To construct the Wordles we have excluded the titles and author names, the abstracts, the questions at the end of each chapter, and the footnotes. Words such as introduction, conclusion and discussion were also eliminated. Section A comprised a total of 28,376 words, Section B – 43,355, Section C – 29,203 and Section D – 14,245 words.

References

Austin, J.E. (2000) *The Collaboration Challenge: How Nonprofits and Businesses Succeed Through Strategic Alliances.* San Francisco, CA: Jossey-Bass.

Austin, J.E. (2010) From organization to organization: on creating value. *Journal of Business Ethics*, 94 (Supplement 1): 13–15.

Austin, J.E. and Seitanidi, M.M. (2012a) Collaborative value creation: a review of partnering between nonprofits and businesses. Part 2: Partnership processes and outcomes. *Nonprofit and Voluntary Sector Quarterly*, 41: 929–68.

Austin, J.E. and Seitanidi, M.M. (2012b) Collaborative value creation: a review of partnering between nonprofits and businesses: Part I: Value creation spectrum and collaboration stages. *Nonprofit and Voluntary Sector Quarterly*, 41: 726–58.

Berger, I.E., Cunningham, P.H. and Drumwright, M.E. (2004) Social alliances: company/nonprofit collaboration. *California Management Review*, 47 (1): 58–90.

Bovaird, T. (2004) Public-private partnerships: from contested concepts to prevalent practice. *International Review of Administrative Sciences,* 70 (2): 199–215.

Branzei, O. and Le Ber, M.J. (2014) Theory-method interfaces in cross-sector partnership research, in M.M. Seitanidi and A. Crane (eds) *Social Partnerships and Responsible Business: A Research Handbook*. London: Routledge: 229–66.

Bryson, J.M., Crosby, B.C. and Stone, M.M. (2006) The design and implementation of cross-sector collaborations: propositions from the literature. *Public Administration Review*, 66: 44–55.

Cashore, B. (2002) Legitimacy and the privatization of environmental governance: how non-state market-driven (NSMD) governance systems gain rule-making authority. *Governance*, 15 (4): 503–29.

Cornelius, N. and Wallace, J. (2010) Cross-sector partnerships: city regeneration and social justice. *Journal of Business Ethics*, 94 (Supplement 1): 71–84.

Crane, A. (1998) Exploring green alliances. *Journal of Marketing Management*, 14 (6), 559–79.

Crane, A. (2011) From governance to Governance: on blurring boundaries. *Journal of Business Ethics*, 94 (Supplement 1): 17–19.

Crane, A., Matten, D. and Spence, L.J. (2013) *Corporate Social Responsibility: Readings and Cases in a Global Context* (2nd edn.). London: Routledge.

Dahan, N.M., Doh, J. and Teegen, H. (2010) Role of nongovernmental organizations in the business-government-society interface: special issue overview and introductory essay. *Business and Society*, 35 (1): 567–9.

Everett, J. and Jamal, T.B. (2004) Multistakeholder collaboration as symbolic marketplace and pedagogic practice. *Journal of Management Inquiry*, 13 (1): 57–78.

Feinberg, J. (2013) Wordle: www.wordle.net

Fransen, L.W. and Kolk, A. (2007) Global rule-setting for business: a critical analysis of multi-stakeholder standards. *Organization*, 14 (5): 667–84.

Glasbergen, P. (2007) Setting the scene: the partnership paradigm in the making, in P. Glasbergen, F. Biermann and A.P.J. Mol (eds) *Partnerships, Governance and Sustainable Development: Reflections on Theory and Practice*: 1–25. Cheltenham: Edward Elgar.

Googins, B.K. and Rochlin, S.A. (2002) Creating the partnership society: understanding the rhetoric and reality of cross-sectoral partnerships. *Business and Society Review*, 105 (1): 127–44.

Gray, B. (1989) *Collaborating: Finding Common Ground for Multiparty Problems*. San Francisco, CA: Jossey-Bass.

Haynes, K., Murray, A. and Dillard, J. (2013) *Corporate social responsibility. A research handbook*. London and New York: Routledge.

Husted, B.W. (2003) Governance choices for corporate social responsibility: to contribute, collaborate or internalize? *Long Range Planning*, 36 (5): 481–98.

Hyatt, D.G. (2012) Collaborating to empower collaboration: an academic approach. *Annual Review of Social Partnerships*, 7: 25–6.

Kolk, A. and van Tulder, R. (2005) Setting new global rules? *Transnational Corporations*, 14 (3): 1–17.

Koschmann, M.A., Kuhn, T.R. and Pfarrer, M.D. (2012) A communicative framework of value in cross-sector partnerships. *Academy of Management Review*, 37 (3): 332–54.

Kotler, P. and Lee, N. (2008) *Corporate Social Responsibility: Doing the Most Good for Your Company and Your Cause*. Hoboken, NJ: John Wiley and Sons.

Kourula, A. and Laasonen, S. (2010) Nongovernmental organizations in business and society, management, and international business research – review and implications from 1998 to 2007. *Business and Society*, 49 (1): 35–67.

Laasonen, S., Fougère, M. and Kourula, A. (2012) Dominant articulations in academic business and society discourse on NGO-business relations: a critical assessment. *Journal of Business Ethics*, 109 (4): 521–45.

LaFrance, J. and Lehmann, M. (2005) Corporate awakening – why (some) corporations embrace public-private partnerships. *Business Strategy and the Environment*, 14 (4): 216–29.

Le Ber, M.J. and Branzei, O. (2010) Towards a critical theory of value creation in cross-sector partnerships. *Organization*, 17 (5): 599–629.

Matten, D. and Crane, A. (2005) Corporate citizenship: towards an extended theoretical conceptualization. *Academy of Management Review*, 30 (1): 166–79.

McNaught, C. and Lam, P. (2010) Using Wordle as a supplementary research tool. *The Qualitative Report*, 15 (3): 630–43.

Ó Riain, S. (2006) Social partnership as a mode of governance: introduction to the special issue. *The Economic and Social Review*, 37 (3): 311–18.

Pattberg, P. (2005) The institutionalization of private governance: how business and nonprofit organizations agree on transnational rules. *Governance*, 18 (4): 589–610.

Pinkse, J. and Kolk, A. (2012) Addressing the climate change-sustainable development nexus: the role of multistakeholder partnerships. *Business and Society*, 51 (1): 176–210.

Richter, J. (2004) Public-private partnerships for health: a trend with no alternatives? *Development*, 47 (2): 43–8.

Rivera-Santos, M. and Rufin, C. (2010) Odd couples: understanding the governance of firm-NGO alliances. *Journal of Business Ethics*, 94 (Supplement 1): 55–70.

Ronit, K. (2001) Institutions of private authority in global governance. *Administration and Society*, 33 (5): 555–78.

Rufin, C. and Rivera-Santos, M. (2012) Between commonweal and competition: understanding the governance of public-private partnerships. *Journal of Management*, 38 (5): 1634–54.

Seitanidi, M.M. (2008) Adaptive responsibilities: non-linear interactions across social sectors. Cases from cross sector partnerships. *Emergence: Complexity and Organization*, 10 (3): 51–64.

Seitanidi, M.M. (2010) *The politics of partnerships: a critical examination of nonprofit-business partnerships*. Dordrecht: Springer.

Seitanidi, M.M. and Crane, A. (2009) Implementing CSR through partnerships: understanding the selection, design and institutionalization of nonprofit-business partnerships. *Journal of Business Ethics*, 85: 413–29.

Seitanidi, M.M. and Lindgreen, A. (2010) Editorial: cross-sector social interactions. *Journal of Business Ethics*, 94: 1–7.

Seitanidi, M.M., Koufopoulos, D.N. and Palmer, P. (2010) Partnership formation for change: indicators for transformative potential in cross sector social partnerships. *Journal of Business Ethics*, 94 (Supplement 1): 139–61.

Selsky, J.W. and Parker, B. (2005) Cross-sector partnerships to address social issues: challenges to theory and practice. *Journal of Management*, 31 (6): 1–25.

Skelcher, C. (2000) Changing images of the state: overloaded, hollowed-out, congested. *Public Policy and Administration*, 15 (3): 3–19.

Skelcher, C. and Sullivan H. (2002) *Working Across Boundaries. Collaboration in Public Services.* Basingstoke: Palgrave Macmillan.

Skelcher, C. and Sullivan, H. (2008) Theory-driven approaches to analysing collaborative performance. *Public Management Review*, 10 (6): 751–71.

Turpin, T. and Fernández-Esquinas, M. (2011) The policy rationale for cross-sector research collaboration and contemporary consequences. *Science and Public Policy*, 38 (2): 82–6.

Viegas, F.B., Wattenberg, M. and Feinberg, J. (2009) Participatory visualization with Wordle. *Visualization and Computer Graphics, IEEE Transactions On*, 15 (6): 1137–44.

Waddock, S.A. (1991) A typology of social partnership organizations. *Administration and Society*, 22 (4): 480–515.

Waddock, S.A. (2010) From Individual to Institution: on making the world different. *Journal of Business Ethics*, 94 (Supplement 1): 9–12.

Walters, G. and Anagnostopoulos, C. (2012) Implementing corporate social responsibility through social partnerships. *Business Ethics: A European Review*, 21 (4): 417–33.

Wettenhall, R. (2003) The rhetoric and reality of public-private partnerships. *Public Organization Review*, 3 (1): 77–107.

Williams, P. and Sullivan, H. (2009) Faces of integration. *International Journal of Integrated Care*, 9: 1–19.

PART A

Partnership for the social good?

Local, national and global perspectives

2

PARTNERSHIPS AS PANACEA FOR ADDRESSING GLOBAL PROBLEMS?

On rationale, context, actors, impact and limitations

Ans Kolk

Introduction

To address complex social and environmental problems that often cross boundaries and cannot easily be solved by one single actor, a multitude of partnerships has emerged, involving government agencies, companies, and non-governmental organizations (NGOs). The past decades have seen a rapid growth and spread of several types of cross-sector[1] collaboration: public-nonprofit, public-private,[2] private-nonprofit, and tripartite partnerships. Particularly tripartite forms of collaboration, that combine the competences, skills and expertise of the three different types of actors, have been regarded as most suitable for the "wicked" issues at stake, because they are supposedly able to overcome their individual limitations (Austin, 2000a; Kolk *et al.*, 2008; Warner and Sullivan, 2004). These include market failures, governance failures and good intentions, failures resulting from respectively single-actor corporate, public and nonprofit activities (Kolk *et al.*, 2008; OECD, 2006). Partnerships have thus been hailed for their ability to address several existing "gaps" related to regulation, participation, implementation, resources, and learning (e.g. Fransen and Kolk, 2007; Pattberg *et al.*, 2012; Pinkse and Kolk, 2012), or, using a twofold categorization that captures comparable aspects, to counter a democratic (or legitimate) as well as an implementation (or effectiveness) deficit (Bäckstrand, 2006a; Schäferhoff *et al.*, 2009).

This chapter presents and discusses research insights from various disciplines, and their limitations thus far in shedding light on the multi-faceted nature of partnerships that aim to address global problems. It exposes the complexities of actor categorizations and collaborations, of partnership contexts, and of impact at different interaction levels. First, however, a more generic overview of the rationale for partnerships is given, considering role, functions and drivers, and advantages for different actors involved in general, not specifically geared to the global context. This helps to set the stage for the further sections that consider partnerships for addressing global problems. It should be noted that partnerships as discussed in this chapter do not need to entail "global" solutions or be comprehensively global in nature (e.g. at the global level); rather the focus is on partnerships that address complex global problems such as climate change, food security, and more broadly poverty and underdevelopment. This means that a single (Northern) company can be involved in such a partnership, e.g. to help reduce child mortality in a developing country, which is a global problem (included in the Millennium Development Goals and prevalent in many countries). Accordingly, with this macro objective, meso and micro considerations of the partnership (embodied, respectively, in the interorganizational collaboration with e.g. an NGO, and the involvement of its employees and customers) are relevant as well, as these are geared to helping address, in the end, a global problem.

The role of partnerships

Partnerships fulfil specific functions, for which many, often slightly different, classifications have been used (see e.g. Andanova *et al.*, 2009; Bäckstrand, 2008; Beisheim, 2012; Pattberg *et al.* 2012; Schäferhoff *et al.* 2009). The range is indicated by Schäferhoff *et al.* (2009: 457) who refer to functions "from advocacy and awareness-raising, knowledge exchange, research and development, standard-setting and implementation, to service provision, and the creation of markets." As an illustration of how this variety had been made concrete for specific academic and/or practical purposes, Table 2.1 contains information from different sources. The top part (A) shows a list of functions of the partnerships for sustainable development that were adopted in the context of the international discussions related to the Millennium Development Goals, while the subsequent part (1B) distinguishes three types of partnerships, also focused on sustainable development in this same realm. C gives an overview of partnership types as identified in surveys amongst practitioners involved in business-NGO collaboration, and D to related motivations for collaboration. Together they exemplify, respectively, a more governance-oriented approach that starts from the role of government (A and B), and a rather practical one focused on concrete partnership foci of companies and NGOs (C and D). They represent perspectives that will be discussed later in this chapter as well, where relevant.

The role of governments, and thus their "failure", deserves specific attention given that they have traditionally been seen as responsible for "solving" societal problems or, put differently, for providing collective goods. One of the oldest definitions of the partnership concept from a management scholar likewise underlines that actors "cooperatively attempt to solve a problem or issue of mutual concern that is in some way identified with a public policy agenda item" (Waddock, 1991: 481–2). Partnerships have thus often emerged in response to inadequate or failed attempts at regulation, for example, because government instruments are too "blunt"/broad for the complex peculiarities of an issue that also frequently covers multiple jurisdictions, with regulatory processes taking very long, sometimes related to political sensitivities that hamper a more effective approach. There may also be situations in which public benefits can be realized much more efficiently through a collaborative involvement

TABLE 2.1 Examples of partnerships' functions, types, motivations

A. Functions of partnerships for sustainable development (as registered at the United Nations)

- Production of knowledge, information, innovation
- Dissemination of knowledge and good practices
- Technical implementation
- Institutional capacity building
- Norm and standard setting, and certification
- Campaigning for public awareness and education
- Lobby and advocacy
- Technology transfer
- Participatory management and community involvement in policy programs
- Training of employees or other actors
- Planning at national or regional levels

B. Types of international partnerships for sustainable development

- *Knowledge partnerships*: generate, pool and transfer expertise, best practices and formulate proposals
- *Standard-setting partnerships*: drawing up voluntary rules in areas where there are none, sometimes also involving certification of the (new) standards
- *Service partnerships:* focus on initiating and realizing project to implement development goals, thus filling operational gaps, and distributing resources and services

C. Types of partnerships in which companies and NGOs are most often involved

- *'Social investment'* type partnerships: providing/receiving support via donations of cash, products, gifts in kind, employee fundraising
- *'Capacity building'* type partnerships: focused on empowerment, sustaining/bringing about behavioral change, via employee engagement, institution building
- *'Business'* type partnerships: advisory services to improve business/organizational practices, social business development, social or commercial, alternative technology or product development
- *'Marketing'* type partnerships: cause-related marketing, product licensing, sponsorship
- *'Advocacy'* type partnerships: issues-driven partnerships/campaigns, aimed at changing business practices or policy
- *'Brokering'* type partnerships: facilitating large-scale initiatives, bringing together a range of players, also at local levels, to e.g. match expertise or other contributions
- *'Other'* partnerships: initiatives that are highly innovative, unexpected and 'ahead of the evidence'

D. Reasons for companies and NGOs to engage in partnerships

- Gain access to knowledge, expertise, skills, networks, contacts
- Gain access to funding
- Improve/renew understanding of challenging issues and possible (innovative) solutions
- Improve stakeholder relations
- Improve reputation and credibility
- Increase operational efficiencies
- Create more appropriate services and products (for-profit or not-for-profit)
- Gain access to and/or knowledge of new (future) markets
- Gain access to and more insight into business operations, current markets, and supply chains
- Increase leverage/impact
- Increase motivation of and attractiveness to (new) staff members and/or volunteers
- Improve risk management

Sources: Compiled from Pattberg *et al.* (2012: 9) (A); Beisheim (2012) (B); C&E (2010, 2011); Tennyson and Harrison (2008) (C); plus, for D, other sources such as Elkington and Fennell (1998); Rondinelli and London (2003).

of companies. On the other hand, particularly companies may engage in partnerships in an attempt to pre-empt regulation, as they tend to prefer voluntary action to externally-imposed (legal) requirements. Concurrently, partnerships can also help cover things that may otherwise have remained "unregulated." Examples include climate change activities for other than the most polluting sectors or in countries that are not part of international agreements; and reduction of water use, which companies now sometimes tackle via voluntary collaboration in their global supply chain and/or with other actors. In this way, partnerships may, if effective, sometimes even reduce the need for (further) regulation, or help reshape the arrangements (to be) put in place.

Hence, specifically vis-à-vis the role government, there is a variety of possible situations: partnerships may "replace" regulation (i.e. instead of having regulation, partnerships function); they can pre-empt regulation, but also precede it (i.e. set the stage); and they can "follow" or supplement regulation (thus have more of an implementation role). In addition, regulation may sometimes be needed to enable partnerships. Finally, partnerships can include regulators, be it as direct participants or through more indirect involvement. The latter may consist of, for example, providing expertise, supporting services, facilitating implementation, brokering, convening, delivery and outreach. The variety of degrees of government involvement has been captured in a continuum of governance forms, with, on one extreme, public regulation (without real involvement of other, private actors[3]), and private self-regulation, without public actors, on the other end (Bäckstrand, 2008). Except for public regulation, partnerships may play a role in all the other variants, in which involvement of government declines with each "step," while those of other actors increases.

Rather separate from the link to government, companies and NGOs may have their own additional reasons for engaging in partnerships, as part of a broad conglomerate of aspects mentioned (e.g. Austin, 2000b; Selsky and Parker, 2005; Van Huijstee *et al.,* 2007). Part D in Table 2.1 summarizes the main motivations that have come to the fore in the business-NGO context, and which relate to types of partnerships in C. For both parties, there are reasons related to increased access to knowledge, experience, networks and resources, that may translate into innovative new products, services or solutions, better abilities to envision future developments or higher operational efficiencies (more optimal use of current resources and methods). Mentioned as well are greater leverage and impact, and a possibly improved reputation and credibility amongst internal and external stakeholders. It should be noted that the importance of the aspects listed in Table 2.1(D) exhibits some differences between companies and NGOs. A recent survey amongst corporate and NGO representatives involved in partnerships in the UK showed that access to funding was the most important reason mentioned by NGOs (95 per cent; this was 7 per cent for business), while companies prioritized reputation and credibility (92 per cent; this was 57 per cent for NGOs) (C&E, 2011). The 2010 version reported comparable figures, except for the higher importance that NGOs then attached to the reputational effects of partnerships: 70 per cent (C&E, 2010). For other motivations, differences were much smaller between business and NGO respondents, with efficiency mentioned as less important, compared to other aspects, by both types of actors (companies only scored access to funding lower).

Factors related to legitimacy, reputation, and credibility figure prominently amongst the reasons for partnering, for governments, business and NGOs. Consecutive global citizen surveys show that trust in all three types has declined in recent years; amongst them, however, government scores consistently lower than business, with NGOs ranking highest (Edelman, 2009, 2011, 2012). Interestingly, while government is the least trusted institution, it is, at the same time, usually seen as most responsible for helping solve global problems, not business or NGOs that are both trusted more (though to varying degrees). When asked explicitly whether business should act alone to help solve global issues, there was overwhelming support for the view that companies have to partner with governments and NGOs, while the option that business would play no role was rejected (Edelman, 2009). In the 2011 survey amongst corporate and NGO representatives in the UK, government was also mentioned to be very often involved in their key partnerships: by acting as a catalyst on the issues involved; by setting frameworks and public policy directions to which partnerships align, or, alternatively, that partnerships try to influence; or by providing (additional) funding (C&E 2011).

Especially tripartite partnerships thus seem to be a route to reckon with different degrees of trust and expectations from society, while generating mutual benefits and reducing or addressing limitations of individual company, government, or NGO action. The need for such collaboration becomes even more pressing if we move away from the generic (usually developed-country) setting to developing countries, in view of missing institutions (institutional gaps) and the much more common prevalence of many problems related to poverty. At the same time, the specific context matters considerably in shaping partnerships as well as their potential impact. Moreover, in case of partnerships for global problems in particular, the wide diversity of actors at the various levels, from "global to local", should be considered as well. The next section draws some attention to the multi-layered nature of governments, companies as well as NGOs once partnerships start to address global problems in a set-up with more partners than just two (the latter can be the case in e.g. a straight-forward 1:1 business-NGO collaboration for a specific project or program). In the process, it will also nuance the straightforward "triad" picture often used for partnerships.

As shown in the upper half of Figure 2.1, it is rather common to visualize partnership options in a tripartite manner, for example, in the form of circles, or as components in a pyramid representing the three types. While perfectly understandable and useful for presentation purposes, it should not be forgotten that this a simplification that does not do justice to the complexity of the separate actors, especially in the international domain, as will be explained below. Moreover, this triad is sometimes mentioned/assumed to embody the "state," the "market," and "civil society," which seems rather problematic. While this chapter is not the place to go into this longer-standing debate, it is worth noting that the state is more than government, the market wider than only companies, and civil society more encompassing than only NGOs (e.g. Bebbington *et al.,* 2008; Fowler and Biekart, 2011; Mitlin *et al.,* 2007). For this reason, rather than mentioning the three broader realms (let alone characterizing them as "sectors," see Note 1), the actor labels are used here.

Differentiating actor categories in the global context

While the complexity of development activities from international ("Northern"-based) to local (as carried out in the "South") and the range of actors involved are known and discussed in fields such as development studies and international management, the partnership literature tends to adhere to broader generalizations of the three types of actors. Publications on partnerships between multinational enterprises (MNE) and NGOs in an international context, for example, have focused on other aspects, such as new business models (Dahan *et al.,* 2010), or firms' legitimacy (Marano and Tashman, 2012), or entrepreneurship process (Webb *et al.,* 2010), with only limited differentiation of within-actor categories (see the chapter by Doh and Boddewyn in this research handbook for some more information on the MNE). In addition to considering differences within the three actor types, it is also important to note that collaboration to further development purposes frequently takes place in areas characterized by institutional voids and missing market actors, which leads to complex partnerships with multiple partners, often considerably more than three (Rivera-Santos *et al.,* 2012).

The lower part of Figure 2.1 sketches a very basic picture to help "disentangle" partnerships, considering the three types of actors and the links between those who operate with an international focus from a base in the North (i.e. Western, OECD countries, labeled as home country) to undertake activities in/for the South (at the national or local level, in so-called host countries). In between the international and the local levels, there may well be a regional center or unit that takes a coordination/control role, as is often the case for MNEs (Rugman and Verbeke 2008), but can also occur to some extent for governments (regional intergovernmental organizations such as the EU or Nafta or regional development banks such as the Inter-American, African or Asian Development Bank) or NGOs, although less frequently (cf. Berger *et al.,* 2004; Yaziji and Doh, 2009).

As the Figure is just a rough indication, Table 2.2 includes some further components for each of the actor types. Below, some explanation will be given for each, respectively companies, governments and NGOs, in view of the fact that each actor can consist of multiple (sub)organizations within the same category. Moreover, it is acknowledged that the use of "North" and "South" (as done for the NGO category in particular) has its limitations, as has the possible "developed"/"developing" alternative. It is not the terminology as such, however, but the underlying phenomena that deserve attention.

Companies that become involved in partnerships to help address global problems will often be MNEs that may have local subsidiaries (or regional centers) that can play a role. In that situation, activities are likely to be instigated from headquarters

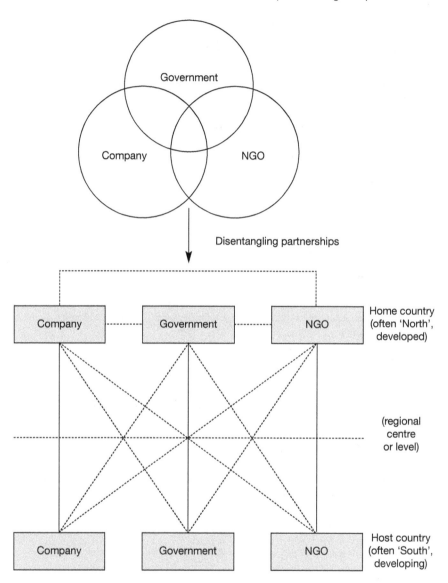

FIGURE 2.1 Distentangling actor categories in partnerships for global problems

in the home country and involve these units at lower levels, although the degree to which these are actually owned and can be controlled from the corporate center may show wide variety, even within one MNE for different business units, or upstream/downstream activities (upstream generally refers to production, downstream to sales). The type of industry is important to consider as well, as global commodities, where many partnerships have emerged in the past decade, are usually characterized by a different set-up, in which MNEs are almost at the end of the value chain, while the

TABLE 2.2 Some peculiarities of actors relevant to an international-to-local (development) perspective

Companies

- Headquarters; via specific (e.g. CSR) department; can also go through geographical or functional (business) units; or ('separate') corporate foundation
- Perhaps via intermediary regional organization to local subsidiaries (fully integrated, partially owned, "independent," with different degrees of "arms' length"); or directly, more "independently" from a corporate foundation to local activities/partners
- Also depends on type of activities, local production and/or sales units in host countries or, in case of commodity-based business more indirect relationship via e.g. buying from traders/exporters

Governments

- "Headquarters" in specific country, particularly notable in case of development assistance, which can be a nested structure with a development agency based in ministry of foreign affairs or dedicated ministry; may also involve one or more inter-governmental organizations
- Usually no regional intermediation, but local presence through embassies or specific dedicated units/officers; regional intergovernmental organizations can be involved
- In addition to donor government also possibility for local (host-country) government representation or involvement; can be at:
  - national level (national government, specific ministry or agency)
  - sub-national/local level (depending on size and governance structure): representatives of national government (agencies) or local government bodies (sub-states/provinces, villages)

NGOs

- "Headquarters" in specific country, can be part of larger international NGO
- Perhaps via intermediary regional organization to local "subsidiaries" (fully integrated, partially owned, "independent," with different degrees of "arms' length"); or directly, more "independently," directly from the home country to local activities/partners
- In addition to "donor" NGO also possibility for local (host-country) NGO representation or involvement; can be at:
  - national level (national NGO), with or without (ownership/network) relationship to home-country NGO
  - regional or local level (depending on size and governance structure); host-country NGOs with or without (ownership/network) relationship to national or home-country NGO
- Also depends on NGOs' types of activities (e.g. advocacy, promotion of transparency, service delivery, assistance in implementation; and whether services are delivered for 'profit'/income generation)

beginning is often in a developing country, with various actors such as traders and exporters in between. An example for the coffee supply chain is given in Figure 2.2 for illustration. MNEs then need to involve and thus "manage" all the steps from the agricultural producer to the end consumer, and relationships are therefore much more indirect (and arms' length) than for those that have local subsidiaries or affiliates.

Still, in the latter case MNEs may also have to involve unrelated (local) companies if they engage in partnerships for development.

Within companies it matters which department is charged with the partnership (and if multiple are involved, how this is coordinated, and which one is leading). Moreover, there is the possibility that a more or less "separate" corporate foundation deals with a partnership, and with the activities carried out in developing countries. While organizational issues within an MNE have been studied extensively in

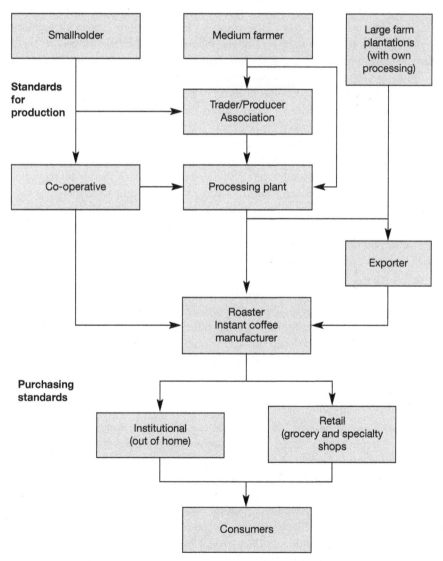

FIGURE 2.2 An overview of the coffee supply chain from bean to cup
Source: Kolk (2011).

international management, this is much less the case for their coordination of partnership activities; the "make-buy-collaborate" spectrum (with "make" as the equivalent of in-house, and "buy" as an "outsourced" mode) has been explored for corporate social responsibility more generally (e.g. Husted, 2003). Corporate foundations have received some attention, but mostly in relation to philanthropy, for which they are seen as responsible for contracting/coordinating charitable contributions hardly related to core business (Husted, 2003; Pedrini and Minciullo, 2010; Westhues and Einwiller, 2006). However, when moving out of the traditional (Northern) settings for foundations in the US or Europe into development issues, corporate foundations sometimes have a different role concerning community development in areas in which the company has operations (e.g. in the mining industry) or from which their agricultural produce originates, thus involving small farmers at the beginning of a global value chain (e.g. in coffee production; Kolk, 2013).

Moving to the *government* perspective in Figure 2.1 and Table 2.2, some things may be comparable to companies in terms of how to organize a partnership from the "home country" (where its "headquarters" are) to the host country; and which ministries/agencies to involve domestically (and which one coordinates/leads) and abroad, where embassies and/or local government agencies may have a role, as well as international organizations (such as the World Bank). The "make-buy-collaborate" decision also applies here, although in an adjusted form given the public nature of the actor and of the goods (cf. Rangan *et al.,* 2006). At the same time, there is always the question to what extent "true" partnerships are involved or whether a contractual mode prevails. As donor, relationships with companies (e.g. in the case of private sector development programs) and with NGOs (in the more traditional official development assistance form) will be peculiar, and frequently close to incentive-based "partnerships" with government aid policies and ideologies shaping recipient activities and approaches (cf. Bebbington *et al.,* 2008; Johansson *et al.,* 2010; Mitlin *et al.,* 2007; Pedersen, 2005). Often, governments will stipulate the involvement of local actors (companies and/or NGOs depending on kind of funding), thus shaping the type of partnerships and the (North-South) relationships involved. The "contractor" role also affects the interaction of donor governments with their local counterparts at the (sub)national levels (ministries, provinces, villages, communities).

Northern development *NGOs* face a difficult position in their attempts to reconcile a variety of pressures and requirements (Bebbington *et al.,* 2008; Derksen and Verhallen, 2008; Mitlin *et al.,* 2007). In addition to their own operational activities for development, they may channel funds with concomitant accountability mechanisms to Southern NGOs that serve as "subcontracted service providers," seek to maintain relationships with those organizations that are more local member-based community (grassroots) and/or advocacy oriented, in connection with their own original objectives for societal and political change as well as improvement in the situation of the poor, while concurrently competing for and generating funding, often also from individual donors, themselves. The way in which international NGOs organize their international activities from their home country in the North all the way to host countries in the South shows a considerable variety, somewhat comparable to MNEs. This can range from collaboration with more or less independent organizations (sometimes under a loose joint umbrella) in the South, via a (con)federate structure, to a unitary "centralized" set-up, with "subsidiaries" (Yaziji and Doh, 2009; cf. Hearn, 2007). Sometimes, and particularly when the same name is used for all units worldwide, those outside the NGO may have difficulty grasping the degree to which local organizations can follow their own approaches or have to adhere to one and the same standard; and also whether and to what extent partnership agreements concluded with a Northern ("holding") NGO (turn out to) apply to their Southern counterparts.

In addition to Southern NGOs more or less related to a Northern one, there are also local NGOs that carry out development assistance (service/contracting) activities, and those involved in advocacy and grassroots activism, but the clarity of the differences between the various types and roles seem to have diminished somewhat over the years. Hearn (2007) raised questions as to the degree to which African NGOs can really be seen as "non-government" (in view of their search for and dependence on government/donor funding) and as representing society (given the apparent and frequent focus to promote their own, entrepreneurial objectives). Using quotes from various sources ("the way to make money is to set up your own NGO," "this is in the first place a business"), the observations by Hearn (2007: 1102–3) illustrate the blurring boundaries between profit and nonprofit. This is also shown in the growth of different types of social entrepreneurs, "benefit corporations" and NGOs that engage in commercial activities – a myriad of forms that is even more difficult to grasp in Southern countries than it is already in the North.

A final aspect to take into account is the complex setting for partnerships for development, which can take place in areas that suffer from weak governance and formal institutional voids, with a prevalence of informal institutions (Rivera-Santos et al., 2012; Webb et al., 2010; see also the chapter by Rufin and Rivera-Santos in this volume).[4] In such a context, tripartite partnerships with multiple parties may help to fill institutional gaps as no single type of actor(s) is likely to be able to provide the whole range of institutions needed. Concurrently, at least some of the partners may be (only or most) familiar with informal governance mechanisms (such as in-kind contributions or community-based personal relationships) that suit the local situation better, to which others (from Northern-base home countries) may not be accustomed as they are used to relying on formal ones (contracts and equity-related property rights) (Rivera-Santos et al., 2012). This co-existence of multiple governance mechanisms and partners' different traditions, and the range of possible and varied institutional contexts, are aspects to be considered as well in assessing the role and impact of partnerships.

The impact of collaborative interactions to address global problems

In recent years, attention has grown for the impact of partnerships, particularly in helping address global problems. Despite the introduction of several tools, such an assessment is very difficult, however, due to the frequently wide diversity and multiple objectives, lack of data, the absence of control groups and baselines, and the phenomenon that partnerships are often "moving targets" that change over the years, with growing experience and "learning by doing." Complexities also stem from the existence of multiple partnerships as well as other initiatives to address the same purpose, and the fact that some activities, such as awareness, advocacy, capacity-building, and empowerment (see Table 2.1), are hard to measure. Compared to ongoing partnerships, it may be easier for new focused collaborative efforts that have clear goals and an in-built evaluation mechanism from the start. Assessing impact also seems less complicated if one takes a more limited view, to consider, for example, only the realization of specific organizational objectives of the participating actors (for example, raising money by NGOs, or an improved reputation for companies). Nevertheless, the type of goal also plays an important role in this respect: the broader and higher the ambitions, the more difficult it may be to achieve them, also because more partners are likely to be involved. Specific projects, programs, or transactions are easier to realize than systemic or societal change (cf. Austin, 2000b; Waddock, 1991); informal, distant settings increase complexities (Rivera-Santos *et al.,* 2012).

What has remained underexposed in this debate are the more indirect effects of partnerships, due to interactions at multiple levels: not only at the macro level, e.g. from North to South, but also within partnering organizations (which can be located in several regions) and by individuals working for or affected by the organizations or the partnership. "Impact" on the social good or the global problem targeted can take place in more subtle ways as well via stakeholder interactions that may "trickle" from micro (individual) to meso (organizational) and macro (societal), or vice versa (cf. Kolk *et al.*, 2010) (see Figure 2.3 for an overview). For example, if an employee of a partnering organization says positive things about a partnership to address a global issue such as poverty to colleagues, customers, family, friends, or acquaintances, then the word about the collaboration and the cause can spread easily, raising awareness and perhaps stimulating others to become active. This is facilitated by the fact that people have multiple roles and belong to several stakeholder groups at the same time (e.g. one can simultaneously be an employee, consumer, voter, and member of a non-governmental organization or political party) (cf. Wolfe and Putler, 2002). In a sense, this is somewhat comparable to the notion of "civic action" that also considers the different capacities of persons who aim to "make society work better for more people" (Biekart and Fowler, 2012: 182). Both approaches in fact showcase micro-level interactions within and across "sectors" that can trickle up and round, and thus further the cause and increase the impact of the partnership on the global problem being addressed.

This chapter argues that it is important to recognize the interlinkages and how micro and meso interactions may have an influence on partnerships that address global problems. Levels have tended to be treated separately in different bodies of literature, as will be explained in the subsections that follow and that offer some reflections on each of them. These are not meant to provide a comprehensive overview, but rather to present some insights on the role of partnerships and the

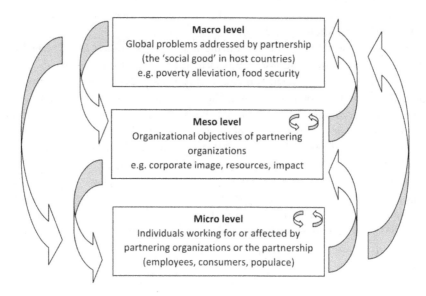

FIGURE 2.3 Trickle effects of partnerships and the various levels

interactions in relation to the rationale, actor, and context issues discussed above. This may also serve as input for further research and for practitioner and scholarly debates about partnerships.

Macro-level perspectives

Most of the discussion at the macro level has focused on the implementation (effectiveness) and democratic (legitimacy) deficits supposed to be addressed by partnerships. Studies that often originate from political science, public policy, and international relations have considered the implications for these governance dimensions (e.g. Bäckstrand, 2008; Liese and Beisheim, 2011; Pattberg *et al.*, 2012; Schäferhoff *et al.*, 2009). What has come to the fore here as well are difficulties of establishing the yardstick against which to assess partnerships (i.e. ideal-type institutions or "real-existing" institutions), and the importance of taking into account institutional design factors as well as "complex" performance that includes unintended side effects, and goes beyond a "simple" benchmarking exercise of an individual partnership and its objective(s). In evaluating effectiveness in terms of realization of overall objectives – or as "aggregate measure of (or judgment about) the merit or worth of an activity" (OECD-DAC, 2002: 21) – the development literature has made a distinction between output, outcome, and impact. Output refers to the first, or immediate result of an intervention or activity; outcome to changes in behaviour of those targeted or in the application/implementation of services, knowledge, or standards; and impact to the most far-reaching of the three, which relates to bringing sustainable and structural solutions to the problem(s) at stake, reckoning with possible negative side effects (Liese and Beisheim, 2011; OECD-DAC, 2002; Schäferhoff *et al.*, 2009).

In view of the difficulties of measuring impact, most studies have focused on assessing output, with mixed results. Especially partnerships for sustainable development that have been registered at the United Nations (UN), following agreements on Millennium Development Goals at the 2002 Johannesburg World Summit on Sustainable Development, turn out to have been often inactive or ineffective, except for some in specific areas such as energy, water, and health (Pattberg *et al.*, 2012; Schäferhoff *et al.*, 2009; Szulecki *et al.*, 2011). The "measure" used to assess this often involved a so-called "function-output fit" to see how the programs, reports, activities or organizational structures related to the functions originally planned (cf. part A in Table 2.1) (Dellas, 2012; Szulecki *et al.*, 2011). As such, this is a rather limited assessment, reflecting lack of data beyond public UN databases. At the same time, it is helpful to consider the specific foci and tasks of partnerships. Another study, on 21 of these international partnerships for sustainable development, aimed to evaluate output, outcome, and impact in a qualitative manner based on documents and interviews, taking the type of partnership into account (see part B in Table 2.1; Liese and Beisheim 2011). The partnerships were broadly categorized as having low, medium, and high overall effectiveness, with almost 60% being placed in the middle group; only two (service) partnerships were labeled highly effective (and the remainder low).

These macro-level studies of effectiveness of partnerships have tended to not only pay most attention to output, based on (often document-based) assessments of globally-oriented partnerships (involving international organizations), but also to skip the organizational and/or individual levels, and the dynamic interactions involved. In some recent management research, these aspects have come to the fore, especially in case of partnerships in contexts characterized by institutional gaps. Examples include Kolk and Lenfant, 2012; Mair and Martí, 2009; Mair *et al.*, 2012; Reffico and Márquez, 2012). The link with the more macro-oriented literature on development impacts has not really been made, however. This was done in the context of supply-chain partnerships (see Figure 2.2), where effectiveness was explored for the case of coffee in (post-)conflict Central African countries. Output was approached as the equivalent of organizational achievements regarding the creation and strengthening of cooperatives for small farmers; outcome as effects on coffee prices, income, and living conditions of these beneficiaries; and impact as broader institutional implications concerning a reduction of conflict or tensions, inter alia, due to more contacts through reconciliation programs and joint cultivation instead of fighting.[5] Based on a range of primary and secondary sources, positive effects were seen for all three aspects. It should be noted, however, that the partnerships in this study took place in (post-)-conflict settings and involved business-NGO partnerships, sometimes supported by Western donor agencies, and were thus rather different in nature from the government-focused international partnerships mentioned in the preceding (and following) paragraphs.

This thus not only points at issues of context but also at different degrees and forms of legitimacy, which is the second component often assumed to be addressed by partnerships (in addition to effectiveness, see the introductory section of this chapter). Particularly in the international partnerships for sustainable development, attention has been paid to input as well as output legitimacy (Bäckstrand 2006b; Dellas 2012). Input refers to a balanced representation of affected stakeholders in decision-making as well as accountability and transparency, while output relates to effectiveness in the sense that legitimacy stems from the realization of results. Dellas (2012) took the function-output function to conclude that output legitimacy of international water partnerships was relatively high, also due to more resources and higher involvement of companies than in other areas. Bäckstrand (2006b) focused on institutional effectiveness (leadership, policy coherence, clear formulation of objectives), given that problem-solving capacity in terms of goal-attainment is difficult to assess. Liese and Beisheim (2011) explored degrees of institutionalization, not so much to assess output legitimacy as such, but to look for possible determinants of effectiveness more generally, for which they also considered process management, governance structures, resources, capacity building, learning and stakeholder inclusion. Schäferhoff et al. (2009) mentioned inclusiveness and accountability as key components of legitimacy.

Regardless of the precise conceptualization, however, studies demonstrate serious concerns regarding legitimacy, with limited inclusiveness and weak accountability mechanisms (Bäckstrand, 2006b; Fransen and Kolk, 2007; Pattberg et al., 2012; Schäferhoff et al., 2009). Partnerships for sustainable development turn out to be most often implemented by international organizations, OECD governments or Northern-based (often donor-funded) NGOs in areas where there are already many activities, not in those where the problems and needs are greatest. They thus do not emerge in low-governance areas and hardly include local communities, with affected stakeholders being underrepresented as well. Business involvement is very limited in the partnerships registered at the UN, although not only there, as this was also found to apply to international partnerships for climate change (Pinkse and Kolk, 2012). Interestingly, while the context of the Millennium Development Goals appeared not to offer a framework for inclusion of business interests across the board, it did lead to the introduction of partnerships on technologies that have sparked some controversy (such as nuclear energy, PVC and water purification chemicals) (Mert and Chan, 2012).

Regarding factors that influence effectiveness, a high degree of institutionalization (which can include clear decision-making processes, rules and monitoring mechanisms, staffing, organizational and financial resources,) appears to play a positive role (Pattberg et al., 2012), but not in the case of knowledge partnerships (see Table 2.1, part B; Liese and Beisheim, 2011). Level and quality of participation seem to matter particularly for standard-setting partnerships, whereas service partnerships require partners with sufficient resources as well as those that are knowledgeable about the local situation and its implementation requirements. It is also mentioned that leadership and management, internal governance structures, and resources and partners need to be arranged to ensure success (Beisheim, 2012); these aspects relate directly to the meso level of partnerships that will be discussed next. Still, it should be noted that these generic conclusions may not hold so much in settings where institutions are weak or non-existent, and/or informal governance mechanisms prevail (Rivera-Santos et al., 2012). Partnerships may be locally-adapted as well, with same international partnerships being implemented rather differently across countries, as Chan (2012) found for China and India, where the degree of government involvement (also in the shape of "official NGOs") was much larger in China, with India showing a much more diverse and larger NGO participation.

Linking macro and meso perspectives

Over the years, there has been large interest in the meso level and the range of aspects related to interorganizational collaboration, from formation and implementation to outcomes (cf. Austin and Seitanidi, 2012; Selsky and Parker, 2005). Except for the few publications mentioned in the preceding section, however, the linkages to the macro level have been limited, as those oriented at the meso level have embedded their work in management and organization studies and marketing, using theoretical frameworks that underexpose the implications for the global problems addressed by the partnerships. Still, insights from this research are potentially relevant for the macro perspective, as the collaborative efforts can trickle to that level, as explained above (see Figure 2.3). Therefore, this section will briefly discuss the main issues of this body of work, which has paid most attention to business-NGO partnerships (e.g. Berger et al., 2004; Dahan et al., 2010; Den Hond et al., 2012; Elkington and Fennell, 1998; Kolk and Lenfant, 2012; Le Ber and Branzei, 2010; Rondinelli and London, 2003; Seitanidi and Crane, 2009; Webb et al., 2010; Yaziji and Doh, 2009). In view of the abundance of studies, it merely presents some insights important for the practice of partnerships, and that help to clarify roles and possible impacts.

Related to the reasons for companies and NGOs to engage in partnerships, as indicated in Table 2.1 (Part D), many publications have explored the actual organizational and operational processes, and the factors that appear to influence "success or failure." Most often evidence is collected from multiple case studies and/or expert interviews with practitioners. Several authors provide guidance to practitioners in decision-making on cooperation. Table 2.3 contains six basic questions on the strategic criteria for assessing whether and, if so, with what intensity parties are recommended to collaborate, and two other questions for appraising the effectiveness of subsequent implementation. Together, these cover especially the initial selection as well as the institutionalization phases of partnerships; in between is a partnership design stage that includes experimentation, adaptation, and operationalization (Seitanidi and Crane, 2009).

Paying most attention to the process of partnering, Berger et al. (2004) identify six "mis-es" that often characterize partnerships: misunderstandings, misallocation of costs and benefits, mismatches of power, mismatched partners, misfortunes of time, and mistrust. These are included and explained in Table 2.4. Following from

TABLE 2.3 Aspects/questions to consider in decision-making on collaboration

---

Six questions on strategic criteria for collaboration

- Can both parties identify specific projects for collaboration and the required internal resources? (with no leading to a no-collaboration approach, and an end of the questions to be answered)
- Have the parties formulated criteria for partner selection? (with no leading to an arm's length, relatively loose, relationship)
- Are both parties willing and able to develop mutually accepted procedures for collaboration? (with no again leading to an arm's length relationship)
- Can both parties define problems clearly and explore feasible and measurable solutions? (with no leading to interactive collaboration, a less intensive form)
- Is the partnership team willing to focus on manageable tasks that can be implemented quickly? (with no again leading to interactive collaboration)
- Can both parties maintain confidentiality? (with no again leading to interactive collaboration, and yes to an intensive partnership)

Two additional questions related to the implementation process

- Is the partnership implementation accountable? (considering accountability mechanisms in the various partnership phases, and the relevant stakeholders)
- Is the partnership institutionalized within the organization? (reckoning with ways in which "crises" in the relationship have been handled, and carrying out an informal audit amongst partnership team members and other staff)

Depending on the outcomes of the review, improvements need to be made or an exit strategy followed.

Source: Compiled from Rondinelli and London (2003) (upper half); Seitanidi and Crane (2009) (bottom half).

this, Table 2.5 contains more information about possible ways to avoid or diminish these predictable problems. The first route is to ensure a good fit between the company and the NGO, in principle on all the nine subdimensions distinguished in the top part of Table 2.5. Still, Berger *et al.* (2004) recognize that this may be rather difficult, and while some fit aspects may increase in the course of the partnership due to learning effects, the ones to prioritize are mission fit, resource fit, management fit, and evaluation fit. The second approach consists of a proper consideration of the best structural configuration of a (potential/candidate) partner organization, for both the company and the NGO in question, and of the partnership itself given the structural characteristics of all three. Each peculiarity has its pros and cons, however, and in that sense there is no optimal "solution."

It might be assumed that the better the various aspects are handled, the higher the likelihood that the objectives of a partnership can be realized, with thus also beneficial effects for the global problem targeted. However, how easy it is to assess overall effectiveness or impact also depends on the degree to which targets are or can be specified, and thus also how ambitious they are. This also applies to efficiency, a measure that especially business partners may want to use to establish a cost/benefit analysis of inputs/resources in relation to results (Gourville and Rangan, 2004; Kolk

TABLE 2.4 Predictable problems in partnerships and ways to avoid/reduce them

---

- *Misunderstandings:* range from misunderstandings about context of partnerships to misunderstandings of each other's objectives (due to lack of familiarity, misconceptions, or unrealistic objectives)
- *Misallocation of costs and benefits:* perceptions of unfair distribution of costs and benefits vis-à-vis other partner (overexploitation of one's own resources, too much risk in relation to value added compared to other partner, overuse for corporate PR, unreasonable demands, insufficient priority, dependence)
- *Mismatches of power:* perceived or real imbalances, leading to (perceived) domination by one of the partners, too much intrusion in partner's affairs, micromanagement, ownership and exclusivity issues
- *Mismatched partners:* insufficient complementarity, lack of overlap in goals, cultures, markets, decision processes, structures, styles or constituencies
- *Misfortunes of time:* due to the fact that novelty diminishes when partnerships last longer, requiring continued commitment and sufficient renewal where necessary, and replacement of key partnership team members if they leave; lack of preparedness for turnover and of an exit strategy
- *Mistrust:* can result from the conglomerate of other "mis-es," and give rise to covert behavior, opportunism, and communication problems

---

Source: Compiled from Berger *et al.* (2004)

et al., 2008; OECD-DAC, 2002). Particularly partnerships that aim to address global problems are likely to suffer from the complexity that outputs and outcomes can be evaluated, but that impact is difficult, as outlined in the previous section on the macro level already. This may also be due to the fact that such partnerships often do not involve a "simple" 1:1 collaboration but that multiple parties are involved, and, especially in the case of international development activities, undertaken in difficult, and often rather different, contexts than the (Northern) home-country setting.

Furthermore, how a partnership actually functions – and thus, can have an impact – also depends on individual factors and the process of interactions, as these can yield not only organizational benefits but also more indirect (trickle) effects within and between the micro, meso, and macro levels (cf. Kolk *et al.,* 2010; Seitanidi and Ryan 2007; see Figure 2.3). Although mission fit, management fit, workforce fit, and cultural fit (see Table 2.5) to some extent relate to these micro-level aspects, Berger *et al.* (2004) appear to treat them more in a one-off manner, not so much in connection with relational processes and interactions. These are aspects that will be discussed somewhat further below.

Adding micro-level perspectives

Partnership research has recently started to pay more attention to the role of individuals and their interactions, but the number of empirical studies is still rather limited. This lack of evidence on the micro level has also been noted more generally in the past few years, in relation to corporate social responsibility (CSR) (Aguinis and Glavas, 2012) and strategic management/organization (Felin and Foss, 2005).

TABLE 2.5 Possible ways to reduce/address predictable problems in partnerships

Ensuring fit on multiple dimensions

- *Mission fit:* creates attention, priority, share of mind
- *Resource fit:* help to gain control of critical assets, skills or resources possessed by the partner
- *Management fit:* involves compatibility on personal level between leaders, creates engagement, support and commitment
- *Evaluation fit:* shared perceptions of success
- *Work force fit:* enhances organizational identification (which may result in job satisfaction, organizational commitment and higher retention) and greater likelihood of volunteer work
- *Target market fit:* demographic, geographic and/or psychographic fit in target markets may lead to differential advantage when customers have affinity for the cause, leading to more support for the NGO and activities on behalf of the cause
- *Product/cause fit:* creates value through co-branding or based on strategic similarity
- *Cultural fit:* if organizational cultures match, then this eases implementation and management
- *Cycle fit:* comparable planning cycles lead to congruence of timing and seasonal complementarity

Careful consideration of structural characteristics of the possible NGO partner

- *Programmatic* versus *grant-making* NGO
- *Autonomy* versus *central control*
- *Large, well-established* versus *small, entrepreneurial* NGO
- *Revenue-generating products/services* versus *none*
- *Inherent cross-sector collaboration* versus *"traditional"* NGO

Careful consideration of structural characteristics of the possible corporate partner

- *Flat* versus *hierarchical* company
- *Broad consumer market* versus *specific target market*
- *Direct sales force/retail presence* versus *business to business*
- *Pre-eminent brand* versus *less eminent brand*

Careful consideration of structural characteristics of the possible partnership

- *Brand-level* versus *company-level* partnership
- *Dedicated partnership manager* versus *none*
- *Dedicated partnership marketing budget* versus *none*
- *Fixed donation* versus *variable donation*
- *Few marketing initiatives* versus *many marketing initiatives*
- *Venues for grassroots engagement of company employees and customers* versus *none*

Source: Compiled from Berger *et al.* (2004).

Building on Figure 2.3 that outlined the links between micro, meso, and macro, Figure 2.4 gives an overview of possible micro-level interactions in relation to partnering organizations. There is a central role for the employee who is involved in (or becomes informed about) the partnership. As such, this builds on broader insights about the importance of employees as facilitators of and possible proponents for

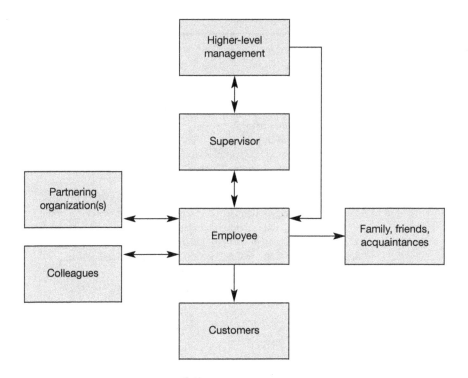

FIGURE 2.4 Micro-level interactions in the context of partnering organizations
Source: Adapted from Kolk *et al.* (2010)

implementation and communication of brand and company activities, also vis-à-vis a range of stakeholders, including customers (Bolton *et al.*, 2011; Burmann and Zeplin, 2005; Du *et al.*, 2010). According to a recent global citizen survey, 50 per cent of respondents regard "regular employees" as highly credible in providing information about a company, a score similar to NGO representatives, and much higher than CEOs or governmental officials/regulators (Edelman, 2012). For such mechanisms to work effectively, however, employees need to have positive job and organizational perceptions (cf. Brown and Lam, 2008; Maxham *et al.*, 2008).

There have been a few recent studies on employees in relation to CSR initiatives more generally, but these have emphasized the need for further investigation, as top-down approaches – focused on managers – have predominated and the active involvement of employees has been largely neglected (Bolton *et al.*, 2010; Van der Voort *et al.*, 2009). This was demonstrated in a partnership context by Seitanidi (2009) who, on the basis of research on NGO employees, showed the missed opportunities due to their too limited involvement in all stages of the partnership. This in turn was said to likely hamper effective implementation and harm the organization's reputation. Drawing on expert interviews from multiple cases, Berger *et al.* (2006) took a somewhat different approach by focusing on the positive effects for employees from partnerships. They found that some employees experienced both intra- and interorganizational identification as well as community and relationship building as a result of the partnership activities. The outreach to partner organizations and the involvement in the partnership created emotional attachments that added to employee learning from cognitive reflections.

Referring to Figure 2.4, Berger *et al.* (2006) thus also considered the link to partner organizations to some extent. This was done in more detail by Le Ber and Branzei (2010), who explored relational processes in business-nonprofit partnerships, particularly how and to what extent roles were (re)calibrated in response to needs of counterparts at partner organizations and the effect for the momentum of success or failure. In this respect, relational attachment to the partner organization played a role as well, but this could be eroded in case of partner complacency and/or disillusionment. This study thus helped to shed some light on relational engagements between organizations, adding to the dimensions discussed under the meso-level heading. However, the implications beyond the individual and organizational levels, and possible trickle effects to macro impacts has not received attention. Most often, partnerships did not really aim to address global problems or target individuals or communities in developing countries.

In addition to employees per se, the possible trickle effects from employees to consumers has been the subject of investigation in a few experimental studies (Vock 2011; Vock *et al.*, 2013). They identified situations in which employee participation in partnerships was perceived positively by consumers, and was accompanied by higher degrees of trust in the company in question, or to increased intentions to buy from the company or recommend it to others. Aspects that turned out to play a role were consumers' perceived self-interest, their personality traits (more pro-social or individualistically-oriented), and the degree of fit between the NGO and the company, with high-fit partnerships exposing the largest effects (though not always necessarily in a positive way for the company). Here as well, however, linkages to other levels, let alone impact on the macro level have remained unexplored. Overall, this can be explained from the fact that the micro level has mostly been studied in areas such as HRM, and organizational and consumer behaviour.

These initial findings thus deserve follow-up investigation to obtain more insight into the micro-interactions and whether and how they influence the overall impact of partnerships, taking the different levels into account. This also applies to more exact diffusion mechanisms between employees, their managers, and colleagues within organizations, to what extent they spread the word about partnerships to families, friends, acquaintances, and customers, if applicable, and whether they relate to individuals or communities targeted by the collaborative efforts. Impact on the ground in developing countries might be furthered by home-host individual interactions. More knowledge about the role of individuals will also be helpful for practitioners involved in partnerships. It seems not so easy to establish the impact of micro-level interactions, however, as they typically involve rather intangible, perception-based aspects. There is a parallel here with some developing-country settings in which informal rather than contractual relations predominate.

Beyond "cross-sector" partnerships: on limitations and possible trends

In 2007, Egels-Zandén and Wahlqvist coined the term "post-partnerships" to indicate a corporate move away from business-NGO partnerships out of frustration with inefficient and unproductive collaboration, also due to conflicts between NGOs. This was based on a case study of the Business Social Compliance Initiative, and while noting the development, the authors warned for possible loss of legitimacy if business would again, like in the pre-partnership period, undertake activities without stakeholder involvement or strict inclusion of internationally accepted standards. Disappointment about multi-stakeholder initiatives has also been expressed by NGOs. Fransen and Kolk (2007) examined 50 standard-setting partnerships and found that some multistakeholder initiatives were characterized by "narrow inclusiveness," with mere consultation instead of real involvement, and concomitant limitations in terms of membership, governance, and implementation processes. This resembles concerns about transparency and accountability as mentioned for international partnerships for sustainable development. Partnerships may face tradeoffs between broad stakeholder involvement and rapid implementation. It has also been noted, in the context of input versus output legitimacy, that different partnerships on a specific issue might balance each other out if one would have relatively even representation (e.g. through more NGO involvement) while another focused more on effectiveness (through more business influence) (Dellas 2012).

As such, the article by Egels-Zandén and Wahlqvist (2007) forms an isolated example that looks at a possible move "beyond partnerships" from a business perspective. Interestingly, if we look at implementation of corporate responsibility initiatives, it turns out that in international supply chains, activities that sometimes started as partnerships, or that used the partnership mechanism as a vehicle for implementation, in reality often seem to be mere business-business collaborations, with NGOs at best in a service-delivery role, rather than a cross-sector cooperation. This may occur in other so-called partnerships as well if governments act as donors; NGOs do the implementation (in a market segment where consultants are similarly active), with business as leading actor. It should be noted that the labeling, and thus the assessment of the "true" nature of the partnerships and the roles of the respective partners, may be a matter of interpretation and perception. Whether this is thus a trend beyond current case-based observations and anecdotal evidence is something that deserves further in-depth investigation.

At the same time, it points at a phenomenon that can be observed in practice. Once companies see the rationale for activities for the social good and if these are close to their core business, they are likely to seek what they perceive as the best and most efficient route to implementation. External funding or support in removing administrative and/or political barriers from governments will be welcomed, and NGO involvement as well if needed. However, the fact that some NGOs increasingly adopt mixed activities accompanied by hybrid income types, a tendency sometimes provoked by diminishing public funding (e.g. declining development assistance), means that their precise role and focus becomes more difficult to assess for outsiders. There are cases in which NGOs act as (semi-)consultants, are involved in trading activities, set up cooperatives, or undertake standard-setting and standard-promoting activities while serving as (partial) auditors of certifiers as well. This might raise questions about their independence, representativeness, legitimacy, "ideological" positioning and key "competences" when engaging in consultancy/advice type of work that "commercial" parties do as well. At the same time, partnerships carried out in the framework of the UN (Millennium Development Goals) are merely government-driven, with very limited business and NGO involvement, thus resembling official development assistance under a different heading.

These observations do not serve to negate the many cases in which partnerships are real and valuable cross-sector interactions, accompanied by learning and effective collaboration for a social good. However, they point at the diffusion of forms as well as the confusion that can be seen to emerge at times, and which is also noted by some practitioners, although not discussed very openly and widely. It may indicate a future trend beyond partnerships in certain instances, or a shake-up of particular actors and collaborative patterns. This may be a "natural" evolution for some issues/countries/ actors for which partnerships were very useful to help set the stage, bring parties together, and clarify roles for further implementation. The need for more insight and precision in terminology and concepts may also be illustrated by the continued existence of "hollow" partnerships, that do not have more than a name and some formalities (such as a list of participants and a website) in place but no (longer) real activities.

Conclusion

What might be concluded is that we have moved beyond the stage of broad assertions about partnerships (as "hype" or "myth" on the one hand; as "panacea" or "the solution to complex global issues in the twenty-first century," on the other). It seems important to recognize the wide variety and the complexities as outlined in this chapter. Given all the insights obtained over the years, there is a need to fine tune further efforts, and assess when and under which conditions which types of partnership do and do not work, and in which cases other mechanisms may be more effective. This chapter has shown that there is a clear set of partnership phenomena that deserves more research attention, based on real-life experiences, so as to also inform the practice of cross-section collaboration to help address global social problems. The current "state of the art" appears to be somewhat fragmented, as different bodies of literature have tended to focus on distinct levels. Combined forces could help to establish a wider view on the impact of partnerships, including the dynamic interactions between and within the different levels, as shown in Figure 2.3 that outlined several trickle effects.

Questions for reflection

1   In which situations are partnerships likely to be effective, and when do single-actor solutions seem more appropriate?
2   Can you think of good examples for both (global problems that require partnerships or for which single-actor solutions might work), or perhaps even categorizations, conditions, and/or contingency factors?
3   How may issue peculiarities (or types of issues) play a role? In other words, are some issues better suitable for certain partnerships or types of collaboration by certain actors?
4   What interaction levels/perspectives (macro, meso, micro) should partnerships for global problems prioritize?
5   Can you think of ways to reduce the complexity of partnerships for global problems (in terms of geographical distance and actors at different levels)?

Notes

1   Implicit in the "cross-sector" label is the notion that there are three "sectors" in society (the state, the market and civil society), which has been subject to controversy. Especially the idea that civil society forms a separate or "third" sector or system (Nerfin 1987), has been debated, in the fields of international relations and development studies in particular (cf. Fowler and Biekart 2011; Kolk, 1996; Mitlin *et al.* 2007). Interestingly, while the notion appeared to have fallen into disuse there, or at least been explicitly recognized for having serious limitations that hamper its further adoption, it has re-emerged in a seemingly rather uncontested manner in critical management studies and a more applied economics stream from a different origin, i.e. related to the US and the UK contexts, most recently (Hull *et al.* 2011; Salamon 2010). While acknowledging the limitations of the "sector" notion, this chapter does not address this debate in detail as such, although the section on context and actors pays some attention to it. It occasionally includes the cross-sector label, however, as this has made some headway to indicate collaboration between different parties and groups in society, and thus seems to fall under the type of analysis for which "a three-sector story is still useful" (Biekart and Fowler 2012: 182), at least to some extent.
2   It should be noted that particularly in the fields of political science, public policy and (international) governance, "private" is often used in the sense of "non-state", thus encompassing both business and NGOs, see e.g. Bäckstrand (2008); Liese and Beisheim (2011); Pattberg *et al.* (2012); Schäferhoff *et al.* (2009). Public-private partnerships are then usually seen as "hybrid" forms of governance as opposed to those that are purely governmental or private. In that context, private consists of business-to-business or NGO, separately or mixed; this is often left unspecified as the focus of debate is elsewhere (i.e. state versus non-state). In the international relations and governance literatures, much attention has been paid to transnational partnerships (usually using the same public versus private dichotomy), building on the long-standing concept of transnational relations: cross-boundary interactions involving at least one non-state actor (see e.g. Andanova *et al.* (2009); Bäckstrand (2008); Schäferhoff *et al.* (2009)). In line with the common terminology in business and management, and to maintain as much conceptual clarity as possible, this chapter clearly distinguishes private (as business) from nonprofit (NGO).

3   As explained in note 2 already, here as well "private" is meant to include both business and civil society representation.

4   Institutional voids have been defined with a focus on the formal aspects as "the absence of specialized intermediaries, regulatory systems, and contract-enforcing mechanisms" (Khanna and Palepu 2005: 62). It should be noted, however, that such "voids" are not "empty" of institutions, as different types of (informal) rules and arrangements may be in place in specific locations, although insufficient to enable the overall proper functioning and development of markets. In that sense, the term 'institutional gaps' might better indicate the varying degrees to which institutions may be present or missing in developing countries. Especially for the latter category, failed or fragile states, or areas of limited statehood have also been used, although terms are not always defined very precisely (for partnerships in limited statehood conditions in South Africa, see the chapter by Hamann).

5   This is part of a broader research project on the role of business in (post-)conflict countries in Central Africa, carried out with François Lenfant. While the paper on coffee partnerships is still in progress at the time of finalization of this chapter, other publications on partnerships in these same contexts are available (Kolk and Lenfant 2012, 2013).

References

Andonova, L.B., Betsill, M.M. and Bulkeley, H. (2009) "Transnational climate governance," *Global Environmental Politics*, 9 (2): 52–73.

Aguinis, H. and Glavas, A. (2012) "What we know and don't know about corporate social responsibility: a review and research agenda," *Journal of Management*, 38 (4): 932–68.

Austin, J.E. (2000a) "Principles for partnership," *Leader to Leader*, 18 (Fall): 44–50.

Austin, J.E. (2000b) "Strategic collaboration between nonprofits and businesses," *Nonprofit and Voluntary Sector Quarterly*, 29 (1) (Supplement), 69–97.

Austin, J.E. and Seitanidi, M.M. (2012) "Collaborative value creation: a review of partnering between nonprofits and businesses. Part 2: partnership processes and outcomes," *Nonprofit and Voluntary Sector Quarterly*, doi: 10.1177/0899764012454685.

Bäckstrand, K. (2006a) "Democratizing global environmental governance? Stakeholder democracy after the World Summit on Sustainable Development," *European Journal of International Relations*, 12 (4): 467–98.

Bäckstrand, K. (2006b) "Multi-stakeholder partnerships for sustainable development: rethinking legitimacy, accountability and effectiveness," *European Environment*, 16: 290–306.

Bäckstrand, K. (2008) "Accountability of networked climate governance: the rise of transnational climate partnerships," *Global Environmental Politics*, 8 (3): 74–102.

Bebbington, A., Hickey, S. and Mitlin, D. (2008) (eds). *Can NGOs Make a Difference? The Challenge of Development Alternatives*, London: Zed Books.

Beisheim, M. (2012) "Partnerships for sustainable development. Why and how Rio+20 must improve the framework for multi-stakeholder partnerships," Berlin: SWP Research Paper 2012/RP 03.

Berger, I.E., Cunningham, P.H. and Drumwright, M.E. (2004) "Social alliances: company/nonprofit collaboration," *California Management Review*, 47 (1): 58–90.

Berger, I.E., Cunningham, P.H. and Drumwright, M.E. (2006) "Identity, identification, and relationship through social alliances," *Journal of the Academy of Marketing Science*, 34: 128–37.

Biekart, K. and Fowler, A. (2012) "A civic agency perspective on change," *Development*, 55: 181–9.

Bolton, S.C., Kim, R.C. and O'Gorman, K.D. (2011) "Corporate social responsibility as a dynamic internal organizational process: a case study," *Journal of Business Ethics*, 101: 61–74.

Brown, S.P. and Lam, S.K. (2008) "A meta-analysis of relationships linking employee satisfaction to customer responses," *Journal of Retailing*, 84 (3): 243–55.

Burmann, C. and Zeplin, S. (2005) "Building brand commitment: a behavioural approach to internal brand management," *Brand Management*, 12 (4): 279–300.

Chan, S. (2012) "Partnerships for sustainable development beyond the OECD world: comparing India and China," in P. Pattberg, F. Biermann, S. Chan and A. Mert (eds). *Public-Private Partnerships for Sustainable Development. Emergence, Influence and Legitimacy*, Cheltenham: Edward Elgar: 115–36.

C&E (2010) "Corporate-NGO Partnerships Barometer 2010," London.

C&E (2011) "Corporate-NGO Partnerships Barometer 2011," London.

Dahan, N.M., Doh, J.P., Oetzel, J. and Yaziji, M. (2010) "Corporate-NGO collaboration: co-creating new business models for developing markets," *Long Range Planning*, 43: 326–42.

Dellas, E. (2012) "Partnerships for sustainable development in the water sector: privatization, participation and legitimacy," in P. Pattberg, F. Biermann, S. Chan and A. Mert (eds). *Public-Private Partnerships for Sustainable Development. Emergence, Influence and Legitimacy*, Cheltenham: Edward Elgar: 183–208.

Den Hond, F., De Bakker, F.G.A. and Doh, J. (2012) "What prompts companies to collaborate with NGOs? Recent evidence from the Netherlands," *Business and Society*, doi: 10.1177/0007650312439549.

Derksen, H. and Verhallen, P. (2008) "Reinventing international NGOs: a view from the Dutch co-financing system," in A. Bebbington, S. Hickey and D. Mitlin (eds). *Can NGOs Make a Difference? The Challenge of Development Alternatives*, London: Zed Books: 219–39.

Du, S., Bhattacharya, C.B. and Sen, S. (2010) "Maximizing business returns to corporate social responsibility (CSR): the role of CSR communication," *International Journal of Management Reviews*, 12 (1): 8–19.

Edelman (2009) "2009 Edelman Trust Barometer." http://edelmaneditions.com/2009/01/trust-barometer-2009/

Edelman (2011) "2011 Edelman Trust Barometer Findings." www.edelmandigital.com/2011/01/25/trust-transformed-results-of-the-2011-edelman-trust-barometer/

Edelman (2012) "2012 Edelman Trust Barometer Executive Summary." http://trust.edelman.com/about-trust/

Egels-Zandén, N. and Wahlqvist, E. (2007) "Post-partnership strategies for defining corporate responsibility: the Business Social Compliance Initiative," *Journal of Business Ethics*, 70: 175–89.

Elkington, J. and Fenell, S. (1998) "Partners for sustainability," *Greener Management International*, 24: 48–60.

Felin, T. and Foss, N.J. (2005) "Strategic organization: a field in search of micro-foundations," *Strategic Organization*, 3: 441–55.

Fowler, A. and Biekart, K. (2011) "Civic driven change: a narrative to bring politics back into civil society discourse," The Hague: International Institute of Social Studies, Working paper No. 529.

Fransen, L. and Kolk, A. (2007) "Global rule-setting for business: a critical analysis of multi-stakeholder standards," *Organization*, 14 (5): 667–84.

Gourville, J.T. and Rangan, V.K. (2004) "Valuing the cause marketing relationship," *California Management Review*, 47 (1): 38–57.

Hearn, J. (2007) "African NGOs: the new compradors?," *Development and Change*, 38 (6): 1095–110.

Hudson, L. (2009) "The enabling state: collaborating for success," Report for the Foreign and Commonwealth Office, London: Foreign and Commonwealth Office.

Hull, R., Gibbon, J., Branzei, O. and Haugh, H. (eds) (2011) *The Third Sector.* Dialogues in Critical Management Studies, Volume 1, Bingley: Emerald.

Husted, B.W. (2003) "Governance choices for corporate social responsibility: to contribute, collaborate or internalize?," *Long Range Planning,* 36: 481–98.

Johansson, K.V., Elgström, O., Kimanzu, N., Nylund, J. and Persson, R. (2010) "Trends in development aid, negotiation processes and NGO policy change," *Voluntas,* 21: 371–92.

Khanna, T. and Palepu, K.G. (2005) "Emerging giants. Building world-class companies in developing countries," *Harvard Business Review,* 84 (10): 60–9.

Kolk, A. (1996) *Forests in International Environmental Politics. International Organizations, NGOs and the Brazilian Amazon.* Utrecht: International Books.

Kolk, A. (2011) "Mainstreaming sustainable coffee," *Sustainable Development,* doi: 10.1002/sd.507.

Kolk, A. (2013) "Contributing to a more sustainable coffee chain: projects for small farmers instigated by a multinational company," in A. Lindgreen, S. Sen, F. Maon and J. Vanhamme (eds). *Sustainable Value Chain Management: Analyzing, Designing, Implementing, and Monitoring for Social and Environmental Responsibility.* Farnham: Gower: 415–32.

Kolk, A. and Lenfant, F. (2012) "Business-NGO collaboration in a conflict setting: partnership activities in the Democratic Republic of Congo," *Business and Society,* 51 (3): 478–511.

Kolk, A. and Lenfant, F. (2013) "Multinationals, CSR and partnerships in Central African conflict countries. *Corporate Social Responsibility and Environmental Management,* 20 (1): 43–54

Kolk, A., van Tulder, R. and Kostwinder, E. (2008) "Partnerships for development," *European Management Journal,* 26 (4): 262–73.

Kolk, A., Van Dolen, W. and Vock, M. (2010) "Trickle effects of cross-sector social partnerships," *Journal of Business Ethics,* 94 (Supplement 1): 123–37.

Le Ber, M.J. and Branzei, O. (2010) "(Re)Forming strategic cross-sector partnerships. Relational processes of social innovation," *Business and Society,* 49 (1): 140–72.

Liese, A. and Beisheim, M. (2011) "Transnational public-private partnerships and the provision of collective goods in developing countries," in T. Risse (ed.). *Governance Without a State. Policies and Politics in Areas of Limited Statehood,* New York: Columbia University Press: 115–43.

Mair, J. and Martí, I. (2009) "Entrepreneurship in and around institutional voids: a case study from Bangladesh," *Journal of Business Venturing,* 24: 419–35.

Mair, J., Martí, I. and Ventresca, M.J. (2012) "Building inclusive markets in rural Bangladesh: how intermediaries work institutional voids," *Academy of Management Journal,* 55 (4): 819–50.

Marano, V. and Tashman, P. (2012) "MNE/NGO partnerships and the legitimacy of the firm," *International Business Review,* 21 (6): 1122–30.

Maxham III, J.G., Netemeyer, R.G. and Lichtenstein, D.R. (2008) "The retail value chain: linking employee perceptions to employee performance, customer evaluations, and store performance," *Marketing Science,* 27 (2): 147–67.

Mert, A. and Chan, S. (2012) "The politics of partnerships for sustainable development," in P. Pattberg, F. Biermann, S. Chan and A. Mert (eds). *Public-Private Partnerships for Sustainable Development. Emergence, Influence and Legitimacy,* Cheltenham: Edward Elgar: 21–43.

Mitlin, D., Hickey, S. and Bebbington, A. (2007) "Reclaiming development? NGOs and the challenge of alternatives," *World Development,* 35 (10): 1699–720.

Nerfin, M. (1987) "Neither prince nor merchant: citizen. An introduction to the third system," *Development Dialogue,* 1: 170–95.

OECD-DAC (2002) "Glossary of key terms in evaluation and results based management," Paris: OECD.

OECD (2006) "Evaluating the effectiveness and the efficiency of partnerships. Workshop on evaluating the effectiveness and efficiency of partnerships," Paris: OECD Environment Directorate, ENV/EPOC (2006) 15.

Pattberg, P., Biermann, F., Chan, S. and Mert, A. (2012) *Public-Private Partnerships for Sustainable Development. Emergence, Influence and Legitimacy*, Cheltenham: Edward Elgar.

Pedersen, E.R. (2005) "Guiding the invisible hand. The role of development agencies in driving corporate citizenship," *Journal of Corporate Citizenship*, 20: 77–91.

Pedrini, M. and Minciullo, M. (2011) "Italian corporate foundations and the challenge of multiple stakeholder interests," *Nonprofit Management and Leadership*, 22 (2): 173–97.

Pinkse, J. and Kolk, A. (2012) "Addressing the climate change – sustainable development nexus: the role of multi-stakeholder partnerships," *Business and Society*, 51 (1): 176–210.

Rangan, S., Samii, R. and Van Wassenhove, L.N. (2006) "Constructive partnerships: when alliances between private firms and public actors can enable creative strategies," *Academy of Management Review*, 31 (3): 738–51.

Reffico, E. and Márquez, P. (2012) "Inclusive networks for building BOP markets," *Business and Society*, 51 (3): 512–54.

Rivera-Santos, M., Rufin, C. and Kolk, A. (2012) "Bridging the institutional divide: partnerships in subsistence markets," *Journal of Business Research*, 65: 1721–7.

Rondinelli, D.A. and London, T. (2003) "How corporations and environmental groups collaborate: assessing cross-sector alliances and collaborations," *Academy of Management Executive*, 17 (1): 61–76.

Rugman, A. and Verbeke, A. (2008) "A regional solution to the strategy and structure of multinationals," *European Management Journal*, 26: 305–13.

Salamon, L.M. (2010) "Putting the civil society sector on the economic map of the world," *Annals of Public and Cooperative Economics*, 81 (2): 167–210.

Schäferhoff, M., Campe, S. and Kaan, C. (2009) "Transnational public-private partnerships in international relations: making sense of concepts, research frameworks, and results," *International Studies Review*, 11 (3): 451–74.

Seitanidi, M.M. (2009) "Missed opportunities of employee involvement in CSR partnerships," *Corporate Reputation Review*, 12 (2): 90–105.

Seitanidi, M.M. and Crane, A. (2009) "Implementing CSR through partnerships: understanding the selection, design and institutionalization of nonprofit-business partnerships," *Journal of Business Ethics*, 85: 413–29.

Seitanidi, M.M. and Ryan, A. (2007) "A critical review of forms of corporate community involvement: from philanthropy to partnerships," *International Journal of Nonprofit and Voluntary Sector Marketing*, 12: 247–66.

Selsky, J.W. and Parker, B. (2005) "Cross-sector partnerships to address social issues: challenges to theory and practice," *Journal of Management*, 31 (6): 849–73.

Szulecki, K., Pattberg, P. and Biermann, F. (2011) "Explaining variation in the effectiveness of transnational energy partnerships," *Governance: An International Journal of Policy, Administration, and Institutions*, 24 (4): 713–36.

Tennyson, R. and Harrison, T. (2008) "Under the spotlight. Building a better understanding of global business-NGO partnerships," International Business Leaders Forum.

Van der Voort, J.M., Glac, K. and Meijs, L.C.P.M. (2009) "Managing' corporate community involvement," *Journal of Business Ethics*, 90: 311–29.

Van Huijstee, M.M., Francken, M. and Leroy, P. (2007) "Partnerships for sustainable development: a review of current literature," *Environmental Sciences*, 4 (2): 75–89.

Vock, M. (2011) "Social interactions for economic value? A marketing perspective," PhD thesis, University of Amsterdam.

Vock, M., Van Dolen, W. and Kolk, A. (2013) "Micro-level interactions in business-nonprofit partnerships," *Business and Society*, doi: 10.1177/0007650313476030.

Waddock, S.A. (1991) "A typology of social partnership organizations," *Administration and Society*, 22 (4): 480–515.

Warner, M. and Sullivan, R. (2004) *Putting Partnerships to Work. Strategic Alliances for Development between Government, the Private Sector and Civil Society*. Sheffield: Greenleaf Publishing.

Webb, J.W., Kistruck, G.M., Ireland R.D. and Ketchen, Jr., D.J. (2010) "The entrepreneurship process in base of the pyramid markets: the case of multinational enterprise/nongovernment organization alliances," *Entrepreneurship Theory and Practice*, 34 (3): 555–81.

Westhues, M. and Einwiller, S. (2006) "Corporate foundations: their role for corporate social responsibility," *Corporate Reputation Review*, 9 (2): 144–53.

Wolfe, R.A. and Putler, D.S. (2002) "How tight are the ties that bind stakeholder groups?," *Organization Science*, 13 (1): 64–80.

Yaziji, M. and Doh, J. (2009) *NGOs and Corporations. Conflict and Collaboration*. Cambridge: Cambridge University Press.

3

INTERNATIONAL BUSINESS AND SOCIAL PARTNERSHIPS

How institutional and MNE capabilities affect collective-goods provisioning in emerging markets

Jonathan Doh and Jean Boddewyn

Introduction

Cross-sectoral collaborations among multinational enterprises (MNEs), governments, and non-governmental organizations (NGOs) are multiplying in emerging markets[1] regarding the provisioning of the collective goods – mainly, security, transportation, communication, utilities, education and basic healthcare – which these countries need for their overall development. Such collaborative arrangements involve establishing, steering, facilitating, operating and monitoring agreements to address public-policy problems that cannot be easily addressed by a single organization or the public sector alone (Tang and Mazmanian, 2009: 7).

Among the factors explaining this cooperative phenomenon are the growing foreign direct investments by MNEs in these countries on account of the latter's rapid growth and very positive business prospects. However, these underdeveloped economies typically suffer from significant "institutional voids" (Khanna and Palepu, 1997) because their government and civil society have proven impotent or ineffective in the provision of collective goods. Such unpropitious circumstances have led MNEs, as part of their global nonmarket strategies, to develop international corporate social responsibility (CSR) programs that respond to the collective-goods needs of the underdeveloped countries in which they do business (Brammer and Pavelin, 2006). We thus have a situation where both commercial and altruistic motives guide MNEs to collaborate with local and international NGOs also involved in the alleviation of institutional deficits in emerging markets (Beck, 2000; Moon and Vogel, 2008; Teegen et al., 2004; Yaziji and Doh, 2009).

Meanwhile, scholarly research on social partnerships in which public, private, and nonprofit organizations join together to address social issues has also grown. For example, a number of recent contributions have explored various aspects of firm-NGO-government interactions (Dahan *et al.*, 2010; Doh and Teegen, 2002; Lucea, 2010; Selsky and Parker, 2005). Yet, despite this growth in practical and scholarly interest in social partnerships, few studies have examined these relationships in the context of international-business theory and research[2] or have explicitly considered how the nature of the missing collective goods in emerging markets interacts with institutional conditions, managerial CSR motivations, and organization structures in determining the choice of governance mode for the provision of these goods. In this section of the book, authors present different perspectives on social partnerships at the local, national, and global levels. This chapter builds on the previous one by offering insights regarding the relevant macro-level and micro-organizational level that can be used to inform questions about roles and responsibilities for collective goods provision – a key contribution of social partnerships – especially in emerging and developing country settings.

Therefore, in this chapter, we leverage several complementary institutional and IB managerial theories to address and respond to the following research questions:

1 What are the challenges associated with the provision of collective goods in emerging markets?
2 How do institutional ordering systems as well as state and NGO capabilities bear on the provisioning of these goods?
3 How do the CSR motivations of MNEs as well as their overall strategy and organization structures affect the choice of governance modes for the provisioning of collective goods in emerging markets?
4 What are the implications of this choice for further research and managerial practice?

The following sections will: (1) distinguish collective goods from private ones and explain the former's shortages; (2) develop the array of governance modes available to supply collective goods; (3) demonstrate how the contractual hazards associated with cross-sectoral partnerships are handled in emerging markets, compared to their treatment in the developed countries from which MNEs originate; (4) analyze the capabilities of governments and NGOs as well as their interactions; (5) investigate the tensions created by the commercial and altruistic motivations of MNEs as well as the impact of MNE international strategies and organization structures on social partnerships, and (6) draw conclusions, implications, and suggestions for further research and managerial practice.

Collective goods and their deficits

We define *collective goods* as these products, functions, and services whose provision has been associated with the state in the form of "public goods" but whose supply has been increasingly assumed by both for-profit and not-for-profit organizations (Boddewyn and Lundan, 2011). They include: (1) *physical infrastructural goods* such as roads, wells, and electricity-generating equipment; (2) *social services* such as education, training, healthcare, and security, and (3) *institutional safeguards* of private-property and citizenship rights (Fisman and Khanna, 2004; Matten and Crane, 2005).

In modern times, the provision of collective goods was progressively assumed to be in the realm of the "public sphere.. That is, political governments were increasingly looked to for provision of "public goods," defined as goods that are accessible to all and for which all can use without reducing their availability to others (Doering, 2007).[3] However, the distinction between the "public" and "private" spheres – the latter referring essentially to the civil society made up of individuals and their associations – has significantly shrunk in recent decades due to the privatization of public agencies, the deregulation of swatches of economic activity and the liberalization or opening of national economies on account of globalization (Sales and Beschorner, 2006) but state over-indebtedness, corruption, and mismanagement have also contributed to the shortage and/or poor quality of public goods. Consequently, such goods are now also provided by non-profit organizations (e.g. NGOs) and for-profit firms (e.g. MNEs, private contractors, and indigenous firms). In this context, Indian business groups are known for their supplying of collective goods in the "underserviced areas" of the country which attract investors on account of their cheap labor, land, and natural resources (Fisman and Khanna, 2004). Thus, in reference to Gurgaon, an Indian city near New Delhi, which "has become a roaring engine of growth, if also a colossal headache as a place to live and work," Yardley (2011: A12) observed:

> To compensate for electricity blackouts, Gurgaon's companies and real estate developers operate massive diesel generators capable of powering small towns. No water? Drill private bore-wells. No public transportation? Companies employ hundreds of private buses and taxis. Worried about crime? Gurgaon has almost four times as many private security guards as police officers.

What distinguishes collective goods from private ones is that, when provided for free by public agencies, NGOs, and/or MNEs, these goods generate *positive externalities* for the local collectivities where these organizations operate. These communities benefit when, for example, firms supply free education, training, health, transportation and housing services to their employees and when they build roads and offer security in and around their facilities. However, this provision by private organizations – including NGOs – is not unlimited and some possible recipients may be excluded so that, in public-economics terms, they amount to "impure public goods" (Kotchen, 2006: 818) because they are either non-rival but excludable (e.g. worker training) or non-excludable and rival (e.g. a public well) in nature. Therefore we refer to them as "collective goods" but will limit our analysis to those provided in *local* communities rather than at the regional or national levels.

Key institutional factors bearing on social partnerships

Active in many countries and involving a variety of economic and non-economic partners, social partnerships are affected by many institutional factors. We will highlight those that particularly bear on the choice of governance modes – namely, the "ordering systems" (see below) that rule relationships among individuals and organizations in emerging markets as well as the capabilities of governments and NGOs because they have been overlooked or minimized in IB studies. Before analyzing them, we will introduce the relevant governance modes bearing on social partnerships – one of which has so far been overlooked (Boddewyn and Doh, 2011; Boddewyn and Lundan, 2011).

Governance modes

According to transaction-costs economics (Williamson, 1985, 1996), the provision of intermediate products – including collective goods – can be assured through one or more of the traditional alternatives of market, alliance, and internalization: (1) MNEs can *contract* with governments and NGOs to buy the goods from the latter and pay for them; (2) MNEs, NGOs, and government agencies can *ally* by setting up public-private partnerships and other types of collaborations for the joint delivery of these collective goods, and (3) MNEs may *internalize* the production of these goods. However, we must consider a fourth governance mode which has been largely ignored in international-business research – namely, that MNEs can *assist* government agencies and/or NGOs through philanthropic and political actions distinguishable from the three traditional governance modes.

Assisting relies on voluntary one-way donations of various kinds – e.g. of money, goods, services, and employees' time and skills – with no direct impact on financial performance (Seifert *et al.*, 2004) and with no explicit *quid pro quo* as in contracting although the donor's power and reputation may benefit from these actions. According to Salamon (1987), assisting reflects the failure of the market system in the provision of collective goods on account of the free-rider problem as well as the failings of governments which can only provide those collective goods which command majority political support. It also permits a degree of diversity and competition among its non-profit recipients, which improves their efficiency and reduces their transaction costs which are lower than those required to mobilize government response to shortages of collective goods.

Assistance is used when contracting would jeopardize the independence of the aid's recipient and raise issues of paternalism (that is, controlling uses and recipients) and particularism (that is, favoring certain uses and recipients). It also includes the "building of government capability" of Valente and Crane (2010) as well as MNEs influencing public policy, which institutional theory considers to be as important as adapting to it (North, 1990, 2005).

Alternative Ordering Systems

Analyses of governance modes have implicitly assumed that they take place in either "well-ordered societies" where property rights and contract enforcement are assured or in "burdened" ones – such as emerging markets – lacking such predictability (Hsieh, 2004; Rawls, 1999). However, even in the latter, means must be found "by which order is accomplished in a relation in which potential conflict threatens to undo or upset opportunities to realize mutual gains" (Williamson, 1996: 12). In developed countries, business transactions and alliances – including social partnerships among MNEs, NGOs, and government agencies – can largely rely on what Williamson (1996: 10) called the "legal centralism" – an assumption that assures enforceable contracts on which exchanges depend. Below we describe what the presence – or absence – of such guarantees would mean for the division of labor in social partnerships. Under such *public ordering*, money – in the forms of taxes, fees, bribes, and donations – is used by firms to obtain the collective goods they need although other "tools" (Kindleberger, 1970: 14) such as force (e.g. the voting out of unfavorable politicians), trust, status, and reputation are also employed for that purpose since economic exchanges are typically embedded in social relations (Granovetter, 1985).

The legal institutions that underlay public ordering are supplemented or replaced in emerging economies by a *private-ordering* system also designed to handle contractual hazards. It is a consensual "bottom-up" system that derives its efficacy and legitimacy from the continuous support of its members and allows many exchanges to take place even when pricing is difficult, property rights are unclear or insecure, and the pursuit of self-interest is insufficient to guarantee orderly transactions free of malfeasance and opportunism (Granovetter, 1985). In lieu of relying on well-defined property rights and contract laws, exchanges are embedded in a broad set of relationships with the same party so that non-performance in one exchange can be penalized in later ones. Deviance from approved behavior is sanctioned through ostracism from the exchange process and/or the withholding of legitimacy, which results in the denial of relevant resources (Ahuja and Yayavaram, 2009; Li and Filer, 2007). For example, if a participant in a social partnership did not live up to its commitments, in an environment of private ordering this failure could be sanctioned through the process of communication and result in that party being excluded from future partnership opportunities due its reputation as an untrustworthy partner.

Societies relying extensively on private ordering are usually characterized by a lower level of generalized public trust and a lack of personal and collective moral values in relations with strangers (Ahuja and Yayavaram, 2009; Brehm and Rahn, 1997; Li and Filer, 2007). Besides, people rely mostly on private information obtained through personal relations and networking with insiders (Li and Filer, 2007: 83). As such, transacting in emerging markets involves few fixed costs but significant marginal ones because one needs to screen, test, and monitor each and every transaction partner. As the market expands from a local to regional, national and international levels, the number of business partners increases and the marginal cost of transactions and relations rises significantly (Li and Filer, 2007: 86).

Private ordering is used everywhere – even in developed economies (Williamson, 1996) – but particularly so in emerging markets where it may co-exist with a strong government that exercises coercive force and tends to favor state enterprises as is the case in China (Peng, 2003) although such *state ordering* differs significantly from the one exercised under public ordering where governments focus on protecting property rights and assisting the enforcement of contracts.

Collaborative arrangements among firms, NGOs and governments must obviously be structured differently under these three distinct ordering systems. Thus, under the public ordering found in developed countries, firms will typically contract or ally with government agencies, NGOs, and private contractors in order to obtain the collective goods they need while internalization and assistance make more sense under the private- and state-ordering systems found in emerging markets.

State and civil-society capabilities

We must also consider the capabilities of state agencies and of such civil-society organizations as NGOs in emerging markets under the above ordering systems, and which can vary from low to high. Thus, when both state and civil-society organizations are absent or ineffective, MNEs with substantial commercial interests in a country's abundant natural resources (e.g. oil, gold, and diamonds in African countries) frequently provide security, transportation, a literate and healthy workforce and other necessary collective goods because the size of the rents generated by these vast MNE projects warrants the internal production of the collective goods necessary for these firms' market activities of innovation, production, and marketing. When shortages of state and civil-society capabilities prevail in poor least-developed countries such as Haiti where MNEs are unlikely to have sizeable investments, assistance in the form of philanthropic donations through cash, food, medical supplies, and the seconding of personnel is more appropriate – together with helping governments build greater development capacity (Valente and Crane, 2010).

High government and weak NGO capabilities are found in such countries as China and Russia where state ordering predominates. Thus, Chinese governmental institutions are reasonably well-developed and able to provide most collective goods – from basic infrastructure to health, education, and communication – although, because of the government's ideological orientation, the civil-society sector is quite underdeveloped. Indeed, the state maintains strict permit and registration requirements for NGOs which, like other non-profit organizations, are, in fact, arms of the government (Peng, 2003). In such environments, MNEs' main role is to assist – whether voluntarily or not – state-sponsored NGOs.

NGOs operate in all types of societies and economies but, under low state capability, these non-profit organizations – often with the support of foreign governments, MNEs, and private foundations – assume primary responsibility for a variety of public functions. This NGO role is most likely to occur within "failing states"

(Fund for Peace, 2010) where basic government institutions are inoperative, and following natural disasters and civil wars. Under such circumstances, MNEs' role is generally limited to providing regular and emergency assistance, and they contract with NGOs for the delivery of their help.

When both government agencies and NGOs can deliver collective goods effectively, as in developed countries, the state may delegate their production and distribution to private firms and non-profit organizations through public-private bi- or tri-partite social partnerships involving private firms and/or NGOs because such collaborative arrangements are more flexible compared to a state bureaucracy and/or more economical in terms of transaction costs (Salamon, 1987).

Nowadays, state and civil-society capabilities can be readily measured through the World Bank Worldwide Governance Indicators (WGI) which provide data about government effectiveness, the rule of law, the control of corruption, and other criteria (Kaufmann *et al.*, 2010) while the United States Agency for International Development's Sustainability Index scores NGOs on such dimensions as organizational capability, financial viability, and public image.

In this section, we analyzed the variety of governance modes available for social partnerships, the impact of ordering systems on the choice of these modes, and the capabilities of state and civil-society organizations. We will now consider the capabilities of MNEs bearing on these choices.

Motivational, strategic and organizational factors bearing on social partnerships

There is little research that explicitly examines the role of MNEs in social partnerships, with most of the contributions being cases and practitioner accounts (see Dahan *et al.*, 2009 for an exception). As such, this research has tended to focus on the reasons *why* MNEs engage with NGOs and governments – for example the benefits they derive from them (Argenti, 2004) – but we must also consider how these motivations are related to the strategic orientations of MNEs as well as to their organizational structures.

MNE motivations

When MNEs supply collective goods to the local communities where they operate, they are effectively exercising their *corporate social responsibility* (CSR) of which we can distinguish two main types (see Doh and Guay, 2004 for a review).

Strategic CSR. This form assumes that a company's social practices are integral to its business- and corporate-level strategies, and that CSR behavior emanates from its economic interests (McWilliams *et al.*, 2006). Baron (2001) coined the expression "strategic CSR" and argued that companies compete for socially responsible customers by explicitly linking their social contributions to product sales. Under this perspective, firms must identify some strategic commercial benefit before engaging in CSR so that one would expect CSR investments to be focused in projects and programs that are self-benefiting, short-term, and asset-specific – that is, to the extent that a firm invests in the provision of a collective good, one would anticipate this good to be directly related to its commercial interests. For example, a firm motivated by strategic CSR would be more inclined to build a road leading to – and only to – its plant and less likely to invest in one for which there may be more general purposes of interest to local communities. In addition to investments in physical assets, firms motivated by strategic CSR may also make ones designed to bolster their legitimacy or reputation (e.g. donations to NGOs) – preferably those with concrete and measurable benefits.

Altruistic CSR. Another potential motivation for firms to engage in CSR emanates from a deeper moral philosophy related to altruism or, more operationally, to philanthropy (Carroll, 1991). This motivation is more consistent with early definitions of CSR such as the one proposed by Bowen (1953: 6) who stated that CSR refers to the "obligations of businessmen to pursue those policies, to make those decisions, or to follow those lines of action which are desirable in terms of the objectives and values of our society." While this conceptualization may appear to rest on the individual preferences and choices of a single or small group of leaders, McGuire (1963: 144) argued that: "The idea of social responsibilities supposes that the corporation has not only economic and legal obligations but also certain responsibilities to society which extend beyond these obligations." Hence, these duties can be organizational as well as individual.

Under this perspective, there is no presumption that the firm is pursuing corporate social responsibility in order to advance its own interests, except perhaps under the longest of time horizons. Rather, the firm is providing collective goods due to some intrinsic moral motivation so that it may be willing to invest in and support collective goods for which it is one of many beneficiaries or not a beneficiary at all. In other words, the positive externalities of such investments would be a paramount factor in their decisions.

Mixed motivations. Obviously, firms – like individuals – have mixed motives for most of their behaviors and, in this regard, we would expect MNEs to pursue CSR in general and collective goods provision in particular for reasons of both altruism and strategy. Hence, we visualize these archetypes as two poles of a continuum, and Carroll (1983: 604) offered a definition of CSR that recognized both strategic and ethical dimensions when he stressed that:

> In my view, CSR involves the conduct of a business so that it is economically profitable, law abiding, ethical and socially supportive. To be socially responsible ... then means that profitability and obedience to the law are foremost conditions to discussing the firm's ethics and the extent to which it supports the society in which it exists with contributions of money, time and talent. Thus, CSR is composed of four parts: economic, legal, ethical and voluntary or philanthropic.

In this regard, Dahan *et al.* (2009) documented how Nestlé's cocoa initiatives in West Africa reflect both strategic and altruistic considerations as it directly engages local NGOs and governments in setting up programs to improve labor conditions and promote sustainable farming practices in this region. Similarly, Nestlé's sponsorship of farmers' field schools in Ivory Coast supports the production of higher-quality cocoa which has obvious benefits for local communities but also ensures that Nestlé has access to these improved labor and production.

Strategic configurations of CSR

We must also consider the strategic organization and administration of CSR activities because a number of scholars have suggested that firms should and do develop international CSR strategies that parallel their core business ones (e.g. Brammer and Pavelin, 2006). In this regard, MNEs face the fundamental question of when to pursue global, regional, or local strategies – an issue commonly referred to as the *global-integration versus national-responsiveness* trade-off. Here, we can leverage the classic Bartlett and Ghoshal (1989) typology to understand at what organizational level(s) MNEs organize and administer their CSR activities under three types of international firms: (1) *multidomestic* (combining low integration and high responsiveness); (2) *global* (combining high integration with low responsiveness), and (3) *transnational* (combining high integration with high responsiveness). Each one of these types affect how a MNE organizes and implements its CSR strategy but we will limit ourselves to focusing on the impact of the levels of global integration and national responsiveness.

Global integration. This strategy favors the production and distribution of products and services of a homogeneous type and quality on a worldwide basis in order to generate cost advantages through economies of scale. Under it, we would expect MNEs to maintain a consistent and standardized approach to their CSR programs and the social partnerships that are part of them in the various markets in which they do business around the world. We would also anticipate MNEs to engage in broad worldwide partnerships with major international NGOs and supranational governmental organizations (e.g. the World Bank and the United Nations) and, to some extent, with national governments. For example, the Coca-Cola Corporation and the World Wildlife Fund – the global conservation organization – have engaged in a broad global initiative related to water conservation, and they use it in a range of markets in which both organizations are active. This project also involves a number of national governments (e.g. that of China) but does not explicitly engage local NGOs or public agencies.

National responsiveness. This strategy reflects the need to understand different consumer tastes in segmented regional markets and to respond to distinct national standards and regulations imposed by autonomous governments. A related perspective on this strategic approach emanates from research on institutional isomorphism and the degree to which MNEs should embed themselves and adjust to the institutional conditions faced in specific local markets (Kostova and Roth, 2002).

Under this strategy, social partnerships between MNEs and NGOs would be comprised of MNEs working with locally embedded organizations, seeking to leverage and maximize the latter's tacit knowledge and insights, and – as Oetzel and Doh (2008) have suggested – devolving considerable responsibilities to those local organizations in the management and implementation of the social partnerships. In this regard, Dahan *et al.* (2009) have illustrated how MNEs and NGOs integrate their respective business models to be especially responsive to local community conditions and contexts. The French company Danone, for example, has partnered with local nonprofit organizations in Africa to promote the development of higher-standard dairy products as part of its marketing of single-serving yogurt drinks in many developing-country markets around the world. Similarly, HSBC Amah has partnered with Islamic Relief to develop financial products that respect Islamic law – the *Sharia* – regarding lending practices.

Organizational factors

The manner in which an MNE organizes and administers its international CSR program bears upon the distribution of responsibilities for the provision of collective goods – particularly, the level of organizational hierarchy where this supply takes place. Thus, globally integrated social partnerships would necessarily require some significant NGO capability – not so much in the local region or country in which an MNE has a particular interest but rather as part of higher-level global programs and initiatives. In other words, all things being equal, the more global the MNE's strategy, the more likely will collective goods provisioning take place at the supranational level – with MNEs, NGOs, and international governmental organizations coming together to plan, coordinate, and administer social partnerships that span national boundaries and reflect some degree of consistency and standardization across the geographies, political systems, and cultures in which those activities take place.

One consequence of such global initiatives is that they would be less likely to reflect the unique and distinctive environments which we discussed in the previous section on institutional factors while MNEs that pursue a more locally adaptive CSR strategy would naturally be more inclined to partner with local organizations as well as state and local governments as they direct their CSR initiatives toward specific social needs within circumscribed geographic boundaries and under specific institutional conditions. These programs would be highly responsive to the unique features and idiosyncrasies of distinct institutional contexts and, therefore, would tend to vary substantially across different locations and contexts.

Implications for social partnerships

The combination of governmental and NGO capabilities, on the one hand, with those of MNEs, on the other hand, has implications for the success of social partnerships that involve all three types of parties. A recent publication by Bhanji and Oxley (2011) is particularly relevant in this regard because they highlighted the need for MNEs to address two important *liabilities* – namely, those of "foreignness" and "privateness" which affect the perceived legitimacy of MNE involvement in public domains such as education and public health.

Foreign investors suffer from their lack of familiarity with host-country institutional and operating environments as well as from a lack of legitimacy where there is high economic nationalism (Zaheer, 1995). This *liability of foreignness* provides a strong motivation for partnering with local organizations – private and public as well as for-profit and not-for-profit bodies – when entering foreign countries. While institutional environments that discourage foreign direct investment also tend to dissuade investing in social partnerships abroad, such investments also serve to enhance the general legitimacy of the MNE and can significantly reduce the risks associated with its foreign status. Hence, partnering with local NGOs, in addition to protection against direct government actions such as expropriation, also offers important knowledge about the development priorities in the host location as well as access to relevant local systems (e.g. in education and health care) for program delivery (Bhanji and Oxley, 2011).

However, in many countries, any significant private investment in the public domain is regarded with suspicion in areas such as education and public health where the government and civil society are viewed as the only legitimate sources of authority. This *liability of privateness* also hampers the legitimacy of MNEs but partnering with a civil-society organization such as a NGO – whether local or international – may help regain it. As Teegen *et al.* (2004: 468) pointed out:

> Many NGOs are adept at providing certain goods and services because they have gained technical expertise and experience by working in difficult settings or with underserved populations. NGOs also tend to enjoy greater public trust than their firm or government counterparts thanks to their social-welfare ideals and relative immunity from pressures to "sell out." Given their expertise and trusted position, they are often best suited to provide high-quality services at low cost to publics with unmet needs.

In partnering with a NGO, MNEs may choose between a local and an international one. As long as the liability of foreignness is relatively low, a partnership with an international NGO may represent the most effective solution but, when the liabilities of foreignness and privateness are both high, linking with a local NGO is the best choice. When both liabilities are low, the MNE may eschew partnerships altogether and internalize the provision of collective goods in order to avoid the contractual hazards inherent to all alliances (Bhanji and Oxley, 2011).

Conclusions, limitations, and further research

In this chapter, we have highlighted some of the major institutional, motivational, strategic and organizational factors that bear upon the relative distribution of responsibilities among states, firms and NGOs in social partnerships. Building on the previous chapter and the overall scope of the book, our analysis was based on the literature on institutional voids and their remedies, international-business organization theory, and insights from research on corporate social responsibilities. While many factors bear on the choice of governance modes, we demonstrated how particular combinations of institutional and firm factors bear on the selection of these modes. Some of these topics are taken up again in latter chapters, especially the contribution of Rufin and Rivera-Santos, who also explore the interaction among institutions and partnership governance, and oversight.

Limitations and further research

Our selectivity forced us to set aside alternative formulations of the problems and solutions associated with social partnerships. Thus, we focused on the *characteristics of firms* in terms of motivational, strategic, and organizational factors although Williamson (1996: 5) argued that it is the *characteristics of transactions* in terms of asset-specificity, external and internal uncertainty, and frequency that matter for the choice of governance modes. Besides, we left out of our analysis the impact of the three pillars of Scott (1992) although social partnerships are often reflective of weak "regulative" institutions that must be compensated by "cognitive" and "normative" ones (Lucea, 2010; Rivera-Santos *et al.*, 2011).[4] Moreover, we focused on the behaviors of MNEs in terms of motivations, strategic perspectives and organizational structures but left out a complementary analysis of the comportments of public agencies and NGOs (Yaziji and Doh, 2009) which differ from MNEs in terms of interests (public over private), incentives (independence and avoidance of compromising ties) and resources (e.g. providing MNEs with legitimacy to help overcome the liabilities of foreignness and privateness). Furthermore, we know that social partnerships evolve over time (Yaziji and Doh, 2009) but we did not consider the dynamic propensities prompted, for example, by changes in government leadership and public policies.

Conclusions

In recent decades, the trend toward greater involvement of MNEs in achieving public goals has been unmistakable (Valente and Crane, 2010: 52) but these firms have discovered that addressing and resolving the institutional voids found in emerging markets often requires partnering with public agencies, NGOs, local community leaders, and private contractors in order to generate positive externalities from their collaborations (e.g. Tang and Mazmanian, 2009).

Social partnerships take many forms whose choice is affected by multiple external and internal factors. We emphasized the importance of ordering systems because many analyses of social partnerships do not take into account the interaction of such systems with the distribution of responsibility for public goods in country settings where governments may be unable or unwilling to provide such goods. Besides, MNEs' contributions to social partnerships are affected by their motivations to engage in CSR programs, which range from the instrumental to the altruistic and are the product of these firms' organization and decision-making structures.

In this context, our analysis has highlighted the governance mode of assistance which has been totally ignored in applications of internalization theory and transaction-cost economics to the study of foreign direct investment in emerging markets. Whether instrumental or altruistic, support and assistance is a phenomenon deserving much greater attention because of the theoretical and practical implications of its existence and impact. Besides, the study of social partnerships can only benefit from the consideration of ordering systems which we have highlighted in this chapter in order to dispel the notion that the institutions of emerging- and developing-market countries are equally and similarly underdeveloped.

Questions for reflection

1 How can social partnerships contribute to economic and social development in emerging markets?
2 What are the supra-institutional, national, regional, sectoral, organizational, and individual variables that contribute to the success or failure of cross-sectoral partnerships?
3 How might social partnerships differ among least developed, developing, and developed markets?

Notes

1 *Emerging markets* are generally viewed as lower-income or middle-income countries that have undertaken substantial liberalization and policy reform (e.g. trade liberalization and the privatization of state-owned enterprise) and have subsequently experience rapid-growth as a result. Some of these countries are treated as "economies in transition" since they have been dominated by business groups now moving toward economic liberalization, are going through the privatization of state enterprises and are engendering more publicly-owned companies and independent intermediaries (Hoskisson *et al.*, 2000: 249; Khanna *et al.*, 2005; Peng, 2003). For our purposes, we focus primarily on emerging markets' level of institutional development so that in the following analyses we will present archetypes even though many countries fall within a continuum rather than into discrete categories.
2 See Dahan *et al.* (2009), Vachani *et al.* (2009), and Valente and Crane (2010) for important exceptions.
3 A *public good* is a commodity or service whose benefits are not depleted by an additional user (that is, they are "non-rival") and from which it is generally difficult or impossible to exclude people (that is, they are "non-excludable) (Doering, 2007: 1126).
4 The *regulative* pillar comprises rule-setting, monitoring, and sanctioning activities, the *cognitive* one focuses on shared conceptions that constitute the nature of social reality and the frames through which meaning is made, and the *normative* introduces a prescriptive, evaluative and obligatory dimension (Scott, 1992).

References

Ahuja, G. and Yayavaram, S. (2011) Explaining influence rents: the case for an institutions-based view of strategy. *Organization Science*, 22 (6): 1631–52.

Argenti, P. (2004) Collaborating with activists: how Starbucks works with NGOs, *California Management Review*, 47 (1): 91–116.

Baron, D.P. (2001) Private politics, corporate social responsibility, and integrated strategy. *Journal of Economics and Management Strategy*, 10 (1): 7–45.

Bartlett, C.A. and Ghoshal, S. (1989) *Managing Across Borders. The Transnational Solution.* Boston, MA: Harvard Business School Press.

Beck, U. (2000) *What is Globalization?* Cambridge: Polity Press.

Bhanji, Z. and Oxley, J.E. (2011) Dancing with the enemy: confronting governance challenges in international corporate citizenship partnerships. Toronto: Rotman School of Management, University of Toronto, April.

Boddewyn, J. and Doh, J. (2011) Global strategy and the collaboration of MNEs, governments and NGOs for the provisioning of collective goods in emerging markets. *Global Strategy Journal*, 1: 345–61.

Boddewyn, J.J. and Lundan, S.M. (2011) The internalization of the production of collective goods by MNEs. Working paper; New York: Baruch College.

Bowen, H.R. (1953) *Social Responsibilities of the Businessman.* New York: Harper & Row.

Brammer, S.J. and Pavelin, S. (2006) Corporate reputation and social performance: the importance of fit. *Journal of Management Studies*, 43 (3): 435–55.

Brehm, J. and Rahn, W. (1997) Individual-level evidence for the causes and consequences of social capital. *American Journal of Political Science*, 41 (3): 999–1023.

Carroll, A.B. (1983) Corporate social responsibility: will industry respond to cutbacks in social program funding? *Vital Speeches of the Day*, 48 (19): 604–8.

Carroll, A.B. (1991) The pyramid of corporate social responsibility: toward the moral management of organizational stakeholders. *Business Horizons*, 34 (4): 39–48.

Dahan, N., Doh, J.P., Oetzel, J. and Yaziji, M. (2009) Corporate-NGO collaboration: creating new business models for developing markets. *Long Range Planning*, 43 (2): 326–42.

Dahan, N., Doh, J.P. and Teegen, H. (2010) Role of nongovernmental organizations in the business-government-society interface: special issue overview and introductory essay. *Business and Society*, 35 (1): 20–34.

Doering, O.C. (2007) The political economy of public goods: why economists should care. *American Journal of Agricultural Economics*, 89 (5): 1125–33.

Doh. J.P. and Guay, T.R. (2004) Globalization and corporate social responsibility: how nongovernmental organizations influence labor and environmental codes of conduct. *Management International Review*, 44 (3): 7–30.

Doh, J.P. and Teegen, H. (2002) Nongovernmental organizations as institutional actors in international business: theory and implications. *International Business Review*, 11 (6): 665–84.

Fisman, R. and Khanna, T. (2004) Facilitating development: the role of business groups. *World Development*, 32 (4): 609–28.

Fund for Peace. (2010) *Failed States Index 2010.* Washington, DC: The Fund for Peace www.fund forpeace.org/web/index.php?option=com_content&task=view&id=99&Itemid=140.

Granovetter, M. (1985) Economic action and social structure: the problem of embeddedness. *American Journal of Sociology*, 91 (3): 481–510.

Hirschman, A.O. (1970) *Exit, Voice and Loyalty: Responses to Decline in Firms, Organizations and States.* Cambridge, MA: Harvard University Press.

Hoskisson, R.E., Eden, L., Lau C.M. and Wright, M. (2000) Strategy in emerging economies. *Academy of Management Journal*, 43 (2): 249–67.

Hsieh, N-h. (2004) The obligations of transnational corporations: Rawlsian justice and the duty of assistance. *Business Ethics Quarterly*, 14 (4): 643–61.

Kaufmann, D., Kraay, A. and Mastruzzi, M. (2010) Governance matters IX: governance indicators for 1996–2009. Washington, DC: World Bank: Working Paper 2196.

Khanna T. and Palepu, K. (1997) Why focused strategies may be wrong for emerging markets. *Harvard Business Review,* 75 (4): 41–9.

Khanna T., Palepu, K. and Sinha, J. (2005) Strategies that fit emerging markets. *Harvard Business Review,* June: 63–76.

Kindleberger, C.P. (1970) *Power and Money.* New York: Basic Books.

Kostova, T. and Roth, K. (2002) Adoption of an organizational practice by subsidiaries of multinational corporations: institutional and relational effects. *Academy of Management Journal,* 45 (1): 215–33.

Kotchen, M. (2006) Green markets and the private provision of public goods. *Journal of Political Economy,* 114 (4): 816–34.

Li, S. and Filer, L. (2007) The effects of the governance environment on the choice of investment mode and the strategic implications. *Journal of World Business,* 42 (1): 80–98.

Lucea, R. (2010) How we see them versus how they see themselves a cognitive perspective of firm-NGO relationships. *Business and Society,* 49 (1), 116–39.

Matten, D. and Crane, A. (2005) Corporate citizenship: toward an extended theoretical conceptualization. *Academy of Management Review,* 30 (1): 166–79.

McGuire, J.W. (1963) *Business and Society.* New York: McGraw-Hill.

McWilliams, A., Siegel, D.S. and Wright. P.M. (2006) Corporate social responsibility: strategic implications, *Journal of Management Studies,* 43 (1): 1–18.

Moon, J. and Vogel, D. (2008) Corporate social responsibility, government and civil society, in A. Crane, A. McWilliams, D. Matten, J. Moon and D. Siegel (eds). *Oxford Handbook of Corporate Social Responsibility.* Oxford: Oxford University Press.

North, D.C. (1990) *Institutions, Institutional Change, and Economic Performance.* New York: Cambridge University Press.

North, D.C. (2005) *Understanding the Process of Economic Change.* Princeton, NJ: Princeton University Press.

Oetzel, J. and Doh, J.P. (2009) Multinational enterprise and development: a review and reconceptualization. *Journal of World Business,* 44 (2): 108–20.

Peng, M.W. (2003) Institutional transitions and strategic choices. *Academy of Management Review,* 28 (2): 275–96.

Rawls, J. (1999) *The Law of Peoples.* Cambridge, MA: Harvard University Press.

Rivera-Santos, M., Rufin, C. and Kolk, A. (2011) Bridging the institutional divide: partnerships in subsistence markets. *Journal of Business Research,* 65: 1721–7.

Salamon, L.M. (1987) Of market failure, voluntary failure, and third-party government: towards a theory of government-nonprofit relations in the modern welfare state. *Journal of Voluntary Action Research,* 16 (1–2): 29–49.

Sales, A. and Beschorner, T. (2006) Societal transformation and business ethics: the expansion of the private sector and its consequences, in N. Stehr, C. Henning and B. Weiler (eds). *The moralization of the markets.* New Brunswick, NJ: Transaction Books, pp. 227–54.

Scott, W.R. (1992) *Organizations: Rational, Natural, and Open Systems.* Englewood Cliffs, NJ: Prentice-Hall.

Seifert, B., Morris, S.A. and Bartkus, B.R. (2004) Having, giving and getting: slack resources, corporate philanthropy, and firm financial performance. *Business and Society,* 43 (2): 135–61.

Selsky, J.W. and Parker, B. (2005) Cross-sector partnerships to address social issues: challenges to theory and practice. *Journal of Management,* 31 (6): 1–25.

Tang, S-Y. and Mazmanian, D.A. (2009) Collaborative governance approached through theory. Working paper; Los Angeles, CA: University of California, Bedrosian Center on Governance and the Public Enterprise.

Teegen, H., Doh, J.P. and Vachani, S. (2004) The importance of nongovernmental organizations (NGOs) in global governance and value creation: an international business research agenda. *Journal of International Business Studies*, 35 (6): 463–83.

Vachani, S., Doh, J.P. and Teegen, H. (2009) NGOs' influence on MNEs' social development strategies in varying institutional contexts: a transaction-cost perspective. *International Business Review*, 18: 446–56.

Valente, M. and Crane, A. (2010) Public responsibility and private enterprise in developing countries. *California Management Review,* 52 (3), Spring: 52–78.

Williamson, O.E. (1985) *The Economic Institutions of Capitalism.* New York: Free Press.

Williamson, O.E. (1996) *The Mechanisms of Governance.* New York: Oxford University Press.

Yardley, J. (2011) Where growth and dysfunction have no boundaries. *New York Times,* June 9: A1, A12–13.

Yaziji, M. and Doh, J.P. (2009) *NGOs and Corporations: Conflict and Collaboration.* Cambridge: Cambridge University Press.

Zaheer, S. (1995) Overcoming the liability of foreignness. *Academy of Management Journal,* 38 (2): 341–63.

4

CROSS-SECTOR SOCIAL PARTNERSHIP IN AREAS OF LIMITED STATEHOOD

Ralph Hamann

Introduction: The state's role in cross-sector partnership

The growing interest in cross-sector collaboration (Seitanidi and Lindgren, 2011) is increasingly giving rise also to research on social partnerships in developing or emerging economies. Dahan *et al.* (2010) describe, for instance, the important role that non-governmental organizations can play in collaboration with multinational enterprises to develop business models with both financial and social benefits in developing markets. Partnerships are particularly helpful because these companies lack knowledge and other resources to respond to challenges brought about by the "cultural, economic, institutional, geographic and other features of these markets" (ibid: 327) (see also Doh and Boddewyn (2014) in this volume). It is clear that context matters in the motivation and implementation of cross-sector social partnerships. This chapter emphasizes the institutional dimension, given that cross-sector partnerships are an institutional response to institutional challenges (see Rufin and Rivera-Santos, and Vurro and Dacin (2014) in this volume).

Hoskisson *et al.* (2000: 252) characterize emerging economies in terms of "missing institutional features (for instance, shortages of skilled labor, thin capital markets, infrastructure problems) as well as political and economic instability." Yet defining emerging markets in terms of what is missing relative to developed economies has been criticized as an "imperialist mindset" (Prahalad and Lieberthal, 1998; London and Hart, 2004). Peng (2003: 283) puts greater emphasis on "institutional transitions," that is, far-reaching changes in the "formal and informal rules of the game," giving rise to the question, "How do organizations play the new game when the new rules are not completely known?" (ibid: 283).

So whether institutions are different (Dahan *et al.*, 2010), absent (Hoskisson *et al.*, 2000) or changing (Peng, 2003), all of these characteristics give rise to challenges for business and other organizations in achieving their objectives. They may be seen as "governance gaps" that provide motivations for different role-players to establish cross-sector collaborations as "new" forms of governance (Moon, 2002). The emerging economy context thus arguably represents the front line of a global phenomenon, as partnerships are being established in response to gaps or deficits in traditional governance models. These gaps appear especially due to the limited – and some argue declining – ability of states to devise and implement rules or to provide public goods in the increasingly global and complex interactions between social, economic, and environmental systems (Benner *et al.*, 2004).

Institutional conditions likely affect *why* cross-sector partnerships are established, because institutional flux or even voids (Mair and Martí, 2009) provide important reasons for organizations to attempt such collaboration (Crosby and Bryson, 2010). At the same time, these institutional conditions influence *how* partnerships are designed and implemented, as well as their likely success (see also Crosby and Bryson, 2010; Vurro *et al.*, 2010). In this chapter, institutional conditions are characterized in terms borrowed from political scientists (bearing in mind Parmigiani and Rivera-Santos' (2011) call for multi-theoretical approaches in the study of cross-sector partnerships). Specific emphasis is placed on the role of the state, a focus that has arguably received inadequate attention among management scholars (Crane, 2010).

Börzel and Risse (2010: 113) consider how governance arrangements are established and maintained in "areas of limited statehood," that is, those geographic or policy areas in which "political institutions are too weak to hierarchically adopt and enforce collectively binding rules." They identify a dilemma in that the same conditions of limited statehood that are likely to motivate for "new," non-hierarchical governance arrangements, including partnerships, are simultaneously likely to make such alternative arrangements difficult to implement because of a lack of a "shadow of hierarchy." This shadow is created when "the state threatens – explicitly or implicitly – to impose binding rules or laws on private actors in order to change their cost–benefit calculations in favor of a voluntary agreement closer to the common good rather than to particularistic self-interests" (ibid: 116).

Figure 4.1 schematically illustrates how the cooperation incentive faced by the government and non-state actors change with varying degrees of state capacity to exert a meaningful shadow of hierarchy. Weak states are likely to be less inclined to cooperate with non-state actors because they fear a loss of autonomy, as basic rules governing the cooperation may not be enforced. Strong states, on the other hand, have little incentive to cooperate because they are ostensibly in a position to provide governance by themselves and are unlikely to want to share authority. According to this argument, there is thus some "middle level" of state capacity that is most likely to give rise to a government incentive to cooperate with non-state actors. This results in the solid curve (a) representing government incentives to engage in partnerships.

Meanwhile, Börzel and Risse (2010) argue that non-state actors are more incentivized to cooperate with the state as the state's ability to exert a "shadow of hierarchy" grows, because they seek to avoid hierarchical mandates in favor of

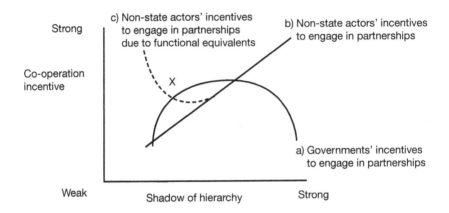

FIGURE 4.1 Governments' and non-state actors' incentives to engage in partnerships depend on the "shadow of hierarchy" and its functional equivalents. Lines a), b) and c) are explained further in the text.

Source: Adapted from Börzel and Risse, 2010: 117

negotiated agreements – this is represented by the straight line in Figure 4.1 (b). However, we have empirical evidence that suggests non-state actors, and businesses in particular, are at least trying to embark on partnerships with the state even if the state is manifestly weak, such as in the Democratic Republic of Congo (Kolk and Lenfant, 2012). Börzel and Risse (2010) explain this with reference to functional equivalents for the state-reliant shadow of hierarchy. These functional equivalents may be premised on the need for companies to maintain some basic level of public service provision and rule enforcement (that is, they fear the "shadow of anarchy"). Alternatively, functional equivalents may arise due to the influence of distant actors, such as investors or NGOs, which exert pressure on companies to engage in corporate social responsibility and associated partnerships (Seitanidi and Crane, 2009; Kolk *et al.*, 2008). A result of considering these functional equivalents to the shadow of hierarchy is an upward curve for non-state actors' interest in cooperation where state capacity is weak – this is indicated by the dashed curve in Figure 4.1 (c).

The implication is that the convergence of governments' and non-state actors' incentives, and thus the likely area of partnership implementation, is stretched horizontally across a broader range of state capacity conditions (as indicated in Figure 4.1 by "X"). However, for partnerships to be successful it is not sufficient for the non-state actors to face incentives for partnership. They also likely need a set of capabilities, including basic human and financial resources and organizational competencies, in order to engage with each other and state organizations. So the case studies below will include not only a consideration of non-state actors' incentives to engage in partnership, but will also consider whether they have the wherewithal to do so. The cases suggest that indeed there is an intermediate level of statehood at which cross-sector partnerships are both necessary and feasible, and this level is influenced by the non-state actors' capacities.

Context and method

The question addressed in this chapter is how varying degrees of statehood affect why cross-sector partnerships are established and how they are designed and implemented, with implications for their likely success. The chapter discusses four case studies in South Africa with a focus on the above propositions with regard to the role of the state in cross-sector partnerships. South Africa pro∞vides a particularly useful context for such a study due to the significant variations in the state's capacity in different geographical and policy areas. It is an emerging economy country characterized by a relatively consolidated state in comparison to other countries on the continent, but it has been experiencing significant institutional changes in the wake of the transition from apartheid and exhibits many features of limited statehood (Börzel and Risse, 2010), particularly in some parts of the country or with regard to particular policy areas. The state struggles to address the many complex social problems associated with widespread poverty and extreme socio-economic inequality, and so there are increasing calls for partnerships to fill some of these gaps (e.g. National Planning Commission, 2012). At the same time the country's social, cultural, and economic diversity is likely to make the implementation of such partnerships particularly challenging (Hamann and April, 2013).

Each of the four cases is an example of partnerships established to respond to complex sustainable development challenges at the local level. Three of the cases involve partnerships between government organizations and non-state actors, including business. The fourth case focuses on a business-NGO partnership and is included here to also explore the role of the state in partnerships, in which it is not a partner. Following guidance by Eisenhardt (1989), the cases were chosen to enhance the potential for comparative analysis against the backdrop of the conceptual discussion above. The cases vary with regard to the relevant state organizations' capacity to establish and enforce rules and to provide public services, as well as the existence of functional equivalents to this state-based shadow of hierarchy. This variation across cases is summarized in Table 4.1 below. In all four cases, the local government is challenged in addressing the complex problems of sustainable development planning and implementation at the local level. But in one of them, the local government has relatively speaking greater capabilities to enforce basic rules, to implement agreements, and to engage in integrative negotiations with non-state actors. Similarly, in all four cases non-state actors face incentives to engage in partnership with the state (or, in the fourth case, with each other) to respond to socio-ecological problems in the area. But the degree to which they are capable to organize themselves and to engage proactively with the state varies across the cases.

Document research and semi-structured interviews (Arksey and Knight, 1999; Kvale, 1996) were the primary data generation methods in the case studies. Interviewees included the leaders or representatives of the various groups and

TABLE 4.1 Summary of cases with regard to the state's and non-state actors' capacity

Case	Relative state capacity	Non-state actors' capacity
1) Cape Town Partnership	The local government is unable to address complex sustainable development problems, but is able to enforce basic rules and implement agreements	Non-state actors are incentivised to engage in partnership, and they have relatively good capabilities to organise themselves and to engage proactively with the state
2) Grabouw Sustainable Development Initiative	The local government is unable to address complex sustainable development problems, and it is also challenged in enforcing basic rules and implementing agreements	Non-state actors are incentivised to engage in partnership, but they lack capacity to organise themselves and to engage proactively with the state
3) Rustenburg Stakeholder Forum	The local government is unable to address complex sustainable development problems, and it is also challenged in enforcing basic rules and implementing agreements	Non-state actors are incentivised to engage in partnership, and they have relatively good capabilities to organise themselves and to engage proactively with the state
4) De Beers–CSA partnership	The local (and national) government is unable to address complex sustainable development prob, and it is also challenged in enforcing basic rules and implementing agreements	Non-state actors are incentivised to engage in partnership, and they have relatively good capabilities to organise themselves and to engage proactively with the state, but they become embroiled in conflict with each other

organizations participating in the multi-stakeholder structures of the initiatives, as well as some non-participating stakeholders. Diversity among interviewees was considered important in order to facilitate triangulation and to ensure that pertinent perspectives are identified. Furthermore, particular attention was given to possible dissenting perspectives. Some focus group discussions were also facilitated along similar lines in three of the cases. Each of the case studies involved between five and 15 interviewees or focus group participants. The data generation period for the case studies was between 2002 and 2011. The Rustenburg case involved data generation in 2002–2003 and again in 2010. Most of the data generation in the Grabouw and Cape Town Partnership case studies was undertaken during 2008–2009.[1] Research on the De Beers–Conservation South Africa partnership was undertaken in late 2011.

Interview quotes used for illustrative purposes in the discussion below generally reflect broader sentiments among interviewees, unless stated otherwise, and the use of quotes was validated by respondents. Data analysis and interpretation was characterized by a process of synthesizing and thematic coding (Strauss and Corbin,

1994). Efforts to enhance the validity of emerging arguments, included respondent validation on the basis of email communication with interviewees or, in the Rustenburg case, a feedback meeting involving interviewees and others.

The Cape Town Partnership

The Cape Town Partnership is focused on the city center of Cape Town, South Africa's third largest city (by population and gross geographic product). The Cape Town municipal government is characterized by relatively significant access to resources and sophistication. Yet these resources and capabilities are limited when compared to the scale and complexity of the social problems facing especially the large low-income settlements in the city.

The Partnership was established in 1999 as a response to the threat of urban decline in the Cape Town central city. As noted by the initiative's CEO: "The Cape Town Partnership was a response to a crisis ... Businesses were divesting, property values were decreasing, crime was increasing, [there was an increase in] litter, graffiti, and anti-social behaviour." Founding partners included in particular the Cape Town municipal government, the property owners' association, and the regional chamber of commerce. According to the initiative's website, its objectives include to "mobilise the public and private sectors and other stakeholders around common development objectives" and to "guide decision-making and direct resources into solving the economic and social challenges facing the Central City."[2] There are a range of programs and projects being facilitated and implemented by the Partnership, including for instance an ambitious residential densification policy. There are tangible outcomes that interviewees were able to point to, which were either directly motivated and developed, or indirectly influenced by the Partnership, such as the decline of "crime and grime" or the design, development, and maintenance of particular public facilities (e.g. the central railway station) or open spaces – though the success of "big ticket" systemic change proposals is as yet uncertain.

The Partnership was established as a non-profit company governed by a Board of Directors, including representatives from local and provincial government, business associations, and civil society organizations. The Board is responsible for strategic decision-making and focuses on broader themes facing the Cape Town central city, but the Partnership also manages the Central City Improvement District (CCID) focusing on "top-up" provision of public services, especially cleansing and security. This two-tier "hybrid" approach was established on the basis of international experiences. At the time of the research, the Partnership employs six full-time staff and a further 18 staff members on behalf of the CCID. Funding for the Partnership itself is provided by municipal and provincial government, as well as the private sector members, and the CCID is supported by a levy contribution from property owners.

For the purpose of this chapter, it is important to note the Cape Town Partnership's emphasis on "topping-up" strained state service delivery capabilities, rather than replacing them. CCID employees highlight their role in ensuring the municipality's accountability to basic service delivery commitments, and augmenting this with additional services supported by the property levy. As explained by the CEO:

> It is important that we do not duplicate or replace the role of the public sector. So the CCID provides only top-up services. Hence the Police Service runs security in the town and is the accountable body. But we say: the police struggles with manpower and vehicles, so we will donate manpower and vehicles, and this is what we've done ... It is also important for the CCID to hold the public sector accountable and to log every problem we come across. We need to withstand the temptation for the public sector to divert its attention and resources elsewhere, because of the work of the CCID. Our deal is for the city to maintain a level of service, and then we top-up on this. This is also important because we want to ensure that this is not about privatization. We are not taking away the role of the public sector.

The point to make here is that this "push and pull" relationship between the Partnership and the municipality has been fruitful because the latter has been able to marshal the resources to respond, even in the context of sometimes overwhelming challenges within its jurisdiction.

Importantly, the state's ability to respond to the Cape Town Partnership's suggestions and projects has not been confined to the delivery of basic services, but has also included an ability to innovate. To illustrate, in about 2005 the partnership broadened its scope from its "base focus on crime and grime" (CEO, interview) to include other key themes, including a social development program. This was partly to respond to criticisms that the partnership was "virtually running a private army in Cape Town, intent mostly on serving the needs of tourists" (Khan, quoted in Klopper, 2004: 228), rather than those of poor citizens. Coinciding with the employment of a new CEO and the invitation of new Board members, a fundamentally different approach to the homeless was adopted. As described by one of these new Board members, Hassan Khan:

> Our common objective was to have a safer city for everyone, with equal application of the law to rich and poor. But there were different strategies. In the early days, the emphasis was on security, which led to homeless people being harassed ... Now we employ a field worker who tries to find the homeless a home ... We also try to help by paying the bus fare back home (because many of them come from elsewhere in the country).

One particular innovation resulting from this revised approach was to establish lower-tier courts that would speedily hear cases of social crimes. These new courts' focus was on finding ways to support the culprits' social integration (e.g. through social service sanctions), rather than confining them to the criminal justice system (where long periods in prison awaiting trial are common). Inter-governmental coordination between the municipality and the national justice department was facilitated to this effect. This underscores not only the importance of capable leadership within the partnership secretariat, but also some minimum level of capability within participating government agencies.

To conclude, the primary state organization involved in the the Cape Town Partnership's activities, the Cape Town municipality, is thus situated near the "X" in Figure 4.1. It experiences governance challenges in the inner city, thus motivating the partnership in the first place. But it does have some minimum level of capacity to participate in and respond to innovations emanating from the cross-sector partnership, and this is a vital aspect in the partnership's overall success. This is furthermore complemented by relatively well organized non-state actors, such as the property owners' association, as well as professional leadership and administration within the partnership secretariat.

The Grabouw Sustainable Development Initiative

The Grabouw Sustainable Development Initiative (SDI) focuses on the small town of Grabouw and its rural surroundings on the outskirts of the Cape Town metropolitan area. It is still within the Cape Town city region (see OECD, 2008), but is administered by another municipality with much fewer resources and managerial and technical capabilities than the Cape Town metropolitan government. It struggles in particular to provide housing and infrastructure to the significant numbers of migrants from poor, rural provinces in search of opportunities in the Cape Town city region.

The SDI was instigated by the Development Bank of Southern Africa, which plays an important role in financing infrastructure in the region. It got underway with a memorandum of understanding signed with the municipality in 2006 and the preparation of a "Strategic Framework" document by the Bank's program team working in conjunction with academics. The need for a close interaction between this initiative and the local municipality was emphasized from the outset, but even at this early stage, municipal officials raised concerns regarding their ability to participate given time and resource constraints.

One of the key objectives was the establishment of a "Social Compact" defined as "a dynamic dialogue on the future of Grabouw and the role that different role players would commit to" (DBSA, 2006: 4). This was based on discussions within a dedicated forum involving diverse groups in the community, in order to identify common interests and develop a shared vision. The resulting document stated, "Our vision is to create, with a sense of urgency, but over the long term, a sustainable community [and] to protect our environment for future generations." This vision is further elaborated upon in specific elements. For instance, with regard to housing: "We are committed to, and support, the integration of human settlement patterns in Elgin/Grabouw. Our vision is that the poor and those more fortunate will be neighbors in this town." This is significant given the persistence of apartheid urban settlement patterns, in which poor, black residential areas are often situated long distances from centers of economic activity and livelihood opportunities.

All interviewees were broadly supportive of the underlying rationale for the forum, and they appreciated the chance for local stakeholders to discuss matters of common concern. Yet, among a number of other concerns, there was some confusion as to how the forum was related to the role of the elected ward councilors and the statutorily required ward committees. Many of these concerns relate to well-worn themes in the literature on community participation processes (e.g. Bloomfield *et al.*, 2001; Holmes and Scoones, 1999; O'Riordan and Stoll-Kleeman, 2002). For the purpose of this discussion, an underlying, more specific constraint was the relatively inert state of the ward committees themselves and hence their inability to engage with the forum in any meaningful way.

Coordination of the project was to be ensured by committees including representatives from public and private sectors, and consultants. These structures were generally considered useful, including important opportunities for intra-governmental coordination, but participants noted that they were time and resource intensive, thwarting the likelihood of establishing such structures in the municipality's eight other towns. Concerns were also raised with regard to limited alignment between the SDI process and the Integrated Development Planning process, which is statutorily required for all municipalities and also requires community participation, at least in principle (Pycroft, 1998; Visser, 2001).

Notwithstanding these concerns, the SDI had the potential to lead to tangible, important outcomes. An especially illustrative example is the SDI's influence on the municipality's housing and infrastructure development strategy (South African government policy provides for subsidised housing to the poor, to be implemented by municipalities). In this domain, large investments by the municipality were imminent, with long-term implications for the town's development trajectory. These included a proposed low-income housing development on a large tract of land some distance from the town center. Even though preliminary agreements had been signed with contractors, the design team emphasized that this development would perpetuate the apartheid city structure, with poor residents confined to the urban fringes far away from livelihood opportunities. Instead they recommended the development of a higher income settlement on the proposed site and the provision of land within the town for low-income residents. The latter was potentially a controversial recommendation, but it received the backing of the stakeholder forum partly because of the explicit commitment to "the integration of human settlement patterns" in the vision quoted above. Eventually in 2008 the municipal council agreed to change its plans for most of the site in question and land closer to the town center was identified for the low-income housing development. However, because the municipality struggled to actually build this low-income settlement in the interim, the intended beneficiaries became impatient and started blaming the SDI and the resulting change in plans for the delay (municipal official, interview).

Yet limited municipal capacity has not been the only constraint in making the SDI effective, as illustrated in another example. With a view to addressing the environmental objectives emphasized by the stakeholder forum, a proposal was developed to build the subsidised low-income houses mentioned above in a different manner in order to enhance their energy efficiency and also their environmental health aspects (specifically by increasing the width of the walls and changing some of the materials used). It was calculated that the longer-term benefits to the town's and the intended beneficiaries' energy accounts would comfortably offset the initial increment in the size of the government subsidy required. This proposal was submitted to the provincial government department, which – after lengthy delays – turned it down. An official from this department argued that the main reason for the rejection was the government's concern that an approval would create a precedent that would preclude rejections of similar proposals from other municipalities, which in turn would lead to a funding crisis. An apparent inability of the government to provide a "ringfenced" space for innovation in the Grabouw SDI and fears of establishing precedents thus constrained the environmental innovation ambitions of the initiative.

Finally, interviewees frequently raised concerns with regard to the perceived lack of continuity between the visioning and planning, on the one hand, and implementation processes, on the other. In the context of the development bank's declining involvement in the SDI after the Social Compact and technical design process (specifically in terms of funding), there were recurring concerns regarding a lack of ownership or capacity to implement among key local role-players, especially the municipality. The municipal manager himself suggested that the SDI might have been more effective if it had been implemented about two years later, and that an assessment of "institutional readiness" might have been an important first step.

In other words, even in the self-assessment by the municipal manager, the municipality was situated to the left of the "X" in Figure 4.1. The incentives and capabilities of the key government organization were insufficient to make this partnership work effectively (at least in its early manifestations). The difficulties were exacerbated by the absence of significantly strong or coordinated action among the non-state actors. The non-state actors in this town are relatively small organizations. Most businesses are small or medium enterprises in agriculture or tourism, and many of them struggle to reach across racial and class divisions. They are thus unable to compensate for the manifestations of limited statehood in the case-study area.

The Rustenburg Stakeholder Forum

The third case is in Rustenburg in the North West Province, a town dominated by the platinum mining industry. A range of initiatives have sought to facilitate improved collaboration among the mining companies and also between the mining companies and the local government and other key role-players, such as the Royal Bafokeng Administration. There continue to be fundamental disagreements regarding responsibility for developing a strategic approach to addressing the informal settlements (or slums) and other infrastructure challenges in the area, such as water provision. Local government has the statutory responsibility for infrastructure planning and development, but it has been constrained by limited capacity, resources, and legitimacy. The municipality's challenges have also been premised on its high-profile conflict with the Royal Bafokeng Administration, which sees itself as the legitimate, traditionally mandated government in this area and furthermore has negotiated lucrative royalty and ownership agreements with some of the mining companies.[3] The Royal Bafokeng Administration seeks to reserve its land for members of the Bafokeng tribe and hence resists the upgrading of the informal settlements, which are predominantly occupied by immigrants from around the country or beyond looking for jobs. This context also contributes to tensions between mining companies and local communities, as there are not always clear representation and accountability channels.

There is the widespread perception that the mines have an important responsibility for social problems and broader development issues around the mines, due to the historical system of migrant labor and given the benefits the mines have reaped from their operations. In the past, the mining houses have only insufficiently addressed these social problems around the mines. Their philanthropic efforts – often referred to as corporate social investment – have not contributed to sustainably addressing the development challenges, partly because of a lack of collaboration among themselves and with other role-players (Hamann, 2004). However, since 2003, mining companies have begun to organize themselves better in the Producers' Forum, which has task teams on water, infrastructure, housing and energy. Participants note that it has taken many years and diligent facilitation for this Forum to give rise to initial suggestions for joint action. Yet the Forum has struggled with the transition from dialogue to implementation, which has brought to the fore numerous challenges, including the realization that additional role-players (such as the national water department) need to be brought into the discussion.

Recognizing that the municipality is the key institution to facilitate better provision of services and coordination between different role-players in the region, some companies have been making targeted contributions to build the capacity of local government through the provision of human and technical resources. However, in some cases this has increased tensions with the traditional authority. For instance, Impala Platinum in 2003 started building an office for local ward councilors, only for the Royal Bafokeng Administration to destroy the structure with reference to a land-use contract.

The municipality also established a mechanism for communicating directly with the mining companies through the Rustenburg Stakeholder Forum. However, rather than facilitate an open and transparent discussion on converging and diverging interests (Austin, 2000; Covey and Brown, 2001), the relevant manager in the municipality described the purpose of this Forum primarily as obtaining mining companies' support (especially financial support) for infrastructure projects that the municipality could not afford. Mining companies' managers thus felt that this was a forum for requesting hand-outs, not a platform for deliberation on overlapping interests and innovative responses to the severe challenges facing all stakeholders in the area.

Relative to Figure 4.1, the Rustenburg case is characterized by influential non-state actors (i.e. the mining companies) with strong incentives to contribute to collaborative governance in cooperation with the municipality and other state actors.

These incentives derive from the mining companies' realization that their operations are negatively impacted by governance gaps, especially with regard to growing social unrest in the informal settlements surrounding the mines[4] and water supply problems. Because they are large, multinational companies, they are also exposed to significant pressures from external agents, such as investors and NGOs. So while the municipality is significantly challenged in dealing with governance challenges in its jurisdiction – thus located to the left of the "X" in Figure 4.1 – the non-state actors' interests are represented by the dashed line in Figure 4.1. The area of convergence between state actors' and non-state actors' interests is hence stretched and there are at least significant, endogenous efforts to establish improved collaboration.

The De Beers–CSA partnership and its demise

The fourth case involves a company-NGO partnership and is included here to consider whether the state plays a role in the motivation and implementation of such a partnership, as well. De Beers, the world's largest diamond mining company, has been mining alluvial diamonds in its Namaqualand Mine on the North-West coast of South Africa for over 80 years. Namaqualand is an area characterized by very low rainfall and entrenched poverty, as well as very high floral and animal diversity and endemism. De Beers has been supporting conservation efforts in the region, for instance by conceding some of its land to the Namaqualand National Park and by investigating and implementing appropriate forms of environmental rehabilitation.

De Beers participated in and supported a series of meetings between 2006 and 2009 organized by Conservation South Africa to discuss options for linking conservation and socio-economic development in the area, with a focus on eco-tourism. (Conservation South Africa is the local branch of the US-based international NGO, Conservation International.[5]) The relationship between De Beers and Conservation South Africa strengthened on the basis of the recognition of the need to link conservation activities to the creation of local livelihood opportunities. This was especially so because the Namaqualand Mine's life was nearing its end and thus post-closure rehabilitation and socio-economic development challenges lay ahead. Inspired by the Eden Project in Cornwall, UK, in which a post-mining landscape is transformed into an eco-tourism attraction,[6] Conservation South Africa proposed a similarly ambitious program of developing eco-tourism and "green industry" projects in Namaqualand under the banner of the "Living Edge of Africa Project" (LEAP).

In 2009 Conservation South Africa was contracted by De Beers to develop the LEAP concept further. This gave rise to a pre-feasibility report published in May 2009, suggesting a number of projects focused on mariculture, wind energy, environmental rehabilitation, and land art. Smuts (2010: 27) argued that this partnership was making "a significant contribution … towards conservation planning in an internationally recognized biodiversity priority area (namely the Succulent Karoo hotspot)," and it "assisted in rehabilitation, job creation and protected area establishment, assisted in realizing the conservation vision."

Yet within months this partnership deteriorated into public acrimony and even threats of legal action. Conservation South Africa's director described how in early 2011 De Beers decided to abandon the LEAP plan. This was triggered, she argued, by a change in corporate- and mine-level leadership. The sale of the mine was perceived by NGO and other critics as a convenient means for De Beers to avoid making the more committed investments in the social and natural environment envisaged in the LEAP document. Furthermore, while the land uses proposed by the company in its amended Environmental Management Plan in preparation for the sale of the mine did include some of the LEAP proposals, they also included arguably incongruent proposals such as a prison and hazardous waste facilities. Conservation South Africa (2011) argued that the sale of the mine had not involved sufficient stakeholder consultation and pertinent information about the social and environmental commitments associated with the sale had not been made available. Specifically, the financial commitment required by law for environmental rehabilitation had not been publicized, in the absence of which, argued Conservation South Africa (2011), the broad principles and commitments contained in the amended Environmental Management Plan for the mine were futile.

De Beers managers described the situation differently, denying that LEAP had been abandoned. They emphasized that the process of developing a pre-feasibility report for the LEAP projects was a success and that some of the proposals were considered feasible in the subsequent De Beers investigations (specifically the wind farm and the abalone mariculture project).

De Beers managers and critics agreed, however, that concerns regarding the mine sale and the subsequent maintenance of social and environmental commitments were exacerbated by the perception of limited capabilities to enforce rules in the responsible national government department, the Department of Mineral Resources. In addition to rule enforcement, there were also fundamental disagreements on the rules themselves – particularly with regard to whether financial provisions in the amended Environmental Management Plan needed to be made public. Little clarity had been given by the Department of Mineral Resources on this and related issues, according to interviewees.

Limited government capacity has also been a constraint at the local level. Mine closure plans were developed according to national regulations, which meant that they would respond to the priorities identified in the local Integrated Development Plans published by the municipalities. Yet a general concern has been the challenges faced by municipalities in actually preparing such plans according to the regulatory guidelines that emphasize community participation, and of course their capacity to then implement the activities and attain the goals envisaged in them (for a discussion on the development and implementation of this policy, see Harrison, 2006). This was also echoed by community interviewees: "The municipality has an IDP but doesn't have the capacity to implement it ... they had IDP meetings, but they're just empty promises." Company interviews emphasized the difficulties in identifying and communicating with legitimate and recognized community representatives, a task apparently made more difficult by local government elections (in May 2011), in which control of the local council moved from African National Congress to Democratic Alliance. "Now previous agreements are questioned all over again … We cannot be seen to be favouring any particularly political party" (De Beers manager, interview).

This case thus illustrates how limited government capacity at both local and national level, as well as institutional changes within government, have provided vital constraints to cross-sector collaboration even between business and civil society. In particular, limited statehood contributed to a partnership between a large corporation and an international NGO deteriorating into conflict because of an absence of clarity on applicable regulations and insufficient implementation of existing state policies. The argument that some limited level of capabilities in the state is required for effective cross-sector collaboration may thus apply even if the state is not one of the partners.

Discussion and conclusion

This chapter focused on how the state's and non-state actors' capacities affect cross-sector partnerships' success. It created a conceptual framework based on Börzel's and Risse's (2010) discussion on the incentives faced by state and non-state actors to cooperate. The preliminary model postulated that, first, partnerships are most likely to be established if both state and non-state actors face sufficient cooperation incentives. Second, it suggested that partnerships are likely to be established with some success when the state has some intermediate level of capabilities, because this means that the partnership is motivated by the existence of governance gaps, while at the same time the state can still play a meaningful role in the partnership.

Non-state actors' incentives to cooperate with the state, meanwhile, are motivated by the potentially detrimental effects of the governance gaps created by limited statehood, or by the expectations of external stakeholders, such as investors or NGOs. But even if non-state actors face such incentives, it is still necessary for them, too, to bring to bear a range of organizational capabilities in order to engage in such partnerships.

Variations in the capabilities of the state and of non-state actors are hence the primary variables of concern in this analysis. Four cases with varying combinations of state and non-state actors' capabilities were discussed in order to substantiate and further develop the conceptual propositions:

- The Cape Town Partnership was implemented in a context, in which the key state organization was overwhelmed by complex challenges associated with potential inner-city decay. This provided a clear motivation for the partnership. At the same time, the state was able to proactively participate in the partnership and fulfil basic responsibilities. It was also able to help implement governance innovations spearheaded by the partnership. Coupled with non-state actors with relatively significant organizational capabilities and financial resources, this context gave rise to a partnership, whose success is widely acknowledged.

- The Grabouw Sustainable Development Initiative was also implemented in a context, in which the local state organization was overwhelmed by complex sustainable development challenges, thus providing a clear motivation for the partnership. However, the local state relied on external role-players to establish and implement the partnership, and it faced various constraints to participate proactively and to implement the outcomes of partnership deliberations. Inter-governmental coordination could not provide for the innovation space that was created in the Cape Town Partnership. In addition, the local non-state actors lacked financial resources and organizational capabilities to compensate for these state weaknesses.
- As in the other cases, the Rustenburg municipality was overwhelmed by complex sustainable development challenges, thus providing a clear motivation for partnership. Like in the Grabouw case, it also struggled to engage non-state actors in integrative negotiation, instead falling back on requests for financial assistance. The Rustenburg case differs from the Grabouw case in that there are large, well-resourced non-state actors present (the mining companies), which face significant incentives to address governance gaps in the area. There are thus some advanced efforts to improve collaboration between the state and these companies, though these are focused particularly on bulk infrastructure and related needs of the companies, rather than broader sustainability challenges in the area.
- Finally, the Namaqualand case is similar to the Rustenburg case, in that state capabilities are low, while there are well-resourced non-state actors (De Beers mining company and Conservation South Africa). It suggested that limited statehood is a constraint even to corporate-NGO partnerships, in which the state is not directly involved. This is because the corporate-NGO partnership was crucially constrained by the lack of clear regulations and "critical rights" (Covey and Brown, 2001).

To develop the preliminary model in more detail, it would be useful to include case studies in contexts, where the state has a higher level of capabilities. The conceptual discussion based on Börzel and Risse (2010) would suggest that partnership formation is then less likely. Indeed, in the Cape Town Partnership case, there were some indications that relatively more consolidated local statehood contributed to tensions, with occasional "turf battles" between the metropolitan government and the partnership. On the other hand, the characteristics of the complex sustainable development challenges facing various jurisdictions suggest that some degree of limited statehood is present in most domains. This is also suggested by the spread of local sustainable development partnerships in countries, such as Canada (see Clarke (2014), this volume).

To conclude, the cases confirm that limited statehood, and in particular challenges faced by key state organizations in addressing complex sustainable development challenges, provide vital cooperation incentives and these underpin the motivation for partnership formation. At the same time, some minimum level of consolidated statehood is necessary for the state to be a proactive participant in the partnership.

This refers not only to the need to contribute to discussions on problem framing and potential solutions, but more especially the capacity to engage in integrative negotiation (Austin, 2000; Covey and Brown, 2001). Furthermore, some level of statehood is necessary for the state to clarify and enforce "critical rights" that underpin the partnership (Covey and Brown, 2001), and to help implement the projects or policy recommendations that arise from the partnership deliberations. The latter also includes a capacity to establish some space for innovation in the way in which public goods and services are provided. It is clear, therefore, that the requirements for effective state participation in partnerships are not trivial. All the more challenging is the identification of the intermediate level of statehood, at which partnerships are both necessary and feasible.

Questions for reflection

1 One of the interviewees quoted in the chapter mentioned the need to assess "institutional readiness" prior to establishing a partnership. What is your view on this suggestion? What might such an analysis look like?
2 One of the implications of the argument of this chapter is that partnerships ought to be approached with caution in contexts where the state is very weak or even absent. Is it possible for non-state actors to contribute to building the minimum level of state capacity mentioned in this chapter, and if so, how?
3 The conceptual framework suggests that there may be circumstances in which the state is well capacitated to address governance problems by itself, and hence partnerships become unnecessary. Are there some governance problems that present inherent difficulties to the state, and hence require partnerships even in areas of consolidated statehood?

Notes

1 By way of disclosure, the author, in mid-2012) joined the Board of the Cape Town Partnership. During the time of this research, however, there was no relationship between the author and the Cape Town Partnership.
2 www.capetownpartnership.co.za, accessed July 2012.
3 The Royal Bafokeng Administration plays an important quasi-governmental role as the traditional authority of the Bafokeng tribe, which owns much of the land in the area. Governance roles for such traditional authorities are catered for in the South African Constitution, but their delineation is still disputed. The Bafokeng tribe received mining royalties and now owns significant stakes in a number of mines in the area, which is one of the reasons the tribe is colloquially referred to as "the richest tribe in Africa" (Manson and Mbenga, 2003).
4 In 2012 these fears were vindicated in the tragic killing of many dozen people in the vicinity of Rustenburg during labor unrests. The difficult living conditions in informal settlements featured prominently in the disputes between workers, labor representatives, and mine management. The so-called Marikana shooting, in which 34 people, mostly striking miners, were killed, was reported in the international press – see for instance, www.bbc.co.uk/news/world-africa-19781993 (accessed October 2012).

5   www.conservation.org/global/ci_south_africa/Pages/conservation-south-africa. aspx (accessed July 2012).
6   www.edenproject.com (accessed July 2012).

References

Arksey, H. and Knight, P.T. (1999) *Interviewing for Social Scientists: An Introductory Resource with Examples.* Thousand Oaks, CA: Sage.

Austin, J.E. (2000) Strategic collaboration between nonprofits and businesses, *Nonprofit and Voluntary Sector Quarterly*, 29 (Suppl. 1): 69–97

Benner, T., Reinicke, W.H. and Witte, J.M. (2004) Multisectoral networks in global governance: towards a pluralistic system of accountability. *Government and Opposition*, 39 (2): 191–210.

Bloomfield, D., Collins, K, Fry, C and Munton, R. (2001) Deliberation and inclusion: vehicles for increasing trust in UK public governance?, *Environment and Planning C: Government and Policy*, 19 (4): 501–13.

Börzel, T.A. and Risse, T. (2010) Governance without a state: can it work? *Regulation and Governance*, 4 (2): 113–34.

Clarke, A. (2014) Designing social partnerships for local sustainability strategy implementation, in Seitanidi, M.M. and Crane, A. (eds) *Social Partnerships and Responsible Business: A Research Handbook.* London: Routledge: 79–102.

Covey, J. and Brown, L.D. (2001) Critical cooperation: an alternative form of civil society-business engagement. *IDR Reports*, 17(1). www.jsi.com/idr/IDRreports.htm

Crane, A. (2011) "From governance to Governance: on blurring boundaries." *Journal of Business Ethics*, 94 (Sup. 1): 17–19.

Crosby, B.C. and Bryson, J. (2010) Integrative leadership and the creation and maintenance of cross-sector collaborations. *The Leadership Quarterly*, 21: 211–30.

CSA (Conservation South Africa) (2011) De Beers avoids best practice protocol n mine sale. Press release, 11 May 2011.

Dahan, N.M., Doh, J.P., Oetzel, J. and Yaziji, M. (2010) Corporate-NGO collaboration: co-creating new business models for developing markets. *Long Range Planning*, 43 (2–3): 326–42.

DBSA (Development Bank of Southern Africa) (2006) Strategic framework and implementation plan for the Grabouw sustainable communities pilots (unpublished document).

Doh, J. and Boddewyn, J. (2014) International business and social partnerships: how institutional and MNE capabilities affect collective-goods provisioning in emerging markets, in Seitanidi, M.M. and Crane, A. (eds) *Social Partnerships and Responsible Business: A Research Handbook.* London: Routledge: 44–59.

Eisenhardt, K. (1989) Building theory from case study research. *Academy of Management Review*, 14 (4): 532–50.

Hamann, R. (2004) Corporate social responsibility, partnerships, and institutional change: The case of mining companies in South Africa. *Natural Resources Forum*, 28 (4): 278–90.

Hamann, R. and April, K. (2013) On the role and capabilities of collaborative intermediary organisations in urban sustainability transition. *Journal of Cleaner Production*, 50: 12–21.

Harrison, P. (2006) Integrated development plans and Third Way politics, in Pillay, U., Tomlinson, R. and Du Toit, J. (eds) *Democracy and Delivery.* Durban: HSRC Press: 186–207.

Holmes, T. and Scoones, I. (1999) *Participatory Environmental Policy Processes: Experiences from North and South,* IDS Working Paper 113, Brighton: Institute for Development Studies.

Hoskisson, R.E., Eden, L., Lau, C.M. and Wright, M. (2000) Strategy in emerging economies. *Academy of Management Journal*, 43 (3): 249–67.

Kvale, S. (1996) *InterViews: An Introduction to Qualitative Research Interviewing.* Thousand Oaks, CA: Sage.

Kolk, A. and Lenfant, F. (2012) Multinationals, CSR and partnerships in Central African conflict countries. *Corporate Social Responsibility and Environmental Management*, doi:10.1002/csr.1277

Kolk, A., van Tulder, R. and Kostwinder, E. (2008) Business and partnerships for development. *European Management Journal*, 26 (4): 262–73.

London, T. and Hart, S.L. (2004) Reinventing strategies for emerging markets: beyond the transnational model. *Journal of International Business Studies*, 35 (5): 350–70.

Mair, J. and Martí, I. (2009) Entrepreneurship in and around institutional voids: a case study from Bangladesh. *Journal of Business Venturing*, 24 (5): 419–35.

Manson, A. and Mbenga, B. (2003) "The richest tribe in Africa": Platinum-mining and the Bafokeng in South Africa's North West Province, 1965–1999. *Journal of Southern African Studies*, 29 (1): 25–47.

Moon, J. (2002) Business social responsibility and new governance. *Government and Opposition*, 37 (3): 385–408.

National Planning Commission (2012), National Development Plan 2030: our Future – make it work: www.npconline.co.za/MediaLib/Downloads/Downloads/NDP%202030%20-%20Our%20future%20-%20make%20it%20work.pdf

OECD (2008) *OECD Territorial Reviews: Cape Town, South Africa*. OECD: http://browse.oecdbookshop.org/oecd/pdfs/product/0408081e.pdf

O'Riordan, T. and Stoll-Kleemann, S. (2002) Deliberative democracy and participatory biodiversity, in O'Riordan, T and Stoll-Kleemann, S. (eds) *Biodiversity, Sustainability and Human Communities: Protecting Beyond the Protected*, Cambridge: Cambridge University Press.

Parmigiani, A. and Rivera-Santos, M. (2011) A path through the forest: a meta-review of interorganizational relationships. *Journal of Management*, 37 (4): 1108–36.

Peng, M.W. (2003) Institutional transitions and strategic choices. *Academy of Management Review*, 28 (2): 275–96

Prahalad, C.K. and Lieberthal, K. (1998) The end of corporate imperialism. *Harvard Business Review*, 76: 68–79.

Pycroft, C. (1998) Integrated development planning or strategic paralysis? Municipal development during the local government transition and beyond, *Development Southern Africa*, 15 (2): 151–63.

Risse, T. (2011) Governance in areas of limited statehood: introduction and overview, in Risse, T. (ed.), *Governance without a State? Policies and Politics in Areas of Limited Statehood*. New York: Columbia University Press.

Rufin, C. and Rivera-Santos, M. (2014) Cross-sector governance: from institutions to partnerships, and back to institutions, in M.M. Seitanidi and A. Crane (eds) *Social Partnerships and Responsible Business: A Research Handbook*. London: Routledge: 125–42.

Seitanidi, M.M. and Crane, A. (2009) Implementing CSR through partnerships: understanding the selection, design and institutionalization of nonprofit-business partnerships. *Journal of Business Ethics*, 85: 413–29.

Seitanidi, M.M. and Lindgreen, A. (2011) Editorial: cross-sector social interactions. *Journal of Business Ethics*, 94: 1–7.

Smuts, R. (2010) Are partnerships the key to conserving Africa's biodiversity? Four partnership case studies between mining companies and conservation NGOs. Conservation International. Arlington, Virginia.

Visser, G. (2001) Social justice, integrated development planning and post-apartheid urban reconstruction, *Urban Studies*, 38 (10): 1673–99

Vurro, C. and Dacin, M.T. (2014) An institutional perspective on cross-sector partnerships, in Seitanidi, M.M. and Crane, A. (eds) *Social Partnerships and Responsible Business: A Research Handbook*. London: Routledge: 306–319.

Vurro, C., Dacin, M.T. and Perrini, F. (2010) Institutional antecedents of partnering for social change: how institutional logics shape cross-sector social partnerships. *Journal of Business Ethics*, 94: 39–53.

5

DESIGNING SOCIAL PARTNERSHIPS FOR LOCAL SUSTAINABILITY STRATEGY IMPLEMENTATION

Amelia Clarke

Introduction

At the local level, much like national and global levels, social problems which are too large for one organization are being addressed through cross-sector social partnerships (CSSPs). One particular approach being used is for a new social partnership to formulate and implement a collaborative strategy (Astley and Fombrun, 1983; Clarke and Fuller, 2011; Huxham and Macdonald, 1992). In regards to the challenge of unsustainable development, in the last twenty years, there has been an emergence of Local Agenda 21s (LA21s) and other collaborative community sustainability strategies (CCSSs). Businesses engage in these LA21s (or other CCSSs) for a number of reasons, including as part of their community engagement and corporate social responsibility efforts (Bowen *et al.*, 2010), and because of the benefits of being involved (Clarke and MacDonald, 2012). In practice, when it comes to the implementation of these collaborative strategic plans, a wide variety of governance structures are being used. Only in the last few years have researchers started theorizing about these implementation structures and the implications of their design for partner organizations (e.g. Barrutia *et al.*, 2007; Clarke, 2011; Fidélis and Pires, 2009; García-Sánchez and Prado-Lorenzo, 2008; Michaux *et al.*, 2011). The focus of this study is to consider the advantages and disadvantages of different governance structures for the implementation phase of a CCSS. This is an important question as practitioners would like to know the best way to design their governance structure to engage partners and achieve desired results, and scholars wish to further theoretical understanding about collaborative governance and about collaborative strategy implementation.

The chapter begins by introducing the role of partnerships for local sustainability, collaborative community sustainability strategies and the Canadian situation. This is followed by a description of the study's methodology. Next, four in-depth cases provide further insight into the perceived advantages and disadvantages of different implementation structures. A cross-case comparison details the CSSP designs in regards to five key structural features. In general, this chapter highlights the emergence and diffusion of cross-sector social partnerships at the local level as a means of solving social problems. It also shows that if partnerships are to be considered as a means to engage responsible businesses in community sustainable development, the design of their implementation structures is important. By considering the advantages and disadvantages of different collaborative governance structures, the chapter introduces some of the challenges faced by social partnerships.

The role of partnerships for local sustainability

Partnerships are increasingly used to address social problems such as unsustainable development (Dienhart and Ludescher, 2010; Geddes, 2008; Glasbergen, 2007). The "problem" is that increased global human population and increased affluence, each, have impacts on ecosystems, social systems and economic systems. There is considerable concern that humans are exceeding the Earth's ecological carrying capacity and depleting its natural capital (Millennium Ecosystem Assessment, 2005). There has also been a trend towards increased urbanization, with more than 50 per cent of the world's population now living in urban centres (UN-Habitat, 2004), and this too has serious implications for the sustainability of human development.

> In industrialized countries, the consumption patterns of cities are severely stressing the global ecosystem, while settlements in the developing world need more raw material, energy, and economic development simply to overcome basic economic and social problems ...
>
> (*UNCED, 1992: Chapter 7.1, Agenda 21*)

According to the United Nations' Sustainable Cities Programme, the problem of environmental deterioration is not necessarily due to urban population growth, but rather from poor planning within urban communities (Sustainable Cities Programme, 1999). A key challenge of managing complex social problems is orchestrating the involvement of not only local authorities and other levels of government, but also businesses, higher education institutions and non-governmental organizations.

The concept of sustainable development (World Commission on Environment and Development, 1987) addresses this challenge by incorporating an intergenerational timeframe, recognizing ecological limits, and integrating ecological, social and economic considerations. Sustainable development is defined as "development that meets the needs of the present without compromising the ability of future generations to meet their own needs" (World Commission on Environment and Development, 1987: 43). Its achievement requires that it be simultaneously tackled at multiple levels and in multiple contexts (Manderson, 2006). Non-governmental organizations, governmental institutions and businesses have roles to play in achieving sustainable development, in part through making their own activities more ecologically sustainable (Jennings and Zandbergen, 1995) and in part by carrying out their role in society with reference to this societal goal (Bowen *et al.,* 2010; Gladwin *et al.* 1995).

Cross-sector social partnerships have been promoted as a way of achieving sustainable development (Glasbergen, 2007). Local authorities have jurisdiction over numerous ecological and social considerations and, therefore, have the potential to play a leadership role in community sustainability (Gibbs *et al.,* 1996). In fact, local "territories are far more than physical spaces: they are communities, systems of relations, and they represent the most suitable level for managing the economy, social cohesion and relations between society and the environment as a whole" (ICLEI, 2012b: 4). Yet local authorities are unable to resolve sustainable development issues alone, as the complexity of these issues necessitates interorganizational collaboration (Biermann *et al.,* 2007b).

The Sustainable Cities Program (SCP) is a program of UN-Habitat and the United Nations Environment Programme (UNEP). These two organizations work to build capacity for urban environmental planning and sustainable development management in cities; the SCP specifically addresses attitudinal change, behavioural change, infrastructure change and organizational change in order to institutionalize sustainable development planning (Sustainable Cities Programme, 1999). The SCP recognizes the importance of collaborations (Sustainable Cities Programme, 1999).

> The SCP does not view environmental deterioration as a necessary or inevitable consequence of rapid urban growth; equally, the SCP does not consider financial resource constraints to be the primary cause of environmental problems. Instead, the SCP considers environmental deterioration to be primarily caused by: 1) inappropriate urban development policies and policy implementation; 2) poorly planned and managed urban growth which does not adequately consider the constraints (and opportunities) of the natural environment; 3) inadequate and inappropriate urban infrastructure, both in terms of investment and especially in terms of operations, maintenance and management; and 4) lack of coordination and cooperation among key institutions and groups.
>
> (*Sustainable Cities Programme, 1999: 76–7*)

The Sustainable Cities Programme emphasizes the development of strategies that recognize ecological limits, ensure cooperation between organizations, integrate traditionally separate issues and consider the long-term implications (Sustainable Cities Programme 1999). The SCP specifically targets both local authorities and their partners and are founded on "broad-based stakeholder participatory approaches" (UN-Habitat 2012). In other words, UN-Habitat and UNEP recommend a partnership approach (Clarke and Erfan, 2007).

A partnership approach (or collaboration approach) is a strategic management process that enables organizational partners to be a part of the formulation and implementation decision-making processes and generally includes formulating collaborative strategic plan (Clarke and Erfan, 2007; Clarke and Fuller, 2011). A participation approach (or consultation approach) is a strategic management process where one focal organization consults other organizations, and thus the decision-making is conducted by that focal organization (e.g. the local authority). This approach generally includes formulating an organizational strategic plan (Clarke and Erfan, 2007). Collaborative community sustainability strategies use a partnership approach; the word "collaborative" indicates this. That said, in practice, it is possible that a strategic plan with community-wide content (and not solely an organizational strategic plan) can be formulated through a partnership approach, but implemented through a partnership approach; and vice versa, a collaborative strategy might be formulated with a partnership approach, but when it comes to implementation, the local authority decides to switch to a participation approach. While in Canada, local authorities are still likely to only use a participation approach, a number of CSSPs are formulating collaborative community sustainability strategies to tackle complex issues such as unsustainable development and climate change mitigation.

Collaborative community sustainability strategies (CCSSs)

Collaborative strategies and collaborative strategic management have been discussed in the literature (Astley and Fombrun, 1983; Clarke and Fuller, 2011; Huxham and Macdonald, 1992). At the local level, the topics that are typically covered in a collaborative community sustainability strategy are integrated social, economic and environmental topics such as adequate housing, natural resource use, infrastructure, carbon and waste management, green economy, and so on (Clarke, 2011). It is important to note relevant differences between collaborative community sustainability strategies and most partnerships theorized in existing management literature. Specifically, CCSSs: 1) can involve a large number of partners from the private, public and non-profit sectors; 2) are very long-term in their vision; and 3) tend to begin with the formulation of a collaborative strategic plan, and therefore have distinct formulation and implementation stages.

In practice, one tool to achieve sustainable development at the local level is termed "Local Agenda 21" (LA21) (Fidélis and Pires, 2009). LA21s are one type of CCSS, and are supported by an international organization called ICLEI – Local Governments for Sustainability. Local Agenda 21 is defined as:

> A participatory, multistakeholder process to achieve the goals of *Agenda 21* at the local level through the preparation and implementation of a long-term, strategic plan that addresses priority local sustainable development concerns.
> *(ICLEI, 2002a: 6)*

A 2012 survey found that about 10,000 local authorities have engaged in LA21s, including involving the local community and local stakeholders (ICLEI, 2012b). In order to qualify in a similar 2002 survey as having undertaken LA21 activity, a community must have engaged in one or more of the following:

a   *multisectoral engagement* in the planning process through a local stake-holder group which serves as the coordination and policy body for moving toward long-term sustainable development;

b   *consultation with community partners* such as community groups, non-governmental organizations, businesses, churches, government agencies, professional groups, and unions in order to create a shared vision and to identify proposals for action;

c   *participatory assessment* of local social, environmental, and economic needs;

d   *participatory target setting* through negotiations among key stakeholders or community partners in order to achieve the vision and goals set out in a community action plan; and/or

e   *monitoring and reporting* procedures, such as local indicators, to track progress and to allow participants to hold each other accountable to a community action plan.

(ICLEI, 2002a: 6)

These quotations make it clear that the LA21 approach involves collaboration in both the planning and the implementation stages. This can be seen from the language in the above quotation; terms such as "stakeholder group which serves as the coordination and policy body", "shared vision" and "community action plan" (instead of local authority's action plan) all indicate that it is a partnership approach and not a participation approach. And while the definition of an LA21 implies a partnership approach, the 2002 survey allowed for initiatives that involved "consultation with community partners" to be included (in other words, a participation approach to the formulation of the shared vision). This indicates that in practice, stakeholder/partner involvement can vary in LA21s. While many local communities still pursue LA21s, many others have chosen to focus on climate change and/or biodiversity planning as their entrance into sustainable development (ICLEI, 2012b). ICLEI's programs for these topics also promote a partnership approach.

Guidance on the planning process is available for communities, as well as information about best practices (ICLEI, 2012a); but absent from LA21 documentation is information on which structures to put in place during the implementation phase (beyond monitoring and reporting). Some recent academic research has been done in this area (Barrutia *et al.,* 2007; Clarke, 2011; Fidélis and Pires, 2009; García-Sánchez and Prado-Lorenzo, 2008; Geissel 2009; Michaux *et al.,* 2011; Owen and Videras, 2008; Peris *et al.,* 2011), but it is still a gap in extant knowledge.

Of particular note for implementation structures, is the work by Clarke (2011). This article offers five criteria by which to evaluate the key structural features of a collaborative governance structure for implementing a collaborative strategy. In particular, the evaluation criteria consider if the structure: engages partner organizations; has a collaborative oversight entity for decision-making and networking; enables individual organizations to implement the collaborative strategy within their own organizations; has a communication system; and has a monitoring system

(Clarke, 2011). Clarke (2011) explains that in order to achieve the collaborative goals outlined in a collaborative strategic plan, all five key structural features are needed as part of the implementation structure. These criteria are used later in this chapter to consider the CSSP implementation structures of the four in-depth case studies. As these are Canadian-based case studies, the next section introduces CCSSs in Canada.

The Canadian situation

Community sustainability strategic plans are still a relatively new concept with wide variations in strategic plan formulation approaches (Devuyst and Hens, 2000). In 1992, Canadian local administration was in a state of flux with departments being renamed, new advisory committees being created, new positions being established and new networks being formed; and, in general, most sustainability initiatives (but not all) had a strictly ecological focus (Maclaren, 1992). By 2012, most local Canadian sustainability initiatives, while still incorporating an ecological focus, also included social and economic topics (Clarke, 2012; Devuyst and Hens, 2000). Most are still limited to issues falling within the local authority's jurisdiction; and involve a participation approach instead of a partnership approach (Clarke and Erfan, 2007). Hence, only a limited number of the Canadian community sustainability strategies are "collaborative" (i.e., involve partners), though this is more common in countries with national LA21 policies (Cartwright, 1997; Eckerberg and Forsberg, 1998; Mehta, 1996; Rotheroe et al., 2003; Sofroniciu, 2005). Indeed, the existence of national-level LA21 policies – as in some countries (but not Canada) – increases the probability of local authorities pursuing a collaborative community sustainability strategy (ICLEI, 2002b).

In Canada, there are a number of government, non-governmental and private organizations that focus on supporting communities becoming more sustainable, many of which promote collaborative community sustainability strategic plan formulation. Each organization has its own approach, which partly explains the wide variance of approaches to formulating CCSSs taken in Canada (Clarke and Erfan, 2007). Recently, there has been a Canada-wide wave of community sustainability strategic plans being formulated, in part due to new funding arrangements. In 2005, Infrastructure Canada, which is federal government department, brought in an initiative called The New Deal for Cities, through which Canadian provinces and territories can access federal "gas tax" money for local water and transportation infrastructure development, so long as recipient local authority commits to developing a long-term integrated community sustainability plan (ICSP) (Infrastructure Canada, 2006). These ICSPs may be developed using either a partnership or participation approach. Over 200 communities in Canada now have or are developing an ICSP (Clarke, 2012). This study uses Canadian case studies to explore the advantages and disadvantages of different structures used by social partnerships to implement their collaborative community sustainability strategy. This is an important question as it is known that implementation structures influence what partners are involved and what outcomes can be achieved (Clarke, 2011; Hood *et al.*, 1993; Huxham and Vangen, 2000).

Methods

This chapter includes empirical research regarding the advantages and disadvantages of different cross-sector social partnership structures for local sustainability strategy implementation. The research design used four case studies. Data were collected through documents and interviews, and inductively analysed through coding, data reduction and cross-case comparison.

When selecting appropriate cases, it is critical that criteria be used (Yin, 2003). In order to qualify as a collaborative community sustainability strategy for this study, the Canadian community must have, as of March 1, 2008, *finalized* a document that: 1) included the words vision/imagine/future/long-term, sustainability, sustainable development, Agenda 21, community or equivalent in the title; 2) included a vision for a sustainable future; 3) addressed economic, social and ecological needs together; 4) was community-wide (i.e., not a neighbourhood); 5) described a cross-sector roundtable, multi-organizational group, multi-sectoral community group, multi-organizational planning committee, partnership team or equivalent that led, or participated as a decision-maker, in the planning process (in other words, the strategy was not developed by only local authority staff and counsellors; or the committee was not only advisory); and 6) included sustainability goals that were relevant for the different organizations within the geographic community (not just the local authority's jurisdiction). These criteria ensured that included in the study were multi-organizational collaborations (i.e., a partnership approach) implementing a CCSS, thus enabling the study of collaborative strategies. In addition, these criteria are consistent with prior research on Local Agenda 21s. From these results, four were selected because they were award winning, had a history of implementation (including reporting), and represented different collaborative governance structures. These cases were: Whistler2020; Montreal's collective sustainable development strategy; Hamilton's Vision 2020, and Greater Vancouver's cities[PLUS]. The case studies considered the time period from the strategy's start (for example, 1992 in the Hamilton case) to 2009. Data was collected in 2008 and 2009, following ethics approval from McGill University.

Interviews were used for data collection. In total, sixty-three interviews were completed with partner organizations. In each case, the partners included the local authority, large corporations, business associations, non-governmental organizations (NGOs), and in three out of four cases there were also university partners and small- and medium-sized enterprises. Each interview was transcribed in its original language (English or French) and inductively coded by a bilingual researcher. In particular, the perceived advantages and disadvantages of the implementation structure were coded. The comments with a single code were clustered and compiled separately for each of the four cases. These were further reduced to key concepts (in English) which are presented in tables in the case descriptions later in this chapter.

In addition, informative quotations were retained to provide a richness in the case descriptions. As promised on the consent form that interviewees signed, all quotations were later verified with interviewees to ensure they agreed to the final wording and agreed to their usage in subsequent presentations and publications. All quotations in this chapter have received this approval from the interviewee.

The coded comments were further reduced by clustering the ideas regardless of case, and presenting them in relation to one of four categories – partners, implementation framework, processes and other. In this situation, other is anything else (the planning process, the content and the interpersonal aspects), as the interest is in the collaborative implementation structure. In addition, a cross-case comparison was completed based on the implementation structure in each case, using the five criteria from Clarke (2011).

In-depth cases

This section details each of the four case studies, including their CCSS implementation structure, and the perceived advantages and disadvantages of interviewees about their structures.

Whistler2020

At the time of the study, the Whistler2020 structure was led by the local authority in an informal partnership with other "early adopter" organizations. The strategic plan formulation was formal, locally driven and resulted in a collaborative strategic plan with a long time horizon (fifty-five years). The main levels at which implementation was carried out are that of joint projects and individual organizations, with fifteen issue-based task forces meeting annually to establish priorities; and Implementing Organizations agreeing to assigned actions. In terms of systems, the structure had centralized decision-making (i.e., action setting) through the task forces, and centralized communication and monitoring managed by a small staff.

Whistler interviewees identified the main advantages of their implementation structure. These are outlined in Table 5.1.

This quotation from Whistler2020 highlights the advantages of this structure,

> Whistler2020 helps us to use community-wide resources in a more coordinated and strategic way to work toward our shared vision. It also helps organizations prioritize actions to better use their internal resources. Rather than requiring new resources, it requires alignment of existing budgets and resources to ensure that all are dedicated to moving toward a shared goal, rather than working inefficiently or at cross-purposes.
>
> (*Frequently Asked Questions. Whistler2020*)

It is interesting to note that the alignment of the local authority's organizational strategy with the collaborative strategy was noted as a real strength (an advantage),

TABLE 5.1 Perceived advantages and disadvantages for Whistler

Perceived advantages (mentioned by more than one interviewee)	Perceived disadvantages (mentioned by more than one interviewee)
• A diversity of organizations involved • An alignment of organizational, joint project and collaborative strategies • An ownership of the CCSS by the organizational partners • A lack of ownership by organizations	• A community with an ability to monitor progress on sustainability • A replicable and on-going process • An increase of costs and workload/ A lack of resources • A lack of alignment of organizational, joint project and collaborative strategies

but the alignment of the other partner organizations' strategies was considered to be inadequately addressed through the CCSS implementation structure. This is also intimately tied to ownership being considered an advantage by some and a disadvantage by others. In terms of addressing the lack of ownership by partner organizations, Whistler2020 employees have identified that there is a perception in the community that this is a local authority plan. The solution has been to create a new NGO to coordinate Whistler2020 task forces, partners, and processes. The trade-off with this decision is the potential loss of control by the local authority, but the gain in ownership and funding from other partners. The move to an NGO also potentially addresses the cost concern as other partners will contribute and other sources of funding can be leveraged. Whistler2020 also addressed the lack of implementation by some partners (those which signed the MOU to become official "Partners") by creating a new mechanism for partners to meet (i.e., distinct from the task forces) and to share progress on their individual implementation efforts, and new programmes targeted at partners and citizens.

Some trade-offs of Whistler2020's implementation structure are that the more partners that are engaged, the more core costs rise. Interviewees also commented on the implications of Whistler being a smaller community; one person thought that the process relies on personal relationships which create a "peer pressure" for businesses to engage. Others thought it is a scalable approach. In summary, this case presents the perceived advantages and disadvantages if the formal implementation structure in the Whistler2020 case.[1]

Montreal's first strategic plan for sustainable development

The strategic plan formulation used a formal process, was locally driven and resulted in a plan with a short time horizon (five years). The implementation of Montreal's First Strategic Plan for Sustainable Development was led by three organizations (Conseil régional de l'environnement de Montréal, the City of Montreal and the Conférence régionale des élus). In terms of its framework, two formal committees were constituted at the full partnership level; individual organizations implemented relevant aspects of the collaborative strategic plan; and there were informal inter-actions among organizations at the joint project level. In terms of processes, decision-making about which collaborative goals to implement and actions to take was left to each individual partner, but CCSS communication and monitoring were centralized with the three lead organizations, with individual partner organizations providing information to these processes. In comparison with Whistler2020, Montreal has no task forces, and instead individual organizations choose actions from a list.

Montreal interviewees identified the main advantages of their implementation structure, and these are presented in Table 5.2. The main trade-off identified was in relation to the number of partners: as the number of partners increases, the quality of interactions decreases; also the need arises to make commitments required of partners easier, and the cost increases due to a need for more capacity.

TABLE 5.2 Perceived advantages and disadvantages for Montreal

Perceived advantages (mentioned by more than one interviewee)	Perceived disadvantages (mentioned by more than one interviewee)
• An opportunity for organizations to network and share resources • A diversity of organizations involved • An on-going autonomy of organizational decision-making • An alignment of organizational joint project, and collaborative strategies • An ownership of the CCSS by the partners	• A lack of focus by some local authority departments and politicians • A broad coverage of topics so lack of consensus and vulnerable to shifts in opinion

This quotation from one of the partner organizations highlights the advantages of this structure:

> The City didn't ask the partners to share in every priority, it allowed partners to identify where they had the most control, the most opportunity for change … there are some things we can't handle right now, but if we know that it's an objective of the greater region, we can plan for it …
>
> (Jim Nicell, Associate Vice-Principal [University Services], McGill University, Montreal)

In summary, this case presents the perceived advantages and disadvantages in the formal implementation structure in the Montreal case.[2]

Hamilton's Vision 2020

Hamilton's Vision 2020 has had three distinct structures at different periods in time. The strategic plan formulation was led by a multi-stakeholder committee and involved a formal process which was designed and led locally and which resulted in a twenty-eight-year CCSS. In terms of implementation, during the 1992–1998 and 2003–2009 time periods, Vision 2020 implementation was led by the local authority, while implementation during the 1999–2003 time period was led by an NGO created by the local authority and other organizations specifically for this purpose. The first time period saw the local authority leading the implementation, with help from the Citizens Steering Committee and informal interactions with a larger number of organizations at the annual Sustainable Community Day. During this time period, the local authority initiated a number of joint projects to complement its own internal activities. Decision-making about Vision 2020 implementation actions, communication about Vision 2020, and monitoring of community sustainability on Vision 2020 themes remained centralized with the local authority.

By the second time period, Action 2020 (the NGO) led the CCSS implementation in close collaboration with the local authority (which also had more than one seat on the Board of Action 2020). Action 2020 initiated a process to engage a large number of partners in issue-based task forces, with the intention that each organization would implement its portion of the thematic Action Plans. During this time period, decision-making about actions to implement Vision 2020 and communication about Vision 2020 were centralized with Action 2020 (and its task forces) and

TABLE 5.3 Perceived advantages and disadvantages for Hamilton

	Perceived advantages (mentioned by more than one interviewee)	*Perceived disadvantages (mentioned by more than one interviewee)*
1992–1998 (Local authority led)	• A diversity of organizations involved • A replicable and on-going structure • An alignment of organizational, joint project and collaborative strategies • An opportunity for organizations to network and share resources	• A lack of sufficient impact/ progress on sustainability
1999–2003 (NGO led)	• A diversity of organizations involved • An ownership of the CCSS by the organizational partners	• Roles not clearly defined • A broad coverage of topics so lack of consensus and vulnerable to shifts in opinion • A lack of ownership by organizations
2004–2009 (Local authority led)	• An alignment of organizational, joint project and collaborative strategies • A replicable and on-going process • A diversity of organizations involved	• A broad coverage of topics so lack of consensus and vulnerable to shifts in opinion • A lack of continuity/freshness • A lack of sufficient on-going engagement, networking and sharing of resources • A lack of resources

could be termed "collaborative" in the sense that they were multi-organizational, although this led to tension with the local authority, and the monitoring (i.e. reporting) and renewal remained with the local authority. By the third time period, Action 2020 was disbanded, and processes were once again centralized with the local authority and the loosely affiliated joint projects in which the local authority was involved. The structure in place during the second time-frame is similar to that of Whistler2020.

Hamilton interviewees identified the main advantages and disadvantages of their implementation structure as it relates to their time involved with the CCSS. See Table 5.3 for the summary.

The advantages mentioned in the first time period were the main reasons that Hamilton won so many awards for their CCSS in the 1990s. The indicators, which were mentioned in only one comment, in particular were very innovative for the time. In Hamilton, the time period of 1999–2003, included the creation and dissolution of the NGO Action 2020. The interviewees commented that the main advantage of the structure during that timeframe was Action 2020's task forces – in particular because they enabled a diversity of organizations to be involved and they provided the opportunity for the CCSS to be owned by many organizational partners. This was not fully implemented before the NGO was dissolved, so the lack of continuity also appears as a disadvantage (in that organizations could not have on-going ownership of the CCSS). It is interesting to note that the two advantages indentified for Hamilton's Action 2020 time period are also reflected in Whistler interviewees' comments; thus this is likely attributable to the structure itself. A disadvantage during this time period was that roles were not clearly defined between the NGO and the local authority; specifically the decision-making process created unresolved tensions. In addition, a problem which perhaps existed from the start emerged during this time period; the broad coverage of topics in Vision 2020 meant that there was a lack of consensus as to what sustainable development really meant, and so implementation was vulnerable to conflicting opinions. The key trade-off identified was the balance between the funders' wishes for the NGO, and the NGO's desire to play a watchdog role.

For the 2004–2009 time period, the disadvantage mentioned about the lack of sufficient on-going engagement, networking and sharing of resources was particularly felt because the Sustainable Community Day from the first time period and Action 2020 from the second time period no longer existed. The on-going implementation by the local authority was identified as having both strengths and weaknesses; the triple bottom-line decision-making had been institutionalized, but it is not taken as seriously as some would like. Other comments were also made about the fact that joint projects are now completely decoupled from Vision 2020, and the process is no longer collaborative; the trade-off in these comments is that while the local authority has maintained control of Vision 2020 and ensured the continuity of the initiative, other institutions, organizations and companies in the community no longer had ownership of the Vision or its implementation, which results in some issues not being implemented.

This quotation summarizes one of the main advantages of Vision 2020, the on-going process.

> There is a fairly good awareness of what Vision 2020 is, and what sustain-ability is; it's truly part of the culture … it has truly engaged the community … the fact that it still has resonance is fairly powerful.
>
> (*Heather Donison, Current Vision 2020 Coordinator, City of Hamilton*)

In summary, this case presents the perceived advantages and disadvantages of the implementation structure in the Hamilton case.[3]

Greater Vancouver cities^PLUS

Greater Vancouver's cities^PLUS had a structure which is predominately informal. It was initiated by a small multi-sector group of organizations who launched a formal process but without a formally constituted entity at the full partnership level to formulate the strategy. It engaged numerous other organizations in the formulation process through formal consultation events and information gathering activities. The efforts resulted in a CCSS with a 100-year time horizon. No formalized imple-mentation effort was ever planned; rather, it was intended that individual organizations would act upon the concepts in the CCSS on their own accord and independently. So organizations made their own decisions about which actions to pursue, and if relevant, conducted their own organizational-level sustainability reporting. Some of the partners continued to informally interact and communicate about implementation through two newsletters, sustainability breakfasts, the PLUS Network, Metro Vancouver's dialogues, QUEST, and the myriad other sustainability initiatives in Greater Vancouver. No monitoring system was created for cities^PLUS, and no renewal was planned. Many legacies have resulted from cities^PLUS, most of which were not deliberate.

Greater Vancouver's cities^PLUS's implementation structure also had its advantages and disadvantages, as outlined in Table 5.4.

Interviewees focused the majority of their comments on the formulation phase as that was the only formal component. In particular, the 100-year timeframe was identified as an advantage for visioning and creativity, but comments were also made that the long time frame was not ideal for facilitating implementation. There was a perception by some that it was the local authority's responsibility to implement, yet the mixed convenor approach meant that the local authority did not have ownership over the plan, and the implementation by local authority was vulnerable to shifts in local political will. Without the local authority leading implementation, the con-sulting firm and the NGO lead organizations were unable to maintain this role as they are both limited by project-based funding. The individual partner implemen-tation and the complementary decentralized decision-making (i.e., decisions made within each organization on what and how they will continue working towards the collaborative strategy's vision) were seen as being a trade-off; while control remained

TABLE 5.4 Perceived advantages and disadvantages for Greater Vancouver

Perceived advantages (mentioned by more than one interviewee)	Perceived disadvantages (mentioned by more than one interviewee)
• A long-term time horizon • A diversity of organizations involved • An opportunity for organizations to network and share resources • An achievement of organizational-level progress on sustainability • An opportunity for individuals	• Roles not clearly defined and no collaborative structure • A lack of mechanism to engage new organizations • A perception that it is only a local authority project (not multi-organizational) • A lack of focus by some local authority departments and politicians • A broad coverage of topics so lack of consensus and vulnerable to shifts in opinion • A timeframe too long for implementation/Vision not action

in the individual organizations enabling them to implement within their mandate, this also limited the issues implemented and the oversight of implementation efforts.

This quotation highlights an advantage of being a partner in cities^PLUS

> The initiatives at BC Hydro were supported by a very vibrant network in Vancouver which included ICSC and many others. The network supported each other and was a critical element in raising the sustainability profile of Vancouver and BC at the time.
>
> *(Bruce Sampson, former VP Sustainability, BC Hydro)*

In summary, this case presents the perceived advantages and disadvantages of the informal implementation structure in the Greater Vancouver case.

Perceived advantages and disadvantages

This section shows the clustered findings from the empirical study about perceived advantages and disadvantages, regardless of implementation structure (i.e., by combining the results from all four cases).

Perceived advantages

Clustering the perceived advantages, fifteen different categories emerged. These are related to specific implementation structure components (partners, framework and processes). These perceived advantages are detailed in Box 5.1.

BOX 5.1 Perceived advantages of interviewee's collaborative implementation structure

Partners (and individuals)

1   A diversity of organizations involved
2   A local authority in the leadership role
3   An opportunity for individuals

Implementation framework

4   An opportunity for organizations to network and share of resources
5   An alignment of organizational, joint projects and collaborative strategies
6   An achievement of organizational-level progress on sustainability
7   A cost effective structure

Processes

8   An on-going autonomy of organizational decision-making
9   A collaborative communication mechanism
10 A community with an ability to monitor progress on sustainability
11 A flexible process
12 A replicable and ongoing structure

Other

13 A broad coverage of sustainability topics
14 A long-term time horizon
15 An ownership of the CCSS by the organizational partners

Perceived disadvantages

Clustering the perceived disadvantages, fifteen different categories emerged. Again these can be related to the implementation structure. The perceived disadvantages are detailed in Box 5.2.

Comparing the four implementation structures

Whistler has the most opportunity for inter-organizational interaction of any of the structures due to the joint projects (i.e., task forces), so provides an opportunity for partner organizations to build relationships, gain knowledge and access marketing opportunities. Both Whistler and Montreal feature implementation by individual organizations, and monitor on their implementation, so are likely to result in partner actions. It was only in the Whistler case that partners complained about increased

---

BOX 5.2 Perceived disadvantages of interviewee's collaborative implementation structure

Partners (and citizens)

1   An inadequacy of involvement of economic organizations in implementation
2   A perception that it is only a local authority project (not multi-organizational)
3   A lack of focus by some local authority departments and politicians
4   A lack of understanding by citizens

Implementation framework

5   A lack of sufficient on-going engagement, networking and sharing of resources
6   A lack of alignment of organizational, joint project and collaborative strategies
7   Roles are not clearly defined or no collaborative structure

Processes

8   An evaluation process which is difficult
9   A lack of sufficient impact/progress on sustainability
10 A lack of continuity/freshness
11 A lack of a mechanism to engage new organizations

Other

12 A broad coverage of topics so lack of consensus and vulnerable to shifts in opinion
13 A timeframe too long for implementation/vision not action/pace too slow
14 An increase of costs and workload/A lack of resources
15 A lack of ownership by organizations

---

demand on their scarce resources, and this likely reflects the situation that task forces require partners to commit the time and effort of human resources to participate in meetings. All the structures enable partners to gain knowledge from their involvement in the CCSS and all also enable partners to make progress on issues related to sustainability (i.e. their sustainability goals). This does not mean they are all equally effective at realizing all collaborative goals, quite the contrary. In Hamilton and Greater Vancouver, progress is only made on the issues that the partners are engaged in, and there are a smaller number of partners in these cases.

TABLE 5.5 Comparison of the implementation structures of the four cases

Criteria (Clarke, 2011:165)	Whistler	Montreal	Hamilton	Greater Vancouver
Engages key organizations from different sectors, and/or has a mechanism to identify them and to add them.	Engages key organizations and has a mechanism to identify and add more.	Organizations can self-engage, invitations can be sent, and new partners can be added. There is no collaborative process to identify missing key partners.	Joint projects can engage key organizations, but do not exist for all issues.	The lead organizations are cross-sector, but there is no mechanism to identify or engage more.
Has collaborative form(s) to oversee the implementation, and identify issue-based short-term actions, and also allows for networking between organizations.	The issue-based joint projects (task forces) serve this purpose.	The framework at the full partnership level and also the joint project(s) oversee the process and allow networking, but do not identify short-term actions. It depends on the timeframe of the strategy itself.	Joint projects allow for networking, action identification and issue-based oversight where they exist.	The informal interactions allow for networking, but not oversight nor action identification.
Has individual organizations implementing within their own organizations.	Yes.	Yes.	No, except for the local authority and perhaps also partners engaged in a joint project.	Yes.
Has a communication system that exists to further networking and to reach citizens.	Yes.	Yes.	Generally only reporting on local authority initiatives and perhaps joint projects, where they exist.	No communication system exists.
Has a monitoring system that exists, including both state and action indicators, which also allows for adjustments to be made to the implementation actions, and renewal to be made to the collaborative strategic plan.	Yes, there is a monitoring system on both indicator types, a mechanism to adjust actions annually, and a renewal process.	Yes, there is a monitoring system on both indicator types and a renewal process that also adjusts actions. There are less frequent adjustments than in Whistler.	Yes, a monitoring system exists that monitors state indicators, particularly in relation to the local authority's jurisdiction. No actions are set, so no adjustment is possible. There may be a renewal process.	Monitoring is conducted by individual partners about their own implementation. Emergent solutions are possible, but no adjustments or renewal of the formal CCSS possible.

Like Whistler, Hamilton has the potential for joint projects so also provides an opportunity for those involved to build relationships. As the joint projects are initiated by the focal organization (e.g. the local authority) in Hamilton, there is less opportunity to access marketing opportunities, i.e. less opportunity to promote their organization, gain visibility and get recognition for their initiatives. Based on interviewee comments, Greater Vancouver is the only one which emphasizes business opportunities as an inherent goal. Partners are informally involved in the implementation in ways that match their mandates, and make progress towards their organizational goals, so it appears they engage in the CCSS implementation when it is also an opportunity to promote their programming or company; thus accessing business and marketing opportunities are a key part of this initiative.

Based on the five criteria developed by Clarke (2011), Table 5.5 demonstrates the comparison of each of the four cases.

Clarke's (2011) five criteria clearly show in Table 5.5 (above) the advantages and disadvantages of each structure for achieving CCSS goals. A practical consideration that was raised during the interviews is particularly important; the commitment of partner organizations to the CCSS (i.e. ownership).

Ownership

In terms of "ownership" (i.e. the commitment of organizations to the CCSS), this was an underlying theme throughout the interviews in all four communities. Whistler struggles with a perception by some that their CCSS is a plan of the local authority; this was one of the motivations for creating the Whistler Centre for Sustainability as the new home. Hamilton also struggled with ownership issues near the end of the time period 1992–1998, which was one of the reasons Action 2020 was created; in order to attempt to share ownership. Hamilton in the time periods 1992–1999 and 2003–2009 places ownership with only the local authority; the disadvantage of this being that without commitment to the CCSS the other potential partners have no implementation responsibility. Greater Vancouver had the opposite challenge from Hamilton in terms of the local authority's role; with the CCSS not being viewed as a plan of just the local authority, and with no on-going formal arrangements at the full partnership level, some felt there was not enough ownership by the local authority (or any of the other partners). In Montreal, having placed the CCSS within one department, there were challenges of ownership by the other parts of local authority, though due to the shared leadership by three lead organizations, there was ownership by these three organizations. In Montreal, those partners more removed from the steering committee still viewed the CCSS as a plan of the local authority as much of the communication and monitoring is centred there. Ultimately, from a local authority perspective, the structures in Whistler, Montreal and Hamilton provide the most ownership, but from the other partners' perspective, Whistler's structure, followed by Montreal's structure, allow for the most ownership. Greater Vancouver's structure also allows for ownership by partners, but does not ensure ownership by any organization.

Related to ownership, was the desire for organizations to retain authority over decisions they believed to be under their jurisdiction. For example, the Board of the local authority for Greater Vancouver was challenged by the partnership committee, and the purpose of that entity, given that decision-making on the local authority's sustainability programs was the responsibility of the Board. This ultimately led to the creation of dialogues instead of a cross-sector decision-making entity.

Conclusion

This chapter details the role and design of cross-sector social partnerships at the local level. In terms of the role, this chapter provides examples of the emergence of local cross-sector social partnerships and collaborative strategies. While the focus is on collaborative community sustainability strategies, the phenomenon of social partnerships also exists for other complex local issues such as economic development, crime prevention, and health services (Dienhart and Ludescher, 2010; Geddes, 2008; Huxham and Vangen, 2005). While collaborative governance is increasingly being used at the local level, in practice, the Local Agenda 21 survey (ICLEI, 2002a) and CCSSs in Canada (Clarke and Erfan, 2007) show that sometimes the same collaborative strategy is formulated and implemented by switching between partnership and participation approaches. The tensions that drive this shift from public to shared authority and back are exemplified through the case studies considered in this chapter, and are also explored in other chapters in Part A of this book. This is also related to the discussion in this chapter about "ownership" of the CCSS by the partners. The tension between autonomy and accountability is inherent in collaborations (Bowen *et al.*, 2010; Huxham, 1996) and these cases help us further how design might help alleviate some of those tensions by providing explicit options.

In terms of the design of CSSPs at the local level, this chapter details four different CCSS implementation structures in order to highlight the management and governance challenges faced by social partnerships. In all of these cases, there were a large number of partners (as many as 180 in the Montreal case). In general, the CSSP literature has been predominantly focused on two or three organization partners, though some more recent studies have considered some large CSSPs (e.g. Babiak and Thibault, 2009; Geddes, 2008; Huxham and Vangen, 2005). There are a number of design implications of these larger CSSPs, including the number of levels of action-taking expanding from just the partnership level and the individual organization level to also include a joint project level (Clarke and Fuller, 2011; Huxham and Vangen, 2005). The Clarke (2011) five criteria were useful in highlighting the different structural features in the four CSSP designs. Having a formal structure with these five features is critical for achieving the goals outlined in the collaborative strategy (Clarke, 2011). Design features in general will determine what value is created for partners and for the society (Austin and Seitanidi, 2012; Elbers and Schulpen, 2011). The interviewee perceptions about the advantages and disadvantages of their own CCSS implementation structure were not as comprehensive and did not have the external perspective of using a framework for analysis (such as Clarke, 2011). That said, it is these perceptions that influence a CSSPs ability to continue to engage the partners over time (Gazley, 2010; Kitchen *et al.*, 1997).

In regards to another focus of this book – partnerships as a means to engage responsible business – this chapter demonstrates that the design of the collaborative governance structure is important for enabling businesses to participate. For example, the structure provides opportunities for new partners to get involved, and it incentivizes engagement through opportunities for learning, marketing and creating real progress on sustainability issues (Clarke and MacDonald, 2012). This is particularly true for these long-term, large partnerships, as new partners can join the implementation efforts without having been a part of the founding efforts, and partners have differing degrees of engagement (Babiak and Thibault, 2009). The design of the implementation structure creates specific advantages and disadvantages for partners. This empirical study found that it was not the organizational type that influenced what partners experienced, but instead the implementation structure. Thus large businesses in Whistler had more in common with other organizations in Whistler, than with large businesses in the other three cases. That said, for the large corporations, one advantage that was consistent across cases was that getting involved in implementing a collaborative community sustainability strategy is an excellent means of conducting community engagement without having to lead the larger process.

As the empirical cases are all related to local sustainable development, the collaborative strategies are long-term in nature, even if their time horizons vary; generally it will take between 20 to 100 years to really achieve the goals. The duration of the CSSP has implications on design; strategy adaptation and renewal opportunities, new partner engagement mechanisms, and avoiding partner fatigue are just of few of the design considerations to consider (Austin and Seitanidi, 2012; Clarke, 2011; Clarke and MacDonald, 2012). Reporting and monitoring mechanisms are one of the key features for longer-term initiatives (Clarke, 2011), yet these are underutilized in practice (Biermann *et al.,* 2007a; Rein and Stott, 2009), and have their challenges (Geddes, 2008). The Greater Vancouver case detailed in this chapter shows how critical formal implementation structures are for ensuring on-going efforts. This topic of design is also covered in some of the other chapters in this book, including the chapter on cross-sector governance (by Rufin and Rivera-Santos, this volume), and the one on future methods of design and decision-making for cross-sector partnerships for sustainable development (by Mangalagiu *et al.*, this volume).

While this study helps contribute to the conversations about cross-sector social partnerships at the local level, collaborative strategy implementation, collaborative governance structures, and Local Agenda 21s, more research is needed in these areas. That said, it is perhaps time for the growing bodies of literature on collaborative governance, collaborative planning, cross-sector social partnerships, inter-organizational relations, cross-sector alliances, and collaborative public management to merge into one "collaboration theory" that can be seen as a theoretical lens of its own with the main unit of analysis being the formal partnership.

Questions for reflection

1   Reflect on a "partnership approach" versus a "participation approach" for tackling sustainability issues at the local level. We know that in theory, social problems that are too large for one organization are being increasingly addressed through cross-sector social partnerships, so why then are most local authorities still using a "participation approach"?

2   Reflect on "designing a CSSP" in order to improve partner engagement. What are the most important structural features for ensuring partners have the opportunity and desire to engage in the collaborative strategy implementation? Why did you choose these features?

3   Reflect on "designing a CSSP" in order to achieve the collaborative goals in the collaborative strategy (and thus help solve the social problem). What are the most important structural features for ensuring that there is a positive impact? Why did you choose these features?

4   What role should the local authority play in the CSSP? In Greater Vancouver, they did not play enough of a role and thus there was no on-going buy-in. In Whistler, it was decided to move the collaborative initiative into an NGO so as to increase the buy-in from other partners. Hamilton experimented with the NGO model and instead decided to move all the decision-making back into the local authority (with no sharing with partners). In Montreal, there are three core partners sharing the decision-making, though the secretariat is housed in the local authority. What are the implications of these approaches and thus what role do you think the local authority should play?

Notes

1   For more information about Whistler2020's implementation structure, see Clarke (2012).
2   For more information about Montreal's implementation structure, see Clarke (2012).
3   For more information about Hamilton's implementation structure, see Clarke (2012).

References

Astley, W.G. and Fombrun, C.J. (1983) "Collective Strategy: Social Ecology of Organizational Environments", *Academy of Management Review*, 8: 576–87.

Austin, J. and Seitanidi, M.M. (2012) "Collaborative Value Creation: A Review of Partnering between Nonprofits and Businesses. Part 2. Partnership Processes and Outcomes", *Nonprofit and Voluntary Sector Quarterly*, (forthcoming).

Babiak, K. and Thibault, L. (2009) "Challenges in Multiple Cross-Sector Partnerships", *Nonprofit and Voluntary Sector Quarterly*, 38: 117–43.

Barrutia, J.M., Aguado, I. and Echebarria, C. (2007) "Networking for Local Agenda 21 Implementation: Learning from Experiences with *Udaltalde* and *Udalsarea* in the Basque Autonomous Community", *Geoforum*, 38: 33–48.

Biermann, F., Chan, M.-s., Mert, A. and Pattberg, P. (2007a) "Multi-stakeholder Partnerships for Sustainable Development: Does the Promise Hold?", in Glasbergen, P., Biermann, F. and Mol, A. P.J. (eds) *Parterships, Governance and Sustainable Development: Reflections on Theory and*

Practice. Northampton, NH: Edward Elgar.

Biermann, F., Mol, A.P.J. and Glasbergen, P. (2007b) "Conclusion: Partnerships for Sustainability – Reflections on a Future Research Agenda", in Glasbergen, P., Biermann, F. and Mol, A. P. J. (eds) *Partnerships, Governance and Sustainable Development.* Cheltenham: Edward Elgar.

Bowen, F., Newenham-Kahindi, A. and Herremans, I. (2010) "When Suits Meet Roots: The Antecedents and Consequences of Community Engagement Strategy", *Journal of Business Ethics,* 95: 297–318.

Cartwright, L. (1997) "The Implementation of Sustainable Development by Local Authorities in the South East of England", *Planning Practice and Research,* 12: 337–47.

Clarke, A. (2011) "Key Structural Features for Collaborative Strategy Implementation: A Study of Sustainable Development/Local Agenda 21 Collaborations", *Revue Management et Avenir,* 50: 153–71.

Clarke, A. (2012) *Passing Go: Implementing the Plan.* Ottawa: Federation of Canadian Municipalities.

Clarke, A. and Erfan, A. (2007) "Regional Sustainability Strategies: A Comparison of Eight Canadian Approaches", *Plan Canada,* 47: 15–18.

Clarke, A. and Fuller, M. (2011) "Collaborative Strategic Management: Strategy Formulation and Implementation by Multi-organizational Cross-sector Social Partnerships", *Journal of Business Ethics,* 94: 85–101.

Clarke, A. and MacDonald, A. (2012) "Partner Engagement for Community Sustainability: Supporting Sustainable Development Initiatives by Reducing Friction in the Local Economy". *State of Knowledge Report.* Ottawa: Sustainable Prosperity.

Devuyst, D. and Hens, L. (2000) "Introducing and Measuring Sustainable Development Initiatives by Local Authorities in Canada and Flanders (Belgium) A Comparative Study", *Environment, Development and Sustainability,* 2: 81.

Dienhart, J.W. and Ludescher, J.C. (2010) "Sustainability, Collaboration, and Governance: A Harbinger of Institutional Change?", *Business and Society Review,* 115: 393–415.

Eckerberg, K. and Forsberg, B. (1998) "Implementing Agenda 21 in Local Government: The Swedish Experience", *Local Environment,* 3: 333–48.

Elbers, W. and Schulpen, L. (2011) "Decision Making in Partnerships for Development: Explaining the Influence of Local Partners", *Nonprofit and Voluntary Sector Quarterly,* 40: 795–812.

Fidélis, T. and Pires, S.M. (2009) "Surrender or Resistance to the Implementation of Local Agenda 21 in Portugal: the Challenges of Local Governance for Sustainable Development", *Journal of Environmental Planning and Management,* 52: 497–518.

García-Sánchez, I.M. and Prado-Lorenzo, J.-M. (2008) "Determinant Factors in the Degree of Implementation of Local Agenda 21 in the European Union", *Sustainable Development,* 16: 17–34.

Gazley, B. (2010) "Why Not Partner With Local Government? Nonprofit Managerial Perceptions of Collaborative Disadvantage", *Nonprofit and Voluntary Sector Quarterly,* 39: 51–76.

Geddes, M. (2008) "Inter-organizational Relationships in Local and Regional Development Partnerships", in Cropper, S., Ebers, M., Huxham, C. and Ring, P.S. (eds) *The Oxford Handbook of Inter-organizational Relations.* Oxford: Oxford University Press.

Geissel, B. (2009) "Participatory Governance: Hope or Danger for Democracy? A Case Study of Local Agenda 21", *Local Government Studies,* 35: 401–14.

Gibbs, D., Longhurst, J. and Braithwaite, C. (1996) "Moving Towards Sustainable Development? Integrating Economic Development and the Environment in Local Authorities", *Journal of Environmental Planning and Management,* 39: 317–32.

Gladwin, T.N., Kennelly, J.J. and Krause, T.-S. (1995) "Shifting Paradigms for Sustainable Development: Implications for Management Theory and Research", *Academy of Management Review,* 20: 874–907.

Glasbergen, P. (2007) "Setting the Scene: The Partnership Paradigm in the Making", in Glasbergen, P., Biermann, F. and Mol, A.P.J. (eds) *Partnerships, Governance and Sustainable Development.* Cheltenham: Edward Elgar.

Hood, J.N., Logsdon, J.M. and Thompson, J.K. (1993) "Collaboration for Social Problem-Solving: A Process Model", *Business and Society,* 32: 1–17.

Huxham, C. (1996) "Collaboration and Collaborative Advantage", in Huxham, C. (ed.) *Creating Collaborative Advantage.* London: Sage.

Huxham, C. and Macdonald, D. (1992) "Introducing Collaborative Advantage: Achieving Inter-Organizational Effectiveness through Meta-strategy", *Management Decision,* 30: 50–6.

Huxham, C. and Vangen, S. (2000) "Leadership in the Shaping and Implementation of Collaboration Agendas: How Things Happen in a (Not Quite) Joined-Up World", *Academy of Management Journal,* 43: 1159–75.

Huxham, C. and Vangen, S. (2005) *Managing to Collaborate: The Theory and Practice of Collaborative Advantage,* New York: Routledge.

ICLEI (2002a) Answers to Survey of Local Authorities – North America. Toronto: International Council for Local Environmental Initiatives.

ICLEI (2002b) Second Local Agenda 21 Survey – Background Paper No. 15. New York: United Nations Department of Economic and Social Affairs – Commission for Sustainable Development.

ICLEI. (2012a) *Local Governments for Sustainability* [Online]. Toronto: International Council for Local Environmental Initiatives. Available: www.iclei.org/ [accessed June 2012].

ICLEI (2012b) Local Sustainability 2012: Taking Stock and Moving Forward. *Global Review, ICLEI Global Report.* Bonn: ICLEI – Local Governments for Sustainability.

Infrastructure Canada (2006) The Path Towards Sustainability: An Evaluation of the "Sustainability-ness" of Selected Municipal Plans in Canada. Ottawa: Research and Analysis Division, Infrastructure Canada.

Jennings, P.D. and Zandbergen, P.A. (1995) "Ecologically Sustainable Organizations: An Institutional Approach", *Academy of Management Review,* 20: 1015–52.

Kitchen, T., Whitney, D. and Littlewood, S. (1997) "Local Authority/Academic Collaboration and Local Agenda 21 Policy Processes", *Journal of Environmental Planning and Management,* 40: 645–60.

Maclaren, V.W. (1992) Sustainable Urban Development in Canada: From Concept to Practice – Volume I: Summary Report. Toronto, ON: Intergovernmental Committee on Urban and Regional Research Press.

Manderson, A.K. (2006) "A Systems Based Framework to Examine the Multi-Contextural Application of the Sustainability Concept", *Environment, Development and Sustainability,* 8: 85–97.

Mehta, P. (1996) "Local Agenda 21: Practical Experiences and Emerging Issues from the South", *Environmental Impact Assessment Review,* 16: 309–20.

Michaux, V., Defelix, C. and Raulet-Croset, N. (2011) "Boosting Territorial Multi-stakeholder Cooperation, Coordination and Collaboration: Strategic and Managerial Issues", *Management and Avenir,* 50: 122–36.

Millennium Ecosystem Assessment (2005) "Preface", in Sarukhan, J. and Whyte, A. (eds) *Millennium Ecosystem Assessment Synthesis Report – Pre-Publication Final Draft.* United Nations Environment Programme.

Owen, A.L. and Videras, J. (2008) "Trust, Cooperation, and Implementation of Sustainability Programs: The Case of Local Agenda 21", *Ecological Economics,* 68: 259–72.

Peris, J., García-Melón, M., Gómez-Navarro, T. and Calabuig, C. (2011) "Prioritizing Local Agenda 21 Programmes using Analytic Network Process: A Spanish Case Study", *Sustainable Development*.

Rein, M. and Stott, L. (2009) "Working Together: Critical Perspectives on Six Cross-Sector Partnerships in South Africa", *Journal of Business Ethics*, 90: 79–89.

Rotheroe, N., Keenlyside, M. and Coates, L. (2003) "Local Agenda 21: Articulating the Meaning of Sustainable Development at the Level of the Individual Enterprise", *Journal of Cleaner Production*, 11: 537–48.

Sofroniciu, O.P. (2005) "Impediments in Implementing Local Agenda 21 in Romania: A Case Study of Ramnicu Valcea Strategy for Sustainable Development", *Journal of Environmental Assessment Policy and Management*, 7: 149–63.

Sustainable Cities Programme (1999) The SCP Source Book Series, Volume 5: Institution-alising the Environmental Planning and Management (EPM) Process. Nairobi, Kenya: United Nations Environment Programme and United Nations Centre for Human Settlements.

UN-Habitat (2004) State of the World's Cities 2004/2005 – Globalization and Urban Culture. Nairobi, Kenya: United Nations Human Settlements Programme.

UN-Habitat. (2012) *Sustainable Cities Programme* [Online]. Nairobi: UN-Habitat. Available: www.unhabitat.org/content.asp?typeid=19&catid=540&cid=5025 [accessed July 2012].

UNCED (1992) Agenda 21. Rio de Janeiro: United Nations Conference on Environment and Development.

World Commission on Environment and Development (1987) *Our Common Future*, Oxford, New York: Oxford University Press.

Yin, R.K. (2003) *Case Study Research: Design and Methods*, Thousand Oaks, CA: Sage.

PART B

Management and governance challenges

6

CREATING PARTNERING SPACE

Exploring the right fit for sustainable development partnerships

Rob van Tulder and Stella Pfisterer

Introduction: the partnering space for sustainable development

The rationale of cross-sector social partnerships (CSSPs) suggests that collaboration has an impact for the society going beyond benefits for the individual partners and creating "new socio-economic developmental models" (Googins and Rochlin, 2000: 127) in which not separate actors, but their relationships shape the relevant change (Glasbergen, 2011). This change is facilitated by "collaborative advantage" (Huxham and Vangen, 2005), or the synergy that is created through organizations bundling their "core complementary competencies" (Warner and Sullivan, 2004). Borrowing from resource dependency literature, we can talk of different types of "organizational fit" between partners in the partnering space. "Organizational fit" describes the internal match or the compatibility between organizations, taking into account "organizational processes, such as culture, human resources, policies, and administrative systems" (Kim *et al.*, 2012; 136, referring to Saxton, 1997). The degree of fit enables the generation of synergistic value – the better the fit, the greater the value creation (Austin and Seitanidi, 2012). From a management perspective this means that the more appropriate roles are aligned, the greater the chance for value creation. From a societal perspective, organizational fit defines the preconditions for sustainable development, which requires a proper alignment between the interests of the three most important institutional spheres: state, market, and civil society. The reverse argument is that the smaller the fit, the bigger the chance of misalignment, role conflicts and skewed development trajectories. In essence, CSSPs can therefore be considered as a necessary institutional innovation to address complex sustainability problems and provide new ways to govern and manage relations in societies. But they – when ill designed and ill-fitted – can also prolong problems or create new ones.

Literature on partnerships has mainly focused on bilateral interfaces, in particular on interfaces between the market and the state (PPPs); the state and civil society (nPPPs) and between the market and civil society (PnPPs). Most of these interfaces have been studied from the perspective of one actor: either the firm, the civil society organization, or the government. The number of studies that actually consider the interaction (the interface) as level of analysis still remains limited. The implication of this is that profit-nonprofit partnership studies concentrate on the question whether cross-sector partnerships produce "social good" or create "shared value" without considering whether this good/value represents a "public" or a "private" good or value and thus a primary responsibility (source of legitimacy) for a specific actor. CSSPs, however, are potentially problematic as the partners assume roles and responsibilities that may be incompatible with their core logics (Glasbergen, 2011 referring to Waddell, 2005). As Glasbergen describes "NGOs are bound by their identification with and loyalty to civic values; the market mechanism forces businesses to act in their own economic interest; governments are responsible for the public good and need to consider implementation gaps in their policies" (2011: 5). Societal identities of actors are restricted; therefore, their roles and responsibilities in a partnership should be aligned to their core complementary competencies. Finding the "golden fit" and developing reciprocal relationships is then the only way for developing effective partnerships.

"Crowding-out" is thereby one of the most recurring effects of misconfiguration of societal roles in a partnership. Ill-conceived bilateral partnerships aim at output that is not in their direct sphere of influence or line of responsibility and legitimacy. Profit-non-profit partnerships (PnPPs) that aim at the provision of public goods may crowd out governments, with the result of inadequate governance. Public-private partnerships that (also) aim at the provision of community goods can remove important incentives of communities and citizens to take up responsibility for their own interests. Government-NGO partnerships (nPPP) aimed at the provision of private goods (often subsidized), disrupt the functioning of markets and thereby can limit efficiency. These examples of misalignment are not theoretical. The various types represent different levels of commitment to engage in mutually dependent positions resulting in different potential collaboration types along the "collaborative continuum" by Austin and Seitanidi (2012). It can be summarized that discussing partnerships is about the debate on public and private responsibilities, profit and nonprofit interests, their relationships and how to configure actors and their roles most effectively for stimulating change for sustainable development (cf. Glasbergen, 2011).

In the management literature, the argument has been put forward for the integration of resource-based (power bases) and institutions-based (societal position) views (Peng, 2002). In the public management and development literature comparable arguments have been used to plead for the integration of various coordination mechanisms in society, based upon the roles taken by their most important agents of change (firms, governments, civil society organizations). Only a minor group of CSSP scholars have however linked the organizational and the institutional perspective and investigated the effects of prevailing institutional logics on the configuration of partnerships (see Vurro et al., 2010). Institutional logics provide a framework of meaning for roles and actions to organizations, which "represents a source of legitimacy and appropriateness for agents to identifying with" (Vurro *et al.,* 2010: 43, referring to March and Olsen, 1989). By introducing the concept of the "partnering space" as a frame in which to consider the positioning games played by actors from different societal sectors in order to contribute to sustainable development, our contribution distinguishes partnership types by focusing on roles and responsibilities of societal actors in CSSPs. Understanding the basic roles of each party in cross-sector partnerships should also lead to a more fine-grained understanding on the "fit" between partners and finally, the "synergistic relationships" based on which partners aim to create value for sustainable development. As our framework identifies a set of different partnering types in the partnering space, we are also able to develop propositions on the possibility of partners to reach a specific stage of the "collaborative continuum" (Austin and Seitanidi, 2012).

With this largely taxonomical activity we aim to contribute to a more comprehensive analytical framework in which to document the nature of the dynamic interactions between organizations (firms, NGOs, governments) and institutions (formal and informal constraints, rules, relationships, and roles) in which strategic choices are created. From an analytical perspective, this exercise should make it possible to link meso-level interactions at the partnership level to macro-level assessments of their contribution to sustainable development. From a managerial perspective, this exercise should inform parties on how to create "organizational fit" for effective sustainable development partnerships.

As an answer to the conceptual and theoretical ambiguities around the concept of "cross-sector partnerships" this contribution first comes up with a relatively simple actor-based classification of four types of cross-sector partnerships and three types of coordination mechanisms (section 2), which consequently define what we can call the "partnering space" for development relevant partnerships. The dynamics of these collaborations that develop in this space and their function for sustainable development can be assessed in a more idealistic and more realistic manner. We argue that balancing these two angles requires a deeper understanding of the roles which societal actors adopt in a partnership (section 3). We develop a framework which leads to a more fine-grained taxonomy of partnership types which captures the natures of the dynamic interactions of organizations and institutions in collaborations for sustainable development. Specific partnerships can be expected to make different contributions to sustainable development.

Framing the partnering space

Present development thinking not only acknowledges the pluralistic idea that more (institutional) "roads can lead to Rome" (cf. Rodrik, 2007), but also that all relevant spheres of society (market, state and civil society) need to be involved in the process. Sustainable development represents a balancing act between the interests and positions of the various sectors, between public and private, and profit and non-profit orientations. The concept of sustainable development is therefore based on an appropriate mix of organizational forms and institutions. The balancing act thereby involves mediation between and/or combination of the interests of each sphere for instance through the creation of societal steering mechanisms, hybrid organizations, and institutions and ... the introduction of partnerships. In the resulting partnering space, key and related issues of sustainable development (poverty, health, education, infrastructure, and ecology) are consequently tackled.

Clashing coordination mechanisms in the partnering space

Each societal sphere represents different interests, power bases, and institutions (rules of the game) and organizes itself on distinct coordination and organization mechanisms (Table 6.1). The legitimacy of each societal sphere is thereby based on a sufficient and equitable production/provision of either public goods and values (state), private goods and values (firms) and community or "club" goods and values (civil society). Sustainable development is consequently built on an intricate combination of various coordination and control mechanisms: market-based, network-based, and hierarchy-based. The extent to which these various mechanisms *complement* or *compete* with each other defines the nature – and probably also the effectiveness – of the (envisaged) change.

Change driven by one interest (either state-driven, market-driven, or civic-driven change) is not likely to create sufficient preconditions for sustained development and is prone to a number of serious "failures" related to each sphere[1] (van Tulder with Van der Zwart, 2006). Partnerships are supposed to tackle the various forms of "failure" attached to unilateral action by either governments or donors, companies

TABLE 6.1 Coordination mechanisms

	State	*Market*	*Civil society*
Primacy of	Politics	Economics	The Social
Goods and values "produced"	Public	Private	Club/community
Core responsibilities	Enforcement of national standards and norms	Production of goods and services	Mobilization of society
Power base: financed by	Taxes	Profits	Donations, contributions
Power base: agency	Voters, political parties	Owners, supervisory boards	Society, members
Parameters	Coercion, codification	Competition	Cooperation, co-optation
Orientation	Public/non-profit	Private/for-profit	Private/non-profit
Coordination and control	Hierarchy-based	Market-based	Network-based

Source: Based on van Tulder with Van der Zwart (2006: 10).

or civil society in addressing sustainable development challenges (OECD, 2006; Kolk *et al.*, 2008; van Tulder with Van de Zwart, 2006). The argument is that "less emphasis is put on the autonomy of the three domains and instead their interdependencies are stressed" (Glasbergen, 2011: 2). The main distinguishing characteristic of such partnerships is the question whether they combine actors from different institutional backgrounds, societal orientations and therefore different power bases and sources of legitimacy, whilst aimed at providing (often pragmatic) solutions to sustainable development problems.

CSSPs are based on the idea of shared responsibility in which no single actor regulates behavior of other actors and in which some form of cooperation is required as one actor and/or one institutional sphere cannot solve the problem alone (Selsky and Parker, 2005; Huxham and Vangen, 2005; Austin, 2000). A true "partnership," as often intended in the sustainable development discourse, is one where both parties share comparable degrees of dependence, with substantial mutual and reciprocal influence. This description builds specifically on the idea of "collaborative advantage" (Huxham and Vangen, 2005) in which partnerships have the potential to address a number of institutional voids that hamper sustainable development (Kolk *et al.*, 2008). Partnerships can thereby broadly be conceptualized as governance arrangements, which have developed against the background of blurring boundaries between the public and the private sector. Verena Bitzer (2011: 28) rightfully argues that the current field of partnership literature discusses partnerships as "manifestation of the structurally changing roles and responsibilities of societal actors in the context of sustainable development, and as a reflection of new styles of organizing the process and interaction among different stakeholders."

An instrumental perspective of CSSPs forces us to identify the specific sectors that the partnership is supposed to bridge. The general nature of the partnership is derived from their position and origins in one of three distinctive institutional spheres in society (Figure 6.1).

This actor-based taxonomy distinguishes partnerships on the basis of the different nature of the actors involved (see also Selksy and Parker, 2005). The societal triangle defines the shape of the *macro-economic "partnering space"* for governments, firms, and civil society organizations first because of overlapping interfaces of their primary coordination circles. These interactions are themselves based on the recognition that no single actor has sufficient potential to address the issue unilaterally. The interaction also defines the objective of the resource allocation of each actor as well as their identity vis-à-vis each other. Four types of specific *meso-partnership interfaces* for sustainable development can consequentially be distinguished:

a) *Public-private partnerships* (PPPs) address in particular the inadequate provision of or underinvestment in public goods; this is also known as the policy rationale for partnerships. Neither the state nor companies invest sufficiently in general provisions that are conducive for sustainable development (Kolk *et al.*, 2008). Key issues in this domain relate to the physical infrastructure, such as roads, water facilities, or telecommunications.

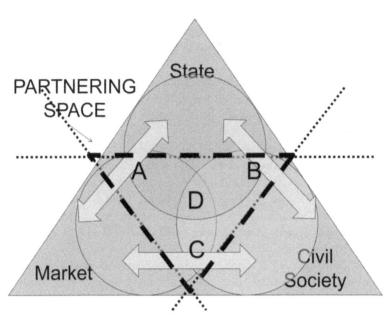

FIGURE 6.1 Partnering space(s)

b) *Non-profit public private partnerships (nPPPs)* aim to increase participation in designing and implementing effective public policies and an adequate provision of common goods. Key development issues in this domain relate to public health (sanitation and disease control) and education (knowledge infrastructure).

c) *Private (for profit)-non-profit partnerships* (PnPPs) address in particular under-provision of relevant private goods/values (for instance in affordable goods for poor people) or the lacking creation of "social capital" resulting from ill-organized civil societies. Key development issues in this domain relate to private health (e.g. access to medicine), empowerment (e.g. access to finance) and hunger (due to unequal distribution of food).

d) *Tripartite partnerships (TPPs)* aim in particular at the problems that result from the "institutional void" that develops due to weak general governance structures (van Tulder with Van der Zwart, 2006) which comes closest to dealing with the macro-economic problems of sustainable development. In most developed countries, tripartite (corporatist) institutions have matured as a means to tackle generic sustainable growth issues. Key issues in this domain are poverty-related such as social security and living wages.

The partnering space is the arena, or the sum of the interfaces, where societal actors can jointly address these complex societal issues and identify opportunities by bundling their core complementary competencies to create (shared) value for sustainable development. This "playing field" between societal actors is characterized by a highly dynamic nature.

Understanding the dynamic nature of the partnering space

How can this playing field be understood? Studies on the dynamics of cross-sector partnerships have adopted a variety of perspectives of the nature of the partnering space, the arena in which the actual process of partnering takes place. Partnering space can be considered in more idealistic or more realistic terms:

1   In more UNCED 1992 terms, partnering space represents ...
   • an area for *collaborative solutions* for wicked problems (Hart and Sharma, 2004) in which new sources of trust can be build up. Trust building will initially be relatively modest – because of the inherent differences between the sectors, but in later stages can develop into more deep trust relations (Austin, 2000). The greater the trust is, the lower the transaction costs are. The arena can also be considered a "value creation spectrum" (Austin and Seitanidi, 2012) in which "collaborative value" or "shared value" (Porter and Kramer, 2006) can be created.
   • an *area of growing interdependencies* as the result of globalization and the related ideologies of privatization, deregulation, liberalization, and decentralization (Bierman *et al.*, 2007: 288). Many studies do not look at the nature of the interdependencies, but either start from the presupposition of interdependence or implicitly suggest that partnerships are based on equality in power and an equal distribution of gains and losses.
   • a *new institutional space* in which the common good can be advanced. New institutional arrangements experimented with in the partnering space can distribute values and resources, or can act as "sources of power to the extent that they are effective, and arenas for power-based conflicts on the distribution of values and resources" (ibid.: 298).
   • a means to *bridge the "institutional divide,"* in particular in case of a co-existence of potentially conflicting institutions, by including multiple partners from multiple sectors (Rivera-Santos *et al.*, 2012).
   • a *novel approach to governance and decision-making* needed to address the "institutional void" that appears in societies. The governance approach that is searched for is also referred to as inclusive-, meta-, transition-, or hybrid governance – but with recurring problems of legitimacy and accountability (cf. Utting and Zammit, 2009) which critically depends on the problem-solving effectiveness of partnerships. In partnerships that have reached a degree of institutionalization (Gray, 2007) power relations are "channeled" through governance mechanisms that guarantee binding decisions and compliance. How to evaluate the effectiveness of partnerships thus becomes increasingly important (Glasbergen, 2011).
   • a *"discursive space"* in which actors collaborate to frame and reframe issues that can be considered of mutual interest. The move into the partnering space forces actors to move out of the existing frames of reference, interest-based positions, or comfort zones (mindset) or homogenous institutional

backgrounds. The power of framing by each actor is brought into the partnership and can lead to a constructive discourse. But this discourse develops only under specific circumstances and has limitations in effectively mitigating power relations (Deetz *et al.*, 2007).

2   In more *realistic* terms, the partnering space represents …

*   a contested *political arena*. Partnerships for sustainable development have been negotiated, endorsed, and implemented in a contested political arena (Mert and Chan, 2012: 21). This idea is very common in critical studies about development partnerships (Utting and Zammit, 2010; Pattberg *et al.*, 2012). In that perspective the term partnership functions as a disguise of unequal relations between the parties (Richter, 2004).

*   a *"bargaining arena"* (van Tulder with Van der Zwart, 2006) in which conflict and power struggles are exercised (Gray, 2007).

*   a *network*, multiple layers of relational structures and the positions therein of actors. In order to understand the structural position of partners it is required to understand power (Ellersiek, 2011: 36). In a network approach, power is generally considered as the inverse of dependence. Influence can be derived from centrality in the network, if combined with sufficient resource to remain independent (the strength of weak ties).

*   as *new opportunity* for the private sector to "exercise power and influence over domains that where the preserve of public-sector organizations" (Buse and Harmer, 2004: 50) or as an action primarily for self-interest and secondarily for social good. Selsky and Parker (2010) in this context use the term "resource dependency platform" to identify the interest base from which transactional collaborations between NGOs and business arise.

*   an *idealized tool and discourse*, initiated in particular by multilateral agencies, that divert "attention from asymmetrical power relations, the struggle for hegemony, participation deficits and trade-off between diverging partnership goals to questions of effectiveness and efficiency" (Bäckstrand, 2012: 169). Partnerships can also crowd out existing roles, functions, and responsibilities of actors. Pattberg *et al.* (2012) argue that international development partnerships are often active in issue areas that "are already densely populated by international law and agreements" (ibid., 2012: 240).

It is easy to consider the idealist perspective on partnerships as "naïve," or the realist perspective as overly skeptical. Both perspectives can and should be considered complementary. Both dimensions need to be taken into account in order to assess the function of cross-sector partnerships for sustainable development – which in itself is a process laden with trade-offs and conflicts. Either perspective of partnerships contains an assessment of the relative dependencies of each partner. Even the search for complementary resources and organizational compatibility – as a condition for co-creation of value – will probably be based on self-interest (Austin and Seitanidi, 2012). The two sets of angles – idealist and realist – towards the partnering space have a bearing on questions of the power bases of actors (as based on resources, roles and institutional background) and the power distribution in partnerships. What kind of resources and roles this is based on becomes an increasingly important question to explore.

Positioning games in the partnering space – toward a taxonomy for understanding the "perfect fit"

As Vurro *et al.* (2010: 48) highlight, "the institutional context dictates conditions that have to be satisfied in order for partnership to be considered appropriate." They highlight that the institutional context provides the preconditions for deciding both to start a CSSP and to configure it according to certain criteria. Therefore, we need to distinguish between the various institutional backgrounds of participating parties (foundation of their power base), and decipher the concrete roles these actors normally have (shape of their influence).

Roles in the partnering space

In society hundreds of different organizational forms exist, which can all influence the nature and effectiveness of partnerships. They generally represent a (combination of) a number of basic institutional characteristics: public or private, profit or non-profit, governmental or non-governmental, aimed at the provision of public or private goods. Each of the three actors bases their legitimacy (and power base) on a specific role in society: governments on their mandating and law enforcement role, CSOs on their mutual support role, and companies on the value they add through competition and profit-seeking (see also Table 6.1). The partnership space of each actor consequently presents a combination of (often accumulated) roles. Partnering space is the result of the "positioning games" played by societal actors along the three societal interfaces (Figure 6.2 a–c).

Government roles. The ideal-type government roles involve a public (governmental) organization, which is aimed at a non-profit oriented provision of public goods. This aim can be achieved by a large number of instruments, related to a variety of roles vis-à-vis business and civil society. Four basic roles are generally distinguished (Fox *et al.*, 2002) which involve increasing levels of dependencies – implying that the effectiveness of government roles becomes dependent on the actions and reactions of the bargaining partners: (1) mandating, (2) facilitating, (3) partnering, and (4) endorsing. In their *mandating* role, governments act primarily as regulators and standard-setters defining minimum behavioral norms. In the various areas of sustainable development, governments can set minimum wages (poverty alleviation), maximum emission standards (ecology), compulsory education ages, or rules for public health. Governments have full autonomy over their inspectors and influence firms and civil society primarily through penalties (either legal or fiscal). Firms and civil society, on their part, can try to influence the (independent) government through lobby activities. In their *facilitating* role, governments search for more enabling instruments to create incentives for firms and citizens to move in the "right"

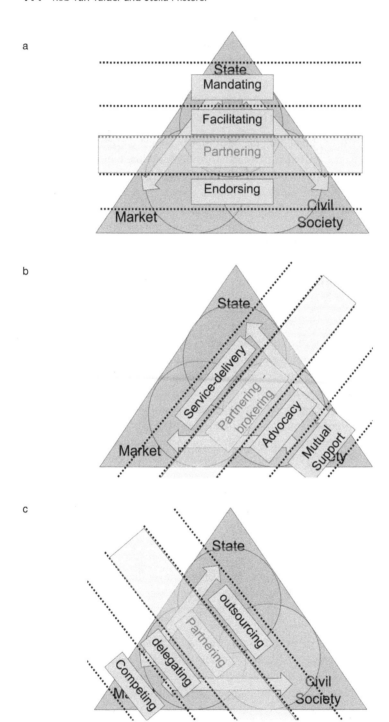

FIGURE 6.2 Roles of societal actors in partnerships

direction and build the appropriate capacities to do so. This could include the use of procurement policies focused on particular goals such as corporate social responsibility or national competitiveness. Other measures are subsidies, but also the set-up of public schools (education), public hospitals (health), child support systems and the like. *Partnering* implies that governments actively seek a combination of resources and stakeholder engagement. This can be done in the form of PPPs, but also in less formal organizational forms such as stakeholder dialogues and shared monitoring activities. The partnering role of government often comes in the form of semi-private regulation and covenants. The *endorsing* role of governments is the least involved and makes governments most dependent on firms and CSOs for achieving particular outcomes. Governments can for instance endorse company initiatives in fair labeling exercises, publish "best practices", support quality control schemes or health campaigns, and/or explicitly support partnerships between firms and CSOs, without providing subsidies.

Civil society roles. The ideal-type civil society role includes a private organization, non-profit and non-governmental oriented. Four roles of civil society organizations can be distinguished: (1) mutual-support, (2) advocacy, (3) partnering, and (4) service provision. The function of civil society organizations is, first and foremost, to organize *mutual support* for groups of citizens, to create so-called "club" or "community" goods and social value or social capital. CSOs are basically "mutual support organizations" (MSOs). All development related CSOs that want to remain independent either from states or firms have to have a solid foundation in membership, contributors, or other autonomous sources of funding. Sustainable development on the basis of mutual support is founded in local communities or international CSOs that transfer money on the basis of "solidarity."

The *advocacy* role of CSOs, requires as much independence as possible, but is defined by the actual influence the organization can exert over other actors. Advocacy towards governments is exerted by human rights organizations like Amnesty International. Advocacy towards firms is exerted by labor unions and other social movement CSOs like ATTAC. Hybrid advocacy CSOs like Greenpeace or Friends of the Earth, try to influence both business and governments. An interesting mixture of roles appears in case a CSO receives funds from governments to engage in advocacy towards firms, or vice versa. For the business-CSO interface the attention for this type of action and advocacy oriented organizations has prevailed in the literature (Kourula and Laasonen, 2010). Many of these CSOs actually seek confrontation and debate in order to draw attention to single issues. They see the partnering space as one of framing through "blaming and shaming" campaigns to highlight corporate responsibilities and inconsistencies. There are also more moderate and less confrontational CSOs in this segment. Other roles taken by CSOs in this segment are taking a supervisory role such as GRI or quality labels. The bulk (i.e. above 50 per cent) of NGO roles at the interface with business relates to this watchdog and discussion oriented role (van Tulder with Van der Zwart, 2006: 124; Laasonen *et al.*, 2012).

CSOs are still experimenting with their *partnering or brokering role* at the interface with business in particular. One of the problems partnering oriented CSOs face is how their strategy is perceived by their members/constituents. A more limited degree of "institutionalization" (Van Huijstee, 2010) of the partnering/brokering role in the own organization limits its power base towards the other organization. New NGOs are increasingly founded that aim at this "mediator" or "broker" in the face of societal conflict. The degree of independence of this NGO is generally low. Contributions of members in the form of donations and memberships fees are accepted on the condition that the donor accepts the independence of the NGO.

The most dependent position in the relationship with firms and governments represents that of *service provision*. At the two interfaces with governments and firms, two additional roles can be discerned: first, the provision of private goods (for instance through social entrepreneurship or labeling) brings it in interaction with the market sector and gives them the identity of a non-profit organization (NPO); second, the provision of public goods defines its interaction with governments and gives them the identity of a non-governmental organization (NGO). Many development NGOs – also referred to as co-financing organizations – appeal to government to obtain additional funding for projects they carry out on behalf of civil society. These are largely local projects for the benefit of the local population. As such, NGOs are taking over part of what is traditionally regarded as government responsibilities. Companies have helped to found a number of NGOs whose sole purpose is to represent their interests. This type of CSOs shares a credibility problem, due their reliance on either government or corporate funding.

Corporate roles at the interface with civil society and governments generally take four shapes: (1) competing, (2) delegating, (3) partnering, and (4) outsourcing. The power basis of companies (and their related fiduciary duty and legitimacy) is derived from their profit-orientation (which generates capital) and is embedded in *competition* (Table 6.1). For this role to develop, society grants substantial freedom and independence – also in terms of power exertion – to companies. Governments use their facilitator role towards firms by checking whether firms do violate the basic principles of free and fair competition. Firms have started to adopt Corporate Social Responsibility (CSR) programs in order to support their wider relationship with society. Corporations have thereby adopted (a combination of) two approaches: first to earn profits and later give part of it back to society through philanthropic initiatives, and second to integrate CSR in the core activities of the corporation. Corporate foundations were created to implement the first strategy. Corporate foundations are often legal independent entities, but their actual independence is often debated, although it has been observed that their relative independence also can create conflicts of interests with the mother company (Westhues and Einwiller, 2006). Corporate foundations are part of a "*delegating*" exercise on CSR themes. Corporations also created business support organizations (BINGOs and BONGOs) to influence the public debate in favor of the company or created for tax reasons. In particular these entities pose a problem for CSSPs: should they be classified as NGOs – and thus representative of civil society – or as corporate entities? It is suggested that in case an organization is 100 per cent dependent on corporate funding, it should be classified as a "delegated" – semi-dependent – entity of the market sphere.

As regards the *partnering* role, it is increasingly acknowledged that partnerships of firms can only contribute to address the problems of sustainable development, in case the initiatives are directly related to the core activities of corporations. CSSPs that are initiated by the foundations of corporations represent a more philanthropic type of engagement. This is changing because companies are increasingly trying to make their corporate foundations more strategic, which makes them more dependent upon their mother company. Most cross-sector partnerships research has not yet distinguished whether or not companies engage in partnerships through their foundations. Herlin and Thusgaard Pedersen (2012) in a case study on one Danish corporate foundation conclude that the corporate foundation has a bridging function towards NGOs (for instance by facilitating dialogues through convening, translating, and mediation). Its effect on securing internal commitment to the topic of the partnership has been more influential on the corporate side than on the CSO side. This illustrates its relative bargaining position, which is stronger towards the corporation than towards the CSOs. Corporate foundations help firms in particular to move forward along the collaboration continuum (Austin, 2000; Austin and Seitanidi, 2012). But they are "fragile bridges", certainly when it comes to partnerships that focus on issues linked to the core competencies of the company (Austin, 2000). They are likely to be primarily effective catalyst for partnerships that are not related to the core business. Corporations can finally *outsource* their (CSR) activities to independent actors. A large number of specialized firms have developed that support firms in their communication and CSR implementation strategies as semi-independent entities. Accountancy firms – in their advisory identity – have become important actors in this area: they take an interesting intermediate position in society as semi-private supervising organizations. In this area also a large number of organizations function as service providers to firms, governments and CSO alike.

Organizational fit in partnering space

Combining these roles creates ten possible positions of partnerships within the core triangle of the partnering space, and six additional combinations in the periphery (Figure 6.3). In practice, all these combinations can and are probably dubbed as "cross-sector partnerships," but from the previous discussion it can be derived that their logic, their dynamics, and their contribution to sustainable development will be substantially different. As our framework identifies a set of different partnering types in the partnering space, we are also able to come up with propositions on the possibility of partners to reach a specific stage of the "collaborative continuum" as introduced by James Austin and May Seitanidi (2012): philanthropic, transactional, transitional and transformational. By doing so, this taxonomy emphasizes the fit between partners based on the role(s) they can adopt in partnerships based on their societal position. The degree of fit defines the conditions of success of partnerships for sustainable development. The better the fit, the more appropriate roles and dependencies are aligned; or the smaller the fit, the bigger the change of misalignment and role conflicts.

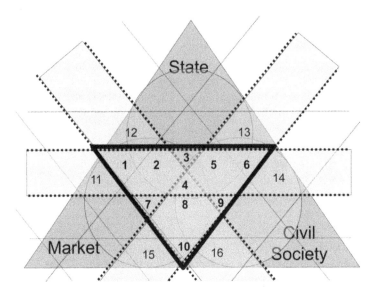

FIGURE 6.3 Positing games in partnering space

1   *Full trilateral fit*: there is only one position in which all relevant societal actors combine wholehearted their partnership strategies (#4). For all parties concerned this involves a first-order partnership, in which none of the parties can mix up intentions and roles. The conditions for such a partnership type are first, that all the parties acknowledge that their failure to address a specific issue is part of the problem. Second, parties are willing to become really interdependent in their approach to the issue. We can hypothesize from the discussion in section one, that sustainable development can best materialize in case we find important representatives of the three societal spheres that are willing to operate in this societal segment and that understand for instance that this type of partnering requires an attitude beyond endorsing or facilitating (governments), delegating or outsourcing (firms), advocacy and service delivery (CSOs). This type of partnership requires important institutional and legal facilitative frameworks. It can be expected that this partnership type – when successfully established – has most capacity to develop a *transformational relationship* between the partners, because the commitment to engage in a mutually dependent relationship with each other is highest.

2   *Partial trilateral fit:* three partnering strategies represent two parties that are fully engaged, while one party is less so: #2 #5 and #8. Take for instance position #5: the partnership represents the willingness to partner from the CSO and the government, but only an effort to outsource from the corporate perspective. This position mirrors a typical educational partnership, in which firms support the project because of "good corporate citizenship" considerations, but not

because they consider themselves dependent upon the outcome of the partnership. We can hypothesize that the latter party will be the least loyal and will experience greater pressure for free-ridership. In case the two other parties have based the feasibility of the partnership on the financial support of the firm, the continuity of the partnership might be hampered. In these configurations, partners will be able to create transition, but will only be able to reach a transformational stage in case they focus on key development issues that can be tackled at this specific societal interface with relatively limited involvement of the third party, for instance: hunger (#8), sanitation (#5), or ecology (#2). The "third party" then serves as support group or sponsor of the bilateral partnership – provided they are also aware of this role.

3   *Weak trilateral fit*: three strategies present a particular challenge for the party that has most capacity to effectively engage in the partnership. In positions #3, #9, and #7, the interdependent strategy of one party is combined with the least dependent position of two other actors. In case of #3, the willingness of the government to partner, is linked to "outsourcing" (firm) and a "service-delivery" (CSO's) strategy. In position #9, the willingness of civil society to partner, is coupled with an "outsourcing" strategy (firm) and an "endorsing" role of the government. It can be hypothesized, that all three positions – in order to be effective – require substantially strict governance measures in order to handle the sizable free-riding possibilities of this partnership. Due to the mixed motives and limited partnership orientation of the majority of the players, it can be expected that these partnership types will develop either a philanthropic or a transactional relationship. Reaching a transformative stage will be very challenging because one of the partners will not be willing to commit for a higher level of interdependency.

4   *Optimal bilateral fit:* bilateral partnerships that have the least risk of "crowding out" are those partnerships that do not represent any major role for the third party. This includes partnerships #1 (no role beyond service-delivery for CSOs), #6 (no role for firms beyond outsourcing) and #10 (no role or responsibilities for governments beyond endorsing). These three bilateral partnership types represent the ideal-typical PPP (#1), nPPP (#6), and PnP (#10) as defined in section 2. We can hypothesize that bilateral partnerships can only be effective for sustainable development – i.e. without compensatory governance measures – in case they belong to this particular constellation of dependencies and roles. These partnerships have the capacity to create an integrative or a transformational collaboration. They are not dependent on the input of the "third societal sector," and have the capacity to reach bilaterally a high level of synergistic value in key areas of sustainable development like infrastructure (#1), private health, (#10) and public education (#6).

5   *Partial bilateral fit:* positions #11–16 represent bilateral partnerships in which only one party is fully committed to the partnership. Positions #12 and #13 for instance show partnerships with the government in which the latter only wants to facilitate the project, rather than act as a partner. This position is taken in

partnerships were the government is subsidizing the partner rather than giving up part of its independence to come to a more shared outcome. The danger of misalignment of roles and expectations looms large in this type of "partnership". In fact it would be analytically unjust to characterize this project as a partnership. For positions #16 and #14 the "partnership" reveals a more limited ambition to partner for the CSO (that will use the partnership as part of an advocacy strategy), for position #11 and #15, the limited ambition is with the firm (that will probably use the partnership for reputational reasons). It can be expected that these partnership types will mainly develop a philanthropic or a transactional relationship between the parties. Achieving an integrative or a transformational collaboration will be almost impossible for these types of "partnerships."

Conclusion – towards an optimal fit?

Social issues differ not only for their intrinsic characteristics and challenges but also in terms of the logics of intervention. Organizations are challenged to adopt approaches to partner appropriately for achieving results for sustainable development (Vurro *et al.*, 2010). In particular the appropriate configuration of actors to address a social issue most effectively is a key challenge in CSSPs. Or with other words – to develop the "perfect fit" between societal actors remains a scant issue in partnership management.

In order to address this issue, this contribution introduced a taxonomy which describes more fine-grained partnership types based on the roles of societal actors. The taxonomy therefore enhances existing classifications based on an actor perspective (Selsky and Parker, 2005) with a relationship perspective (Austin, 2000; Austin and Seitanidi, 2012). Our "relationship perspective" is mainly based on what is often titled the "politics of partnerships". Compared to the original – rough – typology of four cross-sector social partnerships, we now have a more sophisticated taxonomy that can result in a more critical approach towards each type of partnership. It allows us to come up with propositions on the capacity of the partnership type to reach a transformational stage of collaboration and contribute to various domains of sustainable development. For instance as regards the classical public-private partnership for infrastructure (type A in Figure 6.1), we now have identified three different types of elaboration of which only one (#1) can be considered an ideal-type in terms of roles and mutual dependencies. The theoretical and taxonomical exposé on possible positions and their origins in societal partnering space, illustrates how important it is to check for the motivations of parties and their role adoption in a "partnership," whatever its definition is. The taxonomy also makes it clear that some alliances cannot be considered real partnerships, or only skewed partnerships in which only one or two of the three partners also have the intention to partner. This should make parties aware that there can exist a difference between "perception" and "reality" in case they aim at a partnership, but are (only) prepared to adopt one of their possible roles. A government that aims at an equal partnership, but additionally uses its mandating power to influence the parties, creates a less than optimal fit. A firm that uses its philanthropical (delegating) role for an alliance, but presents this as "core business" creates confusion with its partners. A CSO that uses its partnership (with a firm for instance) as input for an advocacy role towards governments is playing with fire.

A role play for creating effective partnerships for development

The taxonomy developed in this contribution can be simulated in a role play in which different parties bring specific "role cards" to the table. From a game theoretical perspective, it then can be considered under what conditions optimal development outcomes can be achieved. This role play supports reflection on role configurations in cross-sector partnerships, the resulting relationships and the degree of organizational fit needed to make the partnership meaningful for sustainable development.

- *Situational sketch:* three parties are represented around the negotiation table – a government, a firm, a development CSO.
- *Occasion:* the parties come together to solve a major sustainable development issue – for instance, poverty, health, education, or infrastructure.
- *Input:* each can choose to bring in one – or a combination – of its roles to address the issue; in case the party chooses to go for a "partnership" role, it should consider what type of complementarities it searches with the other parties.
- *Core competency:* each party defines the extent to which it considers itself responsible for the issue: either being part of the problem and/or part of the solution.
- *Dynamics:* each party should try to anticipate what its answer will be in case the other party(ies) either mix up roles, or come up with a role that they would consider less optimal for the partnership.

Play: a moderator chairs the session, which will be organized in four rounds:

a) Opening statements: what cards (roles) do the parties want to bring to the table and why (failure assessment, dilemma sharing)?
b) Round 1: discuss what is needed to solve the issue at hand; to what extent do the parties consider themselves part of the problem or of the solution (define input and the degree of commitment)?
c) Round 2: define the optimal type of partnership that the parties can design, discuss the governance structure needed to manage the variety of inputs, and define output and outcome ambitions next to the conditions under which parties can "exit" the alliance (establish the degree of organizational "fit" needed to effectively address the issue).
d) Round 3: make appointments on how to measure and monitor progress and impact.

The extent, to which roles are complementary or conflicting, depends on the governance arrangements chosen for each partnership. Defined as such, the governance arrangements can take power inequalities into account, because they affect the relative dependency positions of each actor. The taxonomy of Figure 6.3 shows that different governance arrangements can be needed for each of the five different types of "fit." More fine-grained governance studies will have to take specific issues into account and will distinguish at least 16 different types of partnerships for development.

Questions for reflection

1 Do different development issues require different types of partnerships?
2 In case parties adopt different roles at the same time, can this negatively influence the partnership?
3 Can roles change over time in partnerships and how does this affect the effectiveness of the partnership?
4 Does the degree of fit also define the level and type of governance needed to make the partnership a success?
5 Different roles involve different dependency relations; do partnerships always involve "equal" parties and "mutual dependence"; if not, under what conditions can a skewed partnership be also successful?

Note

1 Knowledge institutes, semi-public, or semi-private regulatory bodies and other hybrid organizations (that combine different roles and coordination mechanisms), serve as important intermediary agencies for sustainable development. If these organizations become too much attached to any one of the societal spheres, they lose their independence and their legitimacy. This happens when knowledge institutes such as universities become too commercial, or semi-private regulatory agencies get underfunded.

References

Austin, J.E. (2000) *The Collaboration Challenge: How Nonprofits and Businesses Succeed Through Strategic Alliances.* San Francisco, CA: Jossey-Bass Publishers.

Austin, J.E. and Seitanidi, M.M. (2012) Collaborative value creation: a Review of partnering between nonprofits and businesses: Part I. Value creation spectrum and collaboration stages. *Nonprofit and Voluntary Sector Quarterly,* 41 (5): 726–58.

Bäckstrand, K. (2012) Are partnerships for sustainable development democratic and legitimate? In Pattberg, P., Biermann, F., Chan, S. and Mert, A. (eds) *Public-Private Partnerships for Sustainable Development. Emergence, Influence and Legitimacy.* Cheltenham: Edward Elgar: 165–83.

Battisti, M. (2009) Below the surface – the challenges of cross-sector partnerships. *Journal of Corporate Citizenship,* 35: 95–108.

Biermann, F., Mol, A.P.J. and Glasbergen, P. (2007) Conclusion: partnerships for sustainability – reflections on a future research agenda, in Glasbergen, P., Biermann, F. and Mol, A.P.J. (eds) *Partnerships, Governance and Sustainable Development. Reflections on Theory and Practice.* Cheltenham: Edward Elgar: 288–300.

Bitzer, V. (2011) *Partnering for Change in Chains. On the Capacity of Partnerships to Promote Sustainable Change in Global Agricultural Commodity Chains.* Published doctoral dissertation, Utrecht: Utrecht University.

Buse, K. and Harmer, A. (2004) Power to the partners? The politics of public-private health partnerships. *Development,* 47 (2): 49–56.

Deetz, S. Newton, T. and Reed, M. (2007) Responses to social constructionism and critical realism in organization studies. *Organization Studies,* 28 (3): 429–30.

Ellersiek, A. (2011) *Same Same but Different. Power in Partnerships: An Analysis of Origins, Effects and Governance.* Published doctoral dissertation, Tilburg: Tilburg University.

Fox, T., Ward, H. and Howard. B. (2002) *Public Sector Roles in Strengthening Corporate Social Responsibility: a Baseline Study.* Washington, DC: World Bank.

Glasbergen, P. (2011) Understanding partnerships for sustainable development analytically: the ladder of partnership activity as a methodological tool. *Environmental Policy and Governance,* 21 (1): 1–13.

Googins, B.K. and Rochlin, S. (2000) Creating the partnership society: understanding the rhetoric and reality of cross-sectoral partnerships. *Business and Society Review,* 105 (1): 127–44.

Gray, B. (2007) The process of partnership construction: anticipating obstacles and enhancing the likelihood of successful partnerships for sustainable development. In Glasbergen, P., Biermann, F. and Mol, A.P. (eds) *Partnerships, Governance and Sustainable Development: Reflections on Theory and Practice.* Cheltenham: Edward Elgar: 29–48.

Hart, S.L. and Sharma, S. (2004) Engaging fringe stakeholders for competitive imagination. *Academy of Management Executive,* 18 (1): 7–18.

Herlin, H. and Thusgaard Pedersen, J. (2012) Corporate foundations: catalysts of NGO-Business Partnerships. Paper presented at Third International Symposium on Cross Sector Social Interactions, Rotterdam: The Partnerships Resource Centre.

Huxham, C. and Vangen, S. (2005) *Managing to Collaborate. The Theory and Practice of Collaborative Advantage.* London: Routledge.

Kim, N., Sung, Y. and Lee, M. (2012) Consumer evaluations of social alliances: the effects of perceived fit between companies and non-profit organizations. *Journal of Business Ethics,* 106 (2): 163–74.

Kolk, A., van Tulder, R. and Kostwinder, E. (2008) Business and partnerships for development. *European Management Journal,* 26 (4): 262–73.

Kourula, A. and Laasonen, S. (2010) Nongovernmental organizations in business and society, management and international business research – review and implications from 1998 to 2007. *Business and Society,* 49 (1): 35–67.

Laasonen, S., Fougère, M. and Kourula, A. (2012) Dominant articulations in academic business and society discourse on NGO-business relations: a critical assessment. *Journal of Business Ethics,* 109 (4): 521–45.

March, J.G. and Olsen, J.P. (1989) *Rediscovering Institutions: The Organizational Basis of Politics.* New York: Free Press.

Mert, A. and Chan, S. (2010) The politics of partnerships for sustainable development, in Pattberg, P., Biermann, F., Chan, S., Mert, A. (eds) *Public-Private Partnerships for Sustainable Development Emergence, Influence and Legitimacy.* Cheltenham: Edward Elgar: 21–43.

OECD (2006) *Evaluating the Effectiveness and Efficiency of Partnerships,* Workshop ENV/EPOC., 12 September 2006. Paris: OCED.

Pattberg, P., Biermann, F., Chan, S. and Mert, A. (eds) (2012) *Public-Private Partnerships for Sustainable Development. Emergence, Influence and Legitimacy.* Cheltenham: Edward Elgar.

Peng, M. (2002) Towards an institution-based view of business strategy. *Asia Pacific Journal of Management,* 19 (2): 251–67.

Porter, M.E. and Kramer, M.R. (2006) Strategy and society: the link between competitive advantage and corporate social responsibility. *Harvard Business Review*, 84 (12): 78–92.

Rein, M. and Stott, L. (2009) Working together: critical perspectives on six cross-sector partnerships in southern Africa. *Journal of Business Ethics*, 90 (1): 79–89.

Richter, J. (2004) Public-private partnerships for health: a trend with no alternatives? *Development*, 47 (2): 43–8.

Rivera-Santos, M., Rufin, C. and Kolk, A. (2012) Bridging the institutional divide: partnerships in subsistence Markets. *Journal of Business Research*, 65 (12): 1721–7.

Rodrik, D. (2007) *One Economics, Many Recipes. Globalization, Institutions and Economic Growth*. Princeton, NJ: Princeton University Press.

Saxton, T. (1997) The effects of partner and relationship characteristics on alliance outcomes. *Academy of Management Journal*, 40 (2): 443–62.

Selksy, J.W. and Parker, B. (2005) Cross-sector partnerships to address social issues: challenge to theory and practice. *Journal of Management*, 31 (6): 849–73.

Selsky, J.W. and Parker, B. (2010) Platforms for cross-sector social partnerships: prospective sensemaking devices for social benefit. *Journal of Business Ethics*, 94 (1): 21–37.

Utting, P. and Zammit, A. (2009) United Nations-business partnerships: good Intentions and contradictory agendas. *Journal of Business Ethics*, 90 (1): 39–56.

Van Huijstee (2010) *Business and NGOs in interaction. A quest for corporate social responsibility*, published doctoral dissertation, Utrecht: Utrecht University.

van Tulder, R. with Van der Zwart, A. (2006) *International Business-Society Management: Linking Corporate Responsibility and Globalization*, London: Routledge.

Vurro, C., Dacin, T. and Perrini, F. (2010) Institutional antecedents of partnering for social change: how institutional logics shape cross-sector social partnerships, *Journal of Business Ethics*, 94 (1): 39–53.

Waddell, S. (2005) *Societal Learning and Change. How Governments, Business and Civil Society are Creating Solutions to Complex Multi-stakeholder Problems*, Sheffield: Greenleaf Publishing.

Warner, M. and Sullivan, R. (2004) *Putting Partnerships to Work. Strategic Alliances for Development between Government, The Private Sector and Civil Society*, Sheffield: Greenleaf Publishing.

Westhues, M. and Einwiller, S. (2006) Corporate foundations: their role for corporate social responsibility, *Corporate Reputation Review*, 9 (2): 144–53.

7

CROSS-SECTOR GOVERNANCE

From institutions to partnerships, and back to institutions

Carlos Rufín and Miguel Rivera-Santos

Introduction

In this chapter, we introduce a conceptual framework that explores the complex link between institutions and social partnerships at the Base of the Pyramid (BoP). The BoP and subsistence marketplace (SM) literatures have underlined the importance of partnerships in BoP settings, while emphasizing the unique challenges associated with these partnerships (e.g. Crawford-Mathis *et al.*, 2010; Dahan *et al*, 2010; London *et al.*, 2006; Rivera-Santos *et al.*, 2012; Seelos and Mair, 2007). As the research on inter-organizational relationships has emphasized in recent years, one of the fundamental challenges for partnerships and alliances is the set of governance arrangements used to regulate the relationship between the partners (Das and Teng, 1998; Parkhe, 1993; Poppo and Zenger, 2002).

At the same time, BoP scholarship has suggested that one of the main characteristics of BoP settings is their institutional diversity and even uniqueness (e.g. De Soto, 2000; Rivera-Santos and Rufín, 2010; Sánchez *et al.*, 2007; Viswanathan *et al.*, 2010; Webb *et al.*, 2010). Hence, the development of effective partnerships at the BoP requires a careful choice of governance mechanisms that takes into account the institutional characteristics of the BoP. Yet, in spite of the fact that social partnerships and institutions overlap in BoP settings, scholars are only beginning to understand the link between the two phenomena (Dahan *et al.*, 2010; Rivera-Santos *et al.*, 2012; Webb *et al.*, 2010). In particular, no study has investigated, to the best of our knowledge, the extent to which partnerships and local institutions influence each other and how this influence evolves over time. A better understanding of this mutual influence and, as a consequence, of the implications of introducing social partnerships into a BoP community, is particularly important as it is likely to have a significant impact on the social and the economic outcomes of the partnership.

We start to fill this gap in this chapter by exploring how the governance of BoP partnerships is influenced by institutions at the BoP, and how these institutions may, in turn, be influenced by the introduction of partnerships in a given BoP setting. Defining micro-level governance as the set of governance mechanisms governing inter-organizational relations in the social partnership, and meso-level governance as the set of governance mechanisms governing transactions at the institutional level, our research question for the chapter is: *How do the micro- and the meso-levels of govern-ance influence each other in BoP settings?* Grounding our reasoning in institutional theory and transaction cost economics, we propose that micro-level governance is embedded in meso-level governance, meaning that the mechanisms available to partners in a given partnership will be determined by the broader characteristics of the BoP institutions surrounding the partnership. We further argue that micro-level decisions have the potential to impact meso-level governance over time, as they introduce novel governance mechanisms into BoP settings. Hence, the social and economic success of BoP partnerships will require a careful understanding of micro-meso linkages, which, to the best of our knowledge, have not been directly explored in the literature so far, with the exception of Vurro and Dacin's chapter in this volume. Like us, Vurro and Dacin focus on "institutional contexts affecting and being affected by the ability of partners to cooperate effectively." Their take on this question, in fact, complements our framework, as Vurro and Dacin largely approach this issue at the macro level of institutional fields.

Our contribution to the literature is threefold. First, we contribute to the BoP and SM literatures by building a conceptual link between two important findings in this literature: the uniqueness of BoP partnerships and the role of local institutions in business transactions at the BoP. Second, we contribute to the partnership literature by emphasizing the link between the availability of partnership governance mechanisms and broader institutional characteristics. Third, we contribute to the development literature by highlighting the role that partnerships may play in facili-tating the evolution from informal to formal institutions in BoP settings.

The structure of the chapter is as follows. A literature review will first allow us to define the key terms and concepts used in our framework; to introduce the main mechanisms of governance that structure social partnerships and institutions; and to discuss the specificities of business in BoP settings. From the main findings presented in this literature review, we will derive implications for BoP governance at the micro and meso levels. After exploring how this analysis fine-tunes our understanding of the social and business objectives associated with cross-partnerships, we will conclude with a discussion of the implications of this framework for future research, as well as for practitioners.

Partnerships and institutions at the BoP: key findings from the literature

For the purpose of this chapter, we define a BoP setting as a market in which con-sumers barely have sufficient resources for day-to-day living (Viswanathan *et al.*,

2010). While we recognize that important conceptual differences exist in the approach emphasized by scholars in the various streams of the literature on poverty alleviation through business, we will use the terms "BoP setting," "subsistence market," and "subsistence marketplace" interchangeably, as they refer to the same populations. These populations include, for instance, slum dwellers in the urban areas of developing countries, living in self-built dwellings without title to their plots or formal access to urban services of any kind, like the well-known districts of Dharavi in Mumbai, Kibera in Nairobi, or Rocinha in Rio de Janeiro; they also include the rural poor, such as the Irula in Southern India, regarded as "untouchables" by their neighbors and relegated to catching rats for a living, or the peasants of Haiti's rural hinterlands, who depend on small plots of largely eroded land for their subsistence.

We define partnerships at the BoP as collaborative ventures between firms, non-profits, and/or public actors, for businesses seeking to establish a presence and to have a positive social impact in BoP settings (e.g. Crawford-Mathis *et al.*, 2010; Dahan *et al.*, 2010; Johnson, 2007; London *et al.*, 2006; Seelos and Mair, 2007; Simanis and Hart, 2008). Our definition is thus slightly more encompassing than Vurro and Dacin's in Chapter 15, since it includes not only those promoted by business "aiming at addressing the social good, as part of their corporate social responsibility programs" but also those that may aim at financial profit in addition or not to the social good. As elsewhere in this book, we use the terms "cross-sector partnerships," "social partnerships," and "partnerships" interchangeably, while referring to relationships only involving business firms as "alliances."

In spite of the limited academic work on the link between partnerships and local institutional environments (e.g. Rivera-Santos *et al.*, 2012), the BoP and SM literatures have independently emphasized both the uniqueness of the BoP's institutional environment – the rules that govern social and business relationships in BoP settings – and the importance of partnerships for successful ventures in BoP settings.

Institutions at the BoP: informal institutions

The literature suggests that BoP settings are characterized by a unique institutional environment, in which informal institutions prevail at the expense of formal institutions. Formal institutions refer to legally valid and enforceable norms, and are characterized by specialization as well as impersonal and transactional relationships (North, 1990). Informal institutions, by contrast, refer to norms with no legal validity, and operate through institutions based on non-specialized kinship, age-group, religious, or other intra-group ties (De Soto, 2000; Rivera-Santos and Rufin, 2010). The prevalence of informal institutions is an important characteristic of BoP settings (De Soto, 2000; Rivera-Santos and Rufin, 2010), even though the relative isolation of the community influences the degree to which informal institutions prevail over formal institutions (Arnould and Mohr, 2005; Rivera-Santos *et al.*, 2012). Over time, as markets develop, informal institutions are typically replaced by formal institutions (Cheater, 2003; Mair, 1962).

This prevalence of informal institutions in BoP settings results from a combination of particularly weak formal institutions and particularly strong informal institutions. BoP settings are characterized by severe institutional gaps, defined as the lack of formal institutions to support economic activities (Khanna and Palepu, 1997), low enforceability of formal laws and regulations (Ricart *et al.*, 2004; Viswanathan *et al.*, 2010) and little legal protection of transactions (World Bank, 2000) – in short, what Hamann (this volume) calls "areas of limited statehood." By contrast, informal institutions are particularly strong and, to a certain extent, substitute for the weakness of formal institutions (De Soto, 2000), although they can contradict formal institutions (Arnould and Mohr, 2005; Johnson, 2007) and the protection they can provide is typically not as complete as the protection provided by fully functioning formal institutions (De Soto, 2000; Khanna and Palepu, 1997). Operating through the traditional ties that bind communities at the BoP (De Soto, 2000; London and Hart, 2004), these informal institutions are significantly stronger within the community than between communities, leading to localized institutions with few bridges across communities (Arnould and Mohr, 2005).

While the prevalence of informal institutions is a characteristic of all communities at the BoP, important variations exist across BoP settings. Research in anthropology and ethnology suggests that there are two main types of informal institutions of community governance, which characterize so-called "acephalous" and "monarchical" communities (Cheater, 2003). In acephalous communities, like the Nuer in Sudan, community norms are based on social capital embedded in the institutions, and these communities lack well-defined authority structures. Punishment of transgressors takes the form of exclusion from the community, a collective punishment made possible by the application of internalized social norms. In other terms, the institutions of acephalous communities are characterized by the absence of a powerful center. By contrast, in monarchical or centralized communities, like the Swazi, a single person, whether a king, a religious leader, or even a gang leader, concentrates most attributes of power. Conflict resolution in these communities takes the form of the exercise of judicial power by the centralized authority. In other terms, the institutions of monarchical communities are characterized by the presence of a powerful center. Intermediate institutional structures can exist between both extremes, as is the case in communities in which decisions are centralized in a council of elders rather than a single person, thus combining centralized institutions with some degree of community involvement.

The prevalence of informal institutions, regardless of their type, leads to a meso-level governance of business transactions embedded in informal, rather than formal, mechanisms, and to business ecosystems characterized by a higher prevalence of structural holes, as institutional gaps prevent the development of supporting industries, such as finance or distribution (Viswanathan *et al.*, 2010; Wheeler *et al.*, 2005). As a result, BoP-based entrepreneurial ventures and firms can be competitively very weak, and at the same time very resilient if they are embedded in the local power structure (Banerjee and Duflo, 2007; Collins *et al.*, 2009; De Soto, 2000). In turn, the government, non-profit, and community sectors take on a particular importance in business ecosystems, as they replace missing actors, supporting industries, or missing portions of the institutional fabric at the BoP (Rivera-Santos *et al.*, 2012).

Partnerships at the BoP: necessary but challenging

Both the BoP and SM literatures highlight the key role of cross-sector partnerships in the success of ventures in BoP settings, both in terms of social impact and economic viability. Prahalad argues that partnering with non-governmental organizations (NGOs) is necessary for the success of any BoP initiative in his foundational book (2005). Building on Prahalad's work, Seelos and Mair (2007) and Simanis and Hart (2008) go as far as to consider that partnerships are an integral component of business models at the BoP. In a similar vein, Gradl *et al.* (2010) analyze how complementary resources and capabilities between the firm and the NGO are crucial to the creation of inclusive business models. Moving beyond the business aspects of BoP ventures, Kolk *et al.* (2008) show how the activities conducted in partnerships are crucial for social and development objectives. Vurro and Dacin, this volume, argue that the pluralistic contexts such as the BoP, where the institutional logics of formal institutions contrast with those of informal institutions, cross-sector partnerships are particularly effective vehicles for assembling coalitions that can effect institutional change. Reports of BoP initiatives by practitioners also emphasize the key role of partnerships in these initiatives. S.C. Johnson explains, for instance, that partnering with the NGO Carolina for Kibera was necessary to be able to enter the slums around Nairobi, Kenya (Johnson, 2007), while Starbucks partnered with the NGO Conservation International to help poor farmers in Mexico produce high-quality coffee in a sustainable way (*Seattle Post-Intelligencer*, 2004). Similar examples abound across the world.

While recognizing the importance of cross-sector partnerships in BoP settings, scholars also emphasize the challenges associated with such partnerships. Rondinelli and London (2003), for instance, highlight the difficulty faced by partners with different governance structures when they communicate and try to solve problems, as they assess the extent to which cross-sector collaboration is necessary in BoP settings. Similarly, McFalls (2007) shows, through the detailed analysis of the challenges faced by HP in Limpopo Province (South Africa), how the tensions that exist between profit seeking, on the one hand, and development and social goals, on the other, can lead to contradictions that are difficult to reconcile. Finally, Pérez-Alemán and Sandilands (2008) find that collaboration between multinationals and NGOs in sustainable and socially inclusive supply chains has in some cases unwillingly resulted in the exclusion of some of the poorest developing country producers within the chain.

Beyond the challenges related to the nature of the relationship between firms and NGOs in cross-sector partnerships, and the difficulties due to the tension between economic and social goals, recent research suggests that the uniqueness of the institutional environment at the BoP adds specific challenges to social partnerships. Dahan and co-authors (2010), for instance, emphasize the need to adapt business models and partnerships to "local markets" cultural, economic, institutional and geographic features." Similarly, Webb and co-authors (2010) emphasize the uniqueness of BoP institutions and link them to the type of resources that NGOs need to bring to social partnerships. Finally, Rivera-Santos *et al.* (2012) argue that one of the major challenges for cross-sector partnerships at the BoP resides in the fact that the partnership's governance structure – the micro-level of governance – needs to be embedded in the local BoP institutions, i.e., the meso-level of governance, leading to a highly complex governance structure. In particular, the authors emphasize the fact that traditional governance mechanisms discussed in the alliance and partnership literature, such as formal contracts and equity, need to be replaced by substitutes better suited to SM contexts, including informal contracts, in-kind contributions, and gifts.

In sum, the BoP and SM literatures emphasize two important and unique aspects of BoP settings. First, meso-level governance at the BoP is characterized by the weakness of formal institutions, and by the prevalence of informal institutions. Contrasting with formal institutions, these informal institutions are non-specialized, meaning that both business and non-business transactions are governed by them, and they can be either mostly monarchical, i.e. with a strong central authority, or mostly acephalous, i.e. with no central authority. Second, while social partnerships are necessary for the success of BoP ventures, they involve significant challenges, which may actually explain why some companies end up abandoning their BoP ventures (Karamchandani *et al.*, 2011).

Micro- and meso-level governance at the BoP

While recent research has started to study the link between these two aspects of BoP settings (e.g. Dahan *et al.*, 2010; Rivera-Santos *et al.*, 2012; Webb *et al.*, 2010), scholars still do not fully understand how different institutions impact partnerships, and, most importantly, how the introduction of partnerships may, in turn, influence the local institutional environment. In this section, we explore these two simultaneous impacts: first, from meso to micro, analyzing the impact of the institutions governing BOP institutions on partnerships between actors from these settings and outside firms that enter BOP communities; and second, from micro to meso, exploring the impact of the introduction of these partnerships on the institutions' structures. Our overall framework is shown graphically in Figure 7.1.

From meso to micro: the impact of local institutions on partnership governance

As recent studies suggest, BoP institutions do not support, or only very imperfectly, the mechanisms of alliance and partnership governance that companies would typically use in more developed settings: equity and contracts (Rivera-Santos *et al.*, 2012). Customary reliance on oral communication and on personal relationships means that written contracts and stipulations are of little use in limiting a partner's behavior or committing to specific actions, as the prevalence of group-based

Timeline of mutual influence

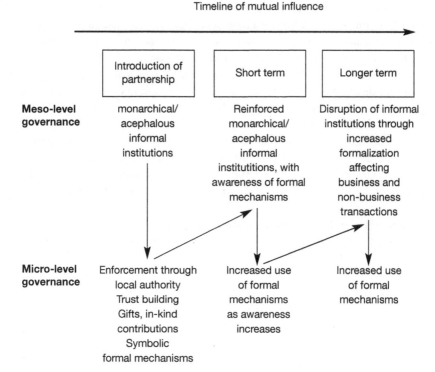

FIGURE 7.1 From institutions to partnership governance, and back to institutions

contracts in microfinance suggests (Cull, *et al.*, 2007). Similarly, the absence of arm's length transactions, in favor of long-term and relationship-based transactions, means that sophisticated accounting systems are not available to monitor complex financial flows (Collins *et al.*, 2009). Individual property rights may not be well defined for many kinds of property, or certain uses of property may be constrained by community norms (De Soto, 2000). In short, the formal mechanisms of governance can be expected to be of limited or no use for partnerships at the BoP.

In such a setting, outside firms and NGOs have no choice but to rely on the local institutions to govern their partnerships, replacing the formal mechanisms of alliance and partnership governance by ones embedded in the community's institutions. In partnerships as much as in alliances, a governance structure can be viewed as a portfolio of mechanisms, and partners can, to a certain extent, use different combinations of these mechanisms to reach an acceptable level of risk and governance costs (Poppo and Zenger, 2002). Similarly, social partnerships at the BoP combine a variety of mechanisms embedded in the local institutions for micro-level governance (Rivera-Santos *et al.*, 2012). Building on previous studies, we argue that this portfolio will include mechanisms to increase protection as well as mechanisms to decrease risk, and that they will be slightly different in acephalous and in monarchical institutions. Our perspective here draws heavily on transaction-cost economics and North's (1990) view of institutions. It thus complements that of Vurro and Dacin in Chapter 15 of this volume, who take a more sociological perspective emphasizing the legitimacy-enhancing consequences of partnership adaptation to local institutions, and with such adaptation, superior access to scarce resources.

The first set of micro-level mechanisms available to partners includes those mechanisms directed at increasing the partners' protection in case of opportunism or conflict, and correspond to equity and contract in alliances (but see also Gray and Purdy's analysis of conflict in social partnerships, in this volume). Given the lack of enforcement of formal contracts or property rights typical of BoP settings (Ricart et al., 2004;Viswanathan et al., 2010), firms and NGOs can seek the support of locally established authority for the enforcement of commitments and the resolution of conflicts, closely paralleling the concept of rule of law in developed countries.

In monarchical institutions, the central authority will be clearly identifiable, so we can expect partners to try to reach a mutually acceptable bargain with the central authority, particularly a bargain that can be expected to last over time. When the cellphone company Celtel Nigeria established cross-sector partnerships to expand into rural markets, for instance, it went to the traditional kings, who do not have official power but whose decisions are widely respected especially in Yoruba areas, not only to get their approval to build towers, but also to be allowed to recruit local entrepreneurs as distributors and ensure safe passage for its staff (Anderson and Kupp, 2008).

In the case of acephalous institutions, seeking the backstop of established authority is a much more complex undertaking, because authority is by definition diffused throughout the community (Cheater, 2003). Social ventures in such settings, however, can incorporate the existing meso-level mechanisms by creating sub-groups within the community, through which enforcement of community-wide relations is manageable. Many micro-finance institutions, for instance, rely on groups to enforce debt repayment commitments, thereby leveraging the monitoring of group members by other group members, which is inherent to acephalous communities, in small and therefore more manageable groups (Cull et al., 2007).

The second set of micro-level mechanisms available to partners includes those mechanisms directed at decreasing the risk of opportunism involved in transactions, and correspond to the development of trust in alliances. Not surprisingly, these mechanisms, which rely heavily on informal institutions, are more clearly compatible with BoP institutions, since trust is built on elements that can be found in BoP settings: unwritten communication, mutual understanding, and the observation of behavior over time (Ariño et al., 2001). In BoP settings, however, developing trust presents major difficulties that go beyond the challenges of cultural and language differences, extensively researched by international business scholars (e.g. Parkhe, 1998). The additional challenges to building trust at the BoP stem from the characteristics of BoP settings discussed above and vary between monarchical and acephalous institutional structures.

In monarchical structures, the centralization of power means that trust will need to be established with actors close to the center of the power structure, who may in principle have little relationship with the transactions sought by the initiators of the partnership (Rivera-Santos and Rufin, 2010). The best local actor to help the introduction of a new product developed by the partnership may be not a local trader, but a locally influential person. Firms and NGOs will thus have to overcome not just differences stemming from cultural barriers, but also from the different social roles of its partners, as in the case of alliances or public-private partnerships. BRAC had to develop trust bonds with religious leaders, for instance, to help establish an inclusive market in rural Bangladesh (Mair *et al.*, 2012).

In acephalous structures, by contrast, the community as a whole enforces the rules of governance of the community, suggesting that establishing trust with a specific member of the community is not sufficient in these settings. In other terms, outside actors, such as firms and NGOs, need to gain broader acceptance under acephalous institutions than under monarchical institutions. NGOs with a local presence may provide partial acceptance to other partners by transferring their legitimacy in the community to the partnership as a whole. Modern Architects for Rural India (MARI), an NGO that promotes strong community based organization of the poor in India, for instance, introduced Solae to the local communities in which it was already present, thereby providing indirect legitimacy to Solae's BoP initiative (Simanis and Hart, 2008). Evidence suggests that this is often not sufficient under acephalous institutions, however. Egypt's Sekem, for instance, had to develop personal and trust-based long-term relationships with the poor farmers from whom it buys fruits and vegetables. By embedding itself in farming communities beyond its connections to local NGOs, Sekem ensured a supply of high-quality grain and produce, often at prices below market level (Elkington and Hartigan, 2008).

Finally, trust, while important, is not the only mechanism that reduces the risk of opportunism available to partners. The development of hostages, which usually takes the form of financial hostages through equity contributions in developed markets (Brouthers and Hennart, 2007), can also be pursued in BoP settings, although the nature of the hostage will reflect the specificities of BoP institutions. Hostages at the BoP thus typically involve in-kind donations as a signal of the outside actors' commitment to the community (Rivera-Santos *et al.*, 2012). The type of donations, and, most importantly, the recipient of the donations, will vary between acephalous and monarchical communities.

In monarchical communities, contributions and gifts are likely to target the person holding power, or the people close to the central power, rather than the community at large. In several monarchical communities of Sub-Saharan Africa, such as the Swazi, for instance, cell-phone service providers have sought to protect their valuable transmission towers from theft and vandalism by providing free cell phones and service to the royal family, and, symbolically, by opening the service on the king's birthday (MTN Swaziland, 2008). If the king or members of the royal family fail to observe their side of the bargain, their cell phones will become useless (at least locally), which gives them an ongoing stake in the cell phone service.

In acephalous communities, by contrast, in-kind contributions and gifts will need to be spread and shared throughout the community. In the Paraisópolis *favela*, for instance, AES Eletropaulo and its NGO partners replaced 9,588 incandescent bulbs with compact fluorescent bulbs, and 497 old refrigerators with new, energy-efficient ones, free of charge. It also rewired the internal electrical cables and fixtures of 496 homes, and placed 505 lights for street lighting (Petersson, 2011).

Building on previous work (Rivera-Santos *et al.*, 2012), we argued in this section that micro-level governance at the BoP will include a portfolio of governance mechanisms that are embedded in the local institutions. As a consequence, these mechanisms will be slightly different under monarchical and acephalous institutions. The portfolio of micro-level governance mechanisms available under monarchical institutions will include increased protection against opportunism through the support of the local power holder, and decreased risk of opportunism through the development of trust with and the contribution of gifts to the local power holder. By contrast, the portfolio of micro-level mechanisms under acephalous institutions will include increased protection against opportunism through the establishment of small groups in which acephalous enforcement is manageable, and decreased risk of opportunism through the development of trust with, and the contribution of gifts to, the community at large. As such, cross-sector partnerships embedding their micro-level governance in these two types of institutions are likely to result in very different social and economic outcomes, as the main beneficiary of the governance mechanisms in the two settings differs. Beyond the direct social and economic impact of the partnership, the very introduction of new micro-level governance mechanisms is likely to impact the local institutions. We explore this little-studied impact in the following section.

From micro to meso: the impact of partnership governance on local institutions

Just as the development of partnerships with actors embedded in BoP institutions will push outside firms and NGOs to rely on local mechanisms for partnership governance, the establishment of these partnerships will have an impact on the local institutions. This impact can be desired by the firm and the NGO and can be one of the goals of the partnership. The creation of inclusive markets or the development of local entrepreneurship, for instance, require changes in the local institutions, in order to allow previously isolated or discriminated members of the community, such as women or youth, to pursue opportunities (Mair *et al.*, 2012; Martí *et al*, forthcoming). As Vurro and Dacin argue in their chapter, cross-sector partnerships can be especially important as catalysts for the formation of coalitions that can alter local institutions. The mere introduction of a partnership, however, is also likely to modify the structure of local institutions, with or without intent on the part of the firm and the NGO. We explore this impact in this section, moving from short-term to long-term impacts, and highlighting the differences that may exist between monarchical and acephalous institutions in this respect.

At time of creation of the partnership, the impact of the partnership on local institutions is likely to be limited, partly due to the resilience of institutional structures. As we discussed in the preceding subsection, the partnership will rely mainly on local, mostly informal, institutions for governance, both in monarchical and in acephalous communities, meaning that the partners will abide by, rather than replace, local meso-governance mechanisms. The fact that the firm and the NGO use locally embedded governance mechanisms is actually likely to reinforce the institutions to some extent, especially in monarchical communities, as the central power becomes recognized by outsiders. When some formal mechanisms, such as contracts, are introduced, they will be of little more than a symbolic nature, as the enforcement of such contracts would be impossible (Rivera-Santos *et al.*, 2012). Evidence suggests that, despite of the lack of enforcement, some firms and NGOs introduce contracts to add a ceremonial element to the commitments mutually undertaken by the parties and to symbolically represent this mutual commitment (e.g. Lutege, 2009).

Over time, however, the impact of the partnership on local institutions is likely to increase. To the extent that the firm and the NGO retain their linkages to outside networks, of which at least a few are governed by formal mechanisms, their BoP partners will gain some exposure to, and increasing familiarity with, these formal mechanisms. As Vurro and Dacin note in Chapter 15 of this volume, "while providing innovative solutions to social problems, collaborators continue to be involved in their regular activities subsuming collaboratively developed solutions under their routinized relational processes, thus fostering the diffusion of local effects beyond original boundaries." In many cases, this exposure will in fact be an integral part of the partnership, and not only for symbolic purposes (such as purely "ceremonial" contract signing). When the partnership involves integration into global supply networks, for instance, local partners interact not only with the outside firm but also with other actors from outside the BoP community (e.g. Perez-Aleman and Sandilands, 2008). In some instances, the actors exposed to formal institutions are likely to perceive these institutions to be superior to local institutions, and seek to use them instead of local institutions, especially in other business transactions. As the partnership between S.C. Johnson and Carolina for Kibera in the slums of Nairobi evolved, for instance, both partners witnessed a high turnover among the entrepreneurs they trained, as the young entrepreneurs realized that there were better opportunities for them outside the partnership in the formal economy (Johnson, 2007). It is important to note that the slow introduction of formal mechanisms into local institutions is likely to have impacts that go beyond business transactions, reflecting the non-specialized nature of these institutions in BoP settings (Vurro and Dacin, this volume). The familiarity with formal mechanisms, and more generally, accountability through the courts of law sometimes lead actors to seek that certain dealings with other BoP actors be placed under the purview of the courts. In the French island of Mayotte, in the Indian Ocean, for instance, there is some evidence that the introduction of formal micro-governance mechanisms in business transactions is actually modifying relationships within families. In the traditional

Muslim society of Mayotte, houses are owned by women, meaning that in case of divorce, the husband needs to leave the house. This ownership, however, is only recognized by the traditional institutions, and not by French courts. Over the last few years, some scholars argue that the introduction of formal micro-mechanisms in business transactions is leading to an increasing number of divorcing husbands going to court to claim ownership of the house, reflecting a new familiarity with formal meso-governance mechanisms (Guyot, 2012).

The slow formalization process will not impact all BoP members in the same way, however. The firm's direct local partners will gain a deeper and earlier acquaintance with formal micro-governance mechanisms than other members of the community. In micro-finance initiatives, for instances, the typically female entrepreneurs helped by the micro-finance institution will gain familiarity with formal accountability standards faster than other members of the community (Cull *et al.*, 2007). Such an asymmetry may be disruptive of the traditional order, as the newly empowered community members seek to leverage their familiarity with formal institutions and challenge local institutions. As a result, the established actors empowered by the local institutions, such as elders, the traditional intermediaries with the outside world, or the male members of the community, to mention a few common categories, are likely to resist formalization efforts. In Northern Tanzania, for instance, the Shanga partnership faced difficulties as locally powerful community members started to resist institutional changes resulting from the introduction of the partnership (Rechsteiner, 2009). Shanga's model is to employ women with disabilities and teach them how to make beads, which are then sold to tourists in Tanzania, thereby providing poor and isolated women with a stable revenue source. Problems started to arise when one of the young women came to Shanga's facilities explaining that her uncle had threatened her at knife point during the night claiming that it was a dishonor for women to earn money in that fashion and asking for all her money. As a result, Shanga ended up building temporary accommodations for threatened women. While this woman's case was an extreme one in Shanga's experience, it shows the possibility of resistance of local institutions to the introduction of new meso-governance mechanisms and to the resulting changes in power structure.

Finally, the local institutional impact following the introduction of a partnership is likely to differ between monarchical and acephalous communities. Overall, formalization is likely to be embraced more quickly by monarchical institutions than by acephalous ones. As we mentioned above, monarchical institutions are similar to formal institutions to the extent that there is a central authority with ultimate decision power in both. As long as the local monarchical power holder believes that formalization will strengthen his or her power, as is the case when traditional kings become wealthier thanks to the partnership, he or she is likely to embrace the process of formalization, even as his or her customary power is eroded. The expansion of cellphone services in rural Yoruba areas of Nigeria, for instance, has reinforced the power of traditional kings as firms and NGOs have sought their permission to operate, and the kings have been eager to hold on to their increased power

(Anderson and Kupp, 2008). By contrast, the introduction of formalization in acephalous communities requires a radical change in the way local institutional frameworks function, suggesting that formalization is likely take longer to permeate through the community.

In sum, the introduction of social partnerships into BoP institutions is likely to impact these institutions over time, and lead to a higher familiarity and use of formal meso-level governance mechanisms. This modification of local institutions may be the goal of the social partnership, but we argue that institutional changes are bound to occur regardless of the intent on the part of the firm and NGO. Although the pace of change will differ between monarchical and acephalous communities, our reasoning shows that these changes will go beyond the way business transactions are governed and may influence social relations and power structures, therefore leading to potentially radical changes in local institutions. In the following section, we discuss the implications of our framework for the social and economic objectives of cross-sector partnerships at the BoP, as well as for scholars and practitioners in the field.

Discussion and conclusion

In the preceding pages, we have introduced a conceptual framework that explores the complex link between institutions and social partnerships at the Base of the Pyramid (BoP). Grounding our reasoning in institutional theory and transaction cost economics, and building on recent work linking partnership governance structures to its surrounding institutions, we argued that firms and NGOs will choose micro-level governance mechanisms that are embedded in the BoP community's institutions for their partnership. In doing so, they will replace the usual alliance governance mechanisms, such as equity or formal contracts, with enforcement mechanisms that leverage local authority, and with risk-reducing mechanisms that emphasize informal and trust-based contracts, gifts, and in-kind contributions. We further argued that monarchical and acephalous institutions will require different micro-level mechanisms. Under monarchical institutions, the firm and the NGO will rely on the central authority for enforcement, and will also focus on the central authority to build trust through gifts and in-kind contributions. By contrast, firms and NGOs active under acephalous institutions will seek enforcement by relying on smaller and more manageable subgroups rather than on the community as whole, and will focus on the community at large to build trust through gifts and in-kind contributions. We also argued that the introduction of the partnership will, over time, modify the local institutions, leading to gradually more formalization. While some partnerships are formed with the intent of changing local institutions to create inclusive markets, for instance, we contended that, with or without intent, local institutions will be modified by the partnership over time and that this change will go beyond business to impact local power structures and social relationships.

This analysis has important implications for social partnerships, as it brings to light the complexity of the link between partnerships and local institutions. In particular, our reasoning suggests that social partnerships can have impacts that neither the firm nor the NGO are fully aware of. In the short term, the partnership will adapt its micro-level governance to fit the characteristics of the meso-level institutions. While this may have few or no implications for acephalous communities, in effect it means reinforcing the power of the central figure in monarchical communities, which may have ethical implications. Indeed, developing trust with a strong central holder, enforcing commitments through his or her authority, and exchanging gifts to build a long-term relationship, may lead the firm and the NGO to strengthen a system that excludes the poor, at least in the short term. South-Africa-based cell phone company MTN, for instance, was strongly criticized for bowing to pressure from Swazi King Mswati III, who demanded that phone records proving that a man in his court had an affair with one his wives be given to him (Hamlyn, 2010). Our framework thus suggests that the type of institutional structure in which a social partnership is created has wide implications for the partnership's social and economic impact on the community. While partnerships may be easier to build under monarchical institutions, the social impact may be great under acephalous institutions, as the firm and the NGO will need to be accepted by the community at large, rather than a small group of power holders.

Our framework also emphasizes the understudied but far-reaching impact that partnerships can have on BoP institutions over time. While some partnerships have the modification of local institutions as an explicit goal, as is the case with inclusive market initiatives or institutional entrepreneurship (Mair *et al.*, 2012; Martí *et al.*, forthcoming), or with partnerships that seek to provide collective goods (Doh and Boddewyn, this volume), many may not recognize their potential long-term impact. Because of the non-specialized nature of BoP institutions, the slow process of formalization will affect not only business relationships but non-business interactions as well. As a consequence, it will be disruptive for the community along many dimensions, which may or may not lead to a more positive environment for the poor or the excluded from the previous system. Even a program often cited as an example of a socially successful BoP venture, Hindustan Lever's Shakti program, which helps rural women become entrepreneurs and distributors of Hindustan Lever products (Chakravarthy and Coughlan, 2012), has a disruptive impact on local networks. Under the program, pre-existing business networks are replaced by a new one, with implications that are likely to go beyond business, given the overlap of business and non-business social relations at the BoP. Our framework therefore urges firms and NGOs in social partnerships to carefully analyze the impact of their activities on pre-existing institutions, be they monarchical or acephalous, and to take into account potentially negative impacts as they develop their partnership, recognizing that the changes brought by the partnership will go beyond the realm of business transactions.

Like any academic study, this chapter has limitations. Our approach, largely based on transaction costs, does not exclude other possibilities. Specifically, Vurro and Dacin argue in Chapter 15 that, given the contested institutional logics that pervade BoP settings, partnerships that deliberately seek to effect institutional change will need to rely on "participatory approaches [to partnership governance], based on negotiated values and community involvement" in order to foster the development of coalitions capable of changing local institutions. We are also aware that our reasoning is conceptual in nature, meaning that the analysis is not based on additional empirical research, but relies on existing theory to develop a stylized framework, and on examples from the SM and BoP literatures to illustrate, rather than prove or disprove, the theoretical argument. The most important extension of the Chapter is therefore the empirical testing of the framework. In-depth case studies across various types of BoP settings could provide at the same time detailed data for each case and necessary variation across cases (Eisenhardt and Graebner, 2007). Alternatively, a longitudinal analysis of a few BoP institutions with partnerships could also provide important and more quantitative insights into the relationship between BoP institutions and micro-level partnership governance.

Beyond this limitation, we believe that this chapter contributes to three main literatures. First, we contribute to the BoP and SM literatures by building a conceptual link between two important findings in this literature: the uniqueness of BoP partnerships and the role of local institutions in business transactions at the BoP. In doing so, we highlight the changes in local institutions that inevitably come with the introduction of a partnership, with or without the intent of the firm and the NGO. Second, we contribute to the partnership literature by emphasizing the link between the availability of partnership governance mechanisms and broader institutional characteristics. Building on previous work, we emphasize the differences that exist between monarchical and acephalous communities, and how these differences impact not only the structure of social partnerships, but also the potential social and economic impact they can achieve. Third, we contribute to the development literature by highlighting the role that partnerships may play in facilitating the evolution from informal to formal institutions in BoP settings. Partnerships can therefore be viewed by national governments as one of the ways through which isolated communities and informal transactions can be integrated into formal institutions.

Finally, we believe that the framework we develop in this chapter has important implications for practitioners. As firms and NGOs develop social partnerships, we urge them to consider the important differences that exist between monarchical and acephalous communities and to take them into account as the objectives and the structure of the partnership are discussed. In this sense, our chapter can be regarded as complementing the methods for partnership design and decision-making examined by Mangalagiu, Selsky, and Wilkinson elsewhere in this book. In addition, our framework highlights an aspect of social partnerships that practitioners working at the BoP in firms and NGOs may overlook: the need for these practitioners to consider the long-term implications of partnership development on the governance of the communities they wish to help. We hope that our framework will prove a first step towards a better understanding of the complex relationships between social partnerships and local institutions at the BoP.

Questions for reflection

1   How can BoP institutions be identified, if they function at a primarily informal level? What capabilities could companies develop in order to identify local institutions?
2   How can companies entering into social partnerships at the BoP recognize the potential positive and negative impacts they can have on local institutions? How could these impacts be anticipated and observed?
3   Should companies consciously attempt to influence BoP institutions?
4   How does your answer to the previous questions change depending on whether the local governance institutions are acephalous or monarchical?

References

Anderson, J. and Kupp, M. (2008) *Celtel Nigeria: Serving the Rural Poor*. Tilburg: TiasNimbas Case Study.

Ariño, Á., De La Torre, J. and Ring, P. S. (2001) Relational quality: managing trust in corporate alliances. *California Management Review*, 44 (1): 109–34.

Arnould, E. J. and Mohr, J.J. (2005) Dynamic transformations for Base-of-the-Pyramid market clusters. *Journal of the Academy of Marketing Science*, 33 (3): 254–74.

Banerjee, A.V. and Duflo, E. (2007) The economic lives of the poor. *Journal of Economic Perspectives*, 21 (1): 141–67.

Brouthers, K.D. and Hennart, J.-F. (2007) Boundaries of the firm: insights from international entry mode research. *Journal of Management*, 33 (3): 395–425.

Chakravarthy, B. and Coughlan, S. (2012) Emerging market strategy: innovating both products and delivery systems. *Strategy and Leadership*, 40 (1): 27–32.

Cheater, A.P. (2003) *Social Anthropology*. New York: Routledge.

Collins, D., Morduch, J., Rutherford, S. and Ruthven, O. (2009) *Portfolios of the Poor – How the World's Poor Live on $2 a Day*. Princeton, NJ: Princeton University Press.

Crawford-Mathis, K., Darr, S. and Farmer, A. (2010) The village network (TM): partnership and collaboration to alleviate poverty in subsistence marketplaces. *Journal of Business Research*, 63 (6): 639–42.

Cull, R., Demirgüç-Kunt, A. and Jonathan, M. (2007) Financial performance and outreach: a global analysis of leading microbanks. *Economic Journal*, 117 (617): F107–F133.

Dahan, N.M., Doh, J.P., Oetzel, J. and Yaziji, M. (2010) Corporate-NGO collaboration: co-creating new business models for developing markets. *Long Range Planning*, 43 (2/3): 326–42.

Das, T.K. and Teng, B.-S. (1998) Between trust and control: developing confidence in partner cooperation in alliances. *Academy of Management Review*, 23 (3): 491–512.

De Soto, H. (2000) *The Mystery of Capital: Why Capitalism Triumphs in the West and Fails Everywhere Else*. New York: Basic Books.

Eisenhardt, K.M. and Graebner, M.E. (2007) Theory building from cases: opportunities and challenges. *Academy of Management Journal*, 50: 25.

Elkington, J. and Hartigan, P. (2008) *The Power of Unreasonable People*. Boston: Harvard Press.

Gradl, C., Krämer, A. and Amadigi, F. (2010) Partner selection for inclusive business models. *Greener Management International*, 56: 25–42.

Guyot, D. (2012) Personal communication with sociologist David Guyot, on April 30, 2012. Mamoudzou, Mayotte.

Hamlyn, M. (2010) MTN warned of all-Africa boycott over Swazi shame. *MSN African News – I-Net Bridge*, August 6 (http://news.za.msn.com/article.aspx?cp-documentid= 154319419 – Accessed on September 28, 2010).

Johnson, S. (2007) SC Johnson builds business at the Base of the Pyramid. *Global Business and Organizational Excellence*, 26 (6): 6–17.

Karamchandani, A., Kubzansky, M. and Lalwani, N. (2011) Is the Bottom Of the Pyramid Really for You? *Harvard Business Review*, 89 (3): 107–11.

Khanna, T. and Palepu, K. (1997) Why focused strategies may be wrong for emerging markets. *Harvard Business Review*, 75: 41–51.

Kolk, A., van Tulder, R. and Kostwinder, E. (2008) Business and partnerships for development. *European Management Journal*, 26 (4): 262–74.

London, T. and Hart, S.L. (2004) Reinventing strategies for emerging markets: Beyond the transnational model. *Journal of International Business Studies*, 35 (5): 350–70.

London, T., Rondinelli, D.A. and O Neill, H. (2006) Strange bedfellows: alliances between corporations and nonprofits, in O. Shenkar and J.J. Reuer (eds) *Handbook of Strategic Alliances*: 353–66. Thousand Oaks, CA: Sage.

Lutege, H. (2009) Personal communication with Helen Lutege, founder of the micro-finance institution BELITA (Better Life for Tanzania), on January 12, 2009. Dar-es-Salaam, Tanzania.

Mair, L. (1962) *Primitive Government*. London: Penguin.

Mair, J., Martí, I. and Ventresca, M. (2012) Building inclusive markets in rural Bangladesh: how intermediaries work institutional voids. *Academy of Management Journal*, 55 (4): 819–50.

Martí, I., Courpasson, D. and Dubard Barbosa, S. (forthcoming). "Living in the fishbowl". Generating an entrepreneurial culture in a local community in Argentina. *Journal of Business Venturing*.

McFalls, R. (2007) Testing the limits of "inclusive capitalism": a case study of the South Africa HP i-Community. *The Journal of Corporate Citizenship*, 28: 85–98.

MTN Swaziland. (2008) Ten years of keeping our kingdom connected. *YelloMagazine* (September).

North, D. (1990) *Institutions, Institutional Change, and Economic Performance*. Cambridge: Cambridge University Press.

Parkhe, A. (1993) Strategic alliance structuring: a game theoretic and transaction cost examination of interfirm cooperation. *Academy of Management Journal*, 36 (4): 794–829.

Parkhe, A. (1998) Building trust in international alliances. *Journal of World Business*, 33 (4): 417–37.

Perez-Aleman, P. and Sandilands, M. (2008) Building value at the top and the bottom of the global supply chain: MNC-NGO partnerships. *California Management Review*, 51 (1): 24–49.

Petersson, I. (2011) One step toward citizenship: the Slum Electrification and Loss Reduction Pilot Project in São Paulo, Brazil, in P. Márquez and C. Rufin (eds) *Private Utilities and Poverty Alleviation: Market Initiatives at the Base of the Pyramid*. Cheltenham: Edward Elgar, pp. 207–41.

Poppo, L. and Zenger, T.R. (2002) Do formal contracts and relational governance function as substitutes or complements? *Strategic Management Journal*, 23 (8): 707–26.

Prahalad, C.K. (2005) *The Fortune at the Bottom of the Pyramid*. Upper Saddle River, NJ: Wharton School Publishing/Pearson Education.

Rechsteiner, S. (2009) Personal communication with Saskia Rechsteiner, near Arusha, Tanznia. Arusha, Tanzania.

Ricart, J.E.J.R., Enright, M.J.M.E., Ghemawat, P.P.G., Hart, S.L.S.H. and Khanna, T.T.K.

(2004) New frontiers in international strategy. *Journal of International Business Studies*, 35 (3): 175–200.

Rivera-Santos, M. and Rufín, C. (2010) Global village vs. small town: understanding networks at the Base of the Pyramid. *International Business Review*, 19: 126–39.

Rivera-Santos, M., Rufín, C. and Kolk, A. (2012) Bridging the institutional divide: partnerships in subsistence markets. *Journal of Business Research*, doi:10.1016/j.jbusres.2012.02.013.

Rondinelli, D.A. and London, T. (2003) How corporations and environmental groups cooperate: assessing cross-sector alliances and collaborations. *Academy of Management Executive*, 17 (1): 61–76.

Sánchez, P., Ricart, J.E. and Rodríguez, M.Á. (2007) Influential factors in becoming socially embedded in low-income markets. *Greener Management International*, 51: 19–38.

Seattle Post-Intelligencer. (2004) Starbucks in alliance to maintain coffee supply. *Seattle Post-Intelligencer*, September 29.

Seelos, C. and Mair, J. (2007) Profitable business models and market creation in the context of deep poverty: a strategic view. *Academy of Management Perspectives*, 21 (4): 49–63.

Simanis, E. and Hart, S.L. (2008) *The Base of the Pyramid protocol: Toward Next Generation BoP Strategy (Version 2.0)*. Ithaca, NY: Cornell University, Center for Sustainable Global Enterprise.

Viswanathan, M., Sridharan, S. and Ritchie, R. (2010) Understanding consumption and entrepreneurship in subsistence marketplaces. *Journal of Business Research*, 63(6): 570–81.

Webb, J.W., Kistruck, G.M., Ireland, R.D. and Ketchen, D.J.J. (2010) The entrepreneurship process in base of the pyramid markets: the case of multinational enterprise/non government organization alliances. *Entrepreneurship Theory and Practice*, 34 (3): 555–81.

Wheeler, D., McKague, K., Thomson, J., Davies, R., Medalye, J. and Prada, M. (2005) Creating sustainable local enterprise networks. *MIT Sloan Management Review*, 47 (1): 33–40.

World Bank. (2000) *World Development Report 2000/2001: Attacking Poverty*. Oxford: Oxford University Press.

8

EVOLUTION OF AN ALLIANCE PORTFOLIO TO DEVELOP AN INCLUSIVE BUSINESS

Jana Schmutzler, Roberto Gutiérrez, Ezequiel Reficco and Patricia Márquez

Introduction

While initially disconnected, the literatures on responsible business on the one hand, and those of inclusive business (Márquez *et al.*, 2010; SNV and World Business Council for Sustainable Development, 2008) and of the "BoP"– after base-of-the-pyramid – on the other (London and Hart, 2011; Prahalad and Hammond 2002), have tended to coalesce in the last years (Reficco, 2010). The prevailing view today, is that "inclusive businesses are entrepreneurial initiatives that are economically profitable and environmentally and socially responsible" (Golja and Požega, 2012: 23). The launching of commercially viable ventures that seek to better serve the needs of the poor is now widely considered to be an integral part of the corporate social responsibility agenda (FOMIN, 2009). Not only can companies increase their potential market but also contribute to poverty alleviation, or as Kofi Annan (2001) put it: "a happy convergence between what shareholders want and what is best for millions of people." However, it has become clear that companies that seek to develop profitable businesses with the BoP face a variety of challenges, ranging from issues of providing access to the areas where the poor live to lack of trust after years of deceit from business and other institutions.

Serving the poor through market mechanisms can be expensive and risky (Karnani, 2007). To create social and economic value at considerable scale is a challenge that goes beyond a single organization or partnership (Selsky and Parker, 2005). As a result, alliances have proven to be quite valuable; when it comes to BoP venture success, "the correct partnership is everything" (Weiser *et al.*, 2006: 6). Partnerships "enable different people and organizations to support each other by leveraging, combining, and capitalizing on their complementary strengths and capabilities" (Lasker *et al.*, 2001: 180). While "the need for building an ecosystem for wealth creation and social development at the BoP is obvious" (Prahalad, 2004: 89), some firms have come to realize that developing a sustainable inclusive business entails configuring a portfolio of alliances. These portfolios include partnerships between organizations in the same sector and others between organizations in different sectors. Thus far, partnerships that include the participation of communities and civil society organizations in these risky businesses appear to be necessary to overcome challenges.

This chapter studies the evolution of alliance portfolios including both cross-sector social partnerships (CSSP) and business-to-business (B2B) alliances established to develop BoP ventures. For this purpose, we examine a Colombian multinational company whose case illustrates different types of partners needed at the initial stages of venture development, and changes that occur as the firm learns about the BoP market and strives to scale operations. The survival and demise of partnerships highlight the different roles of CSSP and B2B alliances in the development of BoP initiatives, as well as ensuing changes in value creation. A steep learning curve and a gain in legitimacy from early success antecede scaling efforts.

We compare the requirements imposed on alliances for setting up the venture, and their management and critical assessment as the business grows. A better understanding of how CSSP and B2B alliances contribute to the promise of generating social and economic value in a BoP venture is crucial, especially in light of the widespread recognition of the difficulties in doing so (Bruni Celli and González, 2010; Olsen and Boxenbaum, 2009; Webb *et al.*, 2010). The analysis of evolution in alliance portfolios raises important questions about social value. At an initial phase of venture development, the impact on community organizations and local promoters can be impressive in terms of increased income, business opportunities, and social capital. Nevertheless, if the number of customers is limited, the viability of the project as a business is threatened. Increasing control and efficiency in the alliance portfolio allows a business to expand and serve many more BoP consumers.

After a literature review highlighting the need to study alliance portfolios that combine different types of partners, we outline the method followed to learn from the experience of one portfolio since its creation. Third, a section describes the role CSSP and B2B alliances played in the development of a BoP venture, and the changes that occurred as the focal company aimed to scale operations. Finally, a section that discusses the evolution of heterogeneous alliance portfolios antecedes an appraisal of the value created by the venture.

Multiple partnerships to serve the poor

Serving low-income citizens is a major challenge for any company. Firms struggle to understand the needs of BoP customers, and often lack the capacity to insert themselves effectively in communities' culture and environment and become truly embedded in the local context (Hart and London, 2005). Companies that have been able to successfully sell to some of the world's most needy consumers address these markets by innovating along four dimensions: affordability, acceptability, availability and awareness (Anderson and Markides, 2007). Offering an affordable product for a population with very low disposable incomes not necessarily translates into cheap products; it rather means understanding the cash flows of customers whose income comes in on a daily or weekly basis. At the same time, offering a product that responds to the specific and unique needs of these consumers is not sufficient. Trust and "business intimacy" needs to be established in order to be able to approach these customers (Simanis and Hart, 2009), and to create acceptability for products and provide legitimacy to businesses. Since many BoP customers cannot be reached through traditional advertising media, awareness has to be created in a different way. Finally, assuring availability is another challenge because traditional distribution channels are extremely fragmented or non-existent in low-income settings.

Alliances can provide companies with relevant expertise, networks, legitimacy, and distribution channels. Most importantly, they enable access to low-income customers. For the challenges that most BoP ventures confront, partners from different sectors contribute in distinct ways because, as Selsky and Parker put it, "they are likely to think about it differently, to be motivated by different goals, and to use different approaches." (2005: 851) A mix of CSSP and B2B alliances in a portfolio has emerged in practice, but our understanding of its characteristics and management is lagging behind.

Extant research has considered the emergence, configuration, and management of alliance portfolios. The comprehensive literature review done by Wassmer (2010) focuses on alliance portfolios established by companies with other for-profit firms. Alliances with different attributes (e.g. governance structure, number of partners, scope) or different types of partners are the two dimensions that have been used to define homo- and heterogeneity in alliance portfolios. Portfolio mix related to partners has been examined by contrasting industry affiliation (Kotabe and Swan, 1995; Nohria and García-Pont, 1991), firm size (Kotabe and Swan, 1995), country of origin (Hagedoorn and Schakenraad, 1994; Kotabe and Swan, 1995), reputation (Saxton, 1997), rivalry (Dussauge *et al.*, 2000), and repeated alliances (Goerzen, 2007; Gulati, 1995). Mixing alliances between private firms with CSSP is an examination that has not been done systematically. Since relatively homogeneous portfolios fail to cohere consistently (Bamford and Ernst, 2002; George *et al.*, 2001), it can be expected that heterogeneous portfolios combining B2B alliances and CSSP will not do better. Problems with individual alliances also bedevil efforts at grouping them in a portfolio. Thus, the study of the difficulties experienced by heterogeneous portfolios can start with the shortcomings of individual alliances.

Research on B2B alliances has focused extensively on the partner selection process as an antecedent of successful partnerships, and three issues that have been identified as key to success: resource complementarity, partner compatibility or fit, and partner commitment and trust (Shah and Swaminathan, 2008). Resource complementarity refers to the extent that each partner is able to contribute resources or capabilities others lack. Firms turn to alliances as an efficient form to acquire necessary resources. Strategic alliances involve voluntary, enduring relationships with partners sharing resources and making joint decisions (Wohlstetter *et al.*, 2005). Apart from potential resource and skill procurement and allocation, firms may also rely on partnerships in order to achieve political advocacy or legitimacy (Galask-iewicz, 1985). Partnerships allow firms to share the risk of an uncertain and unknown environment and thus enable firms to better control their costs. Collaboration contributes to stabilize organizational contexts that are turbulent (Emery and Trist, 1965) or novel (Eisenhardt and Schoonhoven, 1996), and for most companies BoP markets conform to that depiction.

Partner fit is conceived as the extent to which organizational culture and mission, management and work force, target market, product/cause and cycle complement each other. Fit contributes to or even generates a competitive advantage (Drumwright *et al.*, 2000). Fit determines, to a great extent, whether two partners will be able to use their resources to generate the benefits expected from the collaboration. Partner fit among private firms is a key issue, and it is also a strategic imperative for the success of CSSP (Dahan *et al.*, 2010). CSSP "face not only lack of familiarity that B2B alliance partners may encounter, but also the additional lack of familiarity stemming from drastically different goals, organizational processes, and world views" (Rivera-Santos and Rufin, 2011: 62). Sagawa and Segal suggest that, "both business and social sector organizations bring different expectations to these relationships" (2000: 111).

Trust is harder to create and is not to be expected at the outset (Child and Möllering, 2003). Trust develops through a cyclical process of negotiation, interaction, commitment, and execution (Kale and Singh, 2009). Arrow (1974) argues that trust is likely to be the most efficient governance mechanism for economic transactions; trust facilitates coordination. According to Whetten (1981), however, coordination costs increase as a function of differences between partners. Partners in CSSP operate according to different logics. The market logic of a business partner includes "the material practice of accumulation and ownership, where competition and efficiency are part of its symbolic system" (Bryson *et al.*, 2006: 50). The logic of nonprofit organizations (NPO) is influenced by its focus on citizen participation (Friedland and Alford, 1991). As these logics influence organizational behavior by legitimizing actions, processes, norms, and structures, conflicts might arise: "When very different types of organizations work together, the stage is set for clashes of goals, objectives, values, cultures, strategies, management styles, and operating approaches." (Berger *et al.*, 2004: 59) Gray and Purdy (2014) in this volume describe the conflicting logics and frames present in CSSP.

Instead of philanthropic relationships where financial resources are transferred from for profits to NPO, CSSP are forged to achieve separate, yet related, missions (Austin, 2000; Budinich, 2007). Therefore, partners need the alignment of goals, strategies, or values for a CSSP to develop (Austin *et al.*, 2004). However, given the described differences, it takes effort to encounter a CSSP in which a certain level of fit exists. Fit depends on the commitment of both partners; making necessary resources available as well as thinking about long-term benefits, instead of focusing on short-term gains, is needed (Gundlach *et al.*, 1995). Peloza and Ye (2014) in this volume explain different kinds of fit: mission, resource, management, cultural, target market, product/cause and workforce fit. In addition, partnerships face performance risks. An additional risk exists when a partner does not cooperate in good faith due to the rewards of opportunistic behavior. The interests of an organization are not necessarily compatible with those of partners; and as such, they may generate low commitment to common objectives (Das and Teng, 2001).

In CSSP, the strategy of establishing common interests and objectives during initial meetings is a common way to establish cooperative procedures. In BoP ventures, it is increasingly important to establish a formal set of procedures (i.e. the "how" of the cooperation), as the relationships between partners proceed (Rondinelli and London, 2003). Non-cooperative behaviors (i.e. relational risks) and performance risks can actively be managed through trust building mechanisms, but also through the creation of adequate structures and routines (Ariño *et al.,* 2001). It is through the creation of decision processes, as well as information and control systems, that the latent risk of opportunistic behavior by a partner can be diminished. These governance mechanisms align the interests of partners and increase the cost of opportunistic behaviors. In BoP settings, Rufin and Rivera-Santos (2014) in this volume contend that CSSP use trust and sub-groups, where enforcement is manageable, as substitutes for governance mechanisms such as equity and formal contracts.

Firms establish collaboration with different types of partners to face the challenges BoP settings pose. A growing literature on relatively homogeneous alliance portfolios guides the selection of variables to observe as we tried to understand the evolution of a heterogeneous portfolio mix. Pressing issues at the set up and growth stages are the focus of our exploration in this chapter.

Methods and data collection

For this research we followed a case study approach (Yin, 2003), with the positivist aim of generating theory inductively (Eisenhardt, 1989; Eisenhardt and Graebner 2007). This is a single-case, exploratory (Yin, 2003), and instrumental (Stake, 2005) study, as it seeks to provide insight into a larger phenomenon. Such an approach was deemed appropriate, as this is a relatively unexplored topic. Theory-building using cases better answers their "why" and "how" in uncharted areas (as opposed to "how often" or "how many"), when little is known about the phenomenon and where there is few empirical evidence about it (Eisenhardt, 1989).

This study emerged in the context of a multi-year project, one-off papers not embedded in ongoing research projects are sometimes problematic (Gephart, 2004: 459), as part of a wider research project carried out by the Social Enterprise Knowledge Network (SEKN).[1] In that undertaking, 33 BoP initiatives were studied in detail over a three-year period.[2] That project involved multiple investigators, a feature that often enhances the creative potential of the study (Eisenhardt, 1989: 538). During the course of that project, the authors became aware of the acute differences in the trajectory of different alliances, within the context of CSSP. A research protocol was crafted to guide the data collection of the various researchers involved, located in different countries. The result of that effort was a wealth of both qualitative and quantitative data, whose combination can be highly synergistic

(Eisenhardt, 1989: 538). Data sources included interviews and company documents, as well as secondary sources such as industry reports or articles, whenever available.

In this chapter we analyze a Colombian case we have been researching since its creation in 2005. In 2011, after reviewing the literature about partnerships, and those articles and book chapters written about an early stage of this case, we expanded the fieldwork with six targeted and semi-structured interviews to old and new protagonists. An analysis of the transcribed interviews was combined with previous analysis of the primary information in order to identify patterns and themes related to the alliances that were established. We then contrasted these patterns and themes with the identified literature of both strategic alliances and CSSP, and of alliance portfolios.

Our analysis followed two stages. Initially we examined each partnership, to gain familiarity with data and identify unique patterns that may offer leads to preliminary construct generation. We then moved on to a comparison between partnerships (at the individual level and then grouping them as CSSP and B2B alliances), assessing the extent to which findings in one could extrapolate to the rest. Pattern-matching logic, whereby the analyst compares an empirically based pattern with a predicted one, has been judged appropriate for case-study analysis. If the patterns do coincide, the results can help a case study to strengthen its internal validity (Yin, 2003: 116). Our analysis sought to find replications and contrasts among partnerships, and understand their dynamics and roles in the development of a BoP venture.

Case study: a pilot project becomes a business unit of a multinational corporation

Corona began its production of glazed ceramic tiling in 1953 with few competitors in the Colombian market. With the liberalization of the economy in the 1990s, Corona faced increasing competition. In 2005, the company started a pilot project directed at low-income citizens and, a year later, it became a company program within the marketing department. By early 2012, the program constituted a separate, self-sustaining business unit selling in different parts of the country. Corona also considered that the business had a social justification: first, it provided low-income populations with consumer goods for a healthier and dignified life; second, the company began the initiative by including members of the community as sales personnel and giving them the possibility to earn a living; and third, Corona committed itself to reinvest 3 per cent of the venture's profits into community projects.

Colombia has approximately 42 million people, with nearly 12 million living in houses that were built over dirt or cement floors in the poorest neighborhoods. A market study showed that inhabitants, despite their low income, not only had sufficient purchasing power but also showed a surprising financial discipline to fulfil various needs with very few resources. For this population, buying construction materials involves purchasing from traditional small stores, paying cash, and doing everything on their own: design, purchase, pick-up and transportation of materials, and labor. Formal institutions, with a weak enforcement of the rule of law (in this volume, Rufin and Rivera-Santos (2014) describe extreme settings where informal institutions predominate), characterize the settings where the study described in this chapter took place.

How was Corona's BoP initiative set up and achieved scale? We contend that an answer to this question is related to the management of CSSP and B2B alliances throughout the years. What follows is an analysis of the evolution of the company's alliance portfolio.

Commitment and trust building to achieve awareness and acceptability through CSSP

Corona's venture started out as a pilot project that evaluated a new product line for the BoP, a market segment unknown to them. The Director of Mass Marketing, who was assigned to lead this initiative, contacted Ashoka[3] to identify a social entrepreneur who could provide knowledge and establish contact with this low-income community. As this manager recalled: "Ashoka fellows did not believe us. There was a lot of distance; each had a different logic." In the words of the Ashoka fellow who partnered with Corona: "Each had a different language, and we had to arrive to common understandings and find some balance between the social and the economic."

Despite differences, the aim and mission of the project united this social worker and Corona. Commitment was the initial glue; personal commitment between interlocutors somehow compensated for organizational misfit. As the social worker committed to the cause, the company's team members were able to observe her skills: "She was a person who managed serious, very interesting processes, not only with us. This motivated us to really get involved in the project." Commitment, in Corona's case, came from upper management; patient capital, which is often required in order to set up BoP ventures (Márquez *et al.,* 2010), was provided. According to one team member, "if we had calculated PandL from the very first day, we certainly would still be discussing this project."

Apart from commitment, trust was constantly built through information sharing, demonstrating competency, constant human interaction, and following through with the project. Corona invited the social worker and community members to visit their factory while employees went to visit the community and dispelled, according to one manager, "the image that an executive doesn't get his hands dirty."

In the process of launching the venture, Corona's team and the social entrepreneur planned to set up a cooperative within the community in order to assure formal market transactions. The level of community organizing surprised them. As another manager recalled,

> The community questioned why should they create new organizations if they had their own. After hearing from the leaders I asked myself: who are the experts here? We hadn't recognized the real value of their contributions; we had been cocky.

CSSP with the social entrepreneur and her nonprofit, as well as with community organizations, lowered two major barriers that stood in the way of conducting business with BoP consumers. It enabled the entrance into the house of potential customers and it involved community members in such a way that they became aware of their ability to move forward their own development. To support these processes, three per cent of sales from the venture went to community organizations, and another three per cent was allotted to social investments in the community.

It took some time for Corona to really appreciate the different layers of value that its product brought to low-income consumers (beyond its obvious functional advantages), particularly in terms of some intangible dimensions, such as enhanced dignity for the user or its role as a visible symbol of economic progress aimed at fellow dwellers. At that point, community members felt that the company was making an effort to go beyond commercial transactions. In the words of one of their leaders, "Corona could not have made it here only with their Marketing and Sales crew; bringing in people that knew about social and community issues allowed them to get to people and show them it paid to make the effort."

Due to the initial lack of trust, a governance structure was needed. Although no formal contract regarding the partnership was signed, a document containing "binding norms" was written to define the rights and obligations of Corona, of community organizations and of the social worker between them. A project team that included Corona employees, the Ashoka fellow, and community representatives met regularly, and all participated in defining the business model for the project. Services to be provided were clear, but goals and processes were not explicit.

Corona failed to institutionalize the growing mutual trust and relied, instead, on key grass-root individual leaders that had been engaged with the project from the beginning. The lack of supporting structures became evident when a new person took over the management of the BoP venture within Corona, and the hard-won trust soon faded. Without stability and guidance from a formal structure, the number of regular meetings of the alliance team diminished and the content of these meetings concentrated on commercial affairs. This new scenario left social leaders and the communities under the impression that they were no longer consulted. One community leader expressed it in the following terms:

> A lot of the latest activities have not worked out well because we failed to plan them jointly. While the company has technical knowledge of how to market their products, community leaders have a common sense of how things have always been done. Combining these two competencies brought us good results.

Wide access to the community came through organizations such as churches and employee savings funds. These partnerships aggregated demand, thus lowering the cost of sales for Corona. In the case of CSSP with religious leaders, the church community received construction material from Corona. Employee savings funds benefited from an alliance with Corona; namely, they improved their value proposition to its membership. By engaging in these CSSP with clear deliverables, Corona obtained awareness and acceptability for their products. But, as mentioned above, BoP ventures also need products to be affordable and available; to that end, Corona resorted to same-sector alliances.

Structures and routines to achieve affordability and availability through B2B alliances

Corona, the nonprofit and the community organizations – who established CSSP – worked with different logics, structures, and organizational cultures. Contrastingly, Corona's same-sector alliances aligned under the shared objective of profit-seeking, which created a base for mutual understanding. Corona's first effort towards affordability was the design of a new product with better price/performance ratio. The next challenge was to take into account constraints in the cash flows of community members. Since its first sales, the company offered credit but did not rely on the expertise of financial partners. Sales women, recruited within the community, were involved in credit approval and debt collection. Besides not using the time of sales personnel efficiently, overdue payment problems appeared.

Corona's managers painfully realized that financing was not their core business, and that they lacked the capabilities to carry out these functions satisfactorily. One of their discoveries was that it was common for low-income customers to use commercial and cooperative credits. Among the different options, they were taking small loans offered by water, electricity, and gas utilities. From then on, in each zone where the company took its venture, the utility company with the highest acceptability and coverage was chosen as a partner to take over the entire billing and collection processes. Partnerships with commercial banks were not successful for two reasons: one, Corona found out that low-income populations are weary of credits with banks; and two, the business volume that Corona guaranteed was not attractive enough to ensure a certain commitment from commercial banks. Utility companies, by contrast, had extensive experience in providing credits and collecting debt from low-income populations.[4] A common interest and mutual benefit for both partners was clear and unlikely to fade away, as a Corona executive recognized: "Our partners gain a client for their financial products and we gain as well because we have a client who can buy our products." An organizational structure that handled credit approval and debt collection was established from the beginning.

Distribution was another area where Corona tried alliances. After partnering with local hardware stores and establishing procedures for sales to happen, managers realized that leaving it up to the customer to pick up their products was not a good option. As one manager recognized,

> for us, contact with clients is not only during sales, but also when you actually deliver the product. If you leave the product delivery to someone else, they will detect a business opportunity. Delivery is especially important because reselling is key in this business as people remodel their house step by step.

Continuous learning allowed Corona to internalize the whole distribution process. Although product margin was affected, Corona took over the direct delivery of products to customers whose houses were in unpaved and very narrow streets. Beyond issues of availability, this decision gave Corona control over the last mile and allowed it to have direct contact with its clients with a better service.

Despite the focus of B2B alliances on affordability and availability, Corona has also used them to strengthen their attempts in raising awareness and acceptability. For example, partnerships with construction companies of low-income housing allowed these firms to offer their clients a rounder value proposition, as they could choose to have Corona products installed in their low-cost homes. Additionally, Corona is currently seeking to partner with a company that coordinates 20,000 small shop-keepers nationwide and could turn these shopkeepers into promoters of Corona's products in exchange for construction material.

The B2B alliances in which Corona engaged had a relatively low conflict potential. Given their similar logics, mutual understandings were common. Additionally, partners did not have conflicts of interest since they did not compete in the same markets. Favorable conditions at the start of same-sector alliances, however, do not prevent potential conflicts. Trust has to be continually nurtured just as mutual commitment has to be maintained. The institutionalization of routines and structures for each alliance enhances this process. In the case of same-sector alliances, institutionalization with formal procedures took place almost immediately upon their establishment, while CSSP remained informal and were highly dependent on the people involved. While this strategy may work well at the beginning with an emphasis on human interactions and on the alignment of a company with the logic of NPO, this lack of formalization became a hindrance in times of change or crisis.

Scaling imperatives for CSSP

The NPO engaged with Corona aimed not only to provide low-income pop-ulations with products for a better and dignified life, but also to find different ways in which these communities could participate in the business. Hiring community members was one such way. This helped Corona establish itself within the community, but it soon became clear that many of those hired lacked certain abilities for selling tiles and ceramics. NPO insisted that such abilities (e.g. placing orders in square meters) could be acquired and designed a program to develop them. As Corona's managers pushed for efficiency and growth, they guaranteed a basic wage to improve labor conditions and hired people with a basic education and some sales experience. This assured increased control and a general improvement of the sales force:

> If you don't impose a work schedule … a saleswoman with high sales that earns a lot of money one month, might not return the following month. In a business where you need scale to cover costs, that doesn't work for you.

Cost-benefit analyses collided with the civic participation logic and human development objectives of NPO in relation with the sales force: "we are interested in their progressive qualification; we are not only interested in sales, but rather in what these sales mean to them." While Corona's project manager stated that: "NPO did not align with what we wanted because they did not understand the concept of profitability and pursued other objectives"; Ashoka's fellow recalled:

> We are saying no to a sale when it doesn't work structurally; that is something that Corona never does. We aim to have scalable and sustainable sales. This is much more difficult. The questions we ask [potential customers] are not the same, and it is not that one is better than the other.

As a new management team came in with the goal of taking the project to scale, patient and participatory value co-creation came to be perceived not as an asset, but as a shortcoming that impaired standardization and needed to be trimmed (e.g. "We need results now"). In practical terms, growth implied maximizing access to families who would benefit from better living conditions, but at the price of lowering the integration of community members in the value chain. To open operations in other cities, Corona had selected NPO to raise awareness and acceptability, and gave them three per cent of sales to hire saleswomen and provide them with psychological and legal advice. According to the executive in charge of the project:

> In March 2010 we realized that things were not working any longer. We paid NPO in six different regions a large amount of money. In the beginning, they helped us set foot in zones where we hadn't been before. As for contracting saleswomen, they were not as effective due to the quality of the people they sent us. The social services they provided directly to the saleswomen also declined substantially. Basically, we were paying these NPO for being there; so we decided to remove them.

NPO had another task, besides selection and support, in the communities where they operated: namely, to coordinate the social investments to which Corona allotted resources. There was no established procedure as to how these social investments were handled, nor was there a discussion about what to expect from them and how to measure their impact. In time, Corona's managers realized that assuming this task would clarify, for communities, who the donor was. This was one move towards internalizing the functions that were carried out by its social partners. Besides the social benefits of remodeling a public school or park, visibility was expected to raise awareness about Corona's products. This issue was important not only to the project team in Corona, but also to some of its owners: "once we organized this issue of social investment, we were able to have a clear idea of how much was invested and in what. Now we are starting to evaluate the impact of all projects inaugurated last year."

In search of a less costly and more efficient venture, Corona sought to improve every aspect and changed whatever it needed. Once awareness and acceptability existed through their saleswomen, Corona perceived that the alliances with NPO were no longer needed. These organizations did not realize that the resources they initially provided to the cross-sector alliance, trust and the legitimacy, was no longer a complementary resource for Corona. The conflict was aggravated because some NPO did not consider the BoP venture as a strategic project, nor did they continue to show the same commitment that was expected from them as a partner. As distance with Corona grew, some NPO started alliances with other companies. After four years of working together, they had learned and understood the business model. The common goal of improving lives in low-income communities no longer provided the basis for a mutual understanding among partners. Formal mechanisms, such as clear communication channels and an organizational structure that could have helped, were lacking. As each partner pursued its own interest, hardly won mutual trust faded and the demise of these partnerships was accelerated.

Evaluation of the benefits generated by partnerships with religious leaders was undertaken as well. In this case the outcome was the opposite. New customers from a church community were easily identified, and more clients meant more material for that church.

As scaling imperatives appeared, Corona managers tried to secure control in most aspects of the venture. For example, the company wanted to retain partial control of the credit function and they did so by disbursing close to 20 per cent of total loans from their own funds and by not having exclusivity with any of the credit providers. Internalizing the distribution function also increased control on customer information.

Discussion about evolution in heterogeneous alliance portfolios

Alliances are a mechanism to achieve, usually by pooling complementary resources and capabilities, a benefit that could not be achieved alone. A firm can use CSSP and B2B alliances for different purposes, as the studied case illustrates. Both cross- and same-sector alliances need to build trust, adopt formal processes and structures, and evaluate their progress. Sector logics and frames, important from the beginning, have a lasting effect on partnerships (Gray and Purdy, 2014, this volume). As alliances evolve, needs change and alignment has to be reworked.

In new circumstances, the growth imperative for companies and the impact goal for NPO determine the control each partner wants to have on the activities developed jointly. At such points, rational evaluations of costs and benefits take over what once might have been a quick decision to engage in collaboration. It is likely that alliances are formed out of a need or a trend, and not as a result of a rational cost-benefit evaluation that comes with a market transaction or an internal development of a specific capability (Seitanidi and Crane, 2008). Cost-benefit evaluations come in later, especially in times of crisis – either triggered by an internal event such as the failure to scale or an external event such as the entrance of competitors. As the studied case depicts, evaluations can end a partnership for different reasons: e.g. needs change, an organization acquires the resources or develops the capability previously provided by a partner, or a substantial learning curve undermines the sought benefit. Several CSSP and B2B alliances were terminated and others were strengthened as Corona's managers performed evaluations that confirmed, in their words, their discovery of a "blue ocean."

As companies incur in significant costs setting up and managing alliances, it is likely that those will be assessed in relation to their ability to generate a benefit that each partner on its own would not have been able to accomplish. Sustaining the value of an alliance requires continuous efforts. "In the stronger collaborations, the partners are engaged in continual learning about the partnering process and how it can generate more value" (Austin, 2000: 85). Organizations that cease to create benefit for their partners are likely to be replaced, as Corona's CSSP exemplify. In some cases, Corona developed the capabilities its partners had provided. As needs changed, alignment with nonprofit partners waned. In time, Corona acquired legitimacy within the community and gained the access initially provided by CSSP. The increasing need to better control the sales force and achieve scalability became a thorn for those partnerships. Costs for Corona of these CSSP were high, but they had been agreed and quantified from the beginning. Benefits for Corona were, at first, not measureable and when they were, it became clear that they had faded away. CSSP with religious leaders were different: benefits were clear for both sides, and costs for Corona were directly linked to nurturing such relationships. Even though Corona had acquired the capabilities that enabled them to overcome – at least partially – barriers of access and awareness, churches were accelerators of their business at a relatively low cost. Therefore, these more transactional partnerships continued.

Corona's evaluations of their alliances distance them from what the literature reports: i.e. a lack of rigorous performance measurement on the individual alliance level as one of three reasons that explain why most firms are unable to assess the performance of their alliance portfolios (the other two are that "companies often fail to recognize performance patterns across their alliance portfolios," and senior managers lack information to assess whether the portfolio supports the firm strategy) (Bamford and Ernst, 2002: 29). Corona was able to link the strategy of their BoP business, as Hoffmann (2007) suggests, with the objectives of individual alliances and the overall objective of its alliance portfolio. Seeking resource complementarity with CSSP gave Corona awareness and acceptability, and B2B alliances gave them affordability and availability. Clarke and Fuller (2010) ask about appropriate contexts for CSSP; our research points out that these types of partnerships are likely to succeed in environments where companies are seeking awareness and acceptability for their products.

Fit, commitment and trust issues stand out in the comparison of requirements by different types of alliances. As same-sector alliances for distribution and finance exemplify, common logics, similar organizational cultures and shared objectives of profit generation allowed for a closer initial fit than for CSSP. Then, structures and routines were easier to set up. Although fit did not guarantee commitment and trust through time, the need to align partners was less. This situation was different for

CSSP. Diverging logics and the resulting poor fit demanded efforts to build trust. CSSP started by building informal coordination mechanisms. Barriers were lowered through mutual commitment, information sharing, constant personal interaction, and demonstrating skills on the ongoing exchange of the partnership. In same-sector alliances, relations were mediated by contracts and incentives. In CSSP with grass-roots organizations, on the other hand, weak contract enforcement devalued the usefulness of rational incentives in arms-length relations. Thus, there is the need for outsiders to embed themselves in direct, face-to-face relationships, that enhance personal trust and diminish the chances of opportunistic behavior. In both types of alliances, trust needed to be nurtured, and losing it could not be compensated by any formal structure. Table 8.1 summarizes the differences between CSSP and B2B in the alliance portfolio that Corona established for their BoP venture.

While an informal approach can work well at the initial stages of an alliance, it works less when conflicts or scaling needs emerge. The needs of a BoP venture are quite different in the startup and growth phases. In the initial phases, the need to "get the ball rolling" and build legitimacy through results encourage "organic processes": loosely defined tasks and responsibilities, and mobilization through enthusiasm. On the other hand, once the initial uncertainty is dispelled and growth is pursued, the need for "mechanistic processes" emerges involving specialized, differentiated tasks and well-defined responsibilities. Organic processes are best used when conditions are unstable and difficult to predict, when adaptation and change is required. Mechanistic processes are best used when conditions are predictable, and when improvement, efficiency or reliability is the goal (Burns and Stalker, 1961).

So why did CSSP remain informal in Corona's case? As the relationship evolved, the nonprofit partners made concessions. Instead of imposing their logics and frames, they partially adopted an approach that relied more on people than structures. Although this coordinating mechanism was insufficient to deal with arising conflicts,

TABLE 8.1 Comparison of CSSP and B2B alliances for an inclusive business

	CSSP	*B2B alliances*
Set up challenges	Efforts to align partners include: • Commitment by both parties • Acknowledgement of different sector logics and frames • Trust-building processes	Initial fit gives way to the establishment of contracts
Growth challenges	Focus on marketing	Focus on efficiency and control
Management	No formal structure established Reliance on individual commitments	Structures and routines established from the outset
Results	Provide awareness and acceptability for company products	Provide affordability and availability for company products

CSSP were not doomed to fail because of different sector logics. As long as explicit benefits existed and partners evaluated their relationship, changes were incorporated and the survival of the partnership guaranteed.

Expected benefits from partnerships are not always rationally evaluated against possible costs. The tacit character of benefits from CSSP makes evaluations difficult. Same-sector relationships have more explicit costs and benefits. Due to the fact that collaborations are fashionable, it is not common to seriously consider other options when seeking specific resources or capabilities related to unknown low-income markets. However, as crises hit or scaling invites adjustments, each partnership requires careful assessment.

As a company seeks to scale an initiative, it is control, rather than fading mutual benefits or the loss of trust or commitment, that leads to take over important parts of the value chain. Not only do partners need to provide valuable and complementary resources and capabilities; the importance of the activities for the value chain is another factor that needs to be taken into consideration.

Value creation: are involved parties better off?

For Corona, the BoP venture aimed to be a profitable initiative and, at the same time, it included a social component. As one manager expressed, "for us, this is a business that can be a good business, one that gives low-income citizens access to products that improve their quality of life."

In sales, credit, or distribution, Corona sought partners with the capabilities and knowledge they needed to overcome one or more of the four strategic challenges to entering a low-income market. CSSP brought in tacit knowledge, trust, and legitimacy to open the door into a low-income community; in short, the capability to interact with this population. Besides being valuable these capabilities were also rare (i.e. no other competitor had the knowledge needed to sell to the BoP market). At the same time, this capability was not easily imitable or easily replaced.

The combination of four characteristics about an interaction capability – being valuable, rare, not imitable and non-substitutable – provides the basis for a sustained competitive advantage (Barney, 1991). In time, Corona also developed an alliance capability. Corona's unique value system, where internal activities were supported by synergistic same-sector alliances and CSSP, formed a complex (and tightly interwoven) activity system that has proven very difficult to replicate by competitors (Collis and Montgomery, 1995; Porter, 1996). As a Corona manager expressed:

> It is not so easy for other companies to enter this market. The issue is not the product. This market requires a lot of patience and consistency to create trust and legitimacy among community members. Knowledge about these customers is not acquired easily.

Corona could have opted for developing the knowledge about low-income populations on its own. However, it would have been costly and inefficient. As the venture's manager warned, "access to the BoP is impossible to internalize." Partnering with a social entrepreneur allowed Corona to set up and better manage its relationships with the communities. Since such a valuable resource is not available without the commitment generated through a partnership, no other companies can easily enter into the BoP market the way Corona did. Partnering with grass roots organizations allowed Corona to leverage existing leaderships and organizations, as an asset on which to build an ad-hoc value chain. In the words of Corona's Marketing Manager, leader of the BoP venture in its early stages:

> You really need the community on board and you cannot do that just through financial incentives. Grassroots organizations were present on the ground before you arrive, and will be there after you leave. We are outsiders ... they are insiders. You really need that social tissue as a platform upon which to build.

As of the writing of this chapter, Corona's BoP initiative had expanded to 17 councils in Colombia's five main cities. It reached around 170,000 among Colombia's poorest consumers with a high quality product, coupled with technical assistance and affordable credit. It has increased property values and created employment for 200 single mothers. For NPO, the project's impact came through both participation in the value chain and provision of a better life through consumption (i.e. "the poor should not only be considered as customers"). The investment of a percentage of sales in community projects is another source of impact. By 2011, Corona had invested over US$ 330,000 in community-defined projects, from social institutions such as kindergartens, schools, and residences for senior citizens to local infrastructure – like parks or stepped pavements needed to climb steep roads. Has access to this consumer good really improved these citizens' quality of life? Some testimonials from dwellers, gathered during our data-collection, state the following:

- "Never before had I been able to purchase this type of goods on credit ... Corona has given me timely and affordable credit."
- "Having remade my kitchen has motivated me ... It now looks wonderful, and that gives me hope and strength to carry out day-to-day activities ..."
- "Not having to mop my dirt-floor any more makes all the difference; I now use less water, soap, and time."

Perhaps the acid test of the value created for the communities is the fact that grass root organizations – Community Action Boards and Community Mothers – continue to support the initiative. Leveraging these highly credible leaderships brings tangible benefits for all those involved. Conversely, bringing these services to the community can also boost the credibility of local leaders – but only to the extent that these business initiatives deliver real, lasting value to low-income citizens. For local leaders that mediate between the corporation and the community, the stakes are substantial, as their personal credibility is on the line. Had the initiative focused exclusively on extracting short-term financial gains, without tangible gains in quality of life to the community, it would have been short-lived –with leaders' credibility depreciated accordingly. The fact that the initiative continues to be embraced by the leadership of grassroots organizations where it operates suggests a win-win situation, where value is accrued by both the company and low-income consumers.

Our focus on the portfolio of alliances, configured by a multinational corporation to develop a BoP initiative, has allowed us to explore similarities and differences between cross-sector and same-sector alliances. In doing so, we have gotten a glimpse of phenomena that few companies have experienced because of the multiple challenges in scaling BoP ventures. Hopefully, such a glimpse eases the path of many others trying to fulfil the promise of sustainable businesses that contribute to poverty alleviation.

Questions for reflection

1   What factors affect the balance between CSSP and B2B alliances in a portfolio to serve low-income consumers?
2   How does the tension between the formal and informal worlds in which a multinational corporation and the BoP co-exist influence the evolution of an alliance portfolio?
3   In what ways do changes in CSSP in a BoP business affect the creation and appropriation of value?

Notes

1   SEKN is a research and teaching network of ten universities in the Americas and Spain. Learning about partnerships has been a goal of this academic network since its inception in 2001.
2   These 33 cases were selected according to three criteria: first, any private organization with a project that engaged low-income citizens as suppliers, producers or consumers; second, projects that generate profits (subsidies could only exist at initial stages); and third, projects that improve the living conditions of those low-income populations involved.
3   Ashoka "develops the careers of social entrepreneurs throughout the world" by identifying innovative ideas and initiatives. These entrepreneurs receive financial and professional support to advance their projects.
4   Since 2001, utilities in Colombia have taken advantage of their logistics for billing to offer small consumer loans to their customers.

References

Anderson, J. and Markides, C. (2007) "Strategic innovation at the base of the economic pyramid," *MIT Sloan Management Review*, Fall, 49 (1): 83–8.

Annan, K. (2001) "Unparalleled nightmare of AIDS," Address to the United States Chamber of Commerce, Washington, DC: www.un.org/News/Press/docs/2001/sgsm 7827.doc.htm.

Ariño, A., De la Torre, J. and Ring, P.S. (2001) "Relational quality: managing trust in corporate alliances," *California Management Review*, 44 (1): 109–34.

Arrow, K. (1974) "Limited knowledge and economic analysis," *American Economic Review*, 64 (1): 1–10.

Austin, J.E. (2000) "Strategic collaboration between nonprofits and businesses," *Nonprofit and Voluntary Sector Quarterly*, 29 (1): 69–97.

Austin, J.E., Reficco, E. and SEKN (2004) *Social partnering in Latin America: Lessons Drawn from Collaborations of Businesses and Civil Society Organizations*, Inter–American Development Bank, David Rockefeller Center for Latin American Studies. Boston: Harvard University Press.

Bamford, J. and Ernst, D. (2002) "Managing an alliance portfolio," *The McKinsey Quarterly*, 3: 29–39.

Barney, J.B. (1991) "Firm resources and sustained competitive advantage," *Journal of Management*, 17: 99–120.

Berger, I.E., Cunningham, P.H. and Drumwright, M.E. (2004) "Social alliances: company/ nonprofit collaboration," *California Management Review*, 47 (1): 58–91.

Bruni Celli, J. and González, R.A. (2010) "Market-based initiatives for low-income sectors and economic value creation," in P. Márquez, E. Reficco and G. Berger (eds) *Socially Inclusive Business: Engaging the Poor through Market Initiatives in Iberoamerica*, Inter-American Development Bank and David Rockefeller Center for Latin American Studies. Boston: Harvard University Press.

Bryson, J.M., Crosby, B.C. and Stone, M.M. (2006) "The design and implementation of cross-sector collaborations: propositions from the literature," *Public Administration Review*, December: 44–55.

Budinich, V., Reott, K.M. and Schmidt, S. (2007) "Hybrid value chains: social innovations and development of the small farmer irrigation market in Mexico," in K. Rangan, J. Quelch, G. Herrero and B. Barton (eds) *Business Solutions for the Global Poor: Creating Social and Economic Value* (pp. 279–89). San Francisco: Jossey-Bass, San Francisco.

Burns, T. and Stalker, G.M. (1961) *The Management of Innovation*, London: Tavistock Publications.

Collis, D. and Montgomery, C.A. 1995, "Competing on resources: strategy in the 1990s," *Harvard Business Review* 73 (July–August): 118–28.

Child, J. and Möllering, G. (2003) "Contextual confidence and active trust development in the Chinese business environment," *Organization Science*, 14 (1): 69–80.

Clarke, A. and Fuller, M. (2010). "Collaborative strategic management: strategy formulation and implementation by multi-organizational cross-sector social partnerships," *Journal of Business Ethics*, 94: 85–101.

Dahan, N.M., Doh, J.P., Oetzel, J. and Yaziji, M. (2010) "Corporate-NGO collaboration: co-creating new business models for developing markets," *Long Range Planning*, 43: 326–42.

Das, T.K. and Teng, B.S. (2001) "Trust, control, and risk in strategic alliances: an integrated framework," *Organization Studies*, 22 (2): 251–83.

Drumwright, M.E., Cunningham, P.H. and Berger, I.E. (2000) "Social alliances: company/ nonprofit collaboration," Marketing Science Institute Working Paper Series Report No. 100-1.

Dussauge, P., Garrete, B. and Mitchell, W. (2000) "Learning from competing partners: outcomes and durations of scale and link alliances in Europe, North America, and Asia," *Strategic Management Journal*, 21: 99–126.

Eisenhardt, K.M. (1989) "Building theories from case study research," *Academy of Management Review*, 14 (4): 532–50.

Eisenhardt, K.M. and Graebner, M.E. (2007) "Theory building from cases: opportunities and challenges," *Academy of Management Journal*, 50 (1): 25–32.

Eisenhardt, K.M. and Schoonhoven, C.B. (1996) "Resource-based view of strategic alliance formation: strategic and social effects in entrepreneurial firms," *Organization Science*, 7 (2): 136–50.

Emery, F.E and Trist, E.L. (1965) "The causal texture of organizational environments," *Human Relations*, 18: 21–32.

FOMIN. (2009) *Guía de aprendizaje sobre la implementación de responsabilidad social empresarial en pequeñas y medianas empresas*. Washington, DC: Banco Interamericano de Desarrollo.

Friedland, R. and Alford, R.R. (1991) "Bringing society back in: Symbols, practices, and institutional contradictions," in W. W. Powell and P. J. DiMaggio (eds) *The New Institutionalism in Organizational Analysis*. Chicago: University of Chicago Press.

Galaskiewicz, J. (1985) "Interorganizational relations," *Annual Review of Sociology*, 11: 281–304.

George, G., Zahra, S.A., Wheatley, K.K. and Khan, R. (2001) "The effects of alliance portfolio characteristics and absorptive capacity on performance: a study of biotechnology firms," *Journal of High Technology Management Research*, 12: 205–26.

Gephart, R. (2004) "Qualitative research and the academy of management journal," *Academy of Management Journal*, 47 (4): 454–62.

Goerzen, A. (2007) "Alliance networks and firm performance: the impact of repeated partnerships," *Strategic Management Journal*, 28: 487–509.

Golja, T. and Požega, S. (2012) "Inclusive business – what is it all about? managing inclusive companies," *International Review of Management and Marketing*, 2 (1): 22–42.

Gray, B. and Purdy, J. (2014) Conflict in cross-sector partnerships, in M.M. Seitanidi and A. Crane, A. (eds) *Social Partnerships and Responsible Business: A Research Handbook*. London: Routledge: 205–226.

Gulati, R. (1995) "Does familiarity breed trust? The implications of repeated ties for contractual choice in alliances," *Academy of Management Journal*, 38: 85–112.

Gundlach, G.T., Achrol, R.S. and Mentzer, J.T. (1995) "The structure of commitment in exchange," *Journal of Marketing*, 59 (1): 78–92.

Hart, S. and London, T. (2005) "Developing native capability: what multinational corporations can learn from the base of the pyramid," *Stanford Social Innovation Review*, 28–33.

Hagedoorn, J. and Schakenraad, J. (1994) "The effect of strategic technology alliances on company performance," *Strategic Management Journal*, 15: 291–309.

Hoffmann, W.H. (2007) "Strategies for managing a portfolio of alliances," *Strategic Management Journal* 28: 827–56.

Kale, P and Singh, H (1999) "Building alliance capabilities: a knowledge-based approach," Academy of Management Best Paper Proceedings, Chicago.

Karnani, A (2007) "The mirage of marketing to the bottom of the pyramid: how the private sector can help alleviate poverty," *California Management Review*, 49 (4): 90–111.

Kotabe, M. and Swan, K.S. (1995) "The role of strategic alliances in high-technology new product development," *Strategic Management Journal*, 16: 621–36.

Lasker, R.D., Weiss, E.S. and Miller, R. (2001) "Partnership synergy: a practical framework for studying and strengthening the collaborative advantage," *The Milbank Quarterly*, 79 (2): 179–205.

London, T. and Hart, S.L. (2011) *Next Generation Business Strategies for the Base of the Pyramid: New Approaches for Building Mutual Value*, Upper Saddle River, NJ: FT Press.

Márquez, P., Reficco, E. and Berger, G. (eds) (2010) *Socially Inclusive Business: Engaging the Poor Through Market Initiatives in Iberoamerica*, Inter-American Development Bank and David Rockefeller Center for Latin American Studies. Boston: Harvard University Press.

Marx, J. (1999) "Corporate philanthropy: what is the strategy?," *Nonprofit and Voluntary Sector Quarterly*, 28 (2): 185–98.

Nohria, N. and García-Pont, C. (1991) "Global strategic linkages and industry structure," *Strategic Management Journal*, 12: 105–24.

Olsen, M. and Boxenbaum, E. (2009) "Bottom-of-the-pyramid: organizational barriers to implementation," *California Management Review*, 51 (4): 100–25.

Peloza, J. and Ye, C. (2014) How social partnerships build brands, in M.M. Seitanidi and A. Crane, A. (eds) *Social Partnerships and Responsible Business: A Research Handbook*. London: Routledge: 191–204.

Pfeffer, J. and Salancik, G.R. (1978) *The External Control of Organizations: A Resource Dependence Perspective*. New York: Harper.

Porter, M.E. (1996) "What is strategy?," *Harvard Business Review* (November–December): 61–78.

Prahalad, C.K. (2004) *The Fortune at the Bottom of the Pyramid: Eradicating Poverty Through Profits*. Upper Saddle River, NJ: Prentice Hall.

Prahalad, C.K. and Hammond, A. (2002) "Serving the world's poor, profitably," *Harvard Business Review*, 80: 4–11.

Reficco, E. (2010) "Negocios inclusivos y responsabilidad social: un matrimonio complejo," *Debates IESA*, 15 (3): 14–17.

Reficco, E. and Márquez, P. (forthcoming) "Inclusive networks for building BOP markets," *Business and Society*.

Rivera-Santos, M. and Rufin, C. (2011) "Odd couples: understanding the governance of firm–NGO alliances," *Journal of Business Ethics*, 94 (1): 55–70.

Rondinelli, D.A. and London, T. (2003) "How corporations and environmental groups cooperate: assessing CSSP and collaborations," *Academy of Management Executive*, 17: 61–76.

Rufin, C. and Rivera-Santos, M. (2014) Cross-sector governance: from institutions to partnerships, and back to institutions, in M.M. Seitanidi and A. Crane (eds) *Social Partnerships and Responsible Business: A Research Handbook*. London: Routledge: 125–42.

Sagawa, S. and Segal, E. (2000) *Common Interest, Common Good*. Boston: Harvard University Press.

Saxton, T. (1997) "The effects of partner and relationship characteristics on alliance outcomes," *Academy of Management Journal*, 40: 443–60.

Seitanidi, M.M. and Crane, A. (2008) "Implementing CSR through partnerships: understanding the selection, design and institutionalization of nonprofit-business partnerships," *Journal of Business Ethics*, 85: 413–29.

Selsky, B. and Parker, J.W. (2005) "CSSP to address social issues: challenges to theory and practice," *Journal of Management*, 31: 849–73.

Shah, R.H. and Swaminathan, V (2008) "Factors influencing partner selection in strategic alliances: the moderating role of alliance context," *Strategic Management Journal*, 29: 471–94.

Simanis, E. and Hart, S. (2008) "Beyond selling to the poor: building business intimacy through embedded innovation," Working Paper, Cornell University, Ithaca, NY.

SNV and World Business Council for Sustainable Development (2008) "Inclusive Business: Profitable business for successful development," last accessed October 13, 2012, http://wbcsd.typepad.com/wbcsdsnv/wbcsd_snv_alliance_brochure_march_08_web.pdf

Stake, R.E. (2005) "Qualitative case studies" in N.K. Denzin and Y.S. Lincoln (eds) *The Sage Handbook of Qualitative Research* (3rd edn.). Thousand Oaks, CA: Sage.

Wassmer, U. (2010) "Alliance portfolios: a review and research agenda," *Journal of Management*, 36 (1): 141–71.

Webb, J.W., Kistruck, G.M., Ireland R.D. and Ketchen, D.J. (2010) "The entrepreneurship process in base of the pyramid markets: the case of multinational enterprise/nongovernment organization alliances," *Entrepreneurship Theory and Practice*, 555–81.

Weiser, J., Kahane, M., Rochlin, S. and Landis, J. (2006) *Untapped: Creating Value in Underserved Markets*. San Francisco: Berrett-Koehler.

Whetten, D.A. (1981) "Interorganizational relations: a review of the field," *Journal of Higher Education*, 52: 1–28.

Wohlstetter, P., Smith, J. and Malloy, C.L. (2005) "Strategic alliances in action: toward a theory of evolution," *Policy Studies Journal*, 33 (3): 419–42.

Yin, R.K. (2003) *Case Study Research: Design and Methods*. Thousand Oaks, CA: Sage .

9

NGO-INITIATED SUSTAINABLE ENTREPRENEURSHIP AND SOCIAL PARTNERSHIPS

Greenpeace's "Solutions" campaign for natural refrigerants in North America

Edwin R. Stafford and Cathy L. Hartman

Introduction

Sustainable entrepreneurship is an emerging field within the business academic literature defined as "the discovery, creation, and exploitation of opportunities to create future goods and services that sustain the natural and/or communal environment and provide development gain for others" (Patzelt and Shepherd, 2011: 632). Whereas traditional entrepreneurship undertakes innovations, finance, and business acumen in an effort to transform innovations into economic goods (e.g. profitable new products, technologies, etc.) for economic gain for the entrepreneurial individual or business, by contrast, sustainable entrepreneurship leverages innovations, finance, and business acumen to transform environmentally-protective innovations into both economic and non-economic (social) gains that will benefit other groups beyond the individual or business.

The task of sustainable entrepreneurs is to determine "what needs to be sustained" (e.g. preservation of nature, sources of life support, and communities) and "what needs to be developed" (e.g. innovations and business models that provide economic and social gains to other groups in society) to legitimize and establish environmentally-sustainable innovations and practices into the marketplace (Shepherd and Patzelt, 2011). Put simply, *environmentally-sustainable technologies, products, and practices must provide both economic and social gains to relevant market players and constituents* to be accepted and adopted widely in society.

Wind energy, for example, is still a novel technology, and entrepreneurs must not only convince skeptical utilities, government bodies, and citizens about the viability of wind energy as a cleaner, more sustainable alternative to established fossil fuels (i.e.

an innovation that helps sources of life support such as cleaner air and water), but also demonstrate how wind farms can create jobs, lease payments to local land-owners, and property tax revenues for host communities' services, such as the funding of schools, libraries, and fire protection (i.e., economic and social gains) (see Hartman *et al.*, 2011). In short, wind entrepreneurs need to sell constituents on proposed wind farms' economic and social gains to win approval and legitimize the business case for the sustainable technology.

In this chapter, we extend the concept of sustainable entrepreneurship by demonstrating how environmental non-government organizations (NGOs), such as Greenpeace, can initiate similar activities through technology and product development, advocacy, and cross-sector social partnerships.

Greenpeace as "sustainable entrepreneur"

Our case on Greenpeace's efforts to introduce and diffuse natural refrigerants in North America shows how NGOs may be uniquely positioned to engage in successful sustainable entrepreneurship given their traditional roles and competencies, including environmental knowledge, generating public awareness and involvement about environmental issues, lobbying policymakers, and confronting companies and institutions.

Sustainable entrepreneurship, however, also entails considering the needs of businesses and the marketplace (e.g. profits, customer satisfaction), requiring NGOs to *collaborate with businesses* and *engage in business entrepreneurial activities* (e.g. product development, marketing, competitive strategy) so sustainable solutions can compete effectively against incumbent, environmentally-destructive technologies and practices in the marketplace. In short, environmental NGOs have to *think* and *act* as business entrepreneurs, and our analysis shows that Greenpeace has done so, if not without controversy.

Current literature (e.g. Patzelt and Shepherd, 2011; Shepherd and Patzelt, 2011; Hartman *et al.*, 2011) and our analysis herein suggests that NGO-initiated sustainable entrepreneurship entails three stages: (1) recognition of environmental problems and their solutions; (2) determination of the market feasibility of those solutions and the decision to act on that market feasibility; and (3) implementation of those solutions. Our findings indicate that navigating this process to enact change in the marketplace requires sustainable entrepreneurs to undertake more specialized entrepreneurship roles – some of which align effectively with the traditional tactics and strategies used by NGOs whereas business-oriented activities (e.g. product development and marketing) are novel for NGOs and may pose challenges in their execution in terms of social and marketplace acceptance and requiring the cooperation of businesses. We illuminate these roles through our analysis of Greenpeace's campaign to combat climate change by intervening in the refrigeration market.

Why refrigeration? While many people are aware of how the burning of fossil fuels contributes to climate change through carbon dioxide emissions, few may connect the wide use of household refrigerators, vending machines, and commercial cooler cabinets in supermarkets and warehouses as having significant impact. Refrigeration units impact the climate through direct energy use, chemicals used in the machines' insulation foam, and leakage or improper end-of-life disposal of the environmentally-destructive, fluorinated-refrigerant gases (often called F-gases) used in the cooling systems. Some F-gas refrigerants create a global warming potential (GWP), defined as how much a given mass of a chemical contributes to global warming over a given time period compared to the same mass of carbon dioxide, many thousands of times greater than that of carbon dioxide (US Environmental Protection Agency, 2011a). Greenpeace has long recognized this GWP threat and has pursued two principal objectives: (1) elimination of incumbent F-gases from the world; and (2) establishment of natural, ozone- and climate-safe refrigerants as viable, sustainable, and market-accepted "solutions" for replacing F-gas refrigerants through market intervention and partnerships.

Method

As sustainable entrepreneur, Greenpeace has taken on the challenge to help steer the refrigeration and refrigeration-user industries (e.g. food, beverage, grocery retailers, home appliance) onto a more sustainable path through market intervention. With Greenpeace as our primary unit of analysis, we trace the NGO's early experiences beginning in Germany and how over the past two decades its advocacy for natural refrigerants has progressed to North America. We develop our case analysis through two sources of information: (1) depth interviews of campaigners and principals from Greenpeace and one of its corporate partners, conducted in 2012; and (2) the public record. Our case was member-checked by our informants and other Greenpeace campaigners for factual accuracy and interpretation (Yin, 2003). We conclude with a discussion of the implications for NGOs becoming sustainable entrepreneurs and business partners.

Greenpeace and partners honored at Harvard in 2011

On May 4, 2011, Greenpeace Solutions Director Amy Larkin joined high-level officials of Coca-Cola, PepsiCo, McDonald's, Unilever, and the United Nations Environment Programme (UNEP) at Harvard's J.F. Kennedy School of Government to receive the prestigious Roy Family Award for Environmental Partnership for their collaboration called *Refrigerants, Naturally!* The Roy Award honors an outstanding public-private partnership that benefits the environment through creative initiatives, and Greenpeace's unconventional cross-sector social partnership was recognized for championing the replacement of the environmentally-destructive fluorinated gases (called "F-gases") with "natural refrigerants" in commercial refrigeration applications (hydrocarbons, ammonia, carbon dioxide, water, and air[1] – what Greenpeace calls the "gentle five" that have zero or negligible impact on ozone depletion and climate change).

Ellen Roy, a member of the family that established the award stated at the ceremony, "Greenpeace may have been the instigator [for Refrigerants, Naturally!], but the coalition of public and private partnership was essential" (Harvard Kennedy School press release, 2011). Larkin added, "We and they have stayed at the table and have had results." Larkin further explained Greenpeace's work in Refrigerants, Naturally! in her blog:

> Why are we working so closely with these corporations? Because corporations now govern how we live, where we live, what we eat, wear, and desire ... and also whether or not our natural world retains its bounty, its beauty, and it beneficence. For corporations, the greenest possible practices ensure a safer and more secure business environment as well. Environmental actions are now inextricably bound to supply chain, market share and brand loyalty, and businesses either commit to eliminate their pollution or expose themselves to regulatory risk, unpredictable costs, potential liability and Greenpeace scrutiny.
>
> *(Larkin, 2011)*

By December 14, 2011, Greenpeace and Refrigerants, Naturally! celebrated yet another milestone. After many years of lobbying and at the request of Greenpeace's ally, Unilever's Ben and Jerry's, and General Electric (who had been working independent of Greenpeace) – the US Environmental Protection Agency finally approved three hydrocarbon gases (propane, isobutane, and a chemical known as R-441A) as acceptable refrigerants to replace F-gases throughout the United States in household and small commercial refrigerators and freezers (US Environmental Protection Agency news release, 2011b). The approved use of these natural refrigerants was estimated to reduce greenhouse gas emissions by 600,000 metric tons by 2020. While an important development, work still needed to be done to convince appliance manufacturers to adopt the sustainable technology, and Greenpeace was determined to further drive the development of that market, a venture it initiated over two decades earlier.

The beginning – Greenpeace Germany as "accidental" sustainable entrepreneur

Wolfgang Lohbeck, head of the Atmosphere Campaign at Greenpeace Germany in the early 1990s, is widely recognized as the "father" of natural refrigerants via his creation of "Greenfreeze" refrigerators. His pioneering corporate collaboration, technology advocacy, and market development have now become the hallmarks of Greenpeace's "Solutions" advocacy. In a 2009 interview, Lohbeck declared, "Greenfreeze has been my most successful project in my entire working life – by far" (*Hydrocarbons21.com,* 2009). As of this writing, he continues working as a campaigner for Greenpeace Germany and remains an avid advocate of Greenfreeze and other natural refrigerants.

The Greenfreeze story began in 1989 in Germany, when scientists of the Dortmund Institute of Hygiene were seeking an environmentally-responsible refrigerator for their lab (Stafford et al., 2003). Freon and other chlorofluorocarbons (CFCs), the most common commercial refrigerants at the time, posed significant environmental risks. Specifically, CFC leakages from refrigerators and from the mishandling of CFCs during refrigerator servicing depleted the earth's life-protecting ozone shield. Consequently, CFCs were scheduled to be phased out by 1995 in industrialized countries under the globally-binding Montreal Protocol to Control Ozone Depleting Substances.

The chemical industry's proposed replacements for CFCs, however – hydrofluorocarbons (HFCs) and hydrochlorofluorocarbons (HCFCs) – were not environmentally benign. Although the former were ozone-safe, the latter contributed to ozone depletion, and both were believed to contribute to climate change, making them "unsustainable" options for the Dortmund Institute. Looping into past refrigeration technologies, the Dortmund scientists resurrected a butane-propane mix of natural hydrocarbon refrigerants used in the 1930s before the advent of CFCs. The technology was ozone-safe, patent-free (because the gases were common and widely available), and its effect on climate change was negligible, eventually winning the Institute an environmental award.

Meanwhile, Greenpeace Germany campaigner, Wolfgang Lohbeck, was contemplating strategies for the NGO's campaign against ozone depletion and climate change. Lohbeck knew that his NGO could not just say "no" to HFCs and HCFCs when confronting chemical industry representatives and policymakers. Rather, Greenpeace Germany had to show that there were viable ozone- and climate-safe alternatives. Upon learning about the Dortmund scientists' butane-propane mix, Lohbeck studied the technology and became convinced of its feasibility. Dubbing the refrigerant, "Greenfreeze," Lohbeck began championing the technology among German refrigerator manufacturers as the better option to replace CFCs.

Manufacturers, however, scoffed at the idea. Because Greenfreeze consisted of hydrocarbon gases, it was perceived to be unacceptably flammable, even though modern refrigeration advances had virtually eliminated the risk. Moreover, Greenfreeze was incompatible with the standard compressors available from suppliers, and none of the appliance manufacturers made their own compressors. The only exception to this was a former East German manufacturer, DKK Scharfenstein, later renamed Foron Household Appliances.

Verging on bankruptcy due to state-run obsolescence and new western competition after German reunification, Foron was controlled by the German privatization agency, the Treuhand, which was seeking to liquidate the former East German factory's assets. If investors could not be secured, Foron would be dissolved. With Foron's employees eager to protect their jobs, the company agreed to work with Lohbeck's hydrocarbon technology ideas as a last resort (Stafford and Hartman 2001).

In spring 1992, Greenpeace Germany forged a first-of-its-kind partnership with Foron and the Dortmund Institute. Greenpeace paid Foron 27,000 Deutschmarks to produce ten prototype Greenfreeze refrigerators that Lohbeck could exhibit at trade shows to demonstrate the technology's viability. On July 13, however, Lohbeck's prototype plans were threatened when the Treuhand announced that Foron would be dissolved after a failed acquisition offer from Bosch-Siemens. Racing to outwit the Treuhand, Lohbeck and Foron managers announced a press conference for July 16 to display its first Greenfreeze appliances, which were produced virtually overnight. By facsimile, the Treuhand demanded a halt to the press conference. The order was ignored. The Treuhand flew its agents in for a showdown. A debate ensued before the media, resulting in the Treuhand backing down to allow Foron to continue operations and its work with Greenpeace Germany. Eventually, the Treuhand would invest 5 million Deutschmarks in the factory (Stafford and Hartman, 2001).

News of Lohbeck's product development partnership with Foron and the NGO's face-off with the Treuhand to defend the ailing Foron factory sparked a firestorm of controversy throughout Greenpeace's other European offices, including at Greenpeace International based in Amsterdam. Some Greenpeace campaigners and supporters viewed working with Foron as a corporate "sell out." Indeed, Foron was suffering from financial challenges, operational inefficiencies, and environmental problems that placed Greenpeace's credibility as an environmental "attack dog" at significant risk (Stafford *et al.*, 2000).

Lohbeck's rogue moves also derailed Greenpeace International's primary objectives to criticize chemical producers and promote the ozone-depleting effects of CFCs and HCFCs. Lohbeck changed the course of the campaign onto an uncharted path toward backing an ailing company, working to save factory worker jobs, co-producing a commercial product to address the emerging issue of climate change, and forging a market for the product. Playing the role of "accidental" business entrepreneur, Lohbeck was convinced that his unorthodox strategy of promoting an environmentally-preferable technology as a product "solution" and cultivating a market for it could subvert the chemical lobby and sway users.

Greenpeace Germany then turned its grassroots campaign toward selling Foron's refrigerators – procuring advance orders. By appealing to Greenpeace members and supporters, the NGO helped Foron receive over 70,000 orders within three months (Stafford *et al.*, 2003). Alarmed German appliance and chemical companies reacted venomously, denouncing Greenfreeze as "an unacceptable danger" and a "potential bomb" in the kitchen (Vidal, 1992). Ironically, the negative response from industry further promoted Foron's unique refrigerators, and appliance dealers expressed interest. Greenpeace's advocacy also captured the attention of scientific and government groups who tested Greenfreeze refrigerators for product safety, eventually aligning with Foron. In December 1992, Greenfreeze was certified with the Gepruefte Sicherheit (GS) mark by the German Safety Standards Authority, and in February 1993, it earned the prestigious "Blue Angel" ecolabel, becoming the first refrigerator so recognized. Greenpeace's endorsement of the product carried significant clout among consumers.

By March 1993, Foron's first Greenfreeze "Clean Coolers" were rolling off the assembly line. Surprisingly, other major German manufacturers who had bitterly opposed Greenpeace's hydrocarbon technology announced the introduction of their own Greenfreeze appliances and by 1994, all German manufacturers declared that they would abandon HFCs for Greenfreeze, fulfilling Lohbeck's principal objective. Lohbeck's unorthodox entrepreneurial strategy of partnering with an appliance manufacturer to demonstrate the feasibility of Greenfreeze by launching a new refrigerator to convince others in the industry, helped transform Germany's refrigerator industry from the inside out. Lohbeck's victory turned "a heresy to a wisdom" as one Greenpeace insider observed (Stafford and Hartman, 2001), and Greenpeace campaigners sought to build on Lohbeck's philosophy and new-found strategy to promote Greenfreeze worldwide.

In 1994, Lohbeck reflected on his Greenfreeze experience and explained to a reporter that his partnership with Foron, technology advocacy, and market development initiatives were largely directed by a set of auspicious happenstances:

> it wasn't all planned the way it turned out. It was a piece of luck that this firm [Foron] was there, that it was up to its neck in troubles, that Germany reunified … that [Foron] still had its own compressor production and could develop the propane-butane prototype on its own. It was a piece of luck that we could win one company over to our way of thinking and that this firm could turn facts quickly into marketable realities.
>
> (Beste, 1994: 29)

While luck did seem to play a role, Lohbeck's entrepreneurial initiatives to partner with a company to demonstrate the technical and commercial viability of a technology while also engaging in Greenpeace's traditional lobbying and confrontational tactics against both industry and government bodies would emerge as the central elements of what would become trademarks of Greenpeace's "solutions" campaign.

The sustainable entrepreneurship process: a framework for NGOs

Greenpeace Germany's initial venture in business collaboration and market development demonstrates how the environmental NGO leveraged its comprehensive environmental knowledge, policy and government engagement know-how, and expedient business-oriented actions to enact sustainable solutions into the marketplace. The principal task of sustainable entrepreneurs is to determine "what needs to be sustained" (e.g. preservation of nature, sources of life support, and communities) and "what needs to be developed" (e.g. innovations and business models that provide economic and social gains to other groups in society) (Shepherd and Patzelt, 2011). In short, Greenpeace Germany recognized what needed to be sustained (protecting the atmosphere from leaking F-gases) and what needed to be developed (an environmentally-benign refrigerant alternative and a marketing plan to deploy it widely into the marketplace).

Drawing from the emerging sustainable entrepreneurship literature and Greenpeace's initial experiences in developing and promoting Greenfreeze in

Germany, we propose that the sustainable entrepreneurship process for environmental NGOs entails three steps:

Step 1: *Recognition of environmental problems and their solutions* (Shepherd and Patzelt, 2011).
Step 2: *Evaluation of the market feasibility and decision to enact those solutions* (Shepherd and Patzelt, 2011); and
Step 3: *Implementation of those solutions.*

Successful navigation of these three steps warrants environmental NGOs to undertake four more-specialized entrepreneurial roles, often simultaneously, to engage market, social, and political issues that may impact the introduction and diffusion of sustainable business initiatives. These roles include:

- *Business entrepreneur* – traditionally, business-entrepreneurs are individuals or organizations that undertake innovations, finance, and business acumen in an effort to transform innovations into economic goods for economic gains for themselves (Patzelt and Shepherd, 2011). In the context of NGOs, Greenpeace has sought ways to make Greenfreeze (and other natural refrigerants) economically-viable and competitively-advantageous for their corporate partners willing to adopt the technology. As noted in the German experience, Greenpeace's willingness "to act" like a business and help the ailing Foron was the most novel and controversial of Greenpeace's initiatives.
- *Social entrepreneur* – social entrepreneurs are individuals or organizations that seek to discover, define, and exploit opportunities in order to enhance social wealth and benefits (Zahra *et al.,* 2009). While the social benefits of environmental initiatives may seem to go hand-in-hand, Shepherd and Patzelt (2011) assert that social entrepreneurship typically does not include sustaining current states of nature and sources of life support and therefore the two are distinct concepts. Additionally, critics of Greenpeace often fault the NGO for its alleged disregard of the social consequences of its environmentally-focused initiatives. For example, Greenpeace's opposition to genetically-modified plants and foods has been criticized for preventing the proliferation of "Golden Rice," a beta-carotene-enriched food that may aid developing countries socially with improved nutrition and disease prevention (Miller, 2012). By definition, sustainable entrepreneurship warrants the alignment of both economic and social benefits with the implementation of the sustainable technology or practice, and NGOs need to be mindful for how social benefits may be realized for constituents and communities.
- *Policy entrepreneur* – policy entrepreneurs are individuals or organizations that operate from outside the formal positions of government and draw on their resources of expertise, persistence, and skill to achieve certain policies or institutional changes that they favor (e.g. Weissert, 1991). Greenpeace has long engaged in political networks and lobbying to introduce institutional reforms to advance

its sustainable development goals (Rootes, 2006), and this is an important expertise that NGOs can bring to the sustainable entrepreneurship process. That is, NGOs can engage in a two-pronged strategy by (1) engaging in marketing and business strategies to promote their sustainable technologies and products as business entrepreneurs and (2) lobbying government bodies to set policies affecting industry practices, standards, rules, tax incentives, etc., that favor their advocated sustainable technologies and products as policy entrepreneurs.

• *Collaborative entrepreneur* – collaborative entrepreneurs are individuals or organizations that seize opportunities of creating value through the construction of social networks and jointly-generated ideas that emerge from the sharing of information, knowledge, and resources (Ribeiro-Soriano and Urbano, 2009). Forging partnerships may be the most important role for NGOs in the sustainable entrepreneurship process as it is often warranted to initiate other entrepreneurship roles (e.g. need to collaborate with a business to engage in product development or petitioning a government body to consider a regulatory change). The concept of collaborative entrepreneurship recognizes the fact that individuals and organizations (including businesses, government bodies, and NGOs) are resource constrained. Consequently, entrepreneurs must gain access to resources, skills, and capabilities via partnerships to initiate innovation. The concept of collaborative entrepreneur draws attention away from the popularly held conception of the "entrepreneur as an individual hero" to the more nuanced understanding that entrepreneurship and innovation often result from coalition-building and the sharing of knowledge and assets among partners. Social partnerships and coalition-building are key capabilities that NGOs have long accomplished in their advocacy. The engagement of businesses to gain product development, marketing, and distribution acumen in the marketplace extends this capability to the sustainable entrepreneurship process.

Greenpeace's initial experiences with promoting Greenfreeze in Germany illustrate our framework. The first step of NGO-initiated sustainable entrepreneurship is recognition of environmental problems and their solutions. Traditional entrepreneurs recognize and seize opportunities by being able to connect seemingly unrelated events and detect patterns that open the marketplace for new products and services (Baron and Ensley, 2006). Patzelt and Shepherd (2011) argue that sustainable entrepreneurs are those who have an expanded knowledge of the natural environment, recognize threats, and are motivated to address those threats to benefit others. Entities with environmental knowledge and a desire to help others are commonly associated with environmental NGOs. Lohbeck and Greenpeace Germany clearly recognized the threat posed by F-gases proposed by the chemical industry, and as a collaborative entrepreneur, sought out and engaged with scientists working successfully with a hydrocarbon refrigerant alternative that could serve as a viable replacement (or "solution") for those F-gases.

With regard to the second step of the sustainable entrepreneurship process, evaluating the market feasibility and decision to enact sustainable solutions, Lohbeck realized that a demonstration of Greenfreeze's feasibility among industry players was warranted and took the novel role of collaborative entrepreneur with Foron to develop demonstration models that could be showcased at refrigeration conferences. However, "a constellation of forces," as one of our informants explained to us, forced Lohbeck to move well beyond his initial plans.

When the Treuhand threatened to dissolve Foron before Lohbeck's demonstration models were produced, Lohbeck moved out of expediency toward the third step of NGO-initiated sustainable entrepreneurship of working to launch Greenfreeze refrigerators onto the market. Greenpeace Germany took on the role of policy entrepreneur by demanding the Treuhand change its course of action to allow the factory to stay open. The NGO then had to ensure Foron's continued economic viability, negotiating with Treuhand to provide financial support for the factory. As social entrepreneur, Greenpeace even sought consultants to clean up the factory's environmental hazards and adopt safer operating procedures to protect the health and welfare of factory workers and the local community. Finally, as business entrepreneur, Greenpeace acted as a "sales representative" to secure 70,000 pre-production orders for Greenfreeze appliances among Greenpeace members and supporters.

In sum, Lohbeck and Greenpeace Germany engaged in all four specialized entrepreneurial roles to forge partnerships and intervene in the market to transform the German refrigeration industry onto a more sustainable path.

The Solutions campaign: Greenpeace's "brand" of sustainable entrepreneurship

An early proponent of Lohbeck's ideas at Greenpeace UK was Corin Millias, who wrote an article for *Chemistry and Industry* in June 1994 entitled, "Greenpeace's New Solutions," to explain the environmental NGO's emerging market-development campaign philosophy as a new approach to activism. Millias recounted how Greenpeace had historically engaged in "imaginative and daring non-violent direct action" (Millias, 1994: 484) for over two decades that resulted in the ban on dumping nuclear waste at sea and a moratorium on commercial whaling, to name just a few of the NGO's past successes. "We will continue to take such actions," he continued, "Yet times change."

Millias (1994) expressed frustration that although environmental issues had become socially mainstream and accepted, industry and governments appeared to take ownership of environmental issues "only to disown them by leaving "the market" to deliver environmental protections" (p. 484). That is, he saw complicity between industry and government to only deliver partial or token environmental improvements (e.g. introduction of greenhouse-gas HFCs and HCFCs as replacement for CFCs) that preserved "tidy profits" for industry rather than deliver real sustainable solutions for a "tidy environment" (deployment of Greenfreeze and other natural refrigerants industry wide). Millias noted that if "the market" was to prescribe environmental solutions, Greenpeace would then move its direct action into the marketplace as entrepreneur and industry competitor.

As governments currently have neither the will nor the means to prevent future environmental abuse, Greenpeace has decided to take business on and play it at its own game. We have decided to intervene directly in the market by promoting real solutions for environmental problems. For some companies, this may be a dream, for others it may become a nightmare. There is still a long way to go before this game is won. But the early results are going our way.

(*Millias, 1994: 484*)

In addition to Greenpeace Germany's success with Greenfreeze, Millias provided other examples of how the NGO's Solutions campaigns had been disrupting markets and ridiculing corporations among their customers. For example, when the German magazine *Der Speigel* claimed that it was unable to print on chlorine-free paper, Greenpeace mocked the magazine by publishing and distributing a chlorine-free version of *Der Speigel* direct to subscribers. Millias concluded his article by saying, "We will intervene in the boardroom, in the control room, and in the showroom until the environment is safe and the planet is protected" (p. 484).

At the 2000 World Economic Forum in Davos, Switzerland, Greenpeace International's executive director, Thilo Bode, was invited to speak. When attendees complained about Greenpeace protestors outside the building, Bode replied, "If they were not there, I would not be here" (Houlder, 2000). By this time, Greenpeace had fully embraced the need to leverage business-oriented actions as a sustainable entrepreneur across Europe, Asia, and South America, persuading manufacturers to adopt natural refrigerants, including Whirlpool, Sanyo, Haier, and Bosch-Siemens (see Stafford and Hartman, 2001; Stafford *et al.*, 2003). To encourage the technology in developing countries, Greenpeace "open sourced" natural refrigerant technologies, literally giving the know-how to willing entrepreneurs to aid in social and economic development and to avert environmentally-destructive competing technologies from making inroads.

Greenpeace recognized, however, that establishing natural refrigerants in North America was essential, given its leadership in the appliance market and consumer demand. Regulatory and industry barriers have made North America a significantly tougher market to crack.

Breaking into the North American market

Greenpeace seized an opportunity to publicize Greenfreeze in North America with a protest against appliance maker Whirlpool at its 1994 stockholder meeting (Stafford and Hartman 2001). Whirlpool was targeted because it had won the Super-Efficient Refrigerator Program's $30 million contest, sponsored by the Natural Resources Defense Council (a prominent NGO), the US EPA, and 24 electric utilities to develop a CFC-free refrigerator that was 30 per cent more energy efficient than federal standards. Whirlpool's appliance, however, used HCFCs, and Greenpeace questioned the wisdom of "tooling up to use a technology that [was] going to be phased out" (*Ozone Depletion Network Online Today* 1994). Whirlpool dismissed Greenfreeze's flammability as too dangerous. Ironically, Whirlpool was already using Greenfreeze in Europe, and Greenpeace ridiculed the company's apparent double standard at the 1994 Appliance Manufacturers Conference and Exhibition with banners proclaiming, "Whirlpool Profits from Ozone Destruction."

The appliance and chemical industries' position on hydrocarbons was that the technology was inappropriate for large, American-style frost-free refrigerators because they incorporated small heaters, which could ignite if the coolant leaked. This was less of a concern in Europe where refrigerators were smaller and did not have freezers. Consequently, given safety concerns, Underwriter's Laboratories (UL), which is responsible for product design safety, accepted isobutane for refrigerants (and cyclopentane for producing insulation), but at only half the level allowed in Europe.

The US EPA's Significant New Alternatives Policy Program (SNAP), which regulated substitutes for CFCs and other ozone-depleting substances that were phased out under the Clean Air Act, agreed with the industry's flammability concerns and refused to approve of Greenfreeze as a replacement for F-gases in the American market. This made Greenfreeze illegal in the US (and Canada, which often followed the lead of US policy). Greenpeace perceived the safety concerns as smokescreens to protect commercial interests in North America given the successes of the technology in Europe and elsewhere. In a 2009 interview, Lohbeck asserted that the EPA appeared to be unduly influenced from chemical-producer DuPont in keeping Greenfreeze out of the US market (*Hydrocarbons21.com,* 2009).

Given that Greenfreeze did not offer appliance-makers any perceived economic advantages, none was willing to engage in the time and spend the money necessary to petition SNAP to test and approve Greenfreeze nor were they willing to invest in the resources to retool production lines for the technology. Consequently, US appliance-makers and their supply chains were content to design and produce commercial and home refrigerators using HFCs and HCFCs as replacements for CFCs in "a path of least resistance," noted one of the campaigners interviewed for this study.

In protest, Greenpeace Germany declined the EPA's 1995 Stratospheric Ozone Protection Award for its work in natural refrigerants, claiming that it could not accept the award from a government that still promoted F-gases. Greenpeace, did, however accept the United Nation's Environmental Program's Ozone Award in 1997 to further publicize the viability of natural refrigerants around the world (Stafford and Hartman 2001).

Based on interviews we conducted for this study, Greenpeace campaigners explained that given the regulatory roadblock at the US EPA, they took on a more business entrepreneurial approach in 1996 in Canada. In an attempt to replicate the Greenpeace Germany-Foron venture in Canada, Greenpeace Quebec tried to create a niche Greenfreeze market by assembling a partnership to produce small refrigerator and bar-type models for hotel rooms. The partnership included Katz Design (an industrial design company), Hydro-Quebec (the public utility), and FTQ (the province's largest labor union). Greenpeace envisioned consumer demand for the product could force the EPA and other industry players to accept the technology, as had happened earlier in Germany. The partners courted a German manufacturer to spearhead the venture. The manufacturer backed out, however, reluctant to take on the North American market alone.

Greenpeace even considered launching its own "Greenpeace" brand of refrigerators for North America, manufactured by a European partner. The idea was abandoned, however, over concerns that it could offend some of Greenpeace's other business allies who might have seen the product as a competitor. Greenpeace sought to endorse any appliance using natural refrigerants, and a Greenpeace brand might have confused customers.

By the late 1990s, little progress had been made in changing US EPA policy or developing a viable business plan to introduce natural refrigerants in North America. Half a world away, however, Greenpeace Australia was engaged in its own Solutions campaign to promote natural refrigerants in the run up for the 2000 Summer Olympic Games in Sydney. Greenpeace's savvy turns as an Olympic organizer and then Olympic protestor would help turn the tide in Australia, North America, and beyond.

Sydney's 2000 Summer Olympic Games – Greenpeace as organizer and protestor

In the early-1990s, the city of Sydney, Australia, was preparing a bid to host the 2000 Summer Olympic Games and held an open contest for architectural designs for the proposed Athletes' Village (Hartman and Stafford, 2006). In the wake of the successful Greenfreeze campaign in Germany, Greenpeace Australia seized an opportunity to act like a business and submit an anonymous proposal envisioning a bold first "Green Games" architectural concept, incorporating cutting-edge environmental technologies and best practices, including renewable energy, conservation, environmentally-responsible building materials, and natural refrigerants for foods and beverages. Of the over 100 architectural design submissions received, primarily from developers and architectural firms, Greenpeace's Green Games proposal made it into the top five!

Greenpeace was then invited to participate in the official bid proposal to be presented to the International Olympic Committee (IOC); taking on the role of policy entrepreneur, Greenpeace helped draft what ultimately became the document entitled, "Environmental Guidelines for the Olympic Games." The Green Games concept so impressed the IOC that it helped Sydney win the bid to host the 2000 Summer Olympic Games. As an official organizer, Greenpeace Australia played both watchdog and collaborator, ensuring that the Olympic Coordination Authority (OCA) adhered to its environmental promises stated in the Guidelines. The NGO issued an Olympic Report Card every 100 days, praising environmental accomplishments, noting shortcomings, and offering solutions.

By 1998, however, Greenpeace became alarmed that Sydney organizers and sponsors were not keeping their commitments to employ Greenfreeze and other natural refrigerants for food and beverage storage and air conditioning as dictated in the environmental guidelines. Only about 100 of Coca-Cola's 1800 refrigeration units at the site used natural refrigerants. Greenpeace's requests for compliance fell on deaf ears, resulting in Greenpeace filing a lawsuit with the OCA to force adherence (Zemel, 2011). The legal question centered on whether the environmental guidelines were legally binding (as Greenpeace had intended when it helped draft them) or merely discretionary, and Greenpeace worried that a prolonged court battle would drain precious time and resources.

Consequently, Greenpeace Australia moved to a different tack; the NGO would confront Olympic sponsors directly. As the official soft drink of the Sydney Olympics and a primary user of refrigeration, Coca-Cola became the primary target (Hartman and Stafford, 2006). In January 2000, Greenpeace Australia's chief executive, Ian Higgins, wrote to Coca-Cola's top executive, Douglas Daft, asking the soft drink maker to comply with the official Olympic guidelines to use natural refrigerants and volunteering to collaborate with Coca-Cola to achieve genuine environmental outcomes. Coke executives responded that their use of HFCs was in full accordance with the Montreal Protocol and that they were testing natural refrigerants in Europe.

Unhappy with Coca-Cola's response, Greenpeace released the report, *Green Olympics, Dirty Sponsors*, which exposed Cola-Cola and McDonald's use of ozone-depleting and greenhouse gas refrigerants, HFCs and HCFCs at the Sydney Games. The NGO also launched www.CokeSpotlight.org, a spoof web site that detailed the beverage maker's use of environmentally-destructive chemical refrigerants. The site presented satirical images of "Enjoy Climate Change" and "HFCoke" in Coca-Cola's famously-recognizable calligraphy along with Coca-Cola polar bears drifting on melting icebergs at sea. Greenpeace staged protests involving hapless polar bears picketing Coca-Cola to ban HFCs across Australia. Public pressure ensued.

On June 28, 2000, Coca-Cola issued an historic statement. Although it would continue to use HFCs in Sydney, it promised to stop purchasing new HFC appliances where cost-efficient alternatives were available by the 2004 Summer Olympics (Coca-Cola press release 2000). Coca-Cola also pledged to expand its research on alternative refrigerants, to require its suppliers to stop using HFCs by 2004, and to improve its overall energy efficiency by at least 40 per cent by 2010.

Coca-Cola's promises extended beyond what Greenpeace Australia had initially envisioned around the Olympic Games and the NGO declared a victory, congratulating Coca-Cola for its environmental actions in the media and over the Internet. The implication was that Coca-Cola's extensive bottling network and distributors would switch to natural refrigerants, creating significant global demand for change in commercial refrigeration.

A campaigner interviewed for this study said that Coca-Cola executives understood that Greenpeace would keep a close watch to hold the beverage-maker to its promises, and Greenpeace offered its assistance, research, and international network of experts and scientists. In short, Greenpeace's confrontation resulted in collaboration, and eventually Unilever and McDonald's declared that they, too, would join to reduce their dependence on HFC refrigerants. In sum, Greenpeace's engagement with the Sydney Olympics and protest against Olympic sponsors marked a turning point in Greenpeace's Solutions campaign to eliminate F-gases in refrigeration.

Refrigerants, Naturally!

On June 22, 2004, Coca-Cola, Unilever, and McDonald's joined Greenpeace and the United Nations Programme for the Environment at a conference entitled, "Refrigerants, Naturally!," in Brussels to bring together representatives from the food and drink industries, their supply chains, international, and non-government organizations to discuss HFC-free refrigeration solutions. At the conference, Unilever announced that from 2005 onwards, the company would only buy HFC-free refrigeration units, and some 14,000 units had already been put into operation (*Europe Environment,* 2004). McDonald's declared it would transform approximately 30,000 restaurants to convert to alternative refrigerants for air conditioning systems, cold chambers, and other systems for drinks and salads. And Coca-Cola was converting to HFC-free refrigeration for millions of drink distributors worldwide.

All agreed to continue working together, and Refrigerants, Naturally! emerged as the first corporate alliance with the explicit goal of replacing HFC technology in favor of natural refrigerants. Energy efficiency also became a key partnership objective given that refrigeration consumed massive amounts of electricity generated from the burning of fossil fuels, another significant contributor to climate change. As an officially-recognized Partnership for Sustainable Development by the United Nations Commission on Sustainable Development, Refrigerants, Naturally!'s activities have involved regular meetings to share information and technical advances and outreach to suppliers, policymakers, and related companies (Ederberg and Shende 2008).

In 2005, Coca-Cola, McDonald's, and Unilever were awarded the US EPA's Climate Protection Award at a ceremony in Washington, D.C., for their joint efforts. Lauding the achievement, Greenpeace USA's executive director, John Passacantando said of the three corporate partners, "Their commitment shows that some US corporations understand the urgency of global warming and are taking action now... We challenge other companies to follow their lead" (PR Newswire, 2005). In 2006, Carlsberg, IKEA, and PepsiCo Company joined the partnership.

Aside from testing and deploying natural refrigerants worldwide, the partners recognized two principal political and market barriers facing the North American market:

1   The U.S EPA's SNAP program still needed to approve hydrocarbons as legally-acceptable refrigerants to replace CFCs under the Clean Air Act in the United States (and Canada, which often followed US policy).
2   The business case for switching to natural refrigerants needed to be developed for independently-owned food and beverage distributors and cooler cabinet manufacturers. The cost of HFC-free units was about 25 per cent more than HFC appliances, and without significant demand, cooler manufacturers saw little

economic or competitive advantage for re-tooling production lines to HFC-free technologies (Simons, 2008).

"We have the technology, and we know it works," observed Coca-Cola CEO E. Neville Isdell, "The problem is the economic logic doesn't hang together" (Gunther, 2008). Clearly, encouraging other corporations to join Refrigerants, Naturally! was necessary to increase market pressure on suppliers to go HFC-free and decrease the production costs due to economies of scale.

As a policy entrepreneur to encourage the SNAP program's approval of hydro-carbon refrigerants, Greenpeace needed a corporate partner committed to using the technology in the United States. Without a business willing to use the technology, SNAP would not consider Greenpeace's request. Unilever's Ben and Jerry's Home-made Ice Cream, which had worked with Greenpeace before in other environmental initiatives, came forward and petitioned the EPA to allow testing of Greenfreeze freezer cabinets at stores in Washington D.C., Boston, and it its home state of Vermont. Employing state-of-the-art compressors, high efficiency fans, and LEDs, Ben and Jerry's point-of-sale cabinets debuted in September 2008. Though not a part of Refrigerants, Naturally!, General Electric also petitioned the SNAP program about the same time for its intent to use the hydrocarbon isobutane for its premium-grade Monogram-branded household refrigerators that it hoped to launch in 2010 (Tamura, 2010).

To pressure suppliers and expand the scale of HFC-free cooler manufacturing worldwide, Coca-Cola issued a statement in December 2009 that the company was requiring that all of its new vending machines and coolers be HFC-free by 2015, and a major supplier had announced its intention to build a carbon dioxide compressor production facility in order to meet the beverage maker's HFC-free refrigeration needs (*Environmental Leader,* 2009; Westervelt, 2009). Coca-Cola was anxious for others to follow its lead and saw a new opportunity.

Enter Consumer Goods Forum

Coca-Cola executives were members of the Consumer Goods Forum (CGF), a global network of CEOs and senior managers of hundreds of major consumer goods companies and stakeholders that discussed strategic issues facing the industry, including sustainability. Coca-Cola Vice President, Jeff Seabright, who co-chaired CGF's Sustainable Refrigeration Committee, asked Greenpeace Solutions Director, Amy Larkin, to give the keynote speech at the CGF's Sustainable Refrigeration Summit in October 2010. Larkin was encouraged to make a "Greenpeace-style" ask of CGF members.

Larkin challenged the CGF to follow Coca-Cola's lead and made "this 'crazy' objective to eliminate HFCs for 2015," noted a campaigner interviewed for this study. "And they said yes!" The following month, the CGF announced its members' commitment to begin phasing out HFCs as of 2015 and replacing them with non-HFC alternatives (*PR Newswire,* 2010). Greenpeace, with the help of Coca-Cola, now had assembled the largest coalition ever, including many of the world's biggest and most-reputable beverage, food, and consumer goods companies, committed to eliminating F-gases in their refrigeration. Our Greenpeace informant continued:

> That's 400 companies that have resolved to eliminate HFCs ... [Greenpeace has] graduated to such a wholesale impact in working with companies. The jury is still out about what the result will be, but the potential for this work is now so high-impact that it takes most of our resources ... This is where market mechanisms come in. The large companies are making big changes first, which encourages the suppliers to move to HFC-free equipment and also for the development of the maintenance and service infrastructure. This infrastructure is the biggest obstacle for fast transition.

Procuring the CGF's commitment to eliminate F-gases from members' operations and distribution systems marked a significant achievement, but hurdles remained for advancing natural refrigerants across North America.

North America's market in 2012

In December, 2011, the US EPA's SNAP approved three hydrocarbon refrigerants in the US as feasible replacements for CFCs in household and small commercial stand-alone refrigerators and freezers. Greenpeace and Refrigerants, Naturally! saw this approval as an important step for the lagging North American market. The approval, however, was not the breakthrough the partners sought as key barriers remained:

- SNAP limited the amount of hydrocarbon charges in home appliances to 57 grams and in commercial applications to 150 grams. These maximum charge levels were significantly lower than those allowed and proven safe in Japan, Europe, and Australia. Consequently, advocates for hydrocarbon refrigerants were not optimistic about their immediate expanded use in North America.
- Appliance makers were still resistant to hydrocarbons due to on-going concerns over flammability.
- Transition costs (e.g. re-training, re-design of appliances, use of compressors suited to hydrocarbons) and resistance to change without an immediate economic or competitive pay-off remained.
- Development of a service infrastructure to support and maintain hydrocarbon refrigeration units was needed.
- Competing refrigeration chemicals that are not environmentally-benign were more attractive to industry.

The EPA had established recommendations for the safe handling, labeling, and use of hydrocarbons, but with little competitive incentive or government mandate, US transition to hydrocarbons was destined to be slow and incremental. End consumers were unlikely to demand hydrocarbons in their appliances, but growing demand in industrial markets for hydrocarbons and other natural refrigerants via the Consumer Goods Forum could spur change.

A significant factor weighing in favor for hydrocarbons was their proven energy efficiency over HFCs (e.g. Van Gerwen *et al.*, 2008), and this provided an angle for Greenpeace to promote broader use. As one campaigner we interviewed observed:

> This adds to our story. Hydrocarbons are more efficient and have lower operating costs. Lower energy emissions – less coal to burn to keep your beer cold … companies have told us that there's at least a 10 per cent efficiency [using hydrocarbons]. It was easy to get the Energy Star rating [for refrigerators], but the next 10 per cent is going to be that much harder.

Another Greenpeace campaigner added:

> What Greenpeace can do is advocate with the regulators [e.g. EPA's Energy Star program] to push forward tough standards especially when technologies exist to make those standards easy to deploy [e.g. hydrocarbons].

Greenpeace perceives that if increased energy efficiency was demanded by consumers or if EPA's Energy Star standards became more restrictive, European and Chinese appliance imports already using natural refrigerants could gain a competitive advantage over US manufacturers, compelling US manufacturers to follow suit, but come late to the market.

Aside from hydrocarbons, carbon dioxide in commercial applications is also making inroads in North America. Several supermarkets have been experimenting with carbon dioxide, most prominently Sobeys of Nova Scotia, Canada, which plans to install only carbon dioxide systems in new corporate-owned stores and retrofit all their existing stores within the next 15 years; franchised stores are not obligated to switch, though so far, they have all accepted it (Garry, 2012).

One of the barriers facing US implementation of carbon dioxide has been the absence of UL (Underwriters Laboratories) approval for appropriate high-pressure compressors required by carbon dioxide refrigerants, but authorization is expected soon at the request of at least two manufacturers (Garry, 2012). Another issue is energy use. While energy efficiency is well-documented for carbon dioxide units in moderate climates, such as in Canada where Sobeys operates, the question remains whether such efficiencies can be duplicated in warmer climates farther south. Hence, more research is needed.

Finally, the most threatening issue facing North America is the patented fourth-generation F-gases, Hydrofluoroolefins (HFOs) now being promoted by DuPont and Honeywell. A campaigner explained:

> It is basically a "Trojan horse" in that although it is a low GWP [global warming potential], it is terribly toxic in the beginning and at the end of its

> life … There is a large group of people interested in moving to a new technology with a low GWP, but the big money players are pushing an alternative that they can continue to patent, and it is mucking up the work! … In a cradle-to-grave sense, they're horrifying!

Greenpeace has long believed that the chemical industry wants to continue their refrigeration chemical supply businesses. The problem with HFOs is that they produce toxic by-products in their production and decomposition, including trifluoroacetic acid, which in high concentrations is toxic to aquatic ecosystems (Boutonnet *et al.*, 1999). "No one is connecting the dots [with HFOs]," added one of our Greenpeace informants, and Greenpeace is working to engage the EPA and its business partners about the issue.

HFOs' advantage for manufacturers and parts suppliers, however, is that the new F-gases require minimal changes to existing compressors and other components. Hydrocarbons and other natural refrigerants require more significant changes in the supply chain. "Untangling that [supply chain] is the problem," another campaigner added:

> you're not just talking about a refrigerator. There are components – a system of components – that come from different companies. And essentially in refrigerators or air conditioners, [the component suppliers follow] the path of least resistance. Whatever [technology] they will switch to, it needs to be as little trouble as possible – same compressors, same components.

Greenpeace continues seeking opportunities to employ market and policy pressures to encourage adoption of natural refrigerants. The impact of the Consumer Goods Forum is expected to influence North America's appliance industry by mid-decade. In the meantime, Greenpeace seeks to subvert HFOs amongst its business and policy networks, lobby the US EPA to strengthen Energy Star efficiency standards to encourage the use of more-efficient Greenfreeze and other hydrocarbons, and lower the transition and service costs for companies and supply chain manufacturers to switch from HFC-based components to ones amenable for natural refrigerants through partnerships and information exchanges.

NGO-initiated sustainable entrepreneurship and cross-sector social partnerships

Sustainable entrepreneurship is an emerging concept defined as "the discovery, creation, and exploitation of opportunities to create future goods and services that sustain the natural and/or communal environment and provide development gain for others" (Patzelt and Shepherd, 2011: 632). It warrants the leveraging of innovations, finance, and business acumen to transform environmentally-protective innovations into both economic and non-economic (social) gains that will benefit other groups beyond the individual or business. The task of sustainable entrepreneurs is to determine "what needs to be sustained" (e.g. preservation of nature, sources of life support, and communities) and "what needs to be developed" (e.g. innovations and business models that provide economic and social gains to other groups in society) to legitimize and establish environmentally-sustainable innovations and practices into the marketplace (Shepherd and Patzelt, 2011). In short, environmentally-sustainable technologies, products, and practices must provide both economic and social gains to relevant market players and constituents to be accepted and adopted widely in society.

Sustainable entrepreneurship has been conceived primarily as an activity for environmentally-aware individuals and businesses for profit (e.g. Shepherd and Patzelt, 2011; Patzelt and Shepherd, 2011). However, as evidenced by Greenpeace's market interventions to promote natural refrigerants worldwide, we assert that environmental NGOs may be particularly well-positioned to engage in such ventures for the economic and social gain of others given their existing environmental knowledge, lobbying acumen, and partnership experience in their conventional advocacy and confrontational functions in society. We've extended the concept of sustainable entrepreneurship into the context of environmental NGOs, proposing a framework and illustrating it via an overview of Greenpeace's ongoing Solutions campaign to introduce and diffuse natural refrigerants, particularly in North America.

Specifically, we assert that the sustainable entrepreneurship process for NGOs entails three steps: (1) recognition of environmental problems and their solutions; (2) evaluation of market feasibility and decision to enact those solutions; and (3) implementation of those solutions. NGOs need to engage in four more-specialized entrepreneurial functions to navigate that process, including business entrepreneur, social entrepreneur, policy entrepreneur, and collaborative entrepreneur. *Our analysis indicates that the role of collaborative entrepreneur to engage businesses, associations, scientists and other entities in cross-sector social partnerships is the foundation of the sustainable entrepreneurship process for NGOs to gain necessary technical expertise, business acumen, and credibility in the marketplace.*

"Connecting the dots." The first step of NGO-initiated sustainable entrepreneurship is recognition of environmental problems and their solutions (e.g. Shepherd and Patzelt, 2011). Environmental NGOs have a long tradition of recognizing and publicizing environmental issues and their causes (e.g. the impact of HFCs and HCFCs on climate change). As one campaigner we interviewed stated, Greenpeace sees its primary value in society for comprehensively "connecting the dots" regarding environmental problems:

> no one is connecting the dots [in government and business] ... Some of it is inertia. Different regulators have different sets of rules so that leads to no one connecting the dots ... the EPA's concern is Clean Air Act and GWP [global warming potential]. For manufacturers? It [sustainability] is not in their purview... nobody [else] is connecting the dots.

Consequently, in its traditional watchdog role in society, Greenpeace (and other NGOs) have taken on the task of monitoring the long-term environmental

consequences of business practices and government policies and have used confrontation and public awareness to draw attention to potential threats.

The innovation that Greenpeace initiated under Wolfgang Lohbeck in Germany
in the early 1990s was stepping beyond NGOs' traditional watchdog role, recognizing
that NGOs could not just say "no" to unsustainable business actions and government
policies. Rather, they must identify viable alternatives and solutions to environmentally-destructive practices so that businesses may continue to function to make
profits and create a livelihood for their employees and stockholders. Consequently,
taking on the role of collaborative entrepreneur for engaging the scientific and
technology communities for identifying those solutions becomes critical for the first
step of the sustainable entrepreneurship process. For Lohbeck, that entailed searching
for viable alternative refrigerant technologies and ultimately working with Dortmund
Institute scientists for the butane-propane mix they had developed, which became the
basis of Greenfreeze. Further collaborative efforts with refrigeration technical experts
resulted, eventually, in the identification of other natural refrigerants, giving
Greenpeace a portfolio of environmentally-preferable refrigerant options for its
sustainable entrepreneurship efforts around the world and in North America. In short,
proactive efforts to collaborate with the scientific and technical communities gave
Greenpeace the knowledge and credibility in the field of refrigeration.

"You're not just talking about a refrigerator." The second step of NGO-initiated
sustainable entrepreneurship is evaluating the market feasibility of a sustainable
technology or practice and deciding to enact those solutions (e.g. Shepherd and
Patzelt, 2011). In evaluating a market, NGOs need to consider a myriad of industry
issues, including the benefits and competitive positions of existing environmentally-destructive technologies and products vis-à-vis sustainable alternatives,
supply chains, potential commercial buyers and consumers and how they make
buying decisions, regulatory policies governing the industry, needed product
certifications, existing infrastructure, and the nature of how the industry operates
(see Stafford *et al.*, 2003).

Understanding the industry's market structure may then uncover leverage points
on how to disrupt it. "You're not just talking about a refrigerator," explained one of
our informants,

> there are components – a system of components – that come from different
> companies ... if there is a new type of refrigerant that involves new types of
> pressure that needs a new compressor, all those parties have to agree, and
> that's the path forward. So untangling that. Are those compressors UL
> certified? Are they approved for US use? Are they compatible with our
> electric system? All of these things have come up, and all of them can become
> road blocks without a strong profit motive for even the compressor maker to
> step ahead and make a new thing.

Collaboration facilitates an NGO's evaluation of the commercial feasibility of
sustainable technologies and its willingness to intervene in the marketplace. In

Germany, Lohbeck discovered that incompatible compressors in the supply chain were critical barriers facing Greenfreeze. Refrigerator manufacturers outsourced their compressors, and even if manufacturers wanted to try Greenfreeze, none of the existing compressors on the market could accommodate the butane-propane mix developed by the Dortmund Institute. Lohbeck engaged in collaborative entrepreneurship with Foron, an ailing East German appliance factory, that still made its own compressors and was willing to adapt them to demonstrate the alternative refrigerant's market feasibility.

Greenpeace Germany's decision to intervene in the market to sell Greenfreeze appliances was clearly the result of happenstance. When the Treuhand threatened to close down Foron before the Greenfreeze prototypes could be produced, it forced Lohbeck and Greenpeace Germany to defend and keep the factory open by helping to procure 70,000 pre-production orders for Foron's Greenfreeze refrigerators. These actions sent important market signals to Germany's refrigerator industry that not only could Greenfreeze appliances be produced but that there was significant market demand for them as well. This could not have happened, nonetheless, without the NGO's proactive collaborative engagement with Foron and the Treuhand.

In the U.S., the principal barrier facing Greenfreeze has been the protracted process to procure its regulatory authorization as a replacement for CFCs as an alternative to HFCs and HCFCs. Until approval in December 2011, there was no feasible market for Greenfreeze in the US. To open that market, Greenpeace worked with Ben and Jerry's Homemade Ice Cream to petition the US EPA SNAP program to allow testing of Greenfreeze in limited retail settings. Greenpeace's policy entrepreneurial activities to open the US to Greenfreeze were contingent on its collaborative ties with Ben and Jerry's.

"What's Greenpeace doing here?" Clearly, the third step of NGO-initiated sustainable entrepreneurship – market implementation – warrants the proactive collaborative entrepreneurship of businesses to encourage their willingness to adopt sustainable technologies and practices and to leverage their credibility, networks, and market access to facilitate market diffusion.

Although Greenpeace has been engaging in market intervention around the world for over the past two decades, according to one of our informants, a common question raised at industry, technical, and policy meetings in the US is "What's Greenpeace doing here?" Greenpeace campaigners' presence at those meetings, at the request of Coca-Cola or Ben and Jerry's managers, has given Greenpeace the necessary credibility to have a voice among representatives of industrial and government interests (e.g. in Greenpeace's advocacy of natural refrigerants as a replacement for F-gases in US EPA SNAP committee meetings). Sustainability needs a voice in those meetings, continues our informant, and "we have to be the self-interest on behalf of the better solution."

While confrontation in Sydney forced Coca-Cola to take Greenpeace's position on F-gas refrigerants seriously, over the years, the NGO's evolving social partnership work with Coca-Cola has been pivotal. Initially, Coca-Cola opened the opportunity for natural refrigerants to diffuse across its distribution network of bottlers and suppliers. Greenpeace's relationship with Coca-Cola progressed into the partnership of Refrigerants Naturally! and then opened access with the Consumer Goods Forum, whose members are committed to begin eliminating F-gas refrigerants in 2015. As one of our Greenpeace informants added, "Coca-Cola is not only working with us, *they* (Coca-Cola's environmental managers and executives) are the ones (leading the cause of natural refrigerants). We're on speed-dial with them …"

Coca-Cola's motivation to work with Greenpeace and take the corporate lead for eliminating F-gases in the world appears to be two-fold continued our informant,

> Coke decided they wanted to do this by 2015, and the more others do it (adopt natural refrigerants), the cheaper it is for Coke in the supply chain (to use natural refrigerants). That's one incentive – a real one! This would bring about economies of scale, including service and maintenance infrastructure. That's number one. And number two, Muhtar Kent (Coca-Cola's chief executive officer) wants to be the "Green Knight." … I don't doubt for a minute that he wants his company to help change the world in this way. He's got this amazing staff. He's not only pushing them, he's liberating them to do it! … Kent is introducing Coke to a whole new set of new consumers in the developing world, and he would like them to be happy, so the (Coca-Cola) brand and position needs to be positive … So they're pretty serious.

It is remarkable to hear a Greenpeace campaigner talk so positively about a corporation, its chief executive, and his staff. Clearly, Coca-Cola's progressive outlook on sustainability and its willingness to work with Greenpeace may have been serendipitous. Nevertheless, it reflects the impact a single corporation (or a single individual with regard to CEO Muhtar Kent) can have.

The implication for NGO-initiated sustainable entrepreneurship is that engaging in collaborative ties with corporations, especially progressive ones concerned about their global brand image, opens opportunities for NGOs to establish market credibility, engage with other corporations and their supply chains, and partake in policy and regulatory forums to enact change. In sum, collaborative entrepreneurship with business has been instrumental in Greenpeace's efforts to work as a sustainable entrepreneur to enact business initiatives, promote social gains, and institute policy changes in the marketplace.

Conclusion

Over two decades ago, Greenpeace Germany's entrepreneurial actions to pioneer and market an ozone- and climate-safe refrigerator in partnership with Foron sparked a firestorm of controversy. The NGO's leveraging of corporate collaboration with traditional confrontation to intervene in the marketplace, however, encouraged the German refrigeration market to adopt Greenfreeze as a replacement for CFCs, turning a "heresy into a wisdom." The lessons from that experience formed the basis of Greenpeace's "Solutions" campaign, and over the years, the Solutions campaign to eliminate F-gases from the world has helped to sell over 650 million Greenfreeze refrigerators worldwide from leading major manufacturers, including Bosch, Haier, Panasonic, LG, Miele, Electrolux, Whirlpool, and Siemens (see also Davies, 2011). Approximately 40 per cent of global household refrigerator production now employs hydrocarbons instead of F-gases.

We argue that Greenpeace's Solutions campaign has been a prototype of NGO-initiated sustainable entrepreneurship, and our proposed framework suggests how NGOs may help steer industries onto more sustainable paths. Given that sustainable entrepreneurs must determine "what needs to be sustained" (e.g. sustaining the earth's climate by eliminating F-gas refrigerants) and "what needs to be developed" to achieve that goal (replacement of F-gases with natural refrigerants that have a zero- or negligible-impact on the climate), environmental NGOs may be well-positioned to engage in sustainable entrepreneurship given their environmental knowledge, public awareness skills, and experience with engaging in partnerships and lobbying.

The new skill set for NGOs centers on procuring sufficient business acumen to think and act like businesses to analyze markets, develop sustainable technologies and products, and help wage competitive strategies against existing environmentally-destruction technologies and products. NGO-initiated sustainable entrepreneurship does raise some interesting questions: How does sustainable entrepreneurship align with NGOs' traditional advocacy and public awareness campaigns? Does partnering with "junk food" companies such as Coca-Cola and Ben and Jerry's tarnish NGOs' social credibility? Does helping businesses make a profit or build a competitive advantage from sustainable technologies and practices hurt NGOs' social credibility? (Stafford and Hartman, 1996; Hartman and Stafford, 1998). These are questions that warrant further investigation and consideration if NGO-initiated sustainable entrepreneurship, such as Greenpeace's Solutions Campaigns, are to proliferate and help steer industries onto a more sustainable path in the twenty-first century.

Acknowledgements

The authors thank Amy Larkin, Paula Tejon, Wolo Lohbeck, Janos Mate, Kert Davies, and Sultan Latif for their fact checking and comments on an earlier draft of this case analysis.

Questions for reflection

1   What skills and resources do environmental non-government organizations (NGOs), such as Greenpeace, bring to the process of sustainable entrepreneurship?
2   What role does engaging in cross-sector social partnerships play in NGO-initiated sustainable entrepreneurship?

3   What challenges do environmental NGOs, such as Greenpeace who have established "watch dog" roles in society, have to overcome to engage in sustainable entrepreneurship and build trust with business partners?

4   How does sustainable entrepreneurship impact cross-sector social partnerships in terms of achieving economic, social, and environmental gains?

Note

1   Although carbon dioxide is a greenhouse gas and ammonia is a synthetic hazardous substance, Greenpeace's analysis indicates that these substances are "natural" and environmentally-preferable to CFCs, HCFCs, and HFCs. Carbon dioxide, for example, has no impact on ozone depletion and has a negligible impact on climate change when used in closed-cycle refrigeration systems. A Greenpeace fact sheet asserts that typically a car emits five tons of carbon dioxide per year, whereas a refrigerator charged with carbon dioxide may leak only 300 grams over a ten-year period (Carbajal, no publication date). Likewise, ammonia has zero impact on ozone depletion and climate change. It occurs in nature's material cycles and has proven safe for industrial refrigeration uses, including food processing and building air conditioning.

References

Baron, R.A. and Ensley, M.D. (2006) "Opportunity Recognition as the Detection of Meaningful Patterns: Evidence from Comparisons of Novice and Experience Entrepreneurs," *Management Science* (September), 1331–44.

Beste, D. (1994) "The Greenfreeze Campaign," *Akzente*, December, 26–9.

Boutonnet, J.C., Bingham, P., Calamari, D., Rooij, C.d., Franklin, J., Kawano, T., Libre, J.-M., McCulloch, A., Malinverno, G., Odom, J.M., Rusch, G.M., Smythe, K., Sobolev, I., Thompson, R. and Tiedje, J.M. (1999), "Environmental Risk Assessment of Trifluoroacetic Acid," *Human and Ecological Risk Assessment*, 5 (1): 59–124.

Carbalja, P.T. (no date) "Natural Refrigerants: The Solutions," *Greenpeace Fact Sheet*, www.greenpeace.org/international/Global/international/planet-2/report/2009/5/natural-refigerants.pdf (last accessed September 16, 2012).

Coca-Cola press release (2000) "Coca-Cola Unveils Latest Initiatives to Fight Global Climate Change: A Significant Sydney 2000 Legacy," June 28.

Davies, K. (2011) "Greenfreeze F-gas Victory! Greener Refrigerators Finally Legal in US," www.greenpeace.org/usa/en/news-and-blogs/campaign-blog/greenfreeze-f-gas-victory-greener-refrigerato/blog/38405/ (last accessed September 10, 2012).

Ederberg, L. and Shende, R.M. (2008) "Refrigerants, Naturally! Taking Non-HCFC Technologies to the People," *The UN-Business Focal Point*, December 16, available at: www.enewsbuilder.net/focalpoint/e_article001294799.cfm?x=bdS3hTr,bcdVHW2j (last accessed June 26, 2012).

Environmental Leader (2009) "Coke Going to 100% HFC-Free Vending Machines, Coolers," December 3, available at: www.environmentalleader.com/2009/12/03/coke-going-to-100-hfc-free-vending-machines-coolers/ (last accessed June 25, 2012).

Europe Environment (2004) "Coca-Cola, Unilever, and McDonald's Get Involved Against Climate Change," June 24.

Garry, M. (2012) "Refrigeration Systems Chillin' with Carbon Dioxide," *Supermarket News*, April 5, available at: http://supermarketnews.com/technology/refrigeration-systems-chillin-carbon-dioxide (last accessed June 30, 2012).

Gunther, M. (2008) "Coke: The Green Thing," *CNNMoney.com*, April 17, available at: http://money.cnn.com/2008/04/14/news/companies/coca_cola.fortune/ (last accessed June 26, 2012).

Hartman, C.L. and Stafford, E.R. (1998) "Crafting 'Enviropreneurial' Value Chain Strategies through Green Alliances," *Business Horizons*, 41 (March–April): 62–72.

Hartman, C.L. and Stafford, E.R. (2006) "Chilling with Greenpeace, From the Inside Out," *Stanford Social Innovation Review* (Summer): 54–9.

Hartman, C.L. and Stafford, E.R. and Reategui, S. (2011) "Harvesting Utah's Urban Winds," *Solutions Journal*, May–June, 42–50.

Harvard Kennedy School press release (2011) "Belfer Center Awards 2011 Roy Family Award for Environmental Partnership," May 9, available at: www.hks.harvard.edu/news-events/news/articles/belfer-roy-award-may11 (last accessed June 16, 2012).

Houlder, V. (2000) "Inside Track: Power Through Professionalism, Environment Campaigning," *Financial Times*, September 21, 16.

Hydrocarbons21.com (2009) "Exclusive Interview with Father of HC Fridges, Wolfgang Lohbeck from Greenpeace," 13 February 2009, available at: www.hydrocarbons21.com/content/articles/2009-02-13-exclusive-interview-with-father-of-hc-fridges-wolfgang-lohbeck-from-greenpeace.php (last accessed January 23, 2012).

Larkin, A. (2011) "Greenpeace and Business, What's that About?" www.greenpeace.org/usa/en/news-and-blogs/campaign-blog/greenpeace-and-business-whats-that-about/blog/34547/ (last accessed June 25, 2012).

Millais, C. (1994) "Greenpeace's New Solutions," *Chemistry and Industry*, June 20: 484.

Miller, H.I. (2012) "Save the Whales, Forget the Children," *Wall Street Journal*, October 31, A13.

Ozone Depletion Network Online Today (1994) "Greenpeace Encourages Use of 'Greenfreeze' Fridge in US, Not HCFCs," April 21.

Patzelt, H. and Shepherd, D.A. (2011) "Recognizing Opportunities for Sustainable Development," *Entrepreneurship Theory and Practice* (July): 631–52.

PR Newswire (2005) "Coca-Cola Company, McDonald's and Unilever Recognized by US EPA for Leadership in Fighting Global Warming; Commitment to HFC-free Refrigeration Technologies Lauded by Greenpeace," May 4.

PR Newswire (2010) "Consumer Goods Industry Announces Initiatives on Climate Protection," November 29, available at: www.prnewswire.com/news-releases/consumer-goods-industry-announces-initiatives-on-climate-protection-110961494.html (last accessed June 25, 2012).

Ribeiro-Soriano, D. and Urbano, D. (2009) "Overview of Collaborative Entrepreneurship: An Integrated Approach Between Business Decisions and Negotiations," *Group Decision and Negotiation*, 18: 419–30.

Rootes, C. (2006) "Facing South? British Environmental Movement Organizations and the Challenge of Globalization," *Environmental Politics*, 5: 768–86.

Shepherd, D.A. and Patzelt, H. (2011) "The New Field of Sustainable Entrepreneurship: Studying Entrepreneurial Action Linking 'What Is to Be Sustained' with 'What Is to Be Developed'," *Entrepreneurship: Theory and Practice* (January): 137–63.

Simons, C. (2008) "CEO: Coke to Buy More Environmentally-Friendly Coolers," *Atlanta Journal-Constitution*, May 27, available at: www.statesman.com/business/content/shared/money/stories/2008/05/COKE_GREEN28_COX_F5811.html (last accessed June 26, 2012).

Stafford, E.R. and Hartman, C.L. (1996) "Green Alliances: Strategic Relations Between Businesses and Environmental Group," *Business Horizons*, 39 (March–April): 50–9.

Stafford, E.R. and Hartman, C.L. (2001) "Greenpeace's 'Greenfreeze Campaign': Hurdling Competitive Forces in the Diffusion of Environmental Technology Innovation," in *Ahead of the Curve*, K. Green, P. Grownewegen and P. S. Hofman (eds) Dordrecht: Kluwer: 107–31.

Stafford, E.R., Polonsky, M.J. and Hartman, C.L. (2000) "Environmental NGO-Business Collaboration and Strategic Bridging: A Case Analysis of the Greenpeace-Foron Alliance," *Business Strategy and the Environment*, 9: 122–35.

Stafford, E.R., Hartman, C.L. and Liang, Y. (2003) "Forces Driving Environmental Innovation Diffusion in China: The Case of Greenfreeze," *Business Horizons*, March–April: 47–56.

Tamura, L. (2010) "Greener, HFC-free Refrigerator Set to Enter US Market in 2011," *Washington Post*, December 26, available at: www.boston.com/lifestyle/green/articles/2010/12/28/greener_household_refrigerator_set_for_debut_in_us_stores/ (last accessed June 27, 2012).

US Environmental Protection Agency (2011a) *Global Warming Potential of ODS Substitutes,* March 28, available at: www.epa.gov/ozone/geninfo/gwps.html (last accessed October 23, 2012).

US Environmental Protection Agency (2011b) "EPA Approves Three Alternative Refrigerants to Replace Hydrofluorocarbons in Commercial and Household Freezers First Time that Hydrocarbons Substitutes Will be Widely Used in the U.S.," New Release, December 14, available at: http://yosemite.epa.gov/opa/admpress.nsf/0/EED8A9F289E19D3F85 257966005DBF51 (last accessed October 23, 2012).

Van Gerwen, R., Gerrard, A. and Roberti, F. (2008) "Ice Cream Cabinets Using a Hyrdocarbon Refrigerant: From Technology Concept to Global Rollout," Paper presented at Eighth IIR Gustav Lorentzen Conference on Natural Working Fluids, Copenhagen.

Vidal, J. (1992) "The Big Chill," *The Guardian*, November 19: 2.

Weissert, C.S. (1991) "Policy Entrepreneur, Policy Opportunists, and Legislative Effectiveness," *American Politics Research*, 19 (2): 262–74.

Westervelt, A. (2009) "Coke Ices Use of 'Super Greenhouse Gases,'" *SolveClimate.com,* December 9, available at: http://insideclimatenews.org/news/20091203/coke-ices-use-super-greenhouse-gases (last accessed June 27, 2012).

Yin, R. (2003) *Case Study Research: Design and Methods,* 3rd edition, Thousand Oaks, CA: Sage.

Zahra, S.A., Gedajlovic, E., Neubaum, D.O. and Shulman, J.M. (2009) "A Typology of Social Entrepreneurs: Motives, Search Processes, and Ethical Challenges," *Journal of Business Venturing*, 24 (5): 519–32.

Zemel, M. (2011) "How Powerful is the IOC? Let's Talk about the Environment," *Chicago-Kent Journal of Environmental and Energy Law*, 1: 173–220.

10

HOW SOCIAL PARTNERSHIPS BUILD BRANDS

John Peloza and Christine Ye

Introduction

For many who study or advocate responsible business, *marketing* is a term with negative connotations. The term conjures up images of slick sales pitches. Many people associate marketing with attempts to greenwash or otherwise hide irresponsible business practices. This popular opinion is perhaps the result of a small number of high profile attempts by firms to use advertising or sponsorship to engineer their image. Who can forget the criticisms of Philip Morris ads promoting the firm's contributions to charity? The firm came under fire for spending $150 million on advertising in order to promote their $115 donations to charity. Critics charged that the entire effort was designed to use charity donations to detract attention from other activities of the firm (ABC News, 2012).

However, many successful social partnerships have been driven not by a desire to hide some misdeeds or otherwise polish a tainted image. Rather, many successful partnerships have been motivated by (and have resulted in) meaningful social and environmental impacts. The first part of this book examined the trend from public to private authority for many social and environmental problems. In addition, notwithstanding examples like the Philip Morris campaign, many firms have also successfully used social partnerships as part of their overall brand building efforts. In recent years, social partnerships have become a very popular tactic in the corporate social responsibility strategies of many firms. In part because of this rising popularity, and in part due to highly criticized examples such as the Philip Morris campaign, using social partnerships to build brands is more difficult today than in the past. For example, recent data demonstrates that for a sample of global brands, individuals' perceptions of corporate performance on social and environmental issues are not aligned with objective measures of corporate performance (Peloza *et al.*, 2012). In other words, many of the investments made by firms in social responsibility efforts are not providing meaningful differentiation for their brands. The purpose of this chapter is to explore how firms can use social partnerships to strengthen their brands, and their relationships with customers.

In this chapter, social partnership is a term used to describe some relationship between a firm and a nonprofit organization. Importantly, it does not assume a relationship any deeper than simple cash donations. However, as we will see, moving beyond this simple form of partnership is a key ingredient to using social partnerships to build strong brands.

How social partnerships enhance brand image

In order to understand how social partnerships can enhance brands, we first need to understand the concept of customer-based brand equity (Keller 1993). The concept of brand equity refers to how brands deliver value for consumers, and represent, in many cases, the most valuable asset of the firm. Keller (1993) suggests that the associations between the brand and specific attributes, and associations between the brand and perceived benefits, form the image of any brand. This process is depicted in Figure 10.1.

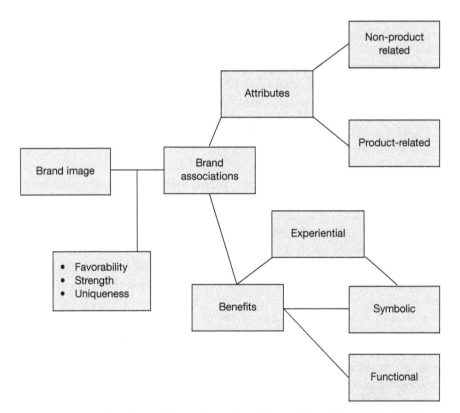

FIGURE 10.1 How brand associations enhance brand image (adapted from Keller 1993)

Brand attributes

Brand attributes include the physical attributes of any product. These include things like style, color, taste, speed, or other attributes related to the performance of a given product. But non-product-related attributes are also an important aspect of brand associations. These non-product-related attributes can include virtually anything that consumers associate with the brand. Over the years, brand managers have increasingly turned to partnerships with nonprofits as one way to enhance the non-product-related attributes of their brands. These associations can develop brand imagery for consumers. For example, consumers may view a brand with strong ties to social partnerships as a brand that is for people who care about social or environmental causes. In turn, if a consumer views caring for social or environmental causes as a positive goal, he or she will favor the brand over others that lack such associations. In this way, social partnerships allow brands to compete on factors beyond actual product performance. One of the first and most recognized examples of a social partnership is the 1982 cause-related marketing campaign between American Express and the Statue of Liberty restoration campaign. Brand managers had previously relied on the product-related attributes of the brand such as acceptance around the world or costs per transaction to compete against other cards such as Visa or MasterCard. By associating the Amex brand with the cause, the brand positioned itself as the card with a social conscience and thus an additional means of differentiation from competitors.

Brand benefits

Keller (1993) outlines three types of benefits consumers receive from any brand. The most obvious benefits related to social partnership are the experiential and social benefits. Experiential benefits are those related to how a consumer feels when they purchase or use a product or service. For many consumers, it feels good to purchase from a company that contributes to social partnerships. Social partnerships can create a high degree of emotional value for many consumers, who enjoy the feeling of contributing to a social or environmental cause through their consumption. Similarly, symbolic benefits are those related to consumers' needs to gain social acceptance or communicate their beliefs to others. Brands tied to social partnerships can provide a high degree of symbolic value by creating "badges" for consumers who support such brands. For example, when companies associated with the Susan G. Komen Foundation sell pink ribbons through retail locations, consumers can wear those ribbons as a means of telling others they support the cause.

Functional benefits include those that relate to the performance of the brand. In some cases, social partnerships can meaningfully increase this benefit for consumers. For example, the development of Greenfreeze by Greenpeace replaced the need for harmful, o-zone destroying chemicals that were previously used in refrigerators. The organization worked with scientists and companies with expertise in the area to develop the product and subsequently integrate it into the manufacture of refrigerators worldwide. This product significantly enhanced the way the product delivered functional value for consumers, and allowed consumers to be more active in the protection of the environment (for an excellent review of the Greenpeace partnership, see Chapter 9 of this book).

In Keller's brand model shown in Figure 10.1, the ability for these brand associations to enhance brand image relies on three factors: *favorability, strength, and uniqueness*. Favorability refers to the degree to which consumers will view the association as positive and congruent with their own values. Strength refers to the degree to which consumers will remember the brand association. Finally, uniqueness refers to the degree to which the brand association is unique from competitors. This last factor has become more important now that the majority of firms engage in some form of social partnership. For example, when Amex launched its Statue of Liberty campaign it was novel within the credit card category, and indeed many other categories. However, today all competitors within this category now engage in various forms of social partnership. Therefore, gaining the same brand benefits has become much more difficult. The remainder of this chapter examines how brand managers can develop and implement social partnerships to maximize their potential for building brand associations with consumers.

Factors impacting brand image enhancement

Many researchers have examined social partnerships from the perspective of the maturity of the partnership. Maturity and partnership development can encompass several issues, and several continua have been developed. For example, Wymer and Samu (2003) outline several forms of potential relationships between a firm and nonprofit, ranging from philanthropy to joint ventures. A defining characteristic of their continuum is the degree of commitment from the firm, ranging from low (philanthropy) to high (joint venture). Our examination of partnership development will use Austin's (2000) model of cross-sector collaboration to examine dimensions of social partnerships that brand managers can use to develop their brands.

Broadly speaking, Austin's continuum includes three stages: philanthropic, transactional, and integrative. His framework is adapted here to focus on three over-riding factors that define social partnerships: operational development, fit, and managerial complexity. Operational development is the degree to which a firm engages with a nonprofit in the implementation of the partnership. Fit is the degree to which the business of the firm and the nonprofit mission align. Generally speaking, greater levels of each of these two factors of social partnerships are positive for brand building. That is, brands benefit from greater levels of operational development and fit. The third factor, managerial complexity, impacts how firms can put their decisions on operational development and fit into practice, and realize their potential for brand building.

Austin argues that social partnerships typically begin at the first stage, and that migration to later stages occurs as the firm and nonprofit gain experience with one another. An example of this migration is found in the partnership between the nonprofit City Year and Timberland. The relationship began with a donation of 50 pairs of boots and now encompasses much higher levels of donation across a range of products, employee volunteerism, and managerial support. Austin also notes that not all relationships develop past the first stage. Much of the research on how social partnerships enhance brand image can be viewed through the lens of the collaboration continuum. The remainder of this chapter examines how the three factors listed on the left side of Figure 10.2 – operational development, fit, and managerial complexity – can create positive brand attributes and benefits.

Operational development

This factor encompasses a range of social partnership characteristics including the level of engagement, interaction level and scope of activities between the firm and nonprofit, and the magnitude of resource allocated by the firm. Researchers have operationalized these elements through the degree of firm commitment and effort to the social partnership. Broadly speaking, greater levels of commitment and effort, exhibited through the items listed in Figure 10.2, provide greater brand associations for the firm. These benefits occur at both the product and non-product-related level, and encompass experiential, symbolic, and functional value.

The primary means by which operational development impacts non-product-related attributes and the associated experiential and symbolic value is through the perception of company motivations. When consumers perceive a firm as motivated by genuine interest for the mission of the nonprofit, as opposed to exploitation of the cause, brand associations are enhanced. Although firms rarely communicate only self-serving motives for social partnerships, consumers make inferences about their motivations based on the operational development of the partnership. When firms engage for only short periods of time, or dedicate only small amounts of resources, consumers are more likely to infer that the firm is seeking to exploit the social partnership. In turn, brand associations may even be negative (e.g. Barone *et al.,* 2000).

Social partnership factor	Stage I Philanthropic	Stage II Transactional	Stage III Integrative
1. Operational development • Level of engagement • Magnitude of resources • Scope of activities • Interaction level	Low Small Narrow Infrequent		High Big Broad Intensive
2. Fit • Importance to mission • Strategic value	Peripheral Minor		Central Major
3. Managerial complexity	Simple		Complex

FIGURE 10.2 Cross-sector collaboration continuum (adapted from Austin 2000)

The type of resources that the firm commits can also impact brand associations and related consumer attributions. For example, a firm that dedicates only financial resources may be seen as less committed or exerting less effort than a firm that dedicates employee resources, expertise, gifts in kind in addition to cash (Ellen *et al.*, 2000; Peloza, 2006). The reason for this is similar to the feeling one gets when one receives a gift of cash on one's birthday. Many people feel as though the gift giver did not care enough to put in real effort to go beyond writing a check, and therefore see the gift as a necessity versus an expression of genuine care.

When consumers infer self-serving motivations, non-product-related brand attributes are negatively affected (Barone *et al.*, 2000). For example, because consumers infer that the company behind the brand doesn't genuinely care, consumers are unlikely to view the brand as the choice for someone who cares about the social and environmental issues. Similarly, experiential and symbolic benefits are diminished. Rather than experiencing a "warm glow" associated with supporting a company involved in a social partnership, consumers may feel a sense of guilt in supporting a company that is more concerned with image and profit than social issues. Similarly, any badges that are created by the firm will carry a negative signal for other consumers (Peloza and Shang, 2011). Consumers who use these products may feel they portray themselves as uncaring through their public association with the brand.

Importantly, while the framework encompasses a magnitude of resources as one element of operational development, research demonstrates that simply dedicating more resources to a social partnership does not necessarily create positive brand associations (Wang *et al.*, 2008). Therefore, brand managers must take care to not merely outspend competitors in social partnerships but instead deploy resources in a fashion that is more likely to build associations. One way that some firms have sought to gain incremental brand building benefits from social partnerships is by branding the nonprofit within the same brand family. For example, Google received significant publicity and brand awareness when it launched Google.org. Although the "nonprofit arm" of the company still works with arm's length nonprofits and companies to support a variety of initiatives, Google.org focuses the philanthropy of the firm on the focal organization and the Google family of brands (e.g. Google Plus, Google Maps, etc.). A similar example is Ronald McDonald's Children's Charities. The organization is tightly linked to the corporate brand, and has even been the recipient of donations from other corporations as their charity of choice (Hoeffler and Keller, 2002).

In addition to the brand associations discussed above, greater levels of operational development in a social partnership gives employees a much greater opportunity to learn from the nonprofit. This experience, in turn, can generate meaningful impacts to the functional value received by consumers and impact product-related attributes of the brand by creating a culture of innovation within the firm (Smith, 2003). Christmann (2000), for example, finds that investments in social responsibility initiatives lead to cost savings in the production process and stimulate a culture of innovation among employees in the firm. This innovative culture can lead to new product development or other process-related improvements that can enhance product-related attributes or the functional benefits received by consumers.

Other researchers have noted similar relationships between firms involved in social responsibility initiatives and process improvements and innovation. For example, Klassen and Whybark (1999) find improvements in production cost, speed, quality and flexibility are associated with firm involvement in social and environmental initiatives. Similarly, Sharma and Vredenburg (1998) use the Canadian oil and gas industry to demonstrate how such initiatives lead to innovation, employee learning, and improved product quality.

The benefits of cultural change that stimulates innovation and related brand benefits are more likely to occur as firms move from philanthropic initiatives to partnerships that are integrative. Deeper engagement with nonprofits over longer periods of time across more touchpoints within the firm is more likely to result in these brand benefits. Conversely, the opportunity for employees to engage within the nonprofit is limited when monetary-based philanthropic initiatives characterize the social partnership (Peloza, 2006; Smith, 2003).

In sum, the degree of operational development in a social partnership impacts the favorability of brand associations by stimulating innovation that can lead to more functional brand benefits, and the perception of prosocial motivations. Operational development impacts the strength of brand associations because consumers are more likely to remember and favor relationships that have a long history. Finally, operational development impacts the uniqueness of brand associations through the potential for new, innovative products and, at least currently, most relationships are characterized by short-term transactions (Austin, 2000). These impacts, as well as those for fit and managerial complexity, are listed in Figure 10.3.

Operational development	Favorability – deeper engagement leads to positive attributions, innovations that create functional value
	Strength – longer term relationships more likely to be memorable for consumers
	Uniqueness – innovations that create new products/solve new consumer needs
Fit	Favorability – greater alignment with target markets
	Strength – integration of partnership into product offering enhances awareness and recall
	Uniqueness – implementation of the partnership across a range of consumer touchpoints, innovation tied to corporate strategy
Managerial complexity	Favorability – participation by multiple actors can enhance reputations of an industry
	Strength – a focused partnership can lead to greater recall and awareness
	Uniqueness – consultation with multiple nonprofits may be the only means by which knowledge can be integrated

FIGURE 10.3 How three factors of social partnerships impact favorability, strength, and uniqueness of brand associations

Fit

Similar to operational development, one of the factors of social partnerships that will generate higher levels of meaningful innovation within the firm is the degree of fit between the firm and the nonprofit. Imagine, for example, the difference in potential for innovation that exists between two hypothetical partnerships: General Motors and the Sierra Club, and a Ford partnership with the Susan G. Komen Foundation. Both firms are in the transportation industry, which is characterized by growing expectations of environmental efficiency within their products. Both nonprofits provide some degree of "warm glow" for consumers, with perhaps even a slight skew toward the Ford partnership from female consumers. However, the ability for the GM partnership to create meaningful innovation for the firm is much greater given the expertise of the Sierra Club and the salience of that expertise to the strategy of the firm. The Sierra Club would have greater exposure to emerging technologies that can be used to protect the environment, for example.

Berger and colleagues (2004) outline the degree of fit between companies and nonprofits across several dimensions. Several of these dimensions are highly relevant to the ability of the partnership to stimulate an innovative firm culture. One dimension is *mission fit*. How aligned are the missions of the two organizations? The greater the social partnership is an expression of the mission of the firm, the greater the potential for an exchange of ideas that will spur innovation that will meaningfully impact firm strategy and performance. They also highlight *resource fit* as the degree to which the two partners have complementary resources that each needs and would otherwise have difficulty accessing. Many nonprofits house expertise that is highly valuable to firms, and managers should seek partnerships with nonprofits that can offer this expertise as part of the relationship. Similarly, Berger and colleagues outline *management and cultural fit*. These again impact the ability of the partnership to generate an innovative culture. The more the two organizations share a participative management style and a personal chemistry between members, the more likely the partnership will spur innovation.

Fit also impacts non-product-related attributes and experiential/symbolic brand benefits. Here again we turn to the dimensions of fit as outlined by Berger and colleagues. Most importantly, they discuss *target market fit*. This type of fit requires the supporters of a given nonprofit to also be within the target market of the brand. This is critically important for enhancement of non-product-related attributes and brand benefits. The associations between the firm and nonprofit are positive if the target market identifies with the nonprofit. Without this identification, the affect transfer to the firm may not occur. In some cases, the affect transfer can even be negative. For example, AT&T faced an intense campaign in the early 1990s from both sides of the abortion debate after their support and then withdrawal of support for Planned Parenthood. The firm angered pro-life activists with their support of the organization, and subsequently faced scrutiny from pro-choice groups who accused the firm of caving into pressure. The result was an organized boycott of AT&T and a group of other major firms (Himmelstein, 1997).

Also important is *product/cause fit*. This type of fit ensures that any co-branding that is done between the partners is logical. Researchers advise marketers to build partnerships that are matched to product lines (e.g. Becker-Olsen *et al.*, 2006; Varadarajan and Menon, 1988). Consumers will be more likely to view the company as possessing expertise in the given area and associate positive emotions for the nonprofit with the firm (Hoeffler and Keller, 2002). Ellen and colleagues (2006), for example, measure the degree of fit between the firm and the cause (in their case, a gas station supporting a transportation service for the elderly versus a wildlife protection agency) predicting whether or not consumers would view the partnership positively. In the high fit scenario, consumers were more likely to view the partnership positively, and more likely to infer motivations of genuine care for the nonprofit.

Another benefit of a high degree of product fit is that it allows for increased opportunities for the firm to integrate the partnership message into its core product offerings. This is beneficial because tying the social and environmental initiatives of the firm to product offerings means they are more likely to be noticed and remembered by consumers. Most consumers have low awareness levels of these partnerships. Du and colleagues (2007) demonstrate that when the message behind the social initiatives of the firm are tied directly to the product itself (in their case, a brand that produces organic yogurt in addition to charity donation, as opposed to brands that only donate) consumers are more likely to be aware of the initiative and recognize the brand as socially responsible. Peloza and colleagues (2012) use communications processing theories to argue that greater "credit" for social responsibility is given to companies that integrate social and environmental attributes into their product offerings. They suggest that this bias occurs because most consumers are more motivated and able to process product-level communications than they are to process information related strictly to social responsibility.

Finally, *workforce fit* represents an opportunity for brands to benefit from social partnerships. Different from cultural fit described earlier, this type of fit deals with the potential for employees of the firm to become engaged with the nonprofit at a grassroots level. Although this may be part of the development of innovation discussed earlier, the larger benefit to the firm is the potential for employee volunteers to aid the brand building effort by enhancing perceptions of commitment and effort on the part of the firm (Peloza, 2006).

In sum, the degree of fit in a social partnership impacts the favorability of brand associations through a greater alignment between markets and taking advantage of positive effect toward the nonprofit. Fit impacts the strength of brand associations because the message of the partnership is more likely to be integrated into the core products of the firm and therefore noticed and remembered. Finally, fit impacts the uniqueness of brand associations through the potential for partnership to reach the consumer at multiple touchpoints (e.g. employee volunteerism, packaging, new products) and greater innovation central to the product strategy of the firm.

Managerial complexity

Inherent in the factors of social partnerships discussed earlier is the complexity of the managerial task. For example, managing a high level of engagement across a wide scope of activities that are highly relevant to the strategy of the firm will take more resources than managing a one-off cash donation that is peripheral to the daily operations of the firm. However, the management and governance of social partnerships does have implications for brand associations when viewed from the perspective of multi-party collaboration. Thus far in this chapter, social partnerships have been examined from the perspective of a single firm/brand and a single nonprofit. However, evidence from the market suggests that many firms have developed partnerships that go well beyond the dyad model to encompass partnerships with multiple firm and/or multiple nonprofits. For example, the Initiative for Responsible Mining Assurance includes a number of firms and nonprofits concerned with social and environmental issues specific to that industry. The examples of social partnerships used throughout other chapters in this book range from single firm/nonprofits to a large number of each organization. In this final section of this chapter we examine the ability for different types of partnership structures to deliver the specific brand building benefits discussed thus far.

Each collaboration structure has its own unique strengths and weaknesses, and offers unique opportunities to build brands. Similar to previous factors of social partnerships, these brand building benefits are present in both non-product-related attributes as well as those more directly tied to the firm's ability to produce specific products with specific functional value. It is important for managers to choose (or develop) the collaboration structure that aligns with the company's brand building objectives. For example, many of the issues at the heart of social partnerships are extremely broad in scope such as community poverty, human rights violations, or dangers to human health. Resolution of these broad issues impacts both product-related and non-product related attributes of the brand. However, they typically require an expanded framework of collaboration from a dyadic collaboration between a single firm and a single nonprofit to network collaborations involving a range of firms and nonprofits.

Peloza and Falkenberg (2009) develop a framework for firm/nonprofit collaboration that includes single and multiple firm and nonprofit actors. Here we use their framework to examine how the firm can build specific brand associations with nonprofits and other firms. Their framework consists of partnerships that include both single and multiple firms, as well as single and multiple nonprofits. As illustrated in Figure 10.4, they delineate between partnerships that involve single versus multiple actors, and argue that specific partnership structures should be pursued that align with the goals of the firm.

We begin with partnerships defined by a single firm and single nonprofit. This type of partnership can be highly effective at stimulating innovation required for firm-specific issues. For example, the partnership between McDonald's and the Environmental Defense Fund has led the company to reduce its waste through

	Single non-profit	Multiple non-profit
Single firm	Visible independence	Remediate footprints
Multiple firm	Share the burden	Communal contribution

FIGURE 10.4 Framework for assessing managerial complexity (Peloza and Falkenberg, 2009)

redesign or reduction of packaging by hundreds of thousands of tons. Environmental Defense provided expertise that guided McDonald's purchasing practices to significantly increase the use of recyclable materials. Similarly, brand building through this form of partnership can provide specific benefits that create differentiation from competitors. For example, Unilever has a partnership with the Rainforest Alliance. The partnership is designed to improve the sustainability of farming, incomes and livelihoods of millions, which provides a meaningful source of differentiation.

An example of a multi-firm and single nonprofit partnership is found in Piracicaba, Brazil, where Caterpillar has its manufacturing operations. Urban migration to the city led to increased unemployment, higher levels of poverty and crime, and a lack of appropriate infrastructure for the bulging population (Griesse, 2007). Managers sought the support of other local firms such as General Motors and White Martins (Brazil's leading supplier of industrial and medical gases) in a partnership with a new NGO, Piracicaba, 2010. This partnership structure is appropriate for firms facing a common threat due to the risk profile of their industry (e.g. energy exploration, mining, chemicals). In essence, the brand building is done at the industry level since the threat is the same for all firms operating within the same industry (Barnett, 2006). Firm innovation can also be stimulated through this approach. For example, Ahuja (2000) demonstrated that network participation in the chemical industry was related to the number of patents secured by the firm.

A third partnership option involves a single firm and multiple nonprofits such as Starbucks working with a range of NGOs working in the coffee growing regions of Mexico. In 2002 Starbucks began a pilot project to work with Oxfam, which is dedicated to fighting hunger and poverty, the Oaxacan State Coffee Producers Network, which represents the thousands of local Mexican farmers and cooperatives, and the Ford Foundation, which supports the promotion of democratic values and international cooperation and fights poverty and social injustice. Through this broader network of NGOs, the firm (and the NGOs) is able to make a broader impact on the local community. Porter and Kramer (2002) argue that a firm can gain economic returns by tackling social and environmental issues that in turn provide advantages for the firm, such as a better educated workforce or a healthier community economy. In this case, the ability to help the firm develop better (or even maintain) production relies on input from multiple nonprofit experts.

An example of the fourth type of partnership (multiple firm/multiple nonprofit) is the Fair Labor Association, which consists of over 20 apparel manufacturers and dozens of nonprofits from various perspectives including Human Rights First and the Federation of Free Workers in the Philippines among others. The Workplace Code of Conduct of the FLA addresses a broad range of issues resulting in comprehensive oversight of a myriad of issues across dozens of nations. Participation by member firms provides the brand building benefits to the entire industry (again, relevant to industry where threats are common) as well as addressing social or environmental issues that are pervasive (Chatterji and Levine, 2006).

In sum, managerial complexity works differently from operational development and fit. Simply adding more managerial complexity doesn't automatically lead to brand image enhancement. Rather, the selection of a partnership structure should be based on the specific brand challenges facing the firm. In particular, partnerships involving multiple firms can create brand building benefits at a collective level, which is highly valuable for firms working in high profile industries under constant threat of sanctions. In addition, the ability for the partnership to spur innovation or otherwise bring expertise to the firm can be enhanced significantly when multiple nonprofits are engaged simultaneously. Therefore, the potential for social partnerships to impact the favorability, strength, and uniqueness of the brand association is contingent upon the specific context and objectives for the brand.

Conclusion

It's been almost 30 years since the first widely discussed social partnership began to generate meaningful academic attention to the field of social partnerships. In that partnership, American Express benefited greatly from their association with the Statue of Liberty restoration effort. However, much has changed in the past three decades. In that time, social partnerships have become ubiquitous. Virtually every major firm has at least one relationship with a nonprofit. This has provided much needed support for social and environmental issues facing our society, but it has also led to increasing calls from some stakeholders to demonstrate the financial value of these partnerships.

Among the primary benefits cited by proponents of social partnerships is the brand building potential of such initiatives. Research demonstrates that relationships with consumers and other stakeholders improve when firms invest in social or environmental causes (Peloza, 2009). However, as this chapter outlines, these benefits are not automatic. In an increasingly competitive market, mere involvement in a social partnership is no longer sufficient to deliver the brand building benefits many managers expect. Managers must carefully select their partnerships, and structure them in a manner that will lead to the desired brand association and image.

Questions for reflection

This chapter highlighted a number of strategies managers can use to ensure their social partnerships contribute to brand building. Here, we provide a series of discussion questions to help stimulate social partnership strategy development:

1   A SWOT analysis can help managers determine where their brands can benefit most from social partnerships. What are the major threats and opportunities facing the firm, and how can social partnerships protect against threats to take advantage of opportunities? For example, does your brand (or industry) suffer reputationally and would therefore benefit from positive affect that many nonprofits can provide? This may dictate a different strategy or specific partnership than if innovation presents an opportunity.

2   What type of fit would benefit your brand the most? Given the many ways fit can be operationalized, managers may need to prioritize one type of fit over another. For example, if employee skill development is a desired outcome, managers may consider prioritizing workforce fit over others to ensure employees have the opportunity to get involved with the charity and engage in team building.

3   Should your firm engage in a portfolio of social partnerships or focus on a handful, or even one? What role can branding play in your social partnership? Is there an opportunity to "vertically" integrate your social partnership and create greater impacts by developing joint ventures or even wholly controlled nonprofits (e.g. Ronald McDonald's Children's Charities)?

4   What is the level of support for the social partnership within senior management? Is the understanding of brand building clear, and does the potential for higher levels of operational development exist? The ability of the firm to allocate specific resources may necessitate a specific social partnership strategy and partner.

References

ABC News (2012) Corporate goodwill or tainted money? Accessed on line from: http://abcnews.go.com/WNT/story?id=131249&page=1#.UHbIsNXjwxU, on October 11, 2012.

Ahuja, G. (2000) Collaboration networks, structural holes and innovation: a longitudinal study. *Administrative Science Quarterly*, 45: 425–55.

Austin, J.E. (2000) *The collaboration challenge*. San Francisco: Jossey-Bass.

Barone, M., Miyazaki, A. and Taylor, K. (2000) The influence of cause-related marketing on consumer choice: does one good turn deserve another? *Academy of Marketing Science Journal*, 28 (2): 248–62.

Barnett, M.L. (2006) Finding a working balance between competitive and communal strategies. *Journal of Management Studies*, 43 (8): 1753–73.

Becker-Olsen, K.L., Cudmore, B.A. and Hill, R.P. (2006) The impact of perceived corporate social responsibility on consumer behavior. *Journal of Business Research*, 59: 46–53.

Berger, I.E., Cunningham, P.H. and Drumwright, M.E. (2004) Social alliances: company/nonprofit collaboration. *California Management Review*, 47 (1): 58–90.

Chatterji, A. and Levine, D. (2006) Breaking down the wall of codes: evaluating non-financial performance measurement. *California Management Review*, 48 (2): 29–51.

Christmann, P. (2000) Effects of "best practices" of environmental management on cost advantage: the role of complementary assets. *Academy of Management Journal*, 43 (4): 663–80.

Du, S., Bhattacharya, C.B. and Sen, S. (2007) Reaping relational rewards from corporate social responsibility: the role of competitive positioning. *International Journal of Research in Marketing*, 24 (3): 224–41.

Ellen, P.S., Webb, D.W. and Mohr, L.A. (2006) Building corporate associations: consumer attributions for corporate socially responsible programs. *Journal of the Academy of Marketing Science*, 34 (2): 147–57.

Griesse, M. (2007) Caterpillar's interactions with Piracicaba, Brazil: a community-based analysis of CSR. *Journal of Business Ethics*, 73: 39–51.

Himmelstein, J.L. (1997) *Looking Good and Doing Good: Corporate Philanthropy and Corporate Power*. Bloomington, IN: Indiana University Press.

Hoeffler, S. and Keller, K.L. (2002) Building brand equity through corporate societal marketing. *Journal of Public Policy and Marketing*, 21 (1): 78–89.

Keller, K.L. (1993) Conceptualizing, measuring, and managing customer-based brand equity. *Journal of Marketing*, 57: 1–22.

Klassen, R.D. and Whybark, C.D. (1999) The impact of environmental technologies on environmental performance. *Academy of Management Journal*, 42 (6): 599–615.

Peloza, J. (2009) The challenge of measuring financial impacts from investments in corporate social performance. *Journal of Management*, 35 (6) 1518–41.

Peloza, J. and Falkenberg, L. (2009) The role of collaboration in achieving corporate social responsibility objectives. *California Management Review*, 51 (3): 95–113.

Peloza, J. and Hassay, D.N. (2006) Intra-organizational volunteerism: good soldiers, good deeds, and good politics. *Journal of Business Ethics*, 64 (4): 357–79.

Peloza, J. and Shang, J. (2011) How can corporate social responsibility activities create value for stakeholders? A systematic review. *Journal of the Academy of Marketing Science*, 39 (1): 117–35.

Peloza, J., Loock, M., Cerruti, J. and Muyot, M. (2012) Sustainability: how stakeholder perceptions differ from corporate reality. *California Management Review*, 55 (1): 74–97.

Porter, M. and Kramer, M. (2002) The competitive advantage of corporate philanthropy. *Harvard Business Review*, 80 (12): 57–68

Sen, S. and Bhattacharya, C.B. (2001) Does doing good always lead to doing better? Consumer reactions to corporate social responsibility. *Journal of Marketing Research*, 38 (May): 225–44.

Sharma, S. and Vredenburg, H. (1998) Proactive corporate environmental strategy and the development of competitively valuable organizational capabilities. *Strategic Management Journal*, 19: 729–53.

Smith, N.C. (2003) Corporate social responsibility: whether or how? *California Management Review*, 45 (4): 52–76

Varadarajan, R. and Menon, A. (1988) Cause-related marketing: a coalignment of marketing strategy and corporate philanthropy. *Journal of Marketing*, 52 (3): 58–74.

Wang, H., Choi, J. and Li, J. (2008) Too little or too much? Untangling the relationship between corporate philanthropy and firm financial performance. *Organization Science*, 19 (1): 143–59.

Wymer, W.W. and Samu, S. (2003) Dimensions of business and nonprofit collaborative relationships. *Journal of Nonprofit and Public Sector Marketing*, 11 (1): 3–22.

11

CONFLICT IN CROSS-SECTOR PARTNERSHIPS

Barbara Gray and Jill Purdy

Introduction

Cross-sector partnerships that bring the public, private sectors, and NGO sectors together to solve problems have become common in arenas including education, urban renewal, research, criminal justice, healthcare, job training, and environmental protection. While many kinds of interactions link these sectors of society, our focus in this chapter is on those that are governed by collaborative or network relations rather than market-based or hierarchical relations (Powell, 1990). We define cross-sector partnerships as dynamic interactions of voluntary participants around shared interests, which stand in contrast to relationships constructed around purely contractual exchange relationships in which one party provides services for another. For example, a nonprofit agency may be retained by a city government to provide shelter, meals, and mental health services for the homeless, but this falls outside our definition of cross-sector partnerships. However, a cross-sector partnership would exist if nonprofit agencies and city leaders jointly developed and implemented a plan to alleviate the problem of homelessness. In this case, the partners engage in a reciprocal interaction that may involve joint information sharing and/or action taking. Bingham (2008) refers to this kind of cross-sector partnership as "governance" and notes that it "may involve multiple organizations and stakeholders from public, private, and nonprofit sectors that combine in a network to address a common and shared problem" (p. 274). Wood and Gray (1991: 11) provide a similar definition of collaborative partnerships but one that emphasizes the processual aspects of partnerships defining collaboration as occurring when "a group of autonomous stakeholders of a problem domain engage in an interactive process using shared rules, norms, and structures, to act or decide on issues related to that domain." Problem domains refer to issues that involve many stakeholders. We believe that identifying a shared problem and attending to the process dynamics of partnership formation and maintenance are both critical for successful partnering.

Cross-sectoral partnerships may be formed for many different reasons. These include managing uncertainty or turbulence within a domain (Trist, 1983; Gray, 1989), pooling scarce resources to tackle societal problems (Gray, 1989; Huxham and Vangen, 2005), gaining collaborative advantage within an industry or network (Huxham and Vangen, 2005), providing public services (Sandfort and Milward, 2008), gaining reciprocity and/or legitimacy (Oliver, 1990), or resolving conflicts that forestall action on critical problems (Susskind *et al.*, 1999; Wondolleck and Yaffee, 2003). However, conflicts often impair partnership formation and functioning (Gray, 1989; Gray, 2004; Lewicki *et al.*, 2003). Attempts at constructing partnerships may fail, for example, if there are few opportunities for parties to trade across issues they value differently, key stakeholders refuse to join, deadlines are unrealistic, stakeholders have strong BATNAs (Best Alternatives to Negotiated Agreements), if large power or other differences exist among the stakeholders (Gray, 1989; Hardy and Phillips, 1998; Susskind and Thomas-Larmer, 1999), or if key identities of partners are threatened (Rothman, 1997; Gray, 2004; Fiol *et al.*, 2009). All these factors will erode potential partners' commitment to collaborate (Gray, 1989) and impede the likelihood that the partners will be successful in deciding on or implementing joint plans.

Types of cross-sector partnerships

Two important bases on which partnerships can be distinguished have been identified: (1) the initial motivation of the partners for joining together and (2) the nature of the desired outcomes (Gray, 1996). Motivations for forming a partnership may stem from a shared perception that an opportunity exists that neither potential partner could capitalize on alone. Alternatively, potential partners may be linked by conflict – that is, they have conflicting views about how a problem domain should be defined and addressed, but often these stakeholders have different and even competing views about the nature of the problem and what to do about it (Trist, 1983; Gray, 1989). Partnerships may also differ with respect to the outcomes the partners desire to achieve, ranging from simple information sharing to formulating (and enacting) joint agreements (Kolk, 2014). By cross-referencing the motivating factors and types of outcomes, four distinct types of partnerships have been identified (Gray, 1996: 61) as shown in Figure 11.1.

Partnerships for *appreciative planning* occur when partners are motivated by opportunities and shared visions and simply seek to share information with each other. These may be one-time events or extended relationships. For example, the Global Reporting Initiative provides information and offers guidelines for sustainable development practices (Glasbergen, 2007). Partnerships motivated by shared visions that lead to joint agreements and action plans to address a problem or opportunity are referred to as *collective strategies*. When partners come together to address a conflict through the exchange of information, Gray (1996) refers to these as *dialogues*. As with appreciative planning, these may be short-lived or continue for months or even years. For example, The Keystone Center sponsored a dialogue on energy futures in 1984 at the request of the Department of Energy to explore critical future energy issues. Similarly, dialogues have been held to find common ground among disputants in the debate over abortion (LeBaron and Carstarphan, 1997; Public Conversation Project, 1999) and others have pursued joint research and learning on sustainable food production (Glasbergen, 2008). In these dialogues, differences are explored, but no decisions are made. When conflicting parties convene try to reach an agreement about how to settle their dispute, these kinds of partnerships are called *negotiated settlements*. These types of partnerships may be temporary or produce long-term cooperation around implementation of the agreements that are reached to provide the kind of governance system referred to above by Bingham (2008).

Partnerships rooted in opportunity

Opportunities abound for shared public-private-nonprofit ventures that enhance education, improve health, advance technology, and serve community interests. However, even when pursuing noble goals, partners may disagree on the exact nature of the desired goal, or differ in their views of how the goal is to be accomplished

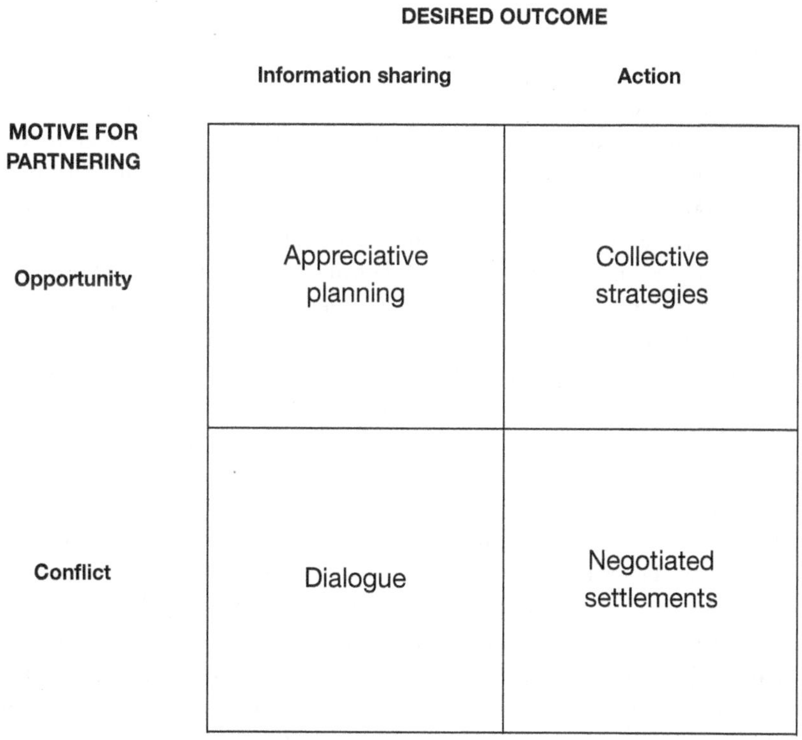

	DESIRED OUTCOME	
MOTIVE FOR PARTNERING	**Information sharing**	**Action**
Opportunity	Appreciative planning	Collective strategies
Conflict	Dialogue	Negotiated settlements

FIGURE 11.1 Types of partnerships

(Huxham and Vangen, 2005). Reaching agreement on how to proceed in such circumstances may give rise to conflict. When shared goals and a common agenda are agreed upon, conflicts still may arise related to the process, substance, or relationships among cross-sector partners. Watershed partnerships are one example of a collaboration that forms around a shared vision – that of protecting and managing natural resources (Wondolleck and Yaffee, 2000). Partners in such situations seek to advance a collective goal that requires ongoing cooperation and agreement among all of them. However conflicts may emerge over the details of such agreements, particularly if one party feels an inequitable burden of responsibility is placed upon it. For example, collaborative efforts to develop habitat conservation plans may limit a landowner's use of the land (Bidwell and Ryan, 2006). In these cases, parties may abandon the collaboration and pursue legal remedies that can block or reverse the progress of the cross-sector partnership (Sousa and Klyza, 2007). Similarly, a company planning to build a hydroelectric power plant in western Mexico found that collaboration with government and community groups was needed to prepare for the social, economic and environmental impacts of the project, including the arrival of more people in the area. Despite substantial support for the project, conflicts regarding project size, compensation to land owners, and natural resource rights arose during the discussions (Chávez and Bernal, 2008). If such conflicts cannot be resolved, the potential partnership may dissolve.

Partnerships rooted in conflict

As noted above, partnerships may also emerge from pitched battles among disputing parties with respect to a problem domain. In some early contests over environmental issues, for example, wrangling parties had been at odds for years (in the courts, on the ground and in the public media), which finally prompted them to explore alternative forms of interaction (Hay and Gray, 1985; Bryan, 2004). For example, environmentalists and loggers in Quincy, California, whose conflicts over clear-cutting of forests had turned violent, decided to meet in their local library (and hence became known as the Quincy Library Group). This partnership, after much negotiation, enabled them to forge an agreement that eventually became the standard practice for the National Forest Service (after much political in-fighting in Washington, D.C.) (Bryan, 2004). Similarly, environmentalists, coal producers, and consumers engaged in a two-year negotiation called the National Coal Policy Project in which they teased out sustainable practices for coal mining (Hay and Gray, 1985). An example of partnerships spawned by social movement activism can be seen in the environmental justice movement that grew up in African American communities in the US that were exposed to disproportionately high levels of toxic chemicals resulting from brownfields. In Chattanooga, TN, for example, protests by two such communities, coupled with strong principles promoting community activism and community visioning processes throughout the city, eventually led to dialogue among industry, city officials, and residents and the federal government that resulted in the clean-up of a Superfund site in the affected areas (Elliott, 2003). These cases represent success stories, but, of course, not all such deliberations produce lasting resolutions or develop institutionalized partnerships even when third-party mediators design and assist the process (Gray, 2004; Gray et al., 2007).

The role of context in shaping conflict among partners

The nature of the context within which a cross-sectoral partnership forms can have important implications for how the partnership develops initially and how it functions over time. In this section we identify several aspects of the context in which partnerships emerge that are important in shaping the degree of conflict. These include the nature of the field(s) or problem domain with which the potential partners are concerned (Dorado, 2005; Wooten and Hoffman, 2008; Vurro and Dacin, this volume), the regulatory structure and politics in which the partnership is embedded (Gray and Hay, 1986; Sharfman et al., 1991), power differences among the partners (Hardy and Phillips, 1998; Lotia and Hardy, 2008) and the scope and timing of the partnership efforts (e.g. whether it is local, national, or transnational). We explore each of these in some detail below.

Nature of the field in which the partnership is emerging

Problem domains ripe for partnerships often emerge within the context of institutional fields that are in transition (Dorado, 2005). A classic definition of institutional fields views them as communities of organizations that are joined by a common meaning system (Scott, 2001), are constructed in terms of physical proximity or issues, or that represent a recognized area of institutional life (DiMaggio and Powell, 1983). This definition suggests that fields are stable and have clear boundaries. A more recent definition of fields, however, stresses that they are "relational spaces that provide an organization with the opportunity to involve itself with other actors" (Wooten and Hoffman, 1998: 138). Several authors have recently advanced the thesis that fields are always in transition and can change over time – often in response to conflicts that arise from within or outside the field (Rao et al., 2002; Rao et al., 2003; Purdy and Gray, 2009) or as collaborations that form solidify new logics for action within of the field in which the collaboration becomes institutionalized (Vurro and Dacin, this volume).

Although fields may initially organize around a similar logic, disruptive events (Wooten and Hoffman, 2008) (e.g. hostile takeovers, new inventions, new social movements) may cause extant fields to reconfigure and field boundaries to shift. For example, social partnerships that form at the base of the pyramid can, over time, trigger shifts in meso-level governance practices (Rufin and Rivera-Santos, this volume). Fields may also be forced to change when two fields intersect and a new field emerges in the interstices or overlapping spaces connecting them (Morrill, 2007; Dorado, 2005). The emergence of new social movements can also force change within a field (Rao et al., 2002; Doh, 2003). Social movement organizations can introduce new issues into existing organizational fields that raise questions about prevailing norms and practices by highlighting them as injust and in need of reform (Zald, 1999; Benford and Snow, 2000). For example, the Environmental Justice Movement raised issues about disadvantaged African Americans whose neighborhoods were disproportionately exposed to environmental contaminants (Bullard, 1990), and social movements also triggered change in health care with respect to AIDS treatment and gave rise to many new partnerships (Maguire *et al.*, 2004). The introduction of new technologies and the search for innovations can also stimulate partnership formation (Nooteboom, 2007; Davis and Eisenhardt, 2011).

When disruptive events occur, the core logic of the field is questioned or even contested (Anand and Watson, 2004; Purdy and Gray, 2009) leaving the field's boundaries uncertain and open to new configurations and relationships among organizations. Within these periods of overlap, transition or contest, partnerships seem most likely to emerge – perhaps out of the necessity to control the resultant field level turbulence (Emery and Trist, 1965; McCann and Selsky, 2012). Trist (1983) refers to this reconfiguration process as structuring of the field, a terms also used by Wooten and Hoffman (2008: 138) who call for additional research to understand "what drives organizations to interact with each other" to engage in field restructuring.

Changes and conflicts related to the logic of an organization field can create opportunities as well as challenges for cross-sector partners as they simultaneously attempt to address a problem domain while implicitly negotiating the field-level logic. As Wooten and Hoffman (2008: 739–40) note:

> While field constituents' actions may be initially conducted in opposition to one another … protracted institutional engagement can yield a gradual merging of interests with a concurrent alternation in the structure of the field itself. However, until that happens, the field is not a collective of isomorphic actors, but an intertwined constellation of actors who hold differing perspectives and competing logics with regard to their individual and collective purpose.
>
> (*McCarthy and Zald, 1977*)

If actors cannot reconcile their divergent logics and no convergent logic emerges, field-level conflict may remain protracted (Purdy and Gray, 2009; Ansari *et al.*, 2013).

The complexity of such processes is multiplied when a problem domain is defined such that it bridges multiple organizational fields, as in the case of affordable housing decisions which may bring together actors from banking/financial services, education, and transportation fields, each of which has its own logic. Social partnerships addressing issues that span two or more organizational fields must address the tensions among partners' logics that arise both within and across fields. As Selsky and Parker (2005) note, multisector partnerships are more prone to reflect these differing aims such as between self-interest and altruism (Pasquero, 1991; Warner and Sullivan, 2004) or between economic and social goals in Base of the Pyramid contexts (Rufin and Rivera-Santos, 2014). While this kind of structural embeddedness has been argued to reduce transactional uncertainty and facilitate coordination among partners by providing a kind of "macrostructure" of shared rules and understandings (Jones and Lichtenstein, 2007: 239), we suggest that when potential partners hail from multiple sectors and interstitial fields, structural embeddedness may actually increase conflict within the partnership (a topic we explore more thoroughly in our discussion of institutional logics below).

Regulations in the problem domain

Whether the context is a regulated one or not can also have important implications for the kinds of conflicts that emerge within a partnership and how they are handled. Effective collaboration among cross-sectoral partners may be hampered in situations where a governmental participant has regulatory authority linked to the opportunity or problem being addressed. Because governmental organizations have legitimate societal authority for certain decisions and accountability to the public, they may be more likely to assert control and attempt to dominate collaborative partnerships even if the partnership is ostensibly "voluntary." For example, Gazley (2008) found that in non-contractual public-private partnerships, local governments were doing most of the decision making. In describing a national effort to redraft the rules for licensing US hydroelectric projects, Purdy (2012) notes that in addition to legal authority over the final rules, government agencies had human and financial resources that allowed them to set the agenda, determine the meeting locations and schedule, and be well-represented at every meeting. Although the process was designed to maximize public impact on the writing of the rules, nongovernmental and private sector participants lacked the ability to reconfigure the process, and the government ultimately had veto authority over the final decision (Purdy, 2012). The presence of regulations or the inclusion of regulators in a partnership can be particularly problematic if the partnership has been formed to revise, challenge, implement, or create substitutes for regulation (Kolk, 2014).

Some scholars have been skeptical about the level of collaboration that is achievable when partnering is mandated (Rodriguez *et al.*, 2007; Genzkow, 2009). When partnerships are generated by a legal mandate or regulatory requirement, at least four possible consequences are likely: either (1) the parties are collaborating perfunctorily or "in name only" just to appear to meet the regulatory requirement; (2) local relevance/ownership is lacking (Taylor and Schweitzer, 2005); (3) the requirements for how to structure the partners' interactions constrain the flexibility with which they can interact; or (4) one partner is able to exert greater power over the others. In the latter situation, Hardy and Phillips (1998) argue that this is no longer collaboration but rather may be compliance, contention, or contestation instead. Another consequence of differential power among potentially collaborative partners is collusion in which some partners withhold effort and information in order to retain their power and avoid exposing their possible vulnerabilities (Gray and Schruijer, 2010).

While mandated collaboration may have the liabilities noted above, in some circumstances it may be necessary and even prove beneficial as it gives regulatory agencies the opportunity to garner input from a wide-array of stakeholders as in regulatory negotiations (Gray and Wondolleck, 2013). Mandated collaborations can force potential partners to get on with addressing problems that need attention. Partnerships for managing natural resource issues at the ecosystem level often warrant mandated approaches to ensure that coordination across the ecosystem occurs (Agranoff, 2007; Wondolleck and Yaffee, 2000).

Recent research suggests the relationship between mandatory participation and partnership effectiveness is not a simple one. Brummela et al.'s (2010) study of mandated collaborations between a wildfire management agency and citizens revealed that the degree of social learning that occurred varied depending on other factors such as number of partners, duration of planning, and quality of the facilitation. Often, learning consisted of enhanced coordination, but not innovation. Additionally, the nature of the mandatory requirements (e.g. annual review by an outside party and use of a standard template) produced different degrees of learning. Finally, these authors raised questions about the longevity of the learning and suggested the need for evaluation beyond the end of the mandated relationship.

Scope of the problem or issue

While partnerships can occur locally, nationally, or globally, in general as the context increases in scope, greater complexity is introduced into the management of the partnership, and the likelihood of conflict also increases. For example, in a mediation over the management of Voyageurs National Park (in the United States), local participants believed that boundaries of the negotiation should include Canadian waters that bordered the park, but the US National Park Service disagreed arguing that the Federal Mediation and Conciliation Service did not have jurisdiction to mediate such a dispute and that adding Canadian officials would turn it a national dispute into an international disagreement, adding more issues to the debate including an entirely different regulatory structure.

A special kind of problem also arises when the presenting conflicts are transnational or global in scope (see also Kolk, 2014). In such cases, there is no government or legitimate overarching authority that sets the norms for negotiations among diverse parties or provides a forum for such debates (Roseneau, 1992; Ansari et al., 2013). Thus, in cases like the Palm Oil Roundtable or the Kyoto Protocol, even if the parties reach a "binding agreement," no explicit means of enforcing the agreement exists. Partnerships formed to wrestle with these complex kinds of issues also comprise hundreds of partners which often makes them unwieldy and subject to dynamics associated with blocking coalitions and with diverse logics and frames which we explore further below. The temporal embeddedness (Jones and Lichtenstien, 2007) of a partnership may also affect its scope and level of conflict, since short-term partnerships may not be able to probe issues in as much depth as protracted ones which may also reduce the level of conflict the partners experience.

Power differences

Differences in power among the potential partners can also fuel conflict within partnerships. These differences may lead them to hold different expectations about the goals of the partnerships and how the process of collaboration will unfold. Thus, although parties may all be concerned about the problem, their vantage points and expectations about what the collaboration will accomplish and why may differ substantially. For example, in analyzing a collaboration about the future of refugees, Lotia and Hardy (2008: 375) noted,

> Although these organizations were working on the same overall problem of refugees and their settlement, their divergent views and asymmetrical power relations led them to define the refugee "problem" in different ways and to advocate for different "solutions" namely those that reinforced the organization's position in the refugee system.

Power differences can also manifest in "representational" disputes over who deserves to have a seat at the table and what invited "experts" were expected to provide in the way of competing views (Laws, 1999). Representational debates may also impact the number and variety of potential partners since when views are exceedingly different, some groups may seek to exclude others from participating in the collaboration to reduce the diversity of perspectives under consideration or to tip the table in their own favor (Gray and Hay, 1986). When the number of stakeholders is large, not only does the complexity of interactions increase, but so do the chances of some stakeholders questioning the presence of others.

The problem of conflicting logics and frames

As described above, the characteristics of the partners (e.g. power differences) or the structure of the situation (e.g. transnational partnerships) may spark conflicts, generate dynamics that make conflicts difficult to resolve, or impair the partnership's ability to achieve resolution. Such barriers can be identified through analysis of the stakeholders and the context, so that they can be acknowledged by the participants and possibly mitigated by mutual agreements about interaction processes and decision making procedures. However, another set of potential barriers exists at a deeper level where fundamental differences between stakeholders are more difficult to recognize. These barriers are derived from the institutional logics held by participants, which are taken-for-granted and thus largely invisible to the parties themselves.

Conflicting logics

Institutional logics are "the socially constructed, historical patterns of material practices, assumptions, values, beliefs, and rules by which individuals produce and reproduce their material subsistence, organize time and space, and provide meaning to their social reality." (Thornton and Ocasio, 1999: 804). When stakeholders agree to join a collaboration, their particular institutional logics may cause them to frame the problem differently (Vaughan and Siefert, 1992; Lewicki *et al.*, 2003; Dewulf and Bouwen, 2012; Dewulf *et al.*, 2011). Participants in cross-sectoral partnerships may be influenced by institutional logics that are derived from (1) the societal sector they represent (private, public, or nonprofit sector), (2) the organizational fields that form around particular problem sets, and (3) the nation-states in which they are situated. We describe each of these types of institutional logics below.

Societal sector logics. Market-based societies can be considered in terms of three sectors – public, private, and non-profit – that can be used to classify the roles of organizations and actors (Bowker and Star, 1999). Each sector is characterized by an institutional logic that helps its members interpret events, create meaning, and experience a sense of identity (Friedland and Alford, 1991). The public sector is characterized by a bureaucratic state logic reflected in a hierarchical system with highly defined roles where interactions are governed by rules. The logic of bureaucracy is to increase efficiency through specialization, and to ensure fairness through oversight and consistent application of rules (Weber, 1947). The private sector is characterized by market logic, which emphasizes individual wealth creation through voluntary exchange. That logic emphasizes economic rationality linked to supply and demand and is reflected in an orientation toward maximization of individual or organizational economic benefit (Friedland and Alford, 1991). The non-profit sector, also known as the social benefit or "third" sector, is characterized by community logic (Thornton *et al.*, 2012). Community logic involves both upholding universal rights and satisfying the particularistic demands of communities (Etzioni, 2004) to address shared concerns for the common good that aren't accounted for through market or governmental mechanisms (Kaghan and Purdy, 2012). An environmental logic is a variant of the community logic (Ansari *et al.*, 2013) but broadens the notion of community reflected in the logic to include non-humans such as animals and plants within the scope of what "community" comprises.

Social partnerships usually include participants from two or three of these sectors who bring with them differing assumptions based on the logics of their sectors (see also Vurro and Dacin, this volume). These logics affect many aspects of the partnership, from the way domains are interpreted to how information is presented and analyzed to preferred solutions for addressing the domain. For example, private sector participants may assume that a cost/benefit approach is the most appropriate approach to evaluating a problem, while public sector participants may interpret the problem in terms of rights and fairness, and a nonprofit sector participant may primarily consider the collective impacts of the partnership on those served by it and how they match up with deeper values such as decency and well-being.

Nation-state logics. Cross-sectoral partnerships may emerge from common concerns that span geography. For example, transnational social movements may arise that bridge countries and are comprised of many different organizations all generally aligned with a common theme such as women's rights or global security (Zald, 1999). The complexity of partnerships increases at the transnational level not only because of differing jurisdictions, but because parties hail from different institutional contexts and national cultures, and thus bring different mental maps or frames to their understanding the issues (Lewicki *et al.*, 2003; Dewulf and Bouwen, 2012). "Institutional building in the transnational sphere involves multiple actors or groups of actors with mental and action maps originating from quite different institutional contexts" (Djelic and Quack, 2008: 309). Especially at this level, in order to forge a partnership, it may first be necessary to explore the potential partners' different frames about the problem.

Conflicting frames

While logics comprise enduring assumptions and practices, frames operate at a more tactical level and are typically more pliable (Ansari *et al.*, 2013). Frames are interpretations we use to make sense of the world around us. "We construct frames by sorting and categorizing our experience – weighing new information against previous interpretations" (Gray, 2003: 12). Frames also shape the actions we are willing to take. For example, we use frames to represent our identities and to characterize others and to justify our actions (Lewicki *et al.*, 2003) and to mobilize others to take action (Benford and Snow, 2000). "Through framing, we place ourselves in relation to the issues or events thereby taking a stance with respect to them (Taylor, 2000) and placing ourselves in concert with or in opposition to other parties" (Gray, 2006: 225).

When domain-related disputes occur, they clearly impede partnership formation despite the fact that the disputants may be concerned about the same problem domain. The institutional orientation of potential partners and their ability to influence the framing of others has a significant effect on the content and outcome of collaborative discussions. For example, in their study of cross-sectoral partnerships organized around watershed management, linking public agencies with nonprofits and citizen groups, Moore and Koontz (2003) identified groups as citizen-based, agency-based, or mixed. Citizen-based groups framed group achievements as linked to lobbying and advocacy, while mixed groups identified achievements as creating a watershed management plan and agency-based groups identified achievements as sustainability activities. In another case, three groups all concerned about homelessness in Massachusetts initially framed the problem differently using a market frame, a social welfare frame, and a social control frame, but eventually they collectively began to reframe their interpretations to incorporate all three perspectives (Schon and Rein, 1994).

Independent partnerships develop their own definitions of problems, while partnerships dominated by a particular partner are likely to develop frames linked to that partner's institutional domain. "Organizational culture and pre-existing constituent relationships may dictate partnerships' definition of the problem and the range of preferred alternatives in agency-affiliated partnerships" (Bidwell and Ryan, 2006). In a natural resource management project in Southern Ecuador in which government engineers were working with indigenous peoples to improve irrigation systems, members of each group framed the complex issues very differently (Dewulf and Bouwen, 2012). The engineers conceptualized it in terms of a theoretical flow rate model whereas the indigenous farmers adopted a practical frame based on years of observation and experience. Dewulf and Bouwen observed that in order to resolve these differences the partners needed to use several conversational techniques that included frame incorporation, accommodation, and reconnection. In many disputes, however, reframing fails or is insufficient, as in the case of climate change in which a lasting partnership to avert global warming fell short despite many shifts in parties' frames over a thirty-year period. These shifts were not sufficient to gain agreement on a hybrid logic that supported reduction and mitigation of carbon emissions (Ansari *et al.*, 2013).

Tactical approaches for addressing conflicts in partnerships

Interventions to promote constructive partnership development have been advanced by many scholars and practitioners. One recent framework proposes eight such intervention tasks and links them to the stages of partnership development (Gray, 2008). These intervention tasks range from the initial imagining of a partnership through implementing an agreement and beyond. The tasks include recognizing a need for partnership (visioning), identifying and enlisting participants (convening), collecting and sharing data to stimulate dialogue (reflective intervening), developing shared meanings of the issues and the options (problem structuring), managing the interactions between partners (process managing), coordinating the exchange among partners (brokering), working through disagreements (conflict handling), and promoting broad acceptance of the outcomes (institutional entrepreneurship) (Gray, 2008). Table 11.1 delineates several specific tactics available to accomplish each of these intervention tasks. For a more detailed descriptions of these tactics (see Gray, 2008).

The specific tactics used for each task differ depending upon whether the partnership is rooted in conflict or opportunity. While this framework identifies a range of tasks and tactics for each type of partnership, it should be noted that partnerships need not proceed through all tasks sequentially nor utilize all tactical interventions to succeed. Partnerships originating from conflict (listed in the center column of Table 11.1) face unique challenges in shifting their interactions from conflict to collaboration, which may necessitate the use of different tactics than partnerships arising from opportunities (listed in the right column of Table 11.1). Below we discuss in further detail the tactics for managing conflict-based cross-sectoral partnerships.

For conflict-rooted partnerships, the use of a *conflict assessment* process may be necessary to determine whether any intervention is possible and might be productive (Susskind *et al.*, 1999). For example, public policy mediators use assessment to "(1) understand the history and background of the conflict, (2) determine the relevant parties and their power relationships, (3) glean the positions and, more importantly, the interests and BATNAs of the parties, and (4) diagnose whether or not a consensus-building process is feasible" (Gray, 2006: 238). In addition to these considerations,

TABLE 11.1 Tasks and tactics for managing cross-sectoral partnerships (adapted from Gray, 2006)

Tasks for constructing partnerships	Tactics for conflict-based partnerships	Tactics for opportunity-based partnerships
Visioning – recognizing interdependence and need for partnership	Acknowledging critical identities Identifying leaders Leveling power differences	Shared strategy maps Search conference
Convening – identifying and enlisting participants	Conflict assessment (including frame analysis)	Feasibility assessment Inviting partners
Reflective Intervening – collecting and sharing data to stimulate dialogue	Telling identity stories	Action research Appreciative inquiry
Problem structuring – developing shared meanings of the issue and the options	Developing shared superordinate identity frames	Analyzing interconnected decision areas Strategic option development and analysis
Process managing – creating and managing the interactions between partners	Setting ground rules that convey safety	Collaborative design Large-scale system interventions
Brokering – coordinating the exchange among partners	Shuttle diplomacy	Liaisons Bridging
Conflict handling – working through disagreements	Synchronized de-escalation Mediation	Mediation Facilitation Consensus building Perspective taking Trust building
Institutional entrepreneurship – promoting broad acceptance of the solution	Addressing the two-table problem	Structuring Replicating

Gray (2006) has suggested that such assessments should also include how the conflicting parties are framing the dispute in order to deepen and sharpen understanding of cognitive and relational impediments to partnership and how they might be overcome. Once forming a partnership is judged to be feasible, another important tactic for moving parties from contentious behavior to a problem-solving orientation is:

> *acknowledging of the parties' critical identities*. Rather than ignoring or smoothing over their different identities, it may be crucial for potential partners to acknowledge each other's prized and distinctive identities in order to minimize feelings that collaboration may threaten these while simultaneously

creating a *superordinate shared identity* (Fiol *et al.*, 2009). Enabling parties to develop a common in-group identity that does not require them to forsake their individual prized identity has been shown to reduce prejudice among groups (Dovidio and Gaertner, 1998) thus enhancing the possibility that the partners will be able to see past their differences in order to collaborate. Gray (2006) has referred to this as frame enlargement since the partners are entertaining a broader conception of their own and their partners' identities.

Another important step in moving from conflict to problem solving is *identifying leaders* who are sufficiently powerful to move a cross-sectoral partnership forward. The structure of a situation may dictate leadership, such as in a regulatory context or when participation is mandatory, however, leadership also occurs through the selection of the process and the participants (Huxham and Vangen, 2000). Cross-sectoral partnerships rooted in conflict may require third-party support to identify a leadership chair or committee that has "the ability to focus people's attention and create a sense of urgency, the skill to apply pressure to stakeholders without overwhelming them, the competence to frame issues in a way that presents opportunities as well as difficulties, and the strength to mediate conflict among stakeholders" (Kania and Kramer, 2011: 40). In the case of the National Coal Policy Project (mentioned earlier), two leaders (one from business and one from the environmental NGOs had the vision to see past the conflict and draw parties into partnership (Hay and Gray, 1985).

Where such leadership is not immediately evident, a third party *mediator* may be needed to help the parties see past their conflicts and forge more collaborative relationships (Gray, 1989; Susskind *et al.*, 1999). By ensuring that *ground rules are established* and agreed to by both partners, a third party can ensure that each partner feels a sense of safety and control over their initial interactions with the other(s). For example, in a dispute between snowmobilers, other citizens and state park officials over maintenance of snow mobile trails, park officials needed to solicit the help of neutral third parties to construct a collaborative table because park officials themselves were too deeply embedded in the conflict to be seen as neutral conveners on their own (Purdy and Gray, 1994).

Third parties can also help to level the playing field when power differences exist and to facilitate listening among the potential collaborators (Gray, 1989). Cross-sector partnerships include parties with different forms of power stemming from the societal sector to which a partner belongs. For example, government agencies may hold decision authority, private-sector organizations may have financial resources, and nonprofit organizations may have representational or grass roots power. Recognizing these different forms of power as valid and significant can assist in *leveling power differences*. Partners may tend to emphasize the power of decision authority, or of having significant human, informational or economic resources, but the relational and perceptual aspects of power are also important in social partnership contexts (Purdy, 2012). For example, power can exist in the ability to catalyze constituents or in the ability to speak on behalf of societally important ideals such as human rights (Purdy, 2012). While government agencies may be reluctant to partner with social movement activists because they consider them as uninformed fanatics (Hanke *et al.*, 2003), the presence of third parties can ensure these agencies that the dialogue will remain civil while enabling access to the decision making forum for the NGOs. Acknowledging different types of power is a means of balancing power among participants which can increase the effectiveness of the partnership by reducing the need for displays of and contests over power. Attending to power differences among partners allows adjustments to be made to the process design, the participants, and the approach to substantive issues, creating a more level playing field on which parties can participate fully and genuinely (Purdy, 2012).

For conflict-initiated partnerships, the task of conflict handling can explicitly be addressed by using the tactic of *synchronized de-escalation* (Osgood, 1962). This tactic helps parties to "step back from the ledge" while saving face and maintaining the integrity of their identity. In synchronized de-escalation, one party decides on a small concession to signal good faith and an intention to improve the relationship. Other parties are invited to reciprocate with their own concessions at a specified time to signal their good faith. The parties commit to make concessions without knowing whether others will follow through, signaling their trust and providing a means for the partners to move into a problem-solving mode.

Telling identity stories is a useful tactic for accomplishing the task of reflective intervening. By telling their own story (and engaging other participants as reflective listeners), each partner can establish their own voice in the dialogue and begin to "hear" the other partners' concerns as well. One specific reflective technique to promote deep listening is the Samoan Circle in which heartfelt concerns are heard and acknowledged by all participants.

Once parties have agreed to participate and have begun to share information, *developing shared frames* is a particularly vital tactic for partnerships rooted in conflict. Participants in cross-sectoral partnerships frame conflicts through their taken-for-granted institutional logics. For reframing to occur, the parties must reassess the stance they are taking in light of the frames proffered by others (Schon and Rein, 1994). Differences in frames may not be immediately evident, but may be exposed by role reversal and imaging processes in which parties share views of themselves and how they appear to others (Alderfer, 1977). By exposing different frames, participants have the opportunity to construct a hybrid shared frame that recombines the extant logics (Djelic and Quack, 2008) and reshapes expectations about outcomes of the partnership (Gray, 2006).

Two other tactics that may prove useful in conflict-initiated partnerships include *shuttle diplomacy* and *addressing the two-table problem*. Shuttle diplomacy is a form of the brokering task that involves the mediator meeting individually with each partner to learn their concerns in order to convey them to the other partner(s) in a subsequent private meeting. This tactic can prove useful when the dynamics among the potential partners are deemed to be initially explosive and likely to escalate the conflict. Through shuttle diplomacy a mediator may be able to diffuse or dampen escalatory tendencies. The two-table problem typically arises toward the end of negotiations when negotiators need to ratify their agreement with back-home constituents (Putnam, 1988). By anticipating this problem and keeping constituents informed about the negotiations and soliciting their input as the negotiations progress, potential partners can prevent eleventh hour rejection of potential partnership agreements.

Although the above tactics have been suggested explicitly for conflict-initiated partnerships, even partnerships that start from opportunities, rather than conflict, may face conflict as they develop. As partnerships move toward creating solutions and making deals, conflicts may emerge that ignite or reignite tensions and move the partnership closer to impasse. In such cases, many of the tactics described here may prove useful for keeping the partnership on track.

Conclusion

Cross-sectoral partnerships draw together stakeholders with varying institutional logics whose interests have clashed or converged around a problem or opportunity. Whether initially rooted on conflict or opportunity, such partnerships are likely to generate conflicts at some point as participants work through the processes needed to try to achieve resolution. Various structural and relational challenges can generate conflict, such as differential power or a mandate to participate. More deeply rooted institutional logics can also drive conflict, such as when participants hail from diverse societal sectors or when the core logic of an organizational field is being negotiated. In this chapter we have offered means by which to understand conflict in cross-sector partnerships and suggested a framework that can be used to support progress toward resolution, unleashing the full potential of such partnerships to create a collective impact (Kania and Kramer, 2011) on society's most daunting challenges and inspiring opportunities.

Questions for reflection

1 How can partnerships evaluate the potential for contention and change in their organizational field? To what degree do participants in a partnership recognize their work as having potential to shift norms and expectations related to the problem domain?

2 What circumstances make it difficult or impossible to bridge power differences among parties? How do the tactics for intervening in partnerships try to overcome such potential impasses?

3 When conveners anticipate that potential partners will approach attempts to collaborate from different institutional logics, what steps can they design in to address the potential conflicts?

4 How and when should participants decide whether to exclude a potential partner because that party is likely to be disruptive to the partnership?

References

Agranoff, R. (2007) *Managing within Networks: Adding Value to Public Organizations.* Washington, DC: Georgetown University Press.

Alderfer, C.P. (1977) Group and intergroup relations, in J.R. Hackman and J.L. Suttle (eds) *Improving Life at Work: Behavioral Science Approaches to Organizational Change.* Santa Monica, CA: Goodyear: 227–96.

Anand, N. and Watson, M.R. (2004) Tournament rituals in the evolution of fields: the case of the Grammy Awards. *Academy of Management Journal,* 47: 59–80.

Ansari, S., Wijen, F. and Gray, B. (2013) Constructing a climate change logic: an institutional perspective on the "Tragedy of the Commons." *Organization Science,* 24: 1014–40.

Benford, R. and Snow, D. (2000) Framing processes and social movements: an overview and assessment. *Annual Review of Sociology,* 26: 611–39.

Bidwell, R.D. and Ryan, C.M. (2006) Collaborative partnership design: the implications of organizational affiliation for watershed partnerships. *Society and Natural Resources,* 19: 827–43.

Bingham, L.B. (2008) Collaborative governance: emerging practices and the incomplete legal framework for public and stakeholder voice. *UC Berkeley Center for the Study of Law and Society Faculty Working Papers.* Accessible at: http://escholarship.org/uc/item/8r99f510

Bowker, G.C. and Star, S.L. (1999) *Sorting things out: classification and its consequences.* Cambridge, MA: MIT Press.

Brummans, B., Putnam, L., Gray, B., Lewicki, R., Weitoff, C. (2008) Making sense of intractable multiparty conflict: a study of framing in four environmental disputes. *Communication Monographs,* 75 (1): 25–51.

Brummela, R.F., Nelson, K.C., Grayzeck Souter, S., Jakes, P.J. and Williams, D.R. (2010) Social learning in a policy-mandated collaboration: community wildfire protection planning in the eastern United States. *Journal of Environmental Planning and Management,* 53 (6): 681–99.

Bryan, T. (2004) Tragedy averted: the promise of collaboration. *Society and Natural Resources,* 17: 881–96.

Bryson, J., Crosby, B.C. and Stone, M.M. (2006) The design and implementation of cross-sector collaborations: propositions from the literature. *Public Administration Review,* 66: S1: 44–55.

Bullard, R.D. (1990) Race, class, and the politics of place, in R.D. Bullard (ed.) *Dumping in Dixie: Race, Class, and Environmental Quality.* Boulder, CO: Westview.

Chávez, B.V. and Bernal, A.S. (2008) Planning hydroelectric power plants with the public: a case of organizational and social learning in Mexico. *Impact Assessment and Project Appraisal,* 26(3): 163–76.

Davis, J.P. and Eisenhardt, K.M. (2011) Rotating leadership and collaborative innovation: recombination processes in symbiotic relationships. *Administrative Science Quarterly,* 56 (2): 159–201.

Dewulf, A. and Bouwen, R. (2012) Issue framing in conversations for change: discursive interaction strategies for "doing differences". *Journal of Applied Behavioral Science,* 48 (2): 168–93.

Dewulf, A., Gray, B., Putnam, L. and Bouwen, R. (2011) An interactional approach to framing in conflict and negotiation, in B. Donohue, R. Rogan and S. Kaufman (eds) *Framing Matters: Perspectives on Negotiation Research and Practice in Communication.* New York: Peter Lang Publishing: 7–33.

DiMaggio P.J. and Powell, W. (1983) "The iron cage revisited" institutional isomorphism and … in organizational fields. *American Sociological Review,* 48: 147–60.

Djelik, M-L. and Quack, S. (2008) Institutions and transnationalism, in R. Greenwood, C. Oliver, K. Sahlin, K. and R. Suddaby (eds) *The Sage Handbook of Organizational Institutionalism*. London: Sage: 299–324.

Djelik, M-L. and Sahlin-Anderson, K. (eds) (2006) *Transnational Governance*. Cambridge: Cambridge University Press.

Doh, J.P. (2003) Nongovernmental organizations, corporate strategy, and public policy: NGOs as agents of change, in J.P.Doh and H.Teegen (eds) *Globalization and NGOs*. Westport, CT: Praeger: 1–18.

Dorado, S. (2005) Institutional entrepreneurship, partaking, and convening. *Organization Studies*, 26 (3): 383–413.

Dovidio, J.F. and Gaertner, S.L. (1998) On the nature of contemporary prejudice: the causes, consequences, and challenges of aversive racism, in J. Eberhardt & S.T. Fiske (eds) *Confronting Facism: The Problem and the Response*. Thousand Oaks, CA: Sage: 3–32.

Elliott, M. (2003) When the parents be cancer-free: community voice, toxics and environmental justice in Chattanooga, Tennessee, in R. Lewicki, B. Gray, and M. Elliott (eds) *Making Sense of Intractable Environmental Conflict*. Washington, DC: Island Press: 303–32.

Emery, F. and Trist, E. (1965) The causal texture of organizational environments, *Human Relations*, 18: 21–32.

Etzioni, A. (2004) *The Common Good*. Cambridge: Polity Press.

Fiol, C., Pratt, M.G. and O'Connor, E.J. (2009) Managing intractable identity conflicts. *Academy of Management Review*, 34 (1): 32–55.

Friedland, R. and Alford, R.R. (1991) Bringing society back in: symbols, practices, and institutional contradictions, in P. DiMaggio and W.W. Powell (eds) *The New Institutionalism in Organizational Analysis*. Chicago, IL: University of Chicago Press: 232–66.

Gazley, B. (2008) Beyond the contract: the scope and nature of informal government–nonprofit partnerships. *Public Administration Review*, 68 (1): 141–54.

Genskow, K.D. (2009) Catalyzing collaboration: Wisconsin's agency-initiated basin partnerships. *Environmental Management*, 43 (3): 411–24.

Glasbergen, P. (2007) Setting the scene: the partnership paradigm in the making, in P. Glasbergen, F. Beirmann, and A.P.J. Mol (eds) *Partnerships, Governance and Sustainable Development: Reflection on Theory and Practice*. Cheltenham: Edward Elgar: 1–25.

Gray, B. (1989) *Collaborating: Finding Common Ground for Multiparty Problems*. San Francisco, CA: Jossey-Bass.

Gray, B. (1996) Cross-sectoral Partners: collaborative alliances among business, government and communities, in C. Huxham (ed.) *In Search of Collaborative Advantage*. London: Sage: 58–99.

Gray, B. (2003) Framing of environmental disputes, in R. Lewicki, B. Gray and M. Elliott (eds) *Making Sense of Intractable Environmental Disputes: Concepts and Cases*. Washington, DC: Island Press: 11–34.

Gray, B. (2005) Strong opposition: frame-based resistance to collaboration. *J. Community and Applied Social Psychology*, 14 (3): 166–76.

Gray, B. (2006) Frame-based intervention for promoting understand in multiparty conflicts, in T. Gössling, L. Oerlemans and R. Jansen (eds) *Inside Networks*. Cheltenham: Edward Elgar: 223–50.

Gray, B. (2008) Intervening to improve inter-organizational partnerships, in S. Cropper, M. Ebers, C. Huxham and P. Smith Ring (eds) *The Oxford Handbook of Inter-Organizational Relations*. New York: Oxford University Press: 664–90.

Gray, B. and Hay, T.M. (1986) Political limits to interorganizational consensus and change. *Journal of Applied Behavioral Science*, 22 (2): 95–112.

Gray, B., Coleman, P. and Putnam, L. (2007) Intractable conflicts: new perspectives on the causes and conditions for change. *American Behavioral Scientist,* 50 (10): 1–15.

Gray, B. and Schruijer, S. (2010) Integrating multiple voices: working with collusion in multiparty collaborations, in C. Staeyert and B. Van Loy *Relational Practices: Participative Organizing.* Bingley: Emerald: 121–35.

Gray, B. and Wondolleck, J. (2013) Environmental negotiations: past, present and future prospects, in M. Olekans and W. Adair (eds) *Handbook of Research in Negotiations.* Cheltenham: Edward Elgar: 445–72

Hanke, R., Rosenberg, A., & Gray, B. (2003) The story of Drake Chemical: a burning issue, in *Making Sense of Intractable Environmental Disputes: Concepts and Cases.* Washington, DC: Island Press: 275–302.

Hardy, C. and Phillips, N. (1998) Strategies of engagement: lessons from the critical examination of collaboration and conflict in an interorganizational domain. *Organization Science,* 9 (2): 217–30.

Hay, T. and Gray, B. (1985) The national coal policy project: an interactive approach to corporate social responsiveness, in L.E. Preston (ed.) *Research in corporate social performance and policy,* Vol. 7, Greenwich, CT: JAI Press: 191–212.

Huxham, C. and Vangen, S. (2000) Leadership in the shaping and implementation of collaboration agendas: how things happen in a (not quite) joined-up world. *Academy of Management Journal,* 43 (6): 1159–75.

Huxham, C. and Vangen, S. (2005) *Managing to Collaborate.* London: Routledge.

Innis, J. (1999) Evaluating consensus building, in L. Susskind, S. MacKearnan and J. Thomas-Larmer (eds) *The Consensus Building Handbook: A Comprehensive Guide to Reaching Agreement.* Thousand Oaks, CA: Sage: 631–75.

Jones, C. and Lichtenstien, B.B. (2008) Temporary inter-organizational projects: how temporal and social embeddedness enhance coordination and manage uncertainty, in S. Cropper, M. Ebers, C. Huxham and P. Smith Ring (eds) *The Oxford Handbook of Inter-Organizational Relations.* New York: Oxford University Press: 231–55.

Kaghan, W.N. and Purdy, J.M. (2012) Capitalism, creative destruction, and the common good. Paper presented at the 2012 ESSEC Business School conference on the role of business in society and the pursuit of the common good. Cergy, France.

Kania, J. and Kramer, M. (2011) Collective impact. *Stanford Social Innovation Review,* Winter, 9 (1): 36–41.

Kolk, A. (2014) Partnerships as panacea for addressing global problems? On rationale, context, actors, impact and limitations, in M.M. Seitanidi and A. Crane (eds) *Social Partnerships and Responsible Business: A Research Handbook.* London: Routledge: 15–43.

Laws, D. (1999) Representation of stakeholding interests, in L. Susskind, S. MacKearnan and J. Thomas-Larmer (eds) *The Consensus Building Handbook: A Comprehensive Guide to Reaching Agreement.* Thousand Oaks, CA: Sage: 241–85.

LeBaron, M. (2003) Cultural and worldview frames, in G. Burgess and H. Burgess, H. (eds) Beyond intractability. Conflict Information Consortium, University of Colorado, Boulder. Posted: August 2003 www.beyondintractability.org/bi-essay/cultural-frames.

LeBaron, M. and Carstarphen, N. (1997) Negotiating intractable conflict: the common ground dialogue process and abortion. *Negotiation Journal,* 13 (4): 341–61.

Lewicki, R., Gray, B. and Elliott, M. (2003) *Making sense of intractable environmental conflict.* Washington, DC: Island Press.

Lotia, N. and Hardy, C. (2008) Critical perspectives on collaboration, in S. Cropper, M. Ebers, C. Huxham and P. Smith Ring (eds) *The Oxford Handbook of Inter-Organizational Relations.* New York: Oxford University Press: 366–89.

Maguire, S., Hardy, C. and Lawrence, T. (2004) Institutional entrepreneurship in emerging fields: HI/AIDS treatment advocacy in Canada. *Academy of Management Journal,* 47: 657–79.

McCann, J.E. and Selsky, J. (2012) *Mastering Turbulence: The Essential Capabilities of Agile and Resilient Individuals, Teams and Organizations.* San Francisco: Jossey-Bass.

McCarthy, J. and Zald, M. (1977) Resource mobilization and social movements: a partial theory. *American Journal of Sociology*, 82: 1212–40.

Morrill, C. (2007) Institutional change through interstitial emergence: the growth of alternative dispute resolution in American law 1965–1995, in W.W. Powell and D.L. Jones (eds) *How Institutions Change.* Chicago: University of Chicago Press.

Moore, E.A. and T.M. Koontz. (2003) A typology of collaborative watershed planning groups: citizen-based, agency-based and mixed partnerships. *Society and Natural Resources,* 16 (5): 451–60.

Nooteboom, B. (2007) Learning and innovation in inter-organizational relationships, in S. Cropper, M. Ebers, C. Huxham and P. Smith Ring (eds) *The Oxford Handbook of Inter-Organizational Relations.* New York: Oxford University Press: 607–34.

Oliver, C. (1990) Determinants of interorganizational relationships: integration and future direction. *Academy of Management Review*, 15 (2): 241–65.

Osgood, C.E. (1962) *An Alternative to War or Surrender.* Urbana, IL: University of Illinois Press.

Pasquero, J. (1991) Supraorganizational collaboration: the Canadian environmental experiment. *Journal of Applied Behavioral Science*, 27 (1): 38–64.

Powell, W.W. (1990) Neither market nor hierarchy: network form of organization. *Research in Organizational Behavior,* Vol. II. Greenwich, CT: JAI Press: 295–336.

Public Conversation Project, 1999. An overview of PCP's work on abortion. www.public-conversations.org/resources/overview-pcps-work-abortion

Purdy, J.M. (2012) A framework for assessing power in collaborative governance processes. *Public Administration Review*, 72 (3): 409–17.

Purdy, J.M. and Gray, B. (1994) Government agencies as mediators in public policy conflicts. *International Journal of Conflict Management*, 5 (2): 379–82.

Purdy, J.M. and Gray, B. (2009) Conflicting logics, mechanisms of diffusion and multilevel dynamics in emerging institutional fields. *Academy of Management Journal*, 52 (2): 355–80.

Putnam, D. (1988) Diplomacy and domestic politics: the logic of two-level games. *International Organization*, 42 (3): 427–60.

Rao, H., Monin, P. and Durand, R. (2003) Institutional change in Toque Ville: nouvelles cuisines an identity movement in French gastronomy. *American Journal of Sociology*, 108: 795–843.

Rao, H., Morrill, C. and Zald, M.N. (2000) Power plays: how social movements and collective action create new organizational forms. *Research in Organizational Behavior,* 22: 239–82.

Rodriguez, C., Langley, A., Beland, F. and Denis, J-L. (2007) Governance, power and mandated collaboration in an interorganizational network. *Administration and Society*, 39 (2): 150–93.

Rosenau, J. (1992) Governance, order and change in world politics, in J. Rosenau and E-O. Czempiel (eds) *Governance without Government: Order and Change in World Politics.* Cambridge: Cambridge University Press.

Rothman, J. (1997) *Resolving Identity-Based Conflict in Nations, Organizations, and Communities.* San Francisco, CA: Jossey-Bass.

Rufin, C. and Rivera-Santos, M. (2014) Cross-sector governance: from institutions to partnerships, and back to institutions, in M. M. Seitanidi and A. Crane (eds) *Social Partnerships and Responsible Business: A Research Handbook.* London: Routledge: 125–42.

Sandfort, J. and Milward, H.B. (2008) Collaborative service provision in the public sector, in S. Cropper, M. Ebers, C. Huxham and P. Smith Ring (eds) *The Oxford Handbook of Interorganizational Relations.* New York: Oxford University Press: 147–75.

Schon, D.A. and Rein, M. (1994) *Frame Reflection: Toward the Resolution of Intractable Policy Controversies.* New York: Basic Books.

Scott, W.R. (2001) *Institutions and Organizations* (2nd edn.). Thousand Oaks, CA: Sage.

Selsky, J.W. and Parker, B. (2005) Cross-sector partnerships to address social issues: challenges to theory and practice, *Journal of Management,* 31 (6): 1–25.

Sharfman, M., B. Gray and A. Yan. (1991) The context of interorganizational collaboration in the garment industry: an institutional perspective. *Journal of Applied Behavioral Science,* 27 (2): 181–208.

Sousa, D.J. and Klyza, C.M. (2007) New directions in environmental policy making: an emerging collaborative regime or reinventing interest group liberalism? *Natural Resources Journal,* 47: 377–444.

Susskind, L. and Thomas-Larmer, J. (1999) Conducting a conflict assessment, in L. Susskind, S. MacKearnan and J. Thomas-Larmer (eds) *The Consensus Building Handbook.* Thousand Oaks, CA: Sage: 99–136.

Susskind, L., MacKearnan, S. and Thomas-Larmer, J. (eds) *The Consensus Building Handbook: A Comprehensive Guide to Reaching Agreement.* Thousand Oaks, CA: Sage.

Susskind, L., McKearnan, S. and Thomas-Larmer, J. (eds) (1999) *The Consensus Building Handbook: A Comprehensive Guide to Reaching Agreement.* Thousand Oaks, CA: Sage.

Taylor, D.E. (2000) Advances in environmental justice: research, theory, and methodology. *American Behavioral Scientist,* 43 (4): 504–80.

Taylor, B.D. and Schweitzer, L. (2005) Assessing the experience of mandated collaborative inter-jurisdictional transport planning in the United States. *Transport Policy,* 12 (6): 500–11.

Thornton, P. and Ocasio, W. (2008) *Institutional Logics,* in R. Greenwood, C. Oliver, K. Sahlin and R. Suddaby (eds) *The Sage Handbook of Organizational Institutionalism.* London: Sage: 99–129.

Thornton, P., Ocasio, W. and Lounsbury, M. (2012) *The Institutional Logics Perspective: A New Approach to Culture, Structure and Process.* New York: Oxford University Press.

Trist, E. (1983) Reference organization and the development of interorganizational domains. *Human Relations,* 36 (3): 247–68.

Vaughan, E. and Siefert, M. (1992) Variability in the framing of risk issues. *Journal of Social Issues,* 48 (4): 119–35.

Vurro, C. and Dacin, T. (2014) An institutional perspective on cross-sector partnerships, in M.M. Seitanidi and A. Crane (eds) *Social Partnerships and Responsible Business: A Research Handbook.* London: Routledge: 306–19.

Warner, M. and Sullivan, R. (2004) *Putting Partnerships to Work: Strategic Alliances for Development Between Government and Private Sector and Civil Society.* Sheffield: Greenleaf Publishing.

Weber, M. (1947) *The Theory of Social and Economic Organization.* Translated by A. M. Henderson and Talcott Parsons. London: Collier Macmillan.

Wondolleck, J. and Yaffee, S. (2000) Making collaboration work: lessons from innovation in *Natural Resource Management.* Washington, DC: Island Press.

Wood, D. and Gray, B. (1991) Toward a comprehensive theory of collaboration. *Journal of Applied Behavioral Science,* 27 (2): 139–62.

Wooten, M. and Hoffman, A. (2008) Organizational fields: past, present and future, in R. Greenwood, C. Oliver, K. Sahli and R. Suddaby (eds) *The Sage Handbook of Organizational Institutionalism.* London: Sage: 130–48.

Zald, M.N. (1999) Transnational and international social movements in a globalizing world: Creating culture, creating conflict, in D. Cooperider and J. Dutton (eds) *Organizational Dimensions of Global Change: No Limits to Cooperation.* Thousand Oaks, CA: Sage: 168–84.

PART C

Reimagining social partnerships

Theory and methods

12

THEORY–METHOD INTERFACES IN CROSS-SECTOR PARTNERSHIP RESEARCH

Oana Branzei and Marlene Janzen Le Ber[1]

Introduction

Cross-sector partnerships are not a new idea. Examples of cross-sector work date back to the beginnings of organizations. Back then, such collaboration was seen as necessary not only for the creation of the private goods that now form the very foundation of our daily lives (steel, automobiles) but also for funding the development and delivery of public goods (day care, pensions, and healthcare and most of the economic and social infrastructure within which we operate). Over time, however, the nature, scope and consequences of cross-sector partnerships have been claimed, and credited, to one of three disciplines – in this order: for-profit organizations, governmental organizations and non-profit organizations.

Pockets of thinking and writing about cross-sector partnerships developed, with organizational studies focusing on profit-making entities and sociology examining public and non-profit institutions. These pockets maintained their original focus on the creation of new public value (Sagawa, 2001) and gradually moved towards cross-disciplinary fertilization (Selsky and Parker, 2005). However, they grew increasingly disconnected from mainstream theories and tests of partnerships more generally – this despite suggestive evidence that cross-sector partnerships remain an active lab for experimenting with new practices, and often help organizations overcome known barriers (Rondinelli and London, 2003), develop new capacities (Crosby and Bryson, 2010), and more generally experiment with novel ideas (Barrett *et al.*, 2000) and unprecedented roles (Simo and Bies, 2007) in ways that other inter-organizational relations might not (Parmigiani and Rivera-Santos, 2011). Our chapter seeks to reduce this disconnect by systematically revealing what the literature on cross-sector partnerships has been adding to our community and to organizational studies scholars more generally.

We start from one beachhead: the subset of studies which coined, claimed and criticized the "cross-sector" aspect of such-named partnerships. For this review, we collected, analysed and reported only on publications that had "cross-sector" in their title. We did not choose this beachhead for its representativeness or comprehensiveness of all the prior work that speaks of or speaks to the thinking and practice of cross-sector partnerships; rather, our intention was to showcase the collective undertaking of a community of scholars' coming of age. Our focus on "cross-sector" titled studies enabled us to explore the unfolding contribution of "cross-sector" thinking for understanding partnerships, across disciplines and time; however, our narrow angle necessarily leaves out the plethora of alternative terms used to describe similar collaborative efforts, especially at higher levels of analysis (for such macro views we recommend the chapters by Kolk, 2014; Hamann, 2014, in Part A; the reflections by Zadek, 2014; Nijhuis, 2014, in Part D; and recent reviews by Kourula and Laasonen, 2010); Branzei *et al.,* 2011; Hull *et al.,* 2011; Austin and Seitanidi, 2012a, b; Laasonen *et al.,* 2012).

Hereon, we focus exclusively on those studies that explicitly and deliberately acknowledged, documented, challenged and extended the "cross-sector" aspects of partnerships. Taken together, this subset affords insights into the unfolding meaning and mandate of cross-sector partnerships since the term was first used in the title of a publication in 1997. To keep pace with a changing and socially impactful phenomenon (Crane and Seitanidi, 2014), the portfolio of theories and methods has grown substantially. Initially, cross-sector studies took on one new theory and/or method at a time. Some scholars borrowed tasks and tools from different disciplines – especially the public, non-profit and for-profit disciplines; others created unexpected interdisciplinary vistas (Hull *et al.,* 2011).

New theory-method combinations pushed against the boundary of the phenomenon to surface new questions and answers. At first, scholars within and across disciplines took singular snapshots; as the perspectives multiplied and diversified, comparisons and contrasts pieced together a more dynamic picture, rife with complexity and conflict (for a review, see Gray and Purdy, 2013 in Part B, also Fiol and O'Connor, 2002) but also rich in possibility (Plowman *et al.,* 2007; Le Ber and Branzei, 2010b). Some interfaces have been generative in their own right – a great example of how a theory-method interface can become generative is the chapter by Selsky *et al*, in Part C of this volume which challenges us to employ forecasting, visioning and scenarios methods so we can "take the future seriously" and deal with it "deliberately". Over time, (ever changing) combinations of theories and methods enabled the growing community of cross-sector scholars to keep pace with ever new possibilities uncovered by practice (especially Bryson, Crosby, Parker, Selsky, and their co-authors; see also the reflection by Stafford and Hartman, 2014 in Part B).

Our chapter is a research synthesis. We

> "seek to summarize past research by drawing overall conclusions from many
> separate investigations that address separate or related hypotheses [with the
> goal] to present the state of knowledge concerning the relation(s) of interest

and to highlight important issues that research has left unresolved […] and to direct future research so that it yields a maximum amount of new information."

(Cooper, 2010: 4)

Our retrospective is systematic: we use the work of others, but do so "as a research in its own right – one using a characteristic set of research techniques and methods" (Feldman, 1971: 86).

This systematic review is comprehensive, but not comparative – so many and so different combinations of theory and method have been applied that it is hardly possible, let alone constructive, to deem some better than rest. However, the whole is now greater than the sum of its parts. We hope to help grow this whole further by explaining how the interface between theories and methods can inform explicit choices about what to ask next and how to answer it. We see at least two forks ahead. On the one hand, cross-sector researchers have used too many theories but claimed too few theories as their own; so we need to stitch and strengthen our theories (especially by theorizing more precisely with data). On the other hand, the toolkit has grown large and heavy to carry. Multiplying and mixing methods is no longer enough. We need to stretch and sharpen our toolkit to keep pace with theory and practice.

In order to classify the theory-method interfaces in use, we retrieve, index and code all prior studies which include the "cross-sector" term in their title using an explicit protocol (Appendix A). We then content- and qualitatively-analyse these studies to discern patterns in these theory-method interfaces. Finally, we look forward to which combinations of theories and methods can further deepen and broaden our collective "cross-sector" work.

Systematic review

Data collection

Given the multiple disciplinary lenses and contributions of cross-sector partnership research (Hull *et al.*, 2011), we conducted a comprehensive, time-unrestricted search of the Google Scholar database. Senior Academic Librarian Mikki (2009) concludes that compared to other searchable databases, Google Scholar offers a wider variety of publications (e.g. books and conference proceedings as well as journal articles), is inclusive of multidisciplinary sources, and provides easier access to full texts beyond library provided portals, while still providing citation counts.

The accessibility and inclusivity of the search were important to us for two key reasons. First, a wider variety of sources in which the term "cross-sector" had been used provided us with the historical overview necessary to identify the full range of theories and methods used to theorize cross-sector partnerships. Second, we wanted to capture the naturally-occurring fluctuation and interaction between theories and methods, in the sources and sequences in which they had occurred. Traditional literature reviews typically include only the most highly ranked journals, often within the confines of a single discipline (see for example, Laplume *et al.*, 2008; Nicholls-Nixon *et al.*, 2011; Aguinis and Glavas, 2012); however, focusing solely on high impact journals would restrict our ability to see which, how and why theories and methods had been used (in different combinations) – and thus bias the answer to our research question (Cooper, 2010).

The only restriction for our search was the explicit use of the "cross-sector" term in the title of the study. We identified 345 publications which included the exact words "cross sector"; of these, 201 used these words to describe comparative studies of multiple industries or sector-specific departments within a single organization (for example, governmental agencies) and were culled from our list. The remaining 144 spanned a 15-year period (1997–2012). Because this is an emerging field of scholarship, with evolving and dynamic focus and boundaries, we were interested in any and all studies focused on "cross-sector" work. We intentionally included both published and unpublished works and looked for different types of scholarly works from conference presentations and masters and doctoral theses to books, book chapters and articles. In addition, we included two special issues which explicitly called for and included "cross-sector" in the title, although not all of the articles therein did so.[2]

Our working set included 144 publications: 74 articles; 12 books and book chapters; 29 conference papers; 6 working papers; 9 PhD dissertations; 7 Master's theses; 3 reports; 1 teaching case, 6 working papers and 3 other publications. The

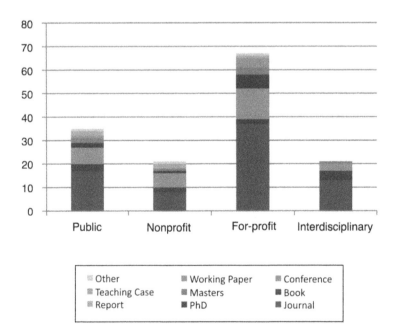

FIGURE 12.1 Fifteen-year composite of publication types by discipline (1997–2012)

types of publications varied across disciplines (Figure 12.1), with the for-profit, public, and interdisciplinary outlets contributing more to journal publications, conferences and PhD theses respectively; interdisciplinary outlets driving books; and for-profit outlets moving on cases, reports and working papers.

Our data collection was unrestricted temporally. This enabled us to reveal patterns of interest within and across disciplines (see Figure 12.2). Over time, the publications shifted gradually from a disciplinary towards a (more) interdisciplinary treatment of cross-sector partnerships. The three disciplines of origin (public, non-profit and for-profit) had single publications in each of the following seven years after the very first "cross-sector" titled publications in 1997. In 2005, cross-sector work became disproportionately more popular in the for-profit literature, which rose quickly to represent more than 50 per cent of all cross-sector publications that year. The predominance of cross-sector works in the for-profit literature was disrupted only once – in 2011. That year *Science and Public Policy* published a special issue on cross-sector partnerships in R&D; the public literature count temporarily rivalled that of the for-profit literature.

Data analysis

We used a two-stage process. We started with a rigorous content analysis, collecting and coding 144 studies that used "cross-sector" in their title, spanning a 15-year window (1997–2012). We then qualitatively analysed the evolution of these studies, qualitatively teasing out themes, types and transitions in theory and methods. We periodically compared and contrasted the content analysis and the qualitative insights to develop an organizing framework. Before turning to our findings, we describe the process and results for the content and the qualitative analysis.

Content analysis

All 144 studies were subjected to content analysis. Content analysis employs structured and systematic protocols for data reduction to facilitate analysis of large quantum of textual data (Laplume *et al.*, 2008: 1156). It can be used both quantitatively (e.g. frequency counts, correlations, trends, and differences over time) and qualitatively (e.g. theme identification, theory elaboration). As recommended by Weber (1990) and Krippendorff (2004), our "protocol" singled out the information we needed to answer our research question. Our codebook helped us capture details about the theory/ies and method(s) used. Each study was coded using this protocol (for the codes and the definitions of the codes please see Appendix A) and cross-referenced tabular summaries were developed by author, type and time of publication, impact (citations), discipline, themes, methods and theories.

We coded each publication as one of three types of study: descriptive (studies that approach and track a phenomenon by providing rich illustrations and inferring lessons or recommendations, but without either theorizing the phenomenon or analysing it empirically); empirical (studies that rely on data and data analyses to test

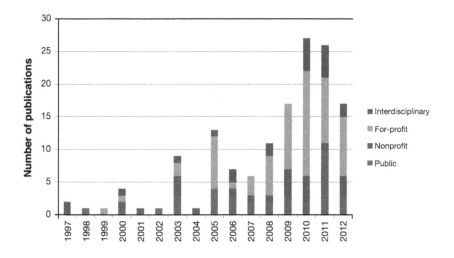

FIGURE 12.2 Publication counts across disciplines by year, 1997–2012

predictions and/or induce new propositions); and conceptual (studies that engage, bridge and build theory without empirical analysis). For example, data-based inferences by Hamann and colleagues, 2009a, b; 2011 and McDonald and Young, 2012 are coded as empirical, while the propositional inventories introduced by Bryson *et al.*, 2006 and Selsky and Parker, 2010 are coded as conceptual. Table 12.1 classifies and clusters our sampled studies in the three types of studies.

We find an almost even balance between the three types of studies (see Table 12.1) – whether we include or exclude special issue publications. This balance holds within the subset of regular journal articles (32 per cent, 35 per cent and 32 per cent respectively). Books and book chapters tilted the balance towards descriptive studies (50 per cent) while PhD dissertations and Master's theses tipped it towards empirical studies. Table 12.2 shows the distribution of publication types for regular journal articles across disciplines. Publications within the public sector are largely descriptive (69 per cent) whereas the nonprofit outlets show preference towards empirical works (63 per cent) and the for-profit outlets show equal favour for empirical and conceptual pieces (46 per cent each). While descriptive and empirical works exceeded conceptual ones in numbers; conceptual pieces were published in top journals and had high citation counts.

Although our search and sampling were agnostic of the ranking (impact) of outlets, we tracked and analysed the impact each article had on the field, both by the outlet of publication and by the aggregate number of citations it received since publication (and before the end of June 2012). Table 12.3 lists the five most cited publications in the public, non-profit, for-profit outlets, and interdisciplinary publications. Even among this set of the "top twenty" we notice significant variance in impact, both within disciplines (with the most cited piece in the public literature receiving almost

TABLE 12.1 Publication types, by contribution

	Descriptive		*Empirical*		*Conceptual*		*Total*
Books	6	*11%*	2	*3%*	4	*8%*	12
Journals	32	*59%*	32	*50%*	32	*67%*	96
Journals, regular issues	24		26		24		74
Journals, special issues	8		6		8		22
Journal of Business Ethics	3		5		6		14
Science and Public Policy	5		1		2		8
Working papers	11	*20%*	12	*19%*	13	*27%*	35
Conference papers	9		9		11		29
Working papers	2		3		1		6
Theses	1	*2%*	15	*23%*			16
PhD dissertations			9				9
Master theses	1		6				7
Other	4	*7%*	3	*5%*			7
Reports	1		2				3
Teaching cases	1						1
Resources (online, bulletins, releases)	2		1				3
Working set total							
(excluding special issues)	**46**		**58**		**40**		**144**
	32%		*40%*		*28%*		
Total	**54**		**64**		**48**		**166**
(including special issues)	*33%*		*39%*		*29%*		

20 times the number of citations of the fifth most cited one, for example), and across disciplines (see Figure 12.3). In the aggregate, conceptual and empirical pieces are similarly impactful – but the former appear only half as frequently in the "top 20".

Only one third of the most cited pieces from each discipline appeared in the traditional top journals:[3] in the non-profit literature *Non-profit and Voluntary Sector Quarterly* published three articles (one in 2000 and two more in 2009 – respectively the first and second most cited from that discipline); and in the public literature *Public Administration Review* published two (in 2006 and 2007 – the first and third most cited to date from that discipline). In the interdisciplinary outlets, *Organization* published one (in 2010, now fourth most cited) and *Leadership Quarterly* published another that same year (the second most cited among the interdisciplinary outlets). In for-profit literature the *Academy of Management Review* only recently published a single study (in 2012), which has yet not rivalled the impact of earlier pieces. The *Journal of Business Ethics* has so far published the largest number of studies on cross-sector partnerships (11 over the time-frame of our review): the first article by Rein and Stott appeared in 2009 and is now the sixth most cited study in the for-profit literature on cross-sector partnerships. A 2010 special issue included a mix of

TABLE 12.2 Distribution of regular issue journal publications across disciplines, by contribution

	Descriptive	Empirical	Conceptual	Total
Public	**11**	**3**	**2**	**16**
	(68.8%)	**(18.8%)**	**(12.5%)**	
Cadernos de Saúde Pública	1			1
Communication Monographs		1		1
Journal of Public Health Management and Practice	1			1
Public Administration and Development	1			1
Public Administration Review	1		1	2
Public Management Review	1			1
Public Productivity and Management Review		1		1
Research in Post-Compulsory Education		1		1
Science and Public Policy	5		1	6
Voices in Urban Education	1			1
Nonprofit	**1**	**5**	**2**	**8**
	(12.5%)	**(62.5%)**	**(25%)**	
International Journal of Nonprofit and Voluntary Sector Marketing	1			1
Journal of Higher Education Outreach and Engagement		1		1
Journal of Nonprofit and Public Sector Marketing			1	1
Nonprofit and Voluntary Sector Quarterly		2	1	3
Nonprofit Management and Leadership		2		2
For-profit	**3**	**17)**	**17**	**37**
	(8.1%)	**(45.9%**	**(45.9%)**	
Academy of Management Executive		1		1
Academy of Management Review			1	1
Business and Society		1		1
Business Ethics Quarterly			1	1
Business Strategy and the Environment			1	1
Development Southern Africa	1	1		2
Emergence: Complexity and Organization		1		1
Hastings Business Law Journal			1	1
Information Technologies and International Development (MIT)	1			1
Innovation: Management, Policy and Practice		1		1
International Journal of Entrepreneurship and Innovation Management		1		1
Journal of Business and Accounting			1	1
Journal of Business Ethics	1	5	5	11
Journal of Business Research		1	1	2
Journal of Cleaner Production		1		1
Journal of Corporate Citizenship		1		1
Journal of Law, Business and Ethics			1	1
Journal of Management			1	1
Journal of Modern Accounting and Auditing			1	1

TABLE 12.2 Continued

	Descriptive	Empirical	Conceptual	Total
Journal of the Australian and New Zealand				
Academy of Management		1		1
R&D Management		1		1
Social Marketing Quarterly			1	1
Stanford Journal of Microfinance			1	1
Supply Chain Management: An International				
Journal			1	1
The Journal of Technology Transfer		1		1
Interdisciplinary	**9**	**1**	**3**	**13**
	(69.2%)	**(7.7%)**	**(23.1%)**	
Canadian Journal of Communication	1			1
IBM Journal of Research and Development	1			1
Journal of Allergy and Clinical Immunology	1			1
Leadership in Health Services	1			1
Metropolitan Universities: An International Forum	1			1
Organization: The Critical Journal of Organization,				
Theory and Society			1	1
Prometheus: Critical Studies in Innovation	2			2
Reflections: The SoL Journal on Knowledge,				
Learning and Change	1			1
The American Journal of Surgery	1			1
The Leadership Quarterly			1	1
The Learning Organization		1		1
Wiley Interdisciplinary Reviews: Climate Change			1	1
Total journals (regular issues)	**24**	**26.9**	**24**	**74**
	(32.4%)	**(35.1%)**	**(32.4%)**	

descriptive, empirical and conceptual articles (please see Table 12.1 for details) that created a critical mass for the term and the content of cross-sector work – although individually their impact has not (at least not yet) rivalled that of earlier works within any of the disciplines.

Qualitative analysis

All 144 articles were also reviewed as a holistic body of work; the set was examined from within (using insights from the content analysis) and from outside (relying on disciplinary reviews of cross-sector partnerships research, e.g. Kourula and Laasonen, 2010; Branzei *et al.*, 2011; Hull *et al.*, 2011). Practice has formed the dynamic core of the literature on cross-sector partnerships. The literature has maintained a "relevance" focus – not in the least by the very legitimization of the entire body of cross-sector research as catching up with, or ushering in, the next frontier of practice. In part because cross-sector practice itself is unfolding and evolving, and in part because prior concepts and frameworks of organizing cannot explain let alone predict the direction of these changes, this revolving door keeps exposing the inadequacy of theories and methods and keeps inviting new efforts, on both fronts.

The radar scan of the literature in Figure 12.4 illustrates how this quest for relevance comes through in four distinct waves: (a) the boundaries that cross-sector partnerships overcome (O'Reagan and Oster, 2000; Rondinelli and London, 2003); (b) the trade-offs and sometimes even paradoxes that cross-sector partnerships hide and reveal (Hayes et al., 2011a); (c) the value cross-sector partnerships create (Le Ber and Branzei, 2010b) and when and why they may fail to create value (Seitanidi, 2008); and (d) the change that cross-sector partnerships can bring about (Selsky and Parker, 2005). These four waves co-evolved, with disciplines, outlets, and scholars switching from one to another. Over time, this revolving door created little convergence or consistence – with one exception. The handful of highly influential pieces celebrates a persistent common core: the shared concern with whether, when and how cross-sector work may offer a response or a remedy to complex problems.[4]

The shared quest for relevance did not, however, result in a critical mass or commonality, in either theories or methods. Overall, we found little overall consistency in either theoretical lenses or methods; our task made even more difficult by the

TABLE 12.3 The five most cited publications in each discipline, by publication and contribution

Discipline	Author(s)	Year	Citation count	Publication	Contribution
Public	Bryson Crosby Stone	2006	278	Journal	Conceptual
	Crosby Bryson	2005	56	Journal	Conceptual
	Simo Bies	2007	36	Journal	Empirical
	Palmer	1998	23	Journal	Empirical
	Rein et al.	2005	17	Book	Descriptive
Nonprofit	O'Regan Oster	2000	50	Journal	Conceptual
	Babiak Thibault	2009	25	Journal	Empirical
	Palmer	1997	17	Journal	Empirical
	Austin	2003	14	Journal	Conceptual
	Sagawa	2001	12	Journal	Descriptive
For-profit	Selsky Parker	2005	195	Journal	Empirical
	Rondinelli London	2003	191	Journal	Conceptual
	Arya Salk	2006	30	Journal	Empirical
	Garrett-Jones et al.	2005	23	Journal	Empirical
	Seitanidi	2008	16	Journal	Empirical
Inter-disciplinary	Jupp	2000	33	Book	Descriptive
	Crosby Bryson	2010	15	Journal	Conceptual
	Couchman Fulop	2004	10	Journal	Descriptive
	Le Ber Branzei	2010b	7	Journal	Conceptual
	Magee	2007	7	Journal	Descriptive

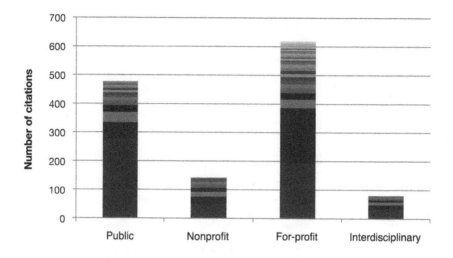

FIGURE 12.3 Citations concentration by discipline, 1997–2012[1]

Note: [1]Gradients represent the total number of citations per publication; publications are ranked order by the number of citations they received in June 2012, with most cited pubications shown at the base and the least cited publications shown at the top of their discipline specific column. Non-cited publications are excluded from the current graph.

wide range of outlets (Table 12.1) and repeated switching of theories and methods across disciplines, even by some of the most cited authors (Table 12.3). Rather the phenomenon anchors and (re)activates a continuous evolution of both theories and methods.

Beyond theories

Theoretical lenses varied, somewhat predictably depending on whether the authors had set out to contribute to one of the three key themes in the literature: emergence (how cross-sector partnerships come into being), evolution (the unfolding and growth/decline of cross-sector partnerships) and governance (how resources are allocated and activities are coordinated and controlled within cross-sector partnerships). (Please see also Crane and Seitanidi (2014) in Part A of this book.) Emergence brought out the most eclectic set of theoretical lenses; while these were applied at different levels of analyses, most studies focused at a specific level. Perhaps not surprisingly, both the for-profit and non-profit literature emphasized organizational and interorganizational theorizing (with a focus on strategic organizational lenses, and only occasional attention to individual and/or societal factors). In contrast, both the public and the interdisciplinary literature took more systemic perspectives – understanding both the problems and the solutions provided by cross-sector

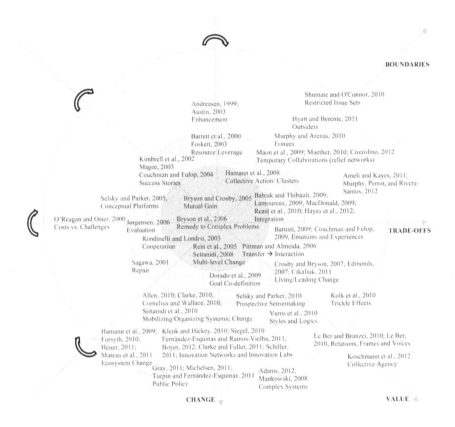

FIGURE 12.4 Radar chart of contributions, 1997–2012

partnerships through larger lenses including risk and hazards, and system failure and resilience, drawing recurrent attention to complexity science.

The evolution of cross-sector partnerships received the lion's share of attention both within and across disciplines, drawing out an impressive range of theoretical perspectives, including: social exchange, resources-based view, change, capacity, and complexity, institutional theory, resource dependency, functionalist and cultural approaches, even paradox. Several uncommon but generative marriages of theories stand out – with complexity and critical perspectives brought to challenge mainstream concepts (borrowed most consistently from the literature on interorganizational alliances and relationships, with frames and sense making coming in as a close second).

Perhaps not surprisingly studies of governance drew attention to power, especially the sharing of power; some focused on social inducements for collaboration; others pointed out biases, frames or processes. Although hardly any of the governance

TABLE 12.4 Overview of theories across disciplines, by theme

	Emergence	Evolution	Governance
For-profit	*Interorganizational:* alliances (Rondinelli and London, 2003); relations (Murphy and Arenas, 2010), relational value creation (Le Ber and Branzei, 2010a)		
	Societal: social issues as platforms (Selsky and Parker, 2005); sensemaking (Selsky and Parker, 2010)		
	Strategic: uncertainty reduction mechanisms (Koljatic and Silva, 2008); collaboration (Clarke, 2010; Clarke and Fuller, 2010) *Individual:* psychoanalytical (Battisti, 2009) *Institutional* (Vurro et al., 2010) *Environmental:* linear vs cyclical models (Maon et al., 2009); disaster relief (Muhammed and Gyimah, 2011); reform (Hyatt and Berente, 2011).	*Social exchange:* attraction–selection–attrition (Kolk, van Dolen and Volk, 2010); social capital; external perspectives (Salk and Arya, 2005); sustainable development (Rein and Stott, 2009); interorganizational relations (Couchman and Fulop, 2007; Garrett-Jones et al., 2010) *Change/Capacity:* intentional change theory (Hyatt and Johnson, 2009); collaboration theory (Lamoureux, 2009); indigenous relations (Murphy, 2012); alliances (Murphy et al., 2012); organizational learning (Arya and Salk, 2006; Reast et al., 2010) *Resource based view* (Turpin et al., 2005); value creation (Le Ber and Branzei, 2010c); social, procedural, distributive justice (Cornelius and Wallace, 2010) *Complexity:* complexity science (Hamann et al., 2009); complex adaptive systems (Seitanidi, 2008)	*Risk* (Garrett-Jones et al., 2005); frames (Le Ber, 2010) *Power:* Weberian and the Parsonian views of power (Ellersiek and Kenis, 2008); legal precedence (Cotten and Lasprogata, 2012); social network theory (Jiang and Cai, 2011) *Development:* Duty of care; Piaget's theory of development (Vachon, 2012); institutional theory; regime theory; social marketing (Heuer and Kumar, 2012); sustainable development (Rein and Stott, 2009); social movements (Heuer, 2011) *Communication:* processes and practices (Koschmann et al., 2012)
Nonprofit	*Legitimacy* (Mendoza, 2009) *Resource dependency:* efficiency, legitimacy, leverage, mutuality (Siegel, 2010; Tien, 2006)	*Institutional theory:* legitimacy; power (Huybrechts and Nicholls, 2010)	*Advantage:* comparative (O'Regan and Oster, 2000); interorganizational (Dorado et al., 2009)

TABLE 12.4 Continued

	Emergence	Evolution	Governance
Public	*Resource dependency and institutional theory* (Bryson and Crosby, 2006, 2012); *Design science* (Bryson et al., 2011)		
	Risk: risk assessment (Turpin and Garrett-Jones, 2003); system failure (Fernández-Esquinas and Ramos-Vielba, 2011); historical (Gray, 2011); resilience (Adams, 2012); stakeholder theory (Shumate and O'Connor, 2010); sustainable development (Rein et al., 2005)	*Functionalist*: network theory, game theory (Jorgensen, 2006); knowledge management (Michelsen, 2011) *Cultural*: managerialism (Palmer, 1998); cultural-based model (Russell, 2011); communities of practice (Pittman and Almedia, 2006)	*Collaborative*: shared power (Crosby and Bryson, 2005); collaborative leadership (Pillsbury et al., 2009); socio-political logics (Sehested, 2003); knowledge transfer (Schiller, 2011)
Inter-disciplinary	*Complexity science* (Bojer, 2012); *Actor network theory* (Klenk and Hickey, 2010)		
	Systems theory (Couchman and Fulop, 2005); Complex systems thinking (Mankowski, 2008)	*Paradox* (Forsyth, 2010; Le Ber and Branzei, 2010b; Messer-Davidow, 2010)	*Success/failure* (Le Ber, 2010); intraorganizational (Ameli and Kayes, 2011); attributional bias (Leigh, 2008)

studies built new theory, as a set they broadened the range of lenses necessary to map and match the requisite variety of the phenomenon.

Beyond methods

Methods also varied widely, showing an overall imbalance between the uniqueness and richness of data and the bluntness of too basic and too disorganized a toolkit. To reveal the richness of methods brought to bear on cross-sector partnerships as well as to uncover the specific combinations in which different methods had been used, our protocol distinguished three categories of studies: single method, multiple method, and mixed method categorization (Table 12.5). At first sight, the designs used to study cross-sector partnerships are predominantly qualitative and focus on either a single-setting or a single-case or a traditional cross-case comparison, and

TABLE 12.5 Overview of methods, by theme

	Emergence	*Evolution*	*Governance*
Single methods	Single case study; multiple case studies (comparative analyses); survey (with or without factor analysis); interviews	Interviews; large N survey; single case study; multiple case studies; survey – quantitative; survey – qualitative	Single case study; multiple case studies. in-depth interviews; secondary quantitative data source
Multiple methods	Action research – semi-structured interviews and multi-stakeholder workshop; grounded theory development using case studies and interviews; archival data and in-depth interviews; case study with interviews, observations, and artifact analysis	Archival data and in-depth interviews; case study with interviews, observations, archival data and artifacts; interviews and written survey; action research; participatory research	Surveys and interviews
Mixed methods	Survey and interviews; questionnaire and case studies; action research with survey, observation, interviews with multiple cases	Qualitative case study with quantitative survey; interviews and social network analysis	Large N network analysis and content analysis

the methods of qualitative inquiry rely predominantly on retrospective interviews (Branzei *et al.*, 2011).

The content analysis painted a finer grained picture. This categorization (single method, multiple methods, and mixed method) brought several realizations. First, the single methods are diverse but coarse. Their lack of sophistication hinders the development of new insights; many of these studies are descriptive rather than analytical. Second, the multiple method studies suffer from too much data and too little design and as a result their contributions often lag the richness of the data collected. Third, even the handful of studies that deliberately employ a mixed method approach are laborious rather than elaborate; the connections among the methods used are insufficiently motivated and thus the gains from the additional data remain largely underexplored. Organizing the methods by theme shows an even greater imbalance between data and insight.

Findings

Throughout this dual process of content analysis and holistic qualitative review, we met regularly and exchanged notes. The findings were fully shared discoveries – revealed by the content analysis and fleshed out by the holistic qualitative review. Collectively the 144 studies employed a dizzying array of theories (Table 12.4) and methods (Table 12.5). The multiplicity and diversity of theory-method combinations motivated us to move beyond inventorying what and how theories and methods have been used to documenting the patterns in which theories and methods have interfaced over time.

Once we conceded that the range, fragmentation and the (often deliberate) increase in eclecticism over time required us to explicitly model the patterns of divergence over time, we undertook two additional steps. We started by inducing three dimensions along which "cross-sector" studies informed their disciplines of origins: *forms* (new configurations of goals or partners); *(trans)formation* (processes of interacting that enable the formation of new relationships or the transformation of prior relationships); and *formulation* (new combinations and evaluations of factors that tilt the balance from failure to success). We then mapped the approach or direction of each contribution, differentiating among *prescriptive* (should do), *proscriptive* (shouldn't do), *prospective* (can do) and *promisive* (will do) contributions. Our overarching framework cross-classifies dimensions and directions to reveal 12 distinct patterns.

Dimensions

"Cross-sector" work invites us to examine new possibilities for social good. Table 12.6 shows a growing concentration of studies in corporate sustainability settings (Arya and Salk, 2006; Seitanidi, 2008; Shumate and O'Connor, 2010; Cotten and Lasprogata, 2012) and environmental/ecosystem challenges more broadly (Austrian and Iannone, 1997; Leigh, 2005; Tafra-Vlahovi , 2007; Mankowski, 2008; Clarke,

2010; Cornelius and Wallace, 2010; Heuer and Kuman, 2012; Ruckelshaus, 2012). Also well represented are poverty and sustainable development (Hamann, Rein and their co-authors); disaster relief organizations (Cozzolino, 2012; Kong, 2012) and organizing in the face of extreme constraints and threats more broadly (Simo and Bies, 2007); healthcare organizations (Le Ber and Branzei, 2010a, b, c; Cikaliuk, 2011) and the provision of health care more broadly (Mendoza, 2009; Davis *et al.*, 2000); education organizations and education interventions more broadly (Edmond, 2007;

TABLE 12.6 Representative studies, cross-classified framework

	Dimensions		
	Forms	*(Trans)formation*	*Formulation*
Prescriptive	Rondinelli and London (2003)	Bryson *et al.* (2006)	Crosby and Bryson (2007)
	Kimbrell *et al.* (2002)	Backes-Gellner *et al.* (2005)	Arya and Salk (2006)
	Heuer and Kumar (2012)	Rein and Stott (2009)	Palmer (1997)
	Andreasen (2009)	Maon *et al.* (2009)	Jorgensen (2006)
	Daniel (2008)	Couchman and Fulop (2004)	Koljati and Silva (2008)
	Bryson *et al.* (2012)	Cotten and Lasprogata (2012)	Bryson and Crosby (2005)
	Maether (2010)	Davis *et al.* (2000)	Reast *et al.* (2010)
	Mishook and Raynor (2010)	Knight (2010)	Hyatt and Berente (2011)
	Adams (2012)	McDonald and Young (2012)	Leigh (2005)
	Mohammed and Gyimah (2011)	Serafin *et al.* (2008)	Edmond *et al.* (2011)
	Murphy *et al.* (2012)	Hamann *et al.* (2009)	Cozzolino (2012)
Proscriptive	Foskett (2005)	Turpin *et al.* (2005)	O'Reagan and Oster (2000)
	Garrett-Jones *et al.* (2010)	Peizer (2003)	Garrett-Jones *et al.* (2005)
	Edmonds (2007)	Foskett (2003)	Palmer (1998)
	Russell (2011)	Flentgel *et al.* (2008)	Turpin (2003)
	Garrett-Jones and Turpin (2003)	Seitanidi (2007)	Coachman and Beckett (2006)
	Ryan (2011)	Klenk and Hickey (2010)	Coachman and Fulop (2009a)
	Yee (2008)	Couchman and Fulop (2009b)	Coachman and Fulop (2005, 2007)
	Koljatic *et al.* (2006)	Vasavada (2007)	Turpin and Fernández-Esquinas (2011)
	Cairns and Harris (2011)	Hyatt and Johnson (2009)	Fernández-Esquinas and Ramos-Vielba (2011);
		Leigh (2008)	Jiang and Cai (2011a,b)

TABLE 12.6 Continued

	Dimensions		
	Forms	*(Trans)formation*	*Formulation*
Prospective	Selsky and Parker (2005)	Jupp (2000)	Simo and Bies (2007)
	Rein *et al.* (2005)	Babiak and Thibault	Le Ber and Branzei
	Sagawa (2010)	(2009)	(2010a)
	Barrett *et al.* (2000)	Seitanidi (2008)	Crosby and Bryson
	Bryson *et al.* (2009)	Dorado *et al.* (2009)	(2010)
	Seitanidi and Lindgreen	Pittman and Almeida	Magee (2003)
	(2010)	(2006)	Le Ber and Branzei
	Heuer (2011)	Le Ber and Branzei	(2010c)
	Clarke (2010)	(2010b)	Vurro *et al.* (2010)
	Sehested (2003)	Selsky and Parker (2010)	Murphy and Arenas
	Siegel (2010)	Kolk *et al.* (2010)	(2010)
	Austrian and Iannone	Seitanidi *et al.* (2010)	Hamann *et al.* (2008)
	(1997)	Le Ber (2010)	Clarke and Fuller (2010)
	Ruckelshaus (2012)	Allen (2010)	Hayes *et al.* (2011)
	Grudinschi *et al.* (2011)	Battisti (2009)	Jamali (2011)
	Kong (2012)	Huybrechts and	Mendoza (2009)
	Ameli and Kayes (2011)	Nicholls (2010)	Cornforth *et al.* (2012)
		Couchman and Fulop	Bryson *et al.* (2011)
		(2005)	Tafra-Vlahovi (2007)
		Rodriguez *et al.* (2005)	
Promisive	Cornelius and Wallace	Ellersiek and Kenis	Schiller (2011)
	(2010)	(2010)	Koschmann *et al.* (2012)
	Forsyth (2010)	Bojer (2012)	Cikaliuk (2011)
	Hamann *et al.* (2009)	Garland *et al.* (2012)	Turpin *et al.* (2011)
	Gray (2011)	Lamoureux (2009)	Messer-Davidow (2010)
	Seitanidi (2010)	Vachon (2012)	Doignon (2003)
	Herman (2009)	Roubos (2008)	Tien (2006)
	Michelsen (2011)	Mankowski (2008)	Fink (2011)
	McDonald (2009)	Murphy (2012)	Fiorentino *et al.* (in
	Pillsbury *et al.* (2009)		press)
	Marcus *et al.* (2011)		Hamann *et al.* (2011)
	Goldsmith (2011)		

Studies are listed in order of their influence, quantified by the number of citations received 1997–2012.

McDonald, 2009; Siegel, 2010); and there are even a handful of studies starting to examine cross-sector work in the arts (Doignon, 2003; Tien, 2006). Surprisingly, traditional organizations and industries remain under-represented in cross-sector partnership research (for exceptions see Hyatt and Johnson, 2009 discussing Walmart; and Cotten and Lasprogata, 2012 discussing Starbucks); perhaps research ethics requirements to disguise key protagonists prevents us from noticing that many of the largest and best known organizations are actively doing "cross-sector" work. Historic, archival or experimental case studies can help scrutinize and publicize such work (great examples are available in the chapter by Stafford and Hartman, in Part B of this volume).

Form

Three qualitatively-induced dimensions piece together a clearer puzzle of when and why and how social good happens (or fails to), across many different issues and contexts. The *form* dimension shown in the first column of Table 12.6 reiterates a need to "move beyond a one-size fits all approach" (Rein and Stott, 2009). Forms that make cross-sector partnerships apt vehicles for poverty reduction (Goldsmith, 2011) are radically different from those than enable image rebuilding for the corporate partner (Sagawa, 2001; see also Peloza and Ye, 2014 in Part B). At the same time, partnerships may take surprisingly similar forms to address rather different practical problems, such as traffic congestion (Bryson *et al.*, 2009) or solid waste (Yee, 2008), rare diseases (Barrett *et al.*, 2000), disaster response (Kong, 2012), public health (Kimbrell *et al.*, 2002) or ecosystem management (Heuer, 2011). City-level initiatives, climate change initiatives, poverty and nutrition interventions or organizing for disaster-relief remind us that despite the great and growing variance of the forms cross-sector partnerships take, we need to pay closer attention to the (dys)function of these forms – especially their (mis)fit to contexts and issues.

(Trans)formation

The *(trans)formation* dimension shown in the second column of Table 12.6 explains when, why and how actors actively (re)shape the contexts in which they operate and/or the issues they set out to address – often in non-trivial ways (examples include the emergence of new capabilities and competencies, Murphy, 2012 for social innovation; Turpin and Garrett-Jones with their co-authors for R&D; Foskett, 2003 and Allen, 2010 for education; Peizer, 2003 for ICT; Roubos, 2008 for microfinance; and new activities such as disaster relief, Maon *et al.*, 2009; or marine conservation, Rodriguez *et al.*, 2005; see also Rufin and Rivera-Santos, 2014 in Part B). Sometimes cross-sector work may change the goals, achievements, even identities of the partners themselves: some may systematically (re)think their responsibilities for creating local, national, and systemic change (Kolk *et al.*, 2010; Seitanidi *et al.*, 2010; Seitanidi and Lindgreen, 2010; Gray, 2011; Bojer, 2012). For a recent review of how such responsibilization processes work, please see the chapter by Martens and Bookman in Part C.

The (trans)formation dimension singles out the importance of impact trajectories as the relationship unfolds (Seitanidi *et al.*, 2010). It also speaks of how role models may inhibit (Seitanidi, 2008), accelerate (Roubos, 2008) or orchestrate (Klenk and Hickey, 2010) impact. Last, it identifies social mechanisms that (re)calibrate impact, especially mutuality (Jupp, 2000; Bryson and Crosby, 2005; Dorado *et al.*, 2009; Le Ber and Branzei, 2010c) and (re)thinking the problem (Pittman and Almeida, 2006).

Taken together, the (trans)formation dimension reminds us that we cannot take responsibility for granted, but rather have to pay closer attention to how partners' responsibility keeps developing over contexts and issues.

Formulation

The formulation dimension shown in the third column of Table 12.6 summarizes which factors, in what combinations, and by what metrics best help partners avoid known risks or at least anticipate unintended consequences. Despite noteworthy variance in empirical settings, from scientific innovation (Turpin and co-authors), R&D commercialization (Couchman and Fulop, 2005a, 2005b, 2007, 2009a) and healthcare organizations (Magee, 2008; Le Ber and Branzei, 2010a,b; Fiorentino *et al.*, 2012) to casinos (Reast *et al.*, 2010) and arts (Doignon, 2003; Tien, 2006), we notice a recurrent preoccupation with risk (from early studies, O'Regan and Oster, 2000 to more recent work, e.g. Koljatic and Silva, 2008); especially the different types of risks partners necessarily encounter in cross-sector work (Couchman and Fulop, 2009; Jiang and Cai, 2011a,b).

The formulation dimensions reminds us that conflicting expectations are not only pervasive but also productive (Le Ber and Branzei, 2010b; Hayes *et al.*, 2011b). However, leveraging conflict is neither easy nor automatic (Hayes *et al.*, 2011b; for a recent review please see the chapter by Gray and Purdy in Part B of this volume). Partners have blind spots (for exceptions see Palmer, 1997; Garrett-Jones *et al.*, 2010); they often favour intended or expected benefits (Serafin *et al.*, 2008; Pillsbury *et al.*, 2009) and overlook unintended consequences (Vurro *et al.*, 2010; Jamali, 2011; Vachon, 2012).

Directions

Most of the early studies were *prescriptive*, that is, telling cross-sector partnerships what they should do; taking lessons from partners who had gone where nobody had been before (especially Rondinelli and London, 2003; Bryson *et al.*, 2006 which rank among the most influential pieces to date). As organizations (public, non-profit and for-profit) met the limits of their own trade in tackling ever more complex problems, how-to advice fell on fertile ground and stirred up demand for more.

However, advice was not always or automatically helpful; both researchers and leaders wondered what went wrong and why. This shifted attention to sources of errors, ways to diagnose them and ways to safeguard against mistakes as the partnerships evolved. A multitude of contextual, cultural and political constraints that got in the way of success were identified. More and more studies shared a preoccupation with explaining, avoiding and warning against what could go wrong. We labelled these studies *proscriptive*, because they warn of mistakes or mishaps and tell partners what they shouldn't do and thereby guiding them to safer or better common ground (e.g. Couchman and co-authors; O'Regan and Oster, 2000; Cairns and Harris, 2011; Jiang and Cai, 2011a,b).

Later studies shifted attention from answers (what cross-sector partnerships should or shouldn't do) to questions (what cross-sector partnerships may do). Paradoxically some of the most complex and complicated examples had few lessons to offer. From 2005–2010 the majority of the studies flying under the cross-sector flag moved away – largely deliberately – from either prescription or proscription, to collectively grapple with why partners may do something as hard but as rewarding as working together for the social good. Some examined first-time instances of cross-sector work in otherwise virgin settings (Le Ber and Branzei, 2010a,b,c) or explored cross-sector work through lenses that had not been so deployed beforehand (Seitanidi, 2007, 2008). We labelled these studies *prospective*: they spoke of what may be (Turpin and co-authors), what the partners may become (Jupp, 2000; Dorado *et al.*, 2009; Seitanidi *et al.*, 2010), or what combinations of goals, motivations, styles, and benefits may be optimal (Selsky and Parker, 2005, for whom and why, Le Ber and Branzei, 2010b).

Much prospection came through doctoral and master theses (Leigh, 2005; Tafra-Vlahovic, 2007; Clarke, 2010; Le Ber, 2010) and the appetite keeps growing. As we confront complex problems at every interface of our daily lives and living, from waste and traffic congestion to educating our children or caring for our elders, we are less interested in judging the outcomes and more vested in their making. Prospective studies acknowledge that although we don't quite know what it takes to get there, or even who or when may have arrived, there is little dispute that the journey is worthwhile in its own right (see also Clarke, 2014 and Doh and Boddewyn in Part A and Schmutzler *et al.*, 2014 and van Tulder and Pfisterer, 2014 in Part B).

Recently a handful of studies, like Koschmann *et al.* (2012),[5] moved beyond looking forward to the possibilities of cross-sector partnerships to examine the promises made and kept, and the processes that enable partners to make and keep such promises when there is little precedent or guidance or safety net. We use the label *promisive* to emphasize the emphasis on what is being promised to whom, and who does what to help partners keep their promises. Promises matter within the partnerships themselves – often they are the only guidepost as partners venture into uncharted territories like social justice and city regeneration (Cornelius and Wallace, 2010) or try new approaches for addressing climate change (Forsyth, 2010), literacy (McDonald, 2009) or poverty (Goldsmith, 2011). Promises become even more important when partners seek new identities, especially in publicly contested and rapidly evolving arenas (e.g. microfinance, Roubos, 2008), or find new ways to enhance the social good (e.g. the arts, Tien, 2006; and drugs for rare diseases, Fiorentino *et al.*, 2012).

Framework

By crossing dimensions with directions, Table 12.6 identifies and illustrates 12 clusters of cross-sector work. The (trans)formation dimension shown in the middle column has attracted the greatest number of studies and researchers; this dimension is bottom heavy, with more prospective and promising studies than prescriptive and proscriptive. The form dimension shown in the left column has been more balanced

– largely due to renewed interest into the possibilities and promises of hybrid forms which evens out the early emphasis on the goals, roles and configurations that are most likely to bring about success or avoid premature failure. The formulation dimension shown in the right column is top heavy on prescription and proscription: there is sustained demand for figuring out which factors in which combinations to add and withhold. There are fewer prospective studies of formulation, but the few studies that engage the prospect and the promise of formulation matter a great deal as they cross levels and integrate disciplines.

Each cluster presents a unique interface between theory and method, as depicted in Figure 12.5. This visual representation shows how far and how fast studies in each

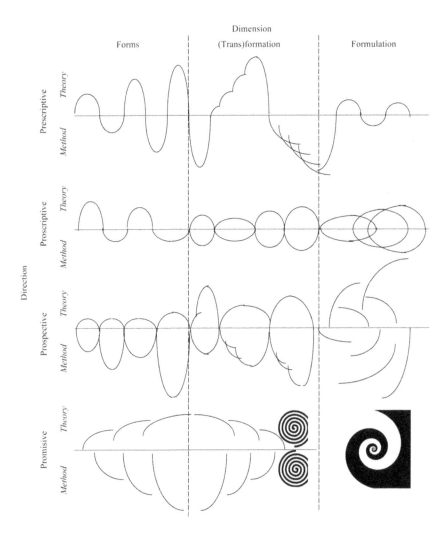

FIGURE 12.5 Theory-method interfaces, by dimension and direction

cluster moved on theory and/or methods. Theoretical moves (above the line) are not always or automatically paired with a methodological one (below the lines); nor are the moves synchronized. Over time, both theory and method contributions shifted horizontally from left to right, and vertically from the top down. However, as we are reminded by the publication list in Table 12.6, each cluster continues to generate new insights, attract new researchers, and influence insights and researchers in the other clusters. Next, we describe the evolving theory-method interface for each of the four rows (by direction), emphasizing key similarities and/or differences among the three columns (by dimension).

Prescriptive

Prescriptive studies started small, from practical problems (Andreasen, 2009) and solutions (Rondinelli and London, 2003), but quickly amplified their impact by moving sequentially between theories (Selsky and Parker, 2005) and methods (Kimbrell *et al.*, 2002). The interface between theory and methods in the *prescriptive-form* cluster is one-sided but progressively daring in its (either) theoretical or empirical contribution (Maether, 2010; Adams, 2012; Murphy *et al.*, 2012).

Similar asynchronicity between theory and method is evident in the *prescriptive-formulation* cluster, although departures on either theory or methods were more modest as well as more cumulative. The interface afforded incremental accumulation of insight which resulted in a few solid and heavily used blocks of theory (Bryson and Crosby, 2005; Arya and Salk, 2006; Crosby and Bryson, 2007). This laid a necessary foundation for the subsequent growth of the field. It also encouraged a dual extension of this foundation, with several recent studies marrying theory and methods to generate a fuller sense of wining formulas (Leigh, 2005; Edmond *et al.*, 2011; Cozzolino, 2012). Methodological departures were also modest (Palmer, 1997; Reast *et al.*, 2010), in great measure because most prescriptive studies were descriptive.

The swollen middle of *prescriptive-(trans)formation* studies was particularly generative – if disproportionately so on methods (Davis *et al.*, 2000; McDonald and Young, 2012; Rein and Stott, 2009). The theoretical development rose much more incrementally (Cotten and Lasprogata, 2012), often by layering multiple perspectives on top of each other rather than extending let alone building new theory. Earlier studies were predominantly descriptive and often used a single method. Later studies were predominantly comparative; they combined and contrasted multiple sources of data and methods of data collection (e.g. Serafin *et al.*, 2008; Hamann *et al.*, 2009; Maon *et al.*, 2009).

Proscriptive

Proscriptive studies developed more common ground. Although advances in theory and method were largely disconnected in the *proscriptive-form* cluster (Foskett, 2003; Peizer, 2003), they became more synchronized in the *proscriptive-(trans)formation* cluster – where theory moves informed method moves and vice-versa. Efforts to marry extensions in theory and methods intensified for the proscriptive-formulation quadrant, in large part because later studies moved beyond descriptions to empirical inductive studies that used novel methods to generate new theory (Vasavada, 2007; Seitanidi, 2008). Once the marriage between theory and method built solid foundations on proscriptions, subsequent studies emphasized connections, even overlaps, in the approach and the findings. Many teams of authors tread the same ground with multiple studies (e.g. Couchman and co-authors; Jiang and Cai, 2011a, b) and their persistence was particularly noteworthy for *proscription-formulation* where growing consensus helped validate previously tentative conclusions across issues and settings.

Prospective

Prospective studies started with a dual approach; albeit, stacking the deck in favour of methods. A majority of the most cited authors converged towards this prospective space, and stretched both theory and method to make room for new ways to understand and use cross-sector partnerships (Dorado *et al.*, 2009; Seitanidi *et al.*, 2010; Selsky and Parker, 2010). A few pushed the phenomenon hard enough to open new avenues of inquiry – especially complexity theory and the combination of institutional theory and political and cultural forces (Clarke and colleagues; Seitanidi and colleagues; Vurro, Dacin and colleagues). Most studies attempted both theoretical and methodological contributions.

Many prospective studies were still descriptive, but the larger empirical undertakings were particularly rewarding; they often generated rich data. But perhaps because the richness of the data afforded so many distinct theoretical lenses, each offered little additional explanatory power. Nonetheless, prospection brought steady if conservative growth in both theory and method. Most of these came by way of authors persisting with their chosen issue or setting for multiple studies, which enabled them to try on different theories or toolkits. Insights were additive more than cumulative because each study asked a different question and/or provided a different answers (even in cases where the same issue and setting are tapped repeatedly).

Studies in the *prospective-(trans)formation* cluster were particularly eclectic in both theory and methods; often extending the methods gradually to make room for a few more theoretical lenses. Notably, this cluster hosts some of the most ambitious empirical undertakings in the cross-sector partnerships literature. A few of these studies open up entirely new empirical contexts (e.g. relief efforts, Simo and Bies, 2007; emerging markets, Hamann and co-authors), right on pace with practice and scholarship as they grapple more explicitly with difference making (www.symposiumprc2012.org/ Third International Symposium on Cross Sector Social Interactions), distinguishing value from impact (Dorado *et al.*, 2009; Seitanidi *et al.*, 2010) and modelling impact trajectories (Branzei and Le Ber, 2012).

Perhaps because of their broad and mixed theoretical foundation, studies in the prospective-(trans)formation cluster contributed even more questions and answers than prospective-form ones, which were geared more modest towards adding precision in explanation. In the prospective-formulation quadrant, the variety in theory and methods was much more aggressive but less cumulative. This cluster remains particularly active. Governance is a dominant theme and institutional theory is widely used (Vurro et al., 2010; see also the recent review by Vurro and Dacin in Part C of this volume). While prospective-formulation studies can also extend institutional theory, current offshoots are more indicative than additive; they flag possibilities about new formulas more than validating existing ones.

Promisive

The *promisive* studies pursue extensions of existing theories and methods. Some studies, particularly those in the *promisive-form* cluster, combine theories and methods that had not been previously paired. For example, Herman (2012) explores affordable housing in an urban-poverty-immigration nexus; Gray (2011) looks at the creation and construction of public goods; and the edited volume by Marcus et al. (2011) stitches a series of bridges between ecosystems and technologies. These endeavours are remarkable because they identify important white spaces – places where cross-sector partnership theorizing or testing has not gone before. They scale these white spaces without illusions of closure; rather they reveal a promise land of forms (and functions) that cross-sector partnerships might take to fit into and fill out complex needs.

The *promisive-(trans)formative* studies pursue compelling and comprehensive theoretical arguments (Bojer, 2012 on systematic social change; Ellersiek and Kenis, 2010 on power dynamics); these create vortexes of interest that concentrate the energy on important topics. When sophisticated methods reach out into these vortexes, cross-sector work unveils radically new promises, such as (re)shaping entire fields like microfinance (Roubos, 2009). Although only a few authors mesh this theoretical energy with the requisite methodological proficiency – promisive-(trans)formation is clearly welcome and influential in quite diverse settings (museums, nutrition program, health leadership). Lastly, promisive-formulation studies leverage deep insights from both theory and method to carve out new collective pursuits. These studies are forward-looking and integrative. They are also co-generative and harness rather avant-garde combinations of theory and methods to foresee and service pressing problems and achieve tangible, immediate social good (the chapter by Selsky et al. in Part C of this volume is a harbinger of what lies ahead).

Discussion

After 15 years of collective work, we believe that the future of cross-sector partnership research is young and full of promise; promise for established researchers whose work has given the topic academic legitimacy and practical relevance; promise for new researchers who can focus on cross-sector work in fields that make them feel alive and connected to society; promise for new theories of business in societies in ways that emphasize, respect, and harness its interdependencies with social actors; and promise for new methods of researching business in ways that shift attention and draw new insight from these interdependencies. In short, we believe cross-sector research helps us see, understand and explain organizations-in-relation, both within their partnerships but also for society at large. We hope this shared cause, deeply rooted in the phenomenon, will continue to energize researchers from different disciplines and stimulate new, bolder, better ways of bringing research to bear on practice and vice-versa.

How do we move forward in a field that has generated such diversity of insight, and done so in such dynamic and diverse ways? How do we stimulate a community that is so interconnected with practice, engaged across disciplines and attracting new members? How do we give advice to peers who already work at intricate interfaces and shy not but rather boldly charge towards ever more complex social problems? We recommend two paths: using new methods to enrich old theories and using new theories to revitalize old methods.

Theory elaboration: using new methods to enrich old theories

The time has come to develop a theory of cross-sector partnerships that allows us to study organizations-in-relation. There are a few precedents for theorizing relationality – critically (Le Ber and Branzei, 2010b), communicatively (Koschmann et al., 2012), and with complexity (Seitanidi, 2007). But none is sufficient. Each offers but a promising beginning for theory elaboration. We have tried on so many theories (Table 12.3) but kept few and redeployed even fewer. We have also borrowed enough; so wide and far that we may have already reached the limits of finding something new out there. It is time for something new – of our own making. There is no shortage of inspiration or role models. Browsing through the diversity of theories and methods is necessary, but not sufficient. As we take a closer look at what we have individually and collectively developed over time, we can find many interesting pieces to puzzle together into a theory that not only fits us better but also one that we can keep adjusting as our models and practices keep unfolding.

Method elaboration: using new theories to revitalize old methods

We have used multiple methods too, starting with the usual suspects: lots of retrospective interviews; some ethnographies; and even a handful of action research projects. But many methods are conspicuously absent. We have few quantitative studies and hardly any experiments. Even systematic research syntheses are hard to come by (to our knowledge this is the first one). Yet we work in a field of dreams. With a phenomenon changing so quickly, we have an embarrassment of natural experiments that could help us study in-situ and in real time emergent forms, functions and formulas. In some cases, we have unprecedented access to the full stream of exchanges or we have access to executives willing to work autobiographically or submit their organizations to transformational interventions. We also see dynamic configurations of partners so we can understand networks as they evolve. And we can study how intractable problems are broken down into manageable pieces, and how these pieces come together into unprecedented solutions. But, you may say, we do not have the methods that do all that. We beg to differ. The set of methods offer us a variety of ways to see, snapshot, record and make sense of how relations are changing organizations. We have an abundance of information too. But our old toolkit is too heavy to carry and too habituated to lose. So it is time to drop old tools and improvise new ones. Tools that would sensitize us to the social good and help us envision new organizational paths to get there.

Conclusion

This chapter is a treasure hunt of 144 studies that deliberately shape and tug at the notion of cross-sector partnerships to unravel multiple theoretical and method-ological threads. While the body of work is diverse, multi-vocal and colourful, finding one's way to the key themes let alone contributions requires a fine-grained map. Scholars interested in cross-sector studies might have missed some of these studies or delved so deep into either the eclectic set of theories or the overwhelming detail of the real-time, real-life interventions that some may have even lost track of key contributions. We hope that our systematic content analysis coupled with iterative qualitative work provides helpful guideposts for finding new treasures at the interface of theories and methods, for rediscovering some forgotten treasures from the broader vantage and longer span of this growing field and community, and especially for rekindling our common search for new forms, (trans)formations and formulations that help further the social good.

Questions for reflection

1   Prescriptions – if we re-imagine partnerships as a vehicle for responsible business, what are the key forms, (trans)formations and formulations that for-profit, non-profit and public organizations should adopt?
2   Proscriptions – what questions can we stop asking because we got the answers we wanted or because the answers we got fell behind the questions we ought to ask next?
3   Possibilities – what possibilities do cross-sector partnerships open for making business a more responsible partner in social innovation, social change and social good?
4   Promises – how do 15 years of examples, explanations and explorations of part-nering across sectors help us recast, rethink and overcome ever more complex social problems?

Appendix

Codebook for content analysis

Code	Definition
Quantitative variables coded	
Year	Year of publication
Authors	Names of authors
Study title	Title of study
# Citations	Number of Citations as listed by Google Scholar (as of June 30, 2012)
Publication title	Title of Publication
Type of publication	Journal article, book or book chapter, conference proceedings, PhD dissertation, master's thesis, report, teaching case working paper, other
	Journal: For journal publications only: journal name
	Sector: Public, non-profit, for-profit sector, interdisciplinary
Qualitative variables coded	
Study type	Descriptive, empirical, or conceptual
Theory	Theory or theories
Method	Single, multiple, mixed
Dependent variables	Dependent variable(s)
Theme	Emergence, evolution, governance as explicitly stated in the publication
Stated questions	Research questions (as explicitly stated in the publication)
Stated contributions	Contributions (as explicitly stated in the publication)

Notes

1 This manuscript is a fully collaborative effort. The authors have contributed equally.
2 Our analyses were robust to the inclusion or exclusion of these 22 special issue articles.
3 We compared the outlets with the current list of top journals in the for-profit literature (*Academy of Management Journal, Academy of Management Review, Strategic Management Journal, Administrative Science Quarterly, Organizational Science, Organizational Studies*); non-profit literature (*Non-profit Management and Leadership, Non-profit and Voluntary Sector Quarterly, Public Administration and Development, World Development*), the public literature (*Administration and Society, American Review of Public Administration, Australian Journal of Public Administration, International Review of Administrative Sciences, Journal of Public Administration, Research and Theory, Policy and Politics, Public Administration*, and *Public Administration Review*). We also included several top interdisciplinary journals (*Organization and Leadership Quarterly*).
4 This concern is explicitly articulated, even mandated, by Bryson, Crosby and Stone in their 2006 piece, which remains the most cited piece in this rapidly growing literature.
5 There are several noteworthy examples of promisive studies which did not use the word cross-sector in their title. Key among these are the Fiol and O'Connor (2002) study that

examines the conflict and the compromise at the interface across sectors; work on discursive practices that bring attention to marginalized plights or actors by Phillips *et al.* (2004), especially their 2005 Academy of Management Review which draws attention to commitments made in conversation (Hardy *et al.*, 2005).

References

Adams, M. (2012) *FEMA Region X: Cross-Sector Collaboration.* Master of Community and Regional Planning. Department of Planning, Public Policy and Management, University of Oregon.

Aguinis, H. and Glavas, A. (2012) What we know and don't know about corporate social responsibility: a review and research agenda. *Journal of Management,* 38 (4): 932–68.

Allen, L. (2010) *Mobilizing a Cross-Sector Collaborative for Systemic Change: Lessons from Project U-Turn, Philadelphia's Campaign to Reduce the Dropout Rate.* [pdf] Boston: Jobs for the Future. Available at: www.jff.org/sites/default/files/PUT_paper_PDF_VERSION_010610.pdf [Accessed 30 June 2012].

Ameli, P. and Kayes, D.C. (2011) Triple-loop learning in a cross-sector partnership: the DC central kitchen partnership. *The Learning Organization,* 18 (3): 175–88.

Andreasen, A.R. (1999) Toward a model of cross sector alliance success. *Social Marketing Quarterly,* 5 (3): 14.

Andreasen, A.R. (2009) Cross-sector marketing alliances, in J.J. Cordes and C.E. Steuerle (eds) *Nonprofits and Business.* Washington, DC: The Urban Institute Press: 155–92.

Arya, B. and Salk, J.E. (2006) Cross-sector alliance learning and effectiveness of voluntary codes of corporate social responsibility. *Business Ethics Quarterly,* 16 (2): 211–34.

Austin, J.E. (2003) Marketing's role in cross-sector collaboration. *Journal of Nonprofit and Public Sector Marketing,* 11 (1): 23–39.

Austin, J.E. and Seitanidi, M.M. (2012a) Collaborative value creation: a review of partnering between nonprofits and businesses: Part I. Value creation spectrum and collaboration stages. *Nonprofit and Voluntary Sector Quarterly,* 41 (5): 726–58.

Austin, J.E. and Seitanidi, M.M. (2012b) Collaborative value creation: a review of partnering between nonprofits and businesses. Part 2: Partnership processes and outcomes. *Nonprofit and Voluntary Sector Quarterly,* 41 (6): 929–68.

Austrian, Z. and Iannone, D. (1997) Cross-sector collaboration: the great lakes environmental finance center. *Metropolitan Universities: An International Forum,* 8 (3): 13–26.

Babiak, K. and Thibault, L. (2009) Challenges in multiple cross-sector partnerships. *Nonprofit and Voluntary Sector Quarterly,* 38: 117–43.

Backes-Gellner, U., Maass, F. and Werner, A. (2005) On the explanation of horizontal, vertical and cross-sector R&D partnerships – evidence for the German industrial sector. *International Journal of Entrepreneurship and Innovation Management,* 5(1–2): 103–16.

Barrett, D., Austin, J.E. and McCarthy, S. (2000) Cross-sector collaboration: lessons from the international trachoma initiative. *Harvard Business School Social Enterprise Series,* 16: 1–17.

Battisti, M. (2009) Below the surface: the challenges of cross-sector partnerships. *Journal of Corporate Citizenship,* 9 (3): 95–108.

Bojer, M. (2012) We can't keep meeting like this: developing the capacity for cross-sector collaboration. *Reflections: The SoL Journal,* 11(4): 25–33.

Branzei, O. and Le Ber, M.J. (2012) In the making: impact evaluation in cross-sector partnerships. Working paper.

Branzei, O., Le Ber, M.J. and Hyatt, D.G. (2011) Cross-sector partnerships for social innovation: processes, perspectives and positioning. A concept note prepared for the PDW of same name at the Academy of Management Annual Meeting in San Antonia, Texas, 12 August 2011.

Bryson, J.M. and Crosby, B.C. (2005) Leadership and the creation of cross-sector regimes of mutual gain, in *Eighth National Public Management Research Conference.* University of Southern California, Los Angeles, CA, 29 September 29–1 October 2005.

Bryson, J.M., Crosby, B.C. and Stone, M.M. (2006) The design and implementation of cross-sector collaborations: propositions from the literature. *Public Administration Review,* 66 (s1): 44–55.

Bryson, J.M., Crosby, B.C., Stone, M.M. and Saunoi-Sandgren, E.O. (2009) Designing and managing cross-sector collaboration: a case study in reducing traffic congestion. *IBM Center for the Business of Government,* Fall/Winter: 78–81. www.businessofgovernment.org

Bryson, J.M., Crosby, B.C., Stone, M.M. and Saunoi-Sandgren, E.O. (2011) Designing and strategically managing cross-sector collaborations propositions from the literature and three longitudinal studies, in *Seventh Transatlantic Dialogue on Strategic Management of Public Organizations.* School of Public Affairs and Administration, Rutgers University, Newark 23–25 June 2011.

Bryson, J.M., Crosby, B.C., Stone, M.M. and Saunoi-Sandgren, E.O. (2012) Dynamics of cross-sector collaboration: Minnesota's Urban Partnership Agreement from start to finish. Technical report to Intelligent Transportation Systems Institute, Center for Transportation Studies, University of Minnesota.

Cairns, D. and Harris, M. (2011) Local cross-sector partnerships tackling the challenges collaboratively. *Nonprofit Management and Leadership,* 21 (3): 311–24.

Cikaliuk, M. (2011) Cross-sector alliances for large-scale health leadership development in Canada: lessons for leaders. *Leadership in Health Services,* 24 (4): 281–94.

Clarke, A. (2010) *Implementing Regional Sustainable Development Strategies: Exploring Structure and Outcomes In Cross-Sector Collaborations.* PhD thesis McGill University, Montreal, QC.

Clarke, A. (2014) Designing social partnerships for local sustainability strategy implementation, in Seitanidi, M.M. and Crane, A. (eds) *Social Partnerships and Responsible Business: A Research Handbook.* London: Routledge: 79–102.

Clarke, A. and Fuller, M. (2010) Collaborative strategic management: strategy formulation and implementation by multi-organizational cross-sector social partnerships. *Journal of Business Ethics,* 94): 85–101.

Cooper, M.H. (2010) *Research Synthesis and Meta-Analysis: A Step-By-Step Approach* (Applied Social Research Methods), 5th edn. Thousand Oaks, CA: Sage Publications.

Cornelius, N. and Wallace, J. (2010) Cross-sector partnerships: city regeneration and social justice. *Journal of Business Ethics,* 94: 71–84.

Cornforth, C., Vangen, S. and Hayes, J.P. (2012) The governance of cross-sector partnerships involving third sector organizations, in The International Society for Third-Sector Research *Tenth International Conference: Democratization, Marketization, and the Third Sector,* Siena, Italy 2012. 10–13 July 2012.

Cotten, M.N. and Lasprogata, G.A. (2012) Corporate citizenship and creative collaboration: best practice for cross-sector partnerships. *Journal of Law, Business and Ethics,* 18: 9–39.

Couchman, P.K. and Beckett, R. (2006) Achieving effective cross sector R&D collaboration: a proposed management framework. *Prometheus: Critical Studies in Innovation,* 24 (2): 151–68.

Couchman, P.K. and Fulop, L. (2004) Managing risk in cross sector R&D collaborations: lessons from an international case study. *Prometheus: Critical Studies in Innovation,* 22 (2): 151–67.

Couchman, P.K. and Fulop, L. (2005a) Bringing innovation to centre stage: the rhetoric of commercialisation and cross-sector collaboration, in APROS 11 2005: Asia-Pacific Researchers in Organization Studies: Eleventh International Colloquium, Melbourne, Victoria: Asia-Pacific Researchers in Organisation Studies: 275–84.

Couchman, P.K. and Fulop, L. (2005b) Engaging in collaborative R&D: an international case study of cross-sector collaboration, in APROS Colloquium (Eleventh: 2005: Melbourne,

Victoria). APROS 11: Asia-Pacific Researchers in Organization Studies: Eleventh International Colloquium, Melbourne, Australia, 4–7 December 2005. Melbourne: Asia-Pacific Researchers in Organization Studies, 2006: 285–95.

Couchman, P.K. and Fulop, L. (2007) Building effective interorganizational relationships in multi-partner R&D collaborations: findings from a study of cross-sector R&D projects, in British Academy of Managment 2007, Conference Proceedings 2007: *Managing Research, Education and Business Success: Is the Future as Clear as the Past?* Warwick Business School UK, 11–13 September, 2007.

Couchman, P.K. and Fulop, L. (2009a) Examining partner experience in cross-sector collaborative projects focused on the commercialization of R&D. *Innovation: Management, Policy and Practice*, 11: 85–103.

Couchman, P.K. and Fulop, L. (2009b) Risk and trust in cross-sector R and D projects, in ANZAM 2009: *Proceedings of the 23rd ANZAM Conference* 2009, Promaco Conventions, Canning Bridge, Western Australia.

Cozzolino, A. (2012) Emblematic example of strategic cross-sector partnership: logistics emergency teams, in A. Cozzolino, ed. *Humanitarian Logistics: Cross Sector Cooperation in Disaster Relief Management, SpringerBriefs in Business*. Heidelberg: Springer, Chapter 4: 39–48.

Crane, A. and Seitanidi, M.M. (2014) Social partnerships and responsible business: what, why and how?, in Seitanidi, M.M. and Crane, A. (eds) *Social Partnerships and Responsible Business: A Research Handbook*. London: Routledge: 1–9.

Crosby, B.C. and Bryson, J.M. (2007) A leadership framework for cross-sector collaboration. *Public Management Review*, 7 (2): 177–201.

Crosby, B.C. and Bryson, J.M. (2010) Integrative leadership and the creation and maintenance of cross-sector collaborations. *The Leadership Quarterly*, 21): 211–30.

Daniel, J.C. (2008) Cross sector partnering between PANDA SOFTWARE INTERNATIONAL (Spain) and GOODWILL (India) in community technology services project for children and young women in Madurai, India – a case study.

Davis, D., DeCristoforo, R., Hege, M. and Griffith, J. (2000) Managing cross-sector partnerships for increasing access to children's health care. The 128th Annual Meeting of American Public Health Association.

Doh, J. and Boddewyn, J. (2014) International business and social partnerships: how institutional and MNE capabilities affect collective-goods provisioning in emerging markets, in Seitanidi, M.M. and Crane, A. (eds) *Social Partnerships and Responsible Business: A Research Handbook*. London: Routledge: 44–59.

Doignon, Y. (2003) Working for the public good through cross-sector partnerships in the arts. University of Oregon theses, Arts and Administration Program, M.A., 2003.

Dorado, S., Giles Jr., D.E. and Welch, T.C. (2009) Delegation of coordination and outcomes in cross-sector partnerships: the case of service learning partnerships. *Nonprofit and Voluntary Sector Quarterly*, 38 (3): 368–91.

Edmond, T.C. (2007) *Cross-Sector Collaborations: A Phenomenological Study of the Nonprofit Sector's Experiences with Successful Cross-Sector Models*. PhD thesis Capella University.

Edmond, T., Raghavan, K. and Smith, P.C. (2011) Cross-sector collaborations and enterprise risk management – strategies for nonprofit organizations to effectively partner with for-profit organizations. *Journal of Business and Accounting*, 4 (1): 24–36.

Ellersiek, A. and Kenis, P. (2007) Power in cross-sector partnerships: an analytical framework and literature review. *Colloquium on Corporate Political Activity*, Paris, 22–24 May, 2008.

Feldman, K.A. 1971. Using the work of others: some observations on reviewing and integrating, *Sociology of Education*, 4: 86–102.

Fernández-Esquinas, M. and Ramos-Vielba, I. (2011) Emerging forms of cross-sector collaboration in the Spanish innovation system. *Science and Public Policy*, 38 (2): 135–46.

Fink, J.H. (2011) Cross-sector integration of urban information to enhance sustainable decision making. *IBM Journal of Research and Development*, 55 (1.2): 12.1–8.

Fiol, C.M. and O'Connor, E.J. (2002) When hot and cold collide in radical change processes: lessons from community development. *Organizational Science*, 13 (5): 532–46.

Fiorentino, R., Liu, G., Pariser, A.R. and Mulberg, A.E. (2012) Cross-sector sponsorship of research in eosinophilic esophagitis: a collaborative model for rational drug development in rare diseases. *Journal of Allergy and Clinical Immunology*, 130 (3): 613–16.

Flentge1, F., Beyel, C. and Rome, E (2008) Towards a standardised cross-sector information exchange on present risk factors, in J. Lopez and B. Hämmerli (eds) *Critical Information Infrastructures Security, Lecture Notes in Computer Science*, 5141: 349–60.

Forsyth, T. (2010) Panacea or paradox? cross-sector partnerships, climate change, and development. *Wiley Interdisciplinary Reviews: Climate Change*, 1: 683–96.

Foskett, R. (2003) Employer and needs-led curriculum planning in higher education: a cross-sector case study of foundation degree development. University of Leeds: Education-line. www.leeds.ac.uk.proxy2.lib.uwo.ca/educol/documents/00003182.htm

Foskett, R. (2005) Collaborative partnership in the higher education curriculum: a cross-sector study of foundation degree development. *Research in Post-Compulsory Education*, 10 (3): 351–72.

Garland, M., Alestalo, S. and Bhatia, S.K. (2012) Cross-sector and interdisciplinary research collaborations as paths for career success for women in academic science and engineering. 2012 WEPAN National Conference, "Getting to the Heart of it All: Connecting Gender Research," WIE Programs, Faculty and Corporate Partners, June 25–27, 2012, Columbus, Ohio.

Garrett-Jones, S. and Turpin, T. (2003) A missing variable: evaluating the institutional impact from participating in government supported cross sector R&D programs, in K. Zinacker and A. Fier (eds) *Evaluation of Government Funded R&D Activities*. Austria: JOANNEUM RESEARCH.

Garrett-Jones, S., Turpin, T. and Diment, K. (2010) Managing competition between individual and organizational goals in cross-sector research and development centres. *The Journal of Technology Transfer*, 35: 527–46.

Garrett-Jones, S., Turpin, T., Burns, P. and Diment, K. (2005) Common purpose and divided loyalties: the risks and rewards of cross-sector collaboration for academic and government researchers. *R&D Management*, 35 (5): 535–44.

Goldsmith, A.A. (2011) Profits and alms: cross-sector partnerships for global poverty reduction. *Public Administration and Development*, 31 (1): 15–24.

Gray, D.O. (2011) Cross-sector research collaboration in the USA: a national innovation system perspective. *Science and Public Policy*, 38 (2): 123–33.

Gray, B. and Purdy, J. (2014) Conflict in cross-sector partnerships, in M.M. Seitanidi and A. Crane, A. (eds) *Social Partnerships and Responsible Business: A Research Handbook*. London: Routledge: 205–26.

Grudinschi, D., Kaljunen, L., Hokkanen, T., Hallikas, J., Sintonen, S. and, Puustinen, A. (2011) Challenges in management of cross-sector collaboration for elderly care, in O. Manninen, (ed.) *Work Among the Elderly*. Kopijyvä Tampere: The ISCES (The International Society for Complex Environmental Studies) Society, (Archives of Complex Environmental Studies (ACES): 32–45.

Hamann, R. (2014) Cross-sector social partnership in areas of limited statehood, in M.M. Seitanidi and A. Crane, A. (eds) *Social Partnerships and Responsible Business: A Research Handbook*. London: Routledge: 60–78.

Hamann, R., Giamporcaro, S., Johnston, D. and Yachkaschi, S. (2011) The role of business and cross-sector collaboration in addressing the "wicked problem" of food insecurity. *Development Southern Africa*, 28 (4): 579–94.

Hamann, R., Giamporcaro, S.,Yachkaschi, S. and Johnston, D. (2009) *On the role of business and cross-sector collaboration in food security in South Africa.*

Hamann, R., Kambalame, D., de Cleene, S. and Ndlovu, N. (2008) Towards collective business action and cross-sector collaboration in responsible competitiveness clusters in southern Africa. *Development Southern Africa,* 25 (1): 99–118.

Hamann, R., Pienaar, S., Boulogne, F. and Kranz, N. (2009) What makes cross-sector partnerships successful? A comparative case study analysis of diverse partnership types in an emerging economy context: 1–33.

Hardy, C., Lawrence,T.B. and Grant, D. (2005) Discourse and collaboration: the role of conversations and collective identity. *Academy of Management Review,* 30 (1): 58–77.

Hayes, J.P., Cornforth, C. and Vangen, S. (2011a) Governance in cross-sector partnerships involving third sector organisations, in *Twenty-fifth British Academy of Management Conference,* 13–15 September 2011, Birmingham.

Hayes, J.P., Cornforth, C. and Vangen, S. (2011b) Tensions: a challenge to governance and cross-sector partnerships, in *Eighteenth Multi-Organisational Partnerships Alliances and Networks,* 4–6 July 2011, University of Strathclyde Business School, Glasgow.

Herman, E.S. (2012) Affordable housing and cross-sector partnerships: improving the bottom line. Working paper posted online at: Scholarly Commons http://repository.upenn.edu/curej/91.

Heuer, M. (2011) Ecosystem cross-sector collaboration: conceptualizing an adaptive approach to sustainability governance. *Business Strategy and the Environment,* 20: 211–21.

Heuer, M. and Kumar, A. (2012) Earth system governance in South Asia: designing cross-sector collaboration. *Journal of Modern Accounting and Auditing,* 8 (1): 128–35.

Hull, R., Gibbon, J., Branzei, O. and Haugh, H. (2011) Cases, configurations, critiques and contributions, in R. Hull, J. Gibbon, O. Branzei and H. Haugh, eds. *Dialogues in Critical Management Studies,Vol. 1:The Third Sector,* Bingley: Emerald: xiii–xxxv.

Huybrechts, B. and Nicholls, A. (2010) Cross-sector collaboration and organizational legitimacy: insights from fair trade. *Third Social Entrepreneurship Research Colloquium,* 19–21 June 2010, Oxford: Skoll Centre for Social Entrepreneurship.

Hyatt, D.G. and Berente, N. (2011) Proactive environmental strategies: an exploration of the effects of cross-sector partnerships. *First International Conference on Engaged Management Scholarship,* 2011. Available at SSRN: http://ssrn.com.proxy2.lib.uwo.ca/abstract=1839826 or http://dx.doi.org.proxy2.lib.uwo.ca/10.2139/ssrn.1839826.

Hyatt, D.G. and Johnson, J. (2009) Cross sector social interaction: leveraging intentional change across the micro, meso and macro.The 2009 *BAWB Global Forum, Manage by Designing in an Era of Massive Innovation,* 2–5 June 2009, Case Western Reserve University.

Jamali, D. (2011) Cross sector social partnerships (CSSPS): prospects and challenges for social change in the Middle East. *Cross Sector Collaboration* organized by New York University in Abu–Dhabi, 24–26 October 2011.

Jiang, L. and Cai, N. (2011a) Cross-sector cooperation and its risk management review. 2011 *International Conference on Business Computing and Global Informatization* (BCGIn 2011). Proceedings of a meeting held 29–31 July 2011, Shanghai, China. Publisher: Institute of Electrical and Electronics Engineers (IEEE): 138–41.

Jiang, L. and Cai, N. (2011b) Risk of cross-sector cooperation based on network structure and relationship, in *Second International Conference on Artificial Intelligence, Management Science and Electronic Commerce* (AIMSEC) [electronic resource]: proceedings. 8–10 August 2011, Zhengzhou, China/IEEE: 3325.

Jørgensen, M. (2006) Evaluating cross-sector partnerships. *CBS Conference Public-private Partnerships in the Post WSSD Context.* Working paper presented at the conference "Public-private partnerships in the post WSSD context" Copenhagen Business School 14 August 2006.

Jupp, B. (2000) *Working Together: Creating a Better Environment for Cross-Sector Partnerships.* London: Demos.

Kimbrell, J.D., Witmer, A. and Flaherty, P. (2002) The Louisiana public health institute: a cross-sector approach for improving the public's health. *Journal of Public Health Management and Practice*, 8 (1): 68–74.

Klenk, N.L. and Hickey, G.M. (2010) Communication and management challenges in large, cross-sector research networks: a Canadian case study. *Canadian Journal of Communication*, 35: 239–59.

Knight, H. (2010) Exploring the fourth sector investigating multi-stakeholder cross-sector social partnerships in societal arts marketing. PhD dissertation proposal. Nineteenth Summer Academy Sorèze, France, July (2010) *Management and Business Administration.*

Koljatic, M. and Silva, M. (2008) Uncertainty reduction mechanisms in cross-sector alliances in Latin America. *Journal of Business Research*, 61: 648–50.

Koljatic, M., Silva, M. and Valenzuela, E. (2006) The development of cross-sector collaboration in a social context of low trust, in S. Shuman, ed. *Creating a Culture of Collaboration.* San Francisco: Jossey-Bass, Chapter 3.

Kolk, A. (2014) Partnerships as panacea for addressing global problems? On rationale, context, actors, impact and limitations, in M.M. Seitanidi and A. Crane, A. (eds) *Social Partnerships and Responsible Business: A Research Handbook.* London: Routledge: 15–43.

Kolk, A., van Dolen, W. and Vock, M. (2010) Trickle effects of cross-sector social partnerships. *Journal of Business Ethics*, 94: 123–37.

Kong, E. (2012) Strategic cross-sector collaboration in disaster response. *Proceedings of the Sixth Asian Business Research.* Novotel Hotel, Bangkok, Thailand, 8–10 April 2012.

Koschmann, M.A., Kuhn, T.R. and Pfarrer, M.D. (2012) A communicative framework of value in cross-sector partnerships. *Academy of Management Review*, 37: 332–54.

Kourula, A. and Laasonen, S. (2010) Nongovernmental organizations in business and society, management, and international business research – review and implications from 1998 to 2007. *Business and Society*, 49 (1): 35–67.

Krippendorff, K. (2004) *Content Analysis: An Introduction to its Methodology.* Thousand Oaks, CA: Sage.

Lamoureux, K. (2009) Success factors of cross-sector volunteer tourism partnerships involving US federal land agencies. PhD thesis, the George Washington University, School of Business.

Laasonen, S., Fougère, M. and Kourula, A. (2012) Dominant articulations in academic business and society discourse on NGO-business relations: a critical assessment. *Journal of Business Ethics*, 109: 521–45.

Laplume, A.O., Sonpar, K. and Litz, R.A. (2008) Stakeholder theory: reviewing a theory that moves us. *Journal of Management*, 34: 1152–89.

Le Ber, M.J. (2010) Cross-sector models of collaboration for social innovation. PhD Richard Ivey School of Business, The University of Western Ontario. Electronic Thesis and Dissertation Repository, Paper 10.

Le Ber, M.J. and Branzei, O. (2010a) (Re)Forming strategic cross-sector partnerships: Relational processes of social innovation. *Business and Society*, 49 (1): 140–172.

Le Ber, M.J. and Branzei, O. (2010b) Towards a critical theory of value creation in cross sector partnerships. *Organization*, 17 (5): 599–629.

Le Ber, M.J. and Branzei, O. (2010c) Value frame fusion in cross sector interactions. *Journal of Business Ethics*, 94: 163–95.

Le Ber, M.J. and Branzei, O. (2011) The dark triangle: hybridization in the third sector, in R. Hull, J. Gibbon, O. Branzei and H. Haugh (eds) *Dialogues in Critical Management Studies: Vol. 1, The Third Sector.* Bingley: Emerald, Chapter 10.

Leigh, J.S.A. (2005) US National Park Service cross-sector partnerships for environmental sustainability and cultural resource preservation. PhD thesis Boston College.

Leigh, J.S.A. (2008) Declining relations: understanding cross-sector partnership failure. MOPAN, *Fifteenth Annual Conference on Multi-Organizational Partnerships, Alliances and Networks*, 25–27 June 2008, Boston.

Maether, J. (2010) The role of global logistics companies in disaster relief efforts: an investigation into benefits, challenges and critical success factors of cross-sector collaborations. A thesis presented in partial fulfilment of the requirements for the degree of Master of Logistics and Supply Chain Management at Massey University, Albany, New Zealand.

Magee, M. (2003) Qualities of enduring cross-sector partnerships in public health. *The American Journal of Surgery*, 185 (1), January 2003: 26–9.

Mankowski, J. (2008) *An Exploratory Study of Alberta Cross-Sector Partnerships Using Complex Systems Thinking*. Master's thesis in Environmental Studies, Dalhousie University, June 2008.

Maon, F., Lindgreen, A. and Vanhamme, N. (2009) Developing supply chains in disaster relief operations through cross-sector socially oriented collaborations: a theoretical model. *Supply Chain Management: An International Journal*, 14 (2): 149–64.

Marcus, A., Shrivastava, P., Sharma, S. and Pogutz, S. (2011) *Cross-Sector Leadership for the Green Economy: Integrating Research and Practice on Sustainable Enterprise*. Basingstoke: Palgrave Macmillan.

McDonald, S. (2009) Cross-sector social partnerships, leading by example: a case study of reading for life. In APABIS 2009: *Strategic Alliances for Sustainable Development: Proceedings of the Annual Conference of the Asia Pacific Academy of Business in Society*, APABIS, Brisbane.

McDonald, S. and Young, S. (2012) Cross-sector collaboration shaping corporate social responsibility best practice within the mining industry. *Journal of Cleaner Production*, 37: 54–67.

Mendoza, X. (2009) Relational strategies for bridging and promoting cross-sector collaboration. *First International Conference on Bridging Knowledge in Long Term Care and Support. Crossing Boundaries between Ageing and Disability*, Barcelona, Spain, 5–7 March 2009. Abstract published in *International Journal of Integrated Care*, 9, 22 June 2009 – ISSN 1568–4156 – www.ijic.org/

Messer-Davidow, E. (2010) Interdisciplinary investigations and cross-sector interventions, in J. Parker, R. Samantrai and M. Romero (eds). *Interdisciplinarity and Social Justice: Revisioning Academic Accountability*. Albany, NY: State University of New York: 301–20.

Michelsen, K. (2011) Practical knowledge in cross-sector settings. EUREGIO III (Work Package 4): Scientific Background Paper Draft, 21.11.2011.

Mikki, S. (2009) Google Scholar compared to Web of Science: a literature review. *Nordic Journal of Information Literacy in Higher Education*, 1 (1): 41–51.

Mishook, J. and Raynor, A.F. (2010) The critical role of data-informed, cross-sector partnerships in smart systems. *Voices in Urban Education* (V★U★E★) Summer 2010, Annenberg Institute for School Reform: 23–32.

Mohammed, K. and Gyimah, N.A.B. (2011) Cross-sector partnership collaboration between humanitarian organizations and the private sector. Master's thesis. Jönköping International Business School.

Murphy, B.M. (2012) Cross-sector social partnerships: value creation and capabilities. PhD Dissertation. ESADE – Escuela Superior de Administración y Dirección de Empresas, Institute for Social Innovation.

Murphy, M. and Arenas, D. (2010) Through indigenous lenses: cross-sector collaborations with fringe stakeholders. *Journal of Business Ethics*, 94: 103–21.

Murphy, M., Perrot, F. and Rivera-Santos, M. (2012) New perspectives on learning and innovation in cross-sector collaborations. *Journal of Business Research*, in press, 10.

Nicholls-Nixon, C.L., Castilla, J.A.D., Garcia, J.S. and Pesquera, M.R. (2011) Latin American management research: review, synthesis, and extension. *Journal of Management*, 37: 1178–227.

Nijhuis, B. (2014) How to co-create opportunities together: CREMOS in Guatemala, in M.M. Seitanidi and A. Crane, A. (eds) *Social Partnerships and Responsible Business: A Research Handbook*. London: Routledge: 349–355.

O'Regan, K.M. and Oster, S.M. (2000) Nonprofit and for-profit partnerships: rationale and challenges of cross-sector contracting. *Nonprofit and Voluntary Sector Quarterly*, 29: 120–40.

Palmer, I. (1997) Arts management cutback strategies: a cross-sector analysis. *Nonprofit Management and Leadership*, 7 (3): 271–90.

Palmer, I. (1998) Arts managers and managerialism: a cross-sector analysis of CEOs' orientations and skills. *Public Productivity and Management Review*, 21 (4): 433–52.

Parmigiani, A. and Rivera-Santos, M. (2011) A path through the forest: a meta-review of interorganizational relationships. *Journal of Management*, 37 (4): 1108–36.

Peizer, J. (2003) Cross-sector information and communications technology funding for development: what works, what does not, and why. *Information Technologies and International Development*, 1 (2): 81–8.

Peloza, J. and Ye, C. (2014) How social partnerships build brands, in M.M. Seitanidi and A. Crane, A. (eds) *Social Partnerships and Responsible Business: A Research Handbook*. London: Routledge: 191–204.

Phillips, N., Lawrence, T.B. and Hardy, C. (2004) Discourse and institutions. *Academy of Management Review*, 29 (4): 635–52.

Pillsbury, J.B., Goddard-Truitt, V. and Littlefield, J. (2009) Cross-sector performance accountability: making aligned contributions to improve community well-being. Preliminary Paper – Presented at the 2009 ASPA (American Society for Public Administration) Conference, Miami, Florida.

Pittman, P. and Almeida, C. (2006) Cross-sector learning among researchers and policy-makers: the search for new strategies to enable use of research results. *Cadernos de Saúde Pública*, 22(suppl): S97–S108.

Plowman, D., Baker, L., Beck, T., Kulkarni, M., Solansky, S. and Travis, D. (2007) Radical change accidentally: the emergence and amplification of small change. *Academy of Management Journal*, 50 (3): 515–43.

Reast, R., Lindgreen, A., Vanhamme, J. and Maon, F. (2010) The Manchester super casino: experience and learning in a cross-sector social partnership. *Journal of Business Ethics*, 94: 197–218.

Rein, M. and Stott, L. (2009) Working together: critical perspectives on six cross-sector partnerships in Southern Africa. *Journal of Business Ethics*, 90: 79–89.

Rein, M., Stott, L., Yambayamba, K., Hardman, S. and Reid, S. (2005) Working together: a critical analysis of cross-sector partnerships in Southern Africa. *The University of Cambridge Programme for Industry*, UK.

Rodriguez, F.D., Carter, A.S. and Rawa, A.D. (2005) Cross sector partnership results in increased marine biodiversity information, awareness, and an initial biodiversity action plan in the Gulf of Paria, Venezuela. Author: Oceans 2005 (2005: Washington, DC) Title: Oceans 2005 MTS/IEEE [electronic resource]: Washington, DC, USA, 18–23 September 2005. Publisher: Columbia, MD: Marine Technology Society; Piscataway, NJ: IEEE, 2005.

Rondinelli, D.A. and London, T. (2003) How corporations and environmental groups cooperate: assessing cross-sector alliances and collaborations. *Academy of Management Executive*, 17: 61–76.

Roubos, K. (2008) The rise of cross-sector partnerships in microfinance: environmental causes and future potential. *Stanford Journal of Microfinance*, 1: 1–15.

Ruckelshaus, M. (2012) I'm with stupid: the power of cross-sector partnerships for conservation. *Growing Pains: Taking Ecology into the 21st century*, The Preliminary Program for Ninety-seventh ESA Annual Meeting (5–10 August 2012).

Rufin, C. and Rivera-Santos, M. (2014) Cross-sector governance: from institutions to partnerships, and back to institutions, in M.M. Seitanidi and A. Crane (eds) *Social Partnerships and Responsible Business: A Research Handbook*. London: Routledge: 125–42.

Russell, L.R. (2011) Identifying complex cultural interactions in the instructional design process: a case study of a cross-border, cross-sector training for innovation program. Middle-Secondary Education and Instructional Technology Dissertations. Paper 80. Georgia State University.

Ryan, J. (2011) Irish experience of cross-sector research collaboration initiatives. *Science and Public Policy*, 38 (2): 147–55.

Sagawa. S. (2001) New value partnerships: the lessons of Denny's/Save the Children partnership for building high-yielding cross-sector alliances. *International Journal of Nonprofit and Voluntary Sector Marketing*, 6 (3): 199–214.

Salk, J.E. and Arya, B. (2005) Social performance learning in multinational corporations: multicultural teams, their social capital and use of cross-sector alliances, in D.L. Shapiro, M.A.Von Glinow and J.L.C. Cheng (eds) *Managing Multinational Teams: Global Perspectives* (Advances in International Management,Volume 18), Emerald Group Publishing Limited: 189–207.

Schiller, D. (2011) Institutions and practice in cross-sector research collaboration: conceptual considerations with empirical illustrations from the German science sector. *Science and Public Policy*, 38 (2): 109–21.

Schmutzler, J., Guitérrez, R., Reficco, E. and Márquez, P. (2014) Evolution of an alliance portfolio to develop an inclusive business, in M.M. Seitanidi and A. Crane (eds) *Social Partnerships and Responsible Business: A Research Handbook*. London: Routledge: 125–42.

Sehested, K. (2003) Cross-sector partnerships as a new form of local governance, in L. Kjaer, (ed.) *Local Partnerships in Europe: An Action Research Project*. Copenhagen: The Copenhagen Centre: 89–95.

Seitanidi, M.M. (2007) The future challenges of cross sector interactions: interactions between nonprofit organisations and businesses. Working Paper Series. http://works.bepress.com/may_seitanidi/3

Seitanidi, M.M. (2008) Adaptive responsibilities: nonlinear interactions in cross sector social partnerships. *Emergence: Complexity and Organization*, 10 (3): 51–64.

Seitanidi, M.M. (2010) Press release "Second International symposium on cross sector social interactions: re-imagining partnerships for the global social good" for immediate release May, 2010. Available at: http://works.bepress.com.proxy2.lib.uwo.ca/may_seitanidi/25

Seitanidi, M.M. and Crane, A. (2014) Conclusion: re-imagining the future of social partnerships and responsible business, in Seitanidi, M.M. and Crane, A. (eds) *Social Partnerships and Responsible Business: A Research Handbook*. London: Routledge: 388–407.

Seitanidi, M.M. and Lindgreen, A. (2010) Editorial: cross sector social interactions. *Journal of Business Ethics*, 94: 1–7.

Seitanidi, M.M., Koufopoulos, D.N. and Palmer, P. (2010) Partnership formation for change: indicators for transformative potential in cross sector social partnerships. *Journal of Business Ethics*, 94: 139–61.

Selsky, J.W. and Parker, B. (2005) Cross-sector partnerships to address social issues: challenges to theory and practice. *Journal of Management*, 31: 849–73.

Selsky, J.W. and Parker, B. (2010) Platforms for cross-sector social partnerships: prospective sensemaking devices for social benefit. *Journal of Business Ethics*, 94: 21–37.

Serafin, R., Stibbe, D., Bustamante, C. and Schramm, C. (2008) *Current practice in the evaluation of cross-sector partnerships for sustainable development*. TPI Working Paper No. 1/2008. London: The Partnering Initiative: 1–15.

Shumate, M. and O'Connor, A. (2010) Corporate reporting of cross-sector alliances: the portfolio of NGO partners communicated on corporate websites, *Communication Monographs*, 77 (2): 207–30.

Siegel, D.J. (2010a) *Organizing for Social Partnership: Higher Education in Cross-Sector Collaboration.* New York: Routledge.

Siegel, D.J. (2010b) Why universities join cross-sector social partnerships: theory and evidence. *Journal of Higher Education Outreach and Engagement,* 14: 33–62.

Simo, G. and Bies, A.L. (2007) The role of nonprofits in disaster response: an expanded model of cross-sector collaboration. *Public Administration Review,* 67 (Ss1): 125–42.

Stafford, E. and Hartman, C. (2014) NGO-initiated sustainable entrepreneurship and social partnerships: Greenpeace's "Solutions" campaign for natural refrigerants in North America, in Seitanidi, M.M. and Crane, A. (eds) *Social Partnerships and Responsible Business: A Research Handbook.* London: Routledge: 164–90.

Tafra-Vlahovi, M. (2007) The value of cross-sector partnership: a case. Master's thesis. Program, Cross-sector Partnership for Sustainable Development, at the University of Cambridge, 2006/2007: 136–53.

Tien, C.C. (2006) Collaboration in museums: the evolution of cross-sector collaboration. Intercom 2006 conference. "New roles and missions for museums." 2–4 November 2006 in Taipei, Taiwan.

Turpin, T. and Fernández-Esquinas, M. (2011) Introduction to special issue: the policy rationale for cross-sector research collaboration and contemporary consequences. *Science and Public Policy,* 38 (2): 82–6.

Turpin, T. and Garrett-Jones, S. (2003) A missing variable: evaluating the institutional impact from participating in government supported cross sector R&D programs. *Conference on Evaluation of Government Funded R&D Activities.*

Turpin, T., Garrett-Jones, S. and Diment, K. (2005) Scientists, career choices and organisational change: managing human resources in cross-sector R&D organisations. *Journal of the Australian and New Zealand Academy of Management,* 11 (2): 13–26.

Turpin, T., Garrett-Jones, S. and Woolley, R. (2011) Cross-sector research collaboration in Australia: the Cooperative Research Centres Program at the crossroads. *Science and Public Policy,* 38 (2): 87–97.

Vachon, C.J. (2012) Scratch my back, and I'll scratch yours: scratching the surface of the duty of care in cross sector collaborations – are for-profits obligated to ensure the sustainability of their partner nonprofits. *Hastings Business Law Journal,* 8 (1): 1–19.

van Tulder, R. and Pfisterer, S. (2014) Creating partnering space: exploring the right fit for sustainable development partnerships, in M.M. Seitanidi and A. Crane (eds) *Social Partnerships and Responsible Business: A Research Handbook.* London: Routledge: 105–24.

Vasavada, T. (2007). *Navigating Networks: An Examination of the Relationship Between Government and Nonprofit Organizations and the Experience of Women Leaders of Nonprofit Organizations in Cross-Sector Partnerships.* PhD thesis Nelson Rockefeller College of Public Affairs and Policy.

Vurro, C., Dacin, M.T. and Perrini, F. (2010). Institutional antecedents of partnering for social change: how institutional logics shape cross-sector social partnerships. *Journal of Business Ethics,* 94: 39–53.

Weber, R.P., 1990. *Basic Content Analysis.* Thousand Oaks, CA: Sage.

Yee, H.W.H. (2008) *Cross-Sector Governance in Solid Waste Management: Making the Most Out of Collaboration and Civic Engagement.* Working paper, School of Policy, Planning and Development, University of Southern California: 1–2.

Zadek, S. (2014) Cross-sector partnerships: prototyping twenty-first-century governance, in M.M. Seitanidi and A. Crane, A. (eds) *Social Partnerships and Responsible Business: A Research Handbook.* London: Routledge: 382–7.

13

USING FUTURES METHODS IN CROSS-SECTOR PARTNERSHIP PROJECTS

Engaging wicked problems responsibly

John W. Selsky, Angela Wilkinson and Diana Mangalagiu

Introduction

In this chapter we bring the body of work on futures methods directly into the debates about the design of and decision making in cross-sector partnerships. Our objectives are to introduce the notion that different, explicit conceptions of the future can be used productively in partnership projects that address wicked problems; and to explore the contingent conditions for using different types of futures methods in such projects. We focus on sustainable development and sustainability projects. We demonstrate how the choice of futures method (e.g. forecasting, visioning or scenarios) shapes the expectations for such projects. Moreover, we argue that the choice of futures method offers a way of understanding the kinds of beneficial outcomes that may be produced and *how* they would be produced. Understanding why explicit attention to the future matters may be useful for business managers seeking to address wicked problems in a responsible manner in today's complex world.

Wicked problems and cross-sector partnerships

Amorphous social-ecological issues with potentially tragic consequences beset many societies today, as many chapters in this volume attest. An example is the unprecedented set of environmental challenges, such as global climate change, and the corresponding social concerns of sustainable development and sustainability (henceforth, SD/S). These twin challenges have been described as a "wicked problem" (Wilkinson and Eidinow, 2008) in that they benefit from a longer term view and more systemic understanding. Yet wicked problems are constrained by irreducible uncertainties, high decision stakes and values disputes (Funtowicz and Ravetz, 1993), such as competing discourses regarding growth, planetary boundaries, sustainable consumption and economic inequality. Wicked problems suggest the need for new types of solutions that bridge different interests and perspectives (disciplines and sectors) and recognize that specific issues are connected to each other and cannot be isolated from the wider contexts in which they originate.

Wicked problems (Rittel and Webber, 1973; see also Waddock's (2014) chapter in this volume) like SD/S have several characteristics. They are: *complex*, with many parts and processes interacting in non-linear ways; *multi-disciplinary and multi-sectoral*, with facets lying in several natural and social sciences and contained in several policy domains; *multi-scalar*, from organizational to local ecosystem to global scales; *equivocal*, with factual uncertainties and multiple interpretations and applications; and *politically intractable* (Voss *et al.*, 2006), with issues fraught with ideological rigidities. By definition, wicked problems have no definitive formulation and no conclusively "best" solutions, and the problems themselves are constantly shifting as events unfold in a complex and volatile world. Wicked problems tend to be entangled with various public policy issues, but also tend to fall through the cracks, or gaps, of prevailing institutional arrangements (Pinske and Kolk, 2012; Selsky and Parker, 2005).

A general sense of dissatisfaction with conventional approaches to governance and decision making regarding wicked problems has stimulated a search for innovative alternative approaches that engage more effectively with such issues and the complexity and uncertainty that come with them. Cross-sector partnerships have become part of that search because they hold the promise of handling the blurring of boundaries between issues and between sectors that often delivers innovative solutions. In response to the tangle of intersecting issues characterizing wicked problems, many concepts and practices have been advanced, such as "anticipatory governance" (Barben *et al.*, 2008), "adaptive management" (Adger *et al.*, 2009; see also Folke *et al.*, 2005) and "participatory politics" (Dryzek, 1999). These new approaches get tried out and refined in projects, programs and policies across the corporate, public and non-governmental sectors, often in partnerships or coalitions.

Framing is important in coping with wicked problems (see Gray and Purdy's chapter in this volume). For example, defining sustainable development is subject to continuing debate and reinterpretation. In recent years, alternative framings of SD/S challenges have emerged, such as "natural capitalism" (Lovins *et al.*, 1999); "green growth" (OECD, 2011), "prosperity without growth" (Jackson, 2009), and "planetary boundaries" (Rockstrom *et al.*, 2009). Each framing highlights different facets of what is arguably the deeper wicked problem in today's "hot, flat and crowded" world (Friedman, 2008), namely, the complex relationships among global environmental change, economic development, democratic process and social justice (see papers in Low, 1999; Eckersley, 2004). We suggest that these alternative framings of wicked problems can be better navigated by more explicit attention to futures thinking and methods.

Wicked problems and the future

Despite a growing literature on cross-sector partnerships – with a proliferation of models, contingencies and suggested benefits – there is limited attention to futures thinking. This is partly due to the challenges in working with "anticipatory know-ledge" (Selin, 2008) in many disciplines. For example, is the problem of the future a deficit of knowledge or a challenge of engaging with and making decisions under irreducible uncertainty? If the former, will a combination of better data and enhanced modelling enable effective change, or do new approaches need to be designed for managing societal transformation rather than just incremental change? If the latter, how can managers, policy makers and researchers determine the rigour and robustness of foresight about an issue or problem when there are no "facts" in the future?

For example, as a practical social challenge SD/S is inherently future-oriented, with its attention focused on future generations and their "needs". Thus, the "longer term" or "*the* future" should be central in the efforts to cope with the wicked problem of SD/S. Yet in organization studies, although the literature on SD/S has grown over the past twenty years, the role of facts and assumptions about the future and how these influence appreciation of today's situation have received limited explicit attention. For example, Pinske and Kolk's (2012) review of seven successful multistakeholder partnership projects around climate change and SD/S do not explicitly mention a futures dimension. Recently, Linnenluecke *et al.* (2012) have pointed to the "critical importance of anticipatory adaptation and organizational resilience in responding to impacts" of extreme weather events. But overall, the proliferation of futures studies, practices and methods has not penetrated the organizational literature on sustainability issues very deeply.

Why does explicit futures work matter for wicked problems like SD/S? The longer term perspective is commonly invoked to expose the effectiveness (or lack thereof) of today's policies and actions by governments and businesses. For example, in SD/S concerns about maintaining human development within a "safe operating space" (Rockstrom *et al.* 2009), without exceeding a "safe level" of climate change (e.g. below 2 degrees Celsius, per the IPCC, or below 350ppm per the 350.org movement) imply the need for long term goals and decision-making horizons that far exceed the normal timescales of political and business decision making. The longer term perspective also opens the space for new issues to be raised, such as intergenerational equity, new systemic risks (e.g. geopolitical resource conflict, ecosystem collapse), and path dependency (potential for lock-in and implications for transition management; see Geels and Schot, 2007). Finally, the long term can also be used to reveal new trade-offs; for example, can global science or global markets be reconciled with national sovereignty and local decision making? Can resilience be managed across multiple scales, from global to local? Because such new issues, like the wicked problems themselves, are often not in the ambit of existing institutions or agencies, cross-sector partnerships can be useful mechanisms for dealing with them (Waddock, 2002: 307).

In this chapter we argue that partnership projects concerned with a wicked problem can benefit by explicitly employing one or several well-established futures methods. Such projects may be concerned with developing corporate strategy or public policy, forging a common industry position, advocating for an environmental cause, restoring an ecosystem, mitigating climate change, or some hybrid of these purposes.

Our argument rests on three premises:

1   *Partnership project participants' assumptions and expectations about the future often remain implicit.* This may constrict decision-making in the present unnecessarily. For example, sustainability narratives include those of climate change, natural capital and sustainable development. Each of these narratives frames the future in a somewhat different way, and calls forth certain decisions and actions to bring about the future, to influence it, and/or to shape it to the interests of the framers and certain other stakeholders.

2   *The future is neither neutral nor passive* (de Jouvenel, 1964). Expectations, hopes and assumptions about the future play an active role in decisions and actions taken in the present. For instance, how participants in a climate change mitigation partnership think about the future shapes what they think should and can be done today. In research, the choice of research methods in studies of wicked problems is similarly consequential. Long-term assessments and forward looking studies often raise and grapple with specific questions about the appropriate time horizon (e.g. how far back into the past, how many years into the future). Also, how is the future conceptualized and how *should* it be – as possible, predictable, probable or preferable, as a linear, continuous evolution of the past or as non-linear, with multiple branch points and with the potential for discontinuities in change trajectories?

3   *The future is a critical "playing field of power"* (van Asselt *et al.*, 2010). Who gets to define, articulate and make sense of the future? Which voices are excluded and thus which futures are excluded from "sensible" consideration? What difference does the stance adopted to the future make to the value and benefits that can be realized in a particular project? These questions have implications for how businesses – often large and powerful in partnership projects – can and should act responsibly toward the future. We focus on the issue of responsible business in the Conclusion.

Technologies for the future: futures methods

Over the past 60 years the search for ways to appreciate, understand and navigate wicked problems and their future uncertainties has generated a diverse range of futures-oriented projects and studies. They take different stances toward the future. Some studies take an *adaptive* stance, that is, the future must be adapted to because it cannot be influenced. They seek to learn *with* futures to ensure effective adaptation. Other studies take an *activist* stance, that is, the future can and should be shaped through human agency. Those studies seek to learn *about* the future to create a better future.

Future-oriented projects and studies employ a diversity of methods, including computer-based modelling and simulation, technological forecasting and backcasting, visioning, scenario planning, environmental and horizon scanning, Delphi techniques, search conferences, and so on (Georghiou *et al.*, 2008). Each method is elaborated in a variety of techniques. Within *scenarios*, for example, Bradfield *et al.* (2005) trace the different origins of scenarios; Van Notten *et al.* (2003) and Borjeson *et al.* (2006) create different scenario typologies; and van der Heijden (2005) parses different scenario building methods. Within *modelling* Kupers and Mangalagiu (2010) analyse differences in climate models, and Epstein (2008) articulates different purposes in modelling. Within visioning van der Helm (2009) lays out seven versions of visions. Sometimes the futures methods cross-fertilize, such as when multiple methods are used in a single project or study. This is discussed in a later section. Finally, futures methods have found new application areas over time; recently they have been extended beyond the single organization into inter-organizational and cross-sectoral settings (Wilkinson and Eidinow, 2008).

The terrain of futures methods in practice may be organized in terms of three dichotomies:

- *Open vs. closed futures thinking*: on the one hand, there is the established method of prediction which emphasizes reducing uncertainty and transforming uncertainty into calculable risk; e.g. forecasting and more sophisticated computer-based probabilistic analysis. These methods close off alternatives to the predicted future. On the other hand, there are practices and approaches such as scenarios and complexity modelling that emphasize engagement with irreducible uncertainties and strive to maintain a more "open" future by encouraging creative and intuitive approaches and thinking in terms of multiple futures. The shift from single to multiple methods suggests there are benefits in iterating between open and closed futures thinking; for example, using scenarios (a set of divergent futures) in combination with visioning (a single convergent future).
- *Normative vs. non-normative attitude*: on the one hand are practices which seek to identify a preferred future and find the best way to achieving it. Such projects tend to take the activist stance mentioned above. On the other hand are practices that deliberately avoid such "normative futures" and instead take either a descriptive (the future that can be expected to occur) or critical (critical reflection on assumptions and beliefs about the future) attitude. Such projects tend to take an adaptive stance. In those cases, critical reflection, enabled by exploring multiple, equally plausible descriptions of the future, may lead to a process of exploration and learning, unlearning and reframing.
- *Inside-out vs. outside-in approaches*: on the one hand, futures thinking can be articulated in terms of a "self" that is, impressions of the future of a specific entity (firm, industry, nation, community, etc.). On the other hand, some practices focus on a/the wider context, such as a policy sector, public issue (e.g. climate change),

institutional field, or simply the task environment in which a specific entity is situated.

Next we describe three futures methods that exemplify these three dichotomies; see Table 13.1. We acknowledge that our characterizations do not do justice to the variety of practices within each method. We include examples of how each method has been used in successful cross-sector partnership projects.

Forecasting

Forecasting as a futures method is concerned with "what the future will look like" based on the assumption that the future continues on an uninterrupted trajectory from the past; that is, the future is predetermined by changes that are already happening and set to continue. A forecast, the product of a forecasting process, refers to a prediction of some future event or set of events. It is a data rich process. Most forecasting processes involve the use of time series data. In the literature, the terms "forecast", "prediction", "projection" and "prognosis" are used almost interchangeably. In terms of the three dichotomies, forecasts and forecasting generate single images of the future, albeit with ranges of sensitivity, which are often *not* preferred or desirable but proferred as "objective" and universal; and forecasts tend to embrace the wider context (outside-in).

While most forecasting processes are future-oriented, some are past-oriented. A major challenge in the forecasting field is to distinguish between purely descriptive and predictive models. A descriptive model is one which can only predict the past. Such models, while useful for understanding retrospective changes and enabling comparability across different models, need to be clearly distinguished from predictive models, which are future-oriented (Strand, 1999). In terms of their timeframe, future forecasts are short-, medium-, and long-term. Depending on the problem to be forecast, the short and medium term timeframes may refer to seconds, days, months or years, and the long term to years, decades or centuries.

Forecasting processes are based on identifying, statistically modelling, and extrapolating the patterns found in historical data, based on the assumption that these historical data exhibit inertia and do not change dramatically very quickly (Montgomery *et al.*, 2008). The main difficulty with forecasting by fitting and extrapolating a deterministic function is that it does not provide reasonable measures of forecast accuracy. "The route to better forecasts does not lie through time series models alone, but through the combination of time series models with subject matter knowledge about the series being forecast" (Bell, 1984: 241). Such combination is usually done using regressions or multivariate time series models.

There are two broad types of forecasting techniques. *Qualitative* techniques are subjective and require experts' judgment. Qualitative forecasts are often used in situations where there is little or no historical data on which to base the forecast. Examples include the Delphi Method, market research, product life-cycle analysis and expert judgment. *Quantitative* techniques use historical data in the form of time

TABLE 13.1 Characteristics of three representative futures methods

Method	Future(s)	Temporal stance	Futures thinking	Attitude (normative stance)	Intervention approach	Epistemology of uncertainty	Output
Forecasting	Single	Linear: past-to-future	Closed	Descriptive: knowing/seeing the future	Outside-in and adaptive	Mathematical treatment of uncertainty	Probable future
Visioning	Single	Backcasting: future-back-to-present	Closed	Normative: responsibility for the future	Inside-out and activist	Choices and values as basis for coping with uncertainty	Preferable future
Scenarios	Multiple	Entangled: multiple temporalities	Open	Descriptive/critical: creating options for the future	Outside-in and can be either activist or adaptive	Cognitive biases, culture and social processes introduce additional uncertainties including ambiguity and ignorance	(set of) Plausible futures

series and a forecasting model. The model is elaborated such that it summarizes patterns in the data and expresses a statistical relationship between previous and current values of variables. Then the model is used to extrapolate the patterns found in the data into the future (Montgomery *et al.*, 2008). Examples include regression models, smoothing models, and general time series models (see Bell, 1984; Montgomery *et al.*, 2008).

Because it assumes no discontinuity with the past, forecasting has a long, positive history in periods of stability and incremental change if the relevant data are available. Perhaps the most well known example of forecasting in the SD/S field is Meadows *et al.*'s *Limits to Growth* report (1972), with its rich data, sophisticated framework and forecasts of trends in five key variables.

Forecasting can be used in a SD/S partnership to align participants' thinking around a shared image of a probable future state, as a prelude to collective action. In dialogue the participants may find the image produced from a forecast-based model undesirable or morally objectionable, such as a ravaged regional ecosystem or a new Ice Age due to the extinction of the Atlantic Current. Data-based models may also lead participants to question the model's parameters and may spur new collaborative initiatives to mitigate the forecast dangers.

An example is the Scottish Climate Change Impacts Partnership (SCCIP), which brings together the Scottish Government, Scottish Environment Protection Agency, Scottish Natural Heritage, Sustainable Scotland Network and the UK Climate Impacts Programme to "help collectively address and prepare for the impacts of Scotland's changing climate" (www.sccip.org.uk). The partnership, now called Adaptation Scotland, was established in 2008 to "increase the resilience of organizations and infrastructure in Scotland to meet the challenges and opportunities presented by the impacts of climate change". Forecasting models were the main source of information for the project, whose results were used and disseminated in "Climate Projections in Practice" informative events, training events throughout Scotland and support to the Scottish Government in the implementation of climate change adaptation policy.

Visioning

Visioning as a futures method implies that the future can be shaped and influenced, rather than being predetermined. A related term, backcasting, "works through envisioning and analyzing sustainable futures and subsequently by developing agendas, strategies and pathways how to get there" (Vergragt and Quist, 2011). A vision, the product of a visioning process, refers to an idealized future, that is, a single image of a future conceived as the most desirable by those producing the vision. In terms of the three dichotomies, visioning represents closed thinking, a normative attitude and inside-out focus.

Those producing one generally believe a vision is needed to help converge actions in a desired direction. As a process, visioning assumes transformational change; it can be driven by a need to trigger change from an undesired status quo or to respond to undesired contextual changes (van der Helm, 2009). For example, visioning and backcasting methods are often used to respond to the now popular normative stance toward sustainability. Thus, such methods may be suitable in SD/S projects because they promise to deliver a potent image of a preferred future toward which people may align their energies going forward.

Most of the literature on visions and visioning focuses on the organizational level (Collins and Porras, 1991; Ackoff, 1993; Larwood *et al.*, 1995; Van der Helm, 2009). Visioning is a relatively recent addition to strategic planning, where a vision may be used to frame the contours of the plan. Corporate visions are also used to align actions, decisions and plans of disparate parts of both small firms and large multinationals. "The magic (and to some extent the confusion) of visions is that like a centrifugal [sic] force, they can still pull organizational members toward a common goal" (Schwarz *et al.*, 2006: 359). Nevertheless, visions can also be controversial, unsettling and divisive, separating insiders from outsiders, believers from non-believers, and those desiring change from vested interests.

"Visions are intriguing phenomena because of what they promise the organization from leadership, motivation, empowerment, cognitive, and change perspectives" (ibid.: 358). Yet the promise often is not realized. Ackoff (1993: 401) believes "corporate visions are frequently illusions or delusions" because they do not contain or consist of an idealized design of the organization, i.e., "an operationally meaningful and commonly held description of the organization all of its stakeholders would have if they could have any organization they wanted – without constraints".

Visioning and backcasting can be useful in a partnership project to help participants think through the kind of future state they want to inhabit. This use of visioning as an explicit futures method often starts with participants sharing different understandings of a current situation from which they want more. Alternative visions may emerge and the method is designed to deliver a consensual, desirable future state. This differs from the "process" sense of visioning discussed in the partnership and collaboration literatures, in which a shared vision is the first phase of a collaborative planning project (see chapters by Gray and Purdy, and Waddock, this volume[1]).

An example is the World Resources Institute's *Safe Climate, Sound Business* initiative, a collaborative effort by General Motors, the World Resources Institute, Monsanto, and British Petroleum. The project addresses "how the Earth's climate can be protected while expanding global economic prosperity" and seeks to engage corporate partners in actively developing and implementing solutions to climate change (World Resources Institute, 1998). The Initiative developed an action agenda of activities that would transform the corporate approach to climate change in the short and long term in such areas as climate performance measurement and reporting; early reductions through efficiency, offsets, and trading; strategic business ventures and alliances; purchasing decisions and leverage; new global investment criteria; education; and dialogue (Cook and Barclay, 2002).

Scenarios

A definition of a scenario used extensively in the IPCC's work is "a coherent, internally consistent and plausible description of a possible future state of the world" (IPCC, 1994). Scenarios always come in sets of two, three or more plausible, relevant and challenging stories of the future. Thus, scenarios are a set of stories about the possible futures contexts of something for some audience for some purpose (Ramírez *et al.*, 2008). Similar to visioning, the majority of literature on scenarios (at least in the English language) focuses at the organizational level. In terms of the three dichotomies, scenario planning works with plausible, multiple futures; are most often open to learning and rethinking the problem in a critical attitude; and are focused on the wider context (outside-in).

Scenarios are not intended to predict the future or even to think about the future. Instead, they encourage learning *with* futures based on four assumptions (Foresight Futures, 2002):

- The future is unlike the past, and is shaped by human choice and action.
- The future cannot be foreseen, but it is possible to reveal and test assumptions about the future. Thus, exploring the future can inform present decisions.
- There are many possible futures: scenarios map a set of "possibility spaces".
- Scenario development combines rational analysis and subjective judgment.

Working with scenarios encourages attention to deeply held assumptions that stem from the worldviews, schemas, theories-in-use and cognitive platforms (Selsky and Parker, 2010) that people harness, often implicitly, to interpret situations and derive "facts". Explorations of those assumptions are often designed to reveal and test conventional wisdom, such as the dominant narrative that shapes a firm's decision making by claiming what the future should or will be. By revealing and testing assumptions about the future, scenarios provide useful insights concerning the outcomes and different pathways along which the present situation might unfold. At the heart of scenario-based approaches is the belief that, although people cannot predict the future, they can create a coherent picture of a number of alternative futures. In contrast to forecasting, which assumes the single future as a continuation of the past, scenarios focus attention on "breaks" with the past, such as the potential for surprise and discontinuity (Ramírez, 2007; van der Heijden, 2005). The emphasis on plausible alternative futures is a deliberate attempt to avoid confusion with forecasting and its focus on repeating events. Plausible scenarios attend to unique future situations that do not lend themselves to statistical analysis or the single handed determination of the client for whom the scenarios matter.

The value of scenario work pivots on their effectiveness in use. In contrast to the universality of forecasts, scenarios are always designed to be fit for a specific purpose. Scenarios may be used in policy making and decision support, crisis management, conflict resolution or collaborative leadership. In any of those uses scenarios are intended to raise awareness, forge shared and more systemic understanding, and enhance sensemaking by revealing and challenging mental maps and models (Jaeger *et al.*, 2007).

An important distinction in recent scenario project research is between "projection-based" and "exploration-based" scenario exercises (Zurek and Henrichs, 2007; Wilkinson *et al.*, 2009). Projection-based scenario studies set out to present one or several probable projections of future developments, often as a reference scenario with variants. This approach is valuable when the impact of a defined set of options is discussed. Conversely, exploratory scenarios aim to widen the scope of discussion about future developments and to identify emerging issues. Hence, exploration-based scenarios are most useful when strategic goals are not settled and critical questions and choices can be developed and tested against a range of plausible futures.

Scenario work may enrich SD/S partnership projects by helping to ensure that the quality of judgment and strategic conversation about such issues as resource use, energy and pollution are informed by systemic and holistic thinking. This allows people to remain open to possible, less comfortable yet plausible futures. Collaborative scenario planning can also help to forge a common vocabulary for strategic conversation between different communities and cultures.

For example, the *Global Scenarios 2000–2050* project of the World Business Council for Sustainable Development (WBCSD, 1999) used a scenario method to articulate and explore three different forms of global governance that might emerge in response to the challenges of sustainable development. The intervention brought together corporate participants from a diverse range of industry sectors with leading scholars and environmental NGOs. The process helped to create a shared vocabulary and promoted more systemic understanding of governance challenges and changes needed. Another example is the WBCSD initiative *Business in the World of Water: Three Scenarios to 2025*. Over a period of nearly two years this project created three scenarios from a workshop-based process structured around open and generative dialogues in which businesses and stakeholders across the public and civic sectors interacted (WBCSD, 2002). This scenario process forged common ground among the stakeholders and prompted further collaboration, resulting in a water footprint analysis tool for firms to use.

In summary, there are many futures methods, and we used forecasting, visioning and scenario work above to illustrate some of the main epistemological differences among them. Next we discuss the growing use of hybrid and multi-method approaches in cross-sector partnership projects and studies.

Hybrid and multiple methods in social partnerships

Grappling with a wicked problem often calls for the application of more than a single futures method (Wilkinson and Eidinow, 2008). Both scholars and practitioners have begun to recognize that more than one futures method might be used productively in the same project, but the methods need to be properly related (Coreau *et al.*, 2009; Fontela, 2000).

Methodological innovation has sparked considerable trialling of multiple futures methods in projects (see Vergragt and Quist, 2011; Kok, 2009). For example, the WBCSD Vision 2050 initiative (WBCSD, 2010; Wilkinson and Mangalagiu, 2012) combined visioning and backcasting with bio-capacity modelling to articulate nine realistic pathways towards a world on track to sustainable development by 2050. These pathways encompass physical resource domains, such as food, fibre and fuel, as well as social resources, such as economic governance, lifestyles and livelihoods. This multi-lateral project involved 29 corporations from various industry sectors along with a set of external stakeholders in the development of the shared vision. During the project, participants adopted two different stances – the projectable and the preferable future – by harnessing visioning and modelling in order to realize the benefits of "more realistic dreaming".

The influential scenario work of the Intergovernmental Panel on Climate Change (IPCC) is a fine example of moving from scenarios to quantitative models. A set of scenarios (first published 1990, updated through 2007) was developed for use in the Assessment Reports – Special Report on Emissions Scenarios (SRES). Four storylines were crafted from the scenarios, identifying driving forces, key uncertainties, possible scenario families, and their logic. Six global modelling teams then quantified the storylines by translating the storylines into a set of quantitative assumptions about the driving forces of emissions, then inputting the assumptions into six integrated, global models that computed the emissions (IPCC, 2001).

The main consideration in using multiple and hybrid futures methods in social partnerships is the appropriate sequencing of methods. This depends largely on the purpose of the wider intervention. For example:

- *Visioning* → *scenarios*. A visioning process followed by the development of scenarios can help to render and test the pathways of action needed to ensure progress towards the desired future. In this sequence, the scenarios tend to focus on "left-field" events and trajectories, that is, what might knock progress toward the vision off track, rather than challenge and inform the elements of the vision.
- *Scenarios* → *visioning*. Developing a set of agreed scenarios followed by visioning can help to clarify the preferred vision as well as inform the pathway(s) to the vision.
- *Forecasting* → *visioning*. The combination of forecasting and visioning can be powerful in exploring why extrapolations of business-as-usual are flawed and often contain the seeds of their own self-destruction. The positivity of visioning can also counterbalance the negativity of extreme forecasts, enabling users to maintain a healthy degree of anxiety without becoming overwhelmed by fear of the future.

Discussion

So far in this chapter we have explored three kinds of futures methods deployed in partnership projects concerned with wicked problems. We showed that these methods have deep epistemological differences in thinking about the future – or futures.

Futures methods may be usefully deployed in a variety of partnership settings and projects and at different scales and scopes. Forecasts can be produced at various geographic as well as temporal scales – local, national, sectoral or global. Research on visioning and scenarios for collaborative multi-lateral initiatives and cross-sector settings has recently started to receive more attention by futures scholars (e.g. Carlsson-Kanyama et al., 2008; Goodier et al., 2010; Wilkinson and Mangalagiu, 2012).

Next, we draw implications for more effective practice and for more responsive research on cross-sector partnerships concerned with wicked problems.

Getting practical: guidelines for project managers and participants

To create more effective partnerships that seek to inform or transform the future, social partnership participants should consider the following practical issues:

1 *Clarify the purpose of the project and the intervention.* The project may be geared to learn, to change or to appreciate (i.e., forge common ground). Identifying the purpose will help to clarify which futures method may be most appropriate. Some questions are:
   - What type of future do you need to accomplish your purpose or fulfil your aspirations?
   - Is your project aiming for shared inquiry or for attempting institutional, social or societal change?
   - Which cognitive platforms do project participants hold (Selsky and Parker, 2010)? That is, is there agreement about what they want the project to do, such as gain resources for participants' home organizations, or address a social issue, or transform institutions? Can you negotiate agreement around these platforms?
2 *Make the choice of futures methods explicit.* The choice of futures methods should be informed by:
   - a clear understanding of the different methods, and their value, benefits and limits
   - the environment that the project will operate in (e.g. scenarios may be a good choice in a turbulent environment but not in a placid environment Ramírez et al., 2008); and
   - behavioural factors such as trust, power and politics of partnerships (Seitanidi, 2010; Huxham and Vangen, 2000; Gray and Purdy, 2014 this volume). See also point 6 below.
3 *Consider the sequencing of futures methods.* This is important if project managers seek to deploy multiple methods within a project. As you make choices regarding sequencing, seek to balance exploration and exploitation of the future.
4 *Respect the integrity and epistemological grounding of each method*, and avoid the traps of hybridization. For example, don't confuse scenarios with an extension of modelling, and don't advance a single scenario as a vision. Carefully navigate the notion of "normative scenarios" (Vergragt and Quist, 2011) in connection with

backcasting practices, and pay attention to the difference in agency (i.e., activist vs. adaptive stance mentioned above) embodied by each.

5   *Clarify the model of governance and mode of participation.* Who needs to be involved in the project, when and how? Conduct an initial stakeholder analysis and remember to refresh it periodically as the project moves forward. It is typical in futures work to identify additional key stakeholders as scenarios and visions are developed. In addition, clarify the mode of participation, that is, the relative roles of the core team and wider stakeholders who participate in the process (see Zurek and Henrichs, 2007).

6   *Mind the implementation gap.* Engagement and communication start early at the design stage of the project, not after scenarios, visions or forecasts have been developed. Important factors in implementation are:

- The value of futures work lies in how it is deployed. Using products like scenarios, visions and forecasts involves linking with other processes and actors in the project. It is helpful to think through who will use the products and for what. Those products are always *part* of a wider intervention for change, not the intervention itself.
- Pay close attention to behavioral dynamics that can hamper progress, such as trust and power (Gray, 1989; Huxham and Vangen, 2000; Selsky and Parker, 2005; Le Ber and Branzei, 2010), and to the powerful role that cognitive platforms can play in sustaining or constraining progress (Selsky and Parker, 2010). Be attentive to different meanings of strategy and planning; don't assume everyone thinks these terms mean the same thing. If possible, probe the theories of learning, action and change that are often implicit in the purpose but pivotal in determining the effectiveness of the intervention. Probing these can help establish metrics that can be used to evaluate impact, effectiveness and success.

Overall, we encourage social partnership practitioners to harness the future in a reflexive way. Futures work can enable more voices to be heard, encourage respect for different perspectives, and generate more and better options that are "future fit." However, remember that the future is not neutral and is a fertile playing field of power. Pay attention to institutional contexts to ensure that the future can be effectively "hosted" in the present and political dynamics are taken into account (Volkery and Ribeiro, 2009).

Implications for research

Researchers studying cross-sector partnerships need to pay attention to how project participants conceive, construct and make sense of the future. This may be a new variable added to the research design. Some considerations for researchers are:

- Be cognizant of the full range of outcomes of a partnership – individual, organizational, shared project, societal/transformative – whether all of those outcomes were intended by project participants or not. It is important to adopt a critical stance toward the production of outcomes, since they are likely to be affected by politics and the mindsets of involved project participants (Seitanidi, 2010). More generally, researchers studying the effectiveness of cross-sector partnerships need to be more reflexive and critical about the role of futures and the choice of futures methods.

- Harnessing scenarios and/or visioning in combination with modelling raises questions about stakeholder participation and modes of participation, given the premise that the future is the playing field of power. In addition, the notion of which stakeholders matter most today is contingent on futures assumptions. Thus the effective governance of cross-sector partnerships might benefit from more explicit consideration of the futures assumptions that underpin stakeholder analysis.

- Be cautious about the knowledge derived from studies of cross-sector partnerships. The knowledge in most instances is situation specific, assuming the research team uses case-study method. If there is opportunity for action research in a partnership project, facilitate the explicit and reflective use of futures methods, based on the analysis provided in this chapter.

- Foster responsible business. Consider adopting a normative attitude in a partnership study that advocates that businesses in their cross-sector engagements authentically nurture wider stakeholder participation. Businesses, especially large ones, often have the resources and clout to reframe the "problem" and seek a transformative solution.

- Futures scholars need to attend to cross-sector partnerships as a new kind of setting, potentially different from their conventional organization-level work. Futures studies currently lack a theory to guide effective practices at the inter-organizational level. New metrics for assessing value/benefit may need to be developed, extending beyond decision support to include indicators of such soft phenomena as social capital building, shared understanding, respect for alternative perspectives and discourses, and quality of judgment.

Illustrative research questions for futures-oriented partnership projects include the following[2] (see also Kolk *et al.*, 2008: 264–5):

- Why did the partnership participants choose visioning, scenarios and/or model-based forecasting? Did they have a history and experience with a particular futures method? To what extent was this choice explicit or implicit? Was it related to the purpose of the intervention?

- Which theory(ies) of the futures method was/were deployed in practice? What is the meaning of a vision, forecast or a scenario set for the partnership participants? How is it expected to add value/impact?

- What criteria or metrics of effectiveness did the partnership participants establish for this project? How did they initially evaluate project effectiveness, and how are they doing so currently?

- How did the partnership participants use the chosen futures method to accomplish a particular goal? Which cognitive platform(s) (Selsky and Parker, 2010) was/were in use?
- Did the use of a futures method increase the likelihood (or capacity) of the partnership for (a) producing a better or broader set of outcomes; or (b) overcoming any governance deficit (regulation, implementation or participation deficit) (Biermann *et al.*, 2007)?

The intersection of futures methods with cross-sector partnerships is in its infancy. We have shed some light on the contents of that space and posed some guiding questions, but much more research is needed. Future research might be directed at a more fine grained analysis of varieties *within* each of the futures methods we examined. This might lead to more detailed guidance for practitioners as to which futures method(s) to use in a particular project. In addition, the difference between bilateral and multi-lateral projects may reward research attention, because more complexity needs to be accommodated and managed in the latter type of projects (e.g. alignments of cognitive platforms, goals, resources and stakeholders needed in order to move forward). Whether and how this makes a difference in terms of using futures methods remains to be explored. Finally, researchers might examine how futures methods developed and designed for intra-organization use could be modified for use in cross-sector partnerships. This could lead to a set of propositions regarding the contingent use of such methods under different sets of conditions.

Conclusion

One of the premises underpinning this chapter is that the choice of futures method is not neutral; partnership projects involving anticipatory knowledge have the potential to colonize the future by reflecting the discourse, preferences or mental model of one dominant stakeholder or some coalition of stakeholders. Opening up the future by learning *with* alternative future contexts (i.e. using scenarios to reveal and test deeply held assumptions) or closing down the future by focusing on an idealized or preferred future state (i.e. visioning) or the probable future (i.e., forecasting) influences the insights that can be developed and subsequent actions that can be taken. In other words, social partnership projects have the potential to overcome a "futures gap", in addition to gaps in regulation, participation, resources and learning (Pinske and Kolk, 2012).

If assumptions about the future are not made explicit in social partnerships, they risk foreclosing the framing of the wicked problem prematurely and overlooking new options that can emerge by designing the issue *for* the future. This has direct implications for businesses trying to respond to social responsibility pressures.

There are many entry points to discussions of responsible business. The entry point relevant to this chapter is the future. Based on our analysis, we argue that business is responsible when it takes seriously not only its own future but also the future of the markets, societies and natural ecosystems on which it ultimately depends. *How* a business or business sector might take the future seriously is an important question: it may mean creating the future, not preserving the status quo. Discounting via net present valuation can be a means to "future-proof" one's firm, immunizing it against a future that may be very different from, and potentially threatening to, the present. In contrast, there is increasing evidence of forward-looking collaborations among businesses, such as the WBCSD's Vision 2050 project, as described above. Some are using futures methods not only to stress test their strategies and plans but also to work together responsibly to create better futures.

In general terms, strategists and executives are advised to appreciate the future not only as a stakeholder that exists in the present that the firm needs to be responsive to, but also as the encompassing context that envelops the present and all of the firm's stakeholders. These appreciations are key to authentic engagements with public-sector and non-governmental partners. The work for businesses to do here is to engage with those in other sectors in co-creating new institutions for a more sustainable future – or futures (see Holling *et al.*, 2002). As Barbara Gray (1989: 271) observed over 20 years ago: "Collaboration assumes that stakeholders share responsibility for formulating and enacting the future direction of their domain". This leads to a sense of "shared stewardship", which "implies a more expansive conception of power than is typically in use". She called it "catalytic power".

Our analysis raises important issues regarding the democratization of futures methods, and indeed, the future itself. Arguably, this invokes a larger sense of business responsibility. For example, in the current debates regarding climate change and sustainable societies (see Pinske and Kolk, 2012; and Waddock, 2014 this volume), who decides and on what basis the quality, relevance and legitimacy of anticipatory knowledge? Do assumptions concerning the proactive or reactive nature of decision-making responses inform the selection of futures method deployed in collaborative engagements? What new epistemological and normative challenges does working with anticipatory knowledge entail?

The future is active in the present; it is not a passive receptacle for our aspirations or our externalities. We are always in a story of change from past to future, but we often bound off this story of change as the present. Futures methods allow more flexibility in temporal thinking, but attending explicitly to the future or raising the audacious prospect of multiple futures presents a challenge to conventional social science research, which is grounded in that present and offers researchers an easy path-dependence for their models and concepts. Because the future is not neutral, it will always be colonized by particular images and particular competing interests. Therefore it is important for organizational scholars of cross-sector partnerships to have a firm grasp of the levers to the future and to build the future explicitly into their research designs.

Questions for reflection

1   What futures methods are available and what are their key characteristics and contingencies?

2   What is the purpose of using futures methods in a CSSP?
3   What kind of environment does the CSSP operate in – turbulent or stable?
4   In a CSSP is it important to know the future, create the future and/or cultivate responsibility for the future?
5   When does the future begin – what is "long term" and who decides and on what basis?

Notes

1   For instance, in Gray's (2007) discussion of the stages of cross-sector collaborations, the first stage, which she calls "appreciation", involves constructing and diffusing a shared vision of how the parties in a partnership project can collaborate.
2   Two of the authors used a very similar set of questions in an evaluation of the WBCSD's Vision 2050 project; see Wilkinson and Mangalagiu (2012).

References

Ackoff, R. L. (1993) "Idealized design: Creative corporate visioning", *OMEGA*, 21(4): 401–10.
Adger, W., Dessai, S., Goulden, M., Hulme, M., Lorenzoni, I., Nelson, D., Naess, L., Wolf, J. and Wreford, A. (2009) "Are there social limits to adaptation to climate change?", *Climatic Change*, 95: 47–51.
Barben, D., Fisher, E., Selin, C. and Guston, D.H. (2008) "Anticipatory governance of nano-technology: foresight, engagement, and integration", in E. J. Hackett, O. Amsterdamska, M. Lynch and J. Wajcman (eds) (2008) *The Handbook of Science and Technology Studies*, 3rd edn, Cambridge, MA: MIT Press.
Bell, W.R. (1984) "An introduction to forecasting with time series models", *Insurance: Mathematics and Economics*, 3: 241–55.
Biermann, F., Chan, M., Mert, A. and Pattberg, P. (2007) "Multi-stakeholder partnerships for sustainable development: does the promise hold?", in P. Glasbergen, F. Biermann and A. Mol (eds) (2007) *Partnerships, Governance and Sustainable Development: Reflections on Theory and Practice*. Cheltenham: Edward Elgar.
Borjeson, L., Hojer, M., Dreborg, K.-H., Ekvall, T. and Finnveden, G. (2006) "Scenarios types and techniques: towards a user's guide", *Futures*, 38 (7): 723–39.
Bradfield, R., Wright, G., Burt, G., Cairns, G. and van der Heijden, K. (2005) "The origins and evolution of scenario techniques in long range business planning", *Futures*, 37: 795–812.
Carlsson-Kanyama, A., Dreborg, K., Moll, H. and Padovan, D. (2008) "Participative back-casting: a tool for involving stakeholders in local sustainability planning", *Futures*, 40 (1): 34–46.
Collins, J. and Porras, J. (1991) "Organizational vision and visionary organizations", *California Management Review*, 34 (1): 30–52.
Cook, E. and Barclay, E. (2002) "Safe climate, sound business" *Corporate Environmental Strategy*, 9 (4): 338–44.
Coreau, A., Pinay, G., Thompson, J.D., Cheptou, P.O. and Mermet. L. (2009) "The rise of research on futures in ecology: rebalancing scenarios and predictions", *Ecology Letters*, 12: 1277–86.
de Jouvenel, B. (1964) *L'Art de la Conjecture*, Monaco: Editions du Rocher.
Dryzek, J. (1999) Global ecological democracy, in N. Low (ed.) *Global Ethics and Environment*. London: Routledge, pp. 264–82.

Eckersley, R. (2004) *The Green State: Rethinking Democracy and Sovereignty.* Cambridge, MA: MIT Press.

Epstein, J. (2008) "Why model?", *Journal of Artificial Societies and Social Simulation*, 11 (4): http://jasss.soc.surrey.ac.uk/11/4/12/12.pdf.

Folke, C., Hahn, T., Olsson, P. and Norberg, J. (2005) "Adaptive governance of social-ecological systems", *Annual Review of Environment and Resources*, 30: 441–73.

Fontela, E. (2000) "Bridging the gap between scenarios and models", *Foresight*, 2 (1): 10–14.

Foresight Futures (2002) *Foresight Futures 2020 – Revised Scenarios and Guidance*, UK Department of Trade and Industry. www.foresight.gov.uk; www.futurestudio.org/scenario%20documents/Foresight%20Futures%202020.pdf, 32 pages.

Friedman, T. (2008) *Hot, Flat and Crowded,* New York: Farrar, Straus & Giroux.

Funtowicz, S. and Ravetz, J.R. (1993) "Science for the post-normal age", *Futures,* 25: 735–55.

Geels, F.W. and Schot, J. (2007) "Typology of sociotechnical transition pathways", *Research Policy*, 36 (3): 399–417.

Georghiou, L., Cassingena, J., Keenan, M., Miles, I. and Popper, R. (eds) (2008) *The Handbook of Technology Foresight*, Cheltenham: Edward Elgar.

Goodier, C.I., Austin, S.A., Soetanto, R., Dainty, A.R.J. (2010) "Causal mapping and scenario building with multiple organizations", *Futures*, 42 (3): 219–29.

Gray, B. (1989) *Collaborating,* San Francisco, CA: Jossey-Bass.

Gray, B. (2007) "The process of partnership construction: anticipating obstacles and enhancing the likelihood of successful partnerships for sustainable development", in P. Glasbergen, F. Biermann and A. Mol (eds) (2007) *Partnerships, Governance and Sustainable Development: Reflections on Theory and Practice,* Cheltenham: Edward Elgar.

Gray, B. and Purdy, J. (2014) Conflict in cross-sector partnerships, in M.M. Seitanidi and A. Crane, A. (eds) *Social Partnerships and Responsible Business: A Research Handbook*, London: Routledge: 205–26.

Holling, C.S., Carpenter, S.R., Brock, W.A. and Gunderson, L.H. (2002) "Discoveries for sustainable futures", in L.H. Gunderson and C.S. Holling (eds) *Panarchy: Understanding Transformations in Human and Natural Systems,* Washington, DC: Island Press: 395–418.

Huxham, C. and Vangen, S. (2000) "Ambiguity, complexity and dynamics in the membership of collaboration", *Human Relations,* 53 (6): 771–806.

IPCC (1994) "IPCC Technical guidelines for assessing climate change impacts and adaptations", T.R. Carter, M.L. Parry, S. Nishioka and H. Harasawa (eds) *IPCC Special Report to the First Session of the Conference of the Parties to the UN Framework Convention on Climate Change, Working Group II, Intergovernmental Panel on Climate Change.* University College London and Center for Global Environmental Research, National Institute for Environmental Studies, Tsukuba.

Intergovernmental Panel on Climate Change (2001) *Climate Change 2001: The Scientific Basis,* Cambridge: Cambridge University Press.

Jackson, T. (2009) *Prosperity Without Growth: Economics for a Finite Planet*, London: Earthscan.

Jaeger, J., Rothman, D., Anastasi, C., Kartha, S. and van Notten, P. (2007) "Training Module 6: scenarios development and analysis", in *GEO Resources Book: A Training Manual on Integrated Environmental Assessment and Reporting.* Nairobi and Winnipeg, Canada: UN Environment Programme and International Institute for Environmental Development.

Kok, K. (2009) "The potential of fuzzy cognitive maps for semi-quantitative scenario development, with an example from Brazil", *Global Environmental Change*, 19 (1): 122–33.

Kolk, A., van Tulder, R. and Kostwinder, E. (2008) "Business and partnerships for development" *European Management Journal*, 26: 262–73.

Kupers, R. and Mangalagiu, D. (2010) Climate change policy positive or negative economic impact? Why?, European Climate Forum Working Paper, No.1.

Larwood, L., Falbe, C.M., Kriger, M.P. and Miesing, P. (1995) "Structure and meaning of organizational vision", *Academy of Management Journal*, 38: 740–69.

Le Ber, M. and Branzei, O. (2010) "(Re)Forming strategic cross-sector partnerships: Relational processes of social innovation", *Business and Society*, 49 (1):140–72.

Linnenluecke, M., Griffiths, A. and Winn, M. (2012) "Extreme weather events and the critical importance of anticipatory adaptation and organizational resilience in responding to impacts", *Business Strategy and the Environment*, 21 (1): 17–32.

Lovins, A., Lovins, L.H. and Hawken, P. (1999) "A road map for natural capitalism", *Harvard Business Review*, 77: 145–58.

Low, N. (ed.) (1999) *Global Ethics and Environment*, London: Routledge.

Meadows, D.H., Meadows, D.L., Randers, J. and Behrens, W.W. (1972) *The Limits to Growth*. New York: New American Library.

Montgomery, D.C., Jennings, C.L. and Murat, K. (2008) *Introduction to Time Series Analysis and Forecasting*, Hoboken, NJ: Wiley.

OECD. (2011, May) *Towards Green Growth*, Paris: OECD.

Pinske, J. and Kolk, A. (2012) "Addressing the climate change – sustainable development nexus: the role of multistakeholder partnerships", *Business and Society*, 51 (1): 176–210.

Ramírez, R. (2007) "Forty years of scenarios: retrospect and prospect", in S. Dopson and M. Earl (eds) *When the Map Changes: Forty Years of Change in Management Research*, Oxford: Oxford University Press.

Ramírez, R., Selsky, J. and van der Heijden, K. (eds) (2008) *Business Planning for Turbulent Times: New Methods for Applying Scenarios*, London: Earthscan.

Rittel, H. and Webber, M. (1973) "Dilemmas in a general theory of planning", *Policy Sciences*, 4: 155–69.

Rockstrom, J. *et al.* (28 co-authors) (2009) "A safe operating space for humanity", *Nature*, 461: 472–75.

Schwarz, G.M., Keer, S., Mowday, R.T., Starbuck, W.H., Tung, R.L. and Von Glinow, M.A. (2006) "Astute foresight or wishful thinking? Learning from visions", *Journal of Management Inquiry*, 15: 347–61.

Scottish Climate Change Impacts Partnership (n.d.) www.sccip.org.uk

Seitanidi, M. (2010) *The Politics of Partnerships: A Critical Examination of Nonprofit-Business Partnerships*, Dordrecht: Springer.

Selin, C. (2008) "The sociology of the future: tracing stories of technology and time", *Sociology Compass*, 2 (6): 1878–95.

Selsky, J. and Parker, B. (2005) "Cross-sector partnerships to address social issues: challenges to theory and practice", *Journal of Management*, 31 (6): 849–73.

Selsky, J. and Parker, B. (2010) "Platforms for cross-sector social partnerships: prospective sensemaking devices for social benefit", *Journal of Business Ethics*, 94 (1): 21–37.

Strand, S. (1999) "Forecasting the future: pitfalls in controlling for uncertainty", *Futures*, 31: 333–50.

Van Asselt, M.B.A., Faas, A., van der Molen, F. and Veenman, S.A. (2010) *Out of Sight: Exploring Futures for Policymaking*, Amsterdam: Amsterdam University Press, Scientific Council for Government Policy (WRR), Explorations 24.

Van der Heijden, K. (2005) *The Art of Strategic Conversation*, Hoboken: Wiley.

Van der Helm, R. (2009) "The vision phenomenon: towards a theoretical underpinning of visions of the future and the process of envisioning", *Futures*, 41: 96–104.

Van Notten, P.W.F., Rotmans, J., van Asselt, M.B.A. and Rothman, D. (2003) "An updated scenario typology", *Futures*, 35 (5): 423–43.

Vergragt, P.J. and Quist, J. (2011) "Backcasting for sustainability: introduction to the special issue", *Technological Forecasting and Social Change*, 78: 747–55.

Volkery, A. and Ribeiro, T. (2009) "Scenario planning in public policy: understanding use, impacts and the role of institutional context factors", *Technological Forecasting and Social Change*, 65: 1198–1207.

Voss, J.P., Bauknecht, D. and Kemp, R. (eds) (2006) *Reflexive Governance for Sustainable Development*, Cheltenham: Edward Elgar.

WBCSD (1999) *Global Scenarios 2000–2050: Exploring Sustainable Development*, Geneva. Retrieved from www.wbcsd.org

WBCSD (2002) *WBCSD Scenarios: Business in the World of Water: Three Scenarios to 2025*, Geneva.

WBCSD (2010) *Vision 2050: The New Agenda for Business*, Geneva. Retrieved from www.wbcsd.org/Plugins/DocSearch/details.asp?DocTypeId=33&ObjectId=Mzc0MDE

Waddock, S. (2002) *Leading Corporate Citizens: Vision, Values, Value Added*, New York: McGraw Hill Irwin.

Waddock, S. (2014) Cross-sector/cross-boundary collaboration: making a difference through practice, in M.M. Seitanidi and A. Crane (eds) *Social Partnerships and Responsible Business: A Research Handbook*, London: Routledge: 335–41.

Wilkinson, A. and Eidinow, E. (2008) "Evolving practices in environmental scenarios: a new scenario typology", *Environmental Research Letters*, 3: 1–11.

Wilkinson, A., Henrichs, T. and Hurley, P. (2009) "Analysing the future of European food systems in a changing world", in *ESF/COST Forward Look: European Food Systems in a Changing World*. A joint report published by the European Science Foundation (ESF) and European Cooperation in Science and Technology (COST).

Wilkinson, A. and Mangalagiu, D. (2012) "Learning with futures to realise progress toward sustainability: The WBCSD Vision 2050 Initiative", *Futures*, 44 (4): 372–84.

World Resources Institute (1998) *Safe Climate, Sound Business*. Retrieved from www.wri.org/publication/safe-climate-sound-business-action-agenda

Zurek, M. and Henrichs, T. (2007) "Linking scenarios across geographical scales in international environmental assessments", *Technological Forecasting and Social Change*, 74 (8): 1282–95.

14

RESPONSIBILIZATION AND GOVERNMENTALITY IN BRAND-LED SOCIAL PARTNERSHIPS

Sonia Bookman and Cheryl Martens

Introduction

At a Starbucks café, it is possible to purchase a bottle of Ethos(R)™ water and play a role in the provision of safe drinking water to communities worldwide via the Ethos(R)Water Fund, a social venture that is part of the Starbucks Foundation. Interacting with MTV's website, young people can become ambassadors of HIV/AIDS awareness, sharing information through blogs and with friends, or donating to specific causes facilitated through social partnerships. Indeed, brands, working in partnership with a wide range of organizations are an increasingly important site for the articulation and performance of social responsibility in contemporary consumer culture, reflecting a growing emphasis on business responsibilities for local communities at a global level (Tichy *et al.*, 1997; Logsden and Wood, 2002).

Partnerships between corporations and non-governmental organizations (NGOs) are progressively becoming central to corporate approaches to social responsibility. In the area of HIV/AIDS education, for example, media involvement in partnerships to promote HIV/AIDS awareness has expanded significantly over the past ten years. This is evidenced by the corporate-led Global Media AIDS Initiative founded in 2004 and corporate media involvement and leadership in creative summits at the United Nations, as well as a wide range of global HIV/AIDS campaigns and projects run by major corporations in collaboration with NGOs and multilateral institutions.

The development of corporate social responsibility (CSR) and social partnerships, particularly from the 1990s onwards is best understood in relation to neoliberalism and the moralization of markets, evidenced in a greater stress on business ethics and corporate citizenship, as well as a rise in consumer activism and NGO involvement in pressuring market actors to adopt more "ethical" behavior (Shamir, 2008; Stehr, 2008). Within this context, it is possible to see a downloading of responsibility for social well-being from public institutions and government to the "private" or "individual" scale. Cross-sector social partnerships (CSSPs) have played an integral role in the implementation of this shift, signaling the emergence of new hybrid forms of societal governance. These are forms of governance that "blend hierarchy, market, and network-based forms of coordination and control" and blur boundaries between traditional sectors such as the "economic" and "civil" sectors of society (Crane, 2011: 18).

There is now a considerable literature in the area of social partnerships, and while it has taken increasingly critical approaches (i.e. Seitanidi, 2010), this work remains largely based in the areas of business and organizational studies. Much of the research into social partnerships has concentrated on matters such as the social objectives of business, cooperative strategy (Seitanidi and Crane, 2008) and intersectoral relationships (Selsky and Parker, 2010), as well as corporate governance (see Crane, 2011). One of the themes in this literature concerns how social partnerships can be used to effectively build brands (see Peloza and Ye, this volume).

In this chapter we attempt to develop new theoretical directions in the literature on brands and social partnerships, with a view to "reimagining" partnerships, by exploring some of their broader social implications. Drawing on recent sociological approaches to brands and branding (i.e. Arvidsson, 2006; Lury, 2004), and a Foucauldian notion of governance (Foucault, 1991), we critically examine how social partnerships, which are integrated with a view to brand-building, are configured to promote the self-monitoring of activities by both employees and consumers. In this regard, we consider the ways in which social partnerships are bound up with particular forms of governance, which involve a process of responsibilization.

Taking the case studies of two global brands, Starbucks and MTV, we examine how these brands are deeply entangled with nonprofit organizations and other partners in the articulation of CSR. Designed to enlist consumers and employees in their performance, we argue that such brand-based social partnerships play an important role in shaping consumer and employee behavior, whereby power is not top-down but "acts through practices that aim at generating particular forms of life" (Rose, 1999). Rather than shaping individual behavior through the use of rules, orders, and norms, from above, this perspective considers how government works from the bottom up and represents a form of power working through practices that make up subjects acting from their own accord (Gordon, 1991; Rose, 1999; Dean, 1999). According to this model, "[O]ne works with and through the freedom of the subject" (Arvidsson, 2006: 74).

In the context of brand-based social partnerships, this entails opportunities for self-realization through the cultivating of cultural skills and capital, as well as socially responsible identities, whilst promoting the brand's philosophy and image. Social risks, are therefore, not left to the state, but become part of the private domain, taken up by individuals who become active participants in becoming responsible citizens.

Responsibilization, from a governmentality perspective can thus be understood as a technology that operates to mobilize individuals to "freely" opt-in and actively perform self-governing tasks, ranging from activities such as participating or taking a leadership role in pro-social programs or campaigns, to simply consumption of certain ethical products and services. Constituted through the framework of social partnerships, with the intention of addressing socio-moral concerns, such practices not only enable employee and consumer ethical expression, but can be understood as strongly orientated to meet corporate objectives.

As part of this process, we argue that the power dynamics of partnerships need to be examined more closely, as it is corporate actors that are most actively shaping configurations and discourses of social responsibility and molding ethical subjects. Nonetheless, as our case studies illustrate, such frames are not taken up straightforwardly and often fail to engage with many of the targeted consumers and brand employees. As such, we look to the open-ended, participatory character of brands and social partnerships as holding potential for the expression of more diverse articulations of social responsibility. The current context of brands as often taking the lead in social partnerships makes these issues a particularly pertinent object of study and discussion.

CSR and social partnerships

In recent years, brands have become a central focus for the articulation of CSR and the elaboration of social partnerships. Evolving from its early inception in the 1950s, CSR began with an emphasis on business leaders giving back to the community (Blowfield and Murray, 2008; see for example, Bowen, 1953) and has now become now an integral aspect of the corporate landscape. Carroll's (1979) influential definition that CSR is comprised of the economic, legal, ethical, and discretionary expectations that society has of an organization at a given moment, has given way to more heterogeneous, generalized definitions. These include concepts such as business ethics, corporate philanthropy, corporate citizenship, sustainability, and environmental responsibility, which are viewed as overlapping and embedded in particular social, political, economic, and institutional contexts (Crane *et al.*, 2008: 5).

The growing influence of CSR in relation to brands can be evidenced in the proliferation of cause-related marketing (CRM) techniques, which have flourished since the 1990s. The main premise of CRM is that it is a process of formulating and implementing marketing activities, "characterized by an offer from the firm to contribute a specified amount to a designated cause when customers engage in revenue providing exchanges that satisfy organizational and individual objectives" (Varadarajan and Menon, 1988: 60). A central vehicle for the implementation of CSR and CRM initiatives is that of the cross-sector social partnership (CSSP). At the same time, such social partnerships are now integrated into brands in ways that extend well beyond CRM, as discussed by Peloza and Ye (this volume).

Social partnerships are conceived as "social problem solving mechanisms" (Waddock, 1989: 79) and platforms for social change (Selsky and Parker, 2010) that address social issues (i.e. health, poverty or the environment) by balancing nonprofit attitudes toward social service with business entrepreneurial orientation (Seitanidi and Ryan, 2007). A significant current of research in this area has been interested in the potential of these partnerships as motors for social change (Seitanidi, 2010). Studies have concentrated on the social benefit of such partnerships for the various actors involved. To a great extent, this body of literature considers social partnerships as a "win-win" situation for both business and non-corporate actors (Tomlinson, 2005). Whilst these authors successfully problematize social benefit, it is important to also consider how social partnerships implicate and impact on people's everyday lives, actions, and subjectivities, as well as how these partnerships themselves are being shaped by those who participate in them.

Social partnerships, especially when integrated extensively as suggested by Peloza and Ye (this volume), enable brands to enroll the participation of multiple actors and auspices with the purpose of performing CSR and putting forth an ethical brand image. Nonprofit-business partnerships (Seitanidi and Crane, 2008) in particular rely to a great extent on the volunteer work of multiple actors and private citizens acting in various locations where the work of these agencies is conducted "on the ground." Our project here is to explore specifically how employees and particularly consumers are enlisted in the articulation and performance of social partnerships through brand-based social responsibility, and what this means for those involved.

Communicating the brand: employees, consumers and social partnerships

Internal branding entails encouraging employees to embrace the company's mission statement or philosophy, and to "live the brand" through their everyday practices and interactions (Mitchell, 2001 in Fan, 2005: 345; Lury 2004). It is associated with a reconfiguration of work, which is perceived by employees as "a means of adding value to themselves" (Lury, 2004: 35; also see du Gay, 1996). With a growing emphasis on CSR and social partnerships as constituting an important aspect of companies' philosophies, "living the brand" increasingly means engaging in ethical performances that reflect socially responsible principles. Opportunities for ethical engagement by employees are increasingly organized through partnerships with nonprofit agencies addressing particular social issues.

Examining this trend, using Foucault's notion of government (1991), Shamir (2004, 2008) considers how social responsibility is bound up with processes and practices of neoliberal corporate governance. He argues that the mobilization of employees' "reflexive moral capacities" through the implementation of CSR facilitates employee responsibilization (2008: 7). Responsibilization is conceptualized by Shamir as an "enabling praxis" that operates to motivate employees to "actively undertake and perform self-governing tasks." It serves as a "practical link" that ties "governance to actual practices on the ground" (Shamir, 2008: 7). Constituted through the framework of CSR, with the intention of addressing socio-moral concerns, these tasks range from self-monitoring of energy use to participation in corporate fundraising efforts in support of a cause. Such practices not only enable employee ethical expression and advance their employability, but are especially linked to corporate performance. As such, social responsibility operates as a tool in the management of employee behavior, linking responsible practices to corporate functioning (Shamir, 2008).

Although not explicitly focused on brands and social partnerships, Shamir's work is instructive in that it provides insight into the relationship between employee CSR performances, responsibilization, and governance. In particular, he directs our attention to the potential use of social partnerships (an aspect of CSR) as a tool of brand management, in which employee performances are coordinated to enhance an ethical brand image. CSR and its articulation via social partnerships, according to this line of argumentation, constitutes a mechanism of governance, by encouraging employees to take responsibility for socio-moral concerns voluntarily as rational, entrepreneurial agents. We extend this analysis to consumers, as they also play an equally significant role in configurations of social responsibility.

Emerging in the context of a "reflexive marketplace," various analysts argue that the growing emphasis on social responsibility and ethical consumption is occurring in response to, and in anticipation of expanded consumer awareness of social and environmental issues, and consumption of goods based on their moral content (Littler and Moor, 2008; see also Stehr, 2008). The communication of socially responsible brand values is attributed in part to the reflexive integration of consumers (and their ethical concerns) into production processes, and particularly branding procedures, through innovations in management and marketing techniques, uses of feedback and consumer data, as well as the framing and incorporation of consumer activity (Lury, 2004; Arvidsson, 2006; Zwick et al., 2008).

The involvement of the consumer as an active participant in the production of products and services as well as brands is now well documented in the management literature by studies on co-creation (e.g. Prahalad and Ramaswamy, 2004; Jenkins 2006; Beer and Burrows, 2010) and the prosumer (Zwick et al., 2008). This view of the consumer is derived in part by a recent emphasis on "value co-creation" in marketing and management, which involves the use and "expropriation of free cultural, technological, social, and affective labour of consumers" in processes of innovation and new product development, and the production of "value-in-use" for goods and services (Zwick et al., 2008: 165–6; also see Prahalad and Ramaswamy, 2004). In this context, consumers are "put to work," making use of their emotional, social, and cultural competence in places previously considered outside the production of monetary value, adding the overall value created for market goods (Arvidsson, 2006; Zwick et al., 2008).

In relation to branding, Arvidsson (2006) suggests that contemporary brand management is concerned with the provision and organization of contexts that will enable consumer productivity to evolve in ways that contribute to (rather than detract from) brand image and value. For Arvidsson (2006: 8), brand management reflects a Foucauldian model of governance, in that it works with the freedom of the subject: "they say not 'You must!' but 'You may'!." This is achieved through the coordination of ambiences or frames designed to enable consumer activity to unfold in particular directions, while deterring unintended uses. We suggest that social partnerships function as a kind of frame that "empowers" consumers in this sense.

Here, we are interested in the specific roles of consumers in the performance of social partnerships and socially responsibly brands. So far, studies have suggested that social responsibility is incorporated into brands as a way of connecting with consumer interests and attitudes (Basil and Herr, 2006; Grau and Folse, 2007). Some have also focused on corporate communications to show how these are configuring consumer responsibility (Caruana and Crane, 2008). Extending this work, we contribute an analysis of the way consumers are implicated in the co-performance of responsible initiatives. Thus while Peloza and Ye (this volume) suggest that social partnerships enhance brand image *for* consumers, we are interested in how social partnerships enhance brand image *with* consumers.

The following case studies explore consumer and employee interactions with two global brands, Starbucks and MTV, both of which have been taking on major leadership roles with regard to social partnerships. The case studies highlight how these relationships may be shaping the meanings and practices of social responsibility, as well as contributing to processes of governance, whereby consumers and employees become involved in their own responsibilization. At the same time, we emphasize the limits of such brand-based social partnerships.

Case studies

The research presented here is excerpted from extensive ethnographic investigations of the branding processes of MTV, which was conducted between 2004–2007 and Starbucks, conducted over the period 2002–2005, and includes supplementary observations and company documentation up to 2011. The Starbucks study, conducted in the cities of Toronto and Vancouver, employed three main qualitative strategies in a multi-pronged research design. These included participant observation of the branded cafés, semi-structured interviews, as well as a visual analysis of various brand materials. The observational component encompassed over forty structured observations in fifteen Starbucks cafés located in a diverse range of Toronto and Vancouver neighborhoods. The visual analysis concentrated on Starbucks' Commitment to Origins™ campaign, which was featured in the cafés. Semi-structured interviews were conducted with twenty-five consumers and brand employees, including those involved in brand marketing and store management.

The MTV research was similarly structured, with participant observation, visual analysis, and semi-structured interviews with MTV employees involved in the production process of the Staying Alive campaigns. In addition, it included six semi-structured focus groups of young people from working- and middle-class backgrounds, including a group of young men with difficulties at school, a group of female café workers, mixed gender groups of a local high school and a community sexual health peer educators group, as well as two groups of HIV positive service group users in a Northeastern city in England. Each focus group was followed up by interviews with key informants. Methods also included visual and discourse analysis of websites, television, and radio announcements as well as electronic campaigns.

Whilst case study methodology is limited with regard to the generalizability of the findings, the case study approach allows an in-depth and multilayered look at how partnerships are articulated and put into practice by consumers and producers of the multinational brands being studied. Starbucks and MTV were selected as noteworthy, iconic brands in that their market power and influence in shaping markets is significant, and they are reflective of cultural currents with regard to CSR. In particular, both Starbucks and MTV are signatories of global social responsibility initiatives (as discussed in the case studies), and may serve as indicators of broader, global trends in analysing social responsibility and partnerships.

Starbucks

In the case of Starbucks, a Seattle-based coffee company with over 17,000 stores worldwide, a program of CSR was instigated in 1991 when it was decided the company was profitable enough (Saporito, 2012; Schultz and Yang, 1997). Beginning with charitable donations, this program has evolved to encompass a vast range of initiatives, from community literacy projects to "green" store design, involving a range of social partnerships. As Peloza and Ye (this volume) discuss, such extensive engagement with social partnerships reflects a high degree of commitment by the firm. To demonstrate leadership in this area, Starbucks joined the voluntary Global Compact, which aims in part to "advance responsible corporate citizenship so that business can be part of the solution to the challenges of globalization" with the intent of achieving "a more sustainable and inclusive global economy" (United Nations, 2005). Starbucks has also established a specially designated CSR department to manage its complex, multiple social partnerships, including Starbucks' more recent partnership with Opportunity Finance Network to support its Create Jobs for USA initiative in the context of a recent economic recession (Saporito, 2012).

A central component of the Starbucks brand experience and culture, coffee has been a crucial locus for the articulation of CSR. Thus, in addition to sponsoring community development organizations working in coffee origin areas through various nonprofit partners, Starbucks has implemented a range of initiatives focused on ethical coffee production and products (Starbucks, 2005). One of these, Starbucks' Commitment to Origins™, comprised a range of specialty coffees premised on social and environmental sustainability (i.e. fair trade and organic), produced through joint ventures with NGOs such as Fairtrade Labeling Organizations International, Conservation International, and Oxfam (Starbucks, 2001, 2002a, 2002b). When asked to comment on the initiative, a marketing agent explained,

> Well, "Commitment to Origins" is not really a campaign; it's a way of doing business … The objective is to ensure that they [coffee farmers] do well, they can provide coffee to us, uh, they provide the best quality coffee, and our commitment is to help them in any way we can to sustain their business.
>
> (*Interview*)

Expressed as a "way of doing business," and with the aim of ensuring sustainability – of both producers and the company – this ethical initiative is illustrative of the way social partnerships are deeply entangled with the brand, reaching the integrative stage as discussed by Peloza and Ye (this volume). Such partnerships are bound up with corporate governance by linking responsible practices to business success.

Starbucks' multiple CSSPs are implemented in part through employee involvement. Referred to as "partners" by the company, baristas are strongly encouraged to incorporate and follow Starbucks' mission statements by participating in brand-sponsored activities such as AIDS Walks, Earth Day events, and local volunteer work with nonprofit agencies (Starbucks, 2002c). This includes involvement in Earthwatch expeditions and volunteer environmental work in coffee growing regions (Starbucks Coffee Company, 2004, 2005). The comments of one employee's experience on a 2005 expedition in Costa Rica were posted on Starbucks' website:

> Planting trees to help restore the rainforest in Agua Buena, Costa Rica was an amazing, life-changing opportunity … I was able to blend all my passions, connecting with others, coffee, conservation, photography and helping others. I actually got to live the Starbucks guiding principle: contributing positively to our communities and environment.
>
> (*Starbucks, 2007*)

While the above quote illustrates enthusiasm for such volunteering and exemplifies employee self-governance, not all employees fully embrace the brand's initiatives. Though generally supportive of its programs, many employee interviewees were nonetheless skeptical of the specific manner in which responsibility was practiced. Several respondents suggested that Starbucks could be doing more in areas such as recycling. For example, a former manager commented:

> I don't know to what extent that is that they're taking it, I'm not sure how well I trust that. I agree that they need to be socially responsible for the effects they're having on communities, but I'm not sure to what extent they could be helping more.
>
> (*Interview*)

In addition to its employee "partners," Starbucks calls on consumers to participate in ethical initiatives. They are provided with various possibilities for involvement, from recycling coffee grounds in their gardens to community service in joint ventures that match volunteer hours with donations to nonprofit organizations. To facilitate consumer involvement, the brand partners with multiple local agencies on a global scale (Starbucks Coffee Company, 2012). Even the act of purchasing is configured as ethical and contributes to the performance of business-nonprofit partnerships. As a paragraph in Starbucks Commitment to Origins™ brochure, titled "You can help make a difference too," declares:

> We try to make a difference to the people and places that produce coffee, to the countries we visit and the families we touch. Every time you purchase Starbucks coffees, you're also making a difference, helping to improve people's lives, and encouraging conservation where our coffee is grown.
>
> (*Starbucks, 2002a*)

More recently, consumers are notified of "green" events and products through social media tools such as Facebook, where they are encouraged to engage in a dialogue with the brand and other consumers about its responsible initiatives.

Interviews conducted with consumers revealed a variety of responses to these programmed prospects. While some regarded Starbucks as an ethical "role model" and actively took up the opportunities afforded by the brand, most were cautiously skeptical. The latter perceived the brand's articulation of social responsibility as a marketing strategy oriented toward a niche market of consumers concerned about social issues. As one consumer asserted, "In terms of global responsibility, I mean, I'm sure that's good, but frankly I see it more as marketing. You know, they have been attacked and criticized, and I think it's one way of responding to that" (Interview). Consumers also pointed to the paradox of brand involvement in social partnerships, especially highlighting what they perceived to be a contradiction between the company's pursuit of profit on the one hand, and its intention to care for communities on the other.

At the same time, consumers were, on the whole, supportive of the fact that the brand is "doing something" even if they were dubious about what it was doing and felt reluctant about being "taxed on your moral responsibilities," as one consumer put it, by paying more for ethical products (Interview). For many consumers, Starbucks' social responsibility did have the effect of helping them justify their relationship with the brand:

> It protects the consumer from being viewed as somebody who supports things like ripping down rainforests …Whether they are or not, nobody knows, none of the consumers go around and do research … Like do the coffee pickers have small children out breaking their backs (pause) probably, but none of us want to come to terms with the fact that that's happening, because none of us would stop going for coffee.
>
> (*Interview*)

As this quote indicates, experiential benefits for consumers are not only a matter of feeling good about purchasing coffee from a company that is involved in social partnerships, but in fact may be more about feeling reassured and justifying their own consumption practices.

MTV

Considered the fastest growing media asset of Viacom and consistently rated by Interbrand within the top fifty global brands today, MTV's success as a cutting-edge entertainment brand is closely related to its branding processes, which strongly implicate its employees, consumers, and stakeholders in co-producing and maintaining its brand image. Over the past ten years, MTV's leadership and sponsorship of HIV/AIDS education campaigns through social partnerships has become increasingly central to their brand positioning. In 2004, MTV and its parent company Viacom were the first of twenty-one signatories for the Global Media AIDS declaration, which promised "to expand public knowledge and understanding about HIV and AIDS through their companies" practices' (Arieff, 2004). MTV's HIV/AIDS partnerships can be seen, however, as more than organizational practices. The partnerships are also part of the brand itself, conditioning the practical outcomes, experiences, and forms of exchange co-produced by employees and consumers.

Employee involvement in MTV's social responsibility mandate takes a wide range of forms, including company inductions, microsites, blogs and internal e-communications. When staff inductions are conducted at MTV, new staff members learn about the pro-social side of the corporation and are subsequently encouraged to use this training to become more responsible for their own behavior, by learning more about how to protect themselves from HIV and by becoming company "volunteers." Internal communications regularly promote the corporation's involvement in relation to HIV/AIDS campaigns, including the promotion of company volunteers for various social partnerships and campaigns. One employee explains how they are involved in the performance of social partnerships:

> On the intranet here, on World AIDS Day, we have stuff here that people can go to. We have any major initiative that we are involved in is on the news here on our intranet system.
>
> *(Interview with employee)*

How is this corporate culture and internal branding through social partnerships being experienced by MTV employees? In relation to his everyday experience at MTV, one employee stressed how he found it important to learn about MTV's pro-social side:

> That is one of the reasons I've been so impressed with MTV. I didn't know that it had that social side. I feel that it is really exciting ... I think it has been important for me to believe that they are doing pro-social work.
>
> *(Interview, MTV writer/contracted worker)*

When interviewed, this employee was skeptical about global brand motives and activities more generally, yet he voiced how it was important for him to *think of* his employer as engaging social issues. An MTV executive producer elaborates on the corporate emphasis on HIV education awareness in relation to employees, and states how this is influencing the MTV brand more generally:

> [S]o that all the employees know what we're about and why we do it, we actually have HIV training sessions going on in the States which we'll be bringing over here; we look to write editorials on it. We've always supported HIV but we never did it on a formal basis. We now, you know, as I said, you ask any employee what is our, you know, what do we support in MTV and everyone will tell you "it's HIV."
>
> *(Interview, MTV Executive Producer)*

A key technique in the management of social partnerships in relation to its brand image is that of the integration of the audience. In MTV's Staying Alive campaign, consumer involvement is a crucial aspect of getting messages about HIV/AIDS across, as consumers become involved in giving feedback about the brand and its campaigns, in creating the content for the website, participating in MTV sponsored events, and using MTV products such as rings and condoms.

The careful internalizing of the consumer in their production processes is now a mainstay of MTV's branding and integration of social partnerships. On a yearly basis, MTV conducts several hundred focus groups globally, which consider what young people want out of the brand. Whether the audience would rather support a socially responsible MTV has been a key point of investigation. According to an MTV production assistant, this feeds into the support and development of partnerships and campaigns, particularly for the Staying Alive campaign and Staying Alive Foundation activities, which are based on a partnership approach and have come to play a leading role in HIV/AIDS education around the world. The integration of consumer information in programming is also effected through a series of sexual health surveys. Much of this research revolves around condom use. In MTV's collaboration with the Body Shop, it found that "When it comes to safe sex, 92% of women do not consider a condom to be a "handbag essential" on a night out" (MTV, 2007). MTV's emphasis on the promotion of condom use amongst women in its various campaigns is thus not only justified, but to a great extent also led by these findings.

MTV has teamed up with many corporations and organizations over the years to promote condom use, including a 2004 partnership with Condomi Condoms to offer branded condoms. Nonetheless, focus group responses to the MTV Staying Alive condoms were varied. The young people in the high school and peer educator groups were very positive towards the initiative. For these groups, the packets were considered "good and effective for selling" and were regarded as appropriately marketed to young couples. The high school focus group also remarked on the MTV Staying Alive logo, quickly coming to the consensus that "Staying Alive means be safe." In contrast, a focus group of young working-class males – the most overtly engaged with brand markers of the groups interviewed – demonstrated the highest level of skepticism of all the interviewees, as well as resistance toward the idea of buying branded condoms: "I wouldn't buy those at a record shop" (Interview, student). However, the resistance was less about the use of condoms than the purchase of the condoms. They stated that they wouldn't personally buy the condoms in record stores (or anywhere) nor did they think others would buy them as they preferred to get condoms for free from local clinics. This response suggests a resistance to responsibilization through processes of branding. It is important to note, however that this resistance is made possible due to state supply of freely available condoms.

Audience involvement in social partnerships is also shaped by the increasingly important role of the audience in the co-creation of socially responsible behavior via web-based and mobile applications. On the Staying Alive website, the audience is invited to actively engage and contribute to blogs. These offer a snapshot of a wide range of sexual health issues facing young people. The content is predominantly targeted at young heterosexuals, and as the cases of two bloggers for the MTV site demonstrate, "discourses of truth" (Foucault, 1986) about sexuality and condom use are being reproduced as sex without condom use is framed as "bad" and sex with a condom is portrayed as "a lot of fun." Candy, a blogger who writes about "putting herself in a guy's shoes" by having a one night stand reflects:

> The thought of being in such a situation is … exhilarating! When he kisses me it is unlike anything I have ever felt … As soon as it's over I begin to panic. He didn't use a condom! … "why spoil the mood – It's just this one time" … but what if I have caught something … My mind fills with things that could go wrong … how could I be so stupid?
>
> (*MTV, 2010*)

Whilst Candy felt at conflict over the choice she made regarding not using condoms, Sarah's blog is forthright in its promotion of condom use first and foremost as she describes how she and her boyfriend became experienced "condom connoisseurs":

> I personally wasn't interested in trying that method – pulling out doesn't even prevent pregnancy effectively let alone catching an STD [sexually transmitted disease] such as HIV. I can't remember what kind of condom we used that first time but by the time our "research" was complete we felt like condom connoisseurs.
>
> (*MTV, 2010*)

Audience interactions with condoms, whether as "condom connoisseurs" or otherwise, may be seen as ethical performances. However, as the frames of discussion are set by MTV on their website at the corporate level, it is important to consider that these ethical performances are thus shaped first and foremost by MTV.

Brands, social partnerships, and responsibility: the making of responsible employees and consumers

As the case studies demonstrate, CSR in the form of brand-led social partnerships is being articulated in part through the coordination of the responsible, voluntary work of employees and consumers. Reflecting deepening levels of entanglement between brands and CSSPs, consumers are no longer just provided with the option to purchase goods or services from brands that demonstrate responsibility, but are actively involved in co-generating socially responsible experiences.

Such involvement includes participation in special events and contributions on websites, which are used to direct branding efforts. Starbucks consumers, for example are offered the choice of extending the brands' ethical expression from the café to the community by participating in recycling programs or volunteering with local nonprofit partner organizations (Starbucks, 2002c, 2003, 2004). MTV audiences are called to participate in responsible brand performances through blogs where they write about their sex lives or the purchasing of cosmetics or condoms distributed and produced via social partnerships. Patterning possibilities for responsible engagement, the brands thus constitute an ethical "frame of action" that enables consumers and employees to feel, be, or act in socially responsible ways (Arvidsson, 2006). Such programmed performances and altruistic practices allow consumers and employees to "feel good" about "doing good," or at least to feel reassured, whether in the context of an imagined global coffee community or a community of bloggers interested in promoting HIV/AIDS awareness.

Active involvement in such ethical practices and social partnerships, from Earth Day events to World AIDS day, we argue, contributes to the responsibilization of both employees and consumers. It is important to note here that while the partnerships may vary, employee and consumer labor is used to embody and communicate the brand's ethical values through volunteerism and entrepreneurial efforts. Configured as a matter of choice, Starbucks consumers are asked to take personal responsibility for complex, global issues such as the trade in coffee through ethical consumption or voluntary pursuits coordinated by the brand. In the case of MTV, individual audience members are encouraged to educate themselves about HIV/AIDS and perform their sexuality in certain ways (i.e. always using condoms), and employees are informed about the benefits of getting themselves tested for HIV. Employees and consumers' ethical interests and orientations are thus channeled in ways that most fit with the brands' image.

Bound up with processes of brand management, responsibilization in this context works to frame and guide the ethical investments and involvement of consumers and employees in a way that positively contributes to brand identity. As Arvidsson notes, the aim of contemporary brand management is to make "the becoming of subjects and the becoming of value coincide" (Arvidsson, 2006: 93).

The responsibilization of employees and consumers takes place through techniques of self-monitoring and self-care (Rose, 1999) and performativity of responsible work in carefully constructed practices. This facilitates on the one hand the development of brand image and ethical reputation, linking responsible action directly to brand value and economic performance. Such tools of responsibilization, in addition reflect a fashioning of the self, drawing on hybrid forms of governance, whereby individuals and other non-state actors assume responsibility for a range of social issues. From a governmentality perspective, using the tool of responsibilization in particular, it is thus possible to see how people's choices, aspirations, needs, desires and lifestyles are being mobilized and shaped through their active participation in social partnerships.

Yet, despite attempts to guide and frame consumer involvement, the brands do not fully determine how this participation takes place. Indeed, consumers have a propensity to co-generate the brand experience in way that exceeds programming efforts. Furthermore, acceptance by employees of the brand's framing of social issues does not occur in a straightforward manner, as reflected in minimal participation and doubts about the brands' motivations by some workers and can also be influenced by other partners, outside the brand. The research presented here points to a level of skepticism by both consumers and employees in relation to brand-based social partnerships. Our case studies support research that has found that consumers may face self-conflict over the choices they are making on a regular basis yet these conflicts are regularly smoothed over and incorporated into "responsible consumer" categories largely defined by the corporation (Caruana and Crane, 2008). Thus although many consumer respondents demonstrated that they were skeptical of the motives of the brands, by participating in the frames of social responsibility defined by the brands some consumers are able to avoid fully considering the impact of their consumption choices. However, it is also evident that skepticism may be translated to resistance, whereby consumers, especially, openly avoid engagement with brand-led programmed possibilities for performing social responsibility.

Furthermore, through their incorporation into branding and the mobilization of their responsible performances in frames of display, from the website to sponsored events and promotional materials, consumers and employees are actively involved in setting the boundaries of what can be considered "responsible" versus irresponsible (Caruana and Crane, 2008). Although their involvement in this sense is tightly managed by the brand, and is incorporated in asymmetrical fashion, there is still room for reconfiguration or reworking of notions and practices of social responsibility by those involved in its performance. Indeed, as Crane (2011: 18) argues, CSSPs, which involve convergences between business and nonprofit sectors and collusions of corporate and individual responsible practice, are also important sites where such partnerships "can be contested, manifested or resisted."

Conclusion

In this chapter we have examined how social partnerships are integrated as part of the articulation of CSR by the brands MTV and Starbucks. Extending the literature on social partnerships and brands, we have drawn attention to the ways in which such partnerships are organized to involve employees and consumers in ethical performances on the platforms of these brands. Concerned with the social implications of brand-based social responsibility, we suggest that it involves a process of responsibilization.

CSR thus operates as a mechanism of governance by enabling employees and consumers to engage in ethical performances; to feel, be, and act responsible, framed as a choice in the construction of socially responsible lifestyles. However, as we also demonstrated, compliance with such programmed possibilities is not always forthcoming, as evident in the skepticism expressed by both consumers and some of the employees involved with the brands.

What is particularly striking about the way social responsibility is constituted as part of the brand-led social partnerships, is how ethical subjects are being molded through the ways in which responsibility is experienced and performed. Guiding branding activity, and formatted as part of the brand, social partnerships are translated into practice in particular ways, constituting specific frames through which responsibility can be enacted. For MTV, the information provided as part of its Staying Alive campaign, now presented at UN Global media summits, frames condom use according to western ideological HIV prevention models, as something that all consumers *should* choose. In the case of Starbucks, consumers' concerns for the well-being of coffee growing communities is given practical expression through the consumption of ethical coffees, promoting a consumerist, market-based response to a much broader global coffee crisis.

Brands can thus be understood to be actively shaping and co-performing, with consumers and employees, specific configurations and discourses of social responsibility, which involve selective engagement with social concerns. Expressed as a "way of doing business," these configurations of social responsibility are thoroughly embedded within, and framed in terms of neoliberal market imperatives (Shamir, 2008).

That brands are constituting social responsibility is significant, particularly in the case of MTV and Starbucks, which are market-shaping, iconic brands that both reflect and contribute to the formation of cultural trends. As leading global brands and powerful actors in the market, they exert significant influence on competitors, constituting a "hegemonic brandscape" through which they not only structure the market, but also shape "consumer lifestyles and identities by functioning as a cultural model that consumers act, think, and feel through" (Thompson and Arsel, 2004: 632). In addition to shaping consumer responsibility, they provide a model through which employees can constitute themselves as socially responsible. Such hegemonic models of social responsibility limit other possibilities for ethical expression and engagement, particularly those that challenge the sustainability of the brand and its business model. These initiatives are thus defined both by the ethical concerns that are selectively supported to fit the brands' images as well as the ideologies and frames of reference used to promote these issues. For this reason, this research points to the need for further investigation of how brands are implicated in limiting the articulation and performance of social responsibility in consumer culture, and are contributing to the shaping of ethical subjects in profound ways.

At the same time, it is possible to see how the brands themselves are being reconfigured through engagement with socially responsible concerns, and interactions with consumers and employees, thus impacting how social responsibility is framed and formatted as part of the brand interface. Indeed, the open-endedness of brands, which are constituted through processes of co-creation, holds potential for responsibility to be articulated in alternative ways with consumers and employees-as-responsible-citizens taking the lead.

Questions for reflection

1   How are cross-sector social partnerships impacting on individual responses to social issues?
2   Think of an example of a social partnership you are familiar with. To what extent are consumers and employees involved in co-generating socially responsible behavior?
3   What are some further benefits or limitations of brand-led social partnerships in addressing social issues (i.e. poverty, environment, health)?
4   Why is it that brands have become such a crucial site for the articulation of CSR through social partnerships?

References

Arieff, X. (2004) *Public Health and Education: U.N. Secretary-General Annan Launches Global Media AIDS Initiative to Educate Public About HIV/AIDS*. (Online). Available: www.kaiser-network.org/daily_reports/rep_index.cfm?DR_ID=21719"www.kaisernetwork.org/daily_reports/rep_index.cfm?DR_ID=21719. (May 16, 2011).

Arvidsson, A. (2006) *Brands: Meaning and Value in Media Culture*. London: Routledge.

Basil, D. and Herr, P. (2006) "Attitudinal balance and cause-related marketing: an empirical application of balance theory." *Journal of Consumer Psychology*, 16: 391–403.

Beer, D. and Burrows, R. (2010) "Consumption, prosumption and participatory web cultures: an introduction." *Journal of Consumer Culture*, (10) 1: 3–12.

Blowfield, M. and Murray, A. (2008) *Corporate Responsibility: A Critical Overview*. Oxford: Oxford University Press.

Bowen, H. (1953) *Social Responsibilities of the Businessman*. New York: Harper.

Carroll, A.B. (1979) "A three-dimensional conceptual model of corporate performance." *Academy of Management Review*, (4) 4: 497–505.

Caruana, R. and Crane, A. (2008) "Constructing consumer responsibility: exploring the role of corporate communications." *Organization Studies*, (29) 12: 1495–1519.

Crane, A. (2011) "From governance to Governance: on blurring boundaries," *Journal of Business Ethics*, 94: 17–19.

Crane, A., Matten, D. and Spence, L.J. (eds) (2008) *Corporate Social Responsibility: Readings and Cases in a Global Context*. New York: Routledge.

Dean, M. (1999) *Governmentality: Power and Rule in Modern Society*. London: Sage.

du Gay, P. (1996) *Consumption and Identity at Work*. London: Sage.

Fan, Y. (2005) "Ethical branding and corporate reputation." *Corporate Communications: An International Journal*, (10) 4: 341–50.

Foucault, M. (1986) "Governmentality." *Ideology and Consciousness*, 6: 5–21.

Foucault, M. (1991) "On governmentality," in Burchell, G., Gordon, C. and Miller, P. (eds) *The Foucualt Effect*. Chicago: The University of Chicago Press: 87–104.

Gordon, C. (1991) "Governmental rationality: an introduction," in Burchell, G., Gordon, C. and Miller, P. (eds) *The Foucault Effect*. Chicago: The University of Chicago Press: 1–35.

Grau, S. and Folse, J. (2007) "Cause-related marketing." *Journal of Advertising*, 36 (4): 19–33.

Interbrand (2009) *Best Global Brands: 2009 Ranking*. (Online). Available: www.interbrand. com/best_global_brands.aspx?year=2009&langid=1000 (June 9, 2010).

Jenkins, H. (2006) *Fans, Bloggers and Gamers: Exploring Participatory Culture*. New York: New York University Press.

Littler, J. and Moor, L. (2008) "Fourth worlds and neo-Fordism," *Cultural Studies*, (22) 5: 700–23.

Logsdon, J.M. and Wood, D.J. (2002) "Business citizenship: from domestic to global level of analysis. *Business Ethics Quarterly*, 12 (2): 155–87.

Lury, C. (2004) *Brands: The Logos of the Global Economy*. London: Routledge.

Mitchell, A. (2001) Rethinking brand thinking: the emperor's new clothes – a backlash against branding? *Market Leader*, no. 15.

MTV (2007) *Staying Alive*. (Online). Available: www.staying-alive.org (July 7, 2010).

MTV (2010) *Staying Alive*. (Online). Available: www.staying-alive.org (September 8, 2010).

Peloza, J. and Ye, C. (2014) How social partnerships build brands, In Seitanidi, M. M. and Crane, A. (eds) *Social Partnerships and Responsible Business: A Research Handbook*. London: Routledge: 191–204.

Prahalad, C.K. and Ramaswamy, V. (2004) "Co-creation experiences: the next practice in value creation," *Journal of Interactive Marketing*, (18) 3: 5–9.

Rose, N. (1999) *Powers of Freedom. Reframing Political Thought*. Cambridge: Cambridge University Press.

Saporito, B. (2012) "Starbucks' big mug," *Time*, 25 June: 53–4.

Schultz, H. and Yang, D. (1997) *Pour Your Heart Into It: How Starbucks Built a Company One Cup at a Time*. New York: Hyperion.

Seitanidi, M.M. (2010) *The Politics of Partnerships*. Berlin: Springer.

Seitanidi, M.M. and Crane, A. (2008) "Implementing CSR through partnerships: understanding the selection, design and institutionalization of nonprofit business partnerships," *Journal of Business Ethics*, 85: 413–29.

Seitanidi, M.M. and Ryan, A. (2007) "A critical review of forms of corporate community involvement: from philanthropy to partnerships," *International Journal of Nonprofit and Voluntary Sector Marketing*, 12: 247–66.

Selsky, J. and Parker, B. (2010) "Platforms for cross-sector social partnerships: prospective sensemaking devices for social benefit," *Journal of Business Ethics*, 94: 21–37.

Shamir, R. (2004) "The de-radicalization of corporate social responsibility," *Critical Sociology*, (30) 3: 669–89.

Shamir, R. (2005) "Mind the gap: the commodification of corporate social responsibility," *Symbolic Interaction*, (28) 2: 229–53.

Shamir, R. (2008) "The age of responsibilization: on market-embedded morality," *Economy and Society*, (37) 1: 1–19.

Starbucks Coffee Company (2001) "Starbucks and conservation international: supporting conservation and coffee farmers," brochure.

Starbucks Coffee Company (2002a) "Commitment to origins™: Starbucks involvement in coffee-origin countries," brochure.

Starbucks Coffee Company (2002b) "Starbucks and fair trade: supporting a better life for coffee farmers," brochure.

Starbucks Coffee Company (2002c) "AIDS walk Toronto 2002," brochure.

Starbucks Coffee Company (2003) "Treat your garden to coffee and watch it grow," brochure.

Starbucks Coffee Company (2004) "Experience the world while making a positive impact on it," brochure.

Starbucks Coffee Company (2005) *Striking A Balance: Corporate Social Responsibility: Fiscal 2004 Annual Report.* (Online). Available: www.starbucks.com /csrannualreport (April 8, 2007).

Starbucks Corporation (2007) *Starbucks Earthwatch Institute and Starbucks Coffee Extend Partnership to Benefit Coffee Farmers in Costa Rica.* (Online). Available: http://news.starbucks. com/article_display.cfm?article_id=121"http://news.starbucks.com/article_display.cfm?article_id=121(May 18, 2010).

Starbucks Corporation (2012) *Community.* (Online). Available: www. starbucks.ca/responsibility/community (June 1, 2012).

Stehr, N. (2008) *Moral Markets: How Knowledge and Affluence Change Consumers and Products.* London: Paradigm Publishers.

Thompson, C. and Arsel, Z. (2004) "The Starbucks brandscape and consumers' (anticorporate) experiences of glocalization," *Journal of Consumer Research*, 31: 631–42.

Tomlinson, F. (2005) "Idealistic and pragmatic versions of the discourse of partnership," *Organization Studies*, (26) 8: 1169–88.

United Nations (2005) *What is the Global Compact?* (Online). Available: www.unglobalcompact.org/Portal/Default.asp? (September 24, 2007).

Varadarajan, P.R. and Menon, A. (1988) "Cause-related marketing: a coalignment of marketing strategy and corporate philanthropy," *Journal of Marketing*, 52: 58–74.

Tichy, N.M., McGill, A.R., St. Clair, L. (1997) *Corporate Global Citizenship: Doing Business in the Public Eye.* San Francisco: The New Lexington Press.

Waddock, S. (1989) "Understanding social partnerships. An evolutionary model of partnership organizations," *Administration and Society*, (21) 1: 78–100.

Wood, D.J. and Jones, R.E. (1995) "Stakeholder mismatching: a theoretical problem in empirical research on corporate social performance," *International Journal of Organizational Analysis*, July 3: 229–67.

Zwick, D., Bonsu, S. and Darmody, A. (2008) "Putting consumers to work: 'co-creation' and new marketing govern-mentality," *Journal of Consumer Culture*, (8) 2: 163–96.

15

AN INSTITUTIONAL PERSPECTIVE ON CROSS-SECTOR PARTNERSHIP

Clodia Vurro and Tina Dacin

Introduction

In an attempt to explain the rise in the number and variety of alliances, both in advanced and developing economies (Berger *et al.,* 2004), an emerging yet growing body of literature has started to analyze the reciprocal interaction between contexts and managerial approaches to cross-sector social partnerships (CSSPs). Building on emerging studies on CSSPs as situated action embedded into a larger institutional environment (Selsky and Parker, 2005; Westley and Vredenburg, 1997; Vurro *et al.,* 2010), in this chapter, we aim to show how CSSPs co-evolve with their specific institutional context of reference (Powell and Di Maggio, 1991; Scott, 2007). As shown in the second section of the book (please refer to Chapter 7 and Chapter 11), partnerships and their drivers do not occur in a vacuum, with institutional contexts affecting and being affected by the ability of partners to cooperate effectively (Lawrence *et al.,* 2002).

Thus, we link ideas from the literature on CSSPs' processes to an institutional perspective, with the aim of detailing the connection between collaboration and the dynamics of institutional fields, defined as sources of rules and resources rooted in material practices and symbolic systems by which individuals and organizations produce and reproduce their material lives and render their experiences meaningful and legitimate (Friedland and Alford, 1991; Fligstein, 2001).

We paint a broad theoretical picture of how institutional fields provide a backdrop of resources and practices that affect the selection and design of collaboration (Holm, 1995). Additionally, we delineate the role of collaboration in the development of institutional fields, showing how partners may act to change the logics for action in a context in which collaboration is institutionalized (Greenwood *et al.,* 2002; Rao *et al.,* 2000). Though recognizing that CSSPs can occur indifferently across business, nonprofit, and government sectors (Selsky and Parker, 2005), we focus purposefully on partnerships promoted by business actors aiming at addressing the social good, as part of their corporate social responsibility programs (Seitanidi and Crane, 2009; Porter and Kramer, 2006; Seitanidi and Ryan, 2007). In other words, we consider CSSPs as part of the portfolio of activities that companies undertake to fulfil perceived duties as members of society (Wood, 1991; Waddock and Smith, 2000). Looking at CSSPs from a corporate perspective offers unique opportunities to study the reciprocal interaction between agency and structure. In fact, companies tend to suffer from the liability of substantial and symbolic foreignness when entering into a social arena (Gardberg and Fombrun, 2006). Despite the growing legitimacy of their social role due to the visibility of their corporate citizenship programs, public opinion continues to be suspicious of the extent to which companies can be considered truly responsible actors in advancing societal interests. As a consequence, the effectiveness of companies in pursuing social targets is shaped by their ability to balance economic approaches with social sensitivity, that is, act across institutional contexts by answering to ever contrasting requests for appropriateness (Sud *et al.,* 2009; Suchman, 1995; Perrini *et al.,* 2011). Moreover, companies potentially have fewer resource constraints and more power to be exchanged in order to produce long-lasting changes into certain contexts, compared to nonprofits and even public authorities (Kistruck *et al.,* 2011). Accordingly, their involvement in CSSPs can be crucial in determining institutional change.

Setting out new theoretical directions in social partnerships, the contribution of our chapter is twofold. First, we emphasize the importance of examining collaboration as embedded in context, in order to be able to predict heterogeneity in organizational approaches to, and the impact of, cross-sector partnerships. Then, we highlight the relevance of collaboration in understanding the dynamics of institutional maintenance and change.

To this end, the remainder of the chapter is organized as follows. First, we advance the idea that inter-organizational collaboration should be analyzed jointly with the characteristics of the fields in which they take place to have a comprehensive picture of the drivers of their effectiveness. Then, a situated view of CSSPs is presented, both focusing on the role of institutions as sources of rules and resources on which to build action and showing institutional change as a possible outcome of collaborative agreements tackling complex social problems. Conclusions are provided, with the aim of setting the stage for future research bridging CSSPs with institutional theory.

The need for an embedded view of inter-organizational collaborations

In an attempt to enrich theoretical and empirical explanations of variation in the dynamics and outcomes of inter-organizational collaborative agreements, research is increasingly recognizing the need for interpreting collaborative governance models in the context in which they occur (Dacin *et al.,* 2007; Phillips *et al.,* 2000).

Spanning from formal rules and regulation (North, 1990) to social norms and taken-for-granted assumptions (Meyer and Rowan, 1977), institutional forces are generally expected to both enable and constrain the dynamics of collaboration in that they motivate actors to conform and search for appropriateness (Scott, 1995; DiMaggio and Powell, 1983; Dacin, 1997). Accordingly, embeddedness in a given social context puts pressure on actors to search for approval for their behavior, particularly from those constituents on whom the actors depend for resource acquisition (Oliver, 1991; Sharfman *et al.*, 1991).

Most of the debate on the importance of examining collaboration in context has explored how the rules and resources associated with the institutional position of potential and actual partners provide the foundation for collaborative action, thus affecting the initial moves and, consequently, the typical pattern of collaborative governance approaches (Westley and Vredenburg, 1997). Accordingly, an inter-organizational collaboration that adapts to institutional pressures and expectations is more likely to obtain access to scarce resources and have higher success rates than those that do not (Meyer and Rowan, 1977; Singh *et al.*, 1986). In sum, collaboration appears as a response to institutional pressures for conformity, such that institutional arrangements shape the way collaboration is set up, operates and strives for efficacy.

Based on observations of the dynamics of opportunity discovery, exploitation and growth in emerging economies and underdeveloped contexts, research on the role of institutions in shaping company behavior has more recently started to complement macro-structural institutional perspectives (North, 1990; Meyer *et al.*, 1997) with an embedded agency view of strategic action (Seo and Creed, 2002; Battilana, 2006; Greenwood and Hinings, 1996). Highlighting the recursive nature of the relationship between action and institutions, studies are focusing attention on how organizations shape institutional contexts, either encouraging particular institutional arrangements and transforming existing institutions or leveraging resources to create new institutions (Fligstein, 1997; Maguire *et al.*, 2004).

This has stimulated an intense debate over the need for a more realistic view of those processes aimed at accomplishing institutional changes involving highly diverse, even contrasting, interests and perspectives (Battilana *et al.*, 2009), as well as occurring in highly complex, fragmented institutional fields (Huxham and Vangen, 2000). As a consequence, a more distributed view of institutional entrepreneurship has emerged as more or less purposive orchestration of resourceful actors spanning from multiple social positions, roles and identities (Wijen and Ansari, 2007; Delbridge and Edwards, 2008) to overcome inaction and succeed in the creation of new institutions or transformation of existing ones (Rao *et al.*, 2000; Vurro *et al.*, 2010).

Research on institutional entrepreneurship as a collective phenomenon has been enlightening in showing both the materiality of institutional impacts associated with collaborative governance models (Lawrence *et al.*, 2002; Phillips *et al.*, 2000) and the antecedents of the ability to set up cooperative actions targeting institutional transformation (Wijen and Ansari, 2007).

Cross-sector partnerships and the dynamics of institutional fields

Institutional antecedents of CSSPs

The quest for an embedded approach to institutional entrepreneurship has clearly raised attention towards less simplistic views of institutional fields, as terrains over which social action takes place to either reproduce or subvert pre-existing order (Fligstein, 2001). While constraining and being constrained by actors belonging to them, fields develop through patterns of social actions that produce, reproduce, and transform established norms, local orders and levels of social acceptance (DiMaggio and Powell, 1983).

Acknowledging the processes through which partnerships develop as directly related to the context in which they are situated, cross-sector collaboration research that has attended to institutional considerations has tended to highlight the degree of institutionalization and heterogeneity as prominent field characteristics that might play a role in enabling or constraining partnership formation and execution (Provan et al., 2004; Webb et al., 2010).

First, fields of action can be described in terms of the extent to which they range along a continuum between low and high levels of institutionalization (Purdy and Gray, 2009; Hinings et al., 2003). Accordingly, highly institutionalized fields correspond to more mature contexts in which collectively agreed upon rules, norms, and behaviors are well established and highly embedded into organizational structures, practices, and role models (Rao et al., 2000). It is in these more or less pluralistic fields that action has to be mainly targeted to gain support from dominant coalitions (Suddaby and Greenwood, 2005). At the opposite extreme, that is, at low levels of institutional development, fragmentation prevails with no norm, rule, or practice having the degree of consensus necessary to guide behavior to conformity (please refer to Chapter 7). When this is the case, contradictions in the field open the way to change agents, so that actors possessing certain characteristics can take advantage of the situation, setting the rules of the game, instead of adhering to existing arrangements (Davis and Marquis, 2005; Markowitz, 2007).

Together with degree of institutionalization, the heterogeneity of institutional arrangements in a field, that is, the variance in the characteristics of different institutional arrangements, has been analyzed in relation to the ease of forming CSSPs and their specific configuration (Bitzer and Glasbergen, 2010). In particular, heterogeneity refers to the extent to which institutional incompatibilities exist, so as to provide sufficient guidance to the behavior of actors in the field (Rein and Stott, 2009). When heterogeneity is low, institutions acting in a field point in the same direction, resulting in a situation in which stability prevails. In these contexts, institutional conflict is not an issue, thus positing both a stronger need for appropriateness and conformity, and a higher resistance to potential change. At the opposite extreme, at high levels of heterogeneity, fragmentation prevails with no institutional arrangement having the degree of consensus necessary to guide behavior towards conformity. When this is the case, contradictions in the field open the way for institutional entrepreneurs and other sources of change, so that actors possessing certain characteristics can take advantage of the situation, setting the rules of the game (please, refer to Chapter 11). In sum, the extent to which an institutional field is more or less under-organized, pluralistic, or inconsistent heavily affects the appropriateness of CSSP-related arrangements and decisions (Vurro *et al.*, 2010).

Institutionalization and heterogeneity have been analyzed at three different levels, corresponding to the components of any institutional setting: the regulatory, the cognitive and the normative components (Scott, 1995).

From a regulatory point of view, existing laws and rules in a field greatly affect the repertoire of acceptable partnering strategies, promoting certain types of behavior while restricting others (Scott, 1995). Especially when CSSPs occur across national and regional environments, variation in the extent to which the legal framework, property rights, information systems or regulatory regimes are developed and efficient establish not only the permissible range of collaborative models but also their effectiveness. Studies on micro-franchising in base-of-the-pyramid markets (please refer to Chapter 7) show how inefficient legal systems, lack of information technology infrastructure, and high unemployment pose significant challenges to franchising's traditional performance drivers, forcing organizations to incur significant expenses in dispute resolution (Kistruck *et al.*, 2011; Deelder and Miller, 2009). Other examples might be related to the existence and content of tax laws regarding the deductibility of philanthropic contributions, restrictions to access to certain forms of capital (e.g. with respect to equity ownership), or the development of a labor market for voluntary work (Gardberg and Fombrun, 2006).

Additionally, widely shared cognitive categories about what constitutes appropriate, credible, or legitimate organizational practices create local expectations about the role of the partners in shaping the collaboration. In fact, the cognitive component of a certain institutional field refers to socially constructed role models to which actors decide to adapt for patterning their actions in a way that they are not sanctioned by the community (Scott, 2007). In this sense, cognitive institutional forces shape how societies accept partners from different sectors, as well as shape the relevance of their collaboration, inculcate values, and even create a cultural milieu whereby cooperation is accepted and encouraged (Bruton *et al.*, 2010). Moreover, the bases for acceptability change as the level of institutionalization ranges in a field between low and high consensus about cognitive boundaries for organizational conformity to expectations (Marquis *et al.*, 2007). Accordingly, in terms of partnering, countries lacking an established infrastructure and facing high levels of unemployment, low levels of education, and low income per capita (contexts typically targeted by social entrepreneurs operating in developing countries) may interpret appropriate CSSPs as catalytic in fostering local development, by actively involving local communities. On the contrary, with high levels of institutionalization characterized by greater uniformity of cultural understandings and greater resistance to change (Zucker, 1991), organizations, in their quest for legitimacy, will generally align their partnering strategies with those sanctioned by the community, searching for adherence to dominant logics in the field (Vurro *et al.*, 2010).

Finally, the social and normative systems that develop in certain contexts set the standards for, and enforce, conformity to accepted collaborative behavior (March and Olsen, 1989). While the cognitive component of the institutional environment shapes the perceptions regarding which role is considered appropriate in a given context, the normative forces specify how that role has to be performed in order to be considered acceptable. Instead of giving a frame of reference, the normative component deals with evaluations regarding the level of appropriateness of practices in a field (Galaskiewicz and Burt, 1991). Additionally, norms in a field provide information about business partners and their likely behavior, which reduces information asymmetries (please, refer to Chapter 11). Emerging economies, for example, are typically characterized by more obscure evaluative criteria, thus having higher partner-related risks and higher costs related to information search for actors deciding to start some sort of collaboration (Peng, 2003; Peng and Health, 1996).

Regardless of the specific component of the institutional environment in which entrepreneurs are embedded, the arguments above point out dynamic views of institutional fields, such that the level of institutionalization sets the context in which partnership approach has to be chosen, as well as which capabilities partners need to develop in order for the strategy to be effective in dealing with quests for acceptability. In more details, research shows how low institutionalization and high heterogeneity are conducive to richer fields in terms of opportunities to cooperate across sector boundaries (Webb *et al.*, 2010). Base of the pyramid markets and contexts in which informality prevail are typical environments in which CSSPs abound, starting from the need for exploiting institutional voids and widespread incongruence (Mair and Martí, 2009) in order to attain developmental goals (please refer to Chapter 7). Beyond the identification of opportunities to cooperate, field characteristics play an important role in determining who has a legitimate case for membership in collaboration. In this sense, institutionalized rules provide the basis for the decision to include some while excluding others, in a way that improves the legitimacy of action while reducing perceived institutional distance (Gardberg and Fombrun, 2006). Finally, the general level of institutional coherence provides the basis for the role to be played by the promoter of the CSSP, while defining leadership and governance requirements more precisely. In fact, when progressing from a low to high level of institutionalization and coherence the potential for setting the rules of the games decreases (Thornton, 2004), and business actors start to benefit from more participative models based on the integration and combination of already consolidated practices (Perrini and Vurro, 2010).

CSSPs as collective institutional entrepreneurs

With the rising complexity of social needs, as increasingly pervasive, multi-scalar, interconnected and evolving, CSSPs have created excitement regarding their potential for social change while addressing societal disequilibria (Seitanidi *et al.,* 2010), in light of the acknowledged superiority of relational approaches in resource-demanding, risky contexts (Austin, 2000). Accordingly, CSSPs are meant to pursue those social problems that exceed the scope of single organizations with the aim of reaching long-lasting, societal-level changes beyond original intentions (Waddock and Smith, 2000; Waddock and Post, 1991). It is in this sense that CSSPs represent an important source of institutional entrepreneurship, that is a collective action purposefully striving for change in established institutional arrangements at the regulatory, cognitive and normative levels (Cornelius and Wallace, 2010; Bitzer and Glasbergen, 2010).

The emerging view of CSSPs as collective institutional entrepreneurs builds on and extends recent studies advancing a distributed view of agency in the description of field dynamics (Lounsbury and Crumley, 2007; Rao *et al.*, 2000; Lawrence *et al.*, 2002). In fact, CSSPs involve different actors with varying access to heterogeneous kind and level of resources who act in a coordinated and purposefully strategic way to enact interaction, build coalitions and exchange information targeting a wider, situated social change objective (DiMaggio and Powell, 1983; Lawrence *et al.*, 2009). Social change objectives are pursued by both sharing complementary assets and through the identification and exploitation of path breaking solutions to address a given social gap (Perrini and Vurro, 2010).

The mechanism by which the collaboratively defined solutions spill over into a wider-level institutional change is twofold. On the one side, while providing innovative solutions to social problems, collaborators continue to be involved in their regular activities subsuming collaboratively developed solutions under their routinized relational processes, thus fostering the diffusion of local effects beyond original boundaries (Esteves and Barclay, 2011). The Global Health Fellows Programs (GHF) launched by Pfizer Corporation in 2002 as an initiative of international corporate volunteering aimed at collaborating with local health organizations in developing countries to develop their capacity is an example of the institutional effects of creativity in collaboratively pursuing social targets. Though framed as a strategic philanthropy initiative, GHF has primarily served as a professional development program, enhancing the personal and professional skills of participating employees through the challenge of working in multicultural and low-resource settings (Vian *et al.*, 2007). On the other side, institutional contexts are affected by the dissemination of rules, norms and cognitive frames across sector boundaries (Lawrence *et al.*, 2002). Collaborators involved in a CSSP are located, by definition, in very different, even contrasting institutional fields, such that each one is pressured by its own quest for conformity. Though the interaction of multiple sets of institutional rules might make collaboration more complex (Googins and Rochlin, 2000), it also sets the basis for reciprocal institutional transfer from one field to the others. A typical example of such a process involves the translation of cultural rules and local norms, as the customs and concepts of large multinational firms move into and are reformulated within the economies of a bottom of the pyramid market, through the actions of local community organizations engaged in a strategic collaboration (Desa, 2011). The case of the joint venture between Grameen Group and Groupe Danone to locally produce and sell nutritionally enhanced yogurt products in Bangladesh is representative of the movement of private-sector concepts and approaches in service of social needs through the launch of innovative models of production, distribution and consumption placed at the interstices between local customs and business norms (Webb *et al,*. 2010).

Yet, any CSSP does not automatically turn into a collective institutional entrepreneur able to affect well-established institutional settings. Several conditions determine the potential for generating long-lasting social change by means of cross-sector collaborations, at both individual and collective levels.

At the actor level, the social position of the collaborators greatly affects their ability to initiate change in a certain field of action (Lawrence, 1999). In fact, both status and control over critical resources are related to the potential for institutional change enactment via their provision of legitimacy in the eyes of stakeholders and power to mobilize action around a common objective (Maguire *et al.,* 2004). Having a good reputation as a partner, as well as a dominant position in a field, represents valuable assets to both gain easier access to further resources to pursue change objectives, and to benefit from greater visibility to induce cooperation beyond the original intent (Wijen and Ansari, 2007). Additionally, the motivations to engage in collaborative efforts have been shown to affect the transformative potential of CSSPs at the community level. Institutional spillovers have been identified in community development projects initiated by corporate actors entering social partnerships moved by strategic intentions rather than purely philanthropic motives (Porter and Kramer, 2011). Also, the history of cross-sector interactions, that is, the interaction experience of each collaborator, has emerged as an indicator of CSSP transformative potential (Seitanidi *et al.,* 2010). Finally, the extent to which actors are involved in possess and enact social skills has been considered to account for institutional change (Fligstein, 2001). Accordingly, socially skilled actors are those who distinguish themselves for having a broad repertoire of bridging tactics to induce cooperation from very diverse allies based on the development of shared visions of the need for change, the management of mobilization activities and the provision of motivation to those in charge of institutionalizing the proposed solution (Battilana and Dorado, 2010; Maguire *et al.,* 2004).

Together with the individual characteristics of the actors involved in collaborations for social change, the structure and the governance of the CSSP represent key levels of analysis for the identification of contingencies affecting the potential to induce institutional transformation. Accordingly, the shift from largely self-interest oriented leadership styles combined with concentrated governance structures to ethical stewardship models based on distributed modes of cooperation has been acknowledged as a relevant driver of the ability to promote societal level changes (Vurro *et al.,* 2010). For example, in the context of community regeneration projects participatory approaches based on negotiated values and community involvement have proven to be the most effective in fostering changes in institutional spillovers (Bitzer and Glasbergen, 2010; Cornelius and Wallace, 2010). Similarly, CSSPs based on joint strategic, decision, and operating processes have been found to be the most appropriate in delivering symbiotic value creation, that is, benefits accruing to all the partners and the context in which the partnership is situated, in terms of opportunities for social change (Esteves and Barclay 2011).

Table 15.1 below summarizes the conditions that influence the potential for generating social change at the actor and organization level.

TABLE 15.1 Drivers of social change

Actor level	Partnership level
Social position of the actors involved	Implementation of participative models
Reputation	Distributed governance styles
Level of commitment to the partnership	Participatory leadership
Collaborative experience	Joint decision processes
Social skills of project leaders and collaborators	

Conclusion

Building on the emerging literature that depicts CSSPs as a collective, situated phenomenon, this chapter examines the dynamics of reciprocal interaction between institutional norms and rules in a field and cross-boundary cooperative model targeting societal change and development. Fields' institutional infrastructures are made of formal and informal regulations, norms and cognitions that dictate conditions that have to be satisfied in order for a CSSP to be considered appropriate and attain expected results. In particular, degree of institutionalization and heterogeneity of the set of rules guiding behavior are paramount in affecting decisions concerning how to structure the partnership in terms of appropriate partners, roles to be played in the partnerships, access to resources, and governance arrangements (Vurro *et al.,* 2010). At the same time, social partnerships are influential in shaping the dynamics of field development, acting as collective social entrepreneurs aimed at introducing social innovations through cross-boundary dissemination of cultural norms, approaches, and cognitions. We have argued that affecting change in an institutional field is not immediate, yet contingent on both individual and organizational factors, with social positions and participative models being the most relevant drivers of transformation (Phillips *et al.,* 2000).

Figure 15.1 summarizes the key mechanisms presented in the chapter on the reciprocal interaction between institutional structure and social partnerships.

The arguments advanced in this chapter have a number of implications for research and practice into collaboration and institutional embeddedness. On the CSSP side, this chapter highlights the importance of considering institutional context when examining the dynamics of cross-sector collaboration. In fact, though perceived as a key factor, institutional embeddedness has rarely been taken explicitly into consideration in predicting the appropriateness conditions that could affect collaborators' effectiveness in pursuing joint missions (Bitzer and Glasbergen, 2010). Moreover, the proposed approach gives a number of suggestions on how to

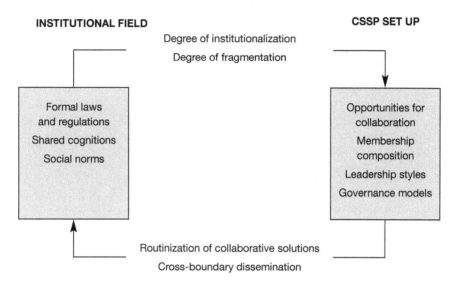

FIGURE 15.1 The institutional context of cross-sector collaboration

effectively manage partnerships across different contexts, characterized by varying levels of institutionalization and heterogeneity. On the institutional change side, our chapter suggests that cross-sector cooperation could be an important form of institutional entrepreneurship, especially in those fields characterized by high multiplicity and a strong collective dimension, such as the social in which high uncertainty and conflicting expectations on appropriateness prevail (Lawrence, 1999; Dorado, 2005). Second, we show how collective institutional entrepreneurship is not immediate but needs to be directed towards expected results, especially through high-involvement relationships and social embeddedness in a field. Third, we comment on the importance of situating studies of institutional entrepreneurship in specific fields of action, so as to account for community-level specificities as the sources of drivers and constraints to entrepreneurial action (Marquis and Battilana, 2009).

Questions for reflection

1   How can partnerships be affected by formal and informal institutions along the collaboration life cycle? And at which stage of institutional development is a social partnership most effective in exploiting change?
2   Are there differences in how fields shape CSSPs in contexts characterized by high levels of informality as compared to highly formalized institutional contexts?
3   What is the impact of resources in affecting the co-evolution of institution and collaboration? Are there specific configurations of resource bundles that are more relevant in affecting institutional change?

References

Austin, J.E. (2000) *The Collaboration Challenge: How Nonprofits and Businesses Succeed through Strategic Alliances.* San Francisco, CA: Jossey-Bass Publishers.

Battilana, J. (2006) "Agency and institutions: the enabling role of individuals' social position," *Organization,* 13 (5): 653–76.

Battilana, J. and Dorado, S. (2010) "Building sustainable hybrid organizations: the case of commercial microfinance organizations," *Academy of Management Journal,* 53 (6): 1419–40.

Battilana, J., Leca, B. and Boxenbaum, E. (2009) "How actors change institutions: toward a theory of institutional entrepreneurship," *Academy of Management Annals,* 3 (1): 65–107.

Berger, I., Cunningham, P. and Drumwright, M. E. (2004)"Social alliances: company/nonprofit collaboration," *California Management Review,* 47 (1): 58–90.

Bitzer, V. and Glasbergen, P. (2010) "Partnerships for sustainable change in cotton: an institutional analysis of African cases," *Journal of Business Ethics,* 93 (Supplement 2): 223–40.

Bruton, G.D., Ahlstrom, D. and Li, H.-L. (2010) "Institutional theory and entrepreneurship: where are we now and where do we need to move in the future?," *Entrepreneurship Theory and Practice,* 34 (3): 421–40.

Cornelius, N. and Wallace, J. (2010) "Cross-sector partnerships: city regeneration and social justice," *Journal of Business Ethics,* 94 (1): 71–84.

Dacin, M.T. (1997) "Isomorphism in context: the power and prescription of institutional norms," *Academy of Management Journal,* 40 (1): 46–81.

Dacin, M.T., Oliver, C. and Roy, J.P. (2007) "The legitimacy of strategic alliances: an institutional perspective," *Strategic Management Journal,* 28 (2): 169–87.

Davis, G.F. and Marquis, C. (2005)"Prospects for organization theory in the early twenty-first century: institutional fields and mechanisms," *Organization Science,* 16 (4): 332–43.

Deelder, W. and Miller, R. (2009) *Franchising in Frontier Markets: What's Working, What's Not, and Why.* Johannesburg, SA: Dalberg Global Development Advisors.

Delbridge, R. and Edwards, T. (2008) "Challenging conventions: roles and processes during non-isomorphic institutional change," *Human Relations,* 61 (3): 299–25.

Desa, G. (2011) "Resource mobilization in international social entrepreneurship: bricolage as a mechanism of institutional transformation," *Entrepreneurship Theory and Practice,* (forthcoming): 1–25.

DiMaggio, P.J. and Powell, W.W. (1983) "The iron cage revisited: institutional isomorphism and collective rationality in organizational fields," *American Sociological Review,* 48 (2): 147–60.

Dorado, S. (2005) "Institutional entrepreneurship, partaking, and convening," *Organization Studies,* 26 (3): 385–414.

Esteves, A.M. and Barclay, M.-A. (2011) "New approaches to evaluating the performance of corporate–community partnerships: a case study from the minerals sector," *Journal of Business Ethics,* 103 (2): 189–202.

Fligstein, N. (1997) "Social skill and institutional theory," *American Behavioral Scientist,* 40 (4): 397–405.

Fligstein, N. (2001) "Social skill and the theory of fields," *Sociological Theory,* 19(2): 105–25.

Friedland, R. and Alford, R.R. (1991) "Bringing society back in: symbols, practices, and institutional contradictions," in Powell, W.W. and DiMaggio, P.J. (eds). *Institutionalism in Organizational Analysis.* Chicago, IL: University of Chicago Press: 232–63.

Galaskiewicz, J. and Burt, R. (1991) "Interorganization contagion in corporate philanthropy," *Administrative Science Quarterly,* 36 (1): 88–105.

Gardberg, N.A. and Fombrun, C.J. (2006) "Corporate citizenship: Creating intangible assets across institutional environments," *Academy of Management Review,* 31 (2): 329–46.

Googins, B.K. and Rochlin, S.A. (2000) "Creating the partnership society: Understanding the rhetoric and reality of cross-sectoral partnerships," *Business and Society Review,* 105 (1): 127–44.

Greenwood, R. and Hinings, C.R. (1996) "Understanding radical organizational change: Bringing together the old and the new institutionalism," *Academy of Management Review,* 21 (4): 1022–54.

Greenwood, R., Suddaby, R. and Hinings, C.R. (2002) "Theorizing change: The role of professional associations in the transformation of institutionalized fields," *Academy of Management Journal,* 45 (1): 58–80.

Hinings, C.R., Greenwood, R. and Suddaby, R. (2003) "The dynamics of change in organizational fields." in Poole, M.S. and Van de Ven, A. H. (eds). *Handbook of Organizational Change and Innovation.* New York: Oxford University Press: 304–23.

Holm, P. (1995) "The dynamics of institutionalization: transformation processes in Norwegian fisheries," *Administrative Science Quarterly,* 40 (3): 398–422.

Huxham, C. and Vangen, S. (2000) "Leadership in the shaping and implementation of collaboration agendas: how things happen in a (not quite) joined-up world," *Academy of Management Journal,* 43 (6): 1159–75.

Kistruck, G.M., Webb, J.W., Sutter, C.J. and Ireland, R.D. *et al.* (2011) "Microfranchising in base-of-the-pyramid markets: institutional challenges and adaptation to the franchise model," *Entrepreneurship Theory and Practice,* 35 (3): 503–31.

Lawrence, T.B. (1999) "Institutional strategy," *Journal of Management,* 25 (2): 161–87.

Lawrence, T.B., Hardy, C. and Phillips, N. (2002) "Institutional effects of interorganizational collaboration: the emergence of proto-institutions," *Academy of Management Journal,* 45 (1): 281–90.

Lawrence, T.B., Suddaby, R. and Leca, B. (eds) (2009) *Institutional Work: Actors and Agency in Institutional Studies of Organization.* Cambridge: Cambridge University Press.

Lounsbury, M. and Crumley, E.T. (2007) "New practice creation: an institutional perspective on innovation," *Organization Studies,* 28 (7): 993–1012.

Maguire, S., Hardy, C. and Lawrence, T.B. (2004) "Institutional entrepreneurship in emerging fields: HIV/AIDS treatment advocacy in Canada," *Academy of Management Journal,* 47 (5): 657–79.

Mair, J. and Martí, I. (2009) "Entrepreneurship in and around institutional voids: a case study from Bangladesh," *Journal of Business Venturing,* 24 (5): 419–35.

March, J. and Olsen, J.P. (1989) *Rediscovering Institutions: The Organizational Basis of Politics.* New York: Free Press.

Markowitz, L. (2007) "Structural innovators and core-framing tasks: how socially responsible mutual fund companies build identity among investors," *Sociological Perspectives,* 50 (1): 131–53.

Marquis, C. and Battilana, J. (2009) "Acting globally but thinking locally? The enduring influence of local communities on organizations," *Research in Organizational Behavior,* 29: 283–302.

Marquis, C., Glynn, M.A. and Davis, G.F. (2007) "Community isomorphism and corporate social action," *Academy of Management Review,* 32 (3): 925–45.

Meyer, J.W. Boli, J., Thomas, G.M. and Ramirez, F.O. *et al.* (1997) "World society and the nation-state," *American Journal of Sociology,* 103 (1): 144–81.

Meyer, J.W. and Rowan, B. (1977) "Institutionalized organizations: formal structure as myth and ceremony," *American Journal of Sociology,* 83 (2): 340–63.

North, D. C. (1990) *Institutions, Institutional Change and Economic Performance.* New York: Cambridge University Press.

Oliver, C. (1991) "Strategic responses to institutional processes," *Academy of Management Review,* 16 (1): 405–25.

Peng, M. (2003) "Institutional transitions and strategic choices," *Academy of Management Review,* 28 (2): 275–96.

Peng, M.W. and Health, P.S. (1996) "The growth of the firm in planned economies in transition: Institutions, organizations and strategic choice," *Academy of Management Review,* 21 (2): 492–528.

Perrini, F., Russo, A., Tencati, A. and Vurro, C. *et al.* (2011) "Deconstructing the relationship between social and financial performance," *Journal of Business Ethics,* 102 (1): 59–76.

Perrini, F. and Vurro, C. (2010) "Collaborative social entrepreneurship." in Tencati, A. and Zsolnai, L. (eds). *The Collaborative Enterprise: Creating Values for a Sustainable World.* Oxford: Peter Lang Academic Publishers.

Phillips, N., Lawrence, T.B. and Hardy, C. (2000) "Inter-organizational collaboration and the dynamics of institutional fields," *Journal of Management Studies,* 37 (1): 23–43.

Porter, M.E. and Kramer, M.R. (2006) "Strategy and society: the link between competitive advantage and corporate social responsibility," *Harvard Business Review,* 84 (12): 78–92.

Porter, M.E. and Kramer, M.R. (2011) "Creating shared value," *Harvard Business Review,* 89 (1/2): 62–77.

Powell, W.W. and Di Maggio, P.J. (1991) *The New Institutionalism in Organizational Analysis.* Chicago, IL: University of Chicago Press.

Provan, K.G., Isett, K.R. and Milward, H.B. (2004) "Cooperation and compromise: a network response to conflicting institutional pressures in community mental health," *Nonprofit and Voluntary Sector Quarterly,* 33 (3): 3.

Purdy, J.M. and Gray, B. (2009) "Conflicting logics, mechanisms of diffusions and multilevel dynamics in emerging institutional fields," *Academy of Management Journal,* 52(2): 355–80.

Rao, H., Morrill, C. and Zald, M.N. (2000) "Power plays: how social movement and collective action create new organizational forms," in Staw, B.M. and Sutton, R.I. (eds). *Research in Organizational Behavior.* New York: JAI Press.

Rein, M. and Stott, L. (2009) "Working together: critical perspectives on six cross-sector partnerships in Southern Africa," *Journal of Business Ethics,* 90 (1): 79–89.

Scott, W.R. (1995) *Institutions and Organizations.* Thousand Oaks, CA: Sage.

Scott, W.R. (2007) *Institutions and Organizations: Ideas and Interests.* Thousand Oaks, CA: Sage.

Seitanidi, M.M. and Crane, A. (2009) "Implementing CSR through partnerships: understanding the selection, design and institutionalization of nonprofit-business partnerships," *Journal of Business Ethics,* 85 (Supplement 2): 413–29.

Seitanidi, M.M., Koufopoulos, D.N. and Palmer, P. (2010) "Partnership formation for change: indicators for transformative potential in cross sector social partnerships," *Journal of Business Ethics,* 94 (Supplement 1): 139–61.

Seitanidi, M.M. and Ryan, A.M. (2007) "A critical review of forms of corporate community involvement: from philanthropy to partnerships," *Journal of Nonprofit and Public Sector Marketing,* 12 (3): 247–66.

Selsky, J.W. and Parker, B. (2005) "Cross-sector partnerships to address social issues: challenges to theory and practice," *Journal of Management,* 31 (6): 849–73.

Seo, M.-G. and Creed, W.E.D. (2002) "Institutional contradictions, praxis, and institutional change: a dialectical perspective," *Academy of Management Review,* 27 (2): 222–47.

Sharfman, M.P., Gray, B. and Yan, A. (1991) "The context of interorganizational collaboration in the garment industry," *Journal of Applied Behavioral Science,* 27 (2): 181–208.

Singh, J.V., Tucker, D.J. and House, R.J. (1986) "Organizational legitimacy and the liability of newness," *Administrative Science Quarterly,* 31 (2): 171–93.

Suchman, M.A. (1995) "Managing legitimacy: strategic and institutional approaches," *Academy of Management Review,* 20 (3): 571–610.

Sud, M., VanSandt, C. and Baugous, A. (2009) "Social entrepreneurship: the role of institutions," *Journal of Business Ethics*, 1 (85): 201–16.

Suddaby, R. and Greenwood, R. (2005) "Rhetorical strategies of legitimacy," *Administrative Science Quarterly*, 50 (1): 35–67.

Thornton, P. (2004), *Markets from Culture: Institutional Logics and Organizational Decisions in Higher Education Publishing.* Stanford, CA: Stanford University Press.

Vian, T., Mccoy, K., Richards, S.C., Connelly, P. and Feeley, F. *et al.* (2007) "Corporate social responsibility in global health: the Pfizer Global Health Fellows International Volunteering Program," *Human Resource Planning*, 30 (1): 30–5.

Vurro, C., Dacin, M.T. and Perrini, F. (2010) "Institutional antecedents of partnering for social change: how institutional logics shape cross-sector social partnerships," *Journal of Business Ethics*, 94 (Supplement 1): 39–53.

Waddock, S. and Post, J.E. (1991) "Social entrepreneurs and catalytic change," *Public Administration Review*, 51 (5): 393–401.

Waddock, S.A. and Smith, N.C. (2000) "Relationships: the real challenge of corporate global citizenship," *Business and Society*, 105 (1): 47–62.

Webb, J.W., Kistruck, G.M., Ireland, R.D. and Ketchen, Jr., D.J. *et al.* (2010) "The entrepreneurship process in base of the pyramid markets: the case of multinational enterprise/nongovernment organization alliances," *Entrepreneurship Theory and Practice*, 34 (3): 555–81.

Westley, F. and Vredenburg, H. (1997) "Interorganizational collaboration and the preservation of global biodiversity," *Organization Science*, 8 (4): 381–403.

Wijen, F. and Ansari, S. (2007) "Overcoming inaction through collective institutional entrepreneurship: insights from regime theory," *Organization Studies*, 28 (7): 1079–00.

Wood, D.J. (1991) "Corporate social performance revisited," *Academy of Management Review*, 16 (4): 691–718.

Zucker, L. (1991) "The role of institutionalization in cultural persistence,." in Powell, W.W. and DiMaggio, P. (eds) *The New Institutionalism in Organizational Analysis.* Chicago, IL: University of Chicago Press: 83–107.

16

TOWARDS A NEW THEORY OF THE FIRM

The collaborative enterprise

Antonio Tencati and Laszlo Zsolnai

Introduction

Several of the previous chapters have underlined the essential role that cross-sector partnerships can play to foster the social good (see Chapter 1 and Part A of the book). But is this enough or, to better explain the point, in the current context, are partnerships really able to change the situation for the better?

The world is facing a multiple (that is, financial, economic, social, environmental) crisis that clearly shows the unsustainability of the current, global pattern of development. After around thirty years of dominance (Friedman, 1970; Porter, 1979; Rappaport, 1986), the still prevailing mainstream business model, characterized by a narrow focus on monetary results, short-termism and a disruptive competitive approach which benefits few (especially financial investors and top managers) at the expense of many (including society as a whole, local communities, ecosystems and ecosystem services, and future generations), is under attack (Castells, 2012; Hardt and Negri, 2012; *The Economist,* 2011; *Time,* 2011).

What is happening challenges also the academy. In particular, alternative approaches are badly needed. In fact, the mainstream theory of the firm, on which much of the partnerships literature is premised and which had and still has a deep influence on real business, public regulations and market functioning, propagates a *negativistic view of human nature*, where agents are always self-interested and want to maximize their own profit or utility without caring for others. Their interactions are based on competition only and their criterion of success is growth measured in monetary terms. Mainstream business organizations generate vicious circles in which agents expect the worst from others and act accordingly (Birkinshaw and Piramal, 2005; Ghoshal, 2005).

If we intend to contribute to the construction of a better world and, so, to make partnerships really agents of change, we need to advance a different paradigm based on a genuine collaborative attitude, where cross-sector partnerships can play a crucial role (Perrini and Vurro, 2010). *Collaborative enterprises* (Tencati and Zsolnai, 2009, 2010) value and develop relationships with their stakeholders and try to generate long-lasting "win-win" solutions. Thus, they display real care about others and themselves and aim to create fitting (social, cultural, economic, institutional, environmental, and so on) values for all the participants in their ecosystems. Therefore, their criterion of success is mutually satisfying relationships with stakeholders and their performance is assessed according to a multiple bottom line perspective (Perrini and Tencati, 2006).

In this perspective, it is also possible to reimagine cross-sector social partnerships. They should overcome a narrow and instrumental view, where they are considered, especially by some firms, a useful tool to get or, sometimes, "buy" consensus and pursue self-interested goals (Perrini and Vurro, 2010: 353–4), to unleash their full potential of change: players (i.e., companies, civil society organizations, and public authorities) with different backgrounds and kinds of expertise work together to advance the common good.

In Table 16.1 the main features of the mainstream and collaborative enterprises are summarized.

TABLE 16.1 Mainstream enterprises versus collaborative enterprises

	Mainstream enterprises	*Collaborative enterprises*
Basic motive	Self-interest	Care about others and themselves
Main goal	Maximizing profit or shareholder value	Creating values for all the participants in the network
Criterion of success	Growth in money terms	Mutually beneficial relationships with the stakeholders

Source: Tencati and Zsolnai (2012).

Elements of a new theory of the firm

The skeptics may think that the collaborative premises of the new view of the firm are misleading. Recent contributions and discoveries in economics, behavioral and social sciences, and biology suggest that this is not the case.

The benefits of collaboration

The world-famous economist Robert Frank challenges the central view of the current prevailing economic models that competitive pressure makes it naïve to expect that people (and organizations) restrain themselves for the common good (Frank 2004). Economic theory suggests that human agents are willing to make sacrifices for the common good only if society penalizes them for doing otherwise. Based on both empirical and theoretical results Frank shows the emergence of prosocial behavior independent of external rewards and sanctions.

One of the main arguments Frank develops is that people who are intrinsically motivated to adhere to ethical norms often prosper in competitive environments. It is a paradoxical phenomenon that people can often promote their own narrow ends more effectively by abandoning the direct pursuit of self-interest (Frank, 2004; Kay, 2010).

According to Frank there is a closer link between rationality and morality than many economists believe. A rational individual will often fail to achieve his or her material ends if the moral emotions are missing from his or her character. An interesting corollary is that the ultimate victims of opportunistic behavior are often those people who practice it.

Frank also shows that socially responsible firms can survive in competitive environments because social responsibility can bring substantial benefits for firms. So it might be good business to sacrifice in the name of ethical concerns.

Frank introduces five distinct types of cases where socially responsible organizations are rewarded for the higher cost of caring (Frank, 2004: 67).

1 Opportunistic behavior can be avoided between owners and managers.
2 Moral satisfaction induces employees to work more for lower salaries.
3 High quality new employees can be recruited.
4 Customers' loyalty can be gained.
5 The trust of subcontractors can be established.

Caring organizations are rewarded for the higher costs of their socially responsible behavior by their ability to form commitments among owners, managers, and employees and to establish trust relationships with customers and subcontractors.

Positive psychology and the emergence of the Homo reciprocans

A relatively new branch of psychology called *positive psychology*, initiated by Martin Seligman and Mihaly Csikszentmihalyi, studies the strengths and virtues that allow individuals, communities, and societies to flourish (Positive Psychology Center, 2007; Seligman, 2011; Seligman and Csikszentmihalyi, 2000).

Positive psychology focuses on three different routes to happiness (Seligman, 2002; Seligman et al., 2005):

1 Positive emotion and pleasure (the pleasant life). This is a hedonic approach, which deals with increasing positive emotions as part of normal and healthy life.
2 Engagement (the engaged life). This constituent of happiness is not merely hedonic but regards the pursuit of gratification (Seligman et al., 2004). In order to achieve this goal, a person should involve himself/herself fully by drawing upon "... character strengths such as creativity, social intelligence, sense of humour, perseverance, and an appreciation of beauty and excellence" (Seligman et al., 2004: 1380).

3   Meaning (the meaningful life). This calls for a deeper involvement of an individual, using the character strengths to belong to and serve something larger and more permanent than the self: "something such as knowledge, goodness, family, community, politics, justice or a higher spiritual power" (Seligman *et al.*, 2004: 1380).

What we need in business and economics is a commitment to helping individuals and organizations to flourish by the use of their strengths to increase and sustain the well-being of others and themselves.

From this point of view, one of the most important recent developments in the behavioral and social sciences is the emergence of the so-called *Homo reciprocans* model which presents a major alternative to the *Homo oeconomicus* model. The *Homo oeconomicus* model suggests that agents are exclusively self-interested and always maximize their utility functions. Overwhelming empirical evidence shows that this is a rather unrealistic description of human behavior (Frank, 2004, 2011; Kahneman, 2011). The model has also been criticized on various normative grounds (Zsolnai, 2002).

The emerging model of Homo reciprocans can be summarized as follows:

> [A] majority of individuals approach strategic interactions involving coordi-
> nation problems with a propensity to cooperate, they respond to the
> cooperation of others by maintaining or increasing their level of cooperation,
> and they respond to defection on the part of others by retaliating against the
> offenders, even at a cost to themselves, and even when they cannot reasonably
> expect future personal gains from such retaliation.
>
> (*Bowles* et al., *1997: 4*)

This approach is consistent with many empirical observations: "people do produce public goods, they do observe normative restraints on the pursuit of self-interest (even when there is nobody watching), and they will put themselves to a lot of trouble to hurt rulebreakers" (Shalizi, 1999).

Insights from evolutionary biology

The crucial importance of the attitude to collaboration is also confirmed by the latest developments in evolutionary biology.

One of the most challenging issues in evolutionary biology is the so-called "paradox of collateral altruistic behaviour" (Wilson, 2005: 159; see also Hölldobler and Wilson, 2009), "that is, when some individuals subordinate their own interests and those of their immediate offspring in order to serve the interests of a larger group beyond offspring."

By observing social behavior of ants and wasps, it seems clearly evident that colonies with altruistic workers "are favored by their superior ability to create and defend nest sites that are stable over extended periods of time, allowing them refuges from which to forage for food." "[T]he critical binding force of colony evolution appears to be ecological natural selection operating at the level of the colony, a level that comprises both colonies versus individuals, and colonies versus other colonies" (Wilson, 2005: 163).

Therefore, not only competition but also collaboration seems to be a crucial force in evolutionary dynamics thanks to the selection forces operating at level of genes, cells, organisms, and groups. That has important implications for humans too. In a recent article Desmond Morris underlines: "In our early evolution, one trait we developed was to survive through co-operation. That quality is built into our genes and can be strengthened genetically as time passes" (Morris, 2012).

Commons and collaboration: beyond market and hierarchy

A good example of the collaborative attitude is provided by the traditional governance practices in the common-pool resources field.

Usually, in order to address the "tragedy of the commons" (Hardin, 1968) the options proposed by the mainstream economics have been privatization or state management with, in the recent decades, a prevailing preference for the market rules.

However, thanks to the extensive and innovative work carried out by the late Elinor Ostrom, awarded with the Nobel Prize in economic sciences in 2009, there is abundant evidence from all over the world that an effective management of the commons can be assured by a polycentric approach rooted in community-based collaborative governance efforts (Nagendra and Ostrom, 2012; see also Ostrom, 1990). The robust, self-organized, and self-governed initiatives demonstrate that collaboration works as a viable, feasible, and desirable alternative to foster really sustainable patterns of production and consumption.

Implications for research

The reflections presented in this chapter are an initial contribution to a research path aimed at reframing the current and prevailing assumptions in economics and business practices. The pivotal idea is that we need to go beyond a disruptive and, after all, self-defeating concept of competition to make collaboration, responsibility, sustainability and a more comprehensive view of the business role and purposes the pillars of an alternative view of management. And it is clear that, in this perspective, the role played by cross-sector social partnerships (Seitanidi, 2010; Seitanidi and Crane, 2009; Seitanidi and Lindgreen, 2010; Seitanidi *et al.*, 2010) is fundamental.

In more detail, the collaborative model opens new research avenues at different levels:

- Individual (individual level).
- Firm (micro level).
- Districts, clusters, industries, and sectors (meso level).
- The economy as a whole (macro level).

Individual level

The emerging paradigm represented by the Homo reciprocans is a major challenge to the mainstream competitive model. We need further studies and empirical support to revise and replace the current behavioral bases of economics. A new positive vision of the human being as a relational and prosocial individual is strongly needed. Psychology, anthropology, and biology (see, for example, Tomasello, 2009), neuroeconomics (Camerer et al., 2005) could provide important contributions to deeply revise the currently dominating negativistic view of the human being (Ghoshal, 2005).

That opens important opportunities for research in the partnerships field. In the current mainstream, cross-sector partnerships have been generally seen as a lucky exception to the prevailing competitive attitude. Furthermore, if forms of collaboration are possible these can be developed especially among similar players, that is, in the business arena (Dyer and Singh, 1998). But if the real nature of persons is relational, then this perspective provides new bases to the feasibility, development, and spread of partnerships for the social good.

Micro level

The firm is the main focus and the starting point of the collaborative enterprise agenda. The current structural crisis and the related sustainability challenges call for innovative business and managerial models. And, as many examples show all around the world (Tencati and Zsolnai, 2009, 2010, 2012), alternative practices are successful. Creating values for the different constituencies thanks to innovation, broad stakeholder engagement and partnerships, and more balanced and democratic mechanisms of governance is the characteristic of the most advanced enterprises. These dispositions also make them more resilient and long-lasting.

Therefore, with regard to the research needs, it is important to study the enabling conditions in terms of institutions, culture, values, managerial approaches, and so on (Campbell, 2007) that allow collaborative enterprises to flourish. Furthermore, we think that especially the investigations on small and medium-sized companies could provide interesting and widespread examples of progressive, locally-based, and community-rooted practices (Spence, 2007). Enabling conditions and practices can be also the focus of the analyses regarding the partnerships in order to understand whether and how firms (and especially small and medium-sized enterprises) consider this tool as a viable, shared, and mutual way of behaving and interacting.

Meso level

The collaborative model considers the firm as part of a broader ecosystem, that is, a stakeholder network of which the firm is one of the components. Therefore, the study of these aggregations, especially at community level, becomes critical and calls for a renewed attention.

In particular, industrial districts (Becattini, 1990, 2004) and clusters (Porter, 1998a;

Sölvell, 2009) are based on the symbiosis between the economic dimension and the social one. In these forms of organization the economic activities foster the local development (Becattini *et al.,* 2003) and, in parallel, the social capital (Bourdieu, 1986; Putnam, 1993, 2000). Social capital which connects local communities and nested firms is one of the most important drivers to explain the long-term success of the involved enterprises (Porter, 1998b; Russo and Perrini, 2010). Furthermore, broader networks emerge at the industry and sector level to address sustainability and competitive issues (Bower *et al.*, 2011).

Therefore, organized networks (Rossiter, 2006), which can include also cross-sector partnerships, are a very important unit of analysis to investigate and understand the current and future dynamics at the social and market level. With regard to this point, according to Ronfeldt after tribes, hierarchical institutions, and markets, collaborative networks are the emerging form of organization, which affects the current stage of social evolution. "Enabled by the digital information-technology revolution, this form is only now coming into its own, so far strengthening civil society more than other realms" (Ronfeldt, 2009).

Macro level

The current pattern of global development is economically, socially, and ecologically unbearable. This calls for enlarged, more participating models of governance to address the sustainability challenge (Crane, 2010), and for the construction of decentralized community-based initiatives connected in global networks, which could constitute feasible and fitting alternatives to the global mainstream.

With regard to this issue, it is important to point out the institutionalization of global action networks such as Global Compact, Global Water Partnership, Forest Stewardship Council, Marine Stewardship Council, Global Reporting Initiative, Microcredit Summit Campaign, International Federation of Organic Agriculture Movements, Fair Labor Association, and Slow Food with Terra Madre which operate in both environmental and social realms (Glasbergen, 2010; Tencati and Zsolnai, 2012; Waddell, 2011). They can be described as "civil society initiated multi-stakeholder arrangements that aim to fulfil a leadership role for systemic change in global governance for sustainable development" (Glasbergen, 2010: 130). In these innovative forms of cross-sector partnership, collaborative efforts are carried on jointly by governments/public institutions, firms, and civil society organizations. Therefore, the collaborative model is gaining ground in the political arena with solutions trying to overcome the conventional public-private partnerships.

Furthermore, the collaborative networks enable local communities to become innovative players on the global scene. Thus, it is crucial to study the emergence of new patterns of governance where coalitions of global players and global alliances of local actors interact to address disequilibria in economic, social, and ecological conditions. A deeper analysis of collaborative models of governance is also needed when they arise to manage the paths of development at local, national and regional levels (Albareda *et al.*, 2008).

Managerial implications

The collaborative enterprise perspective implies a new vision of management.

First of all, it is important to recover the original meaning of the word *compete* that is "to seek together" (from the Latin *cum petere*) (see, on this topic, the Group of Lisbon, 1994). Competition cannot be seen as an end in itself because it leads to detrimental effects on nature, society, and future generations (Zsolnai, 2009), and business should respect the ecological and social limits in which it operates, and embed its activities in the natural and social systems (Zsolnai, 2006).

Thus we need to understand that:

- the real main purpose of the firms is to serve others by providing fitting goods and services;
- markets should be engines for promoting the common good and not a way to reward greedy attitudes;
- treating enterprises as money making machines undermines their license to operate and reduce their real effectiveness (Kay, 2004).

What we are saying here is not that collaboration is a sort of panacea. We recognize that sometimes working together could be hard, frustrating, and not so successful. But because of their crystal clear unsustainability for sure we need to go beyond the current managerial paradigms based on a competitive view of the world and of the life. A collaborative, careful, and responsible attitude in doing business is required. And this also calls for a new vision of partnerships where they are regarded as one of the most important tools to foster advanced and fitting behaviors and policies.

The social and cultural conditions are changing fast and deeply: a general perception is emerging that "a different, more collaborative type of leadership" is needed, "believing multi-sector collaborations will likely provide the best opportunity for future progress on sustainable development" (The Regeneration Roadmap, 2012: 2). And, in fact, just before Rio+20, several cross-sector initiatives have been announced and launched, like the Green Industry Platform, "a global high-level multi-stakeholder partnership intended to act as a forum for catalyzing, mobilizing and mainstreaming action on Green Industry around the world" (UNIDO, 2012).

The same Outcome Document of the Rio+20 Conference recognizes the role of partnerships:

> [T]he implementation of sustainable development will depend on the active engagement of both the public and the private sectors ... [T]he active participation of the private sector can contribute to the achievement of sustainable development, including through the important tool of public-private partnerships. We support national regulatory and policy frameworks that enable business and industry to advance sustainable development initiatives, taking into account the importance of corporate social responsibility. We call on the

private sector to engage in responsible business practices, such as those promoted by the United Nations Global Compact.

(*United Nations Conference on Sustainable Development 2012: Paragraph 46: 8*)

Economic players need to go beyond the dominant competitive paradigm to build progressive economic practices where collaboration for the common good is the key driver and the cross-sector partnerships are a fundamental tool to achieve sustainable patterns of development. Change is possible and feasible, and enterprises that take the lead will thrive and flourish.

Questions for reflection

1 To what extent is the competitive paradigm based on shareholder value really sustainable?
2 What is a collaborative enterprise?
3 Does the collaborative enterprise necessarily call for a new theory of the firm and a new research agenda?
4 What are the implications of the collaborative approach for business and managers?
5 What role can cross-sector social partnerships play in a collaborative perspective?
6 Is the idea of Homo reciprocans a good basis for designing more effective and successful partnerships?

References

Albareda, L., Lozano, J.M., Tencati, A., Midttun, A. and Perrini, F. (2008) "The Changing Role of Governments in Corporate Social Responsibility: Drivers and Responses," *Business Ethics: A European Review*, 17: 347–63.

Becattini, G. (1990) "The Marshallian Industrial District as a Socio-Economic Notion," in F. Pyke, G. Becattini and W. Sengenberger (eds) *Industrial Districts and Inter-Firm Co-operation in Italy*, Geneva: International Institute for Labour Studies.

Becattini, G. (2004) *Industrial Districts: A New Approach to Industrial Change*, Cheltenham: Edward Elgar.

Becattini, G., Bellandi, M., Dei Ottati, G. and Sforzi, F. (2003) *From Industrial Districts to Local Development: An Itinerary of Research*, Cheltenham: Edward Elgar.

Birkinshaw, J. and Piramal, G. (eds) (2005) *Sumantra Ghoshal on Management: A Force for Good*, Harlow: Prentice Hall.

Bourdieu, P. (1986) "The Forms of Capital," in J.G. Richardson (ed.), *Handbook of Theory and Research for the Sociology of Education*, Westport, CT: Greenwood Press.

Bower, J.L., Leonard, H.B. and Paine, L.S. (2011) *Capitalism at Risk: Rethinking the Role of Business*, Boston, MA: Harvard Business Review Press.

Bowles, S., Boyd, R., Fehr, E. and Gintis, H. (1997) "*Homo Reciprocans*: A Research Initiative on the Origins, Dimensions, and Policy Implications of Reciprocal Fairness," 7 June. Available at: www.umass.edu/preferen/gintis/homo.pdf (accessed 4 March 2010).

Camerer, C., Loewenstein, G. and Prelec, D. (2005) "Neuroeconomics: How Neuroscience Can Inform Economics," *Journal of Economic Literature*, 43: 9–64.

Campbell, J.L. (2007) "Why Would Corporations Behave in Socially Responsible Ways? An Institutional Theory of Corporate Social Responsibility," *Academy of Management Review*, 32: 946–67.

Castells, M. (2012) *Networks of Outrage and Hope: Social Movements in the Internet Age*, Cambridge: Polity Press.

Crane, A. (2010) "From governance to Governance: On Blurring Boundaries," *Journal of Business Ethics*, 94 (Supplement 1): 17–19.

Dyer, J.H. and Singh H. (1998) "The Relational View: Cooperative Strategy and Sources of Interorganizational Competitive Advantage," *Academy of Management Review*, 23: 660–79.

Economist (The) (2011) "Rage Against the Machine," *The Economist*, 22 October: 13.

Frank, R.H. (2004) *What Price the Moral High Ground? Ethical Dilemmas in Competitive Environments*, Princeton, NJ: Princeton University Press.

Frank, R.H. (2011) *The Darwin Economy: Liberty, Competition, and the Common Good*, Princeton, NJ: Princeton University Press.

Friedman, M. (1970) "The Social Responsibility of Business Is To Increase Its Profits," *New York Times Magazine*, 13 September; reprinted in L.P. Hartman (ed.) (2005) *Perspectives in Business Ethics*, 3rd edn. New York: McGraw-Hill.

Ghoshal, S. (2005) "Bad Management Theories Are Destroying Good Management Practices," *Academy of Management Learning and Education*, 4: 75–91.

Glasbergen, P. (2010) "Global Action Networks: Agents for Collective Action," *Global Environmental Change*, 20: 130–41.

Group of Lisbon (The) (1994) *Limits to Competition*, Lisbon: Gulbenkian Foundation; international edition: Group of Lisbon (The) (1995). *Limits to Competition*, Cambridge, MA: MIT Press.

Hardin, G. (1968) "The Tragedy of the Commons," *Science*, 162: 1243–8.

Hardt, M. and Negri, A. (2012) *Declaration*, New York: Argo Navis Author Services.

Hölldobler, B. and Wilson, E.O. (2009) *The Superorganism: The Beauty, Elegance, and Strangeness of Insect Societies*, New York: Norton.

Kahneman, D. (2011) *Thinking, Fast and Slow*, New York: Farrar, Straus & Giroux.

Kay, J. (2004) *Everlasting Light Bulbs. How Economics Illuminates the World*, London: The Erasmus Press.

Kay, J. (2010) *Obliquity: Why Our Goals Are Best Achieved Indirectly*, New York: Penguin.

Morris, D. (2012) "The Age of the Urban Ape," *The Telegraph*, 4 May. Available at: www.telegraph.co.uk/science/9245998/The-age-of-the-urban-ape.html# (accessed 26 June 2012).

Nagendra, H. and Ostrom, E. (2012) "Polycentric Governance of Multifunctional Forested Landscapes," *International Journal of the Commons*. Available at: www.thecommonsjournal.org/index.php/ijc/article/view/321/270 (accessed 27 June 2012).

Ostrom, E. (1990) *Governing the Commons: The Evolution of Institutions for Collective Action*, Cambridge: Cambridge University Press.

Perrini, F. and Tencati, A. (2006) "Sustainability and Stakeholder Management: The Need for New Corporate Performance Evaluation and Reporting Systems," *Business Strategy and the Environment*, 15: 296–308.

Perrini, F. and Vurro, C. (2010) "Collaborative Social Entrepreneurship," in A. Tencati and L. Zsolnai (eds) *The Collaborative Enterprise: Creating Values for a Sustainable World*, Oxford: Peter Lang AG, International Academic Publishers.

Porter, M.E. (1979) "How Competitive Forces Shape Strategy," *Harvard Business Review*, 57 (2): 137–45.

Porter, M.E. (1998a) *The Competitive Advantage of Nations*, new edn. New York: Palgrave Macmillan.

Porter, M.E. (1998b) "Clusters and the New Economics of Competition," *Harvard Business Review*, 76(6): 77–90.

Positive Psychology Center (2007) Available at: www.ppc.sas.upenn.edu/ (accessed 4 March 2010).

Putnam, R.D. (1993) *Making Democracy Work: Civic Traditions in Modern Italy*, Princeton, NJ: Princeton University Press.

Putnam, R.D. (2000) *Bowling Alone: The Collapse and Revival of American Community*, New York: Simon & Schuster.

Rappaport, A. (1986) *Creating Shareholder Value: The New Standard for Business Performance*, New York: Free Press.

Regeneration Roadmap (The) (2012) *Down to Business. Leading at Rio+20 and Beyond.* Available at: http://theregenerationroadmap.com/files/reports/TRR_Down-To-Business.pdf (accessed 30 August 2013).

Ronfeldt, D. (2009) "Overview of Social Evolution (Past, Present, and Future) in TIMN Terms," 25 February. Available at: http://twotheories.blogspot.com/2009/02/overview-of-social-evolution-past.html (accessed 4 March 2010).

Rossiter, N. (2006) *Organized Networks: Media Theory, Creative Labour, New Institutions*, Rotterdam: NAi Publications.

Russo, A. and Perrini, F. (2010) "Investigating Stakeholder Theory and Social Capital: CSR in Large Firms and SMEs," *Journal of Business Ethics*, 91: 207–21.

Seitanidi M.M. (2010) *The Politics of Partnerships: A Critical Examination of Nonprofit-Business Partnerships*, Dordrecht: Springer.

Seitanidi M.M. and Crane A. (2009) "Implementing CSR through Partnerships: Understanding the Selection, Design and Institutionalisation of Nonprofit-Business Partnerships," *Journal of Business Ethics*, 85 (Supplement 2): 413–429.

Seitanidi, M.M., Koufopoulos, D.N. and Palmer, P. (2010) "Partnership Formation for Change: Indicators for Transformative Potential in Cross Sector Social Partnerships," *Journal of Business Ethics*, 94 (Supplement 1): 139–161.

Seitanidi M.M. and Lindgreen A. (2010) "Editorial: Cross-Sector Social Interactions," *Journal of Business Ethics*, 94 (Supplement 1): 1–7.

Seligman, M.E.P. (2002) *Authentic Happiness: Using the New Positive Psychology to Realize Your Potential for Lasting Fulfillment*, New York: Free Press.

Seligman, M.E.P. (2011) *Flourish: A Visionary New Understanding of Happiness and Well-being*, New York: Free Press.

Seligman, M.E.P. and Csikszentmihalyi, M. (2000) "Positive Psychology: An Introduction," *American Psychologist*, 55: 5–14.

Seligman, M.E.P., Parks, A.C. and Steen, T. (2004) "A Balanced Psychology and a Full Life," *Philosophical Transactions of the Royal Society B: Biological Sciences*, 359: 1379–81.

Seligman, M.E.P., Steen, T.A., Park, N. and Peterson, C. (2005) "Positive Psychology Progress: Empirical Validation of Interventions," *American Psychologist*, 60: 410–421.

Shalizi, C.R. (1999) "*Homo Reciprocans*. Political Economy and Cultural Evolution," *Santa Fe Institute Bulletin* 14(2): 16–20. Available at: http://cscs.umich.edu/~crshalizi/bulletin/homo-reciprocans.html (accessed 4 March 2010).

Sölvell, Ö. (2009). *Clusters – Balancing Evolutionary and Constructive Forces*, (2nd edn.), Stockholm: Ivory Tower Publishers. Available at: www.cluster-research.org/ (accessed 29 June 2012).

Spence, L.J. (2007) "CSR and Small Business in a European Policy Context: The Five "C"s of CSR and Small Business Research Agenda 2007," *Business and Society Review*, 112: 533–52.

Tencati, A. and Zsolnai, L. (2009) "The Collaborative Enterprise," *Journal of Business Ethics*, 85: 367–76.

Tencati, A. and Zsolnai, L. (eds) (2010) *The Collaborative Enterprise: Creating Values for a Sustainable World*, Oxford: Peter Lang AG, International Academic Publishers.

Tencati, A. and Zsolnai, L. (2012) "Collaborative Enterprise and Sustainability: The Case of Slow Food," *Journal of Business Ethics*, 110: 345–54.

Time (2011) "2011 Person of the Year: The Protester," *Time*, 178 (25), 26 December.

Tomasello, M. (2009) *Why We Cooperate*, Cambridge, MA: MIT Press.

UNIDO (United Nations Industrial Development Organization) (2012) "UNIDO Launches the Green Industry Platform at Rio+20". Available at: www.unido.org/index. php?id=1002609 (accessed 29 June 2012).

United Nations Conference on Sustainable Development (2012) *Outcome Document of the Conference: The Future We Want*. Available at: www.uncsd2012.org/thefuturewewant. html (accessed 29 June 2012).

Waddell, S. (2011) *Global Action Networks: Creating Our Future Together*, Basingstoke: Palgrave Macmillan.

Wilson, E.O. (2005) "Kin Selection as the Key to Altruism: Its Rise and Fall," *Social Research*, 72: 159–66.

Zsolnai, L. (2002) "The Moral Economic Man," in L. Zsolnai (ed.) *Ethics in the Economy. Handbook of Business Ethics*, Oxford: Peter Lang AG, European Academic Publishers.

Zsolnai, L. (2006) "Extended Stakeholder Theory," *Society and Business Review*, 1: 37–44.

Zsolnai, L. (2009) "Nature, Society and Future Generations," in H.-C. de Bettignies and F. Lépineux (eds) *Business, Globalization and the Common Good*, Oxford: Peter Lang AG, International Academic Publishers.

PART D

Reimagining social partnerships

Perspectives on practice

17

CROSS-SECTOR/CROSS-BOUNDARY COLLABORATION

Making a difference through practice

Sandra Waddock

Cross-sector collaboration has been growing as a phenomenon since "public-private partnerships" were first popularized in the early 1980s as a potential means of resolving intractable social problems like primary and secondary education, economic development, and environmental clean ups, to name a few issues (e.g. Austin, 1998; Waddock, 1988, 1989, 1991; Gricar and Brown, 1981; Waddell and Brown, 1997). Today, we can find such partnerships in a wide variety of arenas, ranging from education to sustainability to microfinance, with some even suggesting that we are moving to a "partnership society" (Googins, 2000). Many of these collaborations represent laudable efforts to bridge between profit-making enterprises and those that do social good (Seitanidi, 2008), bringing together business people with business-oriented ideas with social and ecological activists of all stripes, who have a different set of interests, values, and skills.

Bridges from theory to practice are crucially important in the realization of successful cross-sector partnerships. In the contributions that follow you will see short comments from internationally-recognized contributors who take a wide range of perspectives and the role and importance of cross-sector collaboration in practice from around the world. These perspectives include comments from Hadley Archer, vice president of Strategic Partnerships, WWF Canada and Paul Uys, Vice President, Sustainable Seafood, Loblaw Companies Limited Canada; Barbara Nijhuis, an independent profit/charity expert currently based in Amsterdam; Sarah Winchester, Deputy Director of Fundraising, Princes Trust, UK; Surinder Hundal, Owner/Director, Rippleseed Consulting, and Director, Partnership Brokering Association, UK; Lucian J. Hudson, Director of Communications, Open University in the United Kingdom; Steve Waddell, principal, Networking Action, US; and Simon Zadek, Visiting Scholar at Tsinghua School of Economics and Management, Senior Fellow at the Global Green Growth Institute, Senior Advisor at the International Institute for Sustainable Development, the founder and previously the Chief Executive of AccountAbility.

The types of enterprises that constitute cross-sector collaboration are virtually endless. For example, there are now initiatives within the workplace for greater collaboration across functions, and even calls for collaborative processes to replace old hierarchical and conflict-ridden ways of working (e.g. in labor-management relationships, in business-government or business-civil society relationships and practices). Indeed, the Boston Foundation recently launched a new effort called "Toward a New Grand Bargain," which argues for more collaborative labor-management relationships, particularly in the realm of education (Bluestone and Kochan, 2011). Business and government partner in the US Park Service (Leigh, 2005) and US Fish and Wildlife Service,[1] among other places.

Further, in the absence of any kind of global governance mechanism to deal with the impacts of globalization and humanity on the natural and other ecologies as well as other types of problems, there have arisen numerous initiatives that Waddell (2003, 2011) terms global action networks (GANs). GANs bring together actors from multiple sectors to work collaboratively and across sector boundaries on issues in the public policy domain for which no adequate governmental structures exist, often on planetary scale issues. Examples include forest and marine stewardship (e.g. the Forest Stewardship Council and the Marine Stewardship Council), corporate responsibility and transparency (e.g. the UN Global Compact and the Global Reporting Initiative), or disease (e.g. the Global Fund to Fight AIDS, Tuberculosis and Malaria), to name a few.

There are also new initiatives within existing enterprises that break down old distinctions (e.g. social ventures within large corporations that aim for long-term profitability and profit-making initiatives within non-governmental organizations and not-for-profit enterprises to help stabilize revenue flows). Such linkages can potentially provide for disruptive social innovation (Christensen et al., 2006) and can create what has been called collaborative value (Austin and Seitanidi, 2012a, 2012b). Some of these enterprises might not exactly consider themselves, at least at first glance, as cross-sector collaborations; however, their mixed purposes and goals place them squarely in the realm of cross-sector social interaction.

Collapsing boundaries between sectors, functions, and even organization purposes (e.g. Seitanidi, 2010) have created not only a great need for collaboration skills of all sorts, but also an array of new and emerging types of enterprise. Not only do we have traditional boundary-spanners called public-private partnership or cross-sector partnerships (see Austin and Seitanidi, 2012a,b, for a comprehensive review), but we are witnessing the development of new forms of enterprise "born" with a multiple bottom line orientation (e.g. social entrepreneurships, B Corporations, for-benefit corporations), and the rapid emergence into the spotlight of multiple bottom-line enterprises of all sorts – bottom of the pyramid facing enterprises (Prahalad, 2004; Hart, 2005; Prahalad and Hammond, 2002), socially entrepreneurially organizations with both financial and social or ecological goals (Waddock and McIntosh, 2011), benefit or "B" corporations whose purposes and corporate charters bridge the social, ecological, and financial,[2] and large corporations, particularly multinationals, engaging in pro-social or pro-ecological activities that they also hope will provide a future source of revenues (Waddock and McIntosh, 2011).

In addition to the cross-sector partnerships and multi-sector collaborations that have gained popularity in recent years, what have also evolved recently have been numerous new types of enterprises that within rapidly diminishing boundaries attempt to create both social (or ecological) or what can broadly be called "for benefit" purposes, often combined with wealth-generating strategies. Inherently crossing sector boundaries, sometimes functional, and sometimes even the management-worker boundary, these efforts are collaborative by definition. Frequently oriented toward improving the world (or making a positive difference), such enterprises raise many questions related to their capacity to actually solve the difficult problems on which they focus.

All of this activity is part of a phenomenon of change that my collaborator Malcolm McIntosh and I (Waddock and McIntosh, 2011) have called SEE Change – incipient efforts to make a transition to a sustainable enterprise economy in the face of an intractable, highly bureaucratized, and massively scaled set of institutions and enterprises. Yet all of it is fraught with problems of implementation, problems of complexity, and problems associated with doing things differently, simply because the nature of the issues, markets, goals, and purposes of these enterprises are relatively novel – and because frequently the issues with which they are contending are "wicked." Wicked problems are, by their nature, poorly formulated, have confusing or conflicting goals and purposes, multiple stakeholders with different perspectives and values related to the nature and potential solutions of the problem, and indeterminate outcomes (Rittel *et al.*, 1973; Churchman, 1967).

In all of these activities, as is notable in cross-sector collaborations of all sorts, there is an underlying issue of rapidly falling sector, organizational, and even functional boundaries. This collapse of boundaries is combined with a demand for more collaborative forms of leadership – not just at the top of the enterprise, but at all levels. Since wicked problems are increasingly faced today both inside and outside enterprise, and since they do not lend themselves to neat solutions on which all can agree, the growth of interest in collaborative multi-sector interactions to deal with them is not surprising. These same collapsing boundaries also create the need for new skills of management and implementation in collaborative enterprise.

Design, implementation, and leadership issues

Wicked problems create a need to think in new ways, to understand and integrate multiple perspectives, and to work across functions, organizations, or even sectors. Indeed, they demand a capacity for systems thinking and understanding how change processes actually work in practice, which in turn requires a certain degree of sensitivity to human behavior and interactions. Because of their complex, dynamic, and indeterminate nature (Rittel and Weber, 1973), wicked problems require partners with very different perspectives to come together and create some sort of common ground – often a common vision (Waddock, 1988) that somehow abstracts the focal issue and pushes it toward a set of goals or purposes on which diverse collaborators can agree.

Figuring out who should be involved in the collaboration is an important first step – a process called selection by Seitanidi and Crane (2009; also Austin and Seitanidi, 2012b). Sometimes the selection of partners is relatively easy because for one reason or another they have already come to the table or because it is obvious who must be involved. At other times, a complex process of stakeholder analysis is needed to ensure that relevant parties are brought together. A general principle of involvement is to include (representatives of) all stakeholders with significant interest in and perspectives on the particular issue at hand, so that relevant points of view can be included (Waddock, 1988; Austin and Seitanidi, 2012b).

Because the problems associated with collaborative enterprise tend to be wicked, determining the focus, goals, and how the enterprise is to be designed (e.g. Seitanidi and Crane, 2009; Austin and Seitanidi, 2012b) is crucial. Underlying such initiatives tends to be some vision of how things will be better (Waddock, 1988) if the collaboration works, particularly if collaborators allow for adaptation to circumstances (Seitanidi, 2008). But the wicked nature of the problems engaged makes coming to some sort of common understanding – common ground – about goals and design difficult at best, particularly when stakeholder perspectives are widely divergent. Abstracting to higher levels of analysis and attempting to figure out what end goals or values (cf., Burns, 1978) participants share is one way of bringing stakeholders into a degree of agreement about what needs to be done and how. As Seitanidi and Crane (2009) point out, there is likely to be a lot of experimentation (or trial and error) at this stage of any collaboration's development as efforts to find out what works among this particular group advance.

Part of the reason for all of the experimentation in the design stage of collaboration is that wicked problems often have no particular solutions that are likely to satisfy all of the stakeholders. Determining what works as a conceptualization of the problem, though not easy, is crucial because the problem formulation largely determines the priorities, focus, and orientation of implementation steps. Because partners frequently have misconceptions and even stereotypes about others from different types of institutions or sectors, initial experimentations and attempts at problem definition involve a considerable amount of trust and relationship building, negotiation, and efforts to create initial "small wins" (Waddock, 1988; Austin and Seitanidi, 2012b).

Implementation of collaboration is another sticky problem, especially if partners still remain in their original job positions and there are no specific people devoted to monitoring and implementing the collaboration. Partnerships can be expected to change and evolve over time (Waddock, 1988, 1989), making change a constant for collaborations. Further, the characteristics that lead to successful long-term collaborations are still not well understood or researched (Seitanidi and Crane, 2009, albeit see, Leigh, 2005).

We do know some of the things that make for effective partnerships. For example, Austin (2000: 35–7) argues in his "collaboration continuum" that more developed (what he terms integrative) collaborations will experience higher levels of stakeholder engagement with a defined mission that is of central importance. Such integrative collaborations will have high resource levels with broad scope of activity (see also Waddock, 1989), frequent interactions that come from proximity (see also Leigh, 2005), with, has been noted above, trust having developed over time.

Congruent with the centrality of the collaboration to each partner's mission is the notion of high levels of strategic value (also Leigh, 2005) – and the potential for creating shared value (Austin and Seitanidi, 2012a, b; see also Porter and Kramer, 2011). Dissertation research by Leigh (2005) indicates that the ability to manage conflict and managing changing core definitions or "schemata" (Leigh, 2005) were other factors in creating collaboration longevity and success. Regular communications, particularly around strategic alignment and planning, and the ability to cope well with change – particularly expanding ambitions, also seem to differentiate successful from less successful collaborations (Leigh, 2005).

It is, of course, one thing to seek shared collaborative value in dealing with wicked problems and entirely another thing to measure outcomes in a way that satisfies all of the collaborators. Indeed, the way that the problem is defined has a great deal to do with how outcomes will be measured. For example, is a general problem of economic development one of jobs creation, generating more savings and less debt among residents, improving housing stock and values, or improving the education system (or more likely, some combination of these and other factors)? Once the problem is defined, adequate measures for that definition (number of jobs created at a variety of pay ranges, for example) can be established, but only after the fact, and some of these measures are not likely to be satisfying to stakeholders whose definition of the problem did not hold sway. But then, that is the nature of the wicked problems with which cross-sector collaborations almost invariably contend.

If collaborative efforts and enterprises are to create what Austin and Seitanidi (2012a, b) call collaborative value, they need to figure out ways to develop leaders with a huge set of implementation problems. Summarizing, collaborations in practice need to:

- Develop leaders with significant collaborative capabilities at all levels and in all types of enterprise, whether public or private, social or profit-making, government or activist.
- Be able to bring a diverse array of relevant stakeholders into productive and useful dialogue that actually leads to productive outcomes.
- Be able to identify, define, and synthesize a problem situation in ways that stakeholders with multiple perspectives can buy into it.
- Have a capacity to select and then work productively with a set of partners who bring diverse and different interests and perspectives to the situation.
- Become systems thinkers who can understand the dynamics of change and are themselves effective change agents.
- Figure out how to measure outcomes in what are inherently intractable "wicked" problems whose very nature means that different parties will bring different perspectives on what is a reasonable solution – and what a reasonable outcome would be.

Collaboration: central to a sustainable world

Underlying the rapid evolution of collaborative practice is a vision of a new, more sustainable, world in which participation and democracy are truly valued, and where all types of enterprise – and all living creatures – are valued. In this world, collaborations deal with the type of complex problems called "wicked" (Rittel and Weber, 1973) or messes (Ackoff, 1975). The nature of the problems in part dictates the response – collaboration – because no single entity or actor can cope with wicked problems effectively. Collaborative responses also produce the potential for considerably more institutional and enterprise diversity based in a wide range of responses to any given situation. Perhaps that diversity, which inherently underpins healthy social and environmental ecosystems, is our best hope for a sustainable future.

In the quest to create and improve the effectiveness of cross-sector collaborations of all sorts, particularly in the boundary-blurred world that we now face, we clearly need more research and highly developed theory and empirical research. But as the practitioner perspectives included in this section clearly reveal, without reference and relevance to informed practice, theory is unlikely to be useful or particularly helpful. Thus, I believe that this book is doing a great service by bringing together not just the best academic research and thinking about cross-sector collaborations, but also the core ideas of practitioners who have for years been deeply engaged with the development and effectiveness of actual collaborative initiatives.

Notes

1   For example, Conservation through collaboration, www.fws.gov/science/shc/landscape action_200910conservationthroughcollaboration.html, accessed 10/25/11.
2   B Corporation website, www.bcorporation.net/, accessed 10/20/11.

References

Ackoff, R.L. (1974) *Redesigning the Future: A Systems Approach to Societal Problems*. Hoboken, NJ: Wiley.
Austin, J.E. (1998) Business Leadership Lessons from the Cleveland Turnaround. *California Management Review*, Fall, 41 (1): 86–106.
Austin, J.E. (2000) *The Collaboration Challenge: How Nonprofits and Businesses Succeed Through Strategic Alliances*. San Francisco, CA: Jossey-Bass Publishers.
Austin, J. and Seitanidi, M.M. (2012b) Collaborative Value Creation: Partnerships Processes. *Nonprofit and Voluntary Sector Quarterly*, 41 (6): 929–68.
Austin, J. and Seitanidi, M.M. (2012a) Collaborative Value Creation: A Review of Partnering between Business and Nonprofits. *Nonprofit and Voluntary Sector Quarterly*, 41 (5): 723–55.
Bluestone, B. and Kochan, T.A. (2011) *Toward a New Grand Bargain: Collaborative Approaches to Labor Management Reform in Massachusetts*. Boston: The Boston Foundation, available online at: www.northeastern.edu/dukakiscenter/documents/Grand_Bargain_Report.pdf, (accessed 10/20/11).
Burns, J.McG. (1978) *Leadership*. New York: Harper Torchbooks.
Christensen, B., C.M., Ruggles, H., Rudi and Stadtler, Thomas M. (2006) Disruptive Innovation for Social Change. *Harvard Business Review*, December: 94–101.

Churchman, C.W. (1967) Wicked Problems. *Management Science*, 4 (14): 141–2.

Googins, B.K. (2000) Creating the Partnership Society: Understanding the Rhetoric and Reality of Cross-sectoral Partnerships. *Business and Society Review*, Spring, 105 (1): 127–45.

Gricar, B.G. and Brown, L. Dave (1981) Conflict, Power, and Organization in a Changing Community. *Human Relations* 34 (10): 877–93.

Hart, S. (2005) *Capitalism at the Crossroads: The Unlimited Business Opportunities in Solving the World's Most Difficult Problems*. Philadelphia: Wharton School Publishing.

Leigh, Jennifer S.A. (2005) US National Park Service Cross-Sector Partnerships for Environmental Sustainability and Cultural Resource Preservation. Chestnut Hill, MA: Unpublished Boston College Doctoral Dissertation.

Porter, M.E. and Kramer, M.R. (2011) Creating Shared Value: *Harvard Business Review*, January–February.

Prahalad, C.K. (2004) *The Fortune at the Bottom of the Pyramid: Eradicating Poverty through Profits*. New Delhi: Pearson Education/Wharton School Publishing.

Prahalad, C.K. and Hammond, A. (2002) Serving the World's Poor Profitably. *Harvard Business Review*, September, 80 (9): 48–57.

Rittel, W.J. Horst and Webber, M.M. (1973) Dilemmas in a General Theory of Planning. *Policy Sciences*, 4: 155–69.

Seitanidi, M.M. (2008) Adaptive Responsibilities: Nonlinear Interactions in Cross Sector Social Partnerships. *Emergence: Complexity and Organization*, 10 (3): 51–64.

Seitanidi, M.M. (2010) *The Politics of Partnership: A Critical Examination of Nonprofit-Business Partnerships*. Berlin: Springer.

Seitanidi, M.M. and Crane, A. (2009) Understanding the Selection, Design and Institutionalisation of Nonprofit-Business Partnerships. *Journal of Business Ethics*, 85: 413–29.

Waddell, S. and Brown, L. D. (1997) Fostering Intersectoral Partnering: A Guide to Promoting Cooperation among Government, Business, and Civil Society Actors. *IDR Reports*, 13 (3).

Waddell, S. (2003) Global Action Networks: A Global Invention Helping Business Make Globalization Work for All. *Journal of Corporate Citizenship*, Winter, 12: 27–42.

Waddell, S. (2011) *Global Action Networks: Creating Our Future Together*. Basingstoke: Palgrave Macmillan.

Waddock, S. (1986) Public-Private Partnership as Product and Process, *Research in Corporate Social Performance and Policy*, Vol. VII, edited by James E. Post. Greenwich, CT: JAI Press.

Waddock, S.A. (1988) Building Successful Social Partnerships, *Sloan Management Review*, Summer, 29 (4): 17–23.

Waddock, S.A. (1989) Understanding Social Partnerships: An Evolutionary Model of Partnership Organizations. *Administration and Society*, 12 (1), May: 78–100.

Waddock, S.A. (1991) A Typology of Social Partnership Organizations. *Administration and Society*, 22 (4): 480–515.

Waddock, S.A. and McIntosh, M. (2011) *SEE Change: Making the Transition to a Sustainable Enterprise Economy*. Sheffield: Greenleaf.

18

THE NEED FOR A NEW APPROACH TO SUSTAINABILITY

Hadley Archer and Paul Uys

2012 was a milestone year for sustainability. The year marked the twentieth anniversary of the United Nations World Commission on Environment and Development (UNCED), which defined the term "sustainable development" and called for the "Earth Charter" – which aimed to set the context of humanity's relationship with the planet and articulate a vision for how we, as a species, can live in harmony with our natural surroundings. Further, 2012 also marks the tenth anniversary of the World Summit on Sustainable Development, in Johannesburg. Over these past two decades, our brightest minds – award-winning authors, Nobel laureates, visionary political leaders, even Oscar-winning movie stars – have contributed to our understanding of the problems facing our world. Together, we have drafted a roadmap for finding the balance between economic, social, and environmental issues.

But has our roadmap guided us to progress on sustainability goals? 2012 is also the twentieth anniversary of the collapse of the cod fishery in the Grand Banks, off Canada's Atlantic coast: prior to 1992, what most had thought was an inexhaustible population of fish was exploited to the brink of extinction, resulting in thousands of job losses and hundreds of millions in revenue loss. July 2012 marked the hottest month in US history, the latest statistic in a disturbing trend: eighteen of the hottest years on record have occurred in the past two decades.[1] News headlines in 2012 were dominated by record-setting droughts in Canada and the U.S., nationwide power blackouts in India and devastating floods in the UK. Consequently, the key finding of the 2012 *Living Planet Report* – published by the World Wildlife Fund (WWF) – was that humanity's demands exceed our planet's capacity by 50 per cent, a trend that has been going in the wrong direction since WWF began measuring our environmental footprint in the 1990s.

Increasingly, governments are being called upon to address the widening gap between knowledge and action, from environmental, economic, and human rights perspectives. Yet the 2009 United Nations Conference of the Parties meetings in Copenhagen – billed as the most important meeting of world leaders on climate change since the Kyoto Protocol was signed – failed to yield any significant outcomes. The 2012 United Nations Conference on Sustainable Development in Rio was also disappointing – for environmentalists and CEOs alike – because it did not result in a jointly agreed-upon, binding plan to address critical issues such as climate change and deforestation.

With the shared global commitment to improve standard of living in developing countries, along with a burgeoning world population and economic hardship in recent years, it is unlikely that individual citizens can mount a meaningful and coordinated change by voting with their wallet, especially given choices currently at their disposal. And even though government action and binding commitments at national and international levels are critical to any path to sustainability, progress is slow and political deadlocks are prevalent. How, then, are we to address the increasing divide between knowledge and action, and the overshoot in our species' footprint?

Fortunately, a new movement is underway – one that is yielding practical solutions to some of the planet's most challenging sustainability problems and showing tangible results at scale. Companies have genuinely started to tackle the issue of sustainability through the lens of corporate social responsibility, and many are reducing their environmental footprint and bringing "greener" products to market. In recent years, the effort has been building to understand risk and impact as they relate to supply chains, and companies are starting to address risk and impact in a meaningful way. Partnerships between for-profit corporations and civil society groups are arguably one of the most powerful and efficient means of lowering environmental footprint directly while simultaneously paving a way for government action and providing the world's seven billion consumers with sustainable product options.

Corporations influence vast amounts of the world's resources: WWF estimates that approximately 300 to 500 companies control 70 per cent or more in the trade of the world's most essential commodities. Continent-spanning supply chains connect distant environments and communities, influencing massive decisions about how our commodities get produced – how our world's finite "natural capital" gets used. Some environmental non-government organizations (ENGOs) work to understand the science of nature, represent the voices of millions of citizens, and can effectively convene unlikely allies. Working together, these two sectors can and *are* having a significant positive impact. They are writing a new playbook for responsible business by tackling – and indeed, solving – problems at local, national, and international scales.

Global fisheries and the need for sustainable seafood solutions

In one region after another, a long history of relentless overfishing – driven largely by short-term profits – has resulted in excessive pressure on fisheries and ocean ecosystems worldwide. In fact, more than 75 per cent of the world's fish stocks are either fully exploited or overexploited (FAO).[2] With 2.6 billion people currently relying on fish in their diets, and with the global population forecast to reach 9 to 10 billion by 2050, maintaining business as usual is untenable. The cost of doing nothing is – quite clearly – bad business. A 2008 report titled *The Sunken Billions*, jointly published by the United Nations Food and Agriculture Organization and the World Bank, demonstrated that the difference between what is made and what could be made if fisheries were better managed is conservatively estimated to be $50 billion per year. Fisheries are clearly a dramatically underperforming asset, and sadly, our current way of doing business is doing nothing good for our global fish stocks.

Reimagining partnership – a case study

WWF-Canada and Loblaw, Canada's largest grocery retailer, signed a partnership agreement in 2009 with the goal of moving 100 per cent of Loblaw's seafood procurement – wild and farm-caught – to sustainable sources by the end of 2013. For wild-caught fish, this means that the fishing activity of Loblaw's suppliers must be at a level which is sustainable for the fish population, and that fishing operations are managed to maintain the structure, productivity, function, and diversity of the ecosystem on which the fishery depends. For farmed fish, this means that farming is done in a manner that minimizes the environmental and social footprint by addressing key impacts such as biodiversity, water quality, animal health, and the health and safety of workers. To ensure this, both wild and farm-caught seafood will be independently verified by the most rigorous, multi-stakeholder backed certification systems. This bold, transformative commitment sent shockwaves throughout environmental and business communities from Ottawa to Brussels, and on the wharves in Newfoundland.

While the environmental case for WWF's involvement may be obvious, the business case may be less so. For Loblaw, a leader in corporate social responsibility and purchaser of more than 35 per cent of the seafood sold in Canada, the partnership enabled the company to offer its consumers an exciting and sustainable lineup of seafood products well into the future. For WWF-Canada, this partnership provided a market-based solution to addressing unsustainable fishing practices and depleting stocks – a necessary strategy after decades of lobbying federal and provincial governments had yielded modest outcomes. Leveraging Loblaw's purchasing power and visionary commitment meant working with its entire supply chain of 250 vendors and ultimately contributing to the transformation of hundreds of fisheries worldwide. It also meant that one of Canada's largest employers was committing to healthy oceans and sustainable fishing practices and giving a new and powerful voice to this movement. What is so unique about this partnership is that it encompasses nearly every business unit of Loblaw, and is focused on driving change throughout their entire supply chain. The net effect is that fisheries all around the world will be held to a higher standard of practice if they wish to continue doing business with Loblaw. In other words, Loblaw is using its significant buying power to literally transform fishing and farming practices on the ground.

Benefits of partnership

The partnership between WWF-Canada and Loblaw has evolved since 2009, with each partner bringing benefits to the relationship and fostering growth.

At the first stage of the relationship – the "foundational" stage – WWF-Canada stepped into the role of educator. WWF-Canada provided Loblaw with a comprehensive understanding of the issues pertaining to global fisheries, fishing methods and the conservation implications of the status quo, which gave Loblaw a clear picture of the impact of their procurement decisions.

During the "implementation" stage, Loblaw worked with WWF-Canada to cultivate a better understanding of the seafood business – how markets and supply chains work and the impact of decisions at a retail level. Learning the business acumen and how Loblaw engages its vendors – many of whom have worked with Loblaw for decades –was critical for WWF-Canada to be able to provide sound input and advice. WWF-Canada was able to identify practical solutions for Loblaw, ranging from procurement practices to vendor engagement to developing credible communication platforms. WWF-Canada challenged the thinking within Loblaw by encouraging them to commit to the most rigorous certification systems, even when they were still not fully developed, and to develop solutions to address data gaps. This approach helped Loblaw identify new issues and practical solutions.

In the "stakeholder engagement" stage, WWF-Canada leveraged local talent by engaging nearly all of its two dozen marine program staff and by tapping into academic expertise at leading Canadian universities. Additionally, it leveraged its global reach and expertise to inform Loblaw's industry relationships, its commitment and the course to becoming world leader in sustainable practices. Benchmarking the Loblaw commitment against other global leaders helped transform many ideas into practical advice that influenced operational policy.

Through its partnership with Loblaw, WWF-Canada has played a pivotal role in helping the company shift away from traditional retailer-supplier interactions to managing stakeholder relationships and commitments, primarily by helping Loblaw to better understand the complex set of environmental and social issues facing the fisheries and farms they procure from. Six stakeholder groups have been directly impacted by the sustainable seafood partnership: government, fishing communities, business-to-business relationships, consumer, media and other partners, especially NGOs.

Government

Through Loblaw's internal change in government policy engagement and with WWF's guidance, Loblaw has become more proactive in seeking both federal and provincial dialogue and support, which are fundamental to the successful implementation of both local and international policies. One expression of this approach is on World Oceans Day, held each June, when WWF-Canada and Loblaw have jointly met with staff and politicians of the Department of Fisheries and Oceans and other departments to discuss sustainable seafood and healthy oceans.

Fishing communities

Through WWF-Canada's network, Loblaw has become involved in solution-based programs at the fishing community level. This involvement in critical, as Loblaw often buys and sells in these communities. These programs also spur on future fisheries improvement projects that are foundational for developing sustainable management solutions.

Business-to-business

The fundamental business strategy of adopting a sustainable sourcing policy lies in what is referred to as the B2B (business-to-business) practices. WWF-Canada has played an important role in helping Loblaw manage sensitive dialogue with their supply base. Together, the organizations have worked to establish a stepwise approach that gives the company's procurement group a practical way of defining where suppliers sit at any given time, and the tangible next steps needed to show progress towards sustainability.

Consumer

One of the key challenges has been to educate and bring the consumer into the conversation. WWF-Canada's brand has helped to build trust and is a beacon in what is a confusing and sometimes unengaged market. Consumers are understandably suspicious of the intentions of big businesses, and so the use of the WWF-Canada logo in educational and promotional materials, as well as the use of credible certification eco-labels on product, bolsters credibility for the company's commitment and provides consumers with a practical means of supporting sustainable practices through their buying decisions.

Media

Both organizations – together and independently – have played critical roles in supporting various media initiatives. Together, WWF-Canada and Loblaw have launched publicity campaigns designed to educate and encourage consumers to support sustainable seafood practices through their buying decisions. Flyers, signage, online, and social-media advertising has generated engagement with consumers, changed market direction, and reinforced the confidence of Loblaw's suppliers.

Partners

Engaging with WWF-Canada has helped Loblaw create a tide change, one in which the NGO was not just a stakeholder but a partner committed to the same retail sourcing objectives as the company. Thus, the new corporate dynamic is collaborative rather than combative: Loblaw now sees the opportunity in engaging various NGOs and scientific advisors to find solutions. For WWF-Canada, the partnership has been instructive about how to work with a large, complex organization and has set up a model for future corporate partnerships.

The "symbiotic" stage of the partnership involves continuous formal and informal consultation: WWF-Canada and Loblaw have shared ideas, challenged assumptions, and jointly identified solutions, each speaking freely and being heard. Perhaps the most crucial benefit of this enduring stage is that each organization has a thorough understanding of the other, and when solutions are discussed, there is remarkable alignment about context, risks, and opportunities. Ultimately, the partnership has led to stronger, more far-reaching decision-making for both organizations, along with tangible, measureable outcomes, which are transforming the seafood sector in Canada and beyond.

Moving forward, Loblaw and WWF-Canada are exploring ways to leverage their partnership to influence more holistic change related to Oceans' health, and to apply this holistic supply chain approach to tackle additional environmental and social issues such as those associated with palm oil, paper, and water.

The partnership between WWF-Canada and Loblaw has been a powerful agent of change because of three key elements:

- *Openness* – to learn about each partner's business and their stake in the partnership. In the foundational stage, WWF-Canada educated Loblaw about the issues pertaining to global fisheries and conservation; in the implementation stage, Loblaw worked with WWF-Canada to cultivate a better understanding of the seafood business. An effective partnership requires a high level of fluency of client base, market challenges, and broader goals on both sides.
- *Trust and flexibility* – to take on new challenges and grow throughout the partnership. Forging new paths will inevitably yield surprises, no matter how comprehensive the foundation-building is. Without trust and flexibility, WWF-Canada and Loblaw could not have made progress on such a broad scale – among fishing communities, governmental interests, business stakeholders, environmental groups, and consumers.
- *Investment in shared success* – that is bolstered by interdependent goals. WWF-Canada's goal to guide the seafood market towards sustainable practices is dependent on Loblaw maintaining a competitive edge in the marketplace. Thus, both partners are invested in not only in the overall profits of the partnership but also in each other's individual success.

Questions for reflection

1   What obstacles block government and citizen action for sustainable practices? How can partnerships between for-profit corporations and civil society groups overcome these obstacles?
2   What makes corporations influential in pursuing local and global sustainability goals?
3   What is the historical and economic context for the sustainable seafood partnership between WWF-Canada and Loblaw? How does the social context support this partnership?
4   Summarize the business case for the sustainable seafood partnership.
5   What is the significance of the "symbiotic" stage of partnerships between for-profit and civil society groups? How does this stage change decision-making?

Notes

1   NOAA: www.climatewatch.noaa.gov/image/2012/july-2012-hottest-month-onrecord/ United Nations Environment Programme: www.unep.org/GEO/pdfs/Keeping_track.pdf
2   World Bank - FAO Report, "The Sunken Billions," October 8, 2008. http://web.world bank.org/WBSITE/EXTERNAL/NEWS/0,,contentMDK:21932269~pagePK:642570 43~piPK:4373.76~theSitePK:4607,00.html

19

HOW TO CO-CREATE OPPORTUNITIES TOGETHER

CREAMOS in Guatemala

Barbara Nijhuis

As the Executive Director of an extensive charity program in Guatemala I initiated and participated in the growth of several partnerships between nonprofit, public, and commercial organizations. One of those partnerships was between Safe Passage (the nonprofit organization) and CEMACO (a Guatemalan commercial company). The chapter offers an insider's perspective in the origins of the collaborations, how it worked, how it was leveraged and expanded through different levels of involvement. In addition I provide an overview of the relationships with important stakeholder groups.

Partnerships in practice

My first experiences with developing partnerships date back to 2007. That was the year I was appointed as the Executive Director at a non-profit organization called Safe Passage. It was founded in 1999 to support children and families living in one of the largest garbage dump communities in the world, the one in Guatemala City.

As in many developing countries, people from rural areas move to the country's capital in search of work while dreaming of a better life. In many cases, small savings are spent quickly and with limited options for work in sight, people end up working under very difficult conditions at the garbage dump. Here many of them become so-called "guajeros" (recyclers), scavenging waste materials to sell and recycle in order to make a living. The land around the garbage dump is a growing lively community of hard-working people trying to survive. Most of the children I met were born in this extreme poor and at times violent community and had never seen the stunningly beautiful scenery their country is famous for.

In the first years, Safe Passage mainly worked with the children in the dump community. After evaluating the impact it created and could have, we focused more on involving the parents and the community itself. Our professional approach and high impact within the community was well noticed and attracted people and businesses to support us.

Looking back at those years in Guatemala, I consider that one of the main lessons learned is that, from a program and fundraising perspective, partnering strategically with local organizations and businesses is key to the success of any non-profit, either through building strong relationships or by establishing partnerships.

Reorganizing the nonprofit – evaluating the fundraising model

A few years after it was founded, Safe Passage included several buildings, housing an early childhood center and a reinforcement center for hundreds of children. Funding came from visitors and volunteers and an active grass root movement grew around the organization. Back in Guatemala, the garbage dump community was not so well known and certainly not a place to visit. The dirt and dangers were not particularly inviting.

Our funds, needed to meet the annual budget of around 2 million dollars, mostly came from private donors and foundations from the USA and Europe. For years this had been the fundraising model. Although successful, it also was challenging to sustain. When I started working for the organization in 2007, and in the process of evaluating our programmatic impact and fundraising model, it became clear that we needed to connect more to relevant local stakeholders to become more sustainable. From what I have seen around me, I assume that neglecting the importance of connecting with local stakeholders is a common pitfall for many organizations, especially when founded by foreigners. In the flow of starting something new and exciting, the energy goes mostly inwards and sometimes we just forget to notice what is already in place and surrounding us that we could immediately benefit from or collaborate with.

One of the steps we took was to connect strategically with stakeholder groups that would add value to our program in specific areas. These relationships (and in some cases partnerships) were critical in terms of valuable connections and creating new opportunities. Later in this chapter I will give you an overview of the groups of stakeholders we reached out to and the different types of relationships that came out of this.

Strategically connecting to the world around us

In Guatemala, it is not very common yet to donate to "good causes". People support their families, neighbors and friends, but donating cash to a foundation is not so common. In some cases there is a lack of trust and a fear for corruption, in other cases people are not properly asked to contribute and in other cases people simply do not have the means. However, the interest to support us was there and the generated funds locally were growing. Whether we were successful, depended on the way the appeal was asked and the purpose for which the funds were needed.

Overview of relationships with local stakeholders and outcomes (desired and realized)	
Stakeholders	**Outcomes**
Local businesses (for example CEMACO)	*Without these connections our impact would not be as large. After graduation, children need a place to work and generate income. Businesses could help us with this key part of the program.* • *Awareness*: local businesses would help us to raise more awareness, and to inspire people to visit and support us. • *Financial support*: businesses as a source of finance. • *Connections and opportunities*: businesses would open their doors and offer qualified and motivated students an internship or job. • *To avoid the potential risk of "donor fatigue"*: meaning that foreign donors would eventually raise the question why local businesses would not support this program.
Public, private and Nonprofit sectors (with a focus on education and the community)	*It was important to connect with other institutions to strengthen our professional network, which helped us to improve the quality of the overall program.* • *Improving the quality of the program*: sharing knowledge to increase quality and our overall impact. • *Strengthen our (safety) network*: we generated a professional network that would operate efficiently in times of emergency and crises. More stakeholders "close by". • *Impact*: we shared materials and equipment and we could generate more impact with our resources. • *Connections:* through these connections we were able to generate trust and understanding for the specific living conditions of our students.
Private and public universities	*It was important to connect with universities so that our students would be able to continue their education.* • *Connections*: establish relationships to share materials and knowledge and to open academic doors for our students. • *Improving the quality of the program*: local students volunteer to share their knowledge and expertise.
Well-connected Guatemalan professionals	*These contacts would help us to connect strategically within Guatemalan Society.* • *Professional board of directors*: both Guatemalans and foreigners would join the board. Guatemalan Board members bring knowledge in the fields of local law and finances and help to improve our business network. • *Fundraising*: through our connections, we become more efficient in raising funds locally.
Guatemalan volunteers	*We wanted to involve other Guatemalans with the community.* • *Interaction*: students from different social backgrounds would get to know each other and have more interaction. • *Awareness*: more awareness is raised. • *Role models*: connect our students with role models to identify with, especially important in single-mother households.

FIGURE 19.1 Outcomes for the nonprofit as a result of the interactions with stakeholders

Who to connect with – local stakeholders

We connected with public and private schools around us to improve the quality of the program. We invited them to visit our programs, to share knowledge, and discuss the potential risks of safety in the neighborhood. This process was necessary and we noticed the difference. We were taken seriously as important stakeholders during emergencies and crises. More so, because of our interesting international network, we were seen as experts with the ability to get things done. UNICEF invited us to work together in the community especially on children's rights. These stronger relationships did not yet have a huge impact on our finances, but they were critical for our overall impact. They enabled us to connect and to open doors. They helped us to co-create understanding and opportunities for our beneficiaries to break their cycle of poverty.

A local partnership to believe in

Following next is a clear example of one of our cross-sector social partnerships (CSSPs) with impact in multiple areas:

A group of Guatemalan students from a private university needed a social project to collaborate with for their practice. They were interested in collaborating with us, especially with a group of women in our Adult Literacy program. This program was designed for the mothers of the children in our program. These mothers were ambitious and wanted to study to increase their opportunities. Besides going to the literacy classes, they worked at the garbage dump, collecting rubbish under extremely difficult working conditions.

The students and the women developed a plan to generate other sources of income by making beads from recycled materials (in line with the theme of garbage and recycling) and ways on how to market them. The initial partnership was between the private university and Safe Passage, and consisted of dedicating time, resources, and skills. The added value of this partnership lay in the fact that:

1   The women would receive specific support to learn how to generate other sources of income.
2   The students would receive access to and be able to share their skills with a committed group of women and a group of volunteers and professional staff to work with.
3   Safe Passage, an organization which did not specialize in designing business models as such, needed their time, skills, and networking.

The first results of this partnership were beyond expectations. Business skills were developed, a good product was created, and the women were able to generate other income sources. In addition to this, the privileged students, who had never met people from this extreme poor community, learned a lot about their own country from a new perspective.

The key of the successful partnership was that the mutual expectations were well managed. The students delivered in terms of effectiveness, collaboration, support, marketing, and so on. The women were committed and learned a great deal in terms of working together, believing in their own abilities, and fine taste in making the pieces of jewelry and business skills. One of our main challenges was to find a structure for the women to work in. They were used to working on their own at the garbage dump and needed to work as a cooperative and to share profits. The group started to work under the name of CREAMOS ("we create" or "let's believe").

The impact of the initial partnership grew when another – much larger – party became involved. Directors of a well-known Guatemalan A-brand department store called CEMACO visited the program. They were inspired by our professionalism and high impact within the community. They were interested in establishing a long-term partnership. We discussed various ways to leverage their support while using their resources and expertise. Motivations for the partnership included:

1   Shared goal – the company could help us to alleviate poverty by supporting CREAMOS and encouraging the development of entrepreneurial skills.
2   Added value – while utilizing its own resources the the company could support us offering us their platform, brand, good reputation, business skills).
3   Win-win – this partnership would allow benefit and added value for all parties involved.
4   Employee engagement – the employees initiated ideas to support the program and felt proud of being part of the partnership, and hence generated widespread support amongst employees.
5   Clear process to impact – we were transparent, well organized, and able to make the partnership work and hence achieve impact.

Together we developed a wide range of ways to leverage their support and areas to collaborate in.

Added value in practice

In the following account I provide an example of added value in practice.

As a result of the partnership, the women of CREAMOS were invited to participate in CEMACO's well-known annual fair at the stores in Guatemala City's luxurious malls, built to satisfy the needs of the happy few. CREAMOS got a premium spot in the store right in front of the entrance to sell their jewelry and their story as well as the story of Safe Passage.

Added value was found in the reputation and location of the store. CEMACO represented luxury and quality which added value to the beads made by CREAMOS. The prices could increase. The company benefited equally because our (non-profit) presence added value to its fair. Publicity was raised, visitors felt inspired, and CEMACO's employees felt connected and were proud to support the program. For weeks the women had a stand, selling many examples of their handwork, while connecting with people they would normally never talk to due to their social-economic differences. Feeling proud of selling something beautiful they had crafted, they were also able to disseminate information about the program to raise awareness.

Following this fair, employees wanted to do something for the program as well. As mentioned previously, giving cash is not very common in Guatemala, but donations in the form of food and materials is common practice. As we had noticed, in the morning many children came to the program with an empty stomach, and we started to include breakfasts. Eggs are an important source of nutrition for children and the idea was raised to ask the employees to donate eggs! CEMACO doubled the amount of donated eggs and we received hundreds of eggs every week to include in our breakfasts. Pancakes and scrambled eggs were now on the menu!

Another important outcome was that our students, who were often discriminated against and had trouble obtaining work at local companies, were accepted as interns in the CEMACO stores. As a result of this first successful partnership, we could then engage more local companies to open their doors and offer our students internship opportunities.

The partnership made a social impact in the lives of many. One example that I recall very vividly involved the wedding of the son of one of the women of CREAMOS. She did not buy herself a beautiful dress for the occasion, but attended the festivities in the uniform she had worn during the fair at the CEMACO store. There she was in her uniform, in green pants and a blue shirt, next to her son, as proud as she had never been. This uniform represented for her the new world of opportunities, the store, and all that the partnership stood for.

Why this partnership worked

I think that the partnerships with (1) the private university students and (2) the business worked so well because all the parties involved (women, students, organization, company and staff) were taken seriously and treated with respect. All parties could add value from their own perspective. Partners were equally important in co-creating and designing the process. Furthermore, the impact was clear and very inspiring. The story of CREAMOS was presented in the newspapers, as an inspiration for many in Guatemala. The women in the program could spend less time at the garbage dump and started to earn a living under much better conditions. CEMACO got involved and felt inspired to remain active because they saw the impact the partnership generated.

Partnerships should be an inspiration to engage beneficiaries, employees, and customers. In my view just donating money is not an option and does not add any value; instead, partners should feel part of something bigger and something that really matters to someone else. A successful partnership is a continuous process of getting to know each other, while accepting and overcoming the fear of the unknown and of failure (from either side of the partnership). It involves taking the risk of becoming involved in something complicated outside your own expertise and comfort zone to build something together. Both parties need to be willing to listen to each other to understand the mutual needs and expectations. Ideally you should be able to experience yourself the potential impact you can have or are able to co-create.

Western nonprofits operating in developing countries with successful local business can increase their impact and safeguard their sustainability by building local partnerships in addition to the much-appreciated existing international or multi-national public-private partnerships. The social gap between rich and poor in these countries is often large and through partnerships a bridge can be made to encourage the different parties in society to get to know each other, to understand each other's needs and to develop trust. What seems as a simple personal contact has the potential for big impact within particular communities. These connections in developing countries are important and relevant. I think that sustainable development is very much about creating opportunities and opening doors so that people can co-create and fully participate in society to truly make a difference.

Questions for reflection

1   The impact of the partnership as described in this chapter is on a relatively small scale. How could this partnership create a larger impact or be replicated into other areas?
2   What are the potential risks for local businesses to partner with local non-profit organizations? How could these risks be minimized? And vice versa?
3   During what stage in its life cycle (start-up, etc.) should a NGO consider initiating partnerships?

20

CROSS-SECTOR COLLABORATIONS

Challenges in aligning perspectives in partnership committees and co-developing funding proposals

Sarah Winchester

The Prince's Trust exists to help young people aged 13 to 30 who are long-term unemployed, have been in trouble with the law, are educational underachievers or who have started life in the care system. We work across the UK to help these groups of young people to get a job, go into further education or training or become volunteers.

We have over 200 corporate partnerships whose focus, shape and scale vary depending on what the business is looking to achieve through their corporate social responsibility. Our aim is to establish strong relationships that deliver mutual value, over multiple years.

The Prince's Trust has experienced a positive shift in the power dynamics, aspirations and outcomes of our cross-sector partnerships. Using two case studies, one involving over 35 construction companies, the other a global management consultancy and outsourcing company, this contribution will explore how these partnerships developed in practice and what key lessons we learnt for the future. The following themes played a central role in the examples so will be explored in detail: the power balance, overcoming misconceptions between sectors and the importance of trial and error.

The social problem we tackle in collaboration with the construction industry is youth unemployment. Together we train young people aged 16 to 25 who are ready for full-time work but who do not have the skills to access and secure jobs in construction. The focus of the collaboration with the management consultancy firm was to address the skills gaps facing young people leaving education with few or no qualifications. The main aim was to use the business's highly experienced workforce to support our young people, imparting simple but essential work based skills such as CV writing and interview techniques.

Both enterprises had reasons for addressing these problems that benefited their organizations: for the construction industry this approach delivered evidence of their commitment to the communities in which they operated for public sector tenders, at the same time as addressing a need for young, reliable workers entering into the sector. Management consultancy relies on a thriving, dynamic, talented workforce. Their business driver, therefore, was to appeal to existing and new employees, by demonstrating their desire to put something back into society through sharing the talent of their people. The biggest challenge of cross-sector working remains striking a balance and delivering mutual benefit for all involved. Both collaborations have been through a lot of change but are still thriving today.

One of the "wicked problems" (Waddock and McIntosh, 2011) The Trust exists to address is UK youth unemployment. Six years ago we identified the need to close the skills gap for job-ready young people. We wanted to work with industries that needed to find and retain entry-level workers that could also provide career progression. The construction industry was identified as a key partner and so a committee was formed to help us take on the challenge.

In establishing this group The Trust created a new partnership dynamic. The committee meets quarterly and includes very senior figures, often CEOs and in the cases of the biggest companies, very senior representatives. The committee is then managed by our fundraising team. A key incentive for companies in the group was that they would be part of the solution, working alongside The Trust to deliver "Get Into Construction" – a two- to four-week programme that teaches young people the basic industry skills. This meant that some of the committee members representing companies became both funders and delivery partners; working directly with our colleagues across the UK to run Get Into programmes, often with very challenging young people, whilst also financially supporting our work.

Committee meetings became more challenging as the members, representing £2.5m of funding, requested more detailed and closer analysis of every aspect of the initiative – expenditure, operational detail. Used to committees focusing on fundraising and faced with ambitious, highly experienced business leaders, fundraisers agreed to detailed levels of reporting that added layers of complexity to existing systems and pressure to already stretched operational teams.

Over time, The Trust involved the delivery teams and Senior Management in committee meetings. Able to give a far more detailed understanding of operations and supported by Trust Senior Management, discussions became more balanced. In retrospect we should have spent more time explaining our priorities, reporting systems and the role we wanted the committee members to fulfil at the outset. This additional preparation would have ensured a smoother beginning to the partnership journey.

Within this there were times when the different parties misunderstood each other. In the case of the construction industry the committee became hugely frustrated with our relatively unsophisticated levels of reporting. It took a while to explain that charities have different priorities and pressures from corporations. As a charity struggling with public sector cuts and facing critical levels of youth unemployment, it is incredibly difficult to justify high levels of investment in systems and processes when every penny is needed on the "front line".

The idea that the charity sector is a poor relative of the private sector is a recurring misconception. However, conversely not-for-profit organizations can be guilty of perceiving themselves as morally superior because of their focus on a cause or mission versus commercialism. In the worse cases this can translate into inflexibility on the part of the charity to explore the ways of partnership working with a corporate organization. Instead of seeing a genuine desire to help, wrapped in a need to demonstrate business values, charities can lack insight into business practices and pressures and instead take a very cynical view.

In the second case The Trust had been working with one of the world's leading management consultancy firms for a number of years when an opportunity arose to potentially secure hundreds of thousands of pounds' worth of new funding. However, this new opportunity required us to work with a different part of the business. As we tried to identify a partnership package that met everyone's needs it became obvious that there was a barrier caused by the complex and advanced systems and processes the business was adopting. That coupled with the businesses' incredibly high expectations, their insistence that their employees be part of the solution and rigorous due diligence processes began to create divisions.

Knowing the partner well, the fundraising team persisted. However, it took the unwavering commitment and keen judgement of two particular individuals, one from each organization, to identify the right project and secure support from both sides to apply for funding. Even use of language caused problems as the bid was painstakingly co-created. Individual words in some cases had to be scrutinized and debated as each tried to keep the bid straddling both parties' needs.

Eighteen months in the making, the new bid was successful and has provided The Trust with a game-changing perspective on how it should provide young people with the skills they need to excel. There are still elements of the bid which are yet to be delivered; the management consultancy firm requires us to co-create a technology project to be used by its multiple charity partners. Having recently integrated with two other youth charities and completed a nationwide organizational restructure it is proving difficult for The Trust to prioritize this. However, we are exploring options and due to strong foundations our partnership continues to flourish.

Looking back at this extensive process and the development of the "Get Into Construction" programme, it is clear that "trial and error" played a crucial role. The more time we spent with our management consultant partner debating the focus of our partnership, the more we learnt about each other and began to understand the potential value of connecting our organizations.

"Get Into Construction" has evolved brilliantly with businesses shaping the programme alongside our delivery teams to better suit our young people's needs. Initially businesses underestimated the challenges involved in engaging young people who come from the most vulnerable backgrounds in UK society and went through a steep learning curve. Equally The Trust has also recognized the need to spend more time educating keen, open-minded employers about what to expect and how best to support our young people. In both cases there was little tolerance or time built in to allow for these developments. Although unspoken, experience suggests that expectations from both sides were that we would effortlessly understand each other's worlds and immediately work faultlessly together.

Looking forward, The Trust needs to build on its modest successes and pro-actively seek partners who can address specific problems facing our organization and the young people we help. With the constant evolution of funding models, for example Social Impact bonds[1] and the increased requirements to evidence positive outcomes resulting from a charities' intervention, charities need nimble infra-structures that bend and flex to deliver solutions for multiple stakeholders. It is crucial that charities are forward thinking and boundary breaking. We have to remain experts in our field, investing resources in truly understanding the big issues facing humanity in order to guarantee our place in cross-sector collaborations.

The key lessons learnt through the above examples and wider experiences are routed in exceptional communication, mutual respect and a sense of curiosity in each other's sectors. There needs to be a desire to close the gap and to make connections that benefit all involved.

Questions for reflection

1   How much information should you share with partners in order to ensure an understanding of your organization whilst protecting your ability to operate independently?
2   Should charities resist or embrace becoming suppliers to other sectors?
3   How should charities balance financial contributions with other benefits? For example, if a construction company chose to cut their donation to Get Into Construction but wanted to help by offering work placements and jobs how should The Trust engage with them? The company is offering highly valuable opportunities but they would benefit from both a strong corporate social respon-sibility narrative and a recruitment service whilst the Trust would be sourcing enthusiastic young recruits and then playing a central role in their training.
4   How should a charity manage the paradox of its supporters on the one hand demanding that it maintain very high percentages of funding going to front-line delivery work (e.g. over 80 per cent) and on the other hand requesting that it invest in better systems and processes in order to improve long-term efficiency?

Note

1   "Social Impact Bonds are an innovative way of attracting new investment around outcomes-based contracts that benefit individuals and communities. Through a Social Impact Bond, private investment is used to pay for interventions, which are delivered by service providers with a proven track record. Financial returns to investors are made by the public sector on the basis of improved social outcomes. If outcomes do not improve, then investors do not recover their investment." www.socialfinance.org.uk.

Reference

Waddock, S. and McIntosh, M. (2011) *SEE Change: Making the Transition to a Sustainable Enterprise Economy*. Sheffield: Greenleaf.

21

THE ROLE PARTNERSHIP BROKERS PLAY IN CREATING EFFECTIVE SOCIAL PARTNERSHIPS

Surinder Hundal

Partnership brokering is relevant for all three themes of this book. In the development of the kinds of cross-sector partnerships proposed for engendering responsible business and solving social problems at local, national and global levels (see Part A), a skilful partnership broker can take the lead in convening potential partners, helping them to explore possibilities and build/consolidate robust working relationships.

In partnership management and governance (see Part B), the broker can ensure that partners agree suitable governance and operating procedures for their partnership. He/she can help pull it together if it starts to come apart due to conflict or disagreement; and assist the partners in remaining focused on their shared objective when they risk getting distracted by other tasks or by day-to-day challenges. He/she will facilitate the partners through any changes in personnel or partnership tasks during its lifetime. It is worth noting at this point, that partnership brokers who adhere to emerging good practice[1] see their role as temporary and expend considerable effort throughout their relationship to the partnership in coaching and building capacity.

And in terms of re-imagining "social partnerships" for the future (see Parts C and D), the professionalization of partnership brokering and partnership brokers through training and reflective practice combined with action research into validating their value and impact could radically transform the way we design and deliver multi-sector collaboration in the twenty-first century.

These are big claims. How do we know what brokers actually do and how they influence the outcomes of cross-sector partnerships?

Answers can be found from two sources: the partnership brokers themselves and from experienced partnership practitioners and entrepreneurs who have pioneered the partnership brokering movement and led its development as a profession.[2]

In the latter category, Ros Tennyson[3] and Michael Warner[4] have generated a substantive body of practical work and thought leadership around partnership brokering over the past 14 years. In 1998, whilst leading cross-sector partnership work for the International Business Leaders Forum (IBLF) Tennyson drew upon her experience of running a wide range of partnership activities in more than 50 countries to articulate the critical role of "partnership intermediaries" in helping to shape and build successful cross-sector collaboration (Tennyson, 1998). Two years later, Tennyson and Luke Wilde coined the term "partnership broker' (Tennyson and Wilde, 2000), which has been widely adopted by partnership practitioners and many development institutions, companies as well as bi- and multi-lateral agencies. Since 2002, there have been several publications making the case for partnership brokering, identifying key brokering skills, building frameworks and tools essential for good brokering practice (Tennyson, 2003; Tennyson, 2005; Warner, 2003a, b).

In 2003, IBLF and the UK's Overseas Development Institute (ODI) set up a collaborative project – the Partnership Brokers Accreditation Scheme (PBAS) – to offer professional development and skills training and support to a growing cadre of individuals operating as partnership brokers. PBAS was scaled up and launched as an independent international professional entity, the Partnership Brokers Association[5] (PBA), in 2012. The first if its kind, PBA promotes good partnership brokering practice through education and vocational training, networking and action enquiry and participative research.

Going to the source – what partnership brokers say about what they do

Since 2003, more than 800 people from 70 countries and representing all sectors have completed the PBA basic partnership brokers training course with more than 250 going on to qualify as accredited partnership brokers. This community is a rich source of experiential knowledge and insights into the frontline work of a partnership broker, the challenges they face and the difference they make to the partnering process and its outcomes.

A report entitled *What do partnership brokers do? An enquiry into practice* (PBA, 2012) taps into the experiences of the 250 PBA accredited brokers operating in a wide range of contexts and circumstances. It concludes that partnership brokers undertake a number of clearly defined roles which can make a significant difference to multi-stakeholder collaboration. They help partners address a wide range of typical partnering challenges and improve a partnership's efficiency, effectiveness and – sometimes – its capacity for innovation. The partnership broker may have emerged from one particular sector or discipline and they are often located within one of the partner organizations, but in the partnership brokering role, they put aside their own preferences and allegiances to draw out and build on the diverse contributions and values of the partners to help create something far greater in the partnership than the sum of its parts.

Some of the key findings are that partnership brokering is most effective when brokers:

- spend quality time on relationship-building and relationship management, building productive relationships and collaboration between partners and their extended communities;
- exercise a range of specific partnering process management skills that partners can learn from and adopt themselves;
- build stronger partnerships both by pulling partners back together when they fall out with each other and by pushing them systematically to achieve more;
- work as "reflective practitioners" in order to get to the heart of what is needed;
- are confident, capable and professional in what they do whilst empowering partners to the point where they have taken over the partnership brokering function.

Situational brokering – playing several roles in a partnership's lifetime

A partnership broker performs a wide range of activities, determined by the context and needs of the partnership, the type of brokering he/she feels comfortable with and the stage in the evolution of the partnership.

A partnership broker can operate as an "internal" (i.e. from within one of the partner organizations) or "external" (i.e. independent of the partner organizations) broker. They can also be expected to operate in either proactive or reactive mode (see Table 21.1). Individuals operating as internal brokers in companies, international NGOs, public sector organizations, international aid agencies and other development-focused institutions currently constitute the largest group. There is a smaller but growing number of individual external brokers working independently across or within sectors, geographies and thematic areas.

Partnership brokering is not only provided by individuals but, increasingly, by specialist partnership units in corporate, public and NGO organizations and bilateral and international agencies (for instance, Accenture Development Partnerships,[6] the Partnerships and Co-operation Unit, ORRU, of the African Development Bank;[7] the UN Office of Partnerships[8]) as well as a range of newly emerging independent intermediary organizations such as the Partnering Initiative.[9]

Specialist partnership units are the primary interface for any external organization seeking to become a partner and provide a gate-keeping function to ensure that their organization's partnering activities are coordinated and consistent with its stated objectives and guidelines. The range of activities such units might undertake include scoping partner and partnership potential, skilled facilitation, brokering relationships, skills training, research, managing the partnering process, providing methods and tools to enhance the partnership, review and evaluation (Hundal and Tennyson, 2010).

The partnering cycle developed by the Partnering Initiative shows how a typical partnership may progress in four phases during its lifetime and hence, how management priorities and key activities might change for the partners as their partnership develops.

TABLE 21.1 The broker relationship to partners and partnership

---

External broker
An individual working externally to the partner organizations appointed either by one (or more, or all) of the partners to build or develop some aspect of the partnership.

	Animator	*Pioneer*	
	Typically an independent consultant or external organization appointed by the partnership to implement decisions on	Typically an independent consultant or external organization who has seeded the idea and may even have initiated the partnership.	
Reactive mandate	its behalf.		*Proactive mandate*
	Coordinator	*Innovator*	
	Typically a member of staff or internal unit working within one of the partner organizations and assigned a partnership coordinating role.	Typically a member of staff or internal unit working within one of the partner organizations tasked to take initiative in creating and building the relationship.	

Internal broker
An individual operating from within one of the partner organizations with a designated role to build and/or develop the partnership.

Source: *The Brokering Guidebook: Navigating Effective Sustainable Development Partnerships* (Tennyson 2005).

A partnership may not actually go through all the phases because of relevance or as linearly as the framework implies. But the framework provides a useful structure to define and overlay the duties of the broker and the activities he/she might carry out in each phase of the partnering cycle. See Figure 21.1.

Each phase requires the broker to adopt a different set of activities and style of intervention. For instance, taking a more proactive/energizing, awareness raising and capacity building role in the *Scoping and Building* phase; a more coaching, capacity-building and monitoring role in the *Managing and Maintaining* phase; and an advisory/mentoring role as the partnership becomes more established and, at some stage, needs to consider a number of "moving on" options.

During the partnership's life time, the partnership broker may face different challenges, relating to individuals involved in the partnership, or resulting from partner diversity or arising from the partnering process. Typical concerns reported by brokers which get in the way of their contribution to the partnership centre around poor utilization of or over-dependence on a broker; poor understanding of their role; personnel turnover; power imbalances; hidden agendas, conflicting priorities and interests; personality clashes; cross-sectoral or cross-cultural intolerance; difficulties breaking away from hierarchical structures; poor organizational and cultural adaptability; and inappropriate funding and resource allocation.

Potential roles for brokers in the partnering cycle

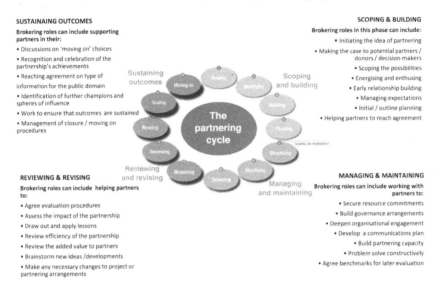

SUSTAINAING OUTCOMES

Brokering roles can include supporting partners in their:

• Discussions on 'moving on' choices
• Recognition and celebration of the partnership's achievements
• Reaching agreement on type of information for the public domain
• Identification of further champions and spheres of influence
• Work to ensure that outcomes are sustained
• Management of closure / moving on procedures

SCOPING & BUILDING

Brokering roles in this phase can include:

• Initiating the idea of partnering
• Making the case to potential partners / donors / decision-makers
• Scoping the possibilities
• Energising and enthusing
• Early relationship building
• Managing expectations
• Initial / outline planning
• Helping partners to reach agreement

REVIEWING & REVISING

Brokering roles can include helping partners to:

• Agree evaluation procedures
• Assess the impact of the partnership
• Draw out and apply lessons
• Review efficiency of the partnership
• Review the added value to partners
• Brainstorm new ideas /developments
• Make any necessary changes to project or partnering arrangements

MANAGING & MAINTAINING

Brokering roles can include working with partners to:

• Secure resource commitments
• Build governance arrangements
• Deepen organisational engagement
• Develop a communications plan
• Build partnering capacity
• Problem solve constructively
• Agree benchmarks for later evaluation

FIGURE 21.1 Potential roles for brokers in the partnering cycle

Source: The Partnering Initiative and the Partnership Brokers Association. Copyright Partnership Brokers Association. Reproduced with permission.

To be effective, the broker needs to be able to rely on more than his/her own competencies, skills and experience. He/she also needs recognition, status and acceptance of his/her role from the partners and their key constituencies; active involvement with and practical support from the partners; supervision with appropriate management and appraisal systems in place as well as clearly defined goals, tasks and timelines.

This in turn has consequences for the selection and appointment of a broker and the subsequent quality of the broker-partner relationship (Tennyson, 2005 – includes guidance on how to appoint a broker).

Careful thought needs to be given to whether an internal or external broker (individual or organizational mechanism) is appropriate for the proposed partnership and its brokering needs and whether those with whom the broker will be working understand the extent and boundaries of his/her role. A mismatch between expectations and the working relationship will undermine both partners and partnership broker(s). For instance, it could lead to frustration, dysfunctional behaviours, inadequate progress or even collapse of the partnership. Two examples of a mismatch are where the broker operates in a highly independent way when what the partners require is low-key, background coordination; or when he/she provides administrative support when the partners are expecting him/her to take more initiative on their behalf.

Multi-faceted skills and attributes define a good broker

Effective partnership brokering requires a radical change of mind-set and behavior together with a willingness to think and act in new ways. Based on experiential evidence from partnership brokers themselves,[10] and on action research into the brokering process, there are five specific areas where good partnership brokers show particular expertise: facilitation, negotiation, record-keeping, coaching and reviewing.[11]

In addition to these core skills, Tennyson (2005) asserts that a good broker is also adept at managing his/her brokering skill as a balance between art and science: that he/she combines attributes such as creativity, envisioning skills, active listening, tact, humility, well-developed people skills, and personal engagement with analytical and administrative skills, diligence, continuous learning, precise speaking and a professional detachment to deliver flexibility and adaptability that characterizes almost every partnership.

One of the most substantive contributions a broker can make is in getting inside different partner perspectives. A broker can see the richness of the contribution in methodologies/approaches, resources or experiences that each partner can bring to the partnership more easily than the partners themselves might do. He/she can then help them tap into such diversity, actively exploring and exploiting sectoral and organizational differences to create something that would be far greater than the sum of its parts. For instance, an effective broker may take the different sectoral approaches to strategy making, planning, performance evaluation and communication and help them mix and match to create a new framework that would suit the partnership as a whole and still satisfy each partner's expectations.

A good broker needs to provide practical, productive and tactful interventions, supporting rather than dominating the partnering process and accepting that you have to be ready and willing to let go when the partners are ready and hand over roles in a systematic way. The broker works on behalf of the partnership. If the broker does too much, the chances are that the partners are doing too little and are overly reliant on the broker. He/she may help the partners to understand the challenges they face and build their capacity to address them collaboratively, but the partners must take ultimate responsibility for finding solutions.

The growing uptake of brokering skills training offered by PBA also highlights another important attribute – a good broker recognizes his/her own professional limitations and takes steps to improve themselves through training courses, learning from doing, coaching and mentoring and through reflective practice.

Re-imagining social partnerships – brokers as tomorrow's leaders?

Over the past 20 years, we have accumulated enough experiential evidence to help position brokers appropriately in the partnership and build a case for how their particular skills and attributes make a difference to the effectiveness of a partnership. We may take this notion further to ask if partnership brokers role model a new form of leadership – one that suits the kinds of responsible business and development paradigms being proposed for the twenty-first century.

Thought leadership and enquiry led by PBA proposes that we can: the attributes of non-directive or facilitative leadership or "servant leadership" (Greenleaf, 1991) fit more closely with the collaborative model and hence, are fundamental to good partnership brokering. Traditional models of leadership do not nurture collaboration, as they tend to be located in single sector paradigms (making cross-sector work difficult); rooted in specific cultural traditions (making international work difficult); hierarchical in nature (making shared decision-making and shared accountability difficult). In comparison, facilitative leadership attributes such as modesty with regard to personal achievements to empower others, willingness to carry a level of risk on behalf of, or for the benefit of others, ability to show some foresight and inspire others with their vision of future possibilities, capacity to manage uncertainty and complexity to create clarity and productive interactions are better suited to collaborative models (Tennyson, 2011).

Although we have gained considerable understanding of the nature and value of partnership brokering in relation to partnership paradigms, there is a great deal more we can do to test the claims made for brokering and build more evidence for the impact of partnership brokers on cross-sector collaboration and how facilitative leadership might work in practice. It is increasingly clear that without the kind of servant leadership that partnership brokers can bring with their emphasis on empowering partners to become servant leaders themselves, many social partnerships – however strong the claims made for them – will fall short of achieving their full potential in creating a better future. In fact, they may simply fail.

Questions for reflection

1 The business, public and non-profit sectors each have their own competencies, priorities, values and attributes. How can this diversity help – or hinder – cross-cultural collaboration? What role should a partnership broker play in harnessing the different sectoral contributions to social partnerships?

2 What kinds of challenges is an internal partnership broker likely to face from within his/her own organization and from the partners?

3 What key skills would you expect a good partnership broker to have in supporting social partnerships?

4 What kinds of personal behaviours and attributes could affect the impact a partnership broker has on his/her brokering work?

5 Why do you think attributes of non-directive or facilitative leadership (also known as "servant leadership") would fit more closely with social partnerships?

6 What do you think stops companies from seeing partnering for social innovation as a viable way of delivering responsible business management? Suggest changes that would be required in the business model and organizational culture of companies to support more cross-sectoral collaboration. Who should lead this change?

Notes

1   See *Principles of Partnership Brokering Good Practice*, Partnership Brokering Association http://partnershipbrokers.org/w/brokering/principles-of-good-practice.
2   Evidence comes from experiential learning, observation and action research. Although there is academic research into cross-sector partnerships including their management, the author is not aware of any notable academic literature on theory or practice of cross-sector partnership brokering.
3   Ros Tennyson, independent partnership broker and social entrepreneur www.rostenny son.info, Co-founder of postgraduate course in cross-sector partnerships (with the University of Cambridge), co-founder of the Partnering Initiative (IBLF's specialist partnership unit), co-founder and director, lead trainer and mentor Partnership Brokers Association
4   Michael Warner, co-founder with Ros Tennyson of the Partnership Brokers Accreditation Scheme; led the development of multi-sector partnerships at ODI and the World Bank's Business Partners for Development programme.
5   Partnership Brokers Association http://partnershipbrokers.org). The website is a comprehensive source on partnership brokering principles and practice, training, and on developments in the brokering movement.
6   Accenture Development Partnerships, www.accenture.com/us-en/consulting/inter national-development.
7   African Development Bank www.afdb.org/en/about-us/structure/complexes/country-regional-programs-policy.
8   UN Office of Partnerships, www.un.org/partnerships.
9   The Partnering Initiative, http://thepartneringinitiative.org.
10 See *What do partnership brokers do? An enquiry into practice* (PBA 2012) Includes extracts from the log books of accredited partnership brokers.
11 See Partnership Brokering Association website – Partnership Broker Roles and Skills page http://partnershipbrokers.org/w/brokering/roles-and-skills.

References

Greenleaf, R.K. (1991) *Servant Leadership*. New York: Paulist Press.
Hundal, S. and Tennyson R. (2010) Partnership Brokering Units and Organizations. A paper developed during a partnership brokering training session with the African Development Bank, Tunis November 2010. Available at: http://partnershipbrokers.org/w/wp-content/uploads/2010/07/Brokering-units-organisations.pdf.
Partnership Brokering Association (2012) What Do Partnerships Do – An Enquiry into Practice. Available at: http://partnershipbrokers.org/w/wp-content/uploads/2010/07/What-do-Partnership-Broker-Do.pdf.
Tennyson R. (1998) *Managing Partnerships – Tools for Mobilizing the Public Sector, Business and Civil Society as Partners in Development*. London: International Business Leaders Forum.
Tennyson, R. (2003) *Institutionalizing Partnerships: Lessons from the Front Line*. London: International Business Leaders Forum.
Tennyson R. (2005) *The Brokering Guidebook – Navigating Effective Sustainable Development Partnerships*. The Partnering Initiative. London: International Business Leaders Forum.
Tennyson, R. (2011) Partnership Broker's Profile: Brokering Archetypes, Personal Attributes, Technical skills and Resources. Partnership Brokering Association. Available at: http://partnershipbrokers.org/w/wpcontent/uploads/2010/07/Partnership-Brokers-Pro file.pdf

Tennyson, R. and Wilde L. (2000) *The Guiding Hand – Brokering Partnerships for Sustainable Development*. New York: United Nations Department of Public Information on behalf of Prince of Wales International Business Leaders Forum and United Nations Staff College.

Warner, M. (2003a) *The New Broker, Brokering Partnerships for Development*. London: Overseas Development Institute.

Warner, M. (2003b) *Partnerships for Sustainable Development: Do We Need Partnership Brokers?* London: Overseas Development Institute.

22

SOCIAL PARTNERSHIPS

A new social contract to deliver value-focused collaboration

Lucian J. Hudson

Social partnerships signal a paradigm-shift in how we as a society combine the principles of a free-market or mixed economy with the need to make practical progress on social problems, many of which are complex and require collaborative resolution. We have yet to realize their potential. By embracing the political role of partnerships, opportunities can be created for more effective cross-sector leadership, especially by business.

Cross-sector collaboration: a revised formula

I argue for a new social contract, based on a 3+2 formula, representing the added value each sector brings to effective cross-sector collaboration, especially business taking the lead role in identifying and exploiting economic opportunity. The three main constituent parts of cross-sector collaboration are government, business, and civil society. Each delivers a distinctive dividend: political (government), economic (business), and social (civil society).

The two other elements are (i) universities and other higher education institutions, especially their access to teaching and research expertise and students as a source for an up-skilled workforce, and (ii) real-time citizen engagement and feedback on social initiatives. The latter becomes increasingly important with the growth of social media networks, and their power in producing fast a virtual ground-up mass collaboration of active citizens. Their potential is not just social, but political and economic.

This is an emerging example of how such an ecosystem might work at a city level. The Open University (OU) is one of the main employers in Milton Keynes, and works in partnership with the local council[1]. The city council sets the strategy for developing a knowledge economy, focused on economic development and harnessing inward investment from British and international companies. Underpinning its plans is a strong presumption that business leads are creating opportunities, working with national and local stakeholders. One of the city's main challenges is up-skilling its workforce. Milton Keynes is attractive to new business because of its close links to London, and land is cheaper. But it does not have enough of a workforce that can meet the needs of a more knowledge-based economy. Collaboration is being taken to a new level: business is planning to commit itself to generating more jobs if universities and other partners deliver the training and development.

The new social contract: four main features

A more strategic mind-set; a more upstream business model

The real value of collaboration is strategic, where the focus is as much on the *public outcomes* produced by the collaboration as on the *interests of the partners*. Collaboration needs to move upstream, so that projects do not just draw on collaboration at implementation stage, but in their strategic intent and design. Following the Rio+20 UN Earth Summit, John Ashton, former Special Representative on Climate Change to three successive British Foreign Secretaries, argues that both business and civil society have yet to tap their strategic role, "Business needs to shift the Amazon River of private capital from unsustainable production and consumption to sustainable production and consumption. Civil society organizations do not realize how much public trust they can build on if they pull together on shared agendas, when trust is fast draining from governments and business."[2]

Collaboration increases the number of stakeholder interests that need to be satisfied, and therefore makes a strategic consideration of options more likely. "Strategic" here includes responding to emerging evidence about the size of the market. Using the Strategy Management Dynamics model developed by Kim Warren[3], as the then head of programming at BBC Worldwide I showed that new cable channels in new (at the time, Latin American) markets may well grow, but will reach saturation point earlier if they do not monitor why at exit stage subscribers fail to renew their cable subscriptions. Without such feedback, we risked deluding ourselves that growth is sustainable. The fact that this was part of a joint venture with US partners Discovery meant that we were under the scrutiny of two parent organizations to manage risk and opportunity.

Greater role clarity and negotiating boundaries

Each social partner needs to be clearer and more explicit about its respective role, and actively manage boundaries to avoid duplication and exploit synergy. Political skill in working with different agendas and styles, particularly managing complexity, uncertainty and difference, is integral all at levels to making partnerships work.

Governments, national, regional, and local, set the macroeconomic, fiscal, and regulatory framework and priorities for concerted action informed by a democratic mandate. Civil society harnesses public trust and passion for a specific social change.

But it is business that is in the best position to act on economic opportunity, especially locally, and lead on securing investment and making a return. Government needs to recognize its role in providing the architecture in which business operates, and in delivering critical infrastructure and public services. This means removing barriers and increasing levers for business to function effectively. For the whole to be greater than the sum of its parts, outcomes must be judged by their measurable impact on citizens. Recent developments in philanthropic investment are instructive: the Civil Society Forum, set up to foster leadership and cross-sector collaboration among civil society organizations, is developing a workstream with donors to encourage blended investment, where return is a mix of interest rate and social impact.

Collaboration and competition

Collaborative leaders understand how decisions impact on a complex system. Interaction between different parts of the system will produce unforeseen consequences, which require a timely and agile response. Effective collaboration puts value on every link in the chain.

Business's ability – when functioning optimally – to be close to the customer is highly relevant to social partnerships, in responding to, and anticipating demand. Another insight of business is that competition and collaboration coexist. Both are needed to deliver quality and continuous improvement.

The collaborative nature of social partnerships is similar to managing complex supply-chains that companies such Toyota have mastered. Toyota created an ecosystem where suppliers were in competition, yet saw themselves at another level as collaborating. Suppliers learnt from competitors and adapted good practice to drive up their own standards. This resulted in Toyota managing an integrated system of suppliers competing to improve quality and cut costs while being given scope to increase their markets because of Toyota's growing demand. Had Toyota just focused on cost, they would not have brought on over time a network of suppliers contributing to quality outcomes. But this meant that suppliers should see themselves as delivering as part of a bigger whole, and adopting common systems, processes, and standards.

Business focus and social purpose

Given the complexity of today's social challenges, the left-right dichotomy of public versus private no longer holds. Top-down direction needs to be complemented by ground-up engagement. Markets are only as efficient as societies allow them to be. Maintaining public trust is essential. Business has a leadership role, but is only as effective as the cross-sector collaboration that exists to legitimize it and support it.

Western capitalism has in its current form failed to deliver long-term, sustainable growth and a better integrated society. But this does not mean that business loses its role in driving economic growth, only that it cannot operate without wider legitimacy. This new contract requires that leadership rests with business, provided it can take an enlarged view of its role, and act as a catalyst for cross-sector collaboration. Business needs to balance the profit motive with social purpose, and work with government and civil society to secure the social and political buy-in and infrastructure support that it requires to succeed.

The heart-transplant test can be applied when considering change in a single organization or across organizations. Many early heart transplants were technically successful: but the host body rejected them. With a better understanding of the body's immunological response, transplants worked because the body accepted them. The same applies to changes in organizations and sectors. We need to create the ecosystems to receive and sustain social partnerships. This means seeing social partnerships as part of a nexus of communities and networks, improving partnership selection, design and institutionalization, and appreciating the politics inside and outside the partnership.[4]

Engagement with multiple stakeholders has consequences. Every "stake" represents potentially another set of power-relations to be negotiated and re-negotiated. The growth in social media networks means that civil society organizations and groups of consumers can lever pressure by harnessing support and influencing perceptions of a business's brand, product, or service.

The British Foreign and Commonwealth Office commissioned me to deliver a report in 2009 assessing for the first time in any Western government how cross-sector collaboration works.[5] My research covered the period before and after the 2008 Global Financial Crisis, which made the theme of collaboration even more relevant at a time of international coordination in response to systemic market failure.

In reviewing what had changed over the past five years, my respondents confirm that cross-sector collaboration had made major inroads. Jim Thompson, leading the US State Department's work on partnerships, says, "The economic downturn in 2008 made partnerships more essential. While many Corporate Social Responsibility dollars disappeared and companies re-evaluated their CSR initiatives and made them aligned better to core business, this made partnering more important. To get an effect, one could no longer afford to go it alone and the partnering world took off."[6]

The advent of a new business legal classification in the United States – benefit corporations – can transform the way business performs, so that business success is measured by commitment to specific social goals, as well as hitting the financial bottom line. Business school courses in entrepreneurship – particularly social entrepreneurship – are of increasing appeal. Public and professional recognition of social entrepreneurs – through the work of the Skoll Foundation and others – is embedding a culture where business and social good are much more closely aligned.

To the extent that capitalism, especially since the Global Financial Crisis and ensuing economic instability, remains in continual crisis, social partnerships offer the promise of delivering what societies in their twentieth-century configuration could not, without deepening ideological divides.

Social partnerships could become more mainstream if their political role is accepted. By "political," I mean their role in producing social outcomes with underpinning public support, a result of finding common ground and embracing difference. With every successful partnership, we create another "fact on the ground" that builds confidence. They are still an inherently "ideological" phenomenon, in the Althusserian sense that ideology at its most effective hides its own agenda, and appears as natural, common sense, or necessary. Whether one is a policy-maker or an entrepreneur, the challenge to overcome is to temper or eliminate the ideological in its raw form, so that social partnerships become a natural feature of how twenty-first century organizes itself.

Questions for reflection

1   What are the implications for leadership in recognizing the political role of social partnerships in affecting social change?
2   How might business leadership adapt to changing priorities that balance the profit motive with social responsibility?
3   What challenges does multiple stakeholder engagement present in keeping social partnerships focused on their business goals?
4   What opportunities do social media networks create in supporting social partnerships?

Notes

1   As part of the city's Economic Development Forum, the Open University facilitates collaboration between local government, business, and civil society, including knowledge economy and inward investment workshops to attract and support employers.
2   Interview with John Ashton, July 8, 2012 (conducted for this chapter, with permission to publish).
3   Warren, K. (2008). *Strategy Management Dynamics.* Chichester: Wiley.
4   Seitanidi, M.M. (2010). *The Politics of Partnerships: A Critical Examination of Nonprofit Partnerships.* London: Springer.
5   Hudson, L.J. (2009). *The Enabling State: Collaborating for Success.* London: FCO. Available at: www.mbsportal.bl.uk/taster/subjareas/strategy/fco/enabling09.aspx.
6   Correspondence with James Thompson, 19 May 2012 (permission to publish).

23
SOCIAL PARTNERSHIPS' DEVELOPMENT CHALLENGE

Comprehensive self-development

Steve Waddell

Competencies

The term "competency" has spurred a number of interpretations (Deist and Winterton, 2005). To expediently advance the discussion of competency with SPs, there are two perspectives that are useful. Hamel and Prahalad defined core competence as "the collective learning in the organization, especially how to co-ordinate diverse production skills and integrate multiple streams of technologies" (Hamel and Prahalad, 1994: 82). This strategic organizational-level view of competencies can be usefully applied to SPs as a specific organizational form. What is the collective learning that a SP must have, to be effective? This can be usefully matched with the individual perspective on competency that often has been associated with three elements:

- Knowledge: through education and experience we gain knowledge about facts and understanding about how something works.
- Skills: these are associated with talent and application of knowledge in an effective way. It can be vis-à-vis a technical skill such as use of a software, or an interpersonal skill as in "diplomatic skills."
- Attributes/behavioral qualities: these are about actions in specific situations. Thoughtfulness, ability to react, inventiveness, and personality are all examples.

The concept of competency is closely associated with expertise. There are three types of expertise that are associated with SPs:

- *Issue expertise:* this is substantive knowledge about the issue the partnership is tackling, e.g. transparency, youth employment, AIDS. For learning and knowledge partnerships, this is core. And all networks must possess participants who have this type of expertise. But most often the core expertise of a partnership is creating an effective partnership that realizes synergies and coordination.

- *Tool expertise:* many partnerships, particularly larger and enduring ones, have one or more core tools that they have to realize their goals. For Transparency International, one is "anti-corruption pacts" such as one between all the stakeholders building the new Berlin airport; for the Forest Stewardship Council one is a certification process; for the Global Fund to Fight AIDS, one is financing mechanisms. SPs must be expert at developing and implementing these.
- *Process expertise:* this is the type of expertise associated with the competency model. Partnerships are well described with biological metaphors: they are living, evolving, conscious entities working as an ecosystem. What is the expertise necessary to ensure the health of the system?

A comprehensive competency framework

Figure 23.1 aims to present a comprehensive competency framework. Some competencies are closely associated with actual staff responsibilities in larger partnerships, and with activities in smaller ones. For example, there is usually need for communication competency, and measurement and evaluation. Some competencies – like those just mentioned – reflect ones needed in non-partnership organizations; however, SPs have very particular spins on these traditions. The importance of a specific competency will vary with partnerships and their tasks.

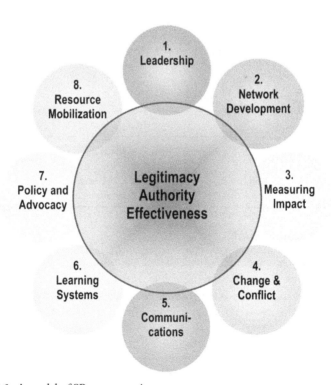

FIGURE 23.1 A model of SP competencies

This framework has already stimulated interest by researchers and practitioners, who are asking questions about how to assess the presence of the competencies and create explicit strategies for their development. It can also be used as a framework for deepening understanding of bottlenecks in a partnership's activities and establish priorities for capacity development.

Leadership

This competency for partnerships is particularly distinctive in comparison to non-partnership organizations. Whereas leadership in the latter is usually associated with an individual and position in a hierarchy, successful partnerships are characterized by "leaderfulness" where "everyone shares the experience of serving as a leader, not sequentially, but concurrently and collectively" (Raelin, 2003). Peter Block earlier described it as "stewardship" (Block, 1993). Ania Grobicki, Global Water Partnership Executive Secretary reflects this in response to key qualities she'd look for in someone to replace her: "The desire to serve … to want really to serve people and lead the organization to achieve our vision and mission through service."

Partnership leaders must know how to lead collaboratively: being mindful of the whole "system" and cultivating leadership throughout to generate alignment and forward movement. One of the most comprehensive analyses of leadership in the network field usefully emphasizes it as a competency of *Levels:* individuals, teams, organizations, communities, and fields of policy and practice; and of *Goals of the Development Effort:* building capacity of individuals, teams, organizations, networks and systems (McGonagill and Pruyn, 2010). Table 23.1 suggests some top skills and attributes.

TABLE 23.1 Leadership

Partnership skills	Partnership attributes
• Connecting	• Systems intelligent
• Stewarding	• Leaderful (Raelin)
• Handling paradox and ambiguity	• Trustworthy
	• Entrepreneurial

Network development

This is the competency usually associated with partnerships: creating a partnership's development cycle of initial investigation, initiation, scaling, and possibly terminating. The partnership requires knowledge about bringing organizations and people into it and creating the needed scale, and about governance structures and decision-making processes. Table 23.2 suggests some top skills and attributes.

TABLE 23.2 Network development

Partnership skills	Partnership attributes
• Systems thinking	• Empathetic
• Community organizing/Network weaving	• Trustworthy
• Strategizing	• Visionary
• Empowering	• Entrepreneurial

Measuring impact

Traditional organizations generally focus on relatively short input-output cycles, with much less focus on the longer term. Sometimes SPs are very task-focused and should use traditional evaluation tools for such cycles. However, they are often working on much more complex, ambiguous issues that require a focus on the longer term impact, while paying attention of course to short-term activities (and using such impact tools for that). The required framework impact measurement tools are more developmental and related to theories of change and social capital (Allee and Schwabe, 2009; IDRC, 2010; Patton, 2010).

TABLE 23.3 Measuring impact

Partnership skills	Partnership attributes
• Measuring and evaluating	• Attentive to detail (but not meticulous)
• Action learning	• Diversity embracing
• Analysing large, complex systems	• Inquisitive
	• Theory-based

Change and conflict

Gray and Purdy (2014), and Stafford and Hartman (2014) addressed these issues earlier in this volume, testifying to their importance. At the very least, forming an SP implies change in the way participants have traditionally worked. It is not simply doing more of the same; it is about doing it differently. Additionally, many SPs are focused on transformational change – a much larger process involving fundamental changes in power, roles, goals, and the way goals are understood (Waddell, 2011). SPs must embrace change theories and be knowledgeable about how to enact them.

TABLE 23.4 Change and conflict

Partnership skills	Partnership attributes
• Stewarding change processes	• Patient
• Systems thinking	• Empathic
• Facilitating/mediating/Negotiating/visioning	• Open
	• Persistent

Communications

SPs must be competent with traditional "telling," pre-social media communication to ensure others know who they are and what they are doing; but even more importantly, they must be competent at generating engaged information flows and conversations to support action. Particularly with respect to the latter, there is a complicated array of tools to master, to develop the cycle of listen-engage-generate buzz-create social content-community building (Kanter, 2010).

TABLE 23.5 Communications

Partnership skills	Partnership attributes
• Listening, writing, speaking, visualizing • Conversing • Creating community platforms	• Creative • Open • Participatory • Empathetic

Learning systems

This competency aims to support all three types of competencies: issue, tool, and process. Learning is done in order to achieve a SP's purposes; learning is shared or distributed by people throughout the SP; and learning outcomes are institutionalized in the processes, systems, and structures of the SP (Snyder, 1996). SPs should know how to create "communities of practice" and a "learning ecology" that comprises a full range of learning activities from learning journeys through classroom learning (Snyder and Wenger, 2004). For some SPs, this will actually be their core work.

TABLE 23.6 Learning systems

Partnership skills	Partnership attributes
• Developing systems • Learning • Teaching • Connecting	• Patient • Empathic • Clear • Wise

Policy development

Here the competency is about policy for all the SP participants, and often for outside "targets" of influence. Stakeholder/organizational "representatives" in an SP almost always must find ways to change their home turf's way of working and policies, simply to realize an SP's goals. This requires knowledge about policy development processes, and how to influence them.

TABLE 23.7 Policy and advocacy

Partnership skills	Partnership attributes
• Action learning	• Legitimate
• Developing policy	• Authoritative
• Connecting cross-sector	• Persuasive

Resource mobilization

SPs almost always are in a resource-constrained situation. There is weak understanding and appreciation for the amount of time and resources required, to make a SP function. Particularly in task-focused SPs, people tend to think of them transactionally like markets, rather than relationally like communities. Funding mechanisms are particularly complicated given the multi-stakeholder nature of SPs and that money is closely associated with power. SP funding strategies generically still require significant development.

Of course resource mobilization involves much more than money. Mobilization of skills, competencies, non-financial resources, and knowledge is often a core purpose of SPs. Knowing how to do this effectively is extremely important.

TABLE 23.8 Resource mobilization

Partnership skills	Partnership attributes
• Developing business models	• Persuasive
• Translating needs into opportunities	• Transparent
• Managing finances	• Accountable

Competency development strategies

This author's view is that SPs, particularly ones of duration and scale, are a new type of organization as different from business as business is from civil society and government organizations. SPs' logic is distinctive: it is about social weaving as opposed to wealth creation, governing, and community health. Shoving SPs into an NGO or non-profit framework retards their development with inappropriate mindsets, mental models, and attitudes; we actually need new legal forms to support their qualities, particularly the transnational and global qualities of large ones.

However, the author's common experience is that there is deep under-appreciation even amongst SP participants of the need for capacity development. There is a naïve attitude often that it is just about getting people together and "it" will happen. And often there is an entrepreneurial spirit of "we're just doing it ... we will learn as we go!"

This is not going to get us to where we have got to go with the level of sophistication and SP scale the world needs. We have developed schools of government, of business and of non-profits to build their competencies and knowledge to support their development. We need something similar for SPs.

However, traditional classroom-based education is only one vehicle in developing competencies. Their development should be integrated into the daily work of SPs, so they do indeed become learning networks. Communities of Practice, learning ecology, and world learning systems provide powerful frameworks for developing SPs as learning networks.

As a first step, there are increasing activities to bring together SP participants to learn collaboratively and to develop new knowledge. For example, there is the Multi-Organizational Alliances, Partnerships and Networks (MOPAN), there are events often sponsored by non-profit schools like Harvard's Hauser Center and Erasmus University's Partnerships Resource Center, there are specialized consultancies like Interaction Institute, and the author has led development of communities of practice and virtual education programs.

All this requires reinforcement through numerous drivers, as described in an excellent report (Baser and Morgan, 2008). For example, one is formal structures, processes and systems. SPs can further reinforce the development of these competencies by creating organizational units and titles and teams associated with them to focus the development of the capacity. Large SPs will often have something like a department for Network Development and for communications, monitoring, and evaluation, something for resource mobilization, often for policy, and sometimes for learning.

Over the past 20 years, tremendous progress has been made in SP development. Increasing their competency is critical for progress in the next 20.

Questions for reflection

1   How does the relative importance of particular competencies vary given such factors as a partnership's goals, size, development stage, and participant profile?
2   How can the presence of a competency be assessed?
3   What are the strategic and structural implications for developing robust levels of competencies? Should partnerships allocate responsibilities for a specific competency? How can competency development be integrated into daily work life?

References

Allee, V. and Schwabe, O. (2009) *Measuring the Impact of Research Networks in the EU: Value Networks and Intellectual Capital Formation*. Haarlem, the Netherlands: European Conference on Intellectual Capital.

Baser, H. and Morgan, P. (2008) Capacity, change and performance. *Discussion Paper No 59B*. Brussels, Belgium, European Centre for Development Policy Management.

Block, P. (1993) *Stewardship: Choosing Service Over Self-Interest*. San Francisco: Berrett-Koehler.

Deist, F.D.L. and Winterton, J. (2005) What is competence? *Human Resource Development International*, 8 (1): 27–46.

Gray, B. and Purdy, J. (2014) Conflict in cross-sector partnerships, in Seitanidi, M. M. and Crane, A. (eds) *Social Partnerships and Responsible Business: A Research Handbook.* London: Routledge: 205–26.

Hamel, G. and Prahalad, C.K. (1994) *Competing for the Future.* Cambridge, MA: Harvard Business School Press.

IDRC (2010) Outcome mapping. Retrieved April 5, 2010, from www.idrc.ca/en/ev-26586-201-1-DO_TOPIC.html.

Kanter, B. (2010) Nonprofit social media strategy map. Retrieved April 5, 2010, from http://bit.ly/9wM9y6.

McGonagill, G. and Pruyn, P.W. (2010) Leadership development in the US: principles and patterns of best practice, in S.Vopel (ed.) *Bertelsmann Stiftung Leadership Series.* Berlin: Bertelsmann Stiftung.

Patton, M.Q. (2010) *Developmental Evaluation: Applying Complexity Concepts to Enhance Innovation and Use.* New York: Guilford Press.

Raelin, J. (2003) *Creating Leaderful Organizations: How to Bring Out Leadership in Everyone.* San Francisco: Berrett-Koehler.

Snyder, W.M. (1996) Organization learning and performance: an exploration of The linkages between organization learning, knowledge, and performance. Dissertation, University of Southern Callifornia.

Snyder, W.M. and Wenger, E. (2004) Our world as a learning system: a communities-of-practice approach, in M.L. Conner and J.G. Clawson (eds) *Creating a Learning Culture: Strategy, Technology, and Practice.* Cambridge: Cambridge University Press: 35–58.

Stafford, E. and Hartman, C. (2014) NGO-initiated sustainable entrepreneurship and social partnerships: Greenpeace's "Solutions" campaign for natural refrigerants in North America, in Seitanidi, M.M. and Crane, A. (eds) *Social Partnerships and Responsible Business: A Research Handbook.* London: Routledge: 164–90.

Waddell, S. (2011) *Global Action Networks: Creating our Future Together.* Bocconi University on Management. Basingstoke, Palgrave Macmillan.

24

CROSS-SECTOR PARTNERSHIPS

Prototyping twenty-first-century governance

Simon Zadek

Blind men and the elephant

Cross-sector partnerships can be all things to all people. Like the parable of the blind men and the elephant, how they are seen depends on which aspect one explores, and explorers' worldly pre-conceptions.

Over time, views of partnerships also evolve, and my views are a case in point. Writing with Jane Nelson in *Partnership Alchemy*, we expressed a widely held view of partnerships as a pragmatic means of blending competencies to get stuff done (Nelson and Zadek, 2000). AccountAbility's *Innovation through Partnership*, on the other hand, hypothesized that partnerships were a source of social, institutional, and business innovation, a perspective that has since taken hold amidst students and practitioners (Sabapathy *et al.*, 2002). *The Logic of Collaborative Governance*, a Harvard publication, raised the stakes further in setting out potential governance roles of partnerships (Zadek, 2006), building on the five-stage corporate responsibility maturity pathway set out in a Harvard Business Review article, *Paths to Corporate Responsibility* (Zadek, 2004). This logic was further developed in the new chapter to *The Civil Corporation* (Zadek, 2007) and transposed into an international development context in a Brookings Institute publication, *Collaborative Governance: The New Multilateralism for the 21st Century* (Zadek, 2008). *Titans or Titanic*, finally, reflects my more recent interest in whether partnerships provide a prototype for an emergent form of corporate governance (Zadek, 2012).

It is this last aspect of our much-studied elephant that is the focus of this short essay. Proposed here is that cross-sector partnerships offer vital signals of how the governance of a new generation of business organizations and public institutions might operate in a manner fit for the twenty-first century.

Limits of intensive accountability

"Corporate responsibility" in its most recent decades has provided a mirror image of the increasingly intensive accountability of businesses to financial capital. Its modern form is a counterpoint to the neoliberal response to perceived shortfalls of many forms of state intervention in our economic affairs, and equally of the observed weaknesses in pluralistic accountability structures such as co-operatives. Corporate responsibility in this sense has provided both a cover for this development and a basis for its contestation.

Cross sector partnerships have been central to this contestation. Overcoming backward-looking markets that continue to externalize social and environmental costs that appear to have no value to business required new rules and new business approaches. Individual companies were in the main unable to achieve either alone, and so sought others to join in such enterprises. Businesses seeking to navigate new waters established temporary alliances with those constituting new potential threats to value creation, notably civil society. Resulting cross-sector partnerships, at least those with more than philanthropic intent, were created with the objective of over-coming so-called "market failures." Some became the purveyors of new standards; some pumped resources into under-funded public goods; yet others lobbied for statutory changes. All sought to improve the alignment of private gain, namely profit making, to some aspect of the public good.

And there has been notable progress, from saving forests to developing vaccines to addressing poor peoples' health problems, to advancing everything from improved workplace conditions to freedom of expression on the internet. Yet whilst such progress has been measurable and at times of astonishing, life-saving value for those impacted directly, partnerships have remained marginal with rare exceptions to the workings of today's global markets. Crucially, the forceful pressure of financial capital has increased. Simultaneously, such capital has become more impatient, with frankly less interest in the fortunes of the real economy. Intensive accountability to finance capital, far from being overcome or even counter-balanced by manifestations of corporate responsibility, including partnerships, has become an ever-greater blight on our economic landscape. Estimates of the economic consequences of the financial crisis vary, for example, but tend to hover around one year's global income, an astronomical sum by any measure. Equally, the environmental costs of our current economic logic are inexorably on the rise, as are levels of income inequality within nations.

Towards a public fiduciary

In today's corporate world, a fiduciary duty is a legal or ethical relationship of confidence or trust regarding the management of money or property between two or more parties (UNEP, 2009). Most commonly, this duty exists between two parties, the principal or intended beneficiary in the relationship, and the fiduciary or agent that acts on the principal's behalf. Framed in these terms, our dilemma is when the principal does not have the capacity to exercise effective oversight over the fiduciary. Today, this is understood to be in exceptional circumstances where the principal is for example a child or disabled or in some other way deemed "unable to act effectively on her or his own behalf." In such instances, there is in many countries the provision in law to allow for a "public fiduciary," essentially a public official or agency appointed to serve as guardian, conservator, or personal representative for those individuals or estates with no one else willing or capable of serving.

A public fiduciary is, then, a helpful frame for understanding the shift from an intensive to a more extensive basis of accountability baked into the fiduciary rules and processes, rather than only the broader legal limitations to the pursuit of financial gains. Asserting the imperative for establishing a public fiduciary is the governing equivalence of demanding that negative social and environmental externalities be internalized into the strategic purpose of the business. The governance of the evolution of business in society can therefore be framed in terms of "the need to build a "public fiduciary" to represent those voices not able to represent themselves, notably natural capital and today's excluded communities and future generations."

There is perhaps no greater sacrilege in the world of corporate governance than to propose the politicization of the governing process. Indeed, many if not most civil society activists in the area of corporate accountability would likewise opt for a reassertion of the state as gamekeeper and the business as poacher approach rather than seek to institutionalize a broader fiduciary goal for business. Yet the facts do get in the way of such conservatism, irrespective of its merits. A second wave of corporate responsibility, unintentionally and using different mechanisms, is seeking to develop extensive accountability beyond the voluntary practice of codes, standards, and partnerships. Such developments are likely to realign the formal rules of corporate governance.

Shifting towards a public fiduciary is not so much a distant wish as self-evident. Most obvious is the extending role of the State in the ownership of economic assets in these countries. Today state-owned oil and natural gas companies, such as Saudi Aramco, Petróleos de Venezuela, and China National Petroleum Corp., own 73 per cent of the world's oil reserves and 68 per cent of its natural gas. Similarly, in 2008, the state-owned share of global mining production value amounts to about 24 per cent (Raw Materials Group, 2011). According to the Inter-American Development Bank, the percentage of state ownership in the banking industry globally by the mid-1990s is over 40 per cent, with the BRIC countries – Brazil, Russia, India, and China – leading the way with its heavy use of public sector banks, comprising about 75 per cent of the banks in India, 69 per cent or more in China, 45 per cent in Brazil, and 60 per cent in Russia.

Classical state ownership of enterprises is, however, only one of several routes through which public interest is being asserted in the matter of business through ownership and governance. Sovereign wealth funds, especially those of China and the Middle East, are rapidly growing in number and size, broadly expected to grow in assets under management from their current level of US$4 trillion to more than US$7 trillion over the course of this decade, powered by a combination of high commodity prices and concentrated trade surpluses. Whilst still representing only a modest fraction of the overall size of today's global capital markets, these funds punch well above their weight during this current period of unstable capital markets, recapitalization seeking companies and countries, and under-priced assets. National and regional development banks are another source of state-controlled investment, and are increasingly active in international markets, including increasingly the huge, state-owned development banks in emerging economies, such as the China Development Bank and Brazil's BNDES.

At a smaller scale, but with significant potential, is the emerging debate and practice of extended social enterprises in developed economies, notably the United States. "Corporation 2020," a US-based initiative, exemplifies this trend, having gathered leading practitioners from around the world in a large-scale co-design exercise focused on modelling the corporations needed for a sustainable future. A parallel but aligned initiative, again in the United States, has been the enactment of legislation to allow companies to register as "B" Corporations that establishes fiduciary arrangements enabling and encouraging multiple accountability holders and interests to be considered in the process of corporate governance. With 500 businesses registered under this regulatory framework worth an annual US$3 billion in revenues, this experiment is clearly still small change. Yet both Corporation 2020 and the B Corporation approach are indications of what the US does best, experimenting in possible futures.

Questions for reflection

1 How do the governing rules enable a clear basis for making governance decisions that effectively mediate between public and private interests, especially in their manner for dealing with conflicts of interest?
2 How is the governance of a cross-sector partnership assessed, and what are the performance criteria that might be applied to ensure effective extended accountability?
3 What are the competencies required for non-executive directors governing cross-sector partnerships if they are to effectively oversee and guide the partnership's purpose?
4 What aspects of the governance of cross sector partnerships have structural durability enabling long term effectiveness, as opposed to their reliance on patronage of the great and good?
5 To what extent are governing arrangements culturally or otherwise biased, whether geographically or by virtue of the founding partners, and so how fair and balanced would they be seen by key stakeholders who have not yet joined?

And last but not least is the emerging practice of cross-sector partnerships. Diverse in their forms, functions, and scope, what they hold in common is a mandate to address a blend of private and public interests. This common feature has in turn driven a generation of experiments in how best to govern such blended and at times conflicting interests. Over time, some of these partnerships have become effectively permanent features of our institutional landscape, including many of the larger global health partnerships such as the Global Fund and GAVI, and the growing number of global sustainability standards initiatives stewarded by partnerships, such as the Forest Stewardship Council and the Extractive Industries Transparency Initiative (Litovsky, 2007; Potts *et al.*, 2010). Whilst rarely if ever conceived of as experiments in new forms of corporate governance, there is no doubt that in practice these partnership governance experiences provide one of the richest sources of data on how blended interest institutions can in practice be governed (Zadek and Radovich, 2006).

Competing futures

Today's business community is simply unable to deliver the required level of public goods from its historically embedded means of creating private value. The challenge is not "to make progress," but to make it rapidly and at scale, something that today's arrangements make difficult, if not impossible. Today's business community will be our collective Titanic unless we change the rules of the game. Three decades of contemporary "corporate responsibility has made a difference, but not enough. We may well have squeezed all we can under the hammer of privileging decisions that benefit private finance capital.

The experience of cross-sector partnerships provide one, competing driver of tomorrow's approach to corporate governance. Whether and if so how this rich experience will inform tomorrow's global economy will depend on how it fares against not only the incumbent's privileged focus on finance capital, but an array of approaches to extended accountability, including state-owned enterprises, state-controlled investment vehicles, and a blooming era of social enterprise models.

The outcome of these competing forces is not a matter of theory, but of practice. Cross-sector partnerships may prove no more than a bridging experience between the old and the new, forgotten by tomorrow's history in the light of more powerful forces, just as were the nineteenth-century romantic socialists. Or else such partnerships could turn out to provide the crucial demonstration that a pluralistic approach to the governance of our economic affairs, involving private and public actors, can be effective in delivering tomorrow's sustainable economy.

Notes

1   http://en.wikipedia.org/wiki/Blind_men_and_an_elephant
2   http://energyseminar.stanford.edu/node/403
3   http://the-tap.blogspot.com/2012/03/state-owned-banks-create-better.html
4   www.corporation2020.org/
5   www.bcorporation.net/
6   www.theglobalfund.org/en/
7   www.gavialliance.org/

References

Litovsky, A., Rochlin, S., Zadek, S. and Levy, B. (2007) *Investing in Standards for Sustainable Development: The Role of International Development Agencies in Supporting Collaborative,* London: AccountAbility.

Nelson, J. and Zadek, S. (2000) *Partnership Alchemy: New Social Partnerships in Europe,* Copenhagen: Copenhagen Centre.

Potts, J., van der Meer, J. and Daitchman, J. (2010) *The State of Sustainability Initiatives Review 2010: Sustainability and Transparency,* Winnepeg: International Institute of Sustainable Development.

Raw Materials Group (2011) *Overview of State Ownership in the Global Minerals Industry,* Washington, DC: World Bank.

Sabapathy, J., Swift, T., Weiser, J. and Polycarpe, M. (2002) *Innovation through Partnership,* London: Accountability.

UNEP (2009) *Fiduciary Responsibility: Legal and Practical Aspects of Integrating Environmental, Social and Governance Issues into Institutional Investment,* Paris: United Nations Environment Programme Finance Initiative.

Zadek, S. (2002) *Working with Multilaterals,* San Francisco: Business for Social Responsibility.

Zadek, S. (2004) "Paths to Corporate Responsibility," *Harvard Business Review,* December 2004.

Zadek, S. (2006) *The Logic of Collaborative Governance: Corporate Responsibility, Accountability, and the Social Contract,* Working Paper 17, Corporate Social Responsibility Initiative, Harvard Kennedy School, Cambridge, MA.

Zadek, S. (2007) *The Civil Corporation,* 2nd edn. London: Earthscan.

Zadek, S. (2008) "Collaborative Governance: the New Multilateralism for the 21st Century," *Global Development 2.0,* Washington, DC: Brookings Institute.

Zadek, S. (2012) "Titans or Titanic: Towards a Public Fiduciary," *Professional and Business Ethics Journal,* 31 (2): 207–2030.

Zadek, S. and Radovich, S. (2006) *Governing Collaborative Governance: Enhancing Development Outcomes by Improving Partnership Governance and Accountability,* Working Paper 23, Corporate Social Responsibility Initiative, Harvard Kennedy School, Cambridge, MA.

25

CONCLUSION

Re-imagining the future of social partnerships and responsible business

M. May Seitanidi and Andrew Crane

Life confronts us with many binary choices. Working in partnership is not one of those. Designing and managing a social partnership is rarely about simple yes/no options, but about including and coordinating in an artful way across multiple constituencies to achieve multiple goals. Consequently it is inevitable to expect significant variation in the way that researchers and practitioners come to understand such a complex phenomenon. This gives rise to a polyphonic representation of social partnerships and, as we have suggested in the introduction, a field in fragmentation (Crane and Seitanidi, 2014).

Our job as editors has been to make sense of this polyphony. As with an orchestra the conductor aims to synchronize the voices and instruments in melody allowing for the unique effect of a well-coordinated ensemble to emerge, while each component preserves its difference. We have sought to do so by drawing on the theme of the "social good" – our own "melody", if you like, to orchestrate perspectives, theories and methods to advance the emerging field of cross-sector social partnerships. This is because, as the world turns into a sea of collaboration, the question is often no longer one of: "To partner or not to partner?" but rather "How to partner in order to maximize the benefits for individuals, organizations and society?" (Austin and Seitanidi, 2012a; Austin and Seitanidi, 2012b).

As demonstrated by the chapters in this book, research and practice around social partnerships is gradually moving from identifying problems, to understanding their components, attempting solutions and is now shifting to the stage of developing more systematic solutions that lead to sustainable outcomes for the social good. Having reached this far does not imply that we fully understand and recognize how to partner and provide solutions to social problems consistently. More likely it means we have a few good templates that can guide us to imagine how to apply the lessons in new problems and different contexts.

However, sustainable outcomes for the social good are not always a clearly articulated focus in social partnerships and responsible business. In this book our aim was to make the connections between social partnerships and responsible business explicit by arriving at a social good articulation within different contexts, on different social issues, across different theories, and on providing a deeper understanding of the "how to" of partnerships. Employing the social good as the underlying intention or "instrumentation" fundamentally assigns *purpose* to social partnerships for theory and praxis; hence our collective proposition espouses a value perspective avoiding the agnostic or value-free viewpoint often associated with management. This requires novel theorizing and methodologizing, as well as new practices, as illustrated in Parts C and D in this book.

It should be said though that although partnerships hold the potential for making a difference at the level of the social good, this is not always the case. Guided by either *a priori* agreed responsibilities or *a posteriori* emerged responsibilities, partnerships aim to achieve in practice what sometimes seems impossible in theory, a compromise of the mutually exclusive economic and ethical viewpoints in responsible business (Windsor, 2006). It is at this point – the very intersection of social partnerships with responsible business – that the greatest challenges, but also the greatest possibilities for positive change are evident.

In this concluding chapter we aim to examine these challenges and opportunities for achieving the social good with a view to reimagining what the future of research and practice in social partnerships and responsible business could or should be like. As such, we review the preceding chapters in terms of the following questions:

1   How do the authors frame social partnerships and responsible business and how do they reframe the phenomenon in terms of the social good?
2   What are the main implications from our contributors regarding how social partnerships might be reimagined in the future?
3   How can we reconceptualize social partnerships in order to advance the social good?

How do authors frame social partnerships and responsible business and how do they reframe the phenomenon in terms of the social good?

Frames, according to Reese (2001: 11), constitute "organizing principles that are socially shared and persistent over time, that work symbolically to meaningfully structure the social world". In the following compilation (Table 25.1) we present our reading of the frames employed by the authors of each chapter of this book. The partnership phenomenon framing in Table 25.1 refers to the content level, i.e. how the author(s) framed social partnerships and responsible business and what the focal social issue was. The context level refers to the industry and country. Finally "reframing the phenomenon" answers to the question of what the suggested social good conceptions were. Our compilation aimed at remaining as close as possible to

TABLE 25.1 Phenomenon framing and re-framing

Authors	*Phenomenon: content level*		*Phenomenon: context level*		*Phenomenon re-framing*
	Understanding of the domain SPRB	*Social problem*	*Industry*	*Country*	*Interpretations of the social good through SP4RB*
Section A: Partnership for the social good? Local, national and global perspectives					
Kolk	Partnerships address complex social and environmental problems that are global and therefore often cross boundaries, cannot easily be solved by one single actor hence a multitude of partnerships emerge, involving government agencies, companies and non-governmental organizations (NGOs).	Multiple: Climate change; poverty	Multiple	Multiple	Social partnerships provide collective goods on the macro level by addressing global problems such as poverty, food security and climate change. Collaboration for the social good takes place through partnerships and trickle effects within and between levels of cross sector interactions.
Doh and Boddewyn	Social partnerships address public policy problems by negotiating roles and responsibilities for the provision of collective goods. MNEs collaborate with local and international NGOs to alleviate the institutional deficits in emerging markets.	Multiple: education, health	Multiple	Emerging markets	Social partnerships can serve the social good through the provision of collective goods in emerging markets.
Hamann	Social partnerships are an institutional response to institutional challenges. Social partnerships are a way for organizations to address their shortages and challenges in order to achieve their objectives; hence they are seen as new forms of governance.	Socio-ecological problems; development including reduction of crime; housing	Mining	South Africa: local and national levels	Social partnerships require a minimum level of consolidated statehood to have the potential to implement projects and/or policy recommendations as a partnership outcome for the delivery of public goods.
Clarke	Social partnerships are considered as a means to engage responsible businesses in community sustainable development.	Sustainability strategies	Multiple	Canada: local level	Local cross sector social partnerships that focus on sustainable development employ collaborative community sustainability strategy as a way to integrate social issues at the local level and serve the social good by prioritizing an ecological focus.

TABLE 25.1 Continued

	Phenomenon: content level		Phenomenon: context level		Phenomenon re-framing
Authors	Understanding of the domain SPRB	Social problem	Industry	Country	Interpretations of the social good through SP4RB
Section B: Management and governance challenges					
Schmutzler, Gutiérrez, Reficco and Márquez	Social partnerships are necessary means in creating inclusive businesses and overcoming the local challenges, increasing efficiency and creating value.	Access to products	Ceramic tiling	Colombia	Social partnerships increase the quality of life (social good) of poor communities by increasing access to products, services and financial resources.
Rufin and Rivera-Santos	Social partnerships are collaborative ventures that address challenges at the BoP (base of the pyramid) settings with the explicit aim to contribute to the financial profit of firms and the social good of urban poor in subsistence markets.	Alleviation of urban poverty	Multiple	Multiple	The positive (or negative) social and economic impact of social partnerships' governance for communities will depend on understanding the linkages between the operational levels at the BoP settings.
van Tulder and Pfisterer	Social partnerships are a necessary institutional innovation addressing complex sustainability problems and consist of new ways to manage societal relations across sectors.	Sustainable development	N/A	N/A	For social partnerships to produce 'social good' optimal fit between the partners should be achieved which will create the 'partnering space'.
Stafford and Hartman	Social partnerships can facilitate the development of environmentally sustainable technologies, products and practices for the economic and social gain of market and non-market constituents.	Climate change	Refrigeration	North America	Social partnership is a process that highlights the role of the collaborative entrepreneur when NGOs engage business, associations, scientists and others in sustainable entrepreneurship in order to sustain, develop and legitimize environmentally-sustainable innovations for the social good.
Peloza and Ye	Social partnerships are used as a tool for brand building demonstrating social and environmental impacts of companies.	Multiple	Multiple	Multiple	Social partnerships can enhance the experiential, symbolic and functional benefits for consumers increasing the 'feel good' factor (a type of social good).

TABLE 25.1 Continued

Authors	Phenomenon: content level		Phenomenon: context level		Phenomenon re-framing
	Understanding of the domain SPRB	Social problem	Industry	Country	Interpretations of the social good through SP4RB
Gray and Purdy	Social partnerships are a common way to address shared problems across sectors with the aim to attend to the potential conflict that either pre-exists or was developed in the course of the interaction.	Multiple	Multiple	Multiple	Social partnerships can resolve a priori or emergent conflict by understanding the role of context and source of difference (logics and frames) in order to create collective impact for the benefit of all.
Section C: Reimagining social partnerships: theory and methods					
Branzei and Le Ber	Social partnerships are a vehicle for responsible business providing insights through cross-sector social interactions and contributing to the creation of public value.	Multiple	Multiple	Multiple	Social partnerships can provide new possibilities of examining the social good through theory or method elaboration informed by answers provided within the dimensions of form, (trans) formation and formulation combined with focus on the possible directions with the aim to re-theorizing the phenomenon.
Selsky, Wilkinson and Mangalagiu	Social partnerships constitute the means of finding solutions to wicked problems in a responsible manner due to their ability to focus on cross cutting issues and interests across sectors providing innovative solutions and informing the long-term decisions of business.	Sustainability/ Sustainable development	Multiple	Multiple	Social partnerships can inform the larger sense of business responsibility for the social good when they focus not only on their own future and that of the markets, but also on the future of societies and natural ecosystems.
Martens and Bookman	Social partnerships consist of a process of CSR articulation hence functioning as a means to achieve brand responsibilization through the direct involvement of consumers and employees while instilling mechanisms of self-governance.	HIV/AIDS	Coffee house TV	Canada UK	Social partnerships can act as a kind of ambience implicating consumers in the performance of responsible initiatives enhancing the brand image with consumers hence promoting social well-being (a type of social good) for the individuals as directed by companies through the enactment of responsibility and hence shaping consumer responsibility.

TABLE 25.1 Continued

	Phenomenon: content level		Phenomenon: context level		Phenomenon re-framing
Authors	Understanding of the domain SPRB	Social problem	Industry	Country	Interpretations of the social good through SP4RB
Vurro and Dacin	Social partnerships as a collectively situated phenomenon are part of the portfolio of activities that companies undertake to fulfil perceived duties as members of society.	Multiple	Multiple	Multiple	Social partnerships addressing the social good co-evolve with the institutional context, the source of rules and resources, functioning as a source of institutional entrepreneurship with the potential for change contingent on both individual and organizational factors.
Tencati and Zsolnai	Social partnerships are considered a tool for consensus building and pursuing in an instrumental way self-interested goals.	N/A	N/A	N/A	Social partnerships can contribute to the social good by fostering a genuine alternative collaborative paradigm on different levels of analysis with a new model of collaborative enterprise at its centre.

Section D: Reimagining social partnerships: perspectives on practice

Waddock	Social partnerships are a potential means of resolving intractable social problems and represent efforts to bridge organizations that make profit with those who aim for the social good.	Multiple	Multiple	Multiple	Social partnerships put forward a new vision for a more sustainable world in which participation and democracy, all types of organizations and living creatures are truly valued for healthy social and environmental ecosystems.
Archer and Uys	Social partnerships are one of the most powerful and efficient means of lowering environmental footprint directly, persuading governments to take action and providing sustainable products to consumers.	Sustainable development/ fisheries	Retail	Canada	Social partnerships can help companies shift their way of doing business and hence be part of the solution in rebalancing oceans and transforming the seafood sector by engaging with government, consumers, fishing communities and the media contributing to sustainable development (social good).

TABLE 25.1 Continued

	Phenomenon: content level		Phenomenon: context level		Phenomenon re-framing
Authors	Understanding of the domain SPRB	Social problem	Industry	Country	Interpretations of the social good through SP4RB
Nijhuis	Social partnerships with local stakeholders including business are key for the success of non-profit organizations if pursued strategically.	Poverty alleviation	Education/ Community Retail	Guatemala	Social partnerships present unexpected opportunities to connect and build bridges between the poor and the rich in communities which can create opportunities to collectively serve the social good.
Winchester	Social partnerships address wicked problems in collaboration with companies in key sectors in order to bridge identified gaps.	Youth unemployment	Construction Management consultancy	UK	Social partnerships can serve the social good if appropriate partners are identified for specific problems, while developing exceptional communication, mutual respect and allowing for appropriate debate to take place in order to understand the true value of the collaboration.
Hundal	Social partnerships engender responsible business and provide solutions to social problems at local, national and global levels.	N/A	N/A	UK	Social partnerships can benefit through facilitative leadership provided by brokers increasing the benefit for all concerned parties.
Hudson	Social partnerships signal a paradigm shift of social problem solving by free-market mechanisms creating opportunities for cross sector leadership by business.	N/A	N/A	UK	Social partnerships offer a promise of twenty-first-century self-organized society delivering social outcomes for the benefit of all through collaboration.
Waddell	Social partnerships are a new type of organization different from business, civil society and government.	N/A	N/A	N/A	Social partnerships can develop new knowledge by reinforcing the development of competences and serving the social good through the associated expertise of the social issue they are serving.

TABLE 25.1 Continued

	Phenomenon: content level			*Phenomenon: context level*		*Phenomenon re-framing*
Authors	*Understanding of the domain SPRB*	*Social problem*	*Industry*	*Country*		*Interpretations of the Social Good through SP4RB*
Zadek	Social partnerships signal the new generation of business organizations and public institution operation for the twenty-first century.	Multiple	Multiple	Multiple		Social partnerships have the potential of changing the rules of the game by extending accountability either as a bridging experience or a pluralistic approach for tomorrow's sustainable economy.

the authors' text, but inevitably we provide our interpretation of their text aiming to allow for comparisons across chapters to inform the above questions.

Looking at the initial positioning frames, social partnerships between business, non-profit organizations and/or government, according to the authors in this Research Handbook, address social and environmental issues (Kolk, 2014; Hundal, 2014; Hudson, 2014), public policy problems (Doh and Boddewyn, 2014) institutional (Hamann, 2014), local/BoP and community challenges (Schmutzler *et al.*, 2014; Rufin and Rivera-Santos, 2014; Clarke, 2014; Hundal, 2014), conflict (Gray and Purdy, 2014), and perceived business duties (Vurro and Dacin, 2014). Such problems are often characterized as intractable, wicked and complex (Waddock, 2014; Selsky *et al.* 2014; Winchester, 2014; Kolk, 2014) but above all they address globally shared problems (Gray and Purdy, 2014; Kolk, 2014; Hundal, 2014).

In terms of responsible business, social partnerships are regarded as a process of CSR articulation (Bookman and Martens, 2014), an institutional response (Hamann, 2014) to engage responsible business (Clarke, 2014; Branzei and Le Ber, 2014), to achieve institutional objectives (Hamann, 2014), provide collective goods, alleviate institutional deficits (Doh and Boddewyn, 2014; Winchester, 2014), achieve community sustainable development (Clarke, 2014), engender inclusive and responsible business (Schmutzler *et al.*, 2014; Hundal, 2014), profitability (Rufin and Rivera-Santos, 2014; Stafford and Hartman, 2014), manage societal relations across sectors (van Tulder and Pfisterer, 2014; Selsky *et al.*, 2014), strengthen brands (Peloza and Ye, 2014), inform long-term decisions of business (Selsky *et al.*, 2014), achieve brand responsibilization (Bookman and Martens, 2014), build consensus to serve self-interested goals (Tencati and Zsolnai, 2014), provide access to products (Schmutzler *et al.*, 2014), lower the environmental footprint of business (Archer and Uys, 2014), assist non-profits to meet their goals (Nijhuis, 2014), and generate a new type of public institution (Zadek, 2014).

Partnerships are also conceptualized as new forms of governance (Hamann, 2014; Zadek, 2014), value creation mechanisms (Schmutzler *et al.*, 2014), collaborative ventures (Rufin and Rivera-Santos, 2014), institutional innovation (van Tulder and Pfisterer, 2014; Selsky *et al.*, 2014), as a collectively situated phenomenon (Vurro and Dacin, 2014), bridges between profit and social good (Waddock, 2014), an opportunity for business leadership (Hudson, 2014) and a new type of organization (Waddell, 2014).

Due to the theoretical nature of the contributions the social problems that provide the focus of the chapters are often classified as multiple, but some chapters provide focus on the content of the phenomenon looking at climate change, socio-ecological problems and sustainability (Kolk, 2014; Hamann, 2014; van Tulder and Pfisterer, 2014; Stafford and Hartman, 2014; Selsky *et al.*, 2014; Archer and Uys, 2014) education and health (Doh and Boddewyn, 2014), poverty (Kolk, 2014; Rufin and Rivera-Santos, 2014; Nijhuis, 2014) crime reduction, housing (Hamann, 2014), product exclusion (Schmutzler *et al.*, 2014), HIV/AIDS (Bookman and Martens, 2014), youth unemployment and education (Nijhuis, 2014).

Moving to the context level of the phenomenon, i.e. the industry and country experience studied, once again, many contributions provide examples across a number of countries and industries (characterized in Table 25.1 as "multiple"). However, the chapters that focus on a particular context examine the following industries: ceramic tiling (Scmutzler *et al.*, 2014), refrigeration (Stafford and Hartman, 2014), media (Bookman and Martens, 2014) retail (Archer and Uys, 2014; Bookman and Martens, 2014; Nijhuis, 2014), construction, and management consultancy (Winchester, 2014). With regards to the countries examined they range from South Africa, Canada, Colombia, North America, Guatemala and the UK. If nothing else this demonstrates that social partnerships have very much become a global phenomenon and one that is hardly constrained to particular sectors such as consumer packaged goods.

So how do the authors frame and re-frame social partnerships? The initial framing of social partnerships provides a wide range of variation demonstrating the polyphony around the phenomenon. It appears to focus on the problems or social issues and often the positioning centres around business and its role in connection to the social issues addressed. Inevitably social partnerships very often are framed as a subservient phenomenon to CSR hence aligning them to responsible business, which we term Social Partnerships *as* Responsible Business (SPRB). In this framing, partnerships are essentially a form of responsible business or a way of implementing responsible business. However, the re-framing under the theme of the social good appears to depart somewhat from this approach and move toward a solutions perspective aimed at rethinking responsible business through a partnerships lens. This we term Social Partnerships *for* Responsible Business (SP4RB). This latter perspective is more concerned with the *adjustments, adaptation or fundamental change* required of business and other actors to achieve the social good. The two perspectives are significantly different as the latter requires action for fundamental change and prioritization of the social good.

Reframing the partnership phenomenon under the domain of the "social good" has the potential of unifying the previous fragmentation of the social partnerships literature (Crane and Seitanidi, 2014), it can provide a thematic critical focus for an emerging scholarly field and in effect move the phenomenon from an episodic focus, usually employing an "instance" or case study, to a thematic focus often concentrating on the outcomes (Iyengar, 1991; Entman, 1993). Employing either frame affects how responsibility is assigned to social issues; episodic framing elicits individualistic, case-by-case responsibility while the thematic framing elicits societal attributions of responsibility hence associates social issues with broader social responsibility and social forces, in effect elevating the "issue" and the phenomenon from the incident level to a social or policy issue (Iyengar, 1991).

By looking at this re-framing it seems possible to align the different social issues, theories and perspectives with the social good (thematic framing). The dominant metaphor that is employed by the authors is that of "the bridge" i.e. a key strength of social partnership is to function as a bridge connecting challenges, social issues, sectors, fields, disciplines and levels of analysis. The connections are expressed through the "trickle effects" of Kolk (2014), the "social issues integration" of Clarke (2014), Rufin and Rivera-Santos's (2014) "linkages", the "enactment of responsibility" of Bookman and Martens (2014) and the "co-evolution of partnerships with the institutional environment" of Vurro and Dacin (2014). The above highlight how interactions take place on different levels of analysis at the same time. In effect it appears that the social good incorporates the ability of people, organizations and institutions to bridge across and identify the in-between unclaimed space, what van Tulder and Pfisterer (2014) call "the partnership space" where the connections make sense and take place. Employing an *a posteriori* perspective of emerged responsibilities could provide focus on the negotiated role during the relationship – in other words focusing on the interaction as the unit of analysis rather than the organizations.

What are the main implications from our contributors regarding how social partnerships and responsible business might be re-imagined in the future?

Given the degree of difficulty of the social issues that social partnerships seek to contend with, it would seem appropriate to look for answers in the realm of alternative desirable outcomes, or what we term "re-imagining". Re-imagining is a mental process usually referred to as counterfactual thinking, a term used in psychology (Tversky and Kahneman, 1974) that describes the tendency of people to imagine alternatives to reality. These usually include "what if" and "if only" state-ments which indicate mental simulations or "cognitive constructions of an event or series of events based on a causal sequence of successive interdependent actions" (Gaglio, 2004: 537). In such cognitive constructions uncertainty is high, hence a type of alternative or counterfactual thinking is required which refers to "logical stateme-nts that stipulate the cause, or antecedent, and the effect also called the consequent or outcome – in other words, these are statements about a means-ends framework" (Gaglio, 2004: 539). We asked the authors of the Handbook to provide educated guesses about what must change and how in social partnerships in order to arrive at their desired future outcomes. In the four subsections that follow we present our interpretation of the re-imaging insights of the authors within each section of the book.

Re-imagining partnerships across geographic contexts

The question of how we should re-think the role, purpose and design of partnerships to focus on the social good given what our contributors have written about the different geographic contexts in Part A gives rise to a number of insights. However, probably the main message to come out of these chapters is that going forward *we need to consider partnerships on multiple levels*. As Kolk (2014) demonstrates in Chapter 2 we have to reimagine partnerships as having significant impacts at macro, meso and micro levels. Even partnerships supposedly aimed at addressing "global" problems have indirect local effects – such as on the family and friends of individuals involved in the partnership. This might give rise to a rather different globalization maxim for globally-oriented partnerships – not so much "think global, act local" as "think local, act global".

In a similar vein, Doh and Boddewyn (2014) urge us in Chapter 3 to rethink how we determine optimal arrangements for public goods provision through international partnerships by considering both country-level factors (ordering systems) and organizational-level capabilities and strategies. To reimagine partnerships we need to take into account the effect of differing economic and institutional settings on how responsibility is arranged among relevant parties. This issue is nowhere more important than in areas with limited statehood. As Hamann (2014) proposes in Chapter 4, partnership practitioners and analysts in such contexts will need to explicitly discuss what capabilities may be required among the state and assess whether these capabilities are adequately present. If not, they will need to consider whether such capabilities can be developed, and indeed this might become an explicit purpose for the partnership. Hamann's analysis suggests that partnership models for the development of state capabilities are likely to become increasingly prominent and crucial in years to come.

Finally, turning to local partnerships within a highly developed state apparatus, Clarke's (2014) case studies in Chapter 5 urge us to reimagine the scope and challenges of the "local". Examining local authority partnerships with a proposed duration of anything up to 100 years, and including large numbers of participants (more than 100 in one case), it is clear that "local" need not equate with small or parochial. Critically though, such partnerships bring with them significant challenges in terms of engagement and governance and Clarke shows that the rhetoric of partnership can easily fall back into the practice of highly asymmetric participation. Partnership scholars and practitioners will have to be attuned to these challenges and seek to determine the realistic conditions under which a real sense of partnership can and should be sustained.

Re-imagining partnerships to address management and governance challenges

Turning now to the management and governance challenges covered in Part B, what insights can be gleaned from these chapters about how we can re-imagine social partnerships to overcome these challenges in the future? In our view, two issues are particularly worthy of note – dealing with *interaction effects* in partnerships, and dealing with *ubiquity*.

Turning to the first aspect, we propose that scholars and practitioners will increasingly need to consider the *interaction effects* of partnerships. For example, van Tulder and Pfisterer in Chapter 6 discuss the dynamics of the "partnering space" and the different roles that actors may play. But as partnerships become more common, the competences, roles and legitimacy-bases of the different actors change, engendering shifts in the partnering space. That is, existing roles inform the partnerships that get formed – but then these partnerships eventually change the original roles into something different. This is well illustrated by the case of Greenpeace's Greenfreeze campaign described by Stafford and Hartman in Chapter 9 which shows that sustainable entrepreneurship on the part of NGOs requires them to become more business-like – e.g. Greenpeace's role and competences have fundamentally shifted because of the various cross-sector partnerships it engaged in. Because of these interaction effects, we will need to reimagine partnerships based not on the current roles of the different sectors but the roles they may eventually come to play.

A similar type of interaction effect is evident in the context of partnership governance as discussed by Rufín and Rivera-Santos in Chapter 7. It would appear that the partnerships of the future will need to be much more mindful not only of their own governance features, but also how of these features then impact upon broader meso-level governance. The interactive effects between these different levels of governance (or what Crane (2010) calls "small g" partnership governance and "big G" societal governance) should become a more prominent feature of the design and assessment of the partnerships of the future.

Relatedly, as Schmutzler *et al.* (2014) show in relation to firms in BOP markets in Chapter 8, organizations should consider partnerships from a portfolio approach. Such a portfolio might include a judicious mix of partners and issues at different stages of learning, and with different risk and return characteristics. Finding the right mix of partnerships will thus become just as important as finding the right partnerships. This means that in the future, the interactions between partnerships will become a critical new site for developing insight and driving value, with smart organizations seeking to derive synergies from combinations of partnerships – and researchers faced with a whole new set of interaction effects which will make impact analysis even more complex.

Our second main issue in the reimagining of management and governance concerns the potential *ubiquity* of social partnerships in the future. Thus far, we have typically discussed partnerships as relatively novel phenomena, but before long it is likely that they will become commonplace, routine, even habitual. Peloza and Ye in Chapter 10 discuss some of the critical ways that organizations can build their brands through social partnerships but the potential for differentiation will become increasingly limited as partnerships become more ubiquitous. Thus, brand building might be replaced by a brand protection approach where, for example, non-profits might wish to partner with firms to develop greater expertise in areas that can help firms mitigate risk. Similarly, the partnerships of the future might feature more collaborations between competing firms looking to reap industry-level brand associations rather than trying to "own" an idea or partnership.

The challenge of managing conflict as discussed by Gray and Purdy in Chapter 11 may also be reshaped by the ubiquity of social partnerships since actors may begin to institutionalize certain features that enable them to manage conflicts in a routinized and peaceful way. We might imagine a scenario where particular types of intra- or inter-sectoral organizations become established with a remit to convene partnerships to ensure that there will be a level playing field with respect to power among the partners, and with clear mechanisms for preventing and handling potential conflicts. Although it is impossible that conflict will be entirely removed from the partnership arena (and indeed may even be necessary to create meaningful change, see Seitanidi, 2010), there are considerable opportunities for managing conflict in a positive and value-adding way as partnership becomes more habitual.

Re-imagining social partnerships in theory and method

Part C of the book is rich in suggestions for the reimaging of theories and methods of social partnership research and practice. Branzei and Le Ber argue, for instance, in Chapter 12 that social partnership researchers "need to stitch and strengthen our theories" and "to stretch and sharpen our [methodological] toolkit to keep pace with theory and practice". The eclecticism they identify in the current literature is both a strength and a weakness in that it continuously brings new perspectives, but often fails to offer sufficient depth to realize a significant enough contribution to theory. Their suggestions for reimagining are to *build a more systematic theory of social partnerships and to better and more extensively apply robust methods* to understand the "field of dreams" of contemporary social partnerships – and thereby contribute to better practice and stronger social outcomes.

With regard to the specific theories and methods discussed in the remainder of this section, the main avenue for reimagining is in *using new theory and method to reset our mindsets.* That is, new theories and methods can help us to evade the cognitive limits imposed by our existing ways of understanding the phenomenon and open up new vistas. For example, the futures methods discussed by Selsky *et al.,* in Chapter 13 offer considerable promise for reimagining social partnerships, helping participants to explicitly envisage alternative, plausible futures and avoiding the trap of the implicit future and premature consensus. Similarly theories of governmentality as discussed in Chapter 14 (Bookman and Martens, 2014) help us to see the limits imposed by the "hedgemonic brandscape" of the big brands often involved in social partnerships and challenge us to conceive of partnerships that open up rather than narrow possibilities for responsible practice beyond the market. Institutional theory, which is the subject of various contributions in the book, but is discussed most fully in Chapter 15 (Vurro and Dacin, 2014) helps diagnose some of the often taken-for-granted contextual forces that influence partnerships' success. Institutional contexts can be sources of fruitful, unexpected opportunities, while presenting a number of hidden constraints, especially at the level of informality and social norms. Finally, Tencati and Zsolnai in Chapter 16 challenge us even further to reimagine not just partnerships but our very theory of the firm. Our existing competitive model of the firm is insufficient, they suggest, to tackle the kind of problems we are now facing, and only a change in the way we conceptualize firms, managers and markets will unleash the full potential of partnerships to foster the common good and change the world for the better.

Re-imagining social partnerships in practice

In the final section of the book, our authors have provided numerous and quite diverse suggestions for how to reimagine partnerships in practice. One way of approaching this is to look at how we could reimagine partnerships tomorrow by *replicating best practice from today*. For instance, Archer and Uys in Chapter 18 recommend three key elements in the success of the WWF-Loblaws partnership: openness; trust and flexibility; and investment in shared success. Winchester in Chapter 20 highlights the importance of a different three factors: dealing with power balance; overcoming misconceptions between the sectors; and the importance of trial and error. Indeed, each of the authors in Part D offers important insight on current practice that can help us design partnerships of the future. We have summarized some of the most important of these in Table 25.2. As can be seen, there is much wisdom to be found here regarding where we should go based on what we have learnt so far.

A second approach is to *envisage new practices of the future*. That is, rather than simply looking to replicate the best of what we know already, to reflect on what we are missing or to forecast how practice might need to evolve in the future to make partnerships more effective. Several of our contributors seek to do this. Hundal in Chapter 21, for instance, extols us to consider whether partnership brokers are a role model for a new form of leadership. Waddell in Chapter 23 highlights the importance of developing the right competences for partnership management and the need to bring partnership practitioners together to learn collaboratively and develop new knowledge – something akin to a "school of social partnership". Finally, and perhaps most challenging of all, Zadek in Chapter 24 questions whether social partnerships can be seen as not just as a way of implementing CSR but as a prototype for twenty-first-century corporate governance that, although imperfect, provides one of the best ways of aligning public and private interests in economic affairs.

How would we then answer the question posed at the outset of this chapter about how partnerships contribute to the social good? It appears that social partnerships have served the social good on many occasions and hold a strong potential to continue in the future. However, it also seems that the more we study these collaborative arrangements the more we realize the multitude of conditions and requirements that play an important role in order to achieve the desirable outcomes.

TABLE 25.2 Insights from practice on success factors for social partnerships

Chapter	Author	Illustrative success factors
17	Waddock	Capable leadership; ability to bring diverse stakeholders into productive dialogue; establishment of buy-in around a common problem definition; capacity to select appropriate partners; system thinking
18	Archer and Uys	Openness; trust and flexibility; investment in shared success
19	Nijhuis	Involving and treating all participants with respect; clear and inspiring impact; overcoming fear of unknown and fear of failure
20	Winchester	Dealing with power balance; overcoming misconceptions between the sectors; trial and error
21	Hundal	Effective brokering, involving: relationship building; partnering process management; partner reconciliation and motivation; reflexivity; empowerment of partners
22	Hudson	Developing a strategic mindset; role clarity and effective management of role boundaries; balancing collaboration and competition; aligning business focus with a social purpose
23	Waddell	Developing social partnership competencies in: leadership; network development; measuring impact; change and conflict; communications; learning systems; policy and advocacy; resource mobilization
24	Zadek	Partnerships as a public fudiciary, requiring: rules for mediating between public and private interests; performance criteria for effective extended accountability; effective oversight by directors; fair, balanced and unbiased governing arrangements.

This would suggest that social partnerships do not necessarily serve the social good yet to the extent required for reaching solutions consistently and inclusively. The chapters of this research handbook, however, present the multitude of conditions that could potentially align social partnerships with the social good in a more systematic way. Inevitably though we need to redefine the success of partnerships by disconnecting the *priority* for profit under all circumstances (but not profit itself) from the notion of responsible business as we discuss next.

How can we re-conceptualize partnerships in order to advance the social good?

One of the central problems in responsible business, most notably in one of its key concepts, corporate social responsibility (CSR) has been how to combine or achieve a compromise between the ethical and economic viewpoints (Windsor, 2006). It is evident that even when CSR is defined in connection to the social good, as in the following extracts from McWilliams and Siegel (2001), it inevitably prioritizes the perspective of the corporation: "we define CSR as actions that appear to further some social good, beyond the interests of the firm and that which is required by law" (p117) yet "we begin our analysis of CSR by relating it to a theory of the firm, in which it is assumed that the management of publicaly held firms attempts to maximise profits" (p119). This instrumentalization of the social good to that which is profitable for companies has received further support recently with the enthusiastic uptake of Porter and Kramer's (2011: 77) "shared value" concept which "focuses companies on the right kind of profits – profits that create societal benefits rather than diminish them."

Despite the good intentions behind these attempts to reconcile the social good with profitability, there is inevitably a tension here with a holistic conception of the social good, often referred "as a broad rubric" desired by many (Windsor, 2001: B2), or as an "improvement" of existing conditions of society (Margolis and Walsh, 2003). Social partnerships that aspire to combine multiple perspectives and address social issues for the social good will potentially need to disassociate from CSR or "shared value" in order to allow for the multifaceted manifestations of what constitutes the "social" (Latour, 2007) to emerge. Hence instead of associating the "social" of responsibility with the mono-dimensional prioritization of "profit" there is a need to re-connect the social and economic through the political process (Banerjee, 2008). CSR may be a vehicle that can be used to approach the "social" in business, but insofar as social partnerships are a bridge to reconceiving the role of business and other actors (SP4RB) the CSR frame, which first and foremost is a function of business, may offer only limited potential.

As suggested by Thucydides "in an alliance the only safe guarantee is an equality of mutual fear…" (Thucydides translated by Warner, 1954). Hence, social problems can be seen as the uniting force for the different perspectives to be aligned under the threat they each pose to one another at the same time. A loosening of the bond with CSR might allow for the shared social good to better emerge as an all-inclusive framing, where business is only one of the actors "equal in fear" rather than the dominant one. Partnerships are one of the emerging ways to co-create social good encompassing the notion of public and private. Hence the notion of what constitutes the "social" is being re-defined under the new set of conditions. As such, old assumptions of the traditional roles of the state, business and non-profits are shifting whilst a new sense of appropriate roles, domains and responsibilities is emerging. In this new understanding the process of connecting becomes the focus, "a trail of associations between heterogeneous elements" (Latour, 2007: 5) in search of the logic of what constitutes the social good. This new terrain requires identifying new rules of interaction in order to govern in an inclusive, fair and efficient way that will accommodate, not have at its centre, profit – but rather will congeal around the collective good and the preservation of our natural resources.

If we are to re-imagine how social partnerships can move forward we need to: (1) prioritize the social good in theory and in practice; and (2) radically re-imagine the social good in praxis through partnerships on multiple levels that require dealing with interaction effects and ubiquity. This will inevitably question not only what constitutes the "social good" but also if the responsibilities of the "I" or individual should be limited or extended for the benefit of the "we" or the collective. Such a rethink may need a more fundamental shift from the existing paradigm to a new direction and in effect abandon the actor perspective and embrace interaction as the new paradigm. This de-centring of actors (most notably the corporation, but also to a lesser degree governments and nonprofits) and refocusing on interactions has the potential to drive our attention, both as researchers and practitioners, towards a more common, inclusive framing around the social good – but at the same time will require a degree of personal and organizational realignment that has yet proved to be elusive.

Conclusion

In this final chapter we have sought to bring together the various strands of the chapters included in this Handbook, and crystallized their insights according to the need to reimagine social partnerships and responsible business for the social good. We showed how the authors view the phenomenon through a wide range of frames in terms of content and context, giving rise to a polyphonic representation. Reframing through the notion of the social good helps provide some coherence to these representations, focusing attention on social partnerships as a bridge between levels, organizations, sectors, fields, and so on. Our analysis of the various insights across the chapters regarding how we need to reimagine the phenomenon raised a number of issues, including: the importance of considering partnerships on multiple levels; dealing with interaction effects and emerging ubiquity; building more systematic theory and robust methods; using new theory and method to reset mindsets; replicating best practice from today; and envisaging new practices for the future. A key element in building these new frames, mindsets and practices, we suggest, will be a rethinking of the underlying relationship between social partnerships and responsible business. To genuinely reimagine social partnerships for the social good, our theories and practice will need to stretch beyond subservience to business self-interest, and perhaps most importantly replace a central focus on actors with a focus on interactions. Returning to the metaphor of the orchestra, our attention has to be on the concert, the moving effect of the music, and not on the musicians.

References

Archer, H. and Uys, P. (2014) The need for a new approach to sustainability, in M.M. Seitanidi and A. Crane (eds) *Social Partnerships and Responsible Business: A Research Handbook*. London: Routledge: 342–8.

Austin, J. and Seitanidi, M.M. (2012a) Collaborative value creation: a review of partnering between business and non-profits. *Non-profit and Voluntary Sector Quarterly*, 41 (5): 726–58.

Austin, J. and Seitanidi, M.M. (2012b) Collaborative value creation: partnerships processes. *Non-profit and Voluntary Sector Quarterly*, 41 (6): 929–68.

Banerjee, S.B. (2008) Corporate social responsibility: the good, the bad and the ugly. *Critical Sociology*, 34 (1): 51–79.

Bookman, S. and Martens, C. (2014) Responsibilization and governmentality in brand-led social partnerships, in M.M. Seitanidi and A. Crane (eds) *Social Partnerships and Responsible Business: A Research Handbook*. London: Routledge: 288–305.

Branzei, O. and Le Ber, M.J. (2014) Theory-method interfaces in cross-sector partnership research, in M.M. Seitanidi and A. Crane (eds) *Social Partnerships and Responsible Business: A Research Handbook*. London: Routledge: 229–66.

Clarke, A. (2014) Designing social partnerships for local sustainability strategy implementation, in M.M. Seitanidi and A. Crane (eds) *Social Partnerships and Responsible Business: A Research Handbook*. London: Routledge: 79–102.

Crane A. and Seitanidi, M.M. (2014) Social partnerships and responsible business: what, why, and how?, in M.M. Seitanidi and A. Crane (eds) *Social Partnerships and Responsible Business: A Research Handbook*. London: Routledge: 1–12.

Crane, A. (2011) From governance to Governance: on blurring boundaries. *Journal of Business Ethics*, 94 (Supplement 1): 17–19.

Doh, J. and Boddewyn, J. (2014) International business and social partnerships: how institutional and MNE capabilities affect collective-goods provisioning in emerging markets, in M.M. Seitanidi and A. Crane (eds) *Social Partnerships and Responsible Business: A Research Handbook*. London: Routledge: 44–59.

Entman, R.M. (1993) Framing: toward clarification of a fractured paradigm. *Journal of Communication*, 43 (4): 51–8.

Gaglio, C.M. (2004) The role of mental simulations and counterfactual thinking in the opportunity identification process. *Entrepreneurship Theory and Practice*, 28 (6): 533–52.

Gray, B and Purdy, J. (2014) Conflict in cross-sector partnerships, in M.M. Seitanidi and A. Crane (eds) *Social Partnerships and Responsible Business: A Research Handbook*. London: Routledge: 205–26.

Hamann, R. (2014) Cross-sector social partnership in areas of limited statehood, in M.M. Seitanidi and A. Crane (eds) *Social Partnerships and Responsible Business: A Research Handbook*. London: Routledge: 60–78.

Hudson, L.J. (2014) Social partnerships: a new social contract to deliver value-focused collaboration, in M.M. Seitanidi and A. Crane (eds) *Social Partnerships and Responsible Business: A Research Handbook*. London: Routledge: 369–73.

Hundal, S. (2014) The role partnership brokers play in creating effective social partnerships, in M.M. Seitanidi and A. Crane (eds) *Social Partnerships and Responsible Business: A Research Handbook*. London: Routledge: 360–8.

Iyengar, S. (1991) *Is anyone responsible? How television frames political issues.* Chicago: Chicago: University Press.

Kolk, A. (2014) Partnerships as panacea for addressing global problems? On rationale, context, actors, impact and limitations, in M.M. Seitanidi and A. Crane (eds) *Social Partnerships and Responsible Business: A Research Handbook*. London: Routledge: 15–43.

Latour, B. (2007) *Reassembling the Social*. Oxford: Oxford University Press.

Margolis, J.D. and Walsh, J.P. (2003) Misery loves companies: rethinking social initiatives by business. *Administrative Science Quarterly*, 48: 268–305.

McWilliams, A. and Siegel, D. (2001) Corporate social responsibility: a theory of the firm perspective. *Academy of Management Review*, 26 (1): 117–27.

Nijhuis, B. (2014) How to co-create opportunities together: CREAMOS in Guatemala, in M.M. Seitanidi and A. Crane (eds) *Social Partnerships and Responsible Business: A Research Handbook*. London: Routledge: 349–55.

Peloza, J. and Ye, C. (2014) How social partnerships build brands, in M.M. Seitanidi and A.

Crane (eds) *Social Partnerships and Responsible Business: A Research Handbook*. London: Routledge: 191–204.

Porter, M.E. and Kramer, M.R. (2011) Creating shared value. *Harvard Business Review,* 89 (January–February): 62–77.

Reese, S.D. (2001) Prologue-framing public life: a model for media research, in *Framing Public Life: Perspectives on Media and Our Understanding of the Social World*. Edited by Reese, S.D., Gandy, Jr., O.H. and Grant, A.E., Mahwah, NJ: Lawrence Erlbaum Associates, 11.

Rufin, C. and Rivera-Santos, M. (2014) Cross-sector governance: from institutions to partnerships, and back to institutions, in M.M. Seitanidi and A. Crane (eds) *Social Partnerships and Responsible Business: A Research Handbook*. London: Routledge: 125–42.

Schmutzler, J., Gutiérrez, R., Reficco, E. and Márquez, P. (2014) Evolution of an alliance portfolio to develop an inclusive business, in M.M. Seitanidi and A. Crane (eds) *Social Partnerships and Responsible Business: A Research Handbook*. London: Routledge: 143–63.

Seitanidi, M.M. (2010) *The Politics of Partnerships: A Critical Examination of Non-profit-Business Partnerships*. Dordrecht: Springer.

Seitanidi, M.M. and Crane, A. (2014) Conclusion: re-imagining the future of social partnerships and responsible business, in Seitanidi, M.M. and Crane, A. (eds) *Social Partnerships and Responsible Business: A Research Handbook*. London: Routledge: 388–407.

Selsky, J., Wilkinson, A. and Mangalagiu, D. (2014) Using futures methods in cross-sector partnership projects: engaging wicked problems responsibly, in Seitanidi, M.M. and Crane, A. (eds) *Social Partnerships and Responsible Business: A Research Handbook*. London: Routledge: 267–87.

Stafford, E. and Hartman, C. (2014) NGO-initiated sustainable entrepreneurship and social partnerships: Greenpeace's "Solutions" campaign for natural refrigerants in North America, in Seitanidi, M.M. and Crane, A. (eds) *Social Partnerships and Responsible Business: A Research Handbook*. London: Routledge: 164–90.

Tencati, A. and Zsolnai, L. (2014) Towards a new theory of the firm: the collaborative enterprise, in Seitanidi, M.M. and Crane, A. (eds) *Social Partnerships and Responsible Business: A Research Handbook*. London: Routledge: 320–31.

Tversky, A. and Kahneman, D. (1974) Judgment under uncertainty: heuristics and biases. *Science*, 185 (4157): 1124–31.

van Tulder, R. and Pfisterer, S. (2014) Creating partnering space: exploring the right fit for sustainable development partnerships, in M.M. Seitanidi and A. Crane (eds) *Social Partnerships and Responsible Business: A Research Handbook*. London: Routledge: 105–24.

Vurro, C. and Dacin, T. (2014) An institutional perspective on cross-sector partnerships, in M.M. Seitanidi and A. Crane (eds) *Social Partnerships and Responsible Business: A Research Handbook*. London: Routledge: 306–19.

Waddell, S. (2014) Social partnerships' development challenge: comprehensive self-development, in M.M. Seitanidi and A. Crane (eds) *Social Partnerships and Responsible Business: A Research Handbook*. London: Routledge: 374–81.

Waddock, S. (2014) Cross-sector/cross-boundary collaboration: making a difference through practice, in M.M. Seitanidi and A. Crane (eds) *Social Partnerships and Responsible Business: A Research Handbook*. London: Routledge: 335–41.

Warner, R. (1954) *Thucydides. Book III: Revolt of Mytiline*. London: Penguin Books.

Winchester, S. (2014) Cross sector collaborations: challenges in aligning perspectives in partnership committees and co-developing funding proposals, in M.M. Seitanidi and A. Crane (eds) *Social Partnerships and Responsible Business: A Research Handbook*. London: Routledge: 356–9.

Windsor, D. (2001) International governance in the twenty-first century: regimes, public goods, and social capital. *Academy of Management Proceedings*, 2001 (1): C1–C6.

Windsor, D. 2006. Corporate social responsibility: three key approaches. *Journal of Management Studies*, 4 (1): 93–114.

Zadek, S. (2014) Cross-sector partnerships: prototyping twenty-first-century governance, in M.M. Seitanidi and A. Crane, A. (eds) *Social Partnerships and Responsible Business: A Research Handbook*. London: Routledge: 382–7.

INDEX

Tables are given with an italic 't'. Figures are given with an italic 'f'. Endnotes are given with an italic 'n' followed by the endnote number.